Charles Benner

DON'T TREAD ON ME

★ ★ ★

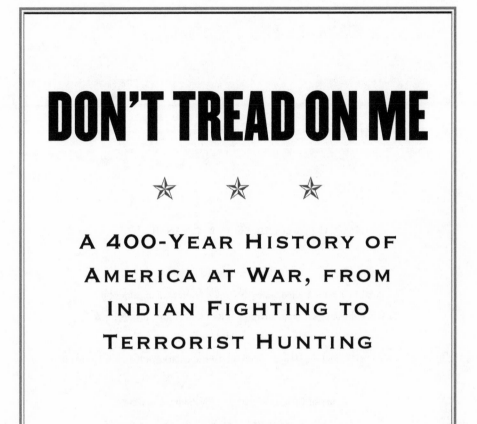

DON'T TREAD ON ME

★ ★ ★

A 400-YEAR HISTORY OF AMERICA AT WAR, FROM INDIAN FIGHTING TO TERRORIST HUNTING

H. W. CROCKER III

CROWN
FORUM
NEW YORK

Published in the United States by Crown Forum, an imprint of the
Crown Publishing Group, a division of Random House, Inc., New York.

www.crownpublishing.com

CROWN FORUM and the Design are registered trademarks of Random House, Inc.

Library of Congress Cataloging-in-Publication Data

Crocker, H. W.

Don't tread on me : A 400-year history of America at war,

from Indian fighting to terrorist hunting / H. W. Crocker III.—1st ed.

Includes bibliographical references and index.

1. United States—History, Military.   I. Title.

E181.C85   2006

355.00973—dc22

2006003964

ISBN-13: 978-1-4000-5363-6

ISBN-10: 1-4000-5363-3

Printed in the United States of America

Design by Leonard Henderson

10   9   8   7   6   5   4   3   2   1

First Edition

For my father,

Harry W. Crocker Jr.

Teacher, Coach, Marine

and the father-in-law I never knew,

Louis J. Maricle

Colonel, U.S. Army

CONTENTS

Our country! In her intercourse with foreign nations,

may she always be in the right; but

our country, right or wrong!

— COMMODORE STEPHEN DECATUR, 1816

THE SUMMONS OF THE TRUMPET

THE MEN OF Merrill's Marauders (code-named GALAHAD) had already endured more than 50 percent casualties—and it would get worse. General Frank Merrill himself had suffered a heart attack. The suffocating tropical heat; the long, exhausting marches through choking jungle; and the biting, stinging insects and leeches that blistered any exposed skin were annoyances. Worse were amoebic dysentery, malaria, scrub typhus, and starvation rations that enfeebled the men. And, yes, there were the Japanese, too.

The Marauders had expected to be withdrawn by now. They had been fought to breaking point. But General "Vinegar Joe" Stilwell needed them. He had to take and hold Myitkyina in northern Burma from the Japanese before the rainy season. President Roosevelt himself was demanding action in Burma. Stilwell knew that only the Marauders could do it: only they—not his Chinese troops—were tough enough, aggressive enough, skilled enough, and had the full support of the Burmese people.

Merrill's remaining effectives, 1,400 men, spearheaded the offensive. What kept them going was Merrill's promise that if they captured the airstrip at Myitkyina, he would have them flown out and "given a party to cause taxpayers a shudder . . . and given furloughs."[1] But the march was worse than could have been imagined. The mountainous trail was a green hell, slippery with mud that sent pack mules sliding down ravines—disappearing with the Marauders' precious supplies. The ravages of bugs, fever, hunger, and thirst swarmed over already debilitated men who were forcing themselves to march into combat. Some of them simply couldn't go on and fell out. But most of them trudged, or even crawled, wearily forward, cursing their luck as men who had volunteered for the Marauders.

But they made it—and on 17 May 1944 easily seized the airstrip and a ferry post on the Irrawaddy River. Yet there was no relief, no party awaiting them.

They were asked to hang on; they had to help the Chinese take the town of Myitkyina, which the Japanese were rapidly reinforcing with thousands of men. The Marauders were so invalided that Stilwell wrote, "GALAHAD is just shot."[2] Merrill called his men "a pitiful but still splendid sight."[3]

With those pitiful, splendid men, the Allies kept the airstrip and captured the town of Myitkyina on 3 August 1944. A week later, the unit was officially disbanded. Every member of Merrill's Marauders—which Marauder Colonel Charles N. Hunter considered "the most beat upon . . . regimental-sized unit that participated in World War II"[4]—was awarded a Bronze Star.

Still, it is reasonable to ask, what were American fighting men doing in Burma at all? Or for that matter, why were they in North Africa in 1805, in Vera Cruz in 1847, in Peking in 1900, in Nicaragua in 1932, or in Afghanistan and Iraq today? This book provides an answer. It is not a blow-by-blow account of every campaign and battle fought by the United States; it does not chart changes in military uniforms, technology, and organization; it is not based on riffling through previously undiscovered papers trying to ferret out new information. It is instead an argument about American history based on America's wars. The argument, briefly stated, is that America is a country of practical, independent-minded people shaped by the frontier, an ambitious and well-meaning people who naturally carved out an "empire of liberty."[5]

It is America's desire for empire that explains her history, and why our founding fathers rebelled against the most liberal country in the world. Had America remained part of the British Empire what sort of future would have awaited us? Well, we might have institutions as repressive as those of Australia—or even Canada. But American leaders living in urban Philadelphia, near the wharves of Boston, and in the plantation houses of Virginia were not content to play second fiddle to bureaucrats, parliamentarians, or even the king in London. Americans wanted an empire of their own, where there would be no proclamation line barring expansion into Indian territory, no restrictions—made in far-off England—governing American trade and law, no shackles placed on what Americans would be allowed to do in furtherance of their own prosperity and self-governance.

The American fighting man has, of course, been the creator and protector of this empire. He began his career in the seventeenth-century Indian Wars—and it is from these wars, and the development of Rogers' Rangers, that American soldiers developed their unheralded strength in small-unit operations. As practical frontiersmen, they showed an early facility for stealthy long marches, ranger combat tactics, and stout fortifications erected overnight. In the War for Independence, American generalship capitalized on British mistakes and halfheartedness and inspired the Patriots to hang on until French intervention at Yorktown secured British defeat. As scions of Great Britain, the naval power par excellence, the muscular Americans took readily to the sea; and the young United States relied heavily on its superlative mastery of seamanship and naval gunnery—strengths that ensured its survival and prosperity in the tumultuous years after independence, when France, Great Britain, and North African pirates tried to circumscribe America's commerce. And the Americans were not humble about carving out a continental empire, pushing aside Indians, Spaniards, and Mexicans. In fact, had America's empire in the Southwest incorporated all of Mexico—as was easily on offer during the Mexican War—the great tragedy of the War Between the States might have been avoided, with sectional friction diverted into continued expansion.

Imperium et libertas, empire and liberty, freedom to grow and expand, was America's eighteenth- and nineteenth-century creed; and the refusal to be trammeled by Indians, the British, or any other impediment to carving out an empire of liberty carried over into the winning of the West, Teddy Roosevelt's charge up San Juan Hill, the U.S. Marines raising the flag over Iwo Jima, and the Ranger patrols that hunt al Qaeda terrorists in Afghanistan. All of this is of a piece; none of it is a dramatic break with previous American history, because Americans have always been an active, expansionist, commercial people, ready to take up arms to defend their interests. Americans refused, from the beginning, to accept restrictions on trading freely with the world. They refuse today to be cowed by terrorism that wants to dictate whom America can befriend, and with whom we can conduct our commerce and broadcast our ideas. America will accept no chains that keep her from being herself and acting freely on the global stage.

Inevitably, the defense of this freedom has required military force. Even that deprecator of a standing army and a blue water navy Thomas Jefferson understood, writing in 1785, that "Our commerce on the ocean . . . must be paid for by frequent war."[6] In winning these wars, it is a commonplace that America's strength has been her enormous industrial, financial, and technological capacity. But in Jefferson's time, America was not the industrial behemoth she would later become. Military hardware, industrial productivity, economic capital, and vanguard technology are all vitally important ingredients of American power. But America's military success relies just as much on something far more basic:

undaunted courage,[7] the sort of courage learned fighting Indians in northern forests, Seminoles in Floridian swamps, Indian horsemen on the Great Plains, and vast numbers of Mexican legions formed up to attack a few Texicans.

The American fighting man reflects the bravery, ingenuity, and grit of a people whose westward expansion required self-confidence, self-reliance, resilience, and determination. His leaders have been above all practical men who know what needs to be done and do it (men like George Washington, Andrew Jackson, and Ulysses S. Grant), who are guided by moral probity (Robert E. Lee, Chester Nimitz, Norman Schwarzkopf), and who operate by dash and daring (Stephen Decatur, George S. Patton, Tommy Franks). As long as America remembers her heritage and retains the best of her own character, she will win her wars.

This book is a debt of gratitude to the fighting men who have made America what she is; who defend her now; and who will defend her in the future. This is their story, and if it can be summed up in a phrase, it is this: *Nemo me impune lacessit,* no one crosses me with impunity.

CHAPTER 1

THE GENTLE ART OF SCALPING

THE AMERICANS were Indian fighters.

At the very first appearance of Englishmen on the shoreline of Virginia "there came the Savages creeping upon all foure, from the Hills, like Beares, with the Bowes in their mouthes, charged us very desperately in faces, hurt Captaine Gabrill Archer in both hands and a sayler in two places of the body very dangerous. After they spent their Arrowes, and felt the sharpnesse of our shot they retired into the Woods with a great noise, and so left us."[1]

The danger was not constant; mostly there was peace. But the few misunderstandings and lethal suspicions could be painful enough. In one case in Virginia, a captain said the wrong thing while negotiating for food with the Powhatan Indians. His savage interlocutors killed thirty-four of the fifty Englishmen and scraped the flesh off the English captain with mussel shells before they threw him into the fire.

The intercourse between Indian and colonist would be full of such cultural exchanges, so that both sides learned to sever heads and limbs and display them from poles to discourage their enemies.[2] The white man learned that a close shave from an Indian could include a shaving of skull and brain. The violent retributions of the Pilgrims in New England earned them the Indian nickname of "cutthroats."[3] Throughout the New World, plagues, either native or imported from Europe, whipped through new settlers and culled native populations. In Virginia, the Indians taught the colonists the use of carcinogenic tobacco, and the colonists taught the Indians the abuse of alcohol. The process of colonization was, thus, a "learning experience" and, like so many such experiences, had a high mortality rate.

It was to the colonists' decided advantage that the Indians of North America, aside from the Five Nations of the Iroquois and the smaller Algonquin confederation of Virginia and North Carolina, were divided into a mosaic of tribal factions, with most of the tribes hostile to one another. Skirmishes between the tribes were common, and most Indians regarded the white man as a potential ally against other Indian enemies.

The Indians were big men, tall and muscular; stoics, stony-faced to pain and torture (hence their reputation as Noble Savages); contemptuous of weakness and, on the whole, oblivious to Christian concepts of mercy. When it came to warfare, they were devious, brutal, and undisciplined. They were masters of ambush and raid, but not of siege or set-piece battle. The American colonists learned to adopt such Indian tactics as were useful but fortified their own efforts with discipline, military science, and strategic campaigning.

Imposing as they were in their fearsome size, blood-chilling howls, and barbaric war paint, the "Red Men" (the colonists thought they were permanently sunburned or indelibly dyed from body painting) did not fill the European colonists with dread and fear. They saw them as human beings—the English even found the Indians' body painting attractive[4]—granted that they had immortal souls, and credited them with ignorance of the true faith rather than hostility toward it, unlike the Muslims of North Africa and the Ottoman Empire.

In the case of the French, the Indians dealt with traders and missionaries. The traders spoke a universal language: I give you worthless beads (or very worthwhile muskets, ammunition, knives, tomahawks, and kettles) and you give me beaver or otter pelts. In the French fashion, these fur traders married into Indian families, and there was little cause for friction between the Indians and the voyageurs. As for the Catholic missionaries to New France, their courage impressed the Indians, even as their vows of chastity and teachings of mercy baffled them.

In Calvinist New England, there was a great emphasis on covenants, compacts, and contracts; and the Pilgrims, as proper men of business, were willing to arrange and sign these with the Indians as much as with anyone. The Pilgrims assumed a monopoly on divine favor, so in principle they had nothing to fear from the Indians. But businessmen often protect their investments with insurance, and the Pilgrims did the same by entrusting their security to a soldier, Miles Standish, a flame-haired fiery bantam, who dominated Pilgrim counsels though he never belonged to their church. Staunchly upright they might be (though they did favor a tipple), and Calvinists, too, but Pilgrim men were practical men.

In Jamestown, in the colony of Virginia, there was another dominant (and short and stocky) soldier, Captain John Smith. As a teenager, Smith enlisted and fought the Spanish in the Netherlands. Afterward, he became a self-taught mercenary. He read the military classics, including Machiavelli's *Art of War* (Miles Standish was a military student, too, partial to Caesar's *Commentaries*), and practiced field exercises with explosives, horses, and signaling equipment. It is not often that the man of action and the man of intellect meet in an integral whole, but in Captain John Smith they did.

His self-taught apprenticeship complete, Smith signed on with the Austrians and fought the Turks in eastern Europe. Wounded in battle in Transylvania, he was captured by the Muslims, sold into slavery, and eventually escaped to become a colonist in Virginia. Smith was not a man easily affrighted: not by Indians and not by noblemen.

Though Americans like to think of themselves as common folk, the New World was blessed by royal charters and developed, in part, by noblemen with coats of arms. Yes, indeed, they invited settlers of a much more common stock and saw the colonies as a convenient dumping ground for religious dissenters, but, especially in the South, the idea of supplementing the riches of lineage with the presumed material riches of the New World, of acquiring vast estates, was very much to the fore in the minds of graduates of Oxford and Cambridge, as well as less well-tutored aristocrats, who decided to stake their claim to America.

Aristocrats of an unfortunately louche and luxurious sort were numerous among the early colonists of Virginia. There were at Jamestown some tough and hardy souls with military experience, but too many had braved a dangerous and hugely uncomfortable journey across the roiling Atlantic to a wild, thickly forested land populated by fearsome savages in order, they imagined, to make a leisured living off the land, easy riches by discovering gold, or effortless wealth through some unspecified trading activity. This mismatch of character, expectation, and reality proved suicidal as effete young blades who preferred starving to working—and who stayed true to that preference—died, dandies to the last, their fingers unsullied by toil, their bellies empty of food. It was Captain John Smith who kept the others alive with his now famous rule of "he that will not work shall not eat."

Smith also impressed the Powhatan Indians. The Indians had assumed that thievery, an art in which they were well practiced, and a few unwelcoming archers' volleys, would convince the English to leave. When that didn't work, they sat back and watched in disdain as the English colony succumbed to starvation and disease. But Smith was too vigorous to succumb. Instead, he began expeditions of hunting, trading, and exploration. On one such, the Indians used a decoy of fair Indian maids to lure Smith and three compatriots into an ambush. Smith and two of his colleagues escaped. The third was scraped clean of his flesh (again by mussel shells) and then burned to death. A second ambush led to the wounding and capture of Smith, who was interrogated by the Indians at length and saved from having his brains beaten out with clubs only by the intervention of Chief Powhatan's daughter Pocahontas, who not only saved the Englishman's life but would marry another Englishman and become a convert to Christianity. Smith was the essential martial colonist and Pocahontas the great maiden of peace and comity between the English and the Indians in Virginia. Both, however, made the passage to England, and in their absence relations between the races deteriorated.

On Good Friday 1622, the Indians came in among the settlers, as they often did, laden with game to trade. The colonists were friendly, relaxed, and unsuspecting of the massacre that would follow. Men, women, and children fell to a sudden Indian onslaught. Anywhere between a quarter and a third of Virginia's colonists were murdered on that day of the Cross.[5] In many cases, they were not only killed, but their dead bodies desecrated.

Before the massacre, the English had seen themselves as colonists of quite a different stripe from their enemies the Spanish, whom they characterized as exterminating inquisitors. But now, English tolerance and phlegm gave way to the English nanny with a blunderbuss. The Indians were to be taught a lesson in manners they would never forget—and kept under a perennial tutelage with the birch always at hand. The Virginia Company, the joint stock company whose investment was the colony, called for "perpetual warre without peace or truce" against the Indians.

Distant, vulnerable plantations were abandoned, arms arrived from England, and a war of explicit, if ineffective, extermination began. It was ineffective because the colonists continued to suffer from diseases and shortages of food (thanks to Indian raids on farms and the killing of farmers), and because the Indians made an elusive prey—prey that was also quite capable of striking back. The colonists did not limit themselves to hunting down warrior parties; they emulated the Indians and attacked native settlements, burning the Indians' huts and making off with their stores of food.

A year and two months after the Good Friday massacre, the English returned the favor of the Indians' initial treachery by gathering to sign a peace treaty with the Powhatan chief Opechancanough. The drinks provided for the Indians' congratulatory toasts were poisoned, and though Opechancanough survived, his colleagues did not, and the English renewed their war against the Indians. Not only did the English see themselves as emulating the Indians' treachery, they also scalped some of the dead. Opechancanough, who had hoped his act of Good Friday terrorism would drive the colonists out, found instead that the English grew in strength. In 1624, Virginia became no longer a private investment but a Crown Colony, an explicit outpost of England's developing empire.[6]

The colonists' skill as Indian fighters also grew. Though they engaged the Indians on unequal terms—the English had fewer men and their muskets were much slower to be reloaded than a bow and arrow—they learned to inflict far heavier casualties on the Red Men. The colonists' secret was the same as that of ancient warfare—steadier discipline. Still, it took ten years for a formal peace to be arranged between the Indians and the Crown Colony of Virginia to end the First Tidewater War in 1632; and the Second Tidewater War began just over a decade later in 1644, when the now hundred-year-old Opechancanough ordered a replay of the Good Friday massacre. He succeeded in killing 500 colonists, more than he had killed twenty years earlier, but a far smaller proportion of the English population. This time it was fatal for him. His tribes were beaten, exiled from the Tidewater, and became vassals of the governor, owing him annual tribute. Opechancanough was captured, and before he could be transported as war booty to England, a soldier killed him.

In Calvinist New England, a similar drama unfolded in the first half of the seventeenth century. The settlers from the good ship *Mayflower* expected and found that Indians would shoot arrows at them. So they proceeded with caution, even disguising from the Indians their harsh losses to disease and cold that first winter in 1620–21, by planting crops over the graves of their dead. Luckily that spring a compact was signed with the neighboring Wampanoag Indians. Pilgrim and Indian pledged themselves to peace, an alliance in case of war with other tribes, and general good behavior. The Pilgrims benefited greatly from the Indians teaching them how to thrive in their new surroundings. Indians and Pilgrims rubbed along well together, even combining to subdue a chieftain who wanted to overturn the peace, and, in general, lived amicably.

The investors in the *Mayflower* expedition, however, were less than pleased because of the lack of return on their investment and trusted that this could be remedied by leavening the settlement of self-proclaimed saints with a good dose of white trash gleaned from the slums of London. The white trash established a new settlement at Wessagusset on Boston Bay and did what they always do:

cause trouble. Unlike the Pilgrims, they were neither hardworking nor moral nor self-respecting. They recklessly sold their belongings, stole from others, became servants to the Indians, and worse still, whined and cried about their lot in front of the Red Men—something that grievously jeopardized white prestige. Indians expected self-possession and had nothing but contempt for those who would whimper or whinge.

Miles Standish, sensing that the Massachusetts Indians around the new settlement would soon make war—not only on the white trash of Wessagusset, but on the Pilgrims of Plymouth and the Puritans of Massachusetts Bay Colony—took preemptive action, murdering four Indians of the Massachusetts tribe (whom he had invited to dinner) and waging a short, sharp attack on any Massachusetts Indians foolish enough to stay in his vicinity. This strike by Standish—and the subsequent disbanding of Wessagusset Colony, with the Pilgrims paying for the white trash to be returned to England—ended any imminent threat of greater war with the Indians. Later, when an aristocrat founded the colony of Merrymount for merrymakers, the Pilgrims used Standish to forcibly squelch it. The Pilgrims dared not compromise the morality that ensured the safety of New England.

The first real Indian war of New England was the Pequot War in 1637. The Pequot tribe was warlike and had been implicated, though without much evidence, in the murder of a white trader. But equally damning in the colonists' eyes was that the Pequots were uninterested in trade, ignored agreements with the colonists that they thought were irrelevant, and stood accused of being "a very false people." Ironically, the precipitant cause of the war was the work of another tribe entirely that killed a group of white traders; the Pequots were a follow-on target because they were considered insufficiently obedient and a potential threat.

The colonists' punitive expedition destroyed abandoned villages of the Block Island Indians, responsible for the murders, and sailed on to attack the Pequots, who kept carefully to the forests, forcing the colonists to inflict vengeance more on property than on people. The Pequots sought allies among the Narragansett tribe. But what would have been a powerful Indian confederacy was foiled when the colonists' deployed their secret diplomatic weapon: the liberal (and banished) minister Roger Williams—further proof that the New England Calvinists were practical men.

If Williams was a heretic from Calvinism, he was nevertheless respected, trusted, and liked by the Indians. The Narragansetts took his counsel, refused to make common cause with the Pequots, and made a present of a severed Pequot hand to the government of the Massachusetts Bay Colony as a pledge of their troth.

With the loyalty of the Narragansetts assured—and another trader tortured to death by the Pequots—the colonial governments of Massachusetts, Connecticut, and Plymouth declared war. The colonists and allied Narragansett and Mohegan Indians launched a surprise attack on the main Pequot settlement alongside the Mystic River, torching the native huts and killing the Indians as they tried to flee. The victorious colonial troops pursued the remnants of the Pequot nation as it fled westward. Most of the remaining Pequots were trapped and killed in a swamp; those who fled farther west were seized—and scalped—by Mohawks, who won colonial approbation for their good deed. The few Pequots who survived were sold into slavery: either to their fellow Indians (to whom they became vassals), or to West Indian planters, or to the colonists themselves.

The formal alliance among the New England colonial governments was made permanent in 1643, so that the English would never be divided, as the Indians were. Roger Williams once explained to an Indian "that all the colonies were subject to one King Charles, and it was his pleasure, and our duty and engagement, for one English man to stand to the death by each other, in all parts of the world."[7] It was to the colonists' great advantage that they did. Though Roger Williams's own freethinking Rhode Island was formally excluded from "the United Colonies of New England," its men would fight on the colonists' behalf. Parochialism in the dangerous New World would have been deadly.

This was proved in King Philip's War in 1675. "King Philip" was the English moniker given to the chief of the Wampanoags.[8] Where Philip's father had been content with peaceful cooperation with the colonists, and saw benefits from the Europeans' advanced skills and knowledge, Philip saw only swarming masses of white men who threatened to overwhelm the Indians.

Informants, one of whom was murdered by King Philip's agents, told the colonists that Philip was conspiring against them. While the colonists captured, tried, and executed a handful of seditious Indians, small-scale raids hit frontier settlements, and Indian tribes—not just Philip's Wampanoags—appeared to be on the move, suggesting the possibility of a general Indian uprising.

The war got off to an uncoordinated start. A variety of skirmishes between distrustful whites and Indians erupted into a New England–wide war. King Philip's initial major strikes were at the Massachusetts settlements of Taunton, Rehoboth, and Dartmouth: houses burned, crops destroyed, livestock stolen, and settlers murdered, scalped, and desecrated to the war whoops of the celebrating Indians. Other raids followed, and the tribes committing them were various.

The psychological effect on the colonists was profound. Even friendly Indians were now viewed with suspicion, and some innocent Red Men were transported into slavery and exile. If war the Indians wanted, war they should have, and war often has little place for subtle distinctions. The war led to the largest army in New England's early history: slightly more than 1,000 men—not counting Indian allies and other volunteers—from Plymouth, the Bay Colony, and Connecticut, out of a colonial population of 40,000, all under the command of Plymouth's governor, Josiah Winslow.

The army was marched, through deep snow, to an elaborate Narragansett fort whose construction had been designed and supervised by a renegade settler—but the construction had not been completed. Winslow's army found the gap in the fort and charged through it. The Indians were ready and met the army with fierce musket fire. Men fell, yet their colleagues kept on until they were among the Indians, fighting hand to hand. Torches flew into Indian huts. As Indian braves tried to protect their families and fled, the battle turned into a rout, with heavy Indian casualties.[9] Winslow attempted a pursuit, but it had to be cut short, because his troops were hurting, sick, weary, and short of supplies and had suffered painful losses themselves.

Though the Narragansetts were nearly destroyed, the Indian raids continued on town after town. Well over a majority of the settlements in New England were attacked, with some abandoned completely to Indian flames and pillage. Indian ambushes obliterated entire colonial military units, numbering dozens of men. A colonist who trusted that his Bible would keep him safe from harm had his belly ripped open and his Bible stuffed inside by an Indian. For the Indians, it was total war.

The colonists of Massachusetts were compelled to retreat from all outlying settlements, but it was the Indians who were tiring of the struggle. The new colonial lines were defensible. The Indians were no longer able to pillage for food and had neglected their own harvests in the interests of war. Now it was they who felt their stomachs sticking to their backbones. And things got worse. Indian allies of the colonists captured hostile chiefs and killed them. The colonial militiamen—the only sort of soldiers the colonies had—kept hostile tribes in flight, pursuing, ambushing, and attacking them, with friendly Indians chasing the hostiles whenever the colonists got tired. Philip's men were so worn down by fighting and fleeing that his once mighty uprising had dwindled to but a few followers, and soon he himself was hunted down and killed by an Indian fighting alongside the colonials.

The Puritans who were opposed to maypoles had no objection to planting King Philip's head on a pole in Plymouth so that passing Indians with thoughts of rebellion would recognize that the wages of rebellion were death. They got the point. The tribes that had joined with King Philip surrendered and, like the Indians who had rebelled in the Pequot War, were sold into slavery. The end of the war meant the end of fear for the colonists—at least with regard to the Indians. Now all they had to worry about were the papists of New France, against whom they nurtured constant dreams of conquest.

BACON'S REBELLION

IN VIRGINIA, THE DESIRED imperial acquisition was not yet Canada, but the vast western frontier—a frontier made dangerous by Indians, Indians who in their warfare made no distinction between combatant and noncombatant; and the colonists and frontiersmen responded in kind. Still, the governor of Virginia, Sir William Berkeley, took the well-balanced, tolerant, English view that a distinction should be made between friendly Indians and hostiles. Frontiersmen found this distinction too subtle and were early exponents of the theory that the only good Indian is a dead Indian.

The frontiersmen, being common people, needed a leader. The aristocratic Nathaniel Bacon stepped forward and became their demagogue, rallying them against the effete, elitist liberalism of Governor Berkeley—though in fact the elderly governor (he was now nearly seventy) had been an Indian fighter himself, albeit one who thought it was important to distinguish friend from foe.

His cousin, Bacon, had no time for such pussyfooting. There was power and influence to be gained in the colony by serving as a tribune of the people and urging Indian extermination. Of particular moment were members of the Doeg Indian tribe who had attacked a plantation, alleging that the planter had not paid his debts. In retaliation, the colonists struck back, and with typical accuracy attacked the wrong tribe—in this case, the Susquehannock. The Susquehannocks retaliated. And Governor Berkeley, hoping to stave off a full-scale Indian war, dispatched Colonel John Washington (great-grandfather of George Washington) and an army of militia—which swelled to 1,000 men when reinforced by militiamen from Maryland—to investigate. Under flag of truce, the chiefs of the Susquehannocks declared their innocence of any wrongdoing. The militia officers refused to believe them and ordered their arrest. They were taken away and immediately killed by their colonial guards. This act of brutality and idiocy (it is uncertain who issued the order) led to a six-week siege of the Susquehannocks' palisaded village. The Indians effectively picked off militia pickets, and the siege ended with the Indians' escape.

The result, in January 1676, was that Virginia's western frontier was aflame with Indian raids. Not just small farmers, but plantation owners withdrew for safety. Among those whose plantation was struck (his overseer was killed) was Nathaniel Bacon. Bacon had been a tearaway at Cambridge University, and once he was married, his father happily bade him farewell to Virginia, in the long tradition of dumping troublesome heirs into the colonies. In Virginia, Bacon's birth, connections, and wealth quickly gained him a place of prominence—indeed, made him one of three councilors to the governor. Black-tempered, imperious, impetuous, and anti-Indian, he took command of the local militia, and in yet another act of murderous incompetence killed the chief of a friendly tribe that he (wrongly) accused of harboring rebellious Susquehannocks.

The Susquehannocks, meanwhile, approached Governor Berkeley with a proposal for peace. They had had their revenge; they asked now only for payment to compensate them for the colonists' crimes. Governor Berkeley was inclined to consider this a reasonable proposal; he did not want Virginia to suffer what the New England colonies were suffering with King Philip's War. So he disbanded his militia force, recalled the House of Burgesses to discuss peace terms, and forbade the sale of gunpowder and ammunition to the Indians. As a further defensive measure, Governor Berkeley asked the frontier settlers to gather within the vicinity of Jamestown. To Berkeley's mind, this offered the settlers protection from Indian attacks and kept the settlers from murdering or otherwise annoying the Indians. To further insulate the colonists, he began building a network of forts to provide a buffer between the two peoples. Moreover, from now on, he declared, the governor and his selected representatives would handle trade with the Indians so that there would be no commercial misunderstandings, and no militia force was to be engaged except on the governor's order.

This did not go down well with the frontiersmen, who saw it as a gubernatorial power grab, a catastrophic and unnecessary sacrificing of their interests to those of the Indians (and of Berkeley), and a clear favoring of Berkeley's wealthy friends over the common settler. Bacon, whom Berkeley denied a militia command, privately bankrolled his own group of Indian fighters to the huzzahs of the frontiersmen, and thus began Bacon's Rebellion against the authority of the governor.

Bacon's war-fighting was of a piece with his earlier efforts. First he engaged the Occaneechee tribe to attack the Susquehannocks—which they did, to bloody effect—then he led his own men against the Occaneechees, slaughtering them and burning down their huts (with Indian families inside). Bacon's strategy and tactics were guided not by murderous whimsy, but by a conscious effort to instigate war between the tribes. This, he reckoned, was the quickest way to dispense with all the Indians. And to the common man, he was right, a hero, and a military genius. To Governor Berkeley, he was an intransigent rebel who must needs be brought to heel. Berkeley called him "Oliver Bacon" after Oliver Cromwell, the unpopular (in Virginia) rebel against the Crown of England.

Though he was officially branded a traitor, Henrico County elected Bacon to the House of Burgesses. He traveled to Jamestown with a company of armed men to take up his seat. The governor responded with cannon fire meant to kill, not to salute, the new member. Bacon tried to withdraw under cover of darkness but was captured by the governor's men. The next day, Berkeley appeared before the House, made the case for honoring peaceful overtures from the Indians, and then, in a coup de théâtre, had Bacon brought to the floor of the House. There Berkeley asked Bacon to acknowledge his guilt of disobedience and to renew his allegiance to himself as governor. Magnanimous in victory, Berkeley pronounced that he (and by the governor's authority, God) forgave Bacon. He even mentioned the possibility of a military commission. So all should have been well.

But it was not. Bacon wielded more power with the burgesses than Berkeley did. His measures were the ones voted through, the governor's were undone, and war with the Indians accelerated to include most every tribe in Virginia. Berkeley distrusted the successful Bacon and never signed his commission papers. His failure to do so roused another rebellion, with angry frontiersmen marching on Jamestown to get justice for their hero. Berkeley met Bacon and demanded that they settle the affair like gentlemen, with swords drawn. Bacon dismissed that option and instead, by threat of force, compelled Berkeley to sign the commission papers; immediately thereafter, he was off to fight the Indians again.

Berkeley tried to raise an army of his own, but even his supporters believed that fighting the Indians was mete and just, while fighting a fellow Virginia settler and an elected member of the House of Burgesses was folly. Bacon learned of Berkeley's scheme and drew up a declaration that the governor was guilty of various wrongs against the commonwealth. He cajoled the burgesses into endorsing the indictment—it must be said, against their better judgment—and thus began a two-front war. Bacon resumed his fight with the Indians, but now also offered a military challenge to the governor. In the classic link between highest and lowest, Governor Berkeley offered indentured servants their freedom and liberation from taxes if they took up arms on his behalf. They did, and the governor regained Jamestown, only to then have it besieged by Bacon, who offered indentured servants the same bribe of freedom (including freedom for black slaves) if they rallied to him.

Bacon took the city and set it aflame (at night, so that its shock value would be the greater), and to finish his victory he set about plundering the estates of the governor's supporters. The plundering stopped when Bacon, debilitated by sickness, died in October 1676. Governor Berkeley was back in command, and he mopped up those few who refused to submit. The rebellion was over.

The consequences, however, were not. Troops arrived from England. Their officers' investigation concluded that there was plenty of blame to go around for the rebellion. Bacon was surely a rebel, but his cause gained support because many of his grievances against the governor were well founded. The Crown supported the governor's efforts for peace with the Indians, thought it shocking and ludicrous that the settlers should fight friendly Indians, and considered it absurd that they should refuse taxes to pay for wars against hostile Indians—a problem that would arise again after the French and Indian War and lead to the unpleasantness of 1776. At the same time, the Crown found fault with the governor's tax regime, which was high even before the Indian Wars, and with the high salaries drawn by Berkeley's administration. In addition, the Crown held Berkeley responsible for alienating the people so that only a small fraction of the colony supported him. The Crown offered amnesty to the rebels and recalled Berkeley to England. It was a typically fair-minded and honest English audit of the situation, a situation that illustrated that the colonies were already well versed in self-government and that the Crown intervened only—and then lightly, as a sort of referee—when the Marquis of Queensbury rules, to use an anachronistic metaphor, were not observed in colonial political disputes.

In the meantime, English settlements continued to expand. South Carolina pushed—that is, fought—against Indians and the Floridian outpost of imperial Spain. Frontiersmen pressed west. But the great challenge was in the north, in New France. The governor-general of New France, Louis de Buade, the Comte de Frontenac, saw Quebec as "the future capital of a great empire." The Anglo-Americans regarded that empire as their own, the French as interlopers on their continent. Conquering Canada remained an American priority for more than a century.

THE RIVALS

THE GREAT NORTH AMERICAN struggle between France and England was a second hundred years' war, spanning King William's War (1689–97), Queen Anne's War (1702–13), King George's War (1744–48), the French and Indian War (1754–63), and even the American War of Independence (1775–83). The Indians, the Iroquois especially, were central to the first four of these wars—indeed, they were wedged directly between the European combatants.

In the south, there were other Indian wars. The most important for English settlers were the wars in the Carolinas: the Tuscarora War (1711–13) in North Carolina, which led to the tribe's defeat and exile north to become the sixth nation of the Iroquois Confederation; and the Yamasee War (1715–17) in South Carolina, which almost drove white settlers from the colony—until they formed an alliance with the Cherokee and the colony of Virginia against the Yamasee. The French had their own skirmishes with hostile Indians throughout the American interior from Alabama to Canada. But the geographical pivot that determined the fate of empires was the Ohio Valley.

If you look at a map of the United States and trace the Allegheny and Blue Ridge mountains, you can see how they form a natural barrier. England's colonists were on the coastal side of that barrier and numbered, by 1754, a million and a quarter settlers. France made claims to the entire interior, via its voyageurs and fur traders who plied the rivers west of the Alleghenies. The white population of French North America was only about 80,000 people, but they were 80,000 mostly single men and fighters, allied with fierce Indians. America's colonists, naturally, refused to recognize French claims to the American wilderness. The Americans already had dreams of a continental empire—dreams that included not just land to settle, but land on which to speculate and make money, land that would make the colonies grow in power and wealth. England was willing to spill its soldiers' blood to achieve these ambitions.

The first French and Indian wars were sideshows of European conflicts, but important enough for those involved. King William's War and Queen Anne's

War (the American fronts of the War of the League of Augsburg and the War of Spanish Succession respectively) followed much the same scenario: French and Indian massacres in New England and, in response, American sieges of Canadian settlements. In Queen Anne's War, Britain acquired Newfoundland, Hudson Bay, and Acadia, and the fighting extended to South Carolina's attacks on Florida, where the Americans destroyed Spanish Catholic mission stations and enslaved the Christian Indians.

In 1733, in the interregnum between Queen Anne's and King George's wars, Georgia was founded by General James Oglethorpe, a military man turned philanthropist. Oglethorpe prudently encouraged Scotch settlers (always good fighters), made alliances with the Cherokees against the Spanish in Spanish Florida, and provided a second chance in his new colony for men and women freed from debtors' prison in England.

The War of Jenkins' Ear (1739–42)—so named because of the parliamentary display of the allegedly Spanish-severed ear of merchant sea captain Robert Jenkins—extended to Georgia, because the war involved a British declaration of war against Spain (and therefore Spain's colonies in Florida and points south). It even led to a British and American joint assault on Cartagena, Colombia. The colonials, both New England and southern, contributed an entire regiment of between 3,000 and 4,000 men for the campaign.[10] Unfortunately, they were defeated—as much by yellow fever as by the Spanish. General Oglethorpe himself battled the Spanish in Georgia and Florida with his Highland Scotch, South Carolinian, and Indian recruits. He could not defeat the Spanish, and they could not obliterate, as they desired to do, the British colonies of Georgia and South Carolina. War's end left the Spanish ensconced in Florida and France holding Louisiana. But England was obviously the coming force.

King George's War (the War of Austrian Succession), which followed two years later, was but a bridge to the cataclysm of the French and Indian War proper (the Seven Years' War). A contemporary observer, the writer Horace Walpole in his history of King George II, noted of the beginning of the Seven Years' War that the "volley fired by a young Virginian in the backwoods of America set the world on fire."[11] That lighter of the global powder keg was the twenty-three-year-old George Washington.

Washington had been a working surveyor from his teenage years and had recently become a major landowner through his inheritance of Mount Vernon. He was tall and powerfully built, with a stolid, determined demeanor that came from the challenges of outdoor life on the frontier. He had the pride and caution of a man seeking to improve himself, an American gentleman seeking parity among more polished gentlemen. And he was a military man—as potentially every able-bodied male was—raised among military men. His half-brother Lawrence, who became his guardian, had served in the campaign against Cartagena. Lawrence Washington's estate, Mount Vernon (later inherited by George), was named after the admiral who had led the assault at Cartagena, Admiral Edward "Old Grog" Vernon.

Coming from an established landowning family, and with his extensive experience of the frontier, Washington was chosen as an imperial agent of Virginia Governor Robert Dinwiddie, who was eager to get the French out of what are now Ohio and parts of Pennsylvania. In the scramble for land, the governor wanted the Ohio Valley for Virginians. The French refused to budge, and in the spring of 1754, the French captured a fort that the British were trying to establish near what is today Pittsburgh. The French built a much larger fort, which they named Fort Duquesne.

Lieutenant Colonel George Washington of the Virginia Regiment was on the march to reinforce the British outpost when he learned of the disaster. He took his men fifty miles short of Fort Duquesne, to Great Meadows, Pennsylvania. Here was fired a shot that was heard as far away as India, if not around the world. Washington and his mixed force of Virginians and Indians sprang an ambush on a small French detachment led by Ensign Joseph Coulon de Villiers de Jumonville. Washington relished his first engagement, writing, "I heard the bullets whistle, and, believe me there is something charming in the sound."[12] Only one American was killed and three wounded, to more than ten Frenchmen dead and more than twenty captured. The French ensign was among the dead, or would be after the leader of Washington's Indians approached the wounded Jumonville, split open his skull, and washed his hands with the ensign's brains before going on to the scalping. Washington led his men and prisoners back to Great Meadow, where he hastily built—on ill-chosen, low, and marshy ground— the marvelously named Fort Necessity.

To the French, Washington's ambush was an unjustifiable massacre and murder. Coming to avenge it was the ensign's brother. With a force outnumbering Washington's by more than two to one, he forced Washington's surrender of Fort Necessity and compelled his signature on a document affirming that Jumonville had been murdered. Washington later explained away this embarrassment as being due to his ignorance of French.[13] On 4 July 1754, Washington led his men on a miserable march home.

In 1755, Major General Edward Braddock arrived from England. His mission: avenge Washington, drive the French from the Ohio Valley, and defeat them in Canada—even though France and England were not officially at war, a formality that was delayed until 1756.

Braddock personally led the expedition to attack the French at Fort Duquesne, taking with him as his aide George Washington. Braddock, sixty, had served in the army since he was fifteen, and he knew how to mount a campaign, though Washington noted Braddock's ignorance of America and Indian fighting, and his choleric refusal to take American advice. Still, the campaign was an impressive affair. Axe men leveled trees, and engineers created roads so that Braddock's vast retinue of 150 Conestoga wagons and 1,400 men—which included 2 British (Irish) regiments, 450 Virginia militia, and Indian allies—could advance, albeit slowly, through the wilderness. He was prudent, too, employing scouts and flankers, and had another 500 men marching in reserve. But Braddock did not fight like an Indian, and that would be his downfall.

The French sent a much smaller force—fewer than 1,000 men; two-thirds of them unreliable Indians,[14] the rest Canadian militia and French *soldats*—to a perfectly placed ambush position along the Monongahela River. But the French Captain Daniel Liénard de Beaujeu, dressed in Indian buckskin, inadvertently marched straight into Braddock's advance, only about seven miles from Fort Duquesne. The initial British volleys met their mark, leaving Captain Beaujeu among the dead and sending the Canadian militiamen fleeing. The French and Indians, however, did not flee. They plunged into the surrounding forest, taking cover in the dense foliage, and fired into the red-coated ranks of the British regiments and the blue-coated ranks of the Virginia militia.

The British had discipline, but it is hard to fight an unseen foe. Some of the Virginians charged into the forest to meet the enemy hand to hand, but friendly fire soon made that too dangerous; others sought cover themselves; still others simply fled. Only the British preferred to fight in the open—or were forced to by their officers, angrier at indiscipline than fearful of crackling French and Indian musket fire. British troops were aligned in firing lines along the road; some, in massed ranks, marched after the invisible enemy, into woods that reverberated with the Indians' blood-chilling war cries and the fearful snap of musket balls clipping foliage, and men. Among those furiously rebuking the troops who tried to break and run or take cover was General Braddock. He and his horse-borne officers were the easiest targets of all, relentlessly picked off by the French and Indians. More than 60 British and American officers—better than two-thirds of those present—were killed or wounded, as were all but 459 of the 1,400 other ranks.

No amount of encouragement, as Washington saw to his disgust, could now prevent a rout—a rout sped by Indian scalping parties who preyed on the wounded and burned at the stake some of the prisoners they captured. Braddock himself was mortally wounded. Courageous throughout the fighting and the retreat—five horses were shot from beneath him (two were shot from beneath Washington)—Braddock confessed his surprise, "Who would have thought it?" He died two days after the battle, his final words those of a gallant officer: "Another time we shall know how better to deal with them."[15] The battle did indeed offer a bloody lesson. But in the short term, the entire campaign, which began in such splendor—and which seemed on the verge of success, with troops and artillery only seven miles from Fort Duquesne—ended as a catastrophe, and as another nightmare retreat for Washington.

CHAPTER 2

WOLFE'S TRIUMPH AND PONTIAC'S REBELLION

BRADDOCK'S DISASTER WAS TYPICAL of British military history—first the calamitous defeat, then the campaign to stunning victory led, preferably, by a memorable commander. That would hold true in the French and Indian War as well. Assisting the British, of course, were the colonials. George Washington was given command of Virginia's troops and spent much of his wartime service again on the frontier, fighting Indians, joining in the capture of Fort Duquesne in 1758, and serving under the command of General John Forbes of the British army.

But for most Americans, the French and Indian War (or Seven Years' War) meant defending the family farm from French and Indian raids. Otherwise life went on as usual. Colonial traders, in the true Yankee spirit, even kept up their trade with their ostensible enemies, the French Canadians. Major combat operations were left to British regulars.

The British army that fought the war on the colonists' behalf was grappling with France across the globe. The Seven Years' War stretched from Canada to the Caribbean, from the European continent to India and even the Philippines. The man guiding America's destiny sat in an office in London. He was a veteran of "the Blues" (the King's Own Regiment of Horse), a member of Parliament known as "the Great Commoner," and, during the war he was secretary of state, holding Churchillian power and portfolio. He was William Pitt, the Elder, later the first Earl of Chatham. He looked to win North America and India for Britain and to defeat Britain's combined enemies on the continent of Europe: France, Austria, Russia, Sweden, and eventually Spain. With Prussia as his sole European ally, he succeeded.

Our story involves only one front of this global war, but it was a front with heroism and drama enough. After Braddock's defeat, the Indians—save for the

Five Nations of the Iroquois, who wavered but leant most often, by tradition, to the British—chose what they saw as the winning side, the French. And at first it appeared they were right. The British attempted to take Fort Niagara and were repulsed. The Irishman William Johnson—the "Mohawk baronet," whose friendship with the tribe helped him acquire huge estates—finally gave the British a victory, and won his baronetcy, by defeating the French at Lake George.[1] He also built Fort William Henry, but he was defeated in his next engagement farther north on Lake Champlain at Crown Point.

While the British, as a wartime measure, exiled the French Catholic Acadians from their home in Nova Scotia,[2] the French continued to chalk up military victories. In 1756 and 1757, the victories went to the Marquis de Montcalm, who captured Fort Oswego (ensuring French domination of Lake Ontario) and then Fort William Henry, where British Lieutenant Colonel George Munro had been left with a holding force of 2,200 men to face Montcalm's 7,000 troops and Indian allies. Munro's men dug trenches in front of the fort and defended these, leaving the fort's walls as a fallback position. Munro's defense was sufficiently stubborn that Montcalm risked running out of ammunition, and he almost ended the siege and withdrew. An intercepted message from the British, however, telling Munro that he would not be reinforced, changed Montcalm's mind. He delivered the message to Munro, who capitulated to what he now assumed was the inevitable. The French offered generous terms—the British soldiers and civilians were granted free passage—and Munro accepted them.

Montcalm extracted a promise from his Indians that they would behave themselves, and his officers extended all the courtesies of gentlemanly warfare. But enraged by drink and lack of booty, the Indians went on a rampage of murder— "the massacre of Fort William Henry"—sparing no one, women or children.[3] How many people were actually killed is open to wide dispute,[4] but what is not disputed is that the French acted quickly and with honor trying to stop the carnage. Perhaps they knew better the danger of their Indian allies, who had inflicted a similar massacre at Fort Oswego the year before. Captain Louis Antoine de Bougainville, for one, seemed to regret having such barbarous allies as the Indians. On the march to Fort William Henry, he wrote this description of his allies: "Indians, naked, black, red, hollowing, bellowing, dancing, singing the war songs, getting drunk, yelling for 'broth,' that is to say blood, drawn from 500 leagues away by the smell of fresh human blood and the chance to teach their young men how one carves up a human being destined for the pot. Behold our comrades who, night and day, are our shadows. I shiver at the frightful spectacles which they are preparing for us."[5] One frightful spectacle that left a mark on the Potawatomi tribe came from their warriors digging up British graves to find more scalps. They found them—on corpses infected with smallpox. The disease did what no British guns had to do, eliminating the tribe.

ROGERS' RANGERS

LACKING MANY INDIAN ALLIES of their own, the British learned to match their field craft—indeed, in many ways to improve upon it. For where the Indian was untrustworthy and lacking in staying power, the Englishman was steady and enduring. It is a myth that the British never adapted from the battlefields of Europe to the North American wilderness. If it were true that the British were so unadaptable, they would never have built the empire that they did, stretching to every conceivable climate and geography: Canada, India, Australia, Malaya, Africa, the Persian Gulf, the Falkland Islands. On the contrary, under the guidance of John Campbell, the fourth Earl of Loudoun, commander in chief of British troops in North America, the redcoats were specifically trained to fire and reload from the prone position and to use forested cover. The first unit of light infantry to be attached to a British regiment was a unit raised during this war. Just as important was the raising of Rogers' Rangers.

Ranger units were not a new idea. The English had deployed them along the border with Scotland, and the English colonists of North America had used them as an early warning system against Indian attacks. But no ranger unit of the colonial period would match the fame of Rogers' Rangers. They were founded, under the command of Captain Robert Rogers, as First Company of the New Hampshire Regiment in 1755.

They were frontiersmen, hard men, and as their numbers grew they even employed such ruffians as Irishmen and Spaniards, to the scandal of Calvinist New England. But they were also valuable men, paid more than a British regular, and at their best they embodied the motto that one of Rogers's lieutenants, John Stark, gave to New Hampshire: "Live Free or Die."

The Rangers saw their first action at Crown Point, serving under William Johnson's command. Johnson was one of the unit's champions; he valued white men who could match the Indians he so highly esteemed. The Rangers equaled the Indians in stealth, skill with canoe and bateau, scouting, taking prisoners, and killing sentries—and Rogers was not above a little scalping, too. He had his military failures against the French and Indians, who could sometimes beat him at his own game. But he overcame them, in part, by his talent for self-promotion, which maintained his unit's reputation. More important, his military successes proved that his few men could, through sheer aggression, disrupt and turn back forces far larger than the Rangers. In fact, Rogers' Rangers are part of an American military tradition that is often overlooked, given the focus on the United States military as an institution that relies on overwhelming firepower and on America's paramount technological, economic, and industrial might. The truth is Americans have always excelled at small-unit operations from the days of Indian fighting to the U.S. Army Rangers, Green Berets, and Navy SEALs of today.

The credo of the Rangers is found in the famous litany of Rogers' Rangers Standing Orders:

1. Don't forget nothing.
2. Have your musket clean as a whistle, hatchet scoured, sixty rounds powder and ball, and be ready to march at a minute's warning.
3. When you're on the march, act the way you would if you was sneaking up on a deer. See the enemy first.
4. Tell the truth about what you see and what you do. There is an army depending on us for correct information. You can lie all you please when you tell other folks about the Rangers, but don't ever lie to a Ranger or officer.
5. Don't ever take a chance you don't have to.
6. When we're on the march we march single file, far enough apart so one shot can't go through two men.
7. If we strike swamps, or soft ground, we spread out abreast so it's hard to track us.
8. When we march, we keep moving till dark, so as to give the enemy the least possible chance at us.
9. When we camp, half the party stays awake while the other half sleeps.
10. If we take prisoners, we keep 'em separate till we have had time to examine them, so they can't cook up a story between 'em.
11. Don't ever march home the same way. Take a different route so you won't be ambushed.
12. No matter whether we travel in big parties or little ones, each party has to keep a scout 20 yards ahead, 20 yards on each flank, and 20 yards in the rear so that the main body can't be surprised and wiped out.
13. Every night you'll be told where to meet if surrounded by superior force.

14. Don't sit down and eat without posting sentries.

15. Don't sleep beyond dawn. Dawn's when the French and Indians attack.

16. Don't cross a river by a regular ford.

17. If somebody's trailing you, make a circle, come back onto your own tracks, and ambush the folks that aim to ambush you.

18. Don't stand up when the enemy's coming against you. Kneel down, lie down, hide behind a tree.

19. Let the enemy come till he's almost close enough to touch. Then let him have it and jump out and finish him up with your hatchet.

At Lord Loudoun's direction, British officers and noncommissioned officers were sent to the Rangers for training before they were assigned to the newly formed light infantry companies. Though this was all to the good—and proved that American Indian fighters had something to teach British regulars—it did not achieve results quickly enough for Loudoun's career. Given the accumulation of French victories and English failures, Pitt recalled Loudoun in late 1757 and replaced him as commander in chief with Colonel Jeffrey Amherst, now promoted to "Major-General in America." It was a fortunate choice. The forty-year-old Amherst had been a soldier since the age of fourteen. The great historian of the British army Sir John Fortescue judged Amherst "the greatest military administrator between Marlborough and Wellington."[6] The key word might be *administrator*. Amherst was methodical, careful, diplomatic, and fair. His first mission for 1758 was the taking of Louisbourg Harbor at Cape Breton, something Loudoun had failed to achieve.[7]

GRAY'S ELEGY

A VICTORY WAS MUCH NEEDED. The British had just suffered another setback, after 4,000 Frenchmen at Fort Ticonderoga (or Fort Carillon, as the French called it) defeated an assault by 16,000 British troops, including the gallant Black Watch Regiment (the 42nd Highlanders) who suffered 50 percent casualties. Amherst would make good their sacrifice. With him was a thirty-one-year-old brigadier general, James Wolfe. Wolfe, like Amherst, had begun his army career young, in his early teens.[8] He was carrot-topped, skinny, with a pointed nose and a weak chin, emotionally volatile to the point that some doubted his sanity,[9] and in poor health—hardly officer material to look at him. But his father had been a major general, and an uncle was a commissioned officer. Wolfe himself was ambitious and extremely capable. He was an ardent student of the military arts (and humane letters and mathematics) and had seen action on the continent and in Scotland from the age of sixteen. He did not indulge his frail constitution; he pushed it. In his own words: "Better to be a savage of some use than a gentle, amorous puppy, obnoxious to all the world."[10] He had, too, that patriotism—one sees it in Nelson and many other heroes of the British Empire—that disdains all discomforts and even death in the name of duty and heroism. He professed his "utmost desire and ambition is to look steadily upon danger," that he was eager "to die gracefully and properly when the hour comes," and that the question is not "what is convenient or agreeable; that service is best in which we are the most useful. . . . For my part, I am determined never to give myself a moment's concern about the nature of the duty which His Majesty is pleased to order us upon. It will be a sufficient comfort . . . to reflect that the Power which has hitherto preserved me may, if it be his pleasure, continue to do so; if not, that is but a few days more or less, and that those who perish in their duty and in the service of their country die honorably."[11] He was, in short, the sort of man produced by a society that values a classical education. It was an education that provided him the moral framework to have that "fear of becoming a mere ruffian and of imbibing the principles of an absolute commander, or giving way insensibly to the temptations of power till I become proud, insolent, and intolerable. . . ."[12] Instead of that, Wolfe became daring.

To make the landing at Louisbourg Harbor, the British had to avoid fierce artillery fire from the French warships in the harbor and overcome the feuding band of French regulars, *troupes de la marine* (Canadian regulars), Canadian militia, landed sailors and marines, and related forces, who manned the fortress and tried to block all landing sites. Wolfe's men in their landing boats were forced back. But Major George Scott of the light infantry secured a foothold, held it against a French force that attempted to repel him (and that outnumbered him more than six to one), and opened the path for the British advance. Of the ten men who first came ashore with Major Scott, five were dead, and Scott's own uniform bore three (nonmortal) bullet holes.

With the men ashore, the siege began and dragged on, as sieges do, for more than six weeks (June–July 1758). There were gentlemanly interludes—Amherst sent Madame Drucour (wife of Louisbourg's governor) pineapples, she sent him champagne—but the fighting was very real. Madame Drucour could even be seen on the battlements, helping the French artillery fire their cannons; French troopers, allegedly liquored up with brandy, charged the British lines shouting, "Kill! Kill!" And the British meted out Indian mercy to the French Indians—that is, none. Rangers scalped them.

The outcome of the siege was inevitable, especially after the French warships fled. Louisbourg, a major French port, was surrendered; and Amherst, under orders from Pitt, destroyed it. Wolfe was sent to demolish other French settlements, clearing the way for a British assault on Quebec. The British made it clear that European conventions would not restrain them; this time they were going to evict France from the continent.

Louisbourg was the turning point, setting in motion a series of British victories. First came Lieutenant Colonel John Bradstreet's destruction of the French supply depot at Fort Frontenac. Then came the campaign against Fort Duquesne.

The expedition was launched from Pennsylvania, despite the vehement opposition of George Washington, now a full colonel. Washington patriotically insisted that the march be made from Virginia, following the trail his men had cleared with General Braddock in 1755. Instead, British Brigadier General John Forbes—leading a force of Scotch Highlanders and colonial regiments, including the Royal American Regiment[13]—ordered another massive feat of engineering. He commanded the building of a road over mountains, through swamps, and into hostile territory, where a detachment of Highlanders and colonial troops were ambushed and badly mauled. Forbes's army reached Fort Duquesne in time to hear it blown up by the retreating French. A ghastly palisade of severed Highlander heads, kilts strung beneath, marked the final path to the fort.[14]

Forbes's campaign was the last of 1758; 1759 would bring further victories, with Pitt setting out the objectives for Amherst. Brigadier General John Prideaux helped deliver the first. With Iroquois allies, who abandoned him until the battle was won and scalps could be taken, he captured Fort Niagara for the British—or actually, Prideaux's second in command, the Mohawk baronet Sir William Johnson, did after General Prideaux's head was blown apart in a friendly-fire accident. Amherst then captured Fort Carillon (Fort Ticonderoga) and seized and built a fort at Crown Point. The French were in retreat and could only hope to delay the methodically successful British commander.

With Amherst were Rogers' Rangers. Lieutenant Colonel Rogers's narrow escapes from death and the ferocity with which his men fought earned him the Indian nickname of *Wobi Madaondo,* or White Devil. The White Devil notched further notoriety into his musket barrel on this campaign when he was sent against the Abanakis Indians at their village of St. Francis. Amherst's orders to

Rogers were "to chastise those savages with some severity."[15] This he did, evading French ships and pursuers, raiding the village—where he found the Indians in a drunken stupor, although a deserter had warned them of the impending raid—and burning it to the ground. The death toll for the Indians has been estimated between 65 and 200.[16] Also killed was the French mission priest. Unbeknownst to Rogers, a group of Rangers, under the direction of Sergeant Benjamin Bradley, raided the mission church for treasure. While Rogers and his men quickly made their escape from Indians pouring out of the forests after them, Bradley's men made a wrong turn. They intended to make their way to Concord, New Hampshire, Bradley's hometown, but found themselves lost in the White Mountains. There, as if accursed, they disappeared along with their treasure, which included a ten-pound silver Madonna. Some of the corpses were later discovered, but the Madonna lies lost, still waiting to be unearthed.

But of more immediate importance was the summit of the main campaign: the city of Quebec, flanked on either side by the wide Saint Lawrence and the thin Saint Charles rivers. For this operation, Amherst chose Wolfe. British naval vessels, dodging French fireships sent to ignite them, navigated toward the city along a route the French thought impossible, bearing a combat force of 9,000 men.[17] The British landed successfully and a siege of bombardment began. Wolfe wanted to bring the French to battle in the open. To goad them out, he rained destruction on civilians, Quebec's cathedral, and all other points in range of his artillery and sent raiding parties against French outposts. But the French trusted to geography, to the bluffs on which the city was perched and which they hoped would make Quebec unassailable.

The French believed that if they could last until winter they would be safe. They had well-positioned forward defenses on the high ground leading up to the city on its eastern side—where the British had landed—that they assumed could hold the British at arm's length. On 31 July 1759, a frustrated Brigadier General Wolfe attempted a breakthrough, sending British Grenadiers and Royal Americans up through the mudflats (exposed at low tide) and against these French positions. The first landing group charged before the other units could assemble. Musket fire cut them down. Then a sudden rainstorm turned the mud into a slippery mess and rendered sodden muskets useless. The British and Americans retreated, having suffered more than 443 casualties, of whom nearly half were killed.

Though Wolfe had sent destruction into the city and devastated the country-side and its farms, it was the British who were in trouble. A third of his men had come down with fever, and he himself was terribly ill. His officers doubted him. Men were deserting. Uncharacteristically unsure of himself—and even considering a retreat—he asked his three subordinate brigadier generals for their plans. They suggested an attack farther up the river, past the forward defenses that currently had them pinned down, landing on Quebec's southwestward side. Wolfe agreed to the plan but developed the details of the assault himself without further consultation.

On reconnaissance he discovered a narrow footpath, which the French had tried to camouflage, up the stark bluffs that led to the Plains of Abraham behind the city.[18] In the days leading up to his planned attack, Wolfe sent ships on aimless journeys up and down the river to distract the French from thinking such movement unusual. On 12 September 1759, he ordered, as a feint, a naval attack and mock landing at the downstream point of Beauport. That night, ships carrying the real assault force headed upstream.

Wolfe's conduct on this night would make him one of Britain's military immortals. He recited Gray's "Elegy in a Country Churchyard," which includes the line: "The paths of glory lead but to the grave." To his brigadiers he said, "Gentlemen, I would rather have written those lines than take Quebec."

Take Quebec he would, through the luck of the brave. French sentries were expecting a supply boat to come and so were not surprised when the waters stirred. They called out a challenge, and a French-speaking Highland officer named Simon Fraser responded that they were Frenchmen from La Reine Regiment. Challenged by a second sentry, another Highlander and a former Jacobite, Captain Donald McDonald, called out in French that they were a supply convoy. The Scotties saw them through, and Wolfe's force landed successfully at the Anse de Foulon (or "Wolfe's Cove"). Wolfe and his men charged up the steep footpath, musket balls chasing the few French who guarded the approach. On the crest of the bluff, known as the Plains of Abraham, the pipers skirled and the British troopers gathered for their march on Quebec, whose defenders were cannonading against the feint at Beauport.

The gifted French commander, the Marquis de Montcalm, immediately recognized that because his artillery batteries and much of his army were deployed against the feint, Quebec was in jeopardy, and if Quebec fell, so too could the empire of New France. With more than two-thirds of his men engaged against the wrong enemy, he had only 4,500 quickly deployable troops at hand, roughly the same number as Wolfe. But where Wolfe had regulars, Montcalm had to rely heavily on less reliable units of Indians and Canadians. Still, he decided to attack and sweep the British from the Plains.

Had Montcalm waited, 3,000 French troops led by Colonel Louis Antoine de Bougainville could have hit Wolfe's thin red line from the rear. But the marquis thought he must act instantly. Bougainville could not possibly arrive from his positions in the north before the afternoon. In the meantime, Montcalm was outflanked. He must act. He acted so quickly he did not even bother to disengage the troops at Beauport.

The British on the Plains of Abraham were already under fire from French sharpshooters and cannon. Wolfe had his men lie on the grass, though he, of course, did not. Strolling behind them, offering encouragement, he was unfazed by shot and shell—or by an officer falling wounded beside him. When the French formed for the attack, Wolfe arranged his men in a two-deep line, telling them to hold their fire. The French marched—regulars to the center, Canadians on the flanks—and fired along the way. The British remained steady and unwavering. With the French only forty yards distant, the order was given—"Fire!"—and British musketry raked the French and Canadians to devastating effect. The British historian Sir John Fortescue wrote that the volley was "the most perfect ever fired on any battlefield, which burst forth as if from a single monstrous weapon, from end to end of the British line."[19] "Fire!" A second crackling volley crashed into the French. Their lines torn, the survivors fled. "Charge!" The British, with bayonet and broadsword, leapt after them.

Wolfe—handkerchief tied around his wrist, which had been shattered by a French musket ball—led the Louisbourg Grenadiers.[20] He was shot again, but he pressed on; a third wound, this one to his chest, brought him down. He was not yet dead, though he knew death was coming. An officer told him, "The enemy, sir. Egad, they give way everywhere!" Wolfe gave further orders to ensure the French defeat and then uttered his last: "Now God be praised, I will die in peace!"[21] His life ended exactly as he would have scripted it.

Also dying was the Marquis de Montcalm, the great gentleman warhorse of New France. He was shot at the gates to the city, riding in the midst of the troops fleeing from the Plains of Abraham. He held his saddle, dismissed the mortal wound as a trifle, but was taken away to recover.

The French troops behind Quebec's rear walls outnumbered the British attackers two to one. But the governor-general of Quebec, the Marquis de Vandreuil, was no Montcalm. In apparent panic, he ordered a retreat from the city.

A French officer reported that the "loss of the Marquis de Montcalm robbed his successors of their senses, and they thought of nothing but flight; such was their fear. . . . The army abandoned the camp in such disorder that the like was never known." A Jacobite Scotchman who served with the French added: "It was not a retreat but an abominable flight, with such disorder and confusion that, had the English known it, three hundred men sent after us would have been sufficient to cut all our army to pieces."[22]

Among those abandoned in the city was Montcalm. Told that he was dying, the marquis replied, "So much the better. I am happy that I shall not live to see the surrender of Quebec." Montcalm wrote to British Brigadier General George Townsend—who had taken command after Wolfe's death and the wounding of Brigadier General Robert Monckton—telling him: "Monsieur, the humanity of the English sets my mind at peace concerning the fate of the French prisoners and the Canadians. Feel toward them as they have caused me to feel. Do not let them perceive that they have changed masters. Be their protector as I have been their father."[23] That the English would do. In fact, they did it so successfully that, in the long term, they alienated the American colonists, especially the Calvinists in New England, who did not understand leniency to papists.

Those unhappy days, however, were still in the future. For now, it was victory, a victory that had fulfilled Wolfe's final orders, which read, in part: "A vigorous blow struck at this juncture may determine the fate of Canada. . . . The officers and men will remember what their country expects of them, and what a determined body of soldiers inured to war are capable of doing."[24] What they were capable of doing was changing the history of an entire continent, or, as a Protestant minister in Boston, Jonathan Mayhew, divined, they offered the American colonies the heaven-sent opportunity to become "a mighty empire."[25]

The troops occupying Quebec now had to endure a Canadian winter. Some took shelter in the city's Ursuline convent, where Montcalm had been buried in a shell hole. The nuns knit stockings for the Highlanders, nursed the sick and wounded at the hospital, and referred to the British as the "most moderate of all conquerors." Lieutenant John Knox returned the compliment, noting that the nuns were, as a rule, "young, handsome, courteous, rigidly reserved, and very respectful."[26]

Brigadier General James Murray, in command of the city after the departure of Brigadier Monckton to New York and Brigadier Townsend to England, ruled true to the gentlemanly code[27] of fair play, and there was little animosity between the French and the British. The British troopers even cooperated in bringing in the harvest—or what was left of it. The British remarked on the cheerfulness of Quebec's inhabitants, and the carefree ladies of the city happily and diligently taught the befuddled British officers French.

The French army was less accommodating, planning a winter campaign—which didn't happen—to retake Quebec, skirmishing with winter foragers, and fighting the British again on the Plains of Abraham in the melting knee-deep snows of a Canadian spring. Though greatly outnumbered, the gallant Murray decided, like Montcalm, to fight in the open. The only real beneficiaries of this encounter—which ended in an inconsequential but bloody draw, with the British losing a thousand killed or wounded and the French perhaps an equal number—were the Indians. They had by now perfected the tactic of not charging the battlefield until the fighting was over; then they could scalp the dead and wounded, friend and foe, without undue risk. They and the French were finally driven off by the British navy, which was beginning to rule Canada's major rivers as Britain ruled the waves. With the breaking of the ice floes, the navy was finally able to resupply Brigadier Murray's beleaguered garrison. Only one-third of his original occupying force was available for active duty. Combat and scurvy had killed or hospitalized many of the rest.

Still, Murray brought his men out to join General Jeffrey Amherst for the last great campaign—to take Montreal. Amherst led 10,000 men from Oswego, Murray came from Quebec, and Lieutenant Colonel William Haviland, commanding 3,000 men, embarked from Crown Point. The careful planner Amherst was thrilled at the professionalism that allowed three armies to cut separate paths through the vast Canadian wilderness to arrive at a single point, Montreal, at a coordinated time. The French were certainly impressed. They agreed to surrender the entirety of Canada. The date was 8 September 1760.

Because the French and Indian War was part of the European Seven Years' War, the surrender of Canada was not the final word. This came with the Peace of Paris on 10 February 1763, which formalized the French capitulation of North America. For the European powers, more notable than the fall of New France were their own casualties. An astonishing 850,000 men had died fighting—mostly in Europe—during the course of this world war.[28] The great prize to the east, India, had fallen to the British. No power could match British strength on the seas. No power could challenge her imperial reach. But power did not bring peace. The French might have had enough fighting, but the Indians had not.

THE CONSPIRACY OF PONTIAC

THE BRITISH CAME WITH FORTS and settlers; the French had limited themselves to missionaries, voyageurs, and traders. While there were some 82,000 Frenchmen in Canada, and a modest string of them down the Mississippi to Louisiana, Britain's American colonies had a combined population of 1,300,000 people—people acquisitive for land. Among the real estate speculators was George Washington, who in 1767 wrote to Captain William Crawford that "any person therefore who neglects the present oppertunity of hunting out good Lands [in the West] & in some measure Marking & distinguishing them for their own (in order to keep others from settling them) will never regain it."[29] Washington advised this in contravention of British policy, which, he knew, was to conciliate the Indians by limiting western expansion. So he advised Crawford to use hunting expeditions as a cover for finding land. Benjamin Franklin, another practical man, was deeply involved in such expansion, acting as an adviser to the Vandalia Company, a large western land development investment group.

The Indians recognized in Washington and Franklin—and in the colonists' expansionist sentiments—a terrible threat to their independence and way of life. The French might want to convert them to Catholicism, but the Americans thought them benighted heathen to be brushed aside; the French offered the Indians trade and annual gifts, but British General Amherst was more judgmental. Indelibly appalled by the Indians' savagery during the French and Indian War, he forbade all trade with the Indians outside of British forts and ended their annual gift subsidies, depriving the Indians of new guns, ammunition, and liquor.

Indian medicine men prophesied for war, and Ottawa Chief Pontiac took up the call. Formerly an ally of the French, Pontiac built a new Indian alliance of Ottawa, Chippewa, Delaware, Erie, Huron, Kickapoo, Miami, Mingo, Mississauga, Ojibwa, Potawatomi, Sauk, Seneca, and Shawnee. His goal was not America for the Indians, but America for the French—because these were white men with whom the Indians could live, and whose firearms and other trade benefited the tribes. So began Pontiac's conspiracy.

Pontiac and several dozen warriors entered Fort Detroit (on the pretense of performing a tribal dance) and gauged the fort's defenses. Pontiac told Major Henry Gladwin, commander of the fort, that he would return with his tribe in order to further good relations—by which Pontiac meant that his braves would smuggle weapons beneath their blankets and slaughter the white men. The attack was set for 8 May 1763.

An Indian maiden, in the mold of Pocahontas, warned the British commander of Pontiac's intended treachery, and Major Gladwin readied his defenses. He had 130 men under arms (and roughly half that many civilians who could be mobilized), six artillery pieces, and two small ships that could offer covering support from the Detroit River. Pontiac, realizing that his plan had been exposed, ordered his braves to kill outlying English settlers, but to spare the French.[30] Pontiac then asked Major Gladwin to send officers with whom he could negotiate; Gladwin sent two and Pontiac seized them as hostages.

Pontiac's warriors encircled Fort Detroit, cutting it off from outside support. Responding to Pontiac's call for rebellion, insurgent Indians stormed a ring of forts along the Great Lakes, from Green Bay, Wisconsin, down through Indiana, Michigan, and Ohio. Fort Pitt (Pittsburgh) and Fort Niagara in New York were besieged. Indian raids made river navigation dangerous. The western frontier of colonial America was aflame with burning arrows and terrorized by Indian hatchets. In two weeks, Pontiac's Rebellion had every fort from the Ohio Valley to the Great Lakes besieged, captured, or threatened.

But relief was coming for Fort Detroit. Shielded by a covering fog, guided by Robert Rogers, and under cover of Ranger fire support, an expedition under the command of Captain James Dalyell slipped past an attacking party of Indians and into Fort Detroit on 28 July 1763. Three days later, at two in the morning, Captain Dalyell, Rogers, and 250 men prepared for a predawn attack on the Indians. The men stealthily moved out for the Indian camps. The British forces had to cross a wooden bridge over Parent's Creek (known as "Bloody Run" after this engagement). The Indians—warned by French settlers of the impending attack—waited under cover of the forest. As the British crossed the bridge, the trap was sprung. Indian war howls pierced the night and musket fire poured into the British. Dalyell and Rogers led units charging uphill into the woods after the enemy, but the Indians melted deeper into the wilderness. Given the threat of ambush, pursuit was too dangerous. Dalyell ordered a withdrawal to the fort, but the Indians were ready for that maneuver, too. The British were ambushed again and Dalyell was killed. Rogers and his Rangers, however, routed a group of Indian snipers, seized their position, and used it to provide cover fire for the British regulars. When the British were safely withdrawn, Rogers pulled his men out. Two bateaus with swivel cannon firing canister rounds covered his retreat.

Though skirmishes continued along the frontier, Pontiac's Francophile dreams were crushed when he was informed that France no longer held any ambitions in North America. The Indians had succeeded with lightning tomahawk strikes against unprepared garrisons. But they had no artillery to maintain effective sieges, no European ally to help them, and no answer to massed ranks of disciplined British musketry, such as was on the march. In Pennsylvania and Ohio, British troops led by Colonel Henry Bouquet relieved Fort Pitt at the Battle of Bushy Run and subdued the Shawnee and Delaware tribes.[31] The Indians might raid and butcher, but they could not hold and consolidate a position. Nor could they fight off smallpox, after the British gave them smallpox-infected blankets.

Pontiac's Indian allies made peace with the British. In November, Pontiac withdrew from Detroit and tried to revive the dream of a new French and Indian War. But the French told him to *ferme la bouche* and the Indians were apathetic. In 1765, Pontiac ended his rebellion on the understanding that the English were mere leaseholders of Indian-owned land. The British agreed to this distinction confident in the knowledge that it would be meaningless in fact, and in 1766 the Mohawk baronet Sir William Johnson arranged a formal peace treaty with Pontiac and his allies at Fort Ontario. Three years later, a Peoria Indian assassinated the famous chief.

Pontiac's Rebellion brought echoes of Nathaniel Bacon's rebellion of a hundred years before. In Pennsylvania, a gang of ruffians known as the Paxton Boys responded to Indian outrages in traditional colonial fashion—lashing out at peaceful, Christianized tribes who happened to be nearby. The British too acted in their traditional fashion—with hopes for a rational, peaceful compromise: in this case, the Proclamation of 1763.

The Proclamation banned colonial settlement west of the Appalachian Mountains, stationed British troops along the frontier to keep the peace, and gave the Mother Country the responsibility for regulating trade with the Indians to reduce Indian-colonist trade friction. The intent was to appease the Indians. It was not the Indians who protested, of course; it was the colonials, who saw their dreams of western trade, empire, and riches being fenced off by redcoats. But as it was British regulars who had largely fought and won the French and Indian War, British regulars who fought Pontiac and his allied tribes, and British taxpayers—whose taxes were *fifty times* higher than those of the average North American colonist[32]—who paid the bill for these colonial engagements, American protests were given short shrift.

The spirit behind such as the Paxton Boys would thus be diverted from animosity against the Indians to resentment against those seen as the Indians' protectors (as well as the protectors of Canadian papists and of imperial rather than strictly American interests)—the British. The Americans had a tradition of reaching for their muskets when they sensed their interests were threatened, but few Britons, if any, worried about war with America. To the British, the interests of economy and peace made the Proclamation sensible legislation. The British were even sensible enough to leave open the prospect of amendment should westward expansion look more inviting in the future.

The colonists, however, were nothing if not self-interested, and the Proclamation of 1763 suited neither their immediate self-interest to be western land barons nor their longer term self-interest of reaching across the continent to create a massive North American empire. John Adams, like many of the leading founding fathers, felt, approvingly, that America was building toward becoming a mighty imperial power, greater than the one centered on London:

> Soon after the Reformation, a few people came over to the new world for conscience sake. Perhaps this apparently trivial incident may transfer the great seat of empire to America.
>
> It looks likely to me: for if we can remove the turbulent Gallicks, our people, according to the exactest computations, will in another century become more numerous than England itself. Should this be the case, since we have, I may say, all the naval stores of the nation in our hands, it will be easy to obtain mastery of the sea; and then the united force of all Europe will not subdue us. The only way to keep us from setting up for ourselves is to disunite us. *Divide et impera.*[33]

The British had subdued the turbulent Gallicks; now America's elite saw the possibility of an empire of their own.

CHAPTER 3

"DISPERSE, YE REBELS!"

BRITAIN LOST AMERICA by winning the French and Indian War. That was the prediction of a Frenchman, Charles Gravier, the Comte de Vergennes: "Delivered from a neighbor they have always feared, your other colonies will soon discover that they stand no longer in need of your protection. You will call on them to contribute toward supporting the burden which they have helped to bring on you, they will answer by shirking off all dependence."[1]

That is exactly what happened. But it was the work of a minority. John Adams estimated that at the beginning of the American War for Independence, one-third of the American colonists were Patriots, one-third were Loyalists, and the remaining third were uncommitted. In other words, in 1776 perhaps two-thirds of Americans thought the war for independence unnecessary or wrong.[2]

So war was not inevitable, nor, on its merits, did it seem likely. England was the most liberal country of its time. The colonies had been treated with the most lenient of supervision, often described as benign neglect, and the colonials enjoyed a higher standard of living and minuscule taxation compared with the average Englishman. The Americans had a long tradition of self-government given them by the British; and the British had, in the past, rarely interfered with colonial assemblies.

Englishmen were famously devoted to liberty—but the Americans were even more so. With the bureaucracy of London far away, and the untrammeled frontier always beckoning, the pursuit of self-interest was an American hallmark. And Americans could be cussedly independent, as displayed in that most admirable flag, the Gadsden Flag, with its coiled rattlesnake and motto "Don't tread on me."[3]

Ultimately, the American War for Independence happened not because the Americans were oppressed but because they were so free—and Patriots saw no reason to subordinate their interests to those of the Mother Country.

"*I* DARE TAX AMERICA!"

THE COLONISTS RIGHTFULLY HATED TAXES of any sort. They were, less rightfully, experienced lawbreakers. A good deal of the colonial economy was based on smuggling, which the British had largely tolerated—until now, when the Mother Country had racked up what at the time seemed like an enormous budget deficit, a debt incurred in the course of the French and Indian War.[4] As Rudyard Kipling wrote, "Our American colonies, having no French to fear any longer wanted to be free from our control altogether. They utterly refused to pay a penny of the two hundred million pounds the war had cost us; and they equally refused to maintain a garrison of British soldiers. . . . When our Parliament proposed in 1764 to make them pay a small fraction of the cost of the late war, they called it 'oppression,' and prepared to rebel."[5] In short, the American War of Independence was, in the eyes of some Britons, the American War of Ingratitude.

When the British tried to enforce the Navigation Acts against American smuggling, the countdown to war began. To American smugglers, cracking down on smuggling was, of course, an outrage. The outrage spread when Parliament passed the Revenue (or Sugar) Act of 1764, which slashed the molasses duty in half. Given that the old molasses duty was rarely paid at all, an enforced halved duty (enforced by Admiralty courts) was more than some liberty-loving Americans could tolerate. In reaction to American protests, the British repealed the Revenue Act.

The British then tried to raise money with the Stamp Act of 1765, requiring a government stamp on newspapers, legal documents, and other items—a pettifogging act that only a bureaucrat or an economist could love. The British Prime Minister George Grenville explained to Benjamin Franklin that he intended to employ respected Americans rather than British agents as tax collectors and by this prestidigitation make the tax not seem like a foreign exaction. It was, after all, a tax to pay for British troops stationed in America for the Americans' benefit. Franklin and the colonists thought that with the French defeated by Wolfe and Amherst, they no longer needed British troops to protect them; nevertheless, Franklin suggested names of possible candidates, and his choices were appointed.

It did no good. In Philadelphia and Boston, mobs attacked the houses of the appointed men before a single stamp could be issued. From New York to Charleston, the "Sons of Liberty" bullied and vandalized the Stamp Act into preemptive oblivion. In Virginia, Patrick Henry used the Stamp Act to declare that as Caesar had his Brutus and King Charles I his Cromwell so too would "some Good American stand up in favor of his country." When burgesses interrupted Henry with calls of "Treason!" he replied, "If this be treason, make the most of it."[6]

Henry proposed the "Virginia Resolves," seven resolutions, of which the burgesses passed five (though all seven were frequently reproduced). The gist of the resolutions was to declare the Stamp Act void within the colony of Virginia. The withdrawn resolves went further, declaring that Virginians were "bound to yield obedience" solely to "the laws or ordinances of the General Assembly," which was a virtual declaration of Virginian independence. Also withdrawn was Henry's resolve declaring "an enemy of His Majesty's Colony" anyone affirming that His Majesty and Parliament—and not solely the General Assembly of Virginia—could levy taxes on Virginians. One assumes the irony was unintended.

The British parliament responded with its usual leniency and liberality. As opposition to the Stamp Act grew ever hotter, the British parliament repealed it. Parliament insisted that it had every right to impose such taxes on the colonies, but chose not to do so now.

The British government noted the uniform resistance of the colonies, which did not often unite in common cause. It noted the extraordinary claim of the Virginia Resolves that the colonies had the sole and exclusive authority to impose taxes on themselves. And it noted that British troops now had to be diverted from facing down Indians to facing down colonial mobs threatening licensed agents of the Crown. Obviously a fuse had been lit. It could be doused or ignite an explosion.

For King George III what was at issue was a clear matter of principle: the Crown had a right to tax Americans to partially cover the costs of defending North America—surely that was simple enough and no injustice. The king's prime minister, Lord Grenville, and the chancellor of the exchequer, Charles Townshend, might have had justice on their side—the colonies surely had a duty to be law-abiding—but as practical politicians, they were floundering. If the goal of the parliamentary acts was to lessen Britain's national debt, they were a colossal failure. The acts had actually *increased* Britain's national debt. American recalcitrance had made the cost of enforcing the acts several times the revenue received.

But in repealing the Stamp Act, the Americans had apparently been appeased. The colonists' immediate reaction was patriotic jubilation. Loyalty to

King George III was cheered. William Pitt, who pushed repeal in the House of Commons, was applauded as the Americans' ever faithful and heroic friend.

But for Charles Townshend, as for King George III, the matter of principle had to be settled, and Townshend had developed a new way to settle it. In the midst of an impressive, hour-long speech, his voice slickly lubricated with a bottle of champagne, Townshend needled Lord Grenville, whose ministry had fallen after the Stamp Act. Grenville barked in reply: "You are cowards, you are afraid of the Americans, you dare not tax America!"

"Fear! Cowards! Dare not tax America! *I* dare tax America!"

"Dare you tax America? I wish to God I could see it!"

"I will! I will!"[7]

Townshend's proud reply was no empty boast powered by bibulousness. He thought he had struck on the expedient to achieve a British victory. He imposed the "Townshend duties" on various goods that Americans imported: glass, tea, paint, paper, and lead.[8] He felt prepared to argue first principles with American tax protestors. They had granted Britain's right to regulate trade across the oceans, for this had always been the case. It was the innovation of "internal" taxation, like the Stamp Act, that was allegedly oppressive.

But like most distinctions of principle when debated before a mass audience, this became a distinction without a difference. Power, will, and statesmanship would decide the outcome, not hoisting the colonists on their own rhetorical petard.[9] Townshend had other levers of power beyond arguing sovereign principles. He granted additional rights of search and seizure to his regulators. He put colonial appointees of the Crown on London's payroll, snipping the influence of colonial legislatures over these officials. As a sweetener, taxes on colonial exports to Britain of grain and whale oil were removed, increasing colonial sales to the Mother Country.

Townshend died before his duties were enforced. The duties' defenders could notice and tout that, despite every colonial protest, revenues to England did indeed rise thanks to the duties. Moreover, New York had capitulated to the Crown's demands that the colony offer British troops barracks and supplies. And it was apparent that some Americans of the propertied and merchant classes were more worried by the mobs of the Sons of Liberty than they were by British duties.

Critics of the taxes, however, could point to other dramatic developments. They pointed to mob riots in radical Boston. They noted that the colonies had drafted statements of support for Boston's rebels and had retaliated—albeit, with inconsistent ardor—against the Townshend duties by refusing to buy British goods. Americans ramped up their grain exports to Britain, yes, but they felt no gratitude for their expanding market. The Americans were men of commerce, but their loyalty could not be bought—at least not with increased grain exports.

Britain folded once more. In 1770, the Townshend duties were repealed on all items save tea on the pretext that tea—unlike glass, lead, paper, and paint—did not come from England but was imported from India. While Parliament could grant that taxing Britain's own goods was nonsensical, taxing trade between colonial territories made sense. Taxation on tea was a reminder to the colonies that Parliament had the right to levy taxes on any part of the British Empire. King George III, and his new prime minister, Lord North, thought that a tax on tea hardly amounted to oppression; and as another bow to conciliation the number of British troops stationed in turbulent Boston was halved.

BOSTON BULLYBOYS

THE "BOSTON MASSACRE" HAPPENED ANYWAY. The massacre was no massacre at all, but the result of a raucous mob's barracking of a British sentry. It started with taunts and snowballs from Bostonians who made a sport of goading the "lobster backs,"[10] until twenty British soldiers were standing off hundreds of hooligans. For half an hour on 5 March 1770, "Negroes and mulattoes, Irish teagues and outlandish jack-tars"[11]—as John Adams described them—hurled insults, snowballs, and stones at the soldiers. One sentry, struck and knocked over by a club, had jolly well had enough. Regaining his feet, he fired his musket into the mob, and—without orders—so did several other soldiers who had been pushed too far. Three members of the mob were killed, and two were mortally wounded. Propagandists like Paul Revere and Samuel Adams turned this measured act of crowd control into a massacre the like of which had not been seen since Rome had salted the earth of Carthage.[12] The more sober-minded John Adams was the defense attorney for the soldiers and got them acquitted of murder, though two of the eight accused had their thumbs branded as punishment.

After the "massacre" came the Boston Tea Party—a protest, ironically, against the lifting of the Townshend duty on tea. Unfortunately for the British, even removing taxes was unpopular in Boston, because the duty-less tea put tea smugglers at a competitive disadvantage. Thankfully, the Sons of Liberty—from Charleston to New York, but most especially in Boston—were on hand to defend the interests of American smugglers over those of the British East India Company. When Massachusetts Governor Thomas Hutchinson—an American devoted to English liberty and law—refused Sam Adams's demand that British ships bearing tea be turned out of Boston Harbor, Sam Adams's ruffians, disguised as Indians, had their celebrated party on 16 December 1773, taking tomahawks to tea crates and dumping so much caffeine into Boston Harbor that if it happened today they would surely be prosecuted by the Environmental Protection Agency.

The tea party forced King George III to recognize that there was no appeasing the Americans. He pressed Lord North for forcible measures to bring them to heel. These forcible measures the Americans would deem the "Intolerable Acts" (1774). The port of Boston was closed; Massachusetts's government was reformed to shift more power into the hands of the governor and royal appointments; throughout America, British troops, who still lacked barracks, were given quartering rights on private property; and, most appalling to Calvinist New England, Parliament passed the Quebec Act, which gave French Catholics freedom of religion and extended Quebec's boundaries to the Ohio and Mississippi rivers.

Americans cried tyranny (as well as no popery)—and were met with an eloquent rebuttal by Dr. Samuel Johnson. In his famous essay, *Taxation No Tyranny* (1775), he noted the hypocrisy of the colonials who railed against English toleration of French Canadian "popery" while simultaneously trying to lure French Canadians into rebellion against England and the Crown.[13] He mocked the Americans as "These lords of themselves, these kings of *Me,* these demigods of independence" who forget that they are "colonists, governed by a charter." He slapped America's parliamentary defenders—a party that included the conservative reformer Edmund Burke—and delivered his closing blow against men like Thomas Jefferson: "We are told, that the subjection of Americans may tend to the diminution of our own liberties; an event, which none but very perspicacious politicians are able to foresee. If slavery be thus fatally contagious, how is it that we hear the loudest yelps for liberty among the drivers of negroes?"[14]

The answer was that liberty was only part of the story; America's rebellion was also about power. As one American historian has noted: "It was not the British Empire that the patriots rejected or even the imperial system, but only America's subordinate place within it."[15] Americans already had bold ideas about their future. Well before 1776, Americans recognized their manifest destiny. *The American Whig* editorialized in 1769: "Courage, then Americans! The finger of God points out a mighty empire to your sons. . . . The day dawns, in which this mighty empire is to be laid by the establishment of a regular American Constitution. . . ."[16] Benjamin Franklin foresaw, in 1767, that "America, an immense territory, favored by nature with all advantages of climate, soil, great navigable rivers and lakes, must become a great country, populous and mighty; and will, in a less time than is generally conceived, be able to shake off shackles that may be imposed on her and perhaps place them on the imposers."[17]

There were of course no shackles on America, aside from the Proclamation Act of 1763, which was likely to collapse under inevitable westward expansion in any event, and the long-standing Navigation Acts, which confined American trade within Britain's mercantile system. There were certainly no shackle marks on Benjamin Franklin's, or Thomas Jefferson's, or John Adams's wrists. Even the nineteenth-century American historian and patriot Francis Parkman debunked the idea that the colonists were oppressed: "The measures on the part of the mother-country which roused their [the colonials'] resentment, far from being repressive, were less burdensome than the navigation laws to which they had long submitted; and they resisted taxation by Parliament simply because it was in principle opposed to their rights as freemen."[18]

But just as the Cavaliers of the English Civil War were "Wrong but Wromantic,"[19] the founders were "wrong but wrighteous." Men like Tom Paine, Patrick Henry, and Sam Adams were wildly effective agitators, propagandists, and radicals who fanned the flames of insurrection, as they were temperamentally suited to do. The founders, however, skillfully detached them—and reserved for themselves—the actual business of creating the new American empire.

The founders were men like John Adams (who opposed Paine's *Common Sense* with his own conservative-constitutional *Thoughts on Government*); George Mason (a conservative who despised Patrick Henry, and whose Virginia Bill of Rights became the model for the Constitution's Bill of Rights); the Federalists James Madison, John Jay, and Alexander Hamilton; and of course George Washington.

They aspired not to overthrow the British constitutional system (which they in fact adapted), but to make America Britain's equal—or superior. George Washington was an Anglophile. He believed in the ideal of an English gentleman: shaping everything from his manners to his suits (imported from London) to his military service. But he was denied a king's commission because he was a colonial. His business interests had to be conducted through an utterly unnecessary British bureaucracy. He considered it an outrage that the British Empire, in whose interests he was an expansionist, would draw a line on a map granting the western frontier to the Indians. In such circumstances, America had to become an empire of its own. The other George, King George III, understood this point very well. On 26 October 1775, he told Parliament that "The rebellious war . . . is manifestly carried on for the purpose of establishing an independent empire."[20]

The time for talk was over. The fighting had begun.

LEXINGTON, CONCORD, AND BUNKER HILL

GENERAL THOMAS GAGE—commander in chief of British forces in the colonies and governor of Massachusetts—had orders to do whatever was necessary to restore the rule of law in Massachusetts. The first step, Gage thought, would be to seize the armory the colonists had established at Concord. Given that the colony was abuzz with militiamen cleaning muskets, making ammunition, and filling powder horns, it made sense to disarm them, if he could.

He was not dismissive of the risks. He assigned 700 to 900 men,[21] grenadiers and light infantry, to do the job, and started them under cover of night. Cavalrymen were sent on forward patrols. One such group captured Paul Revere, who had been disturbing the peace by shouting that the British were coming—hardly news given that the colonies belonged to Britain. On the morning of 19 April 1775, an advance unit of more than 200 British light infantry led by Major John Pitcairn of the Royal Marines found its way blocked by a line of fifty militiamen on the village green at Lexington. The militia commander, John Parker, gave his orders: "Stand your ground. Don't fire unless fired upon. But if they want to have a war, let it begin here."

The British were also under orders not to fire. They continued to advance, the militia to retreat, and the British Major Pitcairn shouted a challenge: "Throw down your arms, ye villains, ye rebels." A musket shot rang out—most likely not from a militiaman or a British regular but from a knave hiding either behind a stone wall or a villager's window. Pitcairn reiterated the order not to fire, but muskets popped and suddenly there were scattered volleys from the light infantry against the retreating militia. The scent of gunpowder in their nostrils, the British troops charged with their bayonets affixed and had to be re-called by a snare drum tattoo.

It was only a skirmish: eight Americans were killed, nine or ten were wounded, and one British soldier and one British horse were wounded—certainly not enough to dissuade the British from marching on Concord. But the bodies that lay on Lexington Green were a rallying point for the Americans.

At Concord the British failed to discover the hidden munitions, but they did discover several hundred militiamen at Concord's North Bridge. The British troops reacted instantaneously, and without orders, firing at the militia. An American volley came back in force—sixteen redcoats were hit; four officers were killed. The British troops abandoned the bridge and joined the main body of redcoats in the town.

Lieutenant Colonel Francis Smith of the 10th Regiment of Foot, in command of the Concord operation, decided the raid was a bust and that it was time to return to Boston. Then the trouble really began. The return march became a scourging of American musketry—muskets fired from behind trees, rocks, fence posts, all along the route—as militiamen from town after town turned out to fight the lobster backs. That these Americans were Indian fighters became apparent when the British troops found one of their own lying by the roadside: he had been scalped, ears severed, and brains removed, perhaps for a stew.

Despite making every tactical effort—sending out flankers, pausing in the retreat to return fire—the points of ambush were so numerous, the hostile forces gathering around them so many, that the British were eventually ordered to simply run through zones of hot fire, a gauntlet of musketry. Their line of retreat took them back through Lexington. Waiting for them were Parker's militia, who got their revenge by picking off the retreating Britons.

Under a constant hail of musket balls and occasional hand-to-hand combat, running much of the way, the British were exhausted, their ammunition nearly spent, while musket-firing Americans kept after them like endless swarms of hornets. Finally, cannon fire smashed into Lexington, announcing the arrival of a British relief column led by Sir Hugh Percy—1,400 men: Royal Marines, Royal Welch Fusiliers, the King's Own Regiment, and the 47th Regiment of Foot. More cannon shots—and an unauthorized charge by the Royal Welch Fusiliers—forced the Americans back.

The combined British forces—about 1,800 men—now had to execute a fighting retreat against 5,000 to 7,000 militiamen, and in executing this maneuver

Lord Percy proved himself a worthy officer indeed. He moved his men slowly, clearing areas of hostiles rather than sprinting through them, and kept his strongest forces on the flanks to make ambushes more difficult and more costly to the enemy. Even so, it was a hard-fought retreat, and British discipline broke down as the angry, frustrated British troops lashed out at the towns that dotted the remaining fifteen miles to Boston. By the time it was over, the British had suffered more than 270 casualties, the Americans one-third that many. Blood had been shed in a way that made reconciliation impossible.

The British were stunned—even more so as they watched 10,000 American militiamen surround Boston, a number that quickly grew to 15,000 as militiamen from Connecticut, Rhode Island, and New Hampshire joined the siege. The British had expected mobs and trouble, but they had not expected battle on this scale. General Gage wrote: "The rebels are not the despicable rabble too many have supposed them to be. . . . In all their wars against the French they never showed such conduct, attention, and perseverance as they do now."[22]

That war had begun was not in doubt. Only a month later, in May 1775, Ethan Allen's Green Mountain Boys of Vermont—about 200 of them, and an ambitious officer from Connecticut, Benedict Arnold—wrested the forts at Ticonderoga and Crown Point from the British. Allen did so, lest there be any doubt about his authority, "in the name of the Great Jehovah and the Continental Congress."[23] The British force opposing him at Ticonderoga amounted to fewer than fifty invalided troops—such were British fears of imminent hostility or action. The Americans seized cannons—that was the big prize—and plentiful stores of arms and ammunition. The Continental Congress decided, in turn, to seize the initiative and in June 1775 ordered the invasion of Canada.

In the meantime, around Boston, the British prepared for a breakout. The Americans learned of the British plan and prepared to block it. They would force the British to confront them directly at two hills: Bunker and Breed's. The Royal Navy shelled these positions, but to little effect. Even at this early stage of the war, the Americans excelled at preparing fortified positions. The Americans were masters of axe, shovel, and engineering—and so quick were they that they had fortified the hills overnight, surprising the British.

The British commander assigned to drive them off was General Sir William Howe, who, with his brother, Admiral Lord Richard Howe, was a reluctant campaigner against the Americans. General Howe had seen duty in North America before. He had fought with Wolfe at Quebec. Another Howe brother had been killed at Ticonderoga during the French and Indian War. Both Sir William, who held a seat in Parliament, and his brother, Admiral Howe, were public advocates of reconciliation with the Americans. But they obeyed their orders, however regretfully, to achieve that reconciliation by force.

From the Mystic River on Boston's north side, General Howe landed a force of 1,500 men, divided into two striking parties, to dislodge an equal number of Americans. The main body of action brought the Welch Fusiliers, the King's Own Regiment, and the 10th Regiment of Foot marching uphill against the American left, where the defenders were New Hampshire militia commanded by Colonel John Stark (formerly of Rogers' Rangers). A cool and resourceful commander—his men had pounded their own musket balls out of lead taken from the pipes of a church organ—he and the other American officers steadied the men. They commanded them to hold their fire and knocked away their muskets if they had nervous trigger fingers. Major General Israel Putnam gave the famous order, "Don't fire until you see the whites of their eyes."[24]

The British landing force, unsupported by artillery—because they had loaded the wrong-sized cannonballs—charged with fixed bayonets. At fifty yards the Americans volleyed with devastating effect on the Fusiliers, then on the King's Own Regiment, and then on the 10th Regiment of Foot. Almost a hundred men had fallen—every member of Howe's staff had been hit—and the diversionary assault force, under General Robert Pigot, had been similarly stymied.

Only one thing had gone according to plan: the British bombardment of Charlestown, which lay just south of the American positions on Breed's and Bunker Hills. The town was a blossom of flame, and its citizens were fleeing. If this was encouraging to British morale, Howe's next attack on the entrenched Americans was not; it too was driven back. But Howe would not be swayed. He prepared for a third attack. This time, he would have artillery support—the proper cannonballs had arrived—reinforcements had come, and his men stripped off their useless packs, which only weighed them down on the charge.

The Americans had one horrible deficiency—they were virtually out of ammunition. Though they were able to volley against the next British charge, this time the British leapt over the parapets, into the American lines, and into hand-to-hand combat. The Americans fell back from Breed's Hill to Bunker Hill and then retreated in the direction of Cambridge. The British were far too exhausted—and bloodied—to pursue them. Of the 2,500 Britons ultimately engaged in the fighting, nearly half were casualties—225 dead, nearly a thousand more wounded. The Americans had suffered 150 dead and 300 wounded. The British claimed victory. They had taken a well-defended and well-placed position from a determined foe and cleared the Americans from the Charlestown peninsula overlooking Boston. But the Americans claimed victory, too, for they had fought the British in a stand-up battle, repulsed repeated attacks, and inflicted plentiful casualties on the redcoats, the finest infantry in the world.

The Americans might have sensed another advantage—it would be the advantage that in the end would win them the war. The British, under Howe, hoped to end the war through negotiations. The Americans' commander in chief was not interested in negotiations; he was prepared to fight until North America belonged to the American colonists.

WASHINGTON

IF BRITAIN WAS DIVIDED about the war—with reluctant generals and admirals like the Howes and strong parliamentary opposition to fighting the Americans—we should remember that American opinion was divided as well, and that a Loyalist can no more be a traitor than a Patriot is. At the outset of the war perhaps as much as 40 percent of the American population was Tory—that is, loyal to the king and opposed to independence (among them was Benjamin Franklin's son William). The Tories were not merely men of station—after all, there were plenty of landed gentlemen who were Patriots—they were fighting men. Among those joining General Howe were Robert Rogers and his Rangers. Rogers became the commander of Rogers' Queen's Rangers, who in 1776 would have the honor of capturing the spy Nathan Hale and handing him over for execution.

The British needed Loyalist support because Britain's army amounted to only 48,000 men since the chancellor of the exchequer's slashing of defense expenditure after the Seven Years' War. These 48,000 men were deployed from Gibraltar to the West Indies and from London to India. Initially, the Crown thought the American insurrection could be put down relatively easily. The idea persisted that the Americans, who had played so little role in the French and Indian War and who lacked the international experience of the British army and navy, would scatter and run at the sound of British cannon and the sight of British redcoats. General Howe had reason to know otherwise, but such facts on the ground were slow to be accepted among the king's men in Parliament.

Edmund Burke—a conservative, Irish-born Whig, sitting on the opposition benches—knew as well as Howe did that the Patriots would put up a stiff fight;

their violent opposition to change had proven that repeatedly. He tried to remind Parliament that prudence is the prime political principle, that established tradition is a law of its own, and that American protests that Americans be taxed through their own representatives were in keeping with the rights of Englishmen. First principles about British sovereignty and the economic calculations of the Treasury, he argued, would not sway the Americans. They would rightly cling to their traditional rights and liberties, and Parliament should act with that understanding. "Magnanimity in politics is not seldom the truest wisdom; and a great Empire and little minds go ill together," he reminded the House of Commons on 22 March 1775.

George Washington understood this better than did King George III. "The indispensable man," as his biographer James Thomas Flexner has so rightly called him,[25] Washington, more than anyone else, determined the outcome of the war and the direction of the American Republic that followed. Washington had come to see English law as, in the words of Mr. Bumble, "an ass." The king might in theory be worthy of American allegiance. But if this meant misrule, cosseting the Indians, and higher taxes; if it meant snobbish and stodgy bureaucratic pettifogging from London that made an annoyance of normal commerce; and if it meant British redcoats policing American cities like Boston, what was the use of being under the Crown? Liberty was an Englishman's—and an American's—first allegiance, not the king; that was the tradition established by the Magna Carta. Kings would come and go, good ones and bad ones, but all must respect the rights of an Englishman; and it was the aristocrat's prerogative most of all—his role in Britain's unwritten constitution—to protect liberty and property.

Washington was no radical like Sam Adams. He had no desire for revolution per se. His, on the contrary, was the jealous guarding of the rights that came to his blood and station. He was a fourth-generation American, a plantation owner, and someone whose presence and character impressed everyone with its dignity and humility. His character was the fruit of gentlemanly ambition and of his broad-minded, but real, religious piety. He was a vigorous man, earning his way in the world from his early teens, inured to an outdoor life, an experienced soldier, a disciplinarian and demanding superior but an intelligent and understanding one as well. He was no scholar, as men like Jefferson and John Adams (who called him "Old Muttonhead") readily acknowledged, but, like many superior military men, he made up for that by solid judgment, fixity of purpose, and sudden lightning flashes of daring.

As commander of the new Continental Army—he was appointed and the army raised by the Second Continental Congress in 1775—Washington was skeptical of the Yankee militias whose muskets had started the war. True, they had mauled the British on the retreat from Concord, but their musket fire had been distressingly inaccurate and ineffective. Had their positions been reversed, the British infantry would have completely annihilated the militia. If the Americans were to defeat the British in what was soon to be a full-scale war, they would need to be a real army like the redcoats. Instead, what Washington saw were filthy camps, an utter lack of discipline (he instituted the lash), and an incompetence of supply and officering. He took care in the design and distribution of uniforms. He mandated yearlong enlistments. He gathered together the colonies' contributions of men and divided them into regiments and companies. By the start of 1776, Washington had 20,000 men under arms, two-thirds of them enlisted in the Continental Army, one-third in the colonial militias.

British recruiting sergeants had been hard at work, too. As Washington raised his army, so the British had recognized the need to send a larger expeditionary force. By the summer, General Howe had received reinforcements of 30,000 troops. Not only had British units arrived, but so had German mercenaries (dubbed "Hessians" because the majority of them came from the German principality of Hesse-Cassel). They were not immediately engaged, for the front was suddenly in Canada.

The first American invasion of a foreign country came at the end of August 1775, approved by General Washington and under the direction of General Philip Schuyler of New York. The American advance was slow—Schuyler was sick; the Americans were stuck in mud besieging Fort St. John for two months; and Ethan Allen, who thought he could take Montreal with 100 men, the way he had taken Fort Ticonderoga and Crown Point in the spring, had been captured. With Schuyler recuperating, General Richard Montgomery led the American main force. Montgomery was an Irish-born veteran of the British army, had served at Quebec with Wolfe, married an American, and was now a Patriot. When Montgomery arrived at Montreal, the British had withdrawn. For the Americans it was a victory; for the British it was only a tactical retreat.

The capture of Montreal was one prong (this one coming from the south end of the St. Lawrence River) of a two-pronged attack. Coming from the northern side of the river was Captain Benedict Arnold of Connecticut, whose objective was the city of Quebec. His route, through the Maine wilderness, was a seven-week rain- and snow-sodden march of horror that reduced men to eating shoe leather, dogs, cartridge boxes, and other meals-unready-to-eat. When they reached Quebec, they were in no condition to fight and waited for relief from Montgomery's column. It took a month. Then, at 5:00 A.M. on New Year's Eve, as the enlistments of many of the men expired, the Americans launched their attack in the midst of a blizzard. It failed, and more than half the American troop strength was lost: dead (about sixty, including General Montgomery), wounded, or captured. Arnold tried to maintain the siege, but its increasing futility finally convinced him to recall his men. By the summer of 1776, the British had whisked all remaining American troops from Canada.

But then again, 1776 would be a very bad year for the Americans.

CHAPTER 4

FORGED IN BATTLE: FROM 1776 TO VALLEY FORGE

ON 31 DECEMBER 1775, American citizen-soldiers packed their gear and headed home. Their enlistments were up. They had done their bit for liberty; now it was someone else's turn. Washington fumed at their lack of patriotism. Men from Connecticut—who in their clever New England way shaved weeks off their service, calculating their time by lunar rather than monthly allotments—received Washington's especial wrath. "Such a dearth of public spirit, and want of virtue, such stock-jobbing, and fertility in all the low arts to obtain advantages of one kind or another, in this great charge of military arrangement, I never saw before, and pray God I may never be witness to again."[1]

Even then southerners and New Englanders were a different breed. During the invasion of Canada, Washington, who came from the Virginia Cavalier and Anglican tradition, thought it wise to warn Benedict Arnold and his New England troops against alienating the Catholic Canadians: "As the Contempt of the Religion of a Country by ridiculing any of its Ceremonies or affronting its Ministers and Votaries has ever been deeply resented, you are to be particularly careful to restrain every Officer and Soldier from such Imprudence and Folly. . . . You are to protect and support the free Exercise of the Religion of the Country and the undisturbed Enjoyment of the rights of Conscience in religious matters."[2]

Washington enjoined religious toleration. He made a point of treating civilians and farmers well—better than the British did. He was a man of personal honor. And he was, as were many Virginians, looking forward to the eventual end of slavery—he would in fact liberate his slaves in his will. But during the war he was also compelled to defend slavery, not just because he was a plantation owner, but because slaves were weapons the British might use against southern Patriots.

The threat came from Virginia's Governor Lord Dunmore. Dunmore shared Washington's vision of colonial expansion. In 1774 he sent the Virginia militia into what is now West Virginia to fight the Mingo and Shawnee Indians in "Lord Dunmore's War." Dunmore, however, was a Loyalist who opposed independence. At the same time, he was reluctant to fight his own Patriot countrymen. Dunmore and Loyalist Governor Josiah Martin of North Carolina eventually resolved to squelch the rebels by emancipating blacks willing to take up arms for the king.

The specter of a Loyalist black uprising was a nightmare for southern Patriots. Blacks were more than 40 percent of the population of Virginia, and more than 60 percent of the population of South Carolina. George Washington said: "If that man [Lord Dunmore] is not crushed before spring, he will become the most formidable enemy America has; his strength will increase as a snowball is by rolling; and faster, if some expedition cannot be hit upon to convince the slaves and servants of the impotency of his designs."[3]

Dunmore was not opposed to slavery. His was purely a military calculation—and it was a political blunder. The colonists were already outraged that Britain had imported Hessians, let alone enrolled Indians to fight the Patriots.[4] Lord Dunmore's "Ethiopian Regiment" was even more alarming.

Dunmore gave his "Ethiopians" their own uniform and kit, but he made relatively few recruits, fewer than a thousand. The vast majority of slaves remained with their masters—either because they had no opportunity to escape or because they accepted their masters' avidly promoted counterclaims that they would be much worse off as freemen than they were as slaves.

In North Carolina, too, the slaves remained quiescent. But the Highland Scotch settlers of the interior—the most Loyalist ethnic group in the Americas—rose up in favor of the king and marched against the Tidewater. On 27 February 1776, with bagpipes skirling, Scotch ferocity roused, haggis digested, they made a typical Highland charge at Moore's Creek Bridge near Wilmington, and suffered a typical Highland fate: cut down by musketry. The Scotties are wonderful soldiers, as a rule, but they need English officers—and they didn't have them here.

Farther south, the colonial assemblies of South Carolina and Georgia held these colonies fast for the Patriots despite significant Loyalist minorities.[5] The British long considered the South potentially friendly territory—at least friendlier than Boston—if they could land in force and begin taming the rebellion.

The British tried a landing at Charleston, South Carolina, but were foiled by Colonel William Moultrie, commander of the fort on Sullivan's Island that guarded the harbor. Moultrie's cannons, and the fort's soft Palmetto log construction that absorbed naval cannonballs, rebuffed the Royal Navy and kept Charleston for the Patriots.

In Boston, meanwhile, the Patriots gained from victories farther north. At Fort Ticonderoga, Ethan Allen had captured artillery pieces, and Henry Knox— a Boston bookseller and military autodidact turned Patriot colonel of artillery (and an extremely capable one)—embarked on an epic winter adventure to drag these cannons through snow and freezing rivers to Boston, where they were used to fortify positions seized by the Americans at Dorchester Heights, east of the city. The Americans established their positions overnight: again astonishing the British with their colonial speed with pickaxe and shovel. General Howe looked about him and saw Patriots everywhere. He and his naval commanders decided that Boston was simply a trap. He packed his men aboard ships and took them away to New York, a much more hospitable place.

THE BATTLE FOR NEW YORK AND NEW JERSEY

NEW YORK, LIKE the South, had a goodly proportion of Loyalists—in fact, New York provided more Loyalist troops than Patriot troops. And it was in New York that General Sir William Howe would nearly destroy Washington's entire army. Howe arrived off Staten Island at the end of June 1776. Over the next two months, he assembled his force: 32,000 soldiers (including 8,000 Hessians) and 10,000 sailors. With the Declaration of Independence of 4 July 1776 the Americans had put into words what was already manifest on the ground—they were in full-fledged rebellion; the British, however, now had an army that threatened to crush the rebels.

Washington held well-fortified positions in Manhattan and Brooklyn, but as Boston had been a trap for the British, New York became a trap for Washington, as Howe outmaneuvered him. On 22 August, the British landed troops on Long Island, where the Americans held two fortified lines. The forward position was along the Heights of Guan, with forces under the command of Generals Israel Putnam (a tough, old Indian fighter who held overall command), John Sullivan of New Hampshire, and "Lord Stirling" (or, given that his claim to the earldom of Stirling was rejected by the House of Lords, William Alexander), the son of a Jacobite and a veteran of the French and Indian War. The second line was at Brooklyn Heights. The Americans hoped for a replay of Breed's and Bunker Hills. Instead, on 27 August, Howe and his subordinate commanders—Generals Sir Henry Clinton, Lord Cornwallis, James Grant, Sir Hugh Percy, and the Hessian Philip de Heister—expertly maneuvered to hit the Americans' position flank, rear, and front. Though the Americans fought hard and well, they were routed from the Heights of Guan, suffering a thousand casualties and two generals—Sullivan and Stirling—captured. Howe had only to execute the same maneuver against the second American line at Brooklyn Heights, and the Continental Army might be decisively destroyed and its commander in chief likely captured.

Washington hurried reinforcements to the Heights, and as he did so, Howe halted his men. Howe was an advocate of conciliation. He had never wanted to fight the Americans—he had even considered refusing his assignment—and he took every opportunity to let the Americans sue for negotiations and peace. He did so now, sending an invitation to the Continental Congress to negotiate, and John Adams, Benjamin Franklin, and Edward Rutledge turned up to refuse all such offers aboard the flagship of his brother, Admiral Lord Howe.

Even if the rebels would not accept a negotiated peace, General Howe had another strong incentive for caution: he knew that Britain's pinchpenny Parliament might not send him reinforcements. Remembering the perilous losses the army had suffered in Massachusetts, he wanted to keep his casualty figures low. So he waited. He could afford to. All that was necessary was for his brother the admiral to sail up the East River and cut the American escape route from Brooklyn Heights to Manhattan and Washington was bagged.

But the weather intervened. A drenching storm made naval operations impossible. A fog followed, calming the waters and giving Washington perfect cover to bring his entire force of 9,500 men and most of his artillery across the now placid East River. Washington's retreat was brilliantly executed—and he was lucky that Howe rejected suggestions to attack. Israel Putnam wrote, "General Howe is either our friend or no general. He had our whole army in his power . . . and yet offered us escape without the least interruption. . . . Had he instantly followed up his victory, the consequence to the cause of liberty must have been dreadful."[6]

If Howe was a reluctant executioner, he was nevertheless an effective general, and he saw that Washington's escape was temporary. Washington was as easily bottled up on Manhattan Island as anywhere else, and Howe set his men to the task. To avoid civilian casualties, the British general did not attack New York City at the southern tip of Manhattan just across the East River. With Washington's men strung along the length of the island, Howe chose to hit them at Kip's Bay on 15 September 1776, sending British and Hessian troops against the defending Connecticut militia. The militiamen had already been battered by the preliminary bombardment. To Washington's furious dismay they now broke at the sight of charging bayonets. Washington smacked the fleeing Patriots with his riding crop and was ready to charge the Hessians himself when a subordinate grabbed the bridle of Washington's horse and saved the Continental Army's commander in chief from riding to his death or capture. Recovering his composure, Washington knew he had no chance. He must quickly evacuate his men from Manhattan. He withdrew them to the northern end of the island at Harlem Heights. Howe, again, could have pursued and perhaps crushed the Continental Army. But, again, he did not. He had the pleasures of New York to enjoy.

New York greeted Howe as a Tory city—greeted him with the sense of Anglo-American brotherhood that he cherished—and he decided to bask in it. On 16 September 1776, the day after he entered the city in triumph and to cheers, a detachment of British light infantry fought the colonials at Harlem Heights. A British bugler sounded a foxhunt signal that the Americans were trapped. Foxhunting Virginians recognized and resented the tune, and perhaps fought the harder because of it. The British were rebuffed, and Patriot soldiers grinned through black-powdered faces.

The skirmish at Harlem Heights was not enough to stir Howe to action. What did was the "Great New York City Fire" of 21 September 1776, which leapt devilishly from street to street, spreading a fiery panic among the New Yorkers. The British suspected—and found plentiful evidence of—Patriot arson. During the chaos of the fire, which consumed a quarter of the city, suspected arsonists and obstructionists were summarily bayoneted or shot by British soldiers or strung up by Tories. When the city stopped burning, Howe took his own vengeance on a captured American spy: hanging the young, handsome, athletic, and religious Nathan Hale without benefit of trial or clergy. The Patriot's last words, uttered with absolute composure, echoed a line from the play *Cato* by the British writer Joseph Addison: "I only regret that I have but one life to lose for my country."[7] The spirit of Anglo-American brotherhood seemed at an end.

For the next two months, Howe sent his redcoats nipping after Washington—never as aggressively as he should have done, but enough to keep the Americans scrambling ignominiously from pillar to post trying to escape. Washington lost 5,000 men in the process, and so humiliated was his army that New York, New Jersey, and Pennsylvania were for all purposes Loyalist colonies again. If the war for America's independence rested with Washington, it was apparently lost. The British strategy was to isolate radical New England—and Parliament believed that had been achieved. The Continental Congress in Philadelphia—only thirty miles from advancing British troops—had fled to Baltimore. The South was said to be rife with Loyalists. Boston could not hold out forever. And thus there remained only Washington's army to destroy—and it seemed well on its way to annihilation.

Washington's original army of 20,000 men was gone. He huddled across the safety of the Delaware River with some 6,000 men, whose enlistments would be up at year's end. There was no reason to think that many would reenlist. After Harlem Heights, the British continued to mock the Americans by blowing hunting horns as they pursued them. The War for Independence seemed begotten in folly, and consigned to doom.

Washington knew that an increasing number of Patriots were seeking to have him replaced—his record was no inspiration to confidence—and the miserable condition of his men would surely make them prey to despair. They might welcome a change of command, if not outright surrender. Washington wrote to his nephew Lund Washington that "many" of his men were "entirely naked and most so thinly clad as to be unfit for service. Ten days more will put an end to the existence of our army. . . . Our only dependence now is upon the speedy enlistment of a new army. If this fails, I think the game will be pretty well up, as, from disaffection and want of spirit and fortitude, the inhabitants, instead of resistance, are offering submission and taking protection from Gen. Howe in Jersey."[8]

Washington had, however, one great advantage: winter. The British, satisfied with their gains, decided it was time to settle into winter quarters; the Continental Army could be left to freeze. Howe had a welcoming mistress in New York. Washington, mistress-less, thought not of warm fires and hot toddies, but of a bold and stunning stratagem—so bold that his subordinate, General Horatio Gates, refused to participate in it. Instead, Gates stormed off to lobby the Continental Congress to have himself appointed Washington's replacement.[9]

On St. Stephen's Day, when good Christian Hessians were sleeping off their Christmas hangovers in Trenton, New Jersey, the Americans were on the move behind the Delaware River. Well informed by his intelligence agents, Washington sent a diversionary force to the south, at Mount Holly, to occupy the attentions of General Carl von Donop and keep him from reinforcing the Hessian garrison at Trenton; the garrison was Washington's target and prize.

The crossing of the ice-clogged Delaware, in the midst of a blizzard—horses and artillery transported along with more than 3,000 men—was one of the great moments in American history. Not everyone made it. Some turned back. But Washington's main force landed at 0800 hours, unlimbered the artillery, and blasted the pajama-clad Hessians with musketry. At small cost in lives—3 American dead, 6 wounded; 22 Hessians dead, 98 wounded—the Americans made 1,000 prisoners and seized valuable stores of muskets, powder, and artillery.

Washington was not done. Lord Cornwallis responded to the provocation by moving 5,000 troops against Washington, pinning him behind Assunpink Creek. But throughout the war, what kept the Americans alive was daring—the daring learned fighting Indians—and what undid the British commanders was caution, the caution learned from fighting regular armies and from the necessity of conserving the men and resources the pinchpenny Parliament allotted them. It was compounded by overconfidence (we can defeat them tomorrow), and for many British commanders, like Howe, no great enthusiasm for the chore. Cornwallis delayed crossing the creek until morning. Washington did not wait for him. He set up fires and highly visible sentries and trench diggers, while he stealthily moved his men north and on 3 January 1777 sprang a surprise attack on British-occupied Princeton, New Jersey. The outnumbered Britons put up a stubborn fight but had to abandon the city. Washington did not press his luck and marched his men farther north, where they established their own winter quarters in Morristown, New Jersey. The Virginian general had won his coup, boosted the morale of his army, and put grousing subordinate generals in their place.

The British remained convinced that victory was near at hand. Parliament rejected General Howe's request for another 20,000 men, giving him only 2,500 and begrudging him even that many. For all Britain's military successes of 1776, Howe could read a map. Regaining the colonies was still an enormous and unachieved task over a vast stretch of geography. In Britain, taxes were rising to pay for a war fought to make the Americans pay tax—an irony that no Briton found amusing. The political answer was a demand for swifter action and a new strategy for victory. The strategy came from "Gentleman Johnny" Burgoyne, a raffish British general who put himself at the head of the British army in Canada. Burgoyne planned to sweep down on New England while General Howe in New York swept up on the rebel stronghold. Together, they would crush it between them.

Howe had other ideas and pursued his own campaign against Philadelphia. His plan was to move against the city, lure Washington to defend it, and destroy the rebel army. Howe sailed his troops from New York to Chesapeake Bay, disembarking in Maryland, and marched them across Delaware into Pennsylvania, where Washington met him at Brandywine Creek on 11 September 1777. Howe again showed himself Washington's superior, diverting the Americans with a frontal artillery barrage while the main British force swept behind the Americans and caught them in the crossfire. More than 1,000 Americans were lost (200 dead, 500 wounded, 400 captured), but Washington's army escaped destruction and he continued to throw up roadblocks, which were brushed aside, to try to slow Howe's advance. On 26 September 1777 Howe's men occupied Philadelphia, which, like New York, was a mostly Loyalist city. Yet again, the Americans appeared defeated.

Washington tried to re-create his success at Trenton. For Washington, the element of surprise was the one advantage his young army could have over the well-trained and disciplined British regulars. He launched his attack, under cover of fog, at 0500 hours on General Howe and his 9,000 British troops at Germantown. Washington had 12,000 troops—9,000 from the Continental Army and 3,000 militiamen. They struck with the necessary surprise and drove the British back—but only temporarily. The fog proved more of a problem for the Americans than the British. The American commander Nathanael Greene's troops arrived late, having lost their way, and got into a confused firefight with their fellow Americans under the command of "Mad Anthony" Wayne. Amid the confusion of his attackers, Howe showed himself a master tactician under fire, successfully rallying his troops for a well-placed counterattack that routed the Americans. "We ran from victory," Wayne wrote afterward of the disaster, which cost the Americans another 1,100 men (650 in killed and wounded, 450 captured). The battle looked less like the bold dash of Trenton and Princeton and more like disorganized desperation that, instead of salvaging something from the loss of Philadelphia, had allowed defeat to follow defeat. But while Howe seemed poised to win the war for the British, "Gentleman Johnny" Burgoyne contributed to the losing of it.

S A R A T O G A

BURGOYNE'S ARMY CONSISTED of 7,000 men: 6 British brigades, 2 German, a few hundred Loyalists, 1,500 Canadians, and 300 Indian scouts. Their first obstacle was Fort Ticonderoga, but this proved no obstacle at all, as the Americans abandoned the position, sacrificing 128 cannon and stores of ammunition and other supplies without a fight. Burgoyne pursued the fleeing Americans, brushed off their raiding parties, and drove them into Connecticut. Burgoyne was a confident man, and so far his campaign had been so easy that he exulted: "I have beaten them—beaten all the Americans."

Nemesis came in the shape of the dense forests of New York. Burgoyne's numbers had been depleted by the necessity of garrisoning Fort Ticonderoga and other diversions, and his progress was slow because trees—felled by the rebels, to whom such sabotage came naturally—were thrown across the already forest-choked roads he had to travel. Burgoyne's lines of supply and communication were badly stretched, his men tired from the heavy labor of clearing the roads. He sent a raiding party of 500 men under the German commander Lieutenant Colonel Friedrich Baum to Bennington, Vermont. But New Hampshire militiamen disguised as Loyalists, and led by General John Stark, ambushed the would-be raiders, forcing Burgoyne to send another 500 men to rescue them. Of the more than 1,000 troops engaged on Burgoyne's side, more than half were killed or captured (Baum was among the dead). American casualties were only 30 men.

Burgoyne was in trouble. Though he could dismiss Baum's defeat as "little more than the miscarriage of a foraging party," he was well aware of the dangers of fighting in the forests of North America, of the ever-present threat of ambush, and of the difficulty of chasing ambushers down and killing them. The Indians read the auguries and many deserted, leaving him with fewer than a hundred tomahawkers.

More bad news: a British force under the command of Colonel Barry St. Leger was no longer marching to meet Burgoyne at Albany. St. Leger's march had begun with military victories, but he was undone by the flightiness of his Indian allies. American commander Benedict Arnold fanned a rumor among the Indians that the British were getting trounced. St. Leger's Indians filled themselves with liquor to better assess the situation, and ran away. Without them, St. Leger had too few men to fight his way to Albany.

That was one propaganda defeat. Burgoyne suffered another with the death of a beautiful American Loyalist named Jane McCrea. Though she was a Tory and indeed had a British officer as her lover, the rebels made a furious to-do about how she had been allegedly tomahawked by Burgoyne's Indian allies—only a depraved and sadistic redcoat commander would employ such brutes. It mattered not that in reality the rebels themselves had shot Jane McCrea;[10] Patriot propagandists turned the incident into another Boston Massacre.

On the British side, the phlegm of the doughty imperial race was also apparent. As one of Burgoyne's officers wrote: "[T]his campaigning is a favourite portion of life: and none but stupid mortals can dislike a lively camp, good weather, good claret, good music and the enemy near. I may venture to say all this, for a little fusillade during dinner does not discompose the nerves. . . . As to numbers of our foes, I believe them great, mais n'importe, what are we not equal to?"[11]

Unfortunately for Burgoyne, he shared the sentiment that his men were equal to anything. Rather than pull back, which he could reasonably do but which vanity denied, he plunged deeper into the forest, farther from his supply lines, trusting he would capture Patriot stores as he had done at Ticonderoga. His military strategy might have been written by Mr. Micawber: "Something will turn up."

On 19 September 1777, Burgoyne's army arrived at Saratoga—and what turned up were the Americans. The initial fight happened at Freeman's Farm, where Benedict Arnold led Daniel Morgan's Virginia riflemen and a New Hampshire regiment against the redcoats. Arnold, as ever, was an aggressive and intelligent commander, and in the daylong fight he pleaded with his ill-bred, English-born Patriot General Horatio Gates to bring reinforcements to the center of his line. Had Gates done so, the Americans would have carried the day. But Gates refused and by the time he changed his mind—and sent the reinforcements to the wrong spot—it was too late. The Germans under General Baron von Riedesel had reinforced the British line, and the British held on, though with heavy casualties that Burgoyne could ill afford. A relief force under British General Henry Clinton was on the way, but poor communications meant that Clinton was not aware how desperate was Burgoyne's position. So Clinton proceeded leisurely, capturing American forts.

Burgoyne attacked again, this time at Bemis Heights on 7 October 1777, where Arnold and the Polish military engineer Tadeusz Kosciuszko had built stout entrenchments. Though Gates had removed Arnold from command, it was Arnold nevertheless to whom the Americans rallied and who stormed from point to point on the battlefield directing American fire until finally he was wounded in the leg. Burgoyne had suffered 600 casualties at Freeman's Farm; at Bemis Heights he lost another 600 men (four times the number of American casualties) and included in his losses was the inspirational General Simon Fraser, whom Arnold had personally pinpointed for an American sniper.

Vanity or no, such losses compelled Burgoyne to retreat, and on 17 October 1777, surrounded and outnumbered at Saratoga, he and 5,000 British troops surrendered.[12] London was shocked, and France, which until now had restrained itself to assisting American smugglers, saw a chance to twist the tail of the British lion. In early 1778, the French signed a formal alliance with the Americans. Spain, the Netherlands, and Russia also looked kindly on the rebels. Burgoyne's failure had emboldened the powers of Europe against England.

VALLEY FORGE

IF WASHINGTON WAS cheered by the news of Saratoga, his immediate prospects were nevertheless bleak. He was a beaten general who had been pushed back to winter quarters at the inhospitable Valley Forge, where there was little food, few supplies, and limited firewood. Neither the Continental Congress nor the quartermaster department could make due the difference. A quarter of the men he brought to Valley Forge would die there. Some of their deaths could be attributed to canny Yankee merchants who thought it more profitable to sell to the British or to sit and watch until shortages drove prices to their preferred gouging levels.

Washington meanwhile dodged an attempt by Samuel Adams and other northerners to get him fired, and watched with approbation as a German professional soldier, General Baron Friedrich von Steuben, taught the American troops how to drill. For the first time, General Washington could see the makings of a real army.

He would also have a new adversary. General Sir William Howe, a skilled if reluctant combatant of the Americans, resigned. Taking his place was General Sir Henry Clinton.[13] Clinton knew well not to underestimate the Americans. He had fought at Bunker Hill—a victory, but an expensive one in British lives— had tried (and failed) to hold South Carolina for the Loyalists, and then had become commander of New York. He was a stolid officer, competent but cautious, and hampered by Britain's downgrading of the war in North America to a secondary theater. The Caribbean had always been more economically valuable to Britain. Now with France in the war, it was also of greater concern—and hope for gain—than rebellious North America; and, serendipitously, it was more susceptible to Britain's great strength: sea power.

Clinton's orders were to withdraw from Philadelphia, send half his men to the West Indies, and remove the remainder to New York. Britain's North American strategy was to draw Washington's army into the open and destroy it entirely. In an area as vast as North America, this seemed the only solution: destroying the enemy army, rather than holding territory. But what really drove the strategy was London's requirement that victory be achieved on the cheap: without reinforcements—indeed, with forces drawn off to other theaters.

Washington had originally assigned the Marquis de Lafayette to pursue Clinton as he withdrew from Philadelphia. But the fabulously wealthy twenty-year-old French aristocrat (and Washington favorite) was muscled aside by the noisome General Charles Lee, who so bollixed the pursuit that Washington, in a rage, took command himself.[14] The resulting battle at Monmouth Court House, New Jersey, on 28 June 1778, is important chiefly because it proved the benefits of von Steuben's training. Washington's army, which had spent most of the previous year fleeing the redcoats, maneuvered and fought two of Britain's best regiments—the Guards and the Black Watch—to a draw.

The war now came to a sort of standstill. Clinton successfully brought his men to New York and then sent troops to the West Indies, as per his orders. A French fleet under Admiral Comte d'Estaing arrived with enormous show, and little effect. It was the British who finally took the initiative. At the very end of 1778, General Clinton shifted Britain's North American strategy. Rather than focus on the northern states, why not mop up Patriots in the southern states, arouse latent Tory sympathies and militia, and give the British army a more promising area of operations?

Initially, the strategy met with success. The British deftly snapped up Georgia and held Savannah against Admiral Comte d'Estaing's French fleet and a Franco-American combined inland assault to retake the city. Francis Marion's 2nd South Carolina Regiment performed particularly well, in the losing cause, as did Pulaski's Legion, a force of American and European cavalry led by the gallant Polish officer Casimir Pulaski, who was killed. The Americans and their allies suffered 1,000 dead—the majority of them Frenchmen; and Admiral Comte d'Estaing was wounded—while the British lost no more than 150 men. Savannah secured, the British looked confidently to retaking South Carolina.

On the Patriot side, with the rebellion being quashed in the South and petering out in the North the Continental Congress returned to its imperial fixation of annexing Canada. Thinking that a Frenchman might appeal to the Quebecois, Congress dispatched Lafayette. He quickly reported that it was a hopeless cause. With Canada unobtainable, fighting in the North was reduced to bloody Indian and Tory raids and Patriot counterraids.

In another international foray, Captain John Paul Jones of the American Navy was far more successful. A Scotchman and former merchant captain, he had fallen into a bit of trouble in the Caribbean, where he had killed a mutineer. So, in 1773, he came to America, changed his name to John Paul Jones (from John Paul), and two years later volunteered for and was granted a commission in the American Navy. In 1778, he made a couple of perfunctory but important raids on the Scotch coast—important because they jolted British fears of a French invasion.

The following year, off the coast of Yorkshire, England, Jones had his triumphant moment of the war: bringing his ship the *Bonhomme Richard* (sneakily flying Britain's flag) against the British frigate the *Serapis*. Unlike his raids, this was a violent clash of arms: the ships strapped together by Jones's grappling hooks; cannons firing at point-blank range; musket fire pouring into the *Serapis* from Jones's French marines (Jones's ship and most of his crew were French). The British fired back with equally murderous vigor, ripping Jones's ship into splinters, awashing its decks with blood so that one of Jones's gunners cried out for surrender. Jones cracked the gunner's skull with a pistol butt—always a sound response—and exclaimed to Captain Richard Pearson of the *Serapis:* "I have not yet begun to fight!" Captain Pearson finally called a halt to the slaughter, but when Jones took possession of the *Serapis*, it was his own victorious ship the *Bonhomme Richard* that sank. Jones's grit made him an American hero.[15]

More American heroes and victories would come.

CHAPTER 5

THE WORLD TURNED UPSIDE DOWN

I N T H E S U M M E R O F 1779, America added a new ally to its war effort:
Spain. With manpower reserves to draw on from Mexico and Cuba, the
Spaniards expanded their holdings in Louisiana, picked off British forts
along the Mississippi River, and took Mobile, forcing the British to fall back on
Pensacola. Britain's claim to what would become the Redneck Riviera was in
serious jeopardy.

But the prize for the British was Charleston, South Carolina, the jewel of
the South. The day after Christmas 1779, General Clinton embarked from New
York with 5,000 men to take it. The Patriots had twice before repelled British
attempts on Charleston. This time the British, knowing the difficulty of attacking from the sea, feinted a sea approach and landed troops to surround and besiege the city. Charleston surrendered to the British on 12 May 1780. Clinton
gave command of the southern theater to Lord Cornwallis, while he returned
(and took 4,000 British regulars with him) to guard New York against the
French fleet.

The British were hawkish on the South, expecting to roll up North Carolina
and Virginia, even though Cornwallis had only 4,000 men, including Tory militia. Far fewer Loyalists than expected were willing to fight, and even when they
did, they were poor substitutes in equipment, officers, and performance for
British regulars. It was hard for the British to navigate Loyalist American sensi-
tivities. On the one hand, General Clinton's generous and conciliatory treatment of the people of Charleston, including the captured Patriot combatants,
angered the Loyalists who wanted to see treason smited. On the other hand,
when the hot-blooded and ruthless British cavalry commander Banastre Tarleton[1] massacred surrendering Patriot troops at Waxhaw, North Carolina, it
did nothing to increase Tory numbers—it only provided substance to the Patriot charge of British oppression (and typified the fierce and brutal partisan
fighting of the southern backcountry).

In the meantime, the British continued to win. The Continental Congress invested General Horatio Gates with command of the Patriots' southern forces and gave him orders to stop the British and retake Charleston—an assignment that might have better suited Washington. Instead, Washington was left at Morristown, where his men froze and starved in the winter of 1779–80.

In August 1780, Gates drove his men through swamps and a southern summer (sharply reducing his numbers through desertion and disease) to fight the British at Camden, South Carolina. Gates had about 3,000 men fit for combat, the British had about 2,000—but the British were mostly regulars, while two-thirds of Gates's men were militia. The battle was a Patriot disaster. The militia fled, Gates thought it wise to flee with them, and only the giant Bavarian "Baron" de Kalb[2] and a detachment of Continental regulars remained to save American honor, fighting with superb tenacity—de Kalb taking eleven wounds, which finally killed him—in a losing cause. Gates, in contrast, covered 180 miles in three days of panic-stricken flight, causing Alexander Hamilton to wonder: "Was there ever an instance of a General running away, as Gates has done, from his whole army? And was there ever so precipitous a flight? . . . It does admirable credit to the activity of a man at his time of life."[3] Two days later, Banastre Tarleton delivered another British victory by surprising and shattering the guerilla force of famed Indian fighter and "Carolina Gamecock" General Thomas Sumter.

The one hope for the Americans was the French, who in July 1780 landed 5,000 men under the command of the Comte de Rochambeau at Newport, Rhode Island. With the arrival of these French, Washington had gained an army, but he simultaneously lost one of his best generals. Benedict Arnold had never fully recovered from his leg wound at Saratoga and was now, after a stint as governor of Pennsylvania, commander of the Patriot fort at West Point. As an officer, Arnold had been aggressive, brave, and resourceful. As governor of a colony rife with Loyalist sentiment, he had ruled with a generous hand and married a beautiful young Tory.

Like Washington, Arnold believed in trying to conciliate Patriot and Loyalist factions. Like Washington, he was a conservative. But Arnold's hatred for the radicals, his bitterness over continually being passed over for promotions, and his belief that America's future was in reconciliation with England rather than alliance with France led him to join the British. If he had done so openly, it would have been one thing; but he did so secretly, demanding money, as a spy—and he was caught.

The shock to Washington, who had long thought Arnold undervalued by the Continental Congress, was profound. That his spying had been discovered was trumpeted as further evidence that Divine Providence watched over the Patriot cause. That he had abandoned his wife and newborn child in trying to make his escape defined him as a cad. But for Washington there was a more somber conclusion: "Who can we trust now!"[4] The British officer with whom Arnold had dealt, Major John André, was captured. He impressed everyone with his looks, cool courage, dignity, intelligence, and charm. General Clinton interceded for his life. Alexander Hamilton, who was extremely impressed by the young British major, thought that at a minimum Washington should grant André's request for a soldier's death by firing squad rather than the gibbet. But Washington was cold and adamant: André was hanged, just as Nathan Hale had been. To many British, Washington had committed an atrocity.

The British advance in the South continued. Major Patrick Ferguson, a Scotch Highlander, and an admirable man and soldier, raised, commanded, and trained a 1,000-strong unit of Loyalist militia. Ferguson sent a message to the American settlements that lived over the Blue Ridge Mountains: stop harboring Patriot partisans or he "would march his army over and lay waste their country."[5] The "Over the Mountain Men" needed no further provocation to take down their rifles[6] from their cabin gun racks and give the British a licking. Ferguson knew they were coming and arranged his men at the summit of a small crest called King's Mountain. He had about 1,000 men; the Over the Mountain Men numbered 1,400. These wildcats from the hinterland approached King's Mountain under the deep cover of the pine trees that led to the summit and used their rifles to pick off Ferguson's militiamen. Ferguson's men were well trained, but not to fight snipers they couldn't see.

When the rebels finally charged, Ferguson's men drove them back—once, twice—but on the third charge, the Over the Mountain Men overwhelmed the Tory line; too many of its men had fallen to the backwoods sharpshooters. Ferguson, waving a sword, bravely rallied his men for a breakout, but he was shot off his horse by an exploding barrage of concentrated rifle fire and killed. Their charismatic commander dead, the Loyalists threw down their arms—and some of the surrendering Loyalists were slaughtered before the Over the Mountain Men were whistled into restraint. They still hanged a few Tories for good measure, mistreated the wounded, and urinated on Ferguson's stripped body. Wolves and pigs gathered to eat the ill-buried dead.

Loyalists learned a terrible, demoralizing lesson from the disaster at King's

Mountain; the lesson was, don't take up arms for the British: you might get killed. Better to go along and get along. Lord Cornwallis, meanwhile, had lost a gifted officer in Patrick Ferguson, and with him he had lost every incentive to advance into North Carolina. Small and highly mobile American forces like "Light Horse Harry" Lee's dragoons and guerilla fighters like "the Swamp Fox" Francis Marion—harried the British and cut their lines of communication to Charleston. Though British officers were foxhunting men, even that dastardly effective British colonel of cavalry Banastre Tarleton groused about Francis Marion: "As to this damn old fox, the devil himself could not catch him."[7]

Banastre Tarleton did catch an American unit at Cowpens, South Carolina. Unfortunately for him, it was led by "the Old Wagoner" Daniel Morgan, a hard-drinking, fist-fighting sort of feller, who had fought throughout this war and the French and Indian War. Though Tarleton slightly outnumbered him, and had better troops to boot, at this engagement Morgan proved himself the superior commander. Morgan got an inadvertent assist from Lord Cornwallis. Cornwallis overruled Tarleton's original plan of attack—that the two British commanders should combine forces to crush Morgan—and told Tarleton to do the job himself. Not for the first time, British overconfidence proved costly.

Morgan played into that overconfidence. His men were arranged with little cover and with the Broad River behind them, cutting off any hope of retreat. Tarleton thought he had Morgan ripe for the squeezing. For his own part, Morgan wanted his men arranged as they were, with no tempting hidey-hole swamp nearby, because he knew the militiamen under his command "would have made for it, and nothing could have detained them from it." Indeed, he even welcomed an attack on his flanks because that was better "than placing my own men in the rear to shoot down those who broke from the ranks."[8] Accurately gauging the cowardice of one's men is as useful to a commander as gauging their courage.

Morgan put his inexperienced militiamen up front as skirmishers. Their job: volley and retreat. He posted riflemen as sharpshooters behind trees and told them to pick off the British officers. Behind these he had his Continental Army regulars on the slope of a hill. And he held a line of cavalry to protect the retreating militia and meet the British charge. Tarleton came on, as expected, but with such alacrity that some of Morgan's militiamen were cut down before they could make their escape. The British infantry, also in pursuit, ran smack dab into the fire of the Continentals, and Tarleton's cavalry quickly found itself outnumbered. Nevertheless, Tarleton maneuvered well and almost turned the right side of the American line, driving it back; the British sensed victory. But Daniel Morgan was there, reorganizing his retreating men, keeping them steady, and stiffening the line. The militiamen who had retreated to the flanks now swung out and tried to cut off the British. Tarleton fought bravely, but the day was lost—indeed, it was a catastrophe. He had entered Cowpens with 1,100 men. He rode away with only 40 cavalry. Eight hundred Britons were captured, the rest killed or wounded.

Cornwallis made fruitless pursuit of the Americans, wearing out his increasingly ragged and hungry troops, marching them farther and farther from any British stronghold. Nathanael Greene, Rhode Island's "Fighting Quaker," was now the Patriot commander of the southern theater. Having amassed an army of 4,500 men—more than double the number under Lord Cornwallis's command—he gathered them at Guilford Court House, North Carolina. Here he planned to defeat the British. With him was Daniel Morgan, and the strategy was essentially the same as at Cowpens: a skirmish line, sharpshooters and cavalry on the flanks, a second militia line, the lines falling back into a pocket of Continental regulars. And the ground at Guilford Court House made it a perfect rebel position: the British would be forced to approach up a road that was flanked by woods, providing cover for the Americans.

No one can fault Lord Cornwallis's bravery. He chose to give battle, despite the disparity in numbers and the rebels' advantage in terrain. This is even more remarkable given the disastrous defeats at Cowpens and King's Mountain and given that Cornwallis's intelligence told him that he was outnumbered not just two to one, but four to one. It was not arrogance that drove him, but determination. British troops, engaged around the world, were often outnumbered yet victorious. His disciplined redcoats, he believed, would carry the day.

On 15 March 1781, they made their attempt. Banastre Tarleton led the way, clearing an advance for Lord Cornwallis's Highlanders. One thousand North Carolina militiamen, the American front line, fired an eviscerating volley into the Scotchmen. But when the Highlanders roared ahead with fixed bayonets, the Tar Heels panicked and ran. It was no orderly retreat, but a humiliating, fleck-mouthed, full-tilt run.

The British advanced into snipers and the second line of militia. British officers sent parties to winkle out the sharpshooters, and the British advance continued like a juggernaut—even when caught by canister fired by their own cannons. With the British apparently unstoppable, Nathanael Greene ordered an immediate retreat. Cornwallis had taken heavy casualties, at least a quarter of his force, but he had sent the Americans, who had every advantage, fleeing the field. Guilford Court House was his. The problem was: it was worth next to nothing. The British defeated Greene again in a smaller action at Camden, South Carolina. Neither engagement, however, seemed to bring victory against the rebels any closer.

Patriot atrocities kept Loyalists quiet; and without open Loyalist majorities that could dominate the Carolinas there was no way that Cornwallis's meager number of troops could tame the rebellion. Victory lay in one thing only: utterly obliterating the Continental Army. But how could Cornwallis do that with 1,400 effectives? The answer, he decided, was to advance into Virginia; compel Washington and Nathanael Greene to combine against him; force General Clinton—who still sat uselessly in New York—to send a substantial number of troops to Virginia (there was no hope of reinforcements from England); and then destroy the American Army.

YORKTOWN

THE BRITISH ROLLED UP Virginia. Baron von Steuben's militiamen were driven from Petersburg. The Marquis de Lafayette was forced to give way at Richmond. George Washington's plantation was threatened. Banastre Tarleton raided Charlottesville and just missed capturing Thomas Jefferson. Lord Cornwallis combined with Benedict Arnold's 4,000-strong American Legion, a unit of Loyalists and deserters from the Patriots, and plotted further victories.

On the Patriot side, Lafayette united with von Steuben and Anthony Wayne and tried to bring the British to battle, now that he could put superior numbers on the field. He did, near Portsmouth, and received a stinging rebuke from the British. Astonishingly, with Cornwallis defeating the enemy in Virginia at will, General Clinton demanded that Cornwallis send 2,000 men to help defend unthreatened New York. He also ordered Cornwallis to cease his Virginia offensive and instead focus on securing a coastal base for the Royal Navy.

If these orders were an absurdity, they were an absurdity exacerbated by Clinton's indecision, which kept a flow of orders with contradictory assignments flying to Cornwallis. The noble lord finally decided that the only answer to Clinton was to move farther away from him, and he marched his men to Yorktown so that they could be embarked for Charleston, South Carolina.

Clinton combined a petty and quarrelsome nature with indecisiveness and a neurotic fear for the safety of his city. Of course, he had something to defend in

New York: his Irish housemaid and mistress, Mrs. Mary Braddely. Mrs. Braddely came from the Irish gentry but had married a common carpenter, immigrated to America, found her husband an adulterer, and so traded tit for tat by succumbing to Sir Henry Clinton. She did what Sir Henry could not do—manage his finances and bear him children—and he was loath to leave her merely to win the war. Perhaps Clinton agreed with the Marquis de Lafayette's flippant dismissal of Lord Cornwallis: "These English are mad. They march through a country and think they have conquered it."[9] Quite right. Far better to stay at home.

Washington meanwhile had suffered through another wretched winter, put down two mutinies among his men, and waited in resigned expectation for news that the British had reduced his home at Mount Vernon to cinder dust (they never did). But in contrasting General Clinton and General Washington one sees forcibly the wisdom that good mistresses make bad generals. The other thing that can make for good generals is good admirals,[10] and the French admiral the Comte de Grasse had decided that he would join an American-French operation if it were directed at Cornwallis on the southern coast of Virginia. Virginia, he calculated from his navigational charts, was close enough to the West Indies that he could strike there and hurry back to the Caribbean, which was far the more important theater for the British and the French.

Washington, whose strategy for the war had been reduced to gloomy tenacity, seized at this chance to do to Lord Cornwallis's army what the noble lord had proposed to do to his: trap it and destroy it. Washington set up an elaborate feint to make it appear as though he were preparing to lay siege to New York, while sprinting his men down to Virginia and ordering Lafayette to Williamsburg to prevent any breakout escape by Cornwallis.

Cornwallis thought he had little to fear. Besting Lafayette was no problem. Sitting as Cornwallis was on the entrance to the Chesapeake, he was in a position to be easily supported and supplied by the Royal Navy. The Navy, however, had uncharacteristically let him down. The British fleet outraced the French to the Chesapeake; finding them not there, the British assumed that New York was the target, and then had to hurriedly beat back when they realized that the French had come up behind them.

The French landed 3,000 soldiers commanded by the Marquis de Saint-Simon at James Island, Virginia. More American and French troops were gathered at Baltimore waiting to be ferried to the battleground. First, though, the

French fleet had to meet the challenge of Admiral Sir Thomas Graves of the Royal Navy, waiting outside Chesapeake Bay. The two-hour battle between Graves and the Comte de Grasse was technically a draw. But Graves proved himself no Lord Nelson. He failed to attack the French ships as they filed out of the bay (waiting instead for them to form a battle line), failed to occupy the bay when he had a chance to do so (he feared it was a trap), allowed Admiral Comte de Barras to slip into the bay with troops and supplies, and thus sealed Lord Cornwallis's fate. After this "Battle of the Capes" on 5 September 1781, Graves spent five days warily maneuvering around de Grasse before finally withdrawing to New York.

Lord Cornwallis was unfazed, abandoned though he was and with French ships on the waters behind him. He had wanted to fight the Americans; soon they would be here. He also received word from Clinton that Admiral Graves would return with a relief column of British troops. Clinton's vain assurance convinced Cornwallis that his best option was not to lash out, fight the enemy, and, if necessary, escape; he had only to hold on, reinforcements would soon be his, and then he could meet and destroy Washington's army.

He withdrew from outer lines to consolidate a poorly fortified position. He had slightly more than 8,000 men. The French and American allied forces had nearly 18,000. Controlling the landward approaches and the sea, the Patriots and the French had no shortage of supplies. Without the assistance of the Royal Navy, Cornwallis certainly did. The siege began on 28 September 1781. Cornwallis had been told the relief column would arrive on 5 October, but on 5 October, no column had even embarked from New York, let alone landed in Virginia.

The Americans bombarded the British positions by day (while the British took cover) and then traded volleys with them at night. Washington hit the British as often as he could; victory was his if he could pound Cornwallis hard enough and fast enough. On 14 October, the French and Americans (the latter under the command of Alexander Hamilton) seized two forward British redoubts in ferocious hand-to-hand fighting. As the Franco-American lines advanced, their artillery fire became all the more devastating. The British earned a brief respite with a night raid that temporarily disabled the Franco-American cannons.

Cornwallis realized now that he was well and truly in trouble. He gathered whatever boats could be found and tried to ferry men across the York River to

Gloucester Point, which was held by Banastre Tarleton, though Tarleton was himself penned in by American militia and the Duke de Lauzon's Legion of hussars. The latter—whose numbers contained plenty of Irish, German, and Polish mercenaries—were turned out with tiger-skin saddle blankets, scarlet trousers, blue coats, and fur hats. These uniforms did not affright the British, but the weather did. A storm swept the bay, forcing the boats back; when the storm cleared, so had Cornwallis's hopes of escape. He was trapped.

The next day, 17 October, Lord Cornwallis opened negotiations with General Washington. The American commander offered no face-saving "convention" such as "Gentleman Johnny" Burgoyne had arranged at Saratoga; he demanded that the British acknowledge they were defeated and prisoners of war. The British capitulated, but included a snub. Cornwallis did not surrender himself. Pleading that he was indisposed, he sent his second in command, Brigadier General Charles O'Hara, to do the surrendering. O'Hara presented Cornwallis's sword not to Washington but to the French commander, the Comte de Rochambeau. The French nobleman directed O'Hara to Washington, who in turn directed him to one of his own subordinates, General Benjamin Lincoln. So did the British and Americans damn each other's eyes in the courtly eighteenth-century fashion. At the traditional postsurrender dinner in which the victor entertained the loser, the British and French officers acted as fellow professionals and noblemen, chatting amiably, sublimely disinterested in distinctions of friend and foe, victory and defeat. At this display of class solidarity, the Americans grumbled. For them, it was personal.

For Sir Henry Clinton, who had left Cornwallis to his fate at Yorktown, it was his mistress that was personal. As for Cornwallis, Baron Ludwig von Closen of the Franco-American forces noted, "His appearance gave the impression of nobility of soul, magnanimity, and strength of character; his manner seemed to say, 'I have nothing with which to reproach myself, I have done my duty, and I held out as long as possible.' "[11] Cornwallis, like General Howe, had been a prewar advocate of conciliating the Americans, but he had accepted his orders as a good soldier. He would find his reward as governor-general of India, where he won the Third Mysore War, and then as lord-lieutenant of Ireland, where he made the conservative case for emancipating Catholics from the restrictive laws against them. Sir Henry Clinton was eventually appointed governor of Gibraltar, a position well suited to someone who liked to stay at home in a fortress. And as for George Washington—well, he had just won the war.

CHAPTER 6

THE FOUNDERS' FOREIGN ENTANGLEMENTS

O F C O U R S E , T H E W A R was not really over. The British had surrendered an army of 8,000 men at Yorktown, a major blow, but
they still held New York and they still held the rest of the South, or
at least the coastal cities of Wilmington, Charleston, and Savannah.[1] The two
Georges—Washington and the king—wished to fight on, but they were increasingly alone. In Parliament, many Whigs rejoiced at liberty's victory in America.
Everyone else, including the king's ministers, thought Britain had far more important interests to attend to than fighting her American cousins. In February
1782, the House of Commons voted for peace; in March, Lord North resigned;
and the new prime minister, Lord Rockingham, pressed for immediate negotiations with the Americans.

In America, the Continental Army considered that its job was done.[2] The
war raged only on the frontier. There, Indian tomahawks continued to split Patriot skulls, and Loyalist attacks were bitterer than ever. The last major engagement of the war was fought in the Ohio Territory against the Shawnee on 10
November 1782. It was the culmination of a punitive expedition led by George
Rogers Clark.[3]

A peace treaty was inevitable, stalled only by Benjamin Franklin's demand
that Britain surrender Canada. When John Jay took over as America's chief negotiator, he dropped this claim and the Treaty of Paris (1783) was soon hammered out, granting the former colonies the North American continent south of
Canada, north of Spanish Florida, and east of the Mississippi River, as well as
free access and fishing rights to Canadian territorial waters. Contrary to the
1778 Treaty of Alliance between France and the United States, the Americans
agreed to peace with Britain without consulting France. The treaty was both an

American triumph in what it achieved and an act of American unilateralism in how it was agreed.[4]

An estimated 4,400 to 6,800 Americans died in battle in the War of Independence. More shocking is that perhaps twice that number (8,000 to 11,600) died in abysmal—indeed horrific—conditions aboard the fifteen or so British prison ships that were docked in New York Harbor. As in most wars of the period, disease was a far more effective killer than were muskets, swords, and artillery—but disease, in this case, was abetted by abuse.

The war, however, was over, the dead were buried, and despite regional differences, jealousies, and independent-mindedness, the former colonies came together as a nation with remarkable ease, sharing, as every American did, a belief that life, liberty, and property were God-given rights to be protected by law. The Articles of Confederation formalized the lineaments of the Continental Congress, and when Congress realized it needed a stronger basis for its authority, the founders met to create a written constitution.

FOUNDING FATHER OF THE ARMY

KING GEORGE III asked the American painter Benjamin West what George Washington would do, having won the war.

"Oh, they say he will return to his farm."

"If he does that," the king replied, "he will be the greatest man in the world."[5]

That was precisely, of course, what Washington did. So did the army, which was disbanded by Congress in June 1783—though some veterans descended on Congress, protesting their arrears in pay. Congress, which had never treated its soldiers terribly well, fled from Philadelphia to Princeton, its fears of a despotic standing army, especially an unpaid one, confirmed. Thus, aside from the state militias, the new republic was now an eagle without talons, though threats remained.

The British, not surprisingly in such circumstances, were slow to leave—they departed from New York just two days before Washington resigned his commission. Canada remained British, and British forts dotted the upper Midwest (or Northwest, as it was then called). There were Indians on the western frontier. Spain owned America west of the Mississippi and had reclaimed "the two Floridas" (East and West) as spoils of war from the British.[6] France and Britain were still regional as well as global powers, with large naval presences in the Caribbean.

Washington had the foresight that Congress lacked. State militias, he believed, had their place, but they were surely insufficient for the new American empire. Immediately after the war, in April 1783, he proposed that America set up frontier garrisons "to awe the Indians, protect our trade, prevent the encroachments of our Neighbours of Canada and Florida's, and guard us at least from surpizes." He wanted to build a navy without which "we could neither protect our Commerce, nor yield that Assistance to each other, which, on such an extent of Sea-Coast, our mutual Safety would require." And he wanted to establish a military-industrial complex of arsenals, military manufacturing, and military academies "for the Instruction of the Art Military; particularly those Branches of it which respect Engineering and Artillery, the knowledge of which, is most difficult to obtain."[7]

Washington's ally on these points was Alexander Hamilton, who had served under him during the war, most especially at the siege of Yorktown. But even Hamilton thought it wise to delete the reference to military academies, which the Catos of Congress regarded as finishing schools for Caesars on white horses.[8] Washington understood that risk—he had actually repudiated an anonymous plan for a military coup in 1783, warning that it would "deluge our rising Empire in blood"[9]—but at the same time, Washington and Hamilton (unlike John Adams, Thomas Jefferson, and James Madison) had actually served in the Continental Army and knew how necessary a regular army was.

Congress's original idea was for an army of . . . well, 80 men should be sufficient, divided between West Point and Fort Pitt to guard the guns there. The number, though, swiftly became 700 regulars. It took Shays's Rebellion in 1786–87 to convince Congress to expand the army to 2,000 men. The chief object of the army was to guard Congress from the mob and to teach the likes of war veteran Daniel Shays and his tax rebels that taxation with representation would be far more onerous and inescapable than it had been without representation under His Majesty King George III.

Shays's Rebellion was an additional encouragement to the creation of the Constitution, which took all of four months, drafted as it was by men who shared a belief in natural law, were schooled in Roman and British history and experienced in colonial government, and lived amid a self-governing Christian people. Maryland-born John Dickinson,[10] who had served both as a member of the Delaware assembly and as governor of Pennsylvania, set the tone when he said: "Experience must be our only guide, reason may mislead us."[11] The founders were, above all, practical men.

Their purpose was to protect an America that Alexander Hamilton in *Federalist One* referred to as "an empire, in many respects, the most interesting in the world."[12] The Constitution was approved in 1787, ratified in 1788, and finally agreed to by Vermont (which had offered itself unsuccessfully to Canada) in 1791. General George Washington was sworn in as America's first president on 30 April 1789 and would serve two terms (1789–97).

President Washington did not get his way in creating a real army and navy of any consequence—at least not at first. Congress refused to cooperate, even while Indians massacred frontier settlers and mauled the militias. Congress mustered an army of only 2,000 men, nearly half of whom were made casualties by the Indians in a single encounter in 1791, at the Battle of the Wabash, about fifty miles from today's Fort Wayne, Indiana. It is called Fort Wayne because in 1794 President Washington sent "Mad Anthony" Wayne and a better-trained army to defeat the Indians who were raiding American settlements.[13]

The disaster at the Wabash (and the Indians' defeat of General Josiah Harmar the year before) proved that even professional officers—like Harmar and the Scotch-born, British and Continental Army veteran Arthur St. Clair, who had commanded the force at the Wabash—could not overcome the handicaps of having such poorly trained and ill-supplied men fighting a ferocious enemy. St. Clair fought bravely, and so did some of his regulars and even a few militiamen. But the army's losses were catastrophic. Every regular officer under St. Clair was either wounded or dead. St. Clair himself gained nine bullet holes in his uniform, but no serious wounds to his body. Washington was furious at St. Clair for destroying his army and at Congress for being so pennywise and blood-foolish. Even Congress was forced to admit that it shared blame with the War Department for so miserably failing to support the army with sufficient numbers of trained men and necessary supplies.

In 1792, Congress authorized a regular army of 5,000 men, which was styled the Legion of the United States. Washington had hoped to put the swashbuckling cavalry officer "Light Horse Harry" Lee in command, but Virginians were so plentiful in high places that Washington had to give diplomatic regard to other states' jealousy.[14] So he chose Pennsylvanian[15] General Anthony Wayne to lead the new American Legion. Wayne's primary recommendations were his extensive experience in the War of Independence and his aggressive spirit. A natural martinet, he drilled, trained, and disciplined the American Army to a level unseen since von Steuben had whipped Washington's men into shape.

Wayne built Fort Recovery at the site of St. Clair's defeat, handily repulsed

Indian attacks, moved on to build Fort Defiance, routed the Indians at the Battle of Fallen Timbers (1794), and then burned the Indians' crops and harried them until their taste for war was forgotten. The British had been the Indians' suppliers and semicovert ally, but from their redcoat redoubt at Fort Miami they did nothing to aid the Indians or obstruct General Wayne's progress. "Mad Anthony" had made his point. In 1795, with Wayne in command of the area, the Indians signed a treaty surrendering most of modern Ohio and eastern Indiana. The combination of Wayne's fighting and John Jay's diplomacy convinced the British to withdraw from their forts in the upper Midwest; and Wayne warned the Spanish not to try to assert their authority east of the Mississippi River. The first great general of the independent Republic died in December 1796, seven months after Congress decided to change the army's name from the Legion of the United States to the United States Army.

THE UNDECLARED WAR

IN 1793, PRESIDENT WASHINGTON reminded Congress that the United States would inevitably have conflict with other states and needed a military capable "of exacting from *them* the fulfillment of *their* duties towards *us*." It was futile to dream that the United States would be spared "those painful appeals to arms, with which the history of every other nation abounds. There is a rank due to these United States among nations, which will be withheld, if not absolutely lost, by the reputation for weakness. If we desire to avoid insult, we must be able to repel it; if we desire to secure peace, one of the most powerful instruments of our rising prosperity, it must be known, that we are at all times ready for war."[16] In December 1793, the American ambassador to Spain gave vent to the same sentiment, writing home that "If we mean to have a commerce, we must have a naval force to defend it."[17]

These calls to arms were, in part, a response to the great European cataclysm of the French Revolution of 1789. On 21 January 1793, the French revolutionaries guillotined King Louis XVI, and the French Republic became the eighteenth-century equivalent of the Communist International, dedicated to spreading atheistic republican revolution. On 1 February 1793, France declared war on Britain and the Netherlands. Though France had, arguably, nullified the Franco-American Treaty of Alliance by guillotining "the Most Christian King" with whom it had been contracted, the French republicans considered the United States their ally and began fitting out privateers in American ports.

Secretary of State Thomas Jefferson agreed with the French. President of the United States George Washington did not. Washington, like Alexander Hamilton (his secretary of the Treasury), shared neither Jefferson's passion for revolution nor his Francophilia. Washington's and Hamilton's foreign policy became that of the Federalist Party; Jefferson's became that of the Republican Party.[18] Washington announced a policy of American neutrality, which Congress gave force with the Neutrality Act of 1794.

Britain responded to France's declaration of war with Orders in Council that made prizes of neutral ships trading with France. As a result, American ships in the Caribbean were targeted and captured by the Royal Navy. Ignoring calls for a trade war, Washington dispatched John Jay to negotiate a treaty with the British. It was another diplomatic triumph. Signed in 1794 and approved by the Senate in 1795, it established limited American trading rights in the British West Indies, granted America most favored nation status in British commerce, included Britain's commitment to withdraw from its "Northwest" forts by 1796, and resolved outstanding disputes about prewar debts and claims from the seizures of American ships. But the Republicans were furious that Washington had negotiated a treaty with Britain and treated revolutionary France as a potential belligerent.

Washington was eager to avoid conflict with Britain not only because he believed in restoring trade and comity with the Mother Country, but because he believed America had a far greater future if it kept its powder dry and bided its time. "Nothing short of self-respect, and that justice which is essential to a national character, ought to involve us in war; for sure I am, if this country is preserved in tranquility twenty years longer, it may bid defiance in a just cause to any power whatever; such in time will be its population, wealth and resources."[19] His objective was to build the United States into a continental colossus. Until that was achieved, America should prepare for war, but remain at peace.

Washington's famous Farewell Address of 1796, written with the assistance of Alexander Hamilton, devotes most of its length to extolling America's constitutional government and warning of sectional and party jealousies,[20] but it is also a paean to the national interest, in which light these famous paragraphs should be read:

> . . . the period is not far off when we may defy material injury from external annoyance; when we may take such an attitude as will cause the neutrality we may at any time resolve upon to be scrupulously respected; when belligerent nations,

under the impossibility of making acquisitions upon us, will not lightly hazard the giving us provocation; when we may choose peace or war, as our interest, guided by justice, shall counsel. . . .

It is our true policy to steer clear of permanent alliances with any portion of the foreign world, so far, I mean, as we are now at liberty to do it, for let me not be understood as capable of patronizing infidelity to existing engagements. I hold the maxim no less applicable to public than to private affairs that honesty is always the best policy. I repeat, therefore, let those engagements be observed in their genuine sense. But in my opinion it is unnecessary and would be unwise to extend them.[21]

This warning against permanent alliances was in large part a warning against the Republicans making a fetish out of loyalty to France. Thomas Jefferson, the leading Republican politician, thought Washington had been "shorn by the harlot England."[22]

Jefferson, however, lost the next presidential election to Washington's vice president, John Adams. Jefferson had the consolation prize of becoming vice president himself.[23] Adams was an enthusiast for building a navy. In his first presidential address to Congress, he noted that "A naval power, next to the militia, is the natural defense of the United States."[24] This was especially true because revolutionary France was now a growing plague on American shipping.

The French considered the United States a de facto ally of Britain and sent privateers against American merchant ships. So divided were Americans on foreign policy that Jeffersonians actually cheered the French on, arguing that the Federalists' tilt toward England justified French depredations against American ships. The Jeffersonians rabidly opposed the creation of an American Navy, which the Federalists wanted to expand and make independent of the Army. And some of the Jeffersonians looked forward to the international triumph of French republican principles. The Federalists called the Jeffersonian Republicans "Jacobins," after the French radicals. The Federalists were horrified by the French Revolution and thought Britain and America should be natural allies against it. The Federalist senator (and briefly first secretary of the Navy) George Cabot of Massachusetts put the Federalist position plainly. England was at war with revolutionary France, and "If England will persevere, she will save Europe and save us; if she yields, all will be lost. . . . She is now the only barrier between us and the deathly embraces of universal irreligion, immorality, and plunder."[25]

The Federalists saw the contagion of the French Revolution spreading into

America through the Republicans and through left-leaning French and Irish immigrants. So in 1798 the Federalist Congress passed the Naturalization Act, which nearly tripled the time—to fourteen years—that an immigrant had to be resident in the United States before he could become a citizen; the Alien Act, so that the president could expel undesirable foreigners; and the Sedition Act, which allowed the prosecution—and fining or brief imprisonment—of anyone (read Republican) who conspired against, slandered, libeled, or impeded the actions of the American government. The Sedition Act carried its own sunset clause, expiring 3 March 1801.[26]

The Federalist majority in Congress also took action to prepare for war. In 1798, it authorized the creation of a Navy Department and reinstated the United States Marine Corps, which had been disbanded after the War for Independence.[27] Moreover, Congress resolved, as reported by the *Times* of London, "that the President should be authorized to employ the Naval Force of the United States as Convoys for the protection of the American Trade, without waiting until there shall exist an actual state of war between that Country and the French Republic. . . ."[28] A de facto state of war already existed, given that French privateers were attacking American merchant ships. The United States Navy now had orders to fight back. So began America's great Undeclared War with France (1798–1800).

Aside from plundering American shipping, France was prepared to drop a giant Camembert on America's presumed manifest destiny to the continent. In Quebec, within the borders of British Canada, France had the makings of a natural seditious movement to establish a Quebecois republic. Spain—France's weak neighbor—could easily be pressured into surrendering Florida and Louisiana to the French. And on the Mississippi River, France had only to revive the old claims of its voyageurs and renew its alliances with the Indians to shut the United States off from the West.

President Adams tried to appease the French with diplomacy, but his overtures were disdainfully rejected. Then in the "XYZ affair" three French agents—code-named X, Y, and Z—introduced American diplomats to Gallic probity by demanding that if America wanted to negotiate with France, she would first have to pay enormous bribes and provide a $10 million "loan." Of the three American envoys who met with Messrs. X, Y, and Z, the Republican Elbridge Gerry of Massachusetts remained in France fearfully trying to negotiate and avert war. But the two Federalists—John Marshall of Virginia and Charles Pinckney of South Carolina—spurned the French, Marshall even letting them know that "America is great, and so far as concerns her self-defence, a powerful nation."[29] Great America might be, but to call her defenses powerful was more Federalist and Virginian pride than naval and military reality. Marshall and Pinckney returned home and their publicly printed dispatches provided that famous American rallying cry: "Millions for Defense, but not One Cent for Tribute!"

The Republicans were shouted down (though they later tried to argue that the XYZ affair was a Federalist plot), and the new Navy Department launched the first six ships of its naval rebuilding program: USS *Constellation,* USS *Constitution,* USS *United States,* USS *Chesapeake,* USS *Congress,* and USS *President.* As the fledgling American Navy built itself up, friendship with Britain was renewed as the Royal Navy provided protection for American merchant ships crossing the Atlantic. The American Navy, however, fought alone, engaging the French in single ship actions. The Americans, using British naval tactics and displaying great skill at gunnery, came out victorious in every engagement save one, when the USS *Retaliation,* a fourteen-gun schooner, was captured by two French frigates with forty guns apiece. One of those frigates, *L'Insurgente,* was made a celebrated capture herself, when Captain Thomas Truxtun of the USS *Constellation* brought her in. In the course of the brief naval hostilities, the American Navy—grown to fifty-four ships—captured more than ninety French combatant ships.

The success of the young American Navy against one of the great powers of Europe was an extraordinary accomplishment, to which the French responded with apologies, protestations that their intentions had been misunderstood, and an end to hostilities. What should have been recognized as a great American victory, the Jeffersonians tried to turn into a Federalist defeat, claiming that the war was completely unnecessary and entirely the fault of the American government.

The Republicans' nightmare statesman was Alexander Hamilton. Hamilton was for war with France—and not just France, but France's ally Spain; and not just Spain, but Spain's colonies in the Floridas and Louisiana; and not just the Floridas and Louisiana, but Mexico; and not just Mexico, but the conquest of all the Americas. All this was possible, he thought, if the United States formed an alliance with England. An Anglo-American empire would divide the American continents as Pope Alexander VI had once divided the world between Spain and Portugal. Such an empire might provide appropriate places to exile Jeffersonians and would inculcate the military discipline the American people so self-evidently needed.[30] Hamilton's eminently sensible and reasonable proposal, however, was undone by Adams's Yankee frugality and suspicion that Hamilton might use his imperial American army not just for foreign adventures, but for domestic ones. Adams settled for a commercial accord with France and an official, much belated dissolving of the Franco-American alliance of 1778. Napoleon Bonaparte had demanded that the old alliance be fulfilled in France's war against Britain. Instead, the United States paid the French an indemnity to officially void it. As soon as this was accomplished, Napoleon acquired Louisiana from Spain—a sour vindication of sorts for Hamilton.

Sourer still, no doubt—though at the eleventh hour Hamilton's intervention helped ensure it—was the election of the flame-haired Thomas Jefferson as president of the United States. Jefferson's party won a thumping majority in Congress, thanks to the Republicans' rousing the libertarian spirit of the American people against the Sedition Act, high taxes, and the allegedly monarchical Federalists. Jefferson's own election, however, was deadlocked in Congress because his Republican vice presidential nominee, Aaron Burr, had tied him for presidential electoral votes. With political violence becoming a possibility, Hamilton guided Federalist votes away from Burr, and the presidency was handed to Jefferson.

Before he left office, John Adams picked the faculty for the United States Military Academy, and Jefferson—in one of the many delicious ironies of his presidency—signed the legislation establishing it in 1802. Jefferson, to put it mildly, was not the "national security candidate." Being in favor of sedition—at least against monarchs and Federalists—he released anyone imprisoned under the Sedition Act; and being opposed to national defense as a mere excuse for Federalist wars he slashed the Army rolls from 4,000 to 2,500 men and planned to completely dismantle the American Navy, even removing from the government payroll every naval contractor.

But in May 1801, Jefferson found to his surprise that Bashaw Yusuf Karamanli of Tripoli had declared war on him. America had, over the course of a decade and a half, paid two million dollars in tribute and ransom to various Barbary Coast pirates as the price of Mediterranean commerce.[31] Now, apparently, it was no longer good enough. Jefferson, to his credit, refused to brook such insolence. Unfortunately, he had already reduced the Navy to a matchstick force of six frigates and a schooner.

TO THE SHORES OF TRIPOLI

SECRETARY OF STATE James Madison understood—indeed the American consuls in Tunis and Algiers had pressed this idea upon him—that the United

States Navy should have a station in the Mediterranean to protect American shipping. The question was finding the ships to station there. While Jefferson's initial strategy was to blockade the Barbary States—with all of two frigates and a sloop, which, it must be said, did as remarkable a job as possible trying to blockade 1,200 miles of coastline—it took three years for a suitable task force to appear off the coast of Tripoli.

Action followed. Commodore Edward Preble of the USS *Constitution* found that running out his guns in the direction of the sultan's palace at Tangier effected a remarkable change in mood on at least one of the pirate-sponsoring rulers. Preble's success, however, was matched by a defeat: the pirate capture of Captain William Bainbridge's ship, the USS *Philadelphia,* which was attempting to single-handedly blockade Tripoli. The *Philadelphia* ran onto a sandbar—at an angle that made its guns worthless—and was surrounded by the Islamic raiders. Thinking his men had successfully scuttled the ship, Captain Bainbridge surrendered, and he and more than 300 crewmen were thrown into the Bashaw's dungeons. The Bashaw scornfully refused ransom and prepared to kit out the *Philadelphia* as a pirate warship. But an enterprising young naval lieutenant, Stephen Decatur—one of the many great men of the young American Navy— had a different idea.

In metaphorical recompense for the shameful Boston Tea Party, Decatur organized the Tripoli pirate party. He disguised his men as Barbary corsairs, snuck into the harbor, leapt aboard the *Philadelphia,* split open pirate skulls with tomahawks, set the *Philadelphia* aflame, and then rowed back to his own ship, the USS *Intrepid,* under the angry belching of the Bashaw's cannons. The whole lovely operation—which no less an authority than Lord Nelson thought was a topper—came off with only one wounded American. The worthy young lieutenant, only twenty-five, was promoted to captain, the youngest ever in the American Navy.[32] He also won the praise of the papacy, which had its own long experience of dealing with the Mussulmen. Pope Pius VII said, "The American Commander, with a small force, and in a short span of time, has done more for the cause of Christianity than the most powerful nations of Christendom have done for ages."[33]

Commodore Preble did good work as well. Though vastly outnumbered, he bombarded Tripoli and fought running engagements with the pirates—engagements that were not standoffish cannon battles, but ferocious hand-to-hand fighting aboard decks. Again, the Navy acquitted itself with admirable vigor and efficiency, teaching the supposedly invincible pirates that the men of the

U.S. Navy were tougher old salts by far when it came to close-quarters combat. America called its new heroes "Preble's Boys."

What Preble's Boys did on the sea, William Eaton attempted to do on land. Eaton, one of the great men of American history, has the honor of being the only American to have personally and publicly horsewhipped a French consul. Eaton was convinced the French were conspiring with the Arabs to shake down Americans. So as America's consul in Tunis, he reached instinctively for the horse-whip. It was a diplomatic necessity, but insufficiently cathartic for the great Eaton.

Eaton burned with resentment and shame—as did American naval officers— at the bribes the American government had been transferring to the pirates. Now, with cannonades erupting and the Navy spilling Barbary blood, Eaton had his chance to do the right thing: acquire a detachment of eight Marines under the command of Lieutenant Presley O'Bannon, hire a mercenary army of Greeks and other ruffians, and employ Arab cavalry under the command of Bashaw Hamet Karamanli—the deposed brother of Bashaw Yusuf—and prom-ise to return him to his throne. Here were the men. This was their moment.

They began their desert crusade at Alexandria, which meant they had to march 1,000 miles across the North African wastes to reach Tunis. Even taking a coastal route, so that the USS *Argus* could cruise alongside, the march was grueling and beset by all the hazards of the desert: heat, sandstorms, sand fleas, and the continual necessity of paying cash bribes to the Arabs to continue the march. O'Bannon's Marines had to put down four attempted mutinies from the raggier of the ragtag force.

As a military tune-up, on 27 April 1805, Eaton had his men attack Derna, the midway point 500 miles between Alexandria and Tunis. O'Bannon led the landward assault. He had one cannon for artillery support—but lost it when the Greek mercenaries fired it with the rammer in the tube, which rather cast doubt on their professionalism. Luckily, it was a combined operation with three American naval frigates offering additional firepower. The Navy, O'Bannon's Marines, and the rest of Eaton's Army took the city, raised the Stars and Stripes over its walls, and defeated the Tripolitan army that tried to wrest it back.

After this glorious action, Eaton learned that even before he had attacked Derna the Bashaw of Tripoli had opened negotiations. With the imprisoned Captain Bainbridge acting as a negotiator—and Eaton's capture of Derna serv-ing as a closing argument—the Bashaw agreed to release the American prison-ers and end all future piracy against American ships in exchange for a $60,000 cash settlement. The war against the Barbary pirates, never declared by the United States, was over.[34]

JEFFERSON'S EMPIRE

SUCH FOREIGN ADVENTURES seemed out of keeping with Jeffersonian principles, but Jefferson was rapidly amending his principles. The fact that Napoleon Bonaparte was looking to reestablish French control of the Mississippi River and the 820,000 square miles of Louisiana—a territory that stretched from New Orleans to Montana—concentrated his mind wonderfully and made him sound like a Hamiltonian. Jefferson wrote: "The day that France takes possession of New Orleans . . . we must marry ourselves to the British fleet and nation."[35] The Spanish governor of New Orleans raised the stakes by closing his ports to American shipping.

Jefferson had the virtue that Napoleon thought essential for all commanders: luck. Napoleon had sent tens of thousands of French troops to defeat the black uprising of Toussaint L'Ouverture in Hispaniola. Jefferson, the Francophile Virginia slaveholder, thought Napoleon's war a just one. But it was also a costly one. With fever stacking up piles of dead Frenchmen, Napoleon decided the Caribbean island was more a burden than a prize; and if France did not need Hispaniola, it did not need New Orleans; indeed, it did not need the New World at all; there was occupation enough in conquering the Old. So, to the astonishment of Jefferson's American negotiators, the French proposed selling America the entire Louisiana Territory. For $15 million and a signature, Thomas Jefferson acquired a continental empire, dismissing opposition from his own strict-constructionist party that the purchase was unconstitutional. He admonished his fellows not to be weighed down by "metaphysical subtleties"[36]— good advice then, and now. Theology is the queen of the sciences, but politics is the art of seizing the main chance. Jefferson understood this; the Federalists, somewhat amazingly, did not, seeing in the Louisiana Purchase a rising populist majority. They were right—it was the majority that would elect Andrew Jackson—but they were wrong to put such sectional interests of the Federalist Party before the interests of the country.

The Federalists, however, were not the most egregious offenders—the Republican Aaron Burr was; he seized the main chance in entirely the wrong way. Though Jefferson dropped him from the presidential ticket as he prepared for his reelection campaign, Burr had greater ambitions—namely, leading the northern states out of the Union.[37] Alexander Hamilton opposed this secessionist plot as well as Burr's subsequent campaign (as a Federalist candidate) for governor of New York. Seeing Hamilton foiling his every scheme—to become president, leader of a new republic, or even governor—Burr challenged Hamilton to a duel, and Hamilton, the man of honor, accepted. Paces drawn, Hamilton obviously and intentionally directed his pistol to miss. Burr acted like the scoundrel he was, took deliberate aim, and killed the greatest president America never had, the greatest of the founding fathers after George Washington.[38] With Hamilton dead, Burr served out the remaining days of his term as vice president and then pursued schemes to, variously, cut a deal with Britain to detach the Louisiana Territory as an independent republic (led by himself), or to make himself emperor of Mexico. Burr was eventually arrested and tried for treason. He was found innocent and resumed the natural office of such a man by practicing law in New York.

Jefferson, meanwhile, was reelected and the Republican Party's hostility to Britain was renewed. The Jeffersonians were incensed that the British routinely stopped American ships to pluck British-born subjects or alleged Royal Navy deserters from the crew.[39] In June 1807, the irritation climaxed when HMS *Leopard* fired broadsides into the USS *Chesapeake* to compel the American ship to let the British board. The action took place immediately off Virginia's coast. Three Americans were killed, twenty were wounded, and four men were impressed by the British.

The popular cry was for war, but Jefferson took pride in responding pacifically and, he thought, cleverly. He imposed a trade embargo of a bizarre sort: no American ship was allowed to dock in a foreign port; in fact there would be no American exports at all. As the embargo tightened, Congress took upon itself the powers to seize any goods suspected as potential exports. London had never enforced—nor even considered—such draconian restrictions on the North American colonies. But the presumed libertarian Thomas Jefferson forbade trade, styling himself a wily progressive who would abolish real wars with trade wars. He assumed that with American goods denied to Britain, the British lion would roar in agony. That didn't happen. Instead, Jefferson's Embargo Act had the obvious downside, from an American point of view, of straitjacketing American commerce, sending America's economy into a recession, giving Napoleon an excuse to impound American ships in French harbors (to help enforce the embargo, *mais naturellement*), and handing world markets to the very

British he meant to punish. Jefferson's idealized self-sufficient agrarian Republic, defended only by a mosquito fleet of coastal gunboats, had little reality outside the reach of his elegant pen. Reality, as it was lived by Americans, was that America was a commercial republic that needed a navy to defend itself. Hamilton would have known better, but Hamilton was dead. Jefferson, at least by the end of his second term, was politically dead, and just before James Madison took over as president, the Embargo Act was repealed.

Now real war would replace trade war.

CHAPTER 7

MADISON'S WARS

THE PARADOX WAS APPARENT at the beginning: a desire for war and a total lack of preparation for it. Jefferson's political heir, James Madison, had been elected president. The Congress was solidly Republican. As befitted Congress's Republican principles, the Army and the Navy budgets were cut, while at the same time, the Republicans beat the drums for war against Spain, the Indians, and the British.

The short, thin, shy Madison (known as "Little Jemmy") was an unlikely war leader. But he was sympathetic to the old alliance with France; he shared Jefferson's dream of "an empire of liberty" on the North American continent; and if he ignored that Britain stood virtually alone against Napoleonic tyranny—well, one has to concede he was a Jeffersonian Republican. At least he jealously guarded American rights, and was eager for American expansion, which he encouraged north, south, and west.

In 1810, American settlers whom the Spanish governor had invited into West Florida declared themselves a republic[1] and petitioned to join the United States. Madison accepted their petition, Spain was powerless to object, and America gained a strip of land that ran from Baton Rouge to Pensacola, and was eventually apportioned between Louisiana (which gained statehood in 1812), Mississippi (1817), Alabama (1819), and Florida (1845). Madison thus rounded out the southern end of Jefferson's Louisiana Purchase.

Madison also advanced Jefferson's Francophile policies. Seizing upon Napoleon's assurances that he welcomed American commerce (while at the same time harassing American shipping at will), Madison embraced trade with France and refused it to France's enemy Great Britain. France had already shut the European continent to British trade. Now that Napoleon had America within his continental system, Britannia felt the pinch.[2] More than a pinch, she found, in 1812, that Madison had won a congressional declaration of war against her.

Backing Madison were members of the congressional class of 1810 known as the "War Hawks," of whom Henry Clay of Kentucky and John C. Calhoun of South Carolina were the most famous. The War Hawks didn't see much point in a navy—they were backwoodsmen after all—but they sure as hell believed in an army that could whup the Indians of the interior and make off with Canada and any other adjacent territories that might be conveniently annexed, most particularly Spanish Florida (East Florida).

In Florida, Madison approved the covert, undeclared, and eventually failed "Patriot War" of Georgians trying to seize the Spanish colony. But it was Canada—and Britain's presumed philo-Redskin policies—that made the War Hawks belligerently anti-British. With the rise of the War Hawks, Jefferson's party of acquisitive continental empire overwhelmed Jefferson's party of peace.

Against the Red Man, the War Hawks scored an early victory through the efforts of William Henry Harrison, governor of the Indiana Territory. Harrison committed himself to sweeping Indians out of the "Old Northwest," opening it up for settlement. Standing against him were two Indian brothers—"The Prophet" Tenskwatawa and the Shawnee chieftain Tecumseh—who were equally committed to stopping the white man's western drive. They preached a return to the old ways, a forswearing of alcohol, a refusal to sell more land to the whites, and a defensive alliance against American expansion. In 1811, while Tecumseh was away in the South, rallying tribes to the tomahawk, Harrison marched toward Prophet's Town on the Tippecanoe River, where Tenskwatawa had gathered his followers. Harrison had 1,000 men: regular soldiers, militia, and frontier Indian fighters. He intended to resolve the issue of American settlement by negotiation or war. A party of Indians approached and told Harrison to wait; on the morrow, they said, peace negotiations could begin. It was a ruse. At first light, the Indians attacked, and though caught by surprise, Harrison's men held on through a desperate fight—so hot that the Indians exhausted their ammunition. The Indians were finally thrown back, and Harrison's men continued their march. Two days later, they destroyed the abandoned Indian village at Tippecanoe.

Tecumseh now sought a new alliance with the British; and the British, as it happened, were next on the War Hawks' agenda; Tecumseh's joining the redcoats was proof that Old England was the old enemy. Though the War Hawks were landsmen who wouldn't know a sloop from a poop deck, they railed against Britain's sins against American ships. These sins included the impressment of American sailors (an outrage to be sure, but American seamen were more agitated about British deserters driving down their wages); Britain's Orders in Council, which tried to prohibit American trade with France (even though these were repealed before Madison asked for a declaration of war[3]); and the Royal Navy's harassment of American shipping (though American merchantmen, who subverted trade embargoes by operating under British trade licenses, argued for peace with Britain). The irony was that New England merchantmen (and the ever-dwindling Federalist Party) believed that the only legitimate war was against Napoleonic France, not Britain, which they considered an ally and vital trading partner.

France, however, did not hold Canada, and given that Henry Clay had declared to Congress, "The militia of Kentucky alone are competent to place Montreal and Upper Canada at your feet,"[4] war with Britain seemed the obvious place to start. The Americans outnumbered the Royal Canadians better than fourteen to one. The War Hawks assumed that French Canadians and American settlers in Ontario might rally to the Stars and Stripes (in the event, they did not). Thomas Jefferson thought acquiring Canada not only a good thing but an easy thing. "The acquisition of Canada this year," he wrote, "as far as the neighborhood of Quebec will be a mere matter of marching."[5] But when it came to matters naval and military, Jefferson was not an authority to be trusted.

The War Hawks had a significant problem: when fighting a war it is generally considered useful to have an army. But while Congress had authorized the enrollment of a 50,000-man volunteer army, there were in fact only 7,000 men in uniform when war was declared. In the first six months of the war, there were 5,000 enlistees—tens of thousands short of the goal—and Congress, as always, found it impossible to support even these few men adequately with uniforms, equipment, and food. Congress treated the Navy, if anything, worse; a bill to increase the Navy's size—and America had declared war against the world's preeminent naval power—was actually voted down, and the War Hawks' plans for invading Canada made no provision for putting American ships on the Great Lakes.

Congress's actions appeared to reflect public opinion: most Americans approved annexing Canada, but they did not want to shoulder a musket or pay higher taxes to achieve it. New England essentially opted out of the war; refused to muster troops, ships, or bond money for it; and traded with the British army. Outside New England, mobs tried to intimidate Federalists who opposed the war. Among those physically attacked—in his case, because he stood up for the Federalists' right to free speech—was "Light Horse Harry" Lee, who was so badly beaten by the mob that he never fully recovered his health. The Republican mob, however, proved fiercer against Federalists than it did against the British.

The British army had 4,450 men in Canada—a small number, minuscule even given the Canadian-American border, but enough to foil Henry Clay's and Thomas Jefferson's boasting. The American strategy against the British was pure War Hawk: it was launched from the western frontier (the Michigan Territory) and the officers commanding the war effort had more bluster than brains—a failing for which the Republicans were fully culpable, not only because they appointed the officers but because they had kept the Army so small that its talent pool was pitifully understocked. Elderly veterans of the War for Independence—long returned to civilian life—were the best that could be had.

The initial invasion of Canada from the west was supposed to be coordinated with attacks in the east, at Niagara and Montreal. But New England's opposition to the war and the tentativeness of sixty-one-year-old General Henry Dearborn, whom the troops called "Granny" (his last employment was at the Customs office in Boston), made the eastern front an inactive front. In the West, the sixty-year-old governor of the Michigan Territory, William Hull, was—at Madison's request and against Hull's protestations—made a brigadier general.[6]

Opposing Hull was British Major General Isaac Brock. Brock was everything his American counterpart wasn't—a professional with the confidence to be effectively aggressive. Hull crossed into Canada, dithered, and then returned to Detroit, taking up defensive positions. What exactly this tiptoe invasion and retreat was supposed to achieve was not clear to Hull's soldiers or anyone else. Brock, however, had both intercepted Hull's orders and taken the measure of the man. He knew that Hull was unnerved, in part because British Captain Charles Roberts had taken a combined force of 45 redcoats, nearly 200 Canadians, and 400 Indians and forced the capitulation of Fort Mackinac on Lake Michigan. The American commander there, Lieutenant Porter Hanks, had, alas, not been informed of the American declaration of war.

Brock, as enterprising as Captain Roberts, assembled a combined force of a few hundred regulars and militia, as well as Tecumseh and his Indians. He then cut off the approaches to Detroit and made a demonstration of force against the Americans, who outnumbered him two to one. Hull, his nerves shattered, and with visions of an Indian massacre that would have included his own daughter and her children, ordered the white flag of surrender raised over Fort Detroit.

More than 2,000 men, as well as the fort's arms and ammunition, were Brock's prize.

Before his surrender, Hull had ordered the evacuation of Fort Dearborn. Captain Nathan Heald, the fort's commander, executed the order reluctantly, thinking he was safer behind the walls of the fort. Coming to assist him was veteran Indian fighter (and a veteran of service under "Mad Anthony" Wayne) Captain William Wells.

Captain Heald bribed the neighboring Indians with goods, rendered useless the ammunition he couldn't carry, dumped all the alcohol in the fort, and solicited the Indians' guarantee of safe passage. Even so, the Americans took no comfort from these precautions. With forebodings of doom, the party of 148—about 50 of them soldiers, the rest being militia, settlers, and women and children—set out. Captain Wells led the column with thirty friendly Miami Indians. The Indians wore war paint. Wells himself was an adopted member of the Miami tribe and didn't trust the professions of peace made by the surrounding Potawatomis. He was right. Hostile Indians, outnumbering the column by almost five to one, sprang an ambush from sand dunes not far away. The Americans fought back hard, but the Indians were butchering them. Finally, with more than half the soldiers dead, Wells scalped and his heart eaten, and beheaded American corpses littering the field, the Indians told the remaining Americans that they would be spared if they surrendered. The Americans agreed. The Indians did spare some—perhaps as many as sixty-two were taken as captives—but a goodly number were also set aside for the Indian sport of torture unto death.

Far from the War Hawks marching into Canada whistling a Jeffersonian tune, the war whoops of hostile Indians were echoing across the West. Madison hadn't counted on this, and his first instinct was an odd one: to appoint his secretary of state, James Monroe—who had last seen active duty in 1779, when he was twenty-one years old—to take command of another army and retake Detroit. The state of Kentucky, however, was closer to the scene and had a militia already armed. Kentucky named the hero of Tippecanoe, William Henry Harrison, to lead the militia and save the frontier from the Indians.[7]

In Canada, the intrepid British Major General Isaac Brock, having disposed of the American threat to the West, now rushed to the East, where he had to be restrained from taking the battle to the Americans who outnumbered him. The British Governor-General Sir George Prevost thought it wiser to play defense.

What happened was sort of a defensive battle of Quebec. Brock (playing the part of Wolfe) was killed leading a countercharge against the Americans who had invaded across the Niagara at Queenstown Heights (13 October 1812). But the American attack—the Americans brought some 6,000 men to the field; the British 2,000—was routed, some men drowning as they tried to recross the Niagara to safety. Worst of all, from the American perspective, was that New York militia units refused to take part in the invasion and sat and watched as their fellow Americans were shot, bayoneted, or captured (among the captured was a giant colonel named Winfield Scott).

A new American commander, Brigadier General Alexander Smyth— a blowhard politician from Virginia—decided to try again. The first step in the plan was executed perfectly. A raiding party sneaked across the river and seized two British batteries. General Smyth then loaded his men into boats, changed his mind, and decided no further action was called for. His inactivity turned his men mutinous. So he proposed another invasion plan. But after further dithering, he finally called the whole thing off. With nothing else to do, the militiamen fired their muskets at General Smyth's tent, and Brigadier General Peter B. Porter called Smyth a coward. Smyth challenged Porter to pistol shots at paces, and, as the military historian John R. Elting has it: "Unfortunately, both missed."[8]

The litany of tragic-comic American failure continued. At Lake Champlain, General Henry Dearborn had his chance for glory with the next big foray into Canada: the planned conquest of Montreal. Outnumbering his British adversaries (actually French and Indians) better than three to one, Dearborn found that his militiamen refused to fight—indeed, they were willing to march only twenty miles from Plattsburgh, New York—and after much squabbling another grand invasion amounted to nothing.

It would be hard to imagine a more embarrassing series of events than this. The War Hawks had a loud squawk, but no talons and few willing fighters— a bad combination to be sure. But on the seas, the U.S. Navy was reclaiming American honor. Here there were no superannuated, unqualified generals and mulish militia pledged solely to the defense of their state; here there were daring, experienced captains—few in number, but excellent in their abilities—leading crews of talented, willing sailors. Their ships were few—survivors of Republican savagery with the naval budget—but powerfully gunned. Facing the greatest naval power in the world, the Americans offered a series of stunning naval jabs. The United States started with a loss—of the brig USS *Nautilus* in July—but quickly recovered. On 19 August 1812, the USS *Constitution* captained by Isaac Hull (nephew and adopted son of William Hull, who had surrendered Fort Detroit three days before) blasted the HMS *Guerrière* into wreckage.

In October, the USS *Wasp* defeated HMS *Frolic* (though while trying to drag the *Frolic* home, the *Wasp,* a sloop of eighteen guns, was taken by the seventy-four-gun HMS *Poictiers*); and Stephen Decatur, commanding the USS *United States,* captured HMS *Macedonia* and delivered it to Newport Harbor—the first and only time an American ship has made a prize of a British ship. In December, William Bainbridge, serving as captain of the USS *Constitution,* turned his cannons on HMS *Java* and pummeled it into driftwood. The winning streak continued into early 1813, when in February the USS *Hornet* sank HMS *Peacock.*

Madison was big enough to confess that the Navy had been wrongly slighted in the initial strategy of the war—that is, if the War Hawks' rodomontade can be elevated to the level of "strategy." Thomas Jefferson, in his retirement at Monticello, sighed that Congress's January 1813 appropriation of $2.5 million to build six forty-four-gun frigates and four ships of the line packing seventy-four guns each was "a sacrifice we must make, as heavy as it is, to the prejudices on the part of our citizens."[9] The main prejudice of America's citizens was to maximize success and minimize failure—and that meant well-armed frigates and ships of the line. Jefferson's harbor patrol gunboats—tattered by poor upkeep in any event—had proved to be nearly worthless, while the seagoing Navy had proved itself of extraordinary worth, valor, and skill.

In 1813, however, the British effectively clamped down on America's small Navy by blockading America's coastline. Congress's parsimony thus ensured that Jefferson got his wish, and ships of the line were relegated to de facto harbor duty. In this capacity, even they could not stop British raiders mauling settlements on the Chesapeake. The British treated New England leniently, because the British were happy to encourage New England's opposition to the war. Still, the British blockade slashed the value of America's exports, which collapsed from $130 million in 1807 to $7 million in 1814.[10] But American privateers gained some vengeance by capturing 2,000 commercial ships.

Inland, the war continued its litany of disaster for the Americans. On 22 January 1813, General James Winchester was encamped at the Raisin River in the Michigan Territory. He had begun with 2,500 men. Winter and disease had halved his command. But his was an eager advance party of William Henry Harrison's new offensive in the West to retake Michigan. He was hurrying—or so he thought—to glorious battle with the British. But British Colonel Henry

Procter[11] was stealing a march on him, looking to destroy this isolated column of William Henry Harrison's army.

Winchester's men were divided, some posted along the north side of the river and others south of it. They had come here to liberate Frenchtown, which they did on 17 January, sweeping away its few Canadian and Indian occupiers. Supremely confident, the Americans slept without bothering to post sentries. So it was that Procter's 1,000 British effectives—half redcoats, half redskins—would have caught the Americans unawares had Procter not paused to get his men into a firing line and unlimber his six artillery pieces.

Now it became a stand-up firefight between Procter's regulars and Winchester's mixed force of regulars, militia, and fighting Kentuckians (the "long knives"). The Indians tipped the balance. Swarming with war whoops, muskets, and tomahawks at the Americans' flanks, they panicked Winchester's greener troops who made the fundamental mistake of trying to outrun Indians in snowdrifts. The result was the drenching of the snow with blood and brains, and happy Indians waving scalps aloft. General Winchester surrendered and ordered the Kentucky Rifles of Major George Madison, whose nearly 400 men still held Frenchtown proper, to surrender as well.

What happened next turned the battle into a notorious massacre. Procter moved quickly, putting the American prisoners of war on the march. As an Englishman, he had a fine regard for his horses; so he rested them and enlisted American prisoners of war to pull the horses' loads, a wonderful form of exercise that the Americans seemed not to have appreciated. In his haste, Procter left behind the American wounded, though one British officer did assure them that the "Indians are excellent doctors."[12] So, they proved, in a rather primitive, purgative fashion: torturing and scalping Americans, and burning down the houses that served as makeshift hospitals—patients and all.[13] Procter's speedy departure was meant to avoid pursuit by William Henry Harrison, but Harrison, receiving news of the massacre, had fled the other way.

Such shame was redeemed once again by the Navy. First, though, came a gallant defeat. British Captain Philip Vere Broke of HMS *Shannon* issued a challenge to Captain James Lawrence of the USS *Chesapeake* to meet him in single ship combat out of Boston Harbor. Lawrence accepted the challenge as a gentleman and set sail to meet his death in a sharp, violent encounter of belching cannon and blood-drenched decks riddled with grapeshot and canister fired at close quarters. In less than fifteen minutes of battle, 146 Americans received death wounds, including Lawrence, whose order to his crew became a Navy standard: "Don't give up the ship. Fight her till she sinks." His crew did as instructed, fighting her until the British boarders overwhelmed them.

If the Navy was bottled up along the Atlantic Coast, it found another outlet for its talents in the Great Lakes, where, belatedly, ships were delivered to another captain of quality, Oliver Hazard Perry. Perry had served in the Navy since the age of thirteen (starting in 1799 as a midshipman), and so was young, experienced, and primed for action.

First, on the shores of Lake Ontario, American General Henry Dearborn bestirred himself to action. He had orders from Secretary of War John Armstrong to invade Canada, striking at the British military base in Kingston, on Lake Ontario. This should have been easy enough to do, as there were fewer than 1,000 British troops there. General Dearborn, however, allowed his fears to magnify their numbers. So instead, he decided to attack the Canadian city of York (today's Toronto), the provincial capital of Upper Canada, which was more a symbolic than a military target. It also offered what America's army most needed—the prospect of victory.

Dearborn, being too flabby to lead men into battle, left that duty to General Zebulon Pike (of Pike's Peak fame), who was killed when a British powder magazine exploded. Resistance to the Americans was light, but that won the Canadians no favors. The Americans sacked the city and burned York's parliament building, an act that would be avenged when the British army invaded Washington.

The next part of the Great Lakes offensive was at Fort George on Lake Ontario across from Fort Niagara on 27 May 1813. Captain Perry and his newly built ships provided a covering naval bombardment under which rowed Colonel Winfield Scott and his men. Scott's troopers took Fort George, but this victory like the victory at York could be seen as a British tactical retreat. The British suffered few losses—their men had merely withdrawn and regrouped to fight again.

By the summer of 1813, however, Captain Perry was prowling Lake Erie with his hastily assembled fleet and amateur crew (which included Kentucky riflemen whom he transformed into Marines). On 10 September 1813, Perry delivered a real victory. He cornered the British Captain Robert Barclay—a veteran of Trafalgar—at Put-in-Bay near Fort Malden at the southern end of Lake Erie and forced him to give battle. Perry had nine ships, Barclay six; Perry had the edge in firepower, but the veteran Barclay—who had lost an arm at

Trafalgar—had professional crews. Perry's flagship was the newly christened USS *Lawrence,* which flew a standard reading "Don't Give Up the Ship."

The battle was three hours of hard pounding, especially of the *Lawrence,* which was so devastated by enemy fire that its crew took 80 percent casualties and the ship was left with only one operable gun. Perry kept it firing to let his other ships know that he was still in the battle. Finally, he evacuated the *Lawrence.* He boarded the USS *Niagara* and continued the fight until Barclay, a third of his men killed and himself badly wounded, agreed that he had had enough. Perry wrote down a message to be delivered to General William Henry Harrison: "We have met the enemy and they are ours. Two Ships, two Brigs, one Schooner, and one Sloop."

Control of Lake Erie meant that Harrison could now land troops to out-flank the British General Henry Procter and his Indian ally Tecumseh. Procter saw the need for another tactical withdrawal; Tecumseh didn't. The Indian chief moved reluctantly, and finally convinced Procter to make a stand on Canada's Thames River. Tecumseh told his braves that his son should inherit his sword (given him by the British, who had granted him the rank of brigadier general) because he would fall on the field of battle.

With Harrison were 1,000 mounted Kentuckians who used tomahawks as cavalry sabres and had muskets slung over their shoulders. They led the American assault at the Battle of the Thames (5 October 1813) with the unlikely war cry: "Remember the Raisin!" (from the Indian massacre of the American wounded at Frenchtown on the Raisin River). The Kentuckians rode like thunder, their tomahawks scything through the redcoats. The thin red line scattered and ran, but Tecumseh's Indians stood firm, even when the Kentuckians leapt from their horses and turned the battle into a melee. The Indians thought they had the Kentuckians well enough in hand to charge the supporting American infantry. Tecumseh, leading the charge, was shot dead—and with that shot, the battle was won. The Indians hurriedly made away with the corpse so that no white man could find it and desecrate it.

With victories securing the upper Midwest, it seemed an opportune moment to launch another invasion of Canada from the east. But the British and the French Canadians easily turned back the tentative probes of America's squabbling elderly commanders. It took the resignation of General Henry Dearborn and the removal of Generals James Wilkinson and Revolutionary War veteran Wade Hampton (grandfather of the much more celebrated Confederate cavalry commander) to break the logjam. Taking command of what would be the final offensive against Montreal was Major General Jacob Brown. Brown and Brigadier General Winfield Scott did take the war into Canada, and did fight hard (both generals were wounded leading their men), but the result of the hard fighting was nothing better than stalemate against the British. Winter, and the seasonal end of yearlong enlistments, left the generals with little choice: they returned to American soil. The captured Fort George was abandoned, too. There would be, contrary to War Hawk brags, no conquest of Canada.

Instead, there was an invasion of the United States, with the British and Indians capturing Fort Niagara, torching Buffalo, and raiding towns along the upper Northeast. That was in the winter of 1813–14. By the spring, things would get much worse.

CHAPTER 8

THE GUNS OF OLD HICKORY

ASHINGTON WAS BURNING, the redcoats making Madison pay for his impertinence.

Until now Britain had been a distracted power: beating Napoleon Bonaparte was the priority; the American war was a sideshow. But on 6 April 1814, Napoleon Bonaparte abdicated, and on 4 May he arrived at his island exile of Elba. With Boney bottled up—at least temporarily—America fell squarely into Britain's gun sights. How could the Americans—who had fared so poorly against a distracted British Empire—succeed now that Britain's baleful glare was upon them?

The answer was deceptively simple. Britain had no real interest in the war, no objectives to gain save those that chance had thrown her way; she was merely defending herself against the arrogance and folly of Madison and the Republicans who had declared war against her. In Congress, John Randolph of Roanoke—a Virginia aristocrat and upholder of the code duello—had been the voice of warning. Not only was there no sense in fighting a country with whom America shared virtually every tie of common culture imaginable, but the War Hawks were hubristic in the extreme.

"I know that we are on the brink of some dreadful scourge," Randolph thundered. "Go to war without money, without men, without a navy! Go to war when we have not the courage, while your lips utter war, to lay war taxes! When your whole courage is exhibited in passing resolutions!"[1] That was a pretty good description of Republican foreign and defense policy as a whole.

The scourge Randolph had predicted, the British delivered. If Britain had no war aims at the outset of the war, now that she had rebuffed the invasion of Canada and blockaded America's coastline, Britain pressed her advantage. The young Republic was not nearly so secure as it thought.

The first terrible shock for the Americans was when British troops came up the Patuxent River, disembarked at Benedict, Maryland, on 21 August 1814, and marched on the capital of the United States. Madison and the War Hawks had wanted a war; now they could fight it themselves—though the War Hawks flew the coop.

British Major General Robert Ross had only 4,000 men, but he marched on a city that was virtually undefended and whose bureaucrats were panic-stricken, fleeing with government papers floating like snowflakes behind them. Six thousand Americans, mostly poorly trained militiamen of the District Brigade, were drawn up at Bladensburg, Maryland, six miles northeast of Washington. This was the only military obstacle Ross had to clear. Secretary of State James Monroe was with the militiamen and monitoring the redcoats' approach. James Madison turned up, too, with dueling pistols; and Secretary of War John Armstrong was at hand. The militiamen were hastily positioned, and Monroe, politician that he was, repositioned them without alerting the commanding brigadier generals William Winder and Tobias Stansbury, making a bad position worse. The generals, meanwhile, wasted their time being interviewed by Madison, Monroe, and Armstrong.

Ross, who had no cavalry and artillery, came head-on with infantry—and with Congreve rockets. American artillery and sharpshooters opened the battle trying to halt the British advance. They had little luck, as the vanguard of British light infantry hustled along. The British were unfazed by shot and shell, and they unnerved the American militia with their cool professionalism. The British fired Congreve rockets as covering fire for their light infantry. The rockets whined and roared as they flew overhead and exploded. They didn't shatter bodies, but they did shatter American morale; and the American militiamen ran from the British as if pursued by furies in what became known as the Bladensburg Races (24 August 1814). As befitted their roles as leaders of the Republic, Madison and his cabinet won the race.

There was one valiant exception to the rout. The handsome and courageous Commodore Joshua Barney with 500 sailors and 150 Marines marched through the fleeing militiamen.[2] Barney placed a row of cannon along the main road a mile from Bladensburg. By a combination of artillery volleys and Marine covering fire, he swept the British from the road in front of him and blunted attempted flanking maneuvers. Noticing 500 militiamen watching the action from the high ground on his right, Commodore Barney ordered a charge, expecting the militiamen to join in. "Board 'em!" he shouted, and the Marines and sailors leapt at the enemy—but the American militiamen simultaneously leapt away; they were watching a show, not fighting a battle.

The British enveloped Barney's sailors; the gunners were cut down at their cannons. Bloody and badly wounded, Barney finally ordered a retreat. He was captured—as he had been captured before, several times, during the War of Independence—but the gallant sea dog had shown himself a hero, inflicting at least three casualties for every one his men suffered. The Navy and the Marines had done their part, but as Barney was dragged from the field, a prisoner of war, there was no other force to stop the British.[3]

General Robert Ross and Admiral Sir George Cockburn entered a city that was virtually deserted (save at least for a sniper who shot Ross's horse from beneath him). At the White House, the redcoats found dinner for forty prepared and waiting. They took their seats and offered a revealing toast: "Peace with America and down with Madison!"

Looting was forbidden (in fact several British soldiers were executed for thievery and disgracing His Majesty's uniform), but disciplined vandalism under orders from proper officers was another thing entirely. Having no sympathy for "Little Jemmy" Madison, they torched the White House. They torched the offices of the secretary of war and the secretary of the Treasury. They torched the Capitol, which held the Library of Congress. They burned down the Navy Yard and all the vessels drawn up along its dock.[4] Their targeted arson ceased only when a thunderstorm blew through the city. But come the morning, the troops went at it again: burning the War Office, the arsenal at Greenleaf's Point (a hundred British soldiers went up with it), and the offices of the *National Intelligencer,* a newspaper much hated by Admiral Cockburn. Again the destruction was cut off by an act of nature—a tornado that stifled the flames—but the British had made their point and decided to move on.[5]

Admiral Sir Alexander Cochrane, who shared naval command with Admiral Cockburn, decided to make his point by taking Baltimore. General Ross led the overland action, and though his troops pushed Baltimore's outlying defenders back, a musket ball struck him down, killing this inspired and gallant officer and gentleman, as noted for his good manners as for his warrior skill. Even veterans groaned and lost heart when they heard the news. At sea, Admiral Cochrane's mortar ships bombarded Baltimore's Fort McHenry (on 13 September 1814) with Congreve rockets and cannonballs for more than twenty-four hours. The bombardment gave the Americans a fabulous fireworks demonstration and inspired Francis Scott Key to pen the "Star-Spangled Banner." From a British military perspective, the bombardment was sound and fury that signified nothing. The British withdrew.

Just two days before the attack on Fort McHenry, disaster threatened America from Lake Champlain. The threat of Canadian invasion had been blunted before—at least along the Niagara River—in July 1814, when American Generals Jacob Brown and Winfield Scott, two of the best, had taken the battle to the enemy at the engagements of Fort Erie (3 July), Chippawa (5 July), and Lundy's Lane (25 July), all fought in Ontario. But in September, Sir George Prevost, governor-general of Canada, assumed military command of a strike force of 10,000 British troops to invade the United States along the route from Lake Champlain. Prevost, however, was so cautious that he could easily have served as one of Madison's incompetents. He clung to his security blanket, the British ships on the lake, and refused to move without them to clear the American forts opposite. That was a great mistake, for the forts were weakly defended. More important, the United States Navy was about to save America again.

The American naval officer on the spot was Captain Thomas Macdonough. Macdonough had seen service against the Barbary pirates, and later been grabbed by a press gang and bound into the Royal Navy, from which he escaped by impersonating a Royal Marine. Macdonough brought fourteen ships against Captain George Downie's fifteen. Downie held every advantage save the size of his guns—Macdonough had loaded monster fifty-two- and forty-pounders—and position, for behind Macdonough were the supporting batteries of Fort Plattsburgh. Downie expected Prevost to lead an assault against the American fort. Once in British hands—and Prevost had more than enough men to seize the fort quickly and easily—the fort's guns could be turned on the Americans, and British victory could be assured. Prevost, however, was a politician by trade, not a professional soldier, and followed the politician's practice of letting Downie do all the fighting for him. The landward assault was called off to watch the British and American ships blast each other, splintering decks and eviscerating men. It was ship versus ship—a naval slugfest that left Downie killed, and Macdonough triumphing by the poundage of his heavy guns. Sir George Prevost scuttled the planned invasion; Macdonough had shut down the British in the North. Meanwhile, in the South, a great hero had arisen to lead America to its final great victory of the war, at the Battle of New Orleans.

JACKSON

HE WAS A RAWBONED, six-foot-one-inch, 145-pound, much-scarred, disease-ridden, Scotch-Irish redheaded fighter named Andrew Jackson. Jackson was a man of the frontier who endured suffering as a matter of course and believed in violence in defense of his rights. Jackson joined the Continental Army at thirteen. Employed as a courier, he and one of his brothers were captured (another brother died in uniform during the War of Independence, probably of fever). As a boy prisoner, Jackson was ordered to polish a British officer's boots. The flame-haired tyro refused, and the officer struck Jackson a sword cut that bit into his head and sliced his raised hand to the bone. These were the first of innumerable wounds Jackson received from war, dueling, and accidents. But few scarred him deeper; he never had any qualms about fighting the British.

Kept in abysmal conditions in a prisoner-of-war camp, he survived smallpox, which killed his brother. His father had died before he was born, and his mother died shortly after the British released him, when he was fourteen. An orphan, alone, Jackson pushed himself to succeed: he became a frontier lawyer—not a pettifogging one, but one who made quick profits in land speculation and brawled against legal opponents. If his formal education was lacking, if he "was imprisoned in his ignorance, and sometimes raged around his little, dim enclosure like a tiger in his den,"[6] he was still a natural leader of men; he had command presence, and he rose to become a congressman, a United States senator, and a pistol-packing judge. But always, he was an Indian fighter.

Proud, prone to rages—yet dignified, too, for he sought to be a southern gentleman, and used his money to acquire the requisite estate and slaves—he was fiercely principled after his own lights. All of which meant he was not a compromiser and not a clubbable man. He resigned his Senate seat after less than a year. Jackson resented wasting the best hours of every day sitting "in a red morocco chair." Sitting was not for him. John Quincy Adams sniffed that Jackson was "a barbarian who could not write a sentence of grammar and hardly could spell his own name"[7]—as if that were an important qualification for someone who would be president of the United States. Thomas Jefferson noted, equally disdainfully, that Jackson could give no speeches because he choked on his fury.

But that fury, properly directed, made him precisely the sort of fighting general America needed. In this, he had something in common with the Navy. The Navy, requiring officers who knew how to manage a ship, was a much more professional service than the Army and was spared political appointments. Jackson was no political favorite in Washington. While many other generals were superannuated politicians appointed because of their loyalty to the Madison administration, Jackson, as major general of the Tennessee militia, was an authentic soldier in every one of his virtues: aggressive, courageous, decisive, dutiful, honorable, a muscular Christian, a practical strategist, and a tactician who kept in martial practice by dueling and fighting Indians. He was, in fact, recovering from a bullet wound—from a follow-up brawl to a duel he had attended as second—when Tennessee called on him again.

While Jackson rested at his estate, the Hermitage (and told his doctors "I'll keep my arm," when they recommended amputation), the Creek nation raised its tomahawks, inspired by Tecumseh's dream of hurling back the white man— at least the American white man, because Tecumseh counted the British and Spanish as allies. Some Creek braves followed Tecumseh north, where they gained experience of massacre. They did so, however, against the wishes of Big Warrior, a great Creek chief, who, with many of the Creek elders, opposed Tecumseh's call for war. When the federal government demanded that the Creeks surrender the killers among them, the tribe fell into war between the Lower Creeks (east of the Chattahoochee River) who repudiated Tecumseh and the Upper Creeks (of northern Alabama) who thirsted for blood, both white and red. The Upper Creek warriors became known as the "Red Sticks" because they painted their war clubs bright red—and they went on a rampage.

Many officers on both sides of this war of Creek against Creek, and Creek against the white man, were half-breeds. Red Stick chiefs included men like Peter McQueen, William Weatherford (Chief Red Eagle), and Paddy Welsh. In late July 1813, Peter McQueen and another Indian chief, High Head Jim, led a Red Stick war party. The Indian braves were well supplied, loaded with ammunition courtesy of the Spanish governor, but were ambushed by Mississippi militiamen under the command of Colonel James Caller and half-breed Captain Dixon Bailey. The Battle of Burnt Corn (or Escambia, 27 July 1813) was in itself inconsequential—the Americans, after gaining the initial advantage were chased away by the Indians—but it led to the Indians' devastating assault on Fort Mims, forty miles from Mobile, Alabama, that would rouse General Jackson from his sickbed.

The Creeks struck Fort Mims on 30 August 1813. Commanding the fort was Major Daniel Beasley, another lawyer appointed to do a soldier's work. He was also a half-breed, as were many of those he sheltered. Beasley discounted warnings from slaves—and even an urgent report from one of his scouts—that Creek war parties were approaching. At noon, while the settlers and soldiers settled down to eating, dancing, card-playing, or in Beasley's case perhaps drinking, the Indians stormed Fort Mims and took its defenders utterly by surprise: the gates were even open to welcome them. Major Beasley was killed almost immediately. Captain Dixon Bailey took command, organizing musket volleys that reaped scores of Indians who were convinced that their medicine men had made them impervious to the white man's guns.

Though they were wrong about that, there were nevertheless between 750 and 1,000 Red Stick braves matched against Captain Bailey's 70 militiamen who had to protect 550 civilians. Even against such odds, Bailey and his men held out for three long hours in the sweltering Alabama heat. Their last defensive positions were two log buildings. The Indians finally set them ablaze. Some defenders and civilians ran outside, where most were seized and killed by the Indians. Others were hideously burned alive. Twenty to forty of the whites managed to escape the carnage. The Indians took the surviving blacks as slaves for themselves, but as many as 400 men, women, and children, half-breed and white, were killed, the women gruesomely butchered.

Andrew Jackson, whose life on the frontier had taught him an inveterate hatred of the Indians and their savagery, summoned his Tennessee militiamen. Though his left arm was still in a sling (with a brawler's bullet embedded in bone), Jackson, in little more than a month's time, would be campaigning against the Red Sticks. He also showed the diplomat's touch with friendly Indians, pledging that he would be the avenger of any peaceful tribe threatened by the enemy. Jackson the Indian hater thereby found himself Jackson the Indian commander.

Jackson marched hard from Tennessee down through northern Alabama and struck his first victory at Tallushatchee. Jackson's men surrounded the Red Sticks and, in the words of Davy Crockett (whose grandparents had been killed by Creeks): "We shot them like dogs."[8] It was revenge for Fort Mims, though Jackson's men spared the women and children; in fact, Jackson actually adopted an Indian orphan from the battle, seeing the lad as an Indian version of himself. He hoped, as the boy grew, to send him to West Point.[9]

Next, Jackson sprang an attack on an army of more than 1,000 Red Stick warriors at Talladega, killing hundreds, and possibly wounding hundreds more; the Indians escaped annihilation by slipping through a gap in Jackson's lines. Though victory seemed well in hand, it was not. Aside from his wounded arm, Jackson had dysentery. His supplies were low. Many militiamen thought they had done their bit and wanted to go home. The governor of Tennessee essentially agreed, telling Jackson there was no point in chasing the Red Sticks through the entire wilderness of Alabama; he urged him to return to Tennessee.

Jackson damned talk of retreat, damned talk of militia enlistments expiring (and backed it up with a gun and an execution), and told the governor that if he gave him the men and supplies he needed, he would vouch for the result. New militiamen at last arrived—just in time to make up for the rest whom Jackson could no longer legally keep in service, which was the vast bulk of his army. Loaded with men once more, he rushed to the attack at Horseshoe Bend, where he knew the Red Sticks were entrenched. The Indians caught him on the march, and in two sharp engagements Jackson dealt them painful losses. But he also recognized that his new recruits needed training and discipline if he were to fight a climactic battle against the Red Sticks. He retreated to Fort Strother and drilled his army into the fighting force he wanted. He was further reinforced with more militia and, better yet, regulars, as the 39th Regiment of United States infantry came under his command.

Now Old Hickory had 5,000 trained men. He marched 3,300 of them, including 600 Indians, against the Red Sticks, who were waiting for him. The rebel Creeks had nearly 900 braves at Horseshoe Bend. Behind them on the Tallapoosa River were canoes that gave them an escape route, though the Indians were confidently entrenched. They had built a log wall in a zigzag pattern with dual gun ports that provided overlapping fields of defensive fire along the approach to the bend. As a defensive pocket, it was, in Jackson's words, "a place well formed by Nature for defence & rendered more secure by Art."[10]

But Old Hickory found a way. He sent his cavalry, under the command of General John Coffee—his closest confidant on the campaign and a fine tactician—across the river along with the allied Indians to prevent a Red Stick escape and pen the rebels in for the slaughter. At 10:30 A.M., on 27 March 1814, Jackson began his frontal attack. He ordered his two field pieces to open fire on the Indian fortifications. He ordered musket volleys fired at a distance of 250 yards. This was no mere softening-up exercise. Jackson had admonished his men to "be cool and collected . . . *let every shot tell.*" He kept the Red Sticks pinned down for two hours, giving Coffee and the allied Indians the chance to go to work. Jackson's Indians slipped across the river on canoes, set alight part of the Red Sticks' fort, and charged into a melee against them.

Now Jackson had his opening. "Charge!" His men sprinted against a torrent of musket balls and arrows, crashing into the log wall and fighting at the gun ports. Major Lemuel Montgomery tried to lead the men over the wall but was shot in the head and killed. Then came Ensign Sam Houston, later to become president of the Republic of Texas, but already at twenty-one a Texas-sized hero (he was taller than Jackson). He led the 39th Regiment over the wall, despite an arrow piercing his thigh, and laid into the Indians with his officer's sword. He received two more wounds—by musket balls—before the end of the day's fighting.

Some Red Sticks fled for the canoes. Coffee's cavalry was waiting with a blast of musketry that ended any hope of escape by the river. The land, however, was forested and the Red Sticks tried to hide within the woods. The soldiers hunted them down. No Red Stick was offered quarter unless a woman or a child, and even some noncombatants were killed. It was a daylong slaughter that ended only with nightfall. When more Indians were found in the morning, they too were dispatched. Jackson estimated that 850 Red Sticks were killed at Horseshoe Bend, and that a few had escaped during the night. Another 350 women and children had been captured and were given as booty to Jackson's allied Indians.

The battle was decisive. The Red Stick rebellion was effectively crushed. Jackson offered the Creek rebels harsh terms, which they accepted on 19 August 1814, turning over 23 million acres to the United States (most of the future state of Alabama and a good part of Georgia). The Red Sticks' only hope had been in British reinforcements—which were in fact on the way to the Gulf Coast. The British were too late to help the Red Sticks, but not too late to give Andy Jackson another great campaign.

THE BATTLE OF NEW ORLEANS

THOUGH THE BRITISH lion hoped to swat the Americans with a big paw, and perhaps gnaw away a larger border for Canada, her allies in Europe were tugging on her tail and reminding her that America was a distraction from keeping the peace that was being negotiated at the Congress of Vienna. The British Prime Minister Lord Liverpool wanted to wrap things up quickly in North America and asked Britain's greatest soldier, the Duke of Wellington, to take command. The Iron Duke declined. He thought the American war best ended, and best ended quickly, with no thought of territorial aggrandizement.

Lord Liverpool did not share the duke's blunt assessment of the war. The United States was weak and vulnerable. Its economy was in shreds. Its military was failing to keep up enlistments and relying on parochial and unreliable militias. And New England was on the verge of secession. A British offensive from Spanish Florida[11] and along the Gulf Coast could capture New Orleans and pry the Louisiana Territory from the United States. Britain might keep the territory, or flip it to Spain, or merely use it as a dandy bargaining chip in the British-American negotiations already under way in Ghent, Belgium. If Wellington thought this a bad strategy and wasting British resources on a sideshow—and he did—Liverpool had another commander in mind, General Sir Edward Michael Pakenham, Wellington's brother-in-law.[12]

Despite Wellington's distaste for a campaign against America, there was no reason to think it would not succeed. Vice Admiral Sir Alexander Cochrane, for one, was convinced it would. He, in fact, had proposed the campaign, arguing that with the assistance of the Indians and freed blacks, Britain could easily seize the entire Mississippi Valley from New Orleans to Canada. If the plan had merit, it neglected one vital point: the newly elevated Andrew Jackson, now a major general in the United States Army, and the regional commander of Tennessee and the Louisiana and Mississippi territories. Jackson stood athwart Cochrane's plans. Indeed, he had his own invasion plan: he wanted to root anti-American Creeks out of Spanish Florida, where they were trained by the British and supplied by the Spanish.

Jackson rushed to Mobile and detached men to restore and defend Fort Bowyer against a British expeditionary force he knew was moving to take it. On 12 September 1814, a landward assault of more than 200 Royal Marines and Indians supported by the Royal Navy failed to take the fort. HMS *Hermes* ran aground, was abandoned, and then set alight by the British. Jackson heard the explosion of its powder magazine thirty miles away. For the British, it was a pitiful performance.

It emboldened Jackson—who hardly needed emboldening—to bring an army of 4,000 men to demand the surrender of the Spanish forts at Pensacola, which were defended by Spanish troops and the Royal Navy. Neither was a match for Jackson, who fooled both into thinking he would attack Pensacola from the west, while he swung round and attacked it from the east. Governor González Manrique surrendered immediately. The British destroyed the most valuable of the forts (Fort Barrancas) and then withdrew.

Jackson withdrew as well, leaving "neutral" Spanish Florida and returning to the charms of Mobile. He also finally took time to read a letter from James Monroe, secretary of war. Written at the behest of President Madison, it forbade Jackson from invading Spanish Florida, but Jackson's actions did far more to win the war than instructions from Washington did. By claiming Mobile for the United States and cleaning out Pensacola, Jackson forced the British to make their invasion through the bayous and swamps of Louisiana. There, at New Orleans, Jackson assembled his defenders.

It is doubtful that there ever was such an apparent rabble put to such good military effect. There was the usual combination of regular army troops, militiamen, and Indians, but also a bouillabaisse of raffish New Orleans blacks, Cajuns, Creoles, and pirates—literally pirates, under the command of Jean Laffite. Jackson set his men to work fortifying the city and making its bayous even tougher treading for the approaching British. The Americans held the Mississippi River—crucial to the battle—but the British had a naval success of their own, sweeping aside the American gunboats on Lake Borgne to the southeast of the city.

Originally, the British had planned to navigate into Lake Pontchartrain and attack New Orleans from the north, through Bayou St. John. But the Royal Navy lacked the shallow draft ships necessary to make the passage. That left them an unexpected alternative that caught Jackson by surprise.

Somehow, the British had stolen a march on him, suddenly appearing at Villére Plantation. The British had landed in the cypress swamps, little more than a dozen miles southeast from the outskirts of New Orleans. But the British made the mistake of pausing their advance. Hot-tempered Jackson lunged to take advantage of it, vowing, "By the Eternal, they shall not sleep on our soil!" He gave his orders: "Gentlemen, the British are below, we must fight them to-night." Jackson quickly assembled about 2,000 men to make good his promise that "I will smash them, so help me God!"[13] Down the Mississippi he sent the fourteen-gun schooner USS *Carolina*.

The *Carolina* anchored directly opposite the British camp. The British were unruffled, assuming it to be a merchant ship, and settled in to make their suppers. Cannonballs became the main course. It was 7:30 P.M., 23 December 1814. After the naval artillery had done its damage, Jackson threw his infantry into the battle.

The disciplined British regulars did not run; instead, they counterattacked so effectively that Jackson drove his horse through enemy fire to order the Marines who were supporting his artillery, "Save the guns, my boys, at every sacrifice."[14] The Marines met the British in hand-to-hand combat, pushing them back, driving deep into the British lines, fighting through falling darkness, fog, and a confusion of gun smoke until nine thirty, when Jackson pulled his men into their defenses outside of New Orleans, though other skirmishes continued until midnight. British Captain John Henry Cooke believed that never "since the invention of gunpowder" had there been "two opposing armies fighting so long muzzle to muzzle."[15] First blood went to the Americans. On Christmas Eve, Jackson fell back to a different defensive line, at Rodriguez Canal, and planned fallback lines behind that. If he could not hold these positions, Jackson was prepared to retreat into the city and set it aflame. There he would battle the British in a blazing winner-take-nothing contest.

Christmas Eve in Ghent, Belgium, was rather less dramatic. The Americans and the British put their signatures to a treaty, agreeing to a peace on the basis of the *status quo ante bellum*, with no resolution of the alleged issues of the war: impressments, settlement of boundaries between Canada and the United States, the rights of neutral shipping, and so forth. These were to be decided by commissions in due course.[16] For the nonce, Lord Liverpool agreed with Wellington, the key thing was to end the war.

The combatants outside New Orleans, however, had no idea the war was over. It would take seven weeks for the news to reach Washington. So they prepared for the greatest battle of the conflict, pitting the finest armed forces in the world against a motley crew of sharpshooting Tennessee frontiersmen (reinforced later by Kentuckians), sailors (only a third of whom spoke English) manning the artillery, pirates, blacks, Indians, and French Louisianans. They were known collectively to the British as "the dirty shirts" who deserved scant respect as soldiers, and who, abominably, failed to abide by the observed decencies of war—killing sentries for sport, among other things.

With the arrival of their commander, General Sir Edward Pakenham, a hero of the Peninsula War, the British regulars felt assured of victory. Pakenham thought General John Keane, who had commanded the army before his arrival, had put them in a damned difficult position, with the Mississippi River on one side, from which they could be and had been raked by American naval artillery, and swampland on the other. His preference was for withdrawing and starting the assault on New Orleans again, from a more promising field of battle. But Admiral Cochrane was bullish, demanding a straight thrust to the prize of New Orleans, where all the redcoats, officers and men, expected to find a wealth of booty.[17] "Captain Dominique," of Jean Lafitte's crew, might have led the pirates proper, but for the Royal Navy and the British army there was such a thing as the spoils of war. The women of Louisiana certainly understood that, and in the manner of Spartan women told their French lovers to come back with their snuffboxes or on them.

First the British brought up artillery against the USS *Carolina,* forcing the

American crew to abandon ship before it exploded. The USS *Louisiana,* farther upriver, pulled back to safety. That same day, 27 December, the British brushed aside minor American resistance to capture the plantations that stood between them and the American line. On 28 December, the redcoats advanced under the cover of artillery and Congreve rocket fire against Jackson's entrenchments at Rodriguez Canal. At 600 yards the British met their nemesis. The American line opened up with an unholy blast of fire and the USS *Louisiana* pitched in with its own cannonades. The British had counted on the Americans panicking at the roar of their rockets and the ominous drumbeat tread of the British regulars. But the Americans didn't panic. They fired their guns with enthusiasm, even glee. One part of the British line, marching through the swampland on the American left, had a chance to turn the American flank, but Pakenham, unable to see them through the smoke of battle, recalled all his men from the hellish slaughter inflicted by the American artillery.

The British were dumbfounded, but those who had predicted an easy victory were almost right. The New Orleans legislature was ready to give the British the keys to the city; it was Jackson who stood in their way. Old Hickory, governing by martial law, disbanded the legislature and locked its members out of the capitol building. This was "Jacksonian Democracy" as it should be.

General Pakenham and Admiral Cochrane withdrew from the range of Jackson's guns and decided to bring up heavier artillery from the British ships in Lake Borgne. Days passed with only minor skirmishes and with the British building gun emplacements. On New Year's Day, even Jackson thought his defenders deserved a celebration and so authorized a parade. His troops lined up in their finest—and British artillery let them have it.

This was the moment. In that instant of American panic, Pakenham should have ordered an immediate charge. But he didn't. He did what seemed sensical, pounding the American positions. But the Americans regained those positions and fired back. The resulting artillery duel was a shameful defeat for the British. The extraordinary mastery that American naval gunners had shown in the past against the Royal Navy was now given a landlubber's display. For Pakenham, it was a disaster.

Despite his losses, Pakenham still held superiority in numbers, perhaps 5,300 men against 4,700 for Jackson. He also developed a plan to make the best of his bad position. On the western side of the Mississippi River, American Brigadier General David Morgan commanded a battery of naval artillery, supported by reinforced militia. Pakenham proposed sending an assault force across the river to seize that position and turn its guns against Jackson. Simultaneously, three columns would hit Jackson's entrenchments.

On paper it worked; in the execution, it did not. Pakenham knew that the plan was unraveling before he launched the attack on the morning of 8 January. Frustrated with delays of getting men into their proper positions with the proper equipment, he refused to wait, as sun pierced through the morning darkness and fog. He fired a rocket signaling the advance—and the cannons, on both sides, roared.

Among the British troops, the fog, miscommunication, and the ill-prepared West Indian and Irish regiments added to the friction of war that makes all plans tenuous. Still, the main thrust of the advance was an eerie and magnificent spectacle as the snap of the drums competed with the thunder of the artillery, and the redcoats marched boldly forward in their columns. American cannons—loaded with grapeshot and firing at close range—ripped into the British lines. The British could not see through the fog, save for the red flashes of cannon and their dead comrades falling before and around them.

Pakenham and his officers tried to rally the men who were faltering under the murderous fire. To their rescue came the skirl of bagpipes and the Highlanders of the 93rd Regiment. But their rescuers merely marched into the hailstorm of death. At 100 yards from the ramparts, even the Highlanders had had enough. Pakenham, his right arm shot through and useless, used his left arm to lift his hat and cheer them on. It only made him a more inviting target. Amid a spattering of grapeshot, he received two more wounds. He ordered that the reserves be thrown into the battle, but it was too late. His wounds were mortal, and the British advance was finished amid a carpet of dead.

There had been two small successes for British arms. A few Britons had successfully crashed into the American lines, but without necessary reinforcements. And the British had taken the position across the river, but only after the Americans had spiked the guns; and those Britons too were recalled with the general retreat. British losses in dead, wounded, and captured numbered about 2,400 men. American casualties amounted to approximately a dozen dead and fifty-eight wounded. For the British, there was no saving grace. They had either been annihilated or humiliated. British soldiers carried General Pakenham's body back to their ships, where the corpse was packed "in a casket of rum to be taken to London. What a sight for his wife who is aboard and who had hoped to be Governess of Louisiana."[18] Another British officer captured by a Tennessean exclaimed: "What a disgrace for a British officer to have to surrender to a chimney sweep."[19]

For Andrew Jackson the field of carnage recalled the New Testament: "I never had so grand and awful an idea of the resurrection as . . . [when] I saw . . . more than five hundred Britons emerging from the heaps of their dead comrades, all over the plain rising up, and coming forward . . . as prisoners."[20] It was victory, and for Old Hickory it was exaltation and glory.

CHAPTER 9

THE EMERGING COLOSSUS

T HE UNITED STATES WAS immediately at war again. In 1814, the Dey of Algiers declared war on the United States. Now, with its British war resolved, America was free to send powder into the faces of Algerians. Two American naval squadrons were dispatched under the commands of Barbary veterans William Bainbridge and Stephen Decatur, but only Decatur saw action. Decatur's squadron blasted the dey's forty-six-gun flagship into submission, and America's naval hero exacted from the pirate king a release of all American prisoners, an end to demands for tribute, and a $10,000 indemnity for the trouble the dey had caused the United States. The swift-sailing Decatur then brought his squadron to Tunis and Tripoli, winning similar pirate surrenders and indemnities. He achieved so much so quickly that he left Commodore Bainbridge, in Bainbridge's sorrowful words, "deprived of the opportunity of either fighting or negotiating."[1] The pirates were beaten; the Americans kept a squadron in the Mediterranean to ensure that fact; and the United States Navy joined with the Royal Navy in ensuring freedom of the seas.

Andy Jackson, meanwhile, was patrolling America's southern borders against the weak Spanish government of Florida, hostile Indians, and runaway slaves (there was a "Negro Fort" in Florida supported by the British). Jackson knew what to do—smash America's enemies with extreme prejudice—but he was obliged to observe the diplomatic niceties of his government. He won agreement from the Spanish governor to destroy the Negro fort, to which task Jackson assigned a joint naval-land task force that quickly reduced the fort and most of its defenders to rubble. But the Indians were the bigger problem, finding sanctuary in Florida from which they could ambush American soldiers and pillage white settlers in Georgia, murdering women and children.

Jackson received the necessary nod from Secretary of War John C. Calhoun[2] to smash the Indians as long as it involved no conflict with Spain. Jackson, whom Thomas Jefferson had thought "a dangerous man,"[3] set about to prove Jefferson's suspicion. For what could be easier, the general decided, than to end the Indian menace by simply annexing Florida? Yes, certainly, there was the small matter of Florida belonging to Spain, but wasn't ownership nine-tenths of the law? If he took it for the United States, would Spain really try to get it back? Jackson wrote to President James Monroe, Madison's successor, that he could make him a prize of the entirety of Florida within sixty days, and he could do it without officially involving Washington.

Jackson raised an army—without congressional authorization—and marched, whether with a wink and a nod from Monroe is a matter of speculation. What is not speculation is that Jackson had embarked on the First Seminole War and the United States had an army of regulars, militia, and friendly Indians scouring Spanish Florida for Seminoles and runaway slaves. Jackson did so while assuring the Spanish governor that he was operating against "our mutual savage enemies." What Jackson did not tell his bullied and bewildered ally was his plan for Florida itself: "I will possess it, for the benefit of the United States, as a necessary position for me to hold, to give peace and security to this frontier, and put a final end to Indian warfare in the South."[4]

Of war there is no end, and Jackson's action carried the risk of a far greater war, not only with Spain—which was a minor risk, given the way Florida's governor bowed, scraped, and acquiesced to the belligerent and unstoppable Jackson—but with Britain, Spain's ally and still a major power in the region; the Royal Navy patrolled the Caribbean and the Atlantic. The Seminoles, Red Stick remnants, and escaped slaves pleaded with the British to support them, as Jackson's troops relentlessly torched their villages on his march along the panhandle. Jackson gave the British every reason to intervene when he ordered executed two British nationals (one a former Royal Marine officer) whom he judged complicit in aiding the Indians and free blacks. The British government, however, did nothing. Indeed, the masterful conservative statesman Lord Castlereagh pursued the same policy he always had done of conciliation with America. He ignored British public opinion and said that while he was sorry the poor chaps had been killed, they had not exactly conducted themselves as law-abiding Britons should, and there was no reason for the Crown's servants to intervene. Nor did President Monroe see any reason to intervene with his hard-charging commander. Nor did he recall Jackson from Florida. So Old Hickory took the next step.

Having satisfactorily cleared the panhandle of hostile Indians and troublesome free blacks, he decided the time was ripe to make Florida his own. He marched into the capital of Pensacola on 24 May 1818. After brief fighting, he won the governor's surrender, and announced that it was not territorial greed that drove him to declare Spanish Florida now American territory, but the responsibility for keeping the peace where Spain could not. He then set up an American government. It took into its hands all legal, military, and tax authority but promised it would protect the traditional rights, laws, and religion of the Spanish settlers. All that remained was to take the last outpost of Spanish power—Fort St. Augustine on the Atlantic coast, at the opposite end of northern Florida—and the entire territory was America's. Oh, and by the way, Jackson added, in a letter to the president, if he could spare a frigate and another regiment of troops, he'd be happy to capture Cuba, too.[5]

What Jackson won by force of arms in 1818, Secretary of State John Quincy Adams confirmed officially by treaty with Spain in 1819. Florida was ceded to America, while America recognized that Texas belonged to Spain, at least for now. Mexico's war for independence was only two years from victory; and Andrew Jackson, for one, believed that Texas belonged to the United States by the preemptive right, well known in international law, of assumed eventual American conquest. Spain also surrendered its claim to the Oregon Territory so that Spain's North American possessions ended at the northern border of California, while the borders separating the United States from Canada remained a matter of dispute. But through Andrew Jackson's fighting and John Quincy Adams's negotiating, the United States and its territories now officially stretched from sea to shining sea.

BLACK HAWK RISING AND THE SECOND SEMINOLE WAR

WITH THE MONROE DOCTRINE, America's hegemony stretched even farther. The doctrine, enunciated by President Monroe in 1823 in his annual address to Congress, was a unilateral declaration that the United States hereby prohibited European colonization of the Americas after the collapse of the Spanish Empire. One might think this was hegemonic impertinence from a power so obviously incapable of enforcing the doctrine. But the Royal Navy could enforce it. Indeed, British foreign secretary George Canning had suggested an Anglo-American declaration along the lines of the Monroe Doctrine,[6] which Monroe eventually rejected, preferring to speak loudly on his own while tacitly relying on Britain's naval stick. The Monroe Doctrine also left open, at John Quincy Adams's insistence, the possibility of further American expansion into what had been Spanish possessions, because Adams was in favor of annexing Cuba as a state.

In the Monroe Doctrine, the United States claimed, as a fundamental foreign policy principle, the right to determine the political fate of an entire hemisphere. It was a tribute to American confidence, if not humility, that typified the "era of good feelings," inaugurated with President Monroe's election in 1816. With the British defeated at New Orleans, with the Barbary pirates actually paying reparations to the United States, with Florida annexed by a resourceful Andrew Jackson, and with the issuance of the Monroe Doctrine—the cost of which would be paid for by the Royal Navy—what was there not to feel good about in a burgeoning continental empire that stretched from the Atlantic to the Pacific?

There were still Indians in the middle, of course, and white settlers sometimes found them troublesome. But the Indians could be dealt with in the usual fashion. The next big Indian war was the Black Hawk War.

By treaty—nefariously negotiated or not—the Sauk and Fox Indians had agreed, in 1804 (and again in 1831), to let white settlers into northern Illinois while the Indians moved west of the Mississippi River into Iowa. In 1832, the Indians divided under two chiefs, Chief Keokuk, who opted for Iowa, and Chief Black Hawk, who repudiated the treaties as unjust. Black Hawk and his followers returned to Illinois, where their very presence scared the hell out of the white settlers and set political sabres a-rattling, militia a-forming, and soldiers a-marching, though Black Hawk had no openly hostile intentions. He did, however, carry a British flag, and the Americans immediately saw the subversive hand of that old Indian friend, the great white father who sat on the throne of the United Kingdom, at this time King William IV. The settlers called Black Hawk's followers the "British Band."

Black Hawk did not, however, speak for Britain. Nor did he speak for any Indians besides his own followers. He led his people up the Rock River where he hoped to be welcomed by other Indian tribes. Instead, he was shunned. If he had hoped to be another Chief Pontiac, he was disappointed. He sent a party under a white flag to negotiate with the Illinois militia commanded by Major Isaiah Stillman. But the nervous militia panicked, seized three of the Indians, and pursued the rest—only to run into an Indian skirmish line that scattered them.

Black Hawk retreated, taking his people north, trying to escape the onrushing tide of soldiers. He was finally brought to battle at Wisconsin Heights, while the Indians attempted to cross the Wisconsin River. Fighting in the rain, the Americans holding the high ground, the Indians taking cover in ravines, Black Hawk successfully brought his people across the river, but at the cost of seventy dead braves to only one dead militiaman. Repeated Indian attempts to negotiate a surrender failed because none of the Americans could understand the Indians.

Black Hawk's willingness to accept a negotiated peace was understood only after the Battle of Bad Axe (1–2 August 1832). Black Hawk had waded out to an armed steamboat, *The Warrior,* carrying a white flag. Unfortunately, again, no one could understand him, and a battle erupted between the Indians, *The Warrior,* and troops on shore commanded by General Henry Atkinson. The Sauks and Foxes were massacred. Sioux scouts, other friendly Indians, and detachments of soldiers tracked Black Hawk's people, scalping them or taking them prisoner. On 27 August Black Hawk and his remaining followers finally found an Indian agent who could understand them, and surrendered. Black Hawk was slapped into jail for eight months, where he became a favorite subject of portrait painters.

As the Black Hawk War ended, war drums began beating in the Florida Everglades. In 1823, after the Treaty of Moultrie Creek, Americans began settling along Florida's coastlines, with the Florida interior left for the Seminole Indians and the runaway slaves who had joined them. Inevitably, conflicts arose between the whites and the Indians over who owned what—including who owned which slaves—and the federal government finally intervened and played real estate agent for the Indians, offering them the splendid lands of Oklahoma with free transport from the malarial swamps of Florida. A group of Seminole leaders visited Oklahoma and didn't like what they saw. The federal government told the Seminoles they were going to be transported anyway. In 1832, the federal government hammered out the Treaty of Payne's Landing, ordering the Seminoles' removal. When the government tried to enforce its decree, it found that seizing the Seminoles was like trying to catch a water moccasin.

The Seminoles were divided. Some went willingly—and risked death at the hands of their fellow Indians, who considered them traitors. Others were imprisoned until they agreed to evacuate Florida for Oklahoma by 1 January 1836. But Osceola, a half-breed warrior and leader (though not a hereditary chief), drove his knife through the treaty. Instead of preparing to leave, he called for war. The Indians who supported him raided settlers and troops for supplies and then coiled into the interior.

The American Army came after them. Militiamen were mustered, regular soldiers were funneled into Florida, and on 28 December 1835 the war erupted with a spectacular opening volley. Seminole warriors under the command of Osceola and Chief Alligator ambushed 107 men of the 3rd U.S. Artillery led by Major Francis Dade. One hundred and seventy-five Indian muskets cracked in unison, striking down Major Dade and more than fifty of his soldiers. With extraordinary courage, the American troops—who, though artillerymen, had been trained to fight as infantry—quickly re-formed, even managing to throw up a log-work defense and bring their single cannon (a small six-pounder) to bear. The Indian musket fire was murderous. At last, a Seminole war whoop went up, the Indians sprang from the swampy undergrowth, and the final killing began. Only three Americans escaped. One died of his wounds, one the Seminoles hunted down and killed, and one lived to tell the tale—telling it for the rest of his life for the edification of generations of Floridian children.

The presumed year of removal, 1836, was a year of setbacks for the United States and the government of the Florida Territory. The Seminoles ambushed— and even besieged—American troops with impunity. The American commanders changed, but the results didn't. In January 1836, the commander of all troops in Florida was General Winfield Scott. In May, it was Governor Richard Call. And in December, the baton was handed to General Thomas Jesup, who was recommended for promotion thanks to an aggressive and successful campaign in western Florida.

Florida became a territory of forts, and Jesup's growing army of roughly 8,000 troops—guided by Indian defectors—pressured the Seminoles, who were running short on supplies and food. The Seminoles needed freedom to plant and harvest, but Jesup's strategy kept the Seminoles so harried that planting and harvesting were near impossible. On 25 October 1837, Osceola and more than seventy warriors entered an American camp, asking to negotiate. The Americans agreed—and immediately imprisoned the Indians. Osceola, the most famous of the Seminole rebels, died at Fort Moultrie, South Carolina, on 30 January 1838.

His imprisonment and death, however, did not break the back of the Seminole rebellion. Jesup used his large army to keep the Seminoles on the run, the constant pressure forcing some to surrender, and pressing the remaining warrior bands to the south. The great battle of the war was fought on Christmas Day 1838 at Lake Okeechobee, where 400 Seminoles and blacks defended their village against 1,100 Americans—800 regulars, 250 Missouri and Florida militia, and 50 Indians—under the command of Colonel Zachary Taylor. The Americans had to cross a half-mile-long patch of sodden mown grass on which the Seminoles trained their muskets. The Seminoles intended this to be their killing field. Zachary Taylor accepted the Indian challenge, threw his men across the field, and dared a frontal assault of fixed bayonets, which, in the event, the Indians found more frightening than the Americans did Indian marksmanship. Twenty-six Americans fell, but when the soldiers' cold steel rammed into the Indians, the Seminoles sprang away, abandoning their village.

The Seminoles now felt desperate and vulnerable—and given that the Army, Navy, Marine Corps, and various militias and Indian scouts were hunting them down, they had every reason to feel vulnerable. Seminole surrenders increased, though the skirmishes continued, extending all the way to the Florida Keys, until hostilities finally ended in 1842. By the end of the war, 4,000 Seminoles had been moved to Oklahoma, several hundred remained in Florida's interior, and perhaps a thousand Seminoles had been killed. In the process, the American military had learned a hell of a lot about guerilla warfare and swamp fighting—always useful skills to have.[7]

LONE STAR REPUBLIC

IN THE MEXICAN TERRITORY of Texas, Americans settlers weren't learning new skills; they were reviving the old ones of creating a new nation as their forefathers had done. In Mexico's dictator, Generalissimo Antonio López de Santa Anna, they saw a new and worse version of George III. Independence was the cry, and war was the result.

The white rebels were, officially, Mexican citizens, though they made a habit of disregarding Mexican law when it suited them. They did not, as a rule, become Catholics, as they were supposed to do. Nor did they forswear slavery[8] as was required by Mexican law. No, instead, they imported the Protestant religion and black chattel slavery as part of who they were; and the Mexican officials, who actively encouraged American settlers into Texas to fill up the sparsely populated province and make it productive, turned a blind eye to such failures to abide by the letter, or for that matter even the spirit, of Mexican law.

The American settlers—adventurers, profit-seekers, debt-dodgers, rogues, and criminals—came from the frontiers of the southern United States, and were, to any eye that could see, sure to make trouble. Their betters in Washington, Monroe's successors as president, John Quincy Adams (1825–29) and Andrew Jackson (1829–37), offered to spare Mexico the trauma of assimilating these rowdies, knowing as these presidents did—Jackson in particular—that they were much better at assimilating the rawboned, hard-swearing, mean-fighting, sharpshooting, whiskey-swilling, lower Protestant classes and diverting them to useful work: killing Indians and bears, providing a large market for distillers and publicans, and enlarging the American empire with their preference for moseying from one land of opportunity to the next.

Adams offered Mexico one million dollars for Texas. Jackson upped the bid to five million dollars. But the pride of Mexico's rulers—these were descendants of imperial Spain, after all—was appalled at the very suggestion that they should offer up huge tracts of Mexico for pieces of silver. Had they known that after the Louisiana Purchase the United States had considered invading Mexico, they might have been less welcoming of American settlers. Had they recognized what sort of man Andrew Jackson was—and what sort of Americans he represented—they might well have shrugged their shoulders at the inevitable and withdrawn from Texas. The Mexicans, however, failed to recognize the danger of Scotch-Irish American frontiersmen on the march.

Mexico had been independent since 1821. The war for independence from Spain—and independence itself—was a disaster for Mexico, an act of self-mutilation.[9] One-tenth of Mexico's population was killed in the years of fighting. Mexico's economy was destroyed. Mexico's cultural achievements, which before independence had rivaled or surpassed those of the United States, were sent into swift decline by the revolution. High ideals about freedom were no substitute for peace and order, which was something that subsequent governments could never quite discover. The dour Yankee John Quincy Adams looked upon the "liberation" of South and Central America from Spain not with the enthusiasm of Henry Clay, who saw Latin Americans breaking chains for freedom, but with the flinty observation that there was "no prospect that they would establish free or liberal institutions of government. Arbitrary power, military or ecclesiastical, was stamped upon their habits, and upon all their institutions."[10]

Mexico had always regarded Texas as a sort of Siberia and that, combined with postindependence turmoil, was another reason the government was untroubled by American settlers. By the end of the 1820s, Americans (only about half of whom had come in with the blessing of the Mexican government) easily outnumbered Mexicans in the province by at least two to one, and in some towns made up virtually the entire population. By 1836, Anglo-Americans would outnumber Mexicans by ten to one.

As the War of 1812 had its War Hawks, the Texas War of Independence had its "War Dogs"—as a rule, young southern lawyers with murky pasts and high, romantic ambitions: men like the venereal William "Buck" Travis and the alcoholic Sam Houston, both of whom left broken marriages to reinvent themselves in Texas, where their taste for personal dissipation, chivalric romance, and dreams of epic grandeur could be fulfilled. In 1830, Mexico handed the War Dogs their flaming torch of an issue. Texas had been "free"—that is, nearly lawless—but now the Mexican government wanted to assert its authority by garrisoning troops in Texas, closing the border with the United States, controlling immigration (the government had come to assume that Europeans would make safer settlers than would Americans), and ending the importation of slaves. Most important, tariffs and Mexican law would finally be enforced.

Quite obviously this was tyranny. Indeed, it reminded the American settlers of the outrageous tyranny of King George III who had tried to enforce the law against smuggling. Texas was so heavily populated with Americans that smuggling was one of its chief economic activities. The arrival of Mexican troops— led by a Kentucky-born officer, Colonel Juan Davis Bradburn, but made up of convict recruits—was the cause of continual friction. As redcoats were baited by the mob in Boston, so were the Mexican convict-recruits accused of crimes against southern women and fomenting slave rebellion against Texas slave owners.

When Colonel Bradburn finally had enough of such goading and jailed Travis and other War Dogs in 1832 for threatening insurrection, the fuse of Texas rebellion was well and truly lit. As a precaution, the Texicans posed at first as Mexican patriots, merely asserting the rights of the liberal 1824 Constitution of Mexico (modeled in part on the American Constitution). They formed militias and fought their first battle against Mexican troops—and beat them. A Mexican colonel, José de las Piedras, stepped forward to negotiate with the rebels. He agreed to free the War Dogs and return to Texas the freedom from Mexican law it had previously enjoyed. He could do this because Mexico's own government was in perpetual upheaval, and as such, Texas returned to being a lawless frontier. Such happiness couldn't last.

But it lasted long enough for wealthy Texans of Mexican blood, the *Tejanos,* to recognize that the Anglo-Americanization of Texas—if one could overlook the frontiersmen's barbaric manners, lack of moral scruples, and heretical religion—was a good thing. Independent Mexico was collapsing into destitution, while the United States was just as obviously booming with people, talent, money, and power. Any true Mexican patriot could recognize that nationalism wasn't what was best for his people; annexation to the United States was.

In 1835, General Santa Anna, now president of the Republic of Mexico, ordered a crackdown on corruption, which meant troops and Mexican law encroaching on Texas. He had revoked the constitution of 1824, declared himself dictator, and was exterminating any remnants of the constitutional federalism of the Mexican Republic. Travis and the War Dogs found plenty of recruits straining at the leash to fight against Santa Anna's tyranny; to fight for Texas freedom; to fight for Texas to be annexed to the United States; to fight for the Mexican constitution of 1824; or frankly just to fight for the hell of it. Even the formerly dovish Texas leader Stephen Austin—hardened after being imprisoned in Mexico for a year (including three months of solitary confinement)—now declared for war.

Mexican cavalry were sent to disarm a rapidly formed Texas militia that boasted a small cannon. The cannon was the centerpiece of the rebels' flag, which bore the legend "Come and Take It."[11] The militia fired on the cavalry, and after a brief pause to parley, renewed the attack and chased the Mexicans from the field. This first battle, the Battle of Gonzalez (2 October 1835), went to the Texans. So did the next battle, a week later and far more important: on 9 October 1835, the Texans seized the Mexican presidio at Goliad, which offered up a treasure trove of military supplies.

Men throughout the South rallied to the Texans' cause—from as far north as Kentucky and as far east as Georgia, tough frontier giants and young would-be cavaliers picked up muskets and mustered themselves for roll calls.[12] The news from Texas was of continuous victories. Slave trader, smuggler, and land speculator Jim Bowie—designer of the famous knife for gutting opponents—led the rebels to victory at the Battle of Concepción (28 October 1835). The Mexican troops had artillery and outnumbered the Texans five to one, but firing from the shelter of a riverbank, the Americans lost only one man while killing sixty Mexican troops, wounding another sixty, and driving the remainder from the field. The Texans then besieged and took San Antonio de Béxar (and the Alamo) on 9 December 1835 after a month and a half of battering.

Dictator and general Santa Anna began amassing troops to crush the Texas rebels. He had fought Americans before. In 1813, nearly a thousand American adventurers had joined a Mexican rebellion and captured San Antonio. Young Lieutenant Santa Anna was with the Mexican army that eliminated the rebellion and inflicted 90 percent casualties on the Americans—by killing those they captured. He thought himself Mexico's Napoleon; his only loyalty was to himself. So he posed, in turn, as a royalist, a revolutionary, a liberal, and a dictator—whatever helped advance the cause of Santa Anna. Most important for the Texans, he was well experienced in warfare and committing atrocities.

When he struck in March 1836, the Texans absorbed three blows, but delivered the knockout blow themselves. On 2 March 1836, the Texans declared themselves independent, raising the Lone Star Flag. At the mission church known as the Alamo—in the epic that would define the war—the Texans were already in the midst of defending their independence. One hundred and eighty American fighters, including William Travis, Jim Bowie, and the frontier legend Davy Crockett, held off Santa Anna's 3,000 troops from 23 February until 6 March 1836. The tenacious defenders killed more than half of Santa Anna's army at the cost of their own lives, but their heroic example was the best recruiter Texas had.

The Americans were defeated again at Coletto Creek (19–20 March 1836), and, in a fateful decision, their commander, Colonel James Fannin, surrendered his army, despite the ardent protests of the hot-blooded—and, as it turned out, right—militias known as the New Orleans Greys and the Alabama Red Rovers, who argued that it was better to die fighting for Texas independence than it was to die in captivity at the hands of the untrustworthy Mexican army. But Fannin and the majority of his men assumed that if they surrendered they would be paroled home.

They were marched to the Goliad presidio. More than 500 American prisoners were packed into its confines, awaiting Santa Anna's verdict on their fate. He had already issued orders that captured Americans were to be killed, and he had enforced these orders on American stragglers. But would he execute an entire army? General José Urrea, who had accepted the Americans' surrender, thought not. General Urrea, a better man than Santa Anna, was wrong. Santa Anna rebuked Urrea for not slaughtering the Texans. Both generals sent letters to the commander at Goliad: Santa Anna ordered the prisoners' immediate execution and sent an officer to witness the killings; Urrea ordered that the prisoners be treated well and put to work on useful projects.

Twenty-eight-year-old Colonel José Nicolás Portilla had to decide. He gave priority to the letter from the generalissimo and dictator of Mexico. The Americans were marched out—still assuming they would be paroled—only to be mortally surprised when the Mexicans formed up in musket lines and raked the lines of American prisoners of war. About 350 Americans were killed at the massacre of Goliad on Palm Sunday, 27 March 1836.

"Remember the Alamo! Remember the Goliad!" became the Texas battle cry, but the Texans themselves, under Sam Houston, seemed in dire straits. Houston had fewer than a thousand men in his army, and Santa Anna had the weight of all Mexico behind him. But at the Battle of San Jacinto on 21 April 1836, Houston's men crept up on Santa Anna's 1,500 troops as they enjoyed their afternoon siesta and opened fire on them. Cavalry under the command of Georgian Mirabeau Buonaparte Lamar charged, as did the Texas infantry, which closed immediately into hand-to-hand combat. The Mexicans fled in terror. They pleaded "Me no Alamo! Me no Goliad" as American troopers clubbed them down; the Americans had no patience with such pleadings. More than half of Santa Anna's army was killed or wounded, and the remainder was swept up and captured, including Santa Anna himself. Only nine Texans had been killed.

Santa Anna was presented to a wounded Sam Houston, who was propped up beneath an oak tree so he could stretch out his wounded leg: a musket ball had shattered his ankle. While he was the victor of the battle, he knew that a larger Mexican army was marching after him. Nevertheless, Santa Anna, eye always on himself, was in no position to negotiate after the Alamo and the Goliad. Houston demanded that he issue an order withdrawing Mexican troops from Texas, pledge never to fight Texas again, and grant Texas independence. Santa Anna, the self-proclaimed "Napoleon of the West," had no choice. His surrender made Sam Houston the inevitable elected president of the Republic of Texas.

The war was won. Independence was had. But what Texans really wanted was statehood within the United States. In that, they suddenly ran up against the unlikely opposition of former president John Quincy Adams—unlikely, because Adams had been a prime architect of American power. He broke with Republican tradition not only by forming the Republicans into a new party, the Whigs, but by wanting to expand the Navy. He was for building roads and canals and sending expeditions to the West (as Jefferson had done with Lewis and Clark). He had been the mind behind the Monroe Doctrine and a practical driving force behind America's assumption of a manifest destiny to rule the continent. But with Texas, a domestic political issue skewed his judgment. The issue was slavery, which had become the paramount dividing line in American politics, first pressed to an extremity in the crisis over Missouri in 1820.

America had banned the slave trade in 1808 and had prohibited slavery north of the Ohio River and east of the Mississippi in 1787, as part of the Northwest Ordinance governing northwestern expansion. But when Missouri applied for statehood as a slave territory in 1820, northern states protested, with New York Congressman James Tallmadge calling for the emancipation of Missouri slaves. Instead, a compromise was hammered out over 1820–21 that barred slavery north of Missouri's southern border—save for Missouri, which was permitted slavery.

When Texas won its independence, there were thirteen slave states and thirteen free states. Florida was not yet a state, but the North had more territories in its quiver than did the South: with Iowa, Wisconsin, and Minnesota lining up for admission to the Union, and more to follow along the Great Plains, while the slave states were blocked by greater Mexico. Adams, the Yankee, pressed his fingers on the scales of power. Just as he wanted American hegemony over two continents, he wanted northern hegemony over the South, and no monkey business with Texas coming in as a slave state or divided into several slave states.

Even more surprising was the hesitance of President Andrew Jackson. Old Hickory regarded Texas as political dynamite and did not grant American recognition of the Lone Star Republic until he had secured the approval of Congress and after the election of 1836—which ensured the election of his vice president, Martin Van Buren, as his successor. New Yorker Martin Van Buren (1837–41), recognizing extreme abolitionist opinion in the North and belligerent proslavery opinion in the South, was content to pass the issue of Texas statehood onto his successor William Henry Harrison (1841), who promptly died, leaving the political hot potato of Texas to his succeeding vice president, John Tyler of Virginia (1841–45). Tyler, a slaveholder, was naturally sympathetic to Texas statehood. Actually, Tyler more than sympathized. He feared that if Texas was not annexed to the United States it might abolish slavery and ally itself to Britain.

The battle lines were clear, if tangled. In his secretary of state, John C. Calhoun, Tyler had an ally; Calhoun's state of South Carolina even threatened to secede and join the Republic of Texas if Texas statehood was denied. But in the northern states, members of Tyler's party, the Whigs, argued that annexation was unconstitutional, while northern states with Jacksonian Democratic majorities (Maine, New Hampshire, and Illinois) approved of Texas statehood. Tyler's annexation treaties failed. But in an expedient of dubious constitutionality, Tyler won simple majorities for a congressional "joint resolution" for annexing Texas as a state of the United States. He had his victory on his last day in office on 26 February 1845.

So the new president, the Democrat James K. Polk of Tennessee (1845–49), inherited Texas not as a political problem, but as a state (as of 29 December 1845), a state he intended to expand. He also had his eye on California, and that as much as Texas led to America's next war of expansion, the biggest by far.

CHAPTER 10

MILITARY HOLIDAY IN MEXICO

T HE UNITED STATES HAD conquered California once before. In 1842, American Navy Commodore Thomas Ap Catesby Jones sailed to Monterey and demanded surrender from the Mexican governor. He did so under the mistaken impression that Mexico and the United States were imminently to be at war. When he was assured this was not the case, he returned the Mexican governor to the seat of power and sailed away.

This interesting precedent did not do much to encourage pro-American feeling in the Mexican government, and the Mexicans spurned President Polk's attempts to buy California. But it would appear that affronted pride rather than practicality guided Mexican policy, for if Commodore Jones could sail into Monterey once, he could do it again. California was sparsely populated with Mexicans and pacific Indians. More important, it already had a few American settlers—and Mexico should have known what that meant.

Polk certainly did. In 1845, he was encouraging the Americans in California to emulate their cousins in Texas and shake the sleepy territory with calls for liberty and annexation by the United States. Urgency was required not so much because of any aspect of Mexican policy, but because Polk feared the intentions of Britain—the Royal Navy appraisingly eyed the California coastline—and the Russian bear, who had established trading posts in California.

Meanwhile, Polk moved Zachary Taylor and the United States Army to protect Texas's southwestern border with Mexico. Mexico had broken off diplomatic relations with the United States because of the annexation of Texas. Polk sent John Slidell to Mexico anyway demanding that Mexico pay off its debts (from bonds and other obligations) owed to the United States. But, of course, Slidell—rather the perfect name for a diplomat—had a deal. The debts could be cancelled if Mexico would affirm the Rio Grande as the Texas-Mexico border. In addition, if Mexico ceded the territories of New Mexico and California to the United States, the American government was willing to pay five million dollars for the former and many more millions of dollars—Mexico could set the price—for the latter.

The Mexican president José Joaquin de Herrera huffily refused to see Slidell, but was swiftly overthrown by General Mariano Paredes. General Paredes was adamant: any more *yanqui* talk about debts and purchases and annexations meant war. Polk's response was: don't mind if I do. He ordered Zachary Taylor across the Mexican-established Texas border (along the Nueces River) to a position 150 miles south along the Rio Grande (the border claimed by Texas). Taylor trained his guns on Matamoras, Mexico, which he blockaded. The American challenge was clear: come and get me. The Mexican army took the bait, ambushing a detachment of American dragoons, killing eleven of them. Polk now had the casus belli he wanted. The president, who noted in his diary that he regretted disturbing his Sabbath reflections working out the proper response, announced that Mexico had precipitated a war against the United States. This was truer than Polk knew, because the war was already under way. Neither the Mexican army nor Zachary Taylor waited for official word from Washington. President Polk requested a congressional declaration of war on 11 May 1846—after two major battles: Palo Alto (8 May) and Resaca de la Palma (9 May).

Much of America—especially the North—was skeptical. Polk, they thought, had manufactured an unnecessary war; it was an act of aggression to add more slave states to the Union. A young congressman from Illinois named Abraham Lincoln was one of the doubters. In the event, congressional authorization for the war passed overwhelmingly in both houses. But it was the southern states closest to Texas that were full of enthusiasts and volunteers. They remembered the heroism of the Alamo, the outrage at Goliad, and the victory at San Jacinto. They brought down their muskets, kissed their sweethearts good-bye (or, if more rustic, packed up a big supply of chewing tobaccy), and mustered themselves into militias or volunteer units. Equally enthusiastic were the generals of the Mexican army, who hankered to repel Zachary Taylor, regain Texas, and even attack Louisiana.

The Mexican army numbered more than 30,000 men, while the American regular army was less than one-fourth that size. But what the Americans lacked in numbers, they made up for in the quality of their units and in the tens of thousands of volunteers who already knew how to handle a gun and weren't afraid of nothin'—neither Indians, nor bears, nor Mexicans—and in fact rather enjoyed the idea of fighting and conquering for the United States.[1] Lieutenant

Ulysses S. Grant—who would become no small judge of soldiers—wrote home proudly that "a better army, man for man," than Zachary Taylor's 2,300 men, "probably never faced an enemy."[2]

The Mexican army, on the other hand, though impressive in numbers, was ill-trained (for one thing, the soldiers nervously fired from the hip) and top-heavy. It had more officers than enlisted men, and its officers stood on their authority while their peon-class troops stood only until it became obvious that survival recommended fleeing in another direction. The best soldiers in the Mexican army were a special class of mercenaries the Mexicans acquired just before and during the hostilities: American deserters, specifically, Catholics—many of them Irishmen, who made up a quarter of the American enlisted ranks—who chafed under the harsh discipline of their commanders and felt drawn to their coreligionists (the Irish Catholic soldiers had no chaplains of their own in the U.S. Army).[3] The Catholic deserters—whom the Mexicans actively recruited with claims that the United States acted as a Protestant power seeking to exterminate the Catholic Church in Mexico—formed the Batallón de San Patricio (Saint Patrick Battalion) under the command of an Irish-born private named John O'Reilly.[4] The fighting Irish, like the tenacious Scotch, are natural-born soldiers; and so it proved here.

Meanwhile, Old Rough and Ready Zachary Taylor lived up to his name by playing rough and ready with martial law, executing a couple of foreign-born rankers (a Frenchman and a Swiss), before the official onset of hostilities, in order to discourage further desertions. In those days, admirable men like Andrew Jackson and Zachary Taylor treated "legality" with the proper respect it deserved: damn little. Practicality before pettifoggery is the law of reasonable men.

Such practicality also induced President Polk to refute the Mexican charge that the United States was fighting a religious war. The president asked American Catholic bishops for help, and two priests were dispatched to provide the sacraments for Catholic soldiers. The priests were officially civilians—there were no chaplain billets open to them—but they shared the hardships of the men. Mexican bandits murdered one of the priests and the other eventually fell prey to sickness and had to be sent home. From Washington, Zachary Taylor received a proclamation to be delivered to the Mexican people: "Your religion, your altars, and churches, the property of your churches and citizens, the emblems of your faith and its ministers shall be protected and remain inviolate. . . . Hundreds of our army, and hundreds of thousands of our people are members of the Catholic Church. . . ."[5] Whether this did much good is open to question.

Mexican priests bemoaned the fact that the barbarian American volunteers were "Vandals vomited from Hell."[6] The American regular officers who had to deal with these violent, recalcitrant, and unwieldy Kentuckian, Tennessean, and Texan frontiersmen—about whom they themselves complained—no doubt sympathized.[7] But focused on their task, the "Vandals vomited from Hell" made excellent soldiers.

The first major engagement was the Battle of Palo Alto (8 May 1846), where Mexican General Mariano Arista, having crossed the Rio Grande and failed to take Fort Texas,[8] drew up his artillery, lancers, and infantry to confront Zachary Taylor's army. In the ensuing artillery duel the American gunners—with the accuracy that was their trademark—got much the better of the Mexicans, and General Arista withdrew his men. At that night's council of war Zachary Taylor seconded the opinion of Captain James Duncan: "We whipped 'em today and we can whip 'em tomorrow."[9] So the Americans pursued General Arista's army and whipped 'em again, despite the Mexicans having well-laid battle lines at Resaca de la Palma and despite the Mexicans outnumbering the Americans by 4,000 men. The Americans whipped the Mexicans all the way back across the Rio Grande. In their flight, the Mexicans left their border town of Matamoros undefended.

In Old California things went even better. The American settlers declared their independence, and the California Bear Flag Republic was born. There was no California Alamo because when the California rowdies knocked on the door of California's Commandante-General Mariano G. Vallejo and arrested him, they discovered he was actually on their side: he favored American annexation. California's status as a great independent republic, a historical memory some of us still honor, lasted all of twenty-four days before Commodore John Sloat repeated Commodore Thomas Ap Catesby Jones's deft, if premature, capture of California by sailing into Monterey on 9 July 1846 and declaring that California was hereby annexed to the United States.

To the east, Colonel Stephen Kearny marched from Fort Leavenworth, Kansas, to New Mexico and took the territory without firing a shot, entering Albuquerque on 18 August 1846. Like the Californians, the New Mexicans welcomed annexation. When Kearny received news of action in California, he decided to rush his troopers across the desert to help the American cause.

He left a detachment of men in Santa Fe to take care of a few troublemaking Indians and Mexicans. He sent another unit south to assist in the invasion of central Mexico and link up with Zachary Taylor's army. Kearny himself took a party of dragoons and, using Kit Carson as his scout, raced across the sands of Arizona and California. His men, hungry and haggard, were met not by California senoritas bearing margaritas (which, alas, had not been invented yet) but by Californio lancers at San Pasqual about forty miles northeast of San Diego. The lancers bloodied Kearny's men in an engagement on 6 December 1846. Three officers were killed, and Kearny himself was among the wounded. But the Americans kept the field through the strength of their artillery. Kearny then withdrew his men to San Diego where the American Navy was already established. In league with Commodore Robert Stockton, Kearny rested, refitted, and reinforced his troops and marched them north, besting the Californios in two consecutive engagements—the Battle of the San Gabriel River (8 January 1847) and the Battle of La Mesa (9 January 1847). That was enough. California was won.

In Texas, fighting continued, and with equal ease Zachary Taylor's men took Matamoros in May and Camargo in July 1846. And there, in what proved to be a pestilential location—full of scorpions, tarantulas, and disease that claimed the lives of one of every eight encamped soldiers, including a disproportionate number of volunteers—Taylor prepared his army for what would be its first testing encounter, at Monterrey.

The city's geography, on high ground backed by the Santa Catarina River to the south, made it easily defended. The city itself was built like a fortress. The streets were blockaded. And the stone houses of the city were miniblockhouses. A thousand yards north of the city was the Citadel, a real fortress that the Americans called the "Black Fort" for its dominating position on the field and the danger it posed to any American attack. In addition, the Mexicans had built two new forts—Fort Tenería and Fort Diablo—to defend the city's eastern flank. To the west, the two hills that straddled the Saltillo Road leading into the city were well defended. Indepedencia Hill had Fort Libertad with 50 men and a couple of guns as well as the fortified ruins of a bishop's palace held by another 200 men and four guns. On Federación Hill was Fort Soldado on its eastern side and a small gun emplacement on its western side. The Mexicans had more than 7,000 regular soldiers and forty-two guns at Monterrey. Against them, Taylor had 6,000 men.

Zachary Taylor faced a daunting military task, but he quickly discerned the hidden weakness of the Mexican position. Fort Tenería, Fort Diablo, the Citadel, the hill forts, and the city itself were so positioned that each could be isolated and unable to support the other. Unless the Mexicans massed to meet him on open ground, the fortifications could be tackled individually. Taylor, a strong believer in directly storming positions with bayonets—it worked against Seminoles, after all—authorized a more creative, if potentially dangerous, plan at Monterrey. He divided his troops for separate simultaneous assaults. The advantage lay in bypassing the Citadel. General William Worth's division would strike the hill forts to the west while the rest of the army hit the newly constructed forts in the east and break into the city. The danger lay in dividing his forces and in trying to coordinate the assaults.

On the morning of 21 September 1846, the attack began. Worth's men advanced on the Saltillo Road, hurling back charging Mexican cavalry and inflicting heavy Mexican losses. By nightfall they had seized—and were celebrating the capture of—Federación Hill. Zachary Taylor, meanwhile, tried to keep the defenders of the Citadel pinned down with artillery fire, while he gave Lieutenant Colonel John Garland ambiguous orders about striking from the east. Taylor had meant Garland's to be a diversionary attack. Garland took it to be the lead of the main attack, and quickly got into trouble. His men got stuck in the sweet spot for the Mexican defenders where he was open to fire from the Citadel, the two eastern forts, and the city. More American units charged in to support him. Mexican fire stubbornly cut them down, but when the Americans didn't withdraw, the Mexicans panicked. The commander at Fort Tenería and half his men ran away.

Colonel Jefferson Davis of the Mississippi Rifles saw his moment: "Now is the time! Great God! If I had 30 men with knives I could take the fort!"[10] Even without those men, he and the other charging volunteers took it. But the reduction of Fort Tenería had taken until noon, and though artilleryman Braxton Bragg had managed to bring artillery up to the very streets of Monterrey, the rest of the day was a stalemate. Four hundred Americans, a quarter of them Tennesseans, were dead or wounded: a high price to pay for the capture of a single supporting fort.

On 22 September, Worth again took the lead, spending the day clearing the defenders from Independencia Hill—a job made easier by the Mexicans in the bishop's palace choosing to charge the Americans rather than sit tight behind their defenses. On the other side of Monterrey, the Americans were disinclined to do anything but reorganize themselves for another try the next day. This was just as well, as the Mexican commander, General Pedro de Ampudia, abandoned Fort Diablo and his other outlying positions and concentrated his defenders in the city and at the Citadel.

The third day of battle did not look auspicious for the Americans. Worth's men, though victors, had spent two nights in drenching rains, had scaled two hills, and had two full days of fighting—all without food. Their one great incentive to assault the city was to hit the larders. At the other end of Monterrey, the Americans began a reconnaissance in force that penetrated the city with minimal opposition. The Americans then cleared the defenders house by house, with tactics very similar to those that would be used today: breaking down doors (or walls), tossing in grenades, and then clearing the rooftops. From there, they provided covering fire for troops attacking the next house. Thus, the Americans methodically and efficiently advanced, with light artillery support, clearing blockaded streets. Worth never received orders, but at the sound of firing led his men into the battle and advanced house by house from the west.

The Americans did not press into the center plaza—where the civilians huddled in the cathedral, which General Ampudia was also using as an ammunition dump—but pulled back and dropped mortar rounds into it. As the shelling came closer to the cathedral, General Ampudia came closer to losing his nerve. Well before dawn, General Ampudia opened communications with Taylor that over the course of the next twenty-four hours led to the surrender of Monterrey. Taylor eventually conceded—under hard Mexican negotiating—extremely generous terms that allowed the Mexican army to evacuate the city with its arms and under cover of an eight-week armistice.

President Polk, when he learned of the terms, privately denounced Taylor for a lack of aggression. The Democrat Polk already suspected Taylor of Whiggish presidential ambitions—a military hero on a literal white horse (Old Whitey). Now he suspected him of being soft on Mexicans, too. It did not help that General Winfield Scott (a Whig) cheered Taylor's "three glorious days," which was how the battle appeared in the popular press. Taylor appointed Worth governor of Monterrey and set about using the armistice to patch up and rebuild his army.

TO THE HALLS OF MONTEZUMA

THE UNITED STATES had secured for Texas the border it wanted. It had seized the territories of California and New Mexico (which included the future states of Arizona, Nevada, Utah, and part of Colorado). So now what was the objective: to hold what had been taken, to demand—again—Mexico's payment of debts, or to march into Mexico City and take over the government of Mexico?

The Mexican government had fallen into the hands of Santa Anna. At the outset of the war he had been in exile in Cuba. The United States connived in smuggling him back into Mexico on the understanding that he would broker a peace. Instead, he saw himself returning from exile, like his hero Napoleon from Elba, to grasp a second chance at glory. Ten years had passed since the Alamo. He was fifty-two years old, and short one leg—blown off by the French when they employed gunboat diplomacy to force Mexico to repay its debts. He did, however, have a seventeen-year-old second wife, which surely made the loss of a limb and the bruising of his ego easier to assuage. And now he had his great chance to defeat the *yanquis* who had wrested Texas from Mexico. He raised an army of 20,000 men and led them on a forced march north. Their goal: crush Zachary Taylor.

Generalissimo Santa Anna had to hurry, because the United States Navy was probing the Gulf of Mexico. In November 1846, the Navy plucked the Mexican port city of Tampico, and Santa Anna knew that the Americans' ultimate goal was taking Vera Cruz and then Mexico City. But he assumed that if he defeated Taylor, he would give strength to antiwar critics in the United States, who derided the American invasion as "Mr. Polk's War." The peace party included such strange bedfellows as Abraham Lincoln, who opposed the war on moral and legal grounds; John C. Calhoun, who opposed it on constitutional ones and because he worried it would exacerbate conflict between the slave and free states; and such elder statesmen as John Quincy Adams, Henry Clay, and Daniel Webster. Most Americans, however, took a more robust view, as captured in this little ditty:

Old Zack's at Monterey,
Bring out your Santa Anner:
For every time we raise a gun,
Down goes a Mexicaner.[11]

General Winfield Scott, "Old Fuss 'n' Feathers" and the most educated soldier in the Army, led the Vera Cruz expedition. He had the honor to inform Zachary Taylor (via letter) that he was taking 9,000 of his men—half of them regulars—plus two batteries of light field artillery, for his campaign. "Providence may defeat me," wrote Scott, "but I do not believe the Mexicans can."[12]

Zachary Taylor's leathery face turned the color of oxblood when he learned Scott intended to steal his men. He consoled himself by preparing to fight Santa

Anna. "Let them come," Taylor growled of the Mexican army. "Damned if they don't go back a good deal faster than they came."[13] Brigadier General John E. Wool spotted the advancing Mexicans. With Taylor's approval, he prepared positions eight miles south of Saltillo near the Hacienda Buena Vista on ground cut by ravines that favored the defense and limited the mobility of Santa Anna's cavalry.[14] On 2 February 1847, Santa Anna sent a messenger to Taylor informing him that he was surrounded and outnumbered, and requesting his surrender. Taylor replied true to form: "Tell Santa Anna to go to hell!"[15]

That first day of battle was taken up with inconsequential skirmishing. The second day, however, was a decisive clash between 15,000 Mexican effectives and 5,000 Americans. Santa Anna made the most of his massed force, drawing them up in sight of the Americans, expecting the ruffians led by Old Rough and Ready to be awed by the Mexicans' numbers, their European-style uniforms, the musical splendor of their bands, and the solemn dignity of the priests who passed through the ranks giving their blessings to the soldiers. But to the American volunteer regiments in particular this was all flummery. They licked their thumbs and moistened their musket sights for good luck, and settled down to do what they had come to do: kill Mexicans.

In the initial fighting, American artillery put a full stop to the Mexican advance on the narrow road to Buena Vista, but in the center-left of the American line on a plateau along the high ground, the Mexicans burst through with such vigor— if confused vigor—that General Wool moaned to Zachary Taylor: "General, we are whipped." To which Taylor responded: "That is for me to determine."[16] He determined, rightly, that Wool was wrong, and he rushed the Mississippi Rifles under Jefferson Davis to plug the line. They did that—and drove the Mexicans back.

Santa Anna threw his lancers around the American left flank, charging to take Buena Vista. But Taylor was ready for that gambit and put his dragoons on the chase. They cut the lancers off and turned them away. Santa Anna thought he saw a new way around the Americans. He hurled another attack against Taylor's left flank, this time farther out. But the Americans repelled it and inflicted heavy losses on the Mexicans.

The Americans, however, were also badly battered. Every American unit, save for the Mississippians, had at one point been forced to give ground. And the Americans had suffered heavy losses—including the desertion of 30 percent of their number when things got hot. Among the dead was a young officer,

Henry Clay Jr., son of the antiwar politician who had campaigned against Polk for the presidency. Clay, cut off, wounded, and surrounded by Mexicans, fired his pistol until it was exhausted and the Mexicans killed him.

Taylor reinforced his lines, and as dawn broke, the Americans made an astonishing discovery: Santa Anna had withdrawn. The Americans were jubilant—and prudent. They returned to Monterrey and safety. Santa Anna, after a decent interval of pretending to wait for Taylor's advance, raced back to Mexico City. By the time he got there, his army—bedraggled by casualties, forced marches, and no supplies—was reduced to 10,500 men.

Meanwhile, to the north, at Chihuahua, an army of Missouri volunteers led by the giant Colonel Alexander Doniphan had marched, and occasionally fought, all the way from Missouri through Santa Fe and El Paso, to prosecute the war across the Rio Grande. Doniphan had fewer than 1,000 fighting men. Drawn up ahead of him, north of the Sacramento River on the road to Chihuahua, was an army of 3,000 Mexican soldiers under the command of General García Condé and 1,000 Mexican volunteers. The Mexicans held the plateaus that stood on either side of the road. But, alerted by his scouts, Doniphan did the unexpected and swung his column wide to the right, unseen by the Mexicans, and came in behind the Mexican lines. Defeating Mexican cavalry that finally found them, Doniphan's men then attacked the Mexican positions from the rear with artillery, cavalry, and infantry that closed to hand-to-hand combat. The American casualties were extraordinary: two killed, seven wounded. The Mexicans lost 300 dead, 300 wounded, and all their artillery pieces. The Battle of Sacramento (28 February 1847) was a triumph, leaving the capture of Chihuahua, fifteen miles south, a mere matter of marching. And after 2,000 miles, Doniphan's men were well practiced at marching.

With Taylor retired to Monterrey and Doniphan set to join him, the focus of operations shifted south to where General Winfield Scott was preparing an unprecedented amphibious operation for the American Army and Navy—one that would not be equaled until the Second World War: the capture of Vera Cruz. The island fortress of San Juan de Ulúa guarded the coastal approach to the city, but Scott located an unguarded beach to the south and, in an operation remarkable not only for its size and complexity but for its lack of mishap, landed 10,000 men on 9 March 1847 at Collada Beach.

The next two weeks were spent throwing out a line of troops isolating Vera Cruz, skirmishing with the enemy, establishing artillery positions (this was done by Captain Robert E. Lee), and preparing the siege. On the late afternoon of 22 March, after General Juan Morales rejected Scott's call to surrender, the bombardment began from Scott's initial gun emplacements. The next day, American naval batteries opened up on the city. Two days later, all of Scott's land-based batteries joined in. The pounding had its effect on the European consuls in the city. They demanded that General Morales stop risking civilian lives and surrender. Morales replied that he felt terribly unwell. He transferred command to his deputy, Brigadier General José Juan Landero, who sent a messenger to Scott requesting a parley. The Americans ceased fire and the Mexican negotiators began haggling. When Scott threatened to open up his guns again, it concentrated Mexican minds on the essentials, and on the evening of 27 March 1847, the City of the True Cross was surrendered to the Americans.

General Scott endeavored to treat it well. Old Fuss 'n' Feathers went out of his way to conciliate the clergy, as a means to reconcile the Mexican people to American rule. With his love of pomp and ceremony, he encouraged his officers to attend the city cathedral in their dress uniforms, where he led a candle-lit procession. If his diplomacy paid him dividends in Heaven, it was certain that it paid dividends in the field, for the Church tilted in favor of the Americans and against Santa Anna. Santa Anna was not a strident anticlerical—in fact, his vice president, who led that faction, had just been deposed in a civil war in Mexico City—but like any dictator he saw the wealth of the Church as a tap house for the state. Given a choice, the Church preferred Old Fuss 'n' Feathers.

Scott did not neglect strictly military matters. He was eager to be on the move, to escape the coastal region of Mexico before the yellow fever season. Santa Anna was just as eager to pen him in there and planned to do so fifty miles inland at Cerro Gordo, blocking one of two main roads that led to Puebla, the key point on the way to Mexico City. Mountains straddled the road, and on them Santa Anna assembled an army of 12,000 men. His position was well chosen, but he had made a fateful mistake. He had assumed that the rocky, mountainous terrain to the Mexican left was impenetrable. But Captain Robert E. Lee penetrated it and directed the carving of a trail behind Santa Anna's batteries, with Cerro Gordo dead ahead.

General David Twiggs led his division along Lee's road with orders to take a position on the plateau of La Atalaya, in preparation for the main assault on Cerro Gordo the next day. But after the tough march and skirmish to dislodge the Mexican pickets, Twiggs's blood was up. "Charge 'em to hell," he ordered his troops, and the Americans charged halfway to Cerro Gordo, where they were finally pinned down by Mexican fire, until they were recovered and brought back to Atalaya. The withdrawn lunge had the drawback of alerting Santa Anna to the American presence, but it had the benefit, for the Americans, of wrongly convincing Santa Anna that he'd just won the battle.

He had not. Winfield Scott was already making plans for the morrow to rout Santa Anna from Cerro Gordo and press on to Jalapa. If the battle did not go entirely to plan—General Gideon Pillow mismanaged his attack on the Mexican right—it went well enough. The main attack—and the only one that mattered—came from Twiggs, whose men charged into Cerro Gordo and spread panic in the Mexican ranks. Cut off from retreat, the Mexicans, including peg-legged Santa Anna, fled down any footpath they could find. An untold number of Mexicans were killed and 3,000 were captured and subsequently paroled by Scott, who could not hold so many prisoners. The next day, 19 April 1847, Scott's army of 8,500 men rested in the city of Jalapa.

Here and at Puebla, Scott's army paused. Some of his volunteers had their enlistments running out—fewer than one in ten re-upped for the duration of the war—and Scott let them go so that they could reach transports at Vera Cruz before the yellow fever season. He waited for new volunteer units to arrive, but he did not wait patiently. Politics, he feared, might do him in. He was traveling the national highway to Mexico City, a road built by Cortez and his conquistadors, and he felt himself a similarly embattled conqueror. "Like Cortez, finding myself isolated and abandoned, and again like him, always afraid that the next ship or messenger might recall or further cripple me, I resolved no longer to depend on Vera Cruz, or home, but to render my little army a self-sustaining machine."[17] Scientific soldier that he was, he could do it.

On 7 August 1847, he was on the march again, looking to close on Mexico City. In England, the Duke of Wellington followed the press accounts and took a keen interest in the campaign, charting Scott's maneuvers on a map. The Iron Duke was pessimistic. "Scott is lost! He has been carried away by his successes! He can't take the city, and he can't fall back on his bases."[18] That was one point of view. But Captain Kirby Smith of Scott's 3rd Infantry undoubtedly put the American soldiers' view about their Mexican opponents: "What a stupid people they are! They can do nothing and their continued defeats should convince them of it. They have lost six great battles; we have captured six hundred and eighty cannon, nearly one hundred thousand stand of arms, made twenty thousand prisoners, have the greatest portion of their country and are fast advancing on their Capital which must be ours,—yet they refuse to treat!"[19] From the infantryman's point of view, there was fighting to be done, but the outcome was inevitable.

Scott's "self-sustaining machine" of an army had restored itself to nearly 11,000 effectives, while Santa Anna's Napoleonic gift for raising armies put more than 25,000 Mexicans in uniform and under arms for the defense of Mexico City. Once again, the Mexicans had the advantage of a solid defensive position: a marshy plain (some of it flooded) before the city, stout defenses around it, and the city itself resting on high ground.

Using Robert E. Lee again as a scout, Scott decided to leave the national highway—and thereby avoid the Mexican defenses at El Peñón—and approach Mexico City from the south on roads that straddled the Pedregal, an allegedly impassable volcanic waste that was five miles wide and three miles deep. On either side of that lava bed, the battles of Contreras and Churubusco were fought. And once again, Captain Robert E. Lee would find a path—this time through the Pedregal—where no path was supposed to be found.

The road on the eastern side of the Pedregal was the San Antonio Road; on the western side was the San Angel Road. The San Antonio Road was the more direct, but the Mexicans had a well-fortified position at San Antonio and not far behind it was Santa Anna's main position along the Churubusco River. On the San Angel Road, the Mexican General Gabriel Valencia was supposed to be defending San Angel, where Santa Anna could easily reinforce him. Instead, Valencia—an officer of dubious reputation and on bad terms with Santa Anna—took up a position farther forward, and off the San Angel Road, across from the southwestern base of the Pedregal.

On 19 August 1847, the Americans launched a two-pronged advance on either side of the Pedregal, with the objective of meeting up to attack Santa Anna at Churubuso. Lee's scout work, and the work of the engineers, broadened the path he discovered on the Pedregal and allowed the Americans to flank the Mexican position at San Antonio. Santa Anna, however, thought the San Antonio Road was secure. What worried him was the western side—the responsibility of General Valencia. The Americans, tying Valencia up in an artillery duel, had slipped 3,500 men onto the San Angel Road. But as evening fell the Americans faced the possibility of being trapped, because coming south to stop them were 3,000 Mexican reinforcements under Santa Anna's personal command.

The American hero of the following morning, at the Battle of Contreras, was General Persifor Smith. Smith's infantry was supporting Captain John Magruder's artillery against Valencia's front. But when he saw the danger to the

American troops on the San Angel Road—potentially trapped between Santa Anna and Valencia—Smith brought his brigade to the rescue. Early on the morning of 20 August, Smith launched the attack he had organized during the night: a demonstration against Valencia's front, while the Americans on the road hurled a three-pronged assault at Valencia's left flank.

The morning was cold and wet, and Valencia's troops, whose hopes rested on Santa Anna's reinforcements, saw to their dismay that Santa Anna's men had withdrawn. (Santa Anna had sent orders to Valencia to withdraw with him, which Valencia had ignored.) The next thing they saw was charging Americans. The Mexicans fled, 700 were killed, more than 800 were taken prisoner, and thousands melted away—and those that fled up the road were met by an infuriated Santa Anna, who struck about him with a riding whip. Valencia's army no longer existed, and if Santa Anna had his way, Valencia would not long exist either—he issued orders for his execution.

Santa Anna now withdrew his men. The San Angel Road was cleared, and the San Antonio Road soon would be. Ahead lay the bridges across the Churubusco leading the way into Mexico City. And it was here that the Mexicans fortified their next line of defense. The Americans had two objectives at Churubusco: seize the bridge across the river and clear the fortified convent of San Mateo.

The bridge looked to be easily taken; the only obstacle was the mass of Mexican troops retreating across it. The convent proved to be the tougher nut; the Mexican defenders—including soldiers from the Batallón de San Patricio—put up a stiff defense. They repelled the hastily organized and sloppily executed initial American assaults, and even defeated the American gunners in an artillery duel.

Meanwhile, the Americans easily took the outer defenses of the bridge. At the heavily fortified *tête du pont,* however, the defenders outnumbered the attackers three to one and blunted two American charges that were made with reckless overconfidence. No engineers had scouted the position first. The mood of the American troops plummeted from enthusiasm to dangerous self-doubt.

But they had help in the shape of a flanking maneuver, with troops crossing the river to the west, bypassing the convent and coming onto the road behind the bridge to cut off the Mexican retreat and pressurize the defenders at the *tête du pont.* Santa Anna saw it developing and reinforced the road, so that the flanking Americans ran not into panicked Mexicans, but into Mexican troops pouring musket balls at them. Now, however, the American troopers at the bridgehead showed the grit that had got them this far. After three hours of fighting, they roused themselves for a mighty bayonet charge that filled their general, William Worth, with "wonder" and "gratitude" as they swept the bridge and saved General Scott's army from stalling out before the great prize of Mexico City. With the bridge in American hands, American artillery bombarded the convent, reducing enough of it to rubble so that the Americans could charge over it and invest the defenders in their final redoubt. Because the San Patricios kept tearing the white flag from the hands of Mexicans trying to surrender, the American Captain James Smith raised a white handkerchief, which the Mexicans gratefully saw as their salvation from certain death, throwing down their arms. Even the eighty-five surviving San Patricios realized their battle was over.

The last remaining job was clearing the road, north of the bridge, where the American flankers were still meeting with murderous resistance. Mounted riflemen and dragoons finally drove the Mexicans back, but in their excitement, a handful of hard-charging dragoons who didn't hear the bugler sound recall charged all the way to the gates of Mexico City. Enemy fire that cost Captain Philip Kearny[20] an arm finally reminded the dragoons to return to their comrades.

The road to Mexico City was open for the taking, but Scott decided his troops had had enough fighting for one day. If Mexico City would not capitulate peacefully, if it had to be taken by force, let it be done with cool consideration, not with ragged men whose blood was up. He had already suffered a thousand casualties, more than 130 of them killed. The Mexicans, however, had done far worse, with 10,000 men killed, wounded, or missing, and with 2,637 men, by Winfield Scott's count (including eight generals and two former presidents), held as prisoners of war.

Santa Anna requested a truce, seeing this as his only means to gain time to shore up the defenses of Mexico City. General Winfield Scott agreed to it, assuming that a spirit of accommodation would lead to peace and conciliate Mexican pride. The Mexicans, of course, were not conciliated but kept busy by Santa Anna, while Scott's men grew restive, wondering why they were waiting and knowing damn well what the high-minded Scott chose to ignore: Santa Anna was playing Scott for a fool. After two weeks, even Scott had to concede that the Mexican peace negotiators were not serious and that Santa Anna was violating the truce. So the battle for Mexico City began.

There were three fortifications blocking Scott's way: the stone fortress and earthworks at Casa Mata; the gathering Mexican cavalry at Molino del Rey (where church bells were suspected of being melted and cast into cannons); and the towering Castle of Chapultepec. The stone buildings at Molino del Rey were only 1,000 yards from Chapultepec. Casa Mata was only 500 yards ahead of Molino del Rey and between them lay an artillery battery. The positions were mutually reinforcing, and the Americans estimated the combined number of Mexican defenders at an imposing 12,000 to 14,000, though it might well have been fewer. If accurate, it meant the Mexicans outnumbered Scott's entire army two to one.

Nevertheless, Scott assumed that Casa Mata and Molino del Rey could be snapped off easily and sent 3,500 men under the command of General William Worth to do the snapping. Worth's plan was sound: cut off the road to Chapultepec and attack Molino del Rey from the right, engage the Mexican batteries with his own and bombard the Molino, deploy dragoons to scare off any Mexican cavalry, and detach separate assault units to storm Casa Mata and the Molino. The Molino was first taken by a bayonet charge, with the Americans seizing the Mexican guns and turning them against the defenders. But when the Mexicans saw how small the assault unit was, they counterattacked and inflicted heavy casualties. American troops striking down from the Chapultepec road came to the rescue of the beleaguered assault unit and took the Molino in fierce close quarters combat.

Now the Americans focused their attack on Casa Mata, and in their haste relied not on bombardment—the American artillery and some badly outnumbered dragoons were holding off Mexican cavalry and other enemy reinforcements—but on another bayonet charge, which succeeded. The price, however, was steep. Reducing the two Mexican positions cost the Americans 800 casualties, more than 100 of them dead. Among the dead were wounded men whom the Mexicans had murdered, in some cases by slitting their throats. The Americans would not forget.

Scott pressed on. He ordered the reduction of Chapultepec. His intrepid engineer Captain Robert E. Lee thought Chapultepec best avoided and Mexico City best attacked directly from the south. Scott overruled him after staff officer Lieutenant Pierre Gustave Toutant Beauregard supported Scott's original plan for investing Chapultepec and then approaching the city from the west. Scott hoped to subdue the castle by bombardment alone, and hoped further that once the castle fell Mexico City might be surrendered without a shot—his constant humanitarian wish.

In the event, the Mexicans did not buckle under the daylong bombardment. It was Scott's men who were in need of hope when they assembled on the morning of 13 September 1847. The bloody battles at Churubusco and Molino del Rey gave them a very sober assessment of what storming Chapultepec—used as a military college, and with 100 cadets among its 1,000 defenders—might mean.

Scott's attack was well designed, with demonstrations to keep Santa Anna guessing where the main attack would be launched, which, in turn, kept him from reinforcing Chapultepec. The Americans were up and over the exterior walls of the castle grounds and advanced steadily uphill to the castle proper. Here they were compelled to wait for a miserably long quarter of an hour, under constant Mexican fire, for their scaling ladders to arrive. Then the ladders were thrown up, a few came falling back—with men attached—but so many ladders went up that the Americans were soon into the castle, forcing the defenders from the ramparts and cutting them down wherever they could find them. The Mexicans surrendered—except for the cadets, six of whom jumped to their deaths rather than become prisoners of the *yanquis*.

As he watched the American flag rise over the castle, Santa Anna sensed his doom: "I believe that if we were to plant our batteries in Hell the damned Yankees would take them from us." One of his despairing officers added: "God is a Yankee."[21] If so, He is a Yankee who made good use of future Confederates—and not just in Captain Robert E. Lee and Lieutenant Pierre G. T. Beauregard, but in Lieutenant James Longstreet, who was wounded here; Lieutenant Thomas Jonathan Jackson, who displayed his oblivious imperturbability under fire; Navy Lieutenant Raphael Semmes, who directed artillery; Artillery Captain John Magruder; Lieutenant Joseph E. Johnston leading four companies of Voltigeurs (self-proclaimed elite light infantry); Colonel Jefferson Davis of the Mississippi Rifles; and Lieutenant George Pickett, who tore down the Mexican flag and ran up the Stars and Stripes. Among those cheering the American flag were thirty condemned Patricios, watching from the plains below. They stood on mule-led wagons. Nooses were round the deserters' necks. Their cheers died when the mules trotted forward.[22]

For the Americans, the cheers were just beginning. Chapultepec had fallen in two hours. Mexico City lay ahead. Brigadier General William Worth led his men against the city from the west, while Major General John Quitman slugged straight up the direct road from Chapultepec. Scott envisioned Quitman's attack as a feint, but Quitman saw himself in a race with Worth to claim the prize. Both forces spent the day smashing through the Mexican barricades, infantry, and artillery that guarded the city approaches, with Quitman's units taking heavy casualties. By evening it was obvious that the Americans were unstoppable and Santa Anna escaped with 5,000 men to Guadalupe Hidalgo in a forlorn, desperate belief that he would fight another day. As his parting gift to the American conquerors he opened the city's prisons, hoping the criminals would do their worst to ruin Scott's dream of a calm and orderly occupation.

On the morning of 14 September 1847 the white flag of surrender flew over Mexico City. General Worth occupied the western quarter of the city, but General Quitman got his wish and marched his men (though the general had lost one of his shoes in the fighting) to the Grand Plaza, claiming the capital. He assigned his accompanying United States Marines the task of rounding up the criminals and shoving them behind bars, something the leathernecks did with their usual dispatch after Marine Lieutenant A. S. Nicholson raised the American flag over the National Palace, known as the Halls of Montezuma. As General Scott rode into the city in the full fig of his dress uniform and with a party of dragoons, he saw that his wish had come true. Not only was Mexico City his, but Mexicans were lining the streets waving white handkerchiefs in honor of the conquering hero.

There was some continued scattered resistance, but it was crushed quickly and in force. The city was put under martial law, the streets were patrolled, and the combination of no-nonsense policing and Scott's orders demanding magnanimity and good discipline had the city well pacified within a month. Meanwhile Santa Anna tried to attack the American garrison at Puebla, but his men would do no more than settle into a lazy siege. Other Mexican officers tried to inspire a guerilla war, aiming at Scott's extended lines of communications. But the American forces were not so vulnerable, the guerillas became bandits (preying largely on the Mexicans themselves), and there was no ignition of partisan guerilla warfare.

Indeed, the obvious answer to Scott's conquest of Mexico, which only a few generous and farsighted men recognized—including some Mexican leaders who tried and failed to convince Winfield Scott to take up their cause—was the incorporation of the entire country into the United States, which would have had the immediate effect of improving Mexican civil and economic life and adding tropical Catholic charm to the industrious Yankee Republic. And by dramatically enlarging the southern states, perhaps some of the steam building up between North and South could have been dissipated.

But if that chance was neglected, it should not detract from what was achieved. Scott's magnificent performance won him plaudits from the Duke of Wellington, who dubbed Scott the "greatest living soldier"—presumably excluding the duke himself, given his retirement from soldiering. Ambassador Nicholas Trist, by negotiating the Treaty of Hidalgo (signed on 2 February 1848), gained every territorial demand President Polk had wanted, and as a consolation to the Mexicans, granted them financial compensations such as had been offered before the war. Polk rewarded his general and his diplomat by sacking them. Such is the prerogative of chief executives who are little men.

Polk the politician, however, knew very well what he was doing: dismissing a potential political rival in Scott and a diplomat whom he thought too easy on the Mexicans and who had ignored a presidential summons recalling him to Washington. (Trist negotiated his treaty with the Mexicans in knowing insubordination.) If Polk was handed a fait accompli in the Treaty of Hidalgo, he did his best to sell it to the Senate, in which passage was in doubt. Polk said, presciently: "If the treaty in its present form is ratified, there will be added to the United States an immense empire, the value of which twenty years hence it would be difficult to calculate."[23]

The treaty, with minor changes, was approved. And then came the irony. President Polk's other general—Zachary Taylor—became the Whig candidate for president in the 1848 election, defeating Polk's fellow Democrat Lewis Cass. Polk left the White House, returned to Tennessee, and promptly died. But his gift to the United States of another great imperial acquisition, as great as the Louisiana Purchase, puts him, neglected as he is in popular memory, in the front rank of American presidents.

CHAPTER 11

WRECKING THE FURNITURE

After the Mexican War, the United States had a brilliant future in front of it as the fulfillment of the founders' dreams of an empire of liberty—an empire of confederated states (a Protestant version of the Holy Roman Empire), each with its own prerogatives, pride, and patriotism; spending its excess acquisitive energies in westward and southern expansion down through the tropics; and enjoying peace (save for smiting the occasional Indian, Mexican, or any other person standing in the way of manifest destiny), prosperity, and a limited and distant federal government.

But there was another vision, that of New England and Northern moralizers—many of whom had lost their religious faith but embraced a gospel of politics. They thought imperialism such as had been practiced against Mexico was a sin. They thought slavery was a sin. And they thought the important thing was rubbing out sin at home—and using the federal government to do it—and not exporting American sinfulness abroad, especially not adding more slave states to the Union.

The immediate result was a congressional logjam that held up the incorporation of the newly acquired western territories until Congress decided whether they should be free states or slave states: the Missouri Compromise, which should have provided the answer to this question (and divided California into North California and South California), no longer held the support of the Northern states, in part because of the "Wilmot Proviso" of Pennsylvania Congressman David Wilmot. He proposed, in 1846, that any territory acquired from Mexico—where slavery was illegal—should by rights enter the United States as a free territory. So future potential states that Southerners thought were theirs were suddenly up for grabs.

The North was not solely to blame for this growing sectional unrest. John C. Calhoun of South Carolina was no more supportive of the Missouri Compromise than the North was. He thought it unconstitutional and wanted *national* (rather than state) protection of slaves as property. An able parliamentarian and parser of legality, he saw his view upheld by the Supreme Court in the *Dred Scott* case of 1857.

Both the Northern moralizers and the Southern legalizers were wrong. In the right were Old Rough and Ready Zachary Taylor (now president) and the settlers of California. They took the view that the territories could do whatever they damned well pleased—and that the important thing was to get them into the Union. Once gold was discovered in 1848, California was flush with treasure seekers who had precious little interest in importing slaves: the California Territory was under military government (which worked in happy accord with the Californio elite), filled with raucous 49ers, and sought to attract a respectable white middle class—not black slaves. So what need for further debate? But Calhoun tried to block California's admission to the Union.

It might be a sad commentary on human affairs, but it is true, that the pursuit of political principle is a terrible thing. In practical politics, pragmatism and compromise—Edmund Burke's politics of prescription—are the levers of peace. The pursuit of political principle becomes the triumph of abstraction over humanity. Northern abolitionists and Southern fire-breathers rushed at one another like wild animals fighting over the bone of principle. But there was no need. There was plenty of fighting to be done elsewhere. Enlightened Americans recognized the need for an invasion and annexation of Cuba, just ninety miles off the coast of Florida; of Baja California, to expedite the introduction of fish tacos into the American diet; and of Nicaragua. One such enlightened American was General John Anthony Quitman. He had fought for Texas independence, served in the Mexican War (and had favored annexing Mexico), and was elected governor of Mississippi in 1849, where he supported the idea of annexing Cuba to the point of aiding former Cuban governor Narciso López's attempted coup. That, unfortunately, led to Quitman's resignation in 1851 after he was indicted for violating federal neutrality laws. He was, however, not convicted, and was elected to Congress in 1855. Another supporter of annexing Cuba was John L. O'Sullivan, coiner of the term "manifest destiny." O'Sullivan— who had a wealthy Cuban brother-in-law—was twice prosecuted for violating federal neutrality laws. He had the consolation, as a New York newspaperman, of knowing that prosecutions make good copy. Not indicted or prosecuted were President James K. Polk, who tried to buy Cuba in 1848, and President Franklin Pierce, who tried to do the same in the 1850s.

Another enlightened American was the Tennessee-born doctor, lawyer, journalist, and fighting gamecock (he was only five feet, two inches tall and 120 pounds) William Walker. Though the United States officially opposed and prosecuted "filibusters" embarked on mercenary adventures, Walker won the approval of Secretary of War Jefferson Davis to try to independently conquer Central America for the United States. In 1853, he sailed to La Paz, organized an army of fewer than 250 men, and declared the independence of the Republic of Lower California, putting it under Louisiana law. After some gunplay in La Paz, he and his troopers retired to the assumed safety of Ensenada, where Walker expanded his annexation to include Baja California and Sonora under the banner of the Republic of Sonora, of which he would be president. The republic, alas, proved to be short-lived, despite the enthusiasm for his exploits among the miners and rowdies of California. Walker lacked men and supplies, and when he returned to California, he surrendered to federal officers. Prosecuted in the federal court in San Francisco, he was acquitted.

More famous was his making himself president of Nicaragua, which he conquered with an army of fifty-eight Americans and a swath of Nicaraguan popular support in 1855. The United States recognized his government, but Walker ran afoul of Cornelius Vanderbilt. Walker foolishly picked a commercial fight with the shipping magnate over transit rights. In retaliation, Vanderbilt sponsored a Latin American coalition (led by Costa Rica) against Walker. After two years of turmoil, Walker abdicated his Nicaraguan presidency and turned himself over to the American Navy, which delivered him to New Orleans.

Before the end of the year 1857, Walker made a return landing in Nicaragua hoping to retake his country. He was foiled by an American naval patrol that arrested him, though he again escaped conviction. He made one last attempt in 1860. This time he landed in Honduras, from which point he planned to march an army to Nicaragua. But the Royal Navy—protecting its own neighboring colonies in Belize (British Honduras) and the Miskito Indian Coast of Nicaragua—captured Walker and turned him over to the Honduran authorities, who ordered him executed by firing squad. Though Walker's glory had led but to the grave, did not such enterprising young men show the way forward?

Apparently not: Walker and his fellow filibusters were little more than a colorful sideshow. The real focus of American politics was internal. When Henry Clay and Daniel Webster hammered out the Compromise of 1850, they brought California into the Union as a free state (a good thing), enacted a fugitive slave law that required Northern compliance with Southern principles (a bad thing—for the South—because it violated states' rights and was sure to annoy the North), settled the borders of Texas (good), avoided the question of slavery in the other western territories (good), and prohibited the slave trade in the District of Columbia (good for making the seat of the federal government a better arbiter between North and South). A wizened, gimlet-eyed Calhoun—who died before the issue was decided—opposed the compromise, as did tub-thumping Northern abolitionists. President Zachary Taylor thought the compromise was unnecessary. He believed the territories could decide for themselves whether they wanted to be slave or free, and anyone who conspired to disrupt the Union out of frustration with the result of states' rights could be hanged, which was the most sensible view of all. But the majority in Congress thought the Union needed something stronger to bind it. When Taylor died in 1850, his successor, Millard Fillmore, signed the compromise, and the Union lived by it for the next ten years.

The Whig Fillmore—who later carried the Know-Nothing banner in an unsuccessful reelection bid—was also responsible for opening up Japan. He sent an armed flotilla under the command of Commodore Matthew Perry, who through a combination of a show of force, a shower of gifts, and shovels full of unctuous diplomatic flummery won a welcome mat for American trade with Nippon. Commodore Perry did not press his luck and try to annex Japan to the United States, though this might have paid dividends later, but he did have the foresight to annex Chichi Jima—only to have Congress void the purchase. In the absence of American annexation of the Ryukyu (including Okinawa) and Bonin (including Iwo Jima) island chains, Japan annexed them—one of the many instances where a failure to embrace imperialism only stored up trouble for the United States later.[1]

But of course the immediate trouble was at home. The instigator was the five-foot-tall Democrat senator from Illinois, Stephen Douglas, who pressed for the repeal of the Missouri Compromise. He did so to win Southern Senate votes for the transcontinental railway that would pass through Kansas and Nebraska.[2] Southerners had expected the transcontinental railway to take a southern route running from New Orleans to San Diego. Secretary of War Jefferson Davis had judged this route the best—it was the shortest route—and the United States had already made the Gadsden Purchase, buying additional Mexican territory through which the railway would run. If the South was to lose this route, it wanted the status of Nebraska and Kansas—which under the Missouri Compromise should have been free states—left open to the will of the people, as in California, which was a bad comparison. Where in California the slave question was really not a question—and should not have been a question in Nebraska and Kansas—what the repeal of the compromise really did was turn Kansas into "bleeding Kansas." Kansas became a battleground as "free-soil" partisans and proslavery partisans rushed not to settle the territory but to unsettle it: Northern "Jayhawkers" on the one side, Southern "border ruffians" on the other.

Northerners held the numerical upper hand—indeed, did so overwhelmingly—because Southerners wealthy enough to own slaves were generally content to stay where they were, and certainly not eager to risk their wealth in a violent new territory. But the border ruffians from Missouri gave the proslavery faction a political head start. They ensured proslavery gunmen staffed the polling places so that Southern rights were respected.

Northern immigration to Kansas became a crusade, attracting men like John Brown. Brown responded to the border ruffians with a declaration of holy war against them—or against innocents who happened to look like ruffians. In Washington, too, bleeding Kansas led to bleeding brawls, with South Carolina Congressman Preston Brooks caning Senator Charles Sumner of Massachusetts nearly to death for insulting Southern honor—not to mention the honor of Brooks's relative Senator Andrew Butler of South Carolina.

Brooks was a typically articulate Southern statesman, devoted to the ideal of honor, and violent in defense of it. On the floor of the House, he explained his assault by referring to Sumner's "uncalled for libel on my State and my blood. Whatever insults my State insults me. Her history and character have commanded my pious veneration; and in her defence I hope I shall always be prepared, humbly and modestly, to perform the duty of a son."[3]

If Brooks's motives could be gilded with honor, Stephen Douglas's motives were base—he stood to reap financial rewards from the development of the West—and unworthy of a statesman, both denying the best route for the railway and ripping open the slavery question yet again. His Kansas-Nebraska Act of 1856 was far more horribly consequential than the beating hammered into Sumner, because it made the transcontinental railway an engine driving the country to war. That juggernaut was fueled by the portrayal of slave-master cruelty in the best-selling novel *Uncle Tom's Cabin* (1852), the enforcement of the Fugitive Slave Act that led to inevitable Northern cries of kidnapping, and the sudden appearance of the Republican Party that sprang almost instantaneously from creation (1854) to a majority in Congress (that same year). A standing principle of the Republican Party was opposition to slavery.[4] The heartland of the Republican Party—the North and the West—was booming in population, and as a consequence the South worried that its previous political dominance was slipping away and its way of life mortally threatened.

The Senate rejected a constitution presented by free-soil Kansans and accepted one submitted by proslavery Kansans. Douglas, however, stood by the idea of popular sovereignty, and the people of Kansas themselves decisively voted down the Senate-approved constitution. Thus the sectional crisis was ratcheted up, and a lanky politician from Illinois began proclaiming that "A house divided against itself cannot stand. I believe this government cannot endure, permanently half slave and half free. . . . Either the opponents of slavery, will arrest the further spread of it, and place it where the public mind shall rest in the belief that it is in the course of ultimate extinction; or its advocates will push it forward, till it shall become alike lawful in all the States, old as well as new—North as well as South."[5] This speech, the first in Republican Abraham Lincoln's 1858 senatorial campaign against Democrat Stephen Douglas, was credited with losing him the election. If it did, it was only because it was too prescient for popular consumption. Lincoln's radical—to the ears of the electorate—prognostication was only drawing out the obvious implications of the *Dred Scott* decision, the Kansas-Nebraska Act, and other political decisions that were de facto voiding states' rights and forcing a national showdown on slavery—a showdown that was as much the legacy of the sternly legalistic John C. Calhoun as of the mad-eyed, Bible-quoting killer John Brown; of the obtuse Stephen Douglas as of the Supreme Court that in its *Dred Scott* decision struck down the Missouri Compromise and erased the right of free states to grant citizenship to black Americans.

In the course of the Lincoln-Douglas debates, Lincoln staked what he held to be the line of his party: that slavery was evil, that its spread was evil, but that every Republican would respect its constitutional guarantees while hoping for the institution's eventual dissolution. To this, Douglas offered a Panglossian rejoinder: as long as the states minded their own business, slave states and free states could coexist in perpetuity. The trouble was, it was not a matter of states anymore; it was a matter of national agitation and policy—even Protestant churches split along North-South divides. Instead of following the course of wisdom and diverting Southern hopes to the Southern tropics, to which a civilization based on slavery (or feudalism) could be exported or in some cases already existed, men like Douglas had made a battleground of Kansas, leaving a gunpowder trail that would explode into wholesale sectional war. The gunpowder led first to the arsenal at Harpers Ferry, Virginia.[6]

FIRST SHOTS

NOT CONTENT WITH MURDER in Kansas, John Brown aimed to foment a slave insurrection in Virginia. His first target, however, was not a slave owner but the slaveless federal arsenal at Harpers Ferry. Brown had twenty men with him. They crept into Harpers Ferry before dawn, killed two men (including a free black), and easily captured the rifle works and an extremely well stocked armory. To strengthen his hand he seized sixty hostages among the townspeople. Then he waited for a wave of slaves to well up and form his Mameluke army with which he would trample out the "peculiar institution" in a purgation of blood.

But his rebellious slaves never came. Instead, the Maryland militia came and trapped Brown and his men within the town's fire-engine house adjacent to the armory. The War Department in Washington summoned Colonel Robert E. Lee[7] to command a detachment of Marines. Lee ordered the Marines to attack the firehouse with sledgehammers (to break into it) and bayonets; their muskets were unloaded in order to avoid civilian casualties. The gentleman and professional soldier Lee, who knew just how horrible a battlefield was from his experience in the Mexican War, was far more mindful of not hurting civilians than was the fanatic Brown, for whom the spilling of blood was the point.

Brown was captured and put on trial—giving him a forum to become a hero to abolitionists—and then hanged. Radicals in the North now had their martyr. The South, which had not been troubled by Brown's crime—Lee had dismissed it as a riot—was shocked at the outpouring of Northern abolitionist rhetoric proclaiming the virtues of a murderer and would-be terrorist, an outpouring that convinced the South that the United States was indeed a house divided, and that the South had better fortify its half of the estate.

That was 1859. There was an election in 1860, and to the South's dismay the Democrat Party nominated Stephen Douglas for president. The South considered Douglas a traitor to its cause. The Republican Party nominated Abraham Lincoln, Douglas's erstwhile foe in Illinois's 1858 senatorial election. For Southerners, this was no choice at all. The lower South rallied behind Kentuckian John C. Breckinridge, James Buchanan's vice president, who ran as a

"National Democrat." In the election of 1860, he swept up the electoral votes of Texas, Louisiana, Arkansas, Mississippi, Alabama, Florida, Georgia, South Carolina, North Carolina, Maryland, and Delaware. The other Southerner (running under the banner of the Constitutional Union Party) was Tennessean John Bell, who won the electoral votes of Tennessee, Kentucky, and Virginia. The Democrats' nominee, Stephen Douglas, won only the border ruffians of Missouri and three of New Jersey's seven electoral votes (the other four went to Lincoln). Abraham Lincoln trounced Douglas in Maine, New Hampshire, Vermont, Massachusetts, Rhode Island, Connecticut, New York, Pennsylvania, Ohio, Michigan, Indiana, Illinois, Wisconsin, Iowa, Minnesota, and Oregon and won more narrowly in California (where the popular vote divided 32.3 percent for Lincoln, 31.7 percent for Douglas, 28.3 percent for Breckinridge).

It was a stunning outcome. In total, Lincoln—who ran on a platform of western development ("Free Speech, Free Home, Free Territory") and tariffs— had more electoral votes (180) than his combined opponents: the defender of Southern "property" rights Breckinridge, 72; the "anti-extremist Old Gentleman's Party" candidate Bell, 39; and the muddled Douglas, 12. Though Lincoln spoke words of moderation, the very election of a president of an explicitly antislavery party, and the electoral crushing of the South, seemed to fulfill every dark dream ever entertained by men who considered themselves Calhoun Southern Democrats. The newly elected president had been elected without the support of a single Southern state. To the South the choice seemed clear: submit to Northern domination and the eventual forcible abolition of slavery or secede and preserve the South. Guns would announce the answer.

THE BIRTH OF THE CONFEDERACY

SOUTHERN REACTION WAS immediate. On 20 December 1860, Calhoun's home state of South Carolina left the Union. On 9 January 1861, Mississippi seceded, and would be followed by Florida (10 January), Alabama (11 January), Georgia (19 January), Louisiana (26 January), and Texas (1 February). Then there was a pause. On 8 February 1861, these states met to elect a president for their new country: the Confederate States of America with its capital in Montgomery, Alabama. They chose for that position Mississippi senator and former secretary of war Jefferson Davis. Though Davis had publicly opposed secession and followed the lead of his state in sorrow, he accepted the call, for he had also believed that secession was constitutionally licit should the states pursue it in extremity. His vice president was the stunted and wizened Alexander Stephens of Georgia, another antisecessionist who accepted secession as a fact (and who was apparently an all-around disagreeable chap).[8] The Confederacy's attorney general (and later secretary of war and secretary of state) Judah P. Benjamin was the first Jew appointed to a cabinet post in North America.

In most respects the Confederate Constitution replicated the Constitution of the United States. It did, of course, set out a republican form of government. It incorporated into its basic structure the Bill of Rights, guaranteeing freedom of speech and religion. It also made an explicit reference, as the United States Constitution did not, to "the favor and guidance of Almighty God." The Confederate Constitution guaranteed the right to slavery, making explicit in the constitution what the Supreme Court had ruled in the *Dred Scott* case: that slavery was a constitutional right. The Confederate Constitution also banned the importation of slaves, so there would be no cranking up again of the African slavery trade with Confederate-flagged merchant ships. The Confederate Constitution granted the president a single six-year term, forbade the Confederate federal government from issuing tariffs or otherwise spending money on "internal improvement" save basic necessities to coastal and river navigation and commerce (such as providing buoys and harbor development), and gave the president a line-item veto to reject pork barrel spending. As a founding document of a new nation, it was merely the founding document of the old nation with a few emendations to fix what the South thought needed fixing. (There was no mention of the right to secession, as this was assumed.) Looking at the two documents by themselves, one does not see a people seriously divided. But that's why documents are an inadequate guide to history. It was human passions that forced secession. As Mary Chestnut, wife of Senator James Chestnut of South Carolina, wrote in her diary: "We separated from the North . . . because we have hated each other so."[9]

It was not, then, an amicable divorce. In his inaugural address on 4 March 1861, Lincoln reiterated that he had no intention of prohibiting slavery in the South. He reaffirmed that one "section of our country believes slavery is *right* and ought to be extended, while the other believes it is *wrong* and ought not to be extended. This is the only substantial dispute." But he also denied the right of secession. The textbook on constitutional law at West Point, where so many Southern leaders had been educated, took this right for granted.[10] But Lincoln was not a West Pointer. As every schoolboy knows, he was a self-educated lawyer whose military experience was limited to a brief spell in the Illinois militia during the Black Hawk War.

Lincoln went further. He asserted his right to execute federal law in every state that participated in the 1860 federal election, and to "possess the property and places belonging to the government, and to collect the duties and imposts. . . ." He then said, rather disingenuously, or at least with a train of thought that no Southerner could follow: "In *your* hands, my dissatisfied fellow-countrymen, and not in *mine,* is the momentous issue of civil war. The government will not assail *you.* You can have no conflict without yourselves being the aggressors. *You* have no oath registered in heaven to destroy the government, while I shall have the most solemn one to 'preserve, protect, and defend' it."[11]

Lincoln's was, in short, a declaration of war that denied it was a declaration of war: for how, without recourse to force, was Lincoln to impose his presidential prerogatives over a Confederacy that had declared itself independent? The Southern Confederacy had not only rejected his authority but had, by its own lights, formed a separate country. And it had already seized federal properties and stores (including the U.S. Mint at New Orleans) that suddenly found themselves within the Confederacy's boundaries.

Lincoln said if the South was dissatisfied with the result of the election, it had two choices: "Whenever they shall grow weary of the existing Government, they can exercise their *constitutional* right of amending it or their *revolutionary* right to dismember or overthrow it." So, bizarrely, Lincoln endorsed revolution against the North as a legitimate political option, but not separation. The only solution held out by Lincoln was a choice of Southern capitulation or war to the death between North and South, with one section resting its foot on the neck of the other, triumphant.

Lincoln closed his inaugural speech saying: "We are not enemies, but friends. We must not be enemies. Though passion may have strained it must not break our bonds of affection. The mystic chords of memory, stretching from every battlefield and patriot grave to every living heart and hearthstone all over this broad land, will yet swell the chorus of the Union, when again touched, as surely they will be, by the better angels of our nature."[12]

This was all very well, but the fact remained that the Southern Confederacy's presumptive right to secession and self-government was far better grounded than was the American declaration of independence from Britain. Not only were the populations of the states of the Confederacy more united on secession than the colonists had been, but they had the *precedent* of the American War of Independence and a clear understanding of the constitutionality of secession, a right that other states (including New England states) had threatened to invoke throughout American history, a right that was recognized too by abolitionist writers like Horace Greeley (editor of the *New York Tribune*) and indeed previously by Abraham Lincoln himself, who had noted secession—specifically Texas's secession from Mexico—as a fundamental, universal political right: "Any people anywhere, being inclined and having the power, have the right to rise up and shake off the existing government and form a new one that suits them better. This is a most valuable,—a most sacred right—a right, which we hope and believe, is to liberate the world. Nor is this right confined to cases in which the whole people of an existing government, may choose to exercise it. Any portion of such people that can, may revolutionize, and make their own, of so much of the territory as they inhabit."[13] Granted, a politician is entitled to change his views. If Lincoln now, as president, took the side of Santa Anna, the rhetoric of Southern fire-breathers should not leave scorched and neglected the fact that secession was a peaceful alternative to war, a war that Lincoln was intent on bringing to the South.

The focal point was Fort Sumter, resting just off the coast of Charleston, South Carolina, the seat of secession. As elsewhere in the Confederacy, the South asserted its right to a fort on Southern land and in Southern territorial waters. It certainly could not abide cannons from a potentially hostile power being pointed at Charleston. On 6 April 1861, Lincoln announced that he was sending men and supplies to Sumter—men who would not fire, he pledged, unless fired upon.

On 11 April, General P. G. T. Beauregard sent a note to Fort Sumter's commander, Kentucky-born Major Robert Anderson, requesting, in the politest possible way, his surrender. Anderson, a Southern-sympathizing Unionist, had been holding out (and buying supplies from Charleston) since well before Lincoln's inauguration. He responded with equal courtesy, deferring surrender, as he had done under orders from Washington in the past, but conceding that unless resupplied—or ordered to hold out—he would feel compelled to surrender on 15 April. South Carolinians did not want to accept the risk of Fort Sumter being resupplied by sea and the standoff continuing. At 4:30 A.M. on the morning of 12 April, the guns of Charleston opened fire on Fort Sumter. On 14 April, Major Anderson surrendered.

Lincoln was pleased; he had drawn the South into firing first. He wrote to

Captain Gustavus Fox, who had advocated trying to resupply Fort Sumter, "You and I both anticipated that the course of the country would be advanced by making the attempt to provision Fort Sumter, even if it should fail; and it is no small consolation now to feel that our anticipation has been justified by the result."[14] Lincoln now had his war—or rather, in his opinion, an open regional insurrection against his presidential authority that he could now put down by force.

Lincoln issued a call for 75,000 volunteers and asked Arkansas, Tennessee, North Carolina, and Virginia—all states that had not seceded—to join in the suppression of the Confederacy. These states, however, refused to wage war on their fellow Southerners. For them, the "mystic chords of memory" were strong indeed. Robert E. Lee spoke for them when he declined command of the Union forces, "stating as candidly and courteously as I could, that though opposed to secession and deprecating war, I could take no part in an invasion of the Southern states."[15] Earlier he had confessed, "a Union that can only be maintained by swords and bayonets . . . has no charm for me. . . . If the Union is dissolved and government disrupted, I shall return to my native state and share the miseries of my people and save in defense will draw my sword on none."[16] He made good on that promise, and took the position that every humane man could echo: "With all my devotion to the Union and the feeling of loyalty and duty as an American citizen, I have not been able to make up my mind to raise my hand against my relatives, my children, my home."[17] So spoke a man who had served the flag of the United States his entire adult life, a West Pointer, a former superintendent at West Point, a veteran of the Mexican War.

Abraham Lincoln, however, a man who had opposed the war with Mexico, now eagerly looked forward to war against his fellow Americans. On 17 April, Virginia seceded, making Robert E. Lee's duty plain. On 19 April 1861, Lincoln ordered Southern ports blockaded, an act of war that the United States Navy was not yet large enough to enforce. Nevertheless, the South, with its typical courtesy, kindly did the Navy's work for it on the idiotic Jeffersonian strategy of refusing to export cotton. This act of economic mortification was supposed to compel Britain to rush to the South's aid, when in the event it only caused phlegmatic British merchants to rewrite their purchase orders to buy Indian rather than American. Southerners were never as clever as Yankees when it came to money.

But the harkening back to Jefferson was telling. Virginians, paramount among the Southern states, saw the War of Northern Aggression as 1776 all over again. The great seal of the Confederacy was Washington on horseback. Robert E. Lee, immediately named major general of all land and naval forces in Virginia, was not only the son of Revolutionary War veteran "Light Horse Harry" Lee, but had married into Washington's family, had rescued Lewis W. Washington (a cousin of George Washington) at Harpers Ferry, where he had been one of John Brown's hostages, and had as one of his early staff officers George Washington's nephew, John A. Washington. Descendants of famous Southern Patriots were now in Confederate butternut and grey.

Virginia, the northernmost of the Southern states that joined the Confederacy, was also the most important. It was the Confederacy's front line, and it held the breadbasket of the Shenandoah Valley, the ironworks at Richmond, munitions works, a network of railways, and brave men and talented officers who would provide so many notable Confederate generals. Richmond became the Confederate capital, though it was just a short hundred miles from Washington.

Also joining the Confederacy were Arkansas, Tennessee, and North Carolina, all of which seceded in May 1861. Most of the tribes of the Indian Territory (Oklahoma) joined the Confederacy as well (many Indians were slaveholders). Delaware, Maryland, Kentucky, and Missouri were slave states but opted to stay neutral. Baltimore, Maryland, was so violently pro-South that its mobs attacked Union troops, burned down bridges, and cut telegraph wires to Washington. That brought Northern martial law (and the suspension of habeas corpus) down on the city, and Maryland thus became a de facto Union state. Robert Anderson (late of Fort Sumter) was returned to his home state of Kentucky to keep its Southern sentiments in check. As the birth state of both Jefferson Davis and Abraham Lincoln, Kentucky was as important symbolically as it was strategically. Meanwhile, John C. Frémont—who had played a role in the conquest of California—was dispatched to ever-dangerous Missouri. Delaware—which had no militia, but which like Kentucky, Missouri, and Maryland, contributed volunteers to both North and South—remained Unionist. So too did a portion of Virginia, behind the Appalachians and without a tradition of slavery, which in 1863 became the pro-Union state of West Virginia.

In the South, there was more excitement than foreboding. A new nation was born, its people were mustering to arms, and the newly elected government of the Confederacy was hurriedly trying to organize its resources for what would be the most strenuous conflict that Americans had yet endured. The

South's chief assets were its pride, its men—for whom military service was a natural calling—and by its own lights, the high moral tone set by Jefferson Davis: "All we ask is to be let alone."[18]

Against that, the Federal forces had a four-to-one advantage in available fighting manpower (counting only white males) and an industrial base that out-weighed the South by an even larger proportion. In terms of manufactured goods, Massachusetts produced 60 percent more than the entire Confederacy. Other Northern states—New York and Pennsylvania—produced double the Confederacy's total. Likewise, banking and ready capital belonged to the North, not the South, by a ratio of three to one.

A liberty-loving, agricultural Sparta, the South might have been. It had a fine overlay of manners and charm in its best and brightest. It had never claimed to be an industrial power like the North, and Southern efficiency was always more of a jest than a reality. Yet when Lincoln's armies crossed the Potomac, the South was ready with serried ranks of armed, equipped, and uniformed men led by more than competent generals. The Federals would find that Southern fighting prowess was no trifling matter.

THE CLASH

EARLY SKIRMISHES HAD gained the Federals the neutral Border States, a strong foothold in western Virginia, and an advance presence across the Potomac in Alexandria and Arlington. But no one thought much of these accomplishments, and no one thought much of soon-to-retire General Winfield Scott's "Anaconda Plan" (the critics' name for it). Scott called for tightening the North's economic grip on the South by blockading the Southern coast and dividing the Confederacy by controlling the Mississippi River. Scott was a Virginian and an enormous admirer of Robert E. Lee, whom he knew well from the Mexican War. He thought Lee's loyalty to the South was worth a good 50,000 men, and he did not underestimate the martial prowess of his Southern compatriots. Scott had developed his strategy to minimize casualties, capitalize on the vast disparities in economic resources between North and South, and play to latent Union sentiment in the upper South. He also warned the Federal government that it would need an army of 300,000 men and two or three years to achieve victory.

But popular opinion—to which politicians had to pay heed—would have none of it. The popular demand, as always, was for a short, sharp shock that would provide quick victory. The challenge would be whether the North would take Richmond—"On to Richmond" was the battle cry—or whether the South would take Washington (always more of a Northern fear than a Southern intention). In June 1861, Confederate troops, under General Beauregard, began drawing up behind the Bull Run River at Manassas, a major railway junction, thirty miles from Washington. Confederate General Joseph E. Johnston, meanwhile, guarded Harpers Ferry forty miles to the northwest.

The Federal foe was amassing the largest army ever seen in North America, and it was confident of victory. With the Confederate Congress preparing to meet in Richmond on 20 July, Lincoln had his timeline set for him. The goal— proclaimed by Northern newspapers—was to take Richmond before then. Federal General Irvin McDowell was given a deadline of 16 July to begin the great march to victory. Northern civilians brought picnics as they came along to watch the colorfully clad Union troops[19]—they included gaily bedecked Zouaves, units dressed on a sort of a French-Moroccan model, as well as others dressed like Highlanders—win the war in a stroke.

General Joseph E. Johnston, whose expertise, as the war would show, was in retreats, fell back from his threatened position at Harpers Ferry to Winchester. At Winchester, cavalry commander J.E.B. ("Jeb") Stuart threw up a deceptive screen that allowed Johnston to slip away again and concentrate his forces at the crucial point: Manassas. Fewer than half of his 9,000 men had arrived, but as senior general Johnston took command from Beauregard, who had 21,000 soldiers on hand. Among Johnston's troops still making the journey was a crucial infantry brigade under the command of General Thomas Jonathan Jackson, which would arrive in time to form part of the Confederate line. The combined Confederates were still outnumbered by McDowell's 39,000 men. If Union General Robert Patterson—who had chased Johnston from Harpers Ferry, but was now fooled by Stuart's cavalry—brought his men to bear, another 18,000 Federal troops could hit Johnston and Beauregard.

McDowell's advance was ponderous, but his men were eager. When his troops struck on the hot, humid morning of 21 July, they stubbornly pushed through Confederate fire and forced back the Confederate left—where Beauregard had hoped, but was too slow, to spring his own assault force. Southern troopers— Georgians, Mississippians, Alabamans, Louisianans, South Carolinians—dazed, smoke-begrimed, and bloody, stumbled in retreat over the ridge of Henry Hill, where they saw Thomas Jonathan Jackson's Virginians waiting to repel the Federals. Inspired by the imperturbable Jackson, South Carolina General Bernard

Bee rallied his men: "There is Jackson standing like a stone wall! Let us determine to die here and we will conquer! Follow me!"[20] Bee fell during the combat, mortally wounded, but "Stonewall" Jackson gained his immortal moniker.

At first, the giving of ground was grudging, but overwhelming Federal numbers—and a perfectly placed attack on the Confederate right flank by Brigadier General William Tecumseh Sherman—broke the Confederate lines. The lines re-formed around Jackson, who coolly appraised the enemy and intended to "give them the bayonet." He also had artillery, which proved useful, as did the fact that the Confederate Army, including cavalry, was sweeping around to his left and closing on this section of the fighting. The Confederate line now held strong—Jackson's men drove the Federals back from Henry Hill with a ferocious charge—but more Federal troops kept coming. So did Confederate reinforcements as they arrived by train and marched to the sounds of musketry and cannon. Finally, in the afternoon, Confederate Colonel Jubal A. Early's men jogged into view and into hearing with their piercing rebel yell. That did it for the Federals. Exhausted, stunned by the rebel charge into their right flank, they broke: at first with good order and covering fire, but when a Confederate artillery shell blew up a wagon along the retreat route, panic insinuated itself among the Federals. So did rumors of Confederate cavalry in pursuit. Some Federal troops ran, and as they fled their confusion waxed. They tumbled into the civilian spectators who were hurriedly gathering up their picnics, and then the whole Northern expedition rolled into a massed flight to the Federal capital.

Stonewall knew what to do. President Jefferson Davis—who could rarely keep himself from a battlefield—rode to Henry Hill, where Confederate wounded, including Jackson, were being treated: "I am President Davis! All of you who are able follow me back to the field!" When Jackson recognized the president, he said: "Give me ten thousand men and I will take Washington tomorrow."[21]

Jackson's counsel was ignored. It had been a long day's fighting for the Confederate Army, and given all the difficulties in getting the men to Manassas, getting them to Washington seemed an overstretch of the young army's capabilities, especially as rain began to fall and impeding mud began to form. In one way, it didn't matter. If shocking the North was the intention, the North was well and truly shocked. The Northern war of aggression would be no picnic.

CHAPTER 12

"WAR IS CRUELTY, YOU CANNOT REFINE IT"

ONE BATTLE DOES NOT a war make. If the Confederacy was going to win not just the Battle of First Manassas but the War for Southern Independence, it needed the weapon that George Washington had: foreign intervention. France was sympathetic, and so was aristocratic opinion in England.[1] To European power politicians, the breaking up of the United States into halves was obviously a good thing. France deftly inserted itself into Mexico, where—in the absence of American colonization—one can only wish it had stayed, bringing Gallic rationality, style, and sound fiscal administration[2] to a land in perpetual political turmoil. Most important, France brought the French Foreign Legion, which pursued its usual *mission civilisatrice,* winning one of its most famous battle honors: the immortal heroism of Camerone, still celebrated annually by all legionnaires.[3]

In the smoking rooms of British baronial estates, meanwhile, there was a conviction that the aristocratic society of the South was far the better model. Southern-sympathizing British aristocrats credited the South with superior generalship. And the British ruling class had learned a lesson from the war of 1776 that it believed Lincoln rather foolishly missed: any settlement of liberty-loving Englishmen that declares itself independent will never be brought to heel. Lincoln's war of suppression, they surmised, was doomed. The South would never submit; its pride and love of liberty were too great.

Such opinions, wafting with cigar smoke over port, were one thing. So too was France's plucking of the Mexican cactus. But actually intervening on the side of the South—well, that was something far different, potentially very costly and dangerous, and given Southern military prowess most likely unnecessary. Why not simply let the Americans go at it and diplomatically nod approvingly at both sides?

That, in any event, was the calculation. Ever the realist, Robert E. Lee believed that "We must make up our minds to fight our battles and win our independence alone. No one will help us." The European powers would pursue their own self-interest. The North, he predicted, "would be shrewd enough to make the war appear to be merely a struggle on our part for the maintenance of slavery; and we shall thus be without sympathy, and most certainly without material aid from other powers."[4] Later in the war, he reminded President Davis of this hard fact: "As far as I have been able to judge, this war presents to the European world but two aspects. A contest in which one side is contending for abstract slavery and the other against it. The existence of vital rights involved does not seem to be understood or appreciated. As long as this lasts," he concluded, the Confederacy "can expect neither sympathy or aid." To Lee the conclusion was simple: "Our safety depends on ourselves alone."[5]

Still, many of the advantages European observers noticed were true. Southerners were patriots, their soldiers fierce, their commanders able and bred to the saddle, and their slaves freed the aristocratic class to fight, while the womenfolk ran the plantations (and, incidentally, suffered no slave insurrections). If the South was hindered by a lack of material resources and by states-rights' jealousies that complicated a national war effort, it didn't seem to matter much. For while Lincoln was irrevocably committed to the forcible reunification of the United States at whatever cost in blood and destruction, his generals seemed singularly ill-equipped to perform the task.

Lincoln had no shortage of officers, though many of them appeared better drilled in "self-esteem" than in military science. Nevertheless, he did have his stockpile of West Pointers, and at his disposal was the man who was presumed to be, at least by himself, the next Napoleon: the thirty-four-year-old wunderkind, George McClellan, fresh from victories in West Virginia. Everything about McClellan seemed to indicate success. He was the well-educated son of a surgeon and had attended the University of Pennsylvania before he graduated second in his class at West Point. He had seen action as a staff officer with General Scott in Mexico, taught at West Point, and was sent as a military observer to the Crimea. He even devised the McClellan saddle, a modification of the Prussian and Hungarian cavalry saddles he had admired during his travels in Europe. The McClellan saddle became standard U.S. Army issue until horses were made redundant in the service. A few years before the war, McClellan resigned his commission to apply his engineering skills for a railroad company—where he met a lawyer named Abraham Lincoln—and then became a railroad company president. He had, it appeared, a golden touch at military affairs, engineering, and business. He was a superb organizer, inspired loyalty among enlisted men, and had no doubts about his genius. Indeed, he thought *he* was the one essential man of the Northern war effort—certainly not Lincoln, and surely not any other politician or general. The "Young Napoleon" had arrived to meet his destiny; Lincoln brought it to him on a salver: command of the Army of the Potomac. "Little Mac," however, would prove a big flop.

McClellan kept his newly formed army drilling and marching and polishing boots to the pride of his new recruits and the approbation of all observers save those who thought that armies were for fighting. Before taking over the Army of the Potomac, McClellan had extracted a presidential promise that there would be no hurrying along the shaping of the army. McClellan warned that only the ignorant would call for haste in the forming and training of his *grande armée*. He must be given a free hand and all due time. But even Lincoln—a well-practiced apologist for McClellan's hauteur and careful preparations—eventually felt compelled to say, "If General McClellan does not want to use the army I should like to *borrow* it."[6]

While McClellan shared General Winfield Scott's love of pomp, he did not share his former commander's daring. Scott designed bold plans and executed them with speed. In that respect, Robert E. Lee—who Winfield Scott remarked was "the very best soldier I ever saw in the field"[7]—was Scott's true pupil, not McClellan. As 1861 passed into 1862, McClellan celebrated his thirty-fifth birthday and continued to busy himself dressing and redressing his army, as though destiny were the foot-tapping young man and he the attractive young belle.

In the South, Jefferson Davis staked out the pegs of his new nation. Missouri and Kentucky were granted stars in the Confederate battle flag and seats in the Confederate Congress. They along with Maryland were considered states to be liberated from Northern tyranny. The Confederates also organized in the West, claiming the Arizona Territory. Further western expansion was countenanced. Davis looked at a map and saw the South as having vast borders that must be defended at all points and territory to be reclaimed. As a reluctant secessionist, he, like Lee, was well aware that the war would be neither short nor easy. He also shared his countrymen's—and his generals'—preference for the offensive. But while the Southern spirit was willing, after the Battle of First Manassas sober minds recognized that organization was weak and trained manpower was short. Thus the great opportunity to seize the initiative—invading Maryland

or Ohio and upsetting the Union before McClellan's men had achieved the requisite sheen on their bayonets—was lost. Such plans were put forward. It wasn't
lack of desire or lack of recognition of their advantage that ruled them out—it
was their logistical impossibility at this stage in the war.

Even so, the Confederates kept active. In the West, on 10 August 1861,
Confederate forces under General Ben McCulloch threw back and defeated an
attack by Union General Nathaniel Lyon at Wilson's Creek, a dozen miles
southwest of Springfield, Missouri. Within a month, most of Missouri was
under Confederate control. In neutral Kentucky, Confederate Generals Gideon
Pillow, Leonidas Polk, and Albert Sidney Johnston advanced into the state and
set up a defensive line along the longitude of Columbus through Bowling Green
to the Cumberland Gap. And in the far West, the Confederacy had invaded
New Mexico (in July), fostering dreams of a desert empire that would extend
into southern California.

Another empire builder, Union General John C. Frémont, late of the California conquest, was dispatched to put a stopper in Confederate ambitions in
Missouri. He proved himself a western McClellan. Like McClellan, he mistook
bold words for action. Like McClellan, he was deeply impressed with himself.
And as McClellan had traveled among the militaries of Europe, Frémont surrounded himself with a court of European military advisers. They provided
elaborate European costumery and perhaps helped raise the tone—or at least
the level of foreign languages—at his headquarters, but they seemed to serve
little other purpose.

Unfortunately for his ego, Frémont was more easily dismissed as a preten-
tious nincompoop than was McClellan. The classic pen portrait comes from
Ulysses S. Grant, then a brigadier to Major General Frémont: "He sat in a room
in full uniform with his maps before him. When you went in he would point out
one line or another in a mysterious manner, never asking you to take a seat. You
were left without the least idea of what he meant or what he wanted you to do."[8]

On 30 August 1861, Frémont made the mistake of announcing what he
wanted to do. He issued a proclamation of martial law. Union troops were authorized to confiscate the property of all active Confederates, including their
slaves, who would be freed. Confederate guerillas found behind Union lines
were to be executed. Lincoln was aghast. In his efforts to court the Border
States, he was explicit that his war aim was to restore the Union, not to abolish
slavery. Lincoln asked Frémont to revise the proclamation and take a more conciliatory tone. Frémont refused. He would not alter one word unless he received

a direct presidential order to do so. He even sent his wife, Jessie (daughter of the late senator from Missouri, Thomas Hart Benton), to Washington to lobby on his behalf—a ridiculous maneuver that, predictably, backfired. Lincoln responded with a public order to Frémont that the proclamation must be changed, and then issued a second order removing Frémont from command in Missouri. If Lincoln felt he had to endure McClellan, he felt no such compunction about Frémont.

But while Frémont postured and McClellan primped, another Union commander, whom McClellan had refused to consider for a staff appointment, showed some initiative. On 28 August 1861, Ulysses S. Grant became commander of Union forces in southeastern Missouri. On 6 September, he made a swift occupation of Paducah, Kentucky, to gain a foothold against the developing Confederate line in the state; he then moved to the attack with gunboats and infantry: striking a Confederate camp on the Missouri side of the Mississippi River at Belmont. The Confederates were rousted out of their position, but counterattacked so hard that Grant and his men barely escaped. Grant kept a cool head, telling his nervous subordinate officers, "we had cut our way in and could cut our way out just as well."[9]

While other Union generals stood on their alleged dignity and continually demanded more time and more troops, Grant was of a mind to keep quiet and take action with the troops he had. On 6 February 1862, he was in the field again, taking gunboats, under the command of the "Gunboat Commodore" Andrew Foote, up the Tennessee River to capture the Confederate Fort Henry, something his military superiors (but not Lincoln) had thought too difficult an operation to conduct at this time. Grant used his infantry to cover the rear of the fort and the gunboats to bombard it. The Confederate commander, Brigadier General Lloyd Tilghman, successfully evacuated most of his men to Fort Donelson farther south, and then capitulated.

Having taken one fort, Grant set out methodically to take the next. Fort Donelson proved the harder nut. Albert Sidney Johnston, Confederate commander of the western theater, was divided in his counsels between withdrawing to Tennessee (his actual preferred option) and defending Fort Donelson. He split the difference and gave the fort reinforcements, but not as many as he could have. Nor did he go to the fort to assume command himself. This decision, so obviously bad—halfhearted measures only ensure the defeat of both halves—should have put paid to Johnston's reputation, which before the war had him ranked as one of the nation's finest officers. And he was no mere paper soldier, either. A West Point graduate, he had fought for Texas independence, been secretary of war for Texas, fought in the Mexican War, and made a show of force in the bloodless Mormon War of 1857–58 in the Utah Territory, which President Buchanan had declared was in a state of war against the United States, though it wasn't. Nevertheless, Albert Sidney Johnston, like his namesake Joseph E. Johnston, seemed to find virtue in perpetual retreat.

Holding command at Fort Donelson were General John Floyd, a former secretary of war; General Gideon Pillow; and General Simon Buckner, a West Pointer. Buckner was the youngest man, yet by right of military talent and experience should have been in charge. But Floyd, "one of the greatest rogues ever to serve in high position in both the U.S. and Confederate governments," and Pillow, "one of the most reprehensible men ever to wear the three stars and wreath of a Confederate general,"[10] were both lawyers and politicians whose connections granted them seniority to the professional soldier Buckner.

Despite the Confederates' command disabilities in Floyd and Pillow, Grant's hope of reenacting the capture of Fort Henry met with a reverse when Confederate guns hammered Commodore Foote's improvised force of ironclads and wooden gunboats. Foote had carried the bulk of the battle at Fort Henry, and he stubbornly kept his battered fleet's guns in action on the river. While Foote was embattled on the river, Grant had the Confederates outnumbered on land (there were 27,000 Federal troops to 21,000 Confederates). He used his infantry to invest the fort on three sides and then assumed he had the Confederates trapped. He did, but on the morning of 14 February, in the midst of wind and snow, the Confederates launched an unexpected breakout attack, plowed through the Union line in hard fighting, and cleared the road to Nashville. Inexplicably, General Pillow, leading the attack, didn't take the road. Over Buckner's protests, Pillow conferred with Floyd, and the lawyer-politicians agreed that they'd be safer behind their entrenchments. So the breakout had succeeded, but the commanders acted as though it hadn't, making the engagement serve no purpose at all.

Grant, rushing from a conference with Foote to the scene of the fighting, came to exactly the right conclusion: "Some of our men are pretty badly demoralized, but the enemy must be even more so, for he has attempted to force his way out, but has fallen back: the one who attacks first now will be victorious and the enemy will have to be in a hurry if he gets ahead of me."[11]

Pillow, having marched his men out and back again, decided that more of the same was called for, though even Floyd doubted this. He and Buckner realized that having failed to seize their chance, surrender was now inevitable. But in the well-practiced manner of a public official, Floyd decided that it was time for him to pass command of the fort to Pillow, who could more ably conduct the surrender, and Pillow in turn thought that in this extremity command at last well and truly belonged to the professional Buckner. And very thoughtfully, to avoid having them look over his shoulder, Floyd slipped downriver, past the crippled Union gunboats, and Pillow followed Floyd's stalwart example. More than 1,500 Confederates escaped with them. If Floyd and Pillow were cowards, there was another commander who evacuated Fort Donelson not out of fear, but out of seething anger at their craven stupidity. The fearless cavalry officer—a rags-to-slave-trader millionaire and instinctive military genius—Nathan Bedford Forrest had no intention of surrendering; he had not brought out his boys (he had raised and equipped his battalion himself) to freeze to death in a prison camp; he would beat a retreat to fight again. "Boys," he said, "these people are talking about surrendering, and I am going out of this place before they do or bust hell wide open."[12] Forrest took 700 men with him and slid past the Yankees.

Buckner asked Grant for terms. Grant was blunt: No negotiations. No terms. Only unconditional and immediate surrender would prevent him from attacking. Stung by Grant's reply, Buckner nevertheless had no choice. At Fort Donelson, the Union won its first major victory; and with this single blow, the Confederacy's hold on the western theater was endangered, Kentucky was lost, and Tennessee teetering. The evacuation of Nashville was already accepted as a necessity. President Lincoln, recognizing a fighting soldier, promoted "Unconditional Surrender" Grant to major general.

In the West, the Confederate picture was grim. Where little was at stake—New Mexico—the Confederacy was advancing, though it would be stopped at the Battle of Glorieta Pass in late March 1862. Where much was at stake—Kentucky, Tennessee, Missouri, Arkansas, and Louisiana—sudden reverses put the Confederacy at risk of being divided by the Mississippi River. In Missouri and Arkansas, Confederate hopes rested on General Earl van Dorn, a Mississippian, West Pointer, Mexican War veteran, and Indian fighter. He assembled around him General Ben McCulloch, a Tennessee-born Texas Ranger and fellow Mexican and Indian slayer; former Missouri governor turned general, Sterling Price, who like so many Confederate leaders was a reluctant secessionist; and General Albert Pike, another reluctant secessionist—indeed a Bostonian. Pike was also a scholar, poet, writer, and lawyer, an opponent of slavery, and a grand panjandrum of the Freemasons. He had come West seeking adventure for his large, bearlike frame, and fought in the Mexican War, become an Arkansan, and was noted as a cultivator of Indian alliances, which made him both valuable to the Confederacy, and also controversial, as he didn't prohibit scalping. This fantastical crew of generals and their men, including Indians, marched through a blizzard of snow to regain lost ground in Missouri.

Union General Samuel Custis's scouts—who included Wild Bill Hickok—warned him that the Confederates were coming. He arranged his troops at Elkhorn Tavern, three miles south of Pea Ridge, Arkansas. Van Dorn maneuvered to flank him, but Custis expertly reoriented his men, and when the Confederates came on they ran into a perfectly prepared defensive position. The Confederates outnumbered the Federals, but in the two-day battle they were completely outgeneraled and outfought by the Union's disciplined soldiers and were forced to withdraw. With their retreat, Missouri was lost to the Confederacy, and Arkansas too was wide open for the Federals to attack. That occurred in March. A month later, on 6 and 7 April 1862, the biggest clash of arms in the history of the eighty-year-old American republic occurred at Shiloh, Tennessee, in a battle of American against American.

SHILOH

AFTER HIS VICTORY at Fort Donelson, Grant had been held waiting. Major General Henry Halleck was his superior officer—and Halleck, a lawyer and military intellectual (trained at West Point), was yet another general who was far more keen on organization, letter-writing, and politicking than he was on leading men into battle. Instead of congratulating Grant on the capture of Fort Donelson, he had Grant arrested (with approval from McClellan, as commander of the Army) for failing to keep him informed of his movements. He also passed along a rumor that Grant was drunk and hinted at other allegations of impropriety. In fact, Grant was sober, the telegraph operator had decamped with Grant's dispatches (which was why Halleck hadn't heard from him), and the fighting general had traveled to Nashville to coordinate his movements with Union General Don Carlos Buell. Buell had occupied Tennessee's capital nine days after the fall of Fort Donelson. Grant had done nothing wrong except achieve victories. When pressed by Washington for details on Grant's alleged failings, Halleck restored Grant to command. Lincoln went one better and gave Grant command of the "Department of Mississippi" and stripped McClellan of his role as general in chief, pushing him to focus on leading a campaign into Virginia.

On the Southern side, Albert Sidney Johnston watched the blue lines forming up in Tennessee. Grant's forces, the Union Army of the Tennessee, had swelled to 42,000 men. At Nashville, General Buell had the Army of the Ohio: 50,000 Union troops. The Confederate government of Tennessee had fled from Nashville to Memphis in the southwest corner of the state and didn't feel at all secure there, either. Johnston's army was even farther south, regrouping in Corinth, Mississippi. The one bright spot was Johnston's new second in command: P. G. T. Beauregard. Pulling together his retreating forces and gathering additional ones, by the end of March, Johnston had 40,000 men assembled for offensive operations.

Johnston knew he had to move quickly. If Grant and Buell's forces combined, he would be crushed. Johnston's hope was to defeat Grant—whose men were gathered at Shiloh, near Pittsburgh Landing on the Tennessee River—before turning to Buell. Grant, meanwhile, thought the initiative was all his and was expecting to move on Corinth as soon as Buell's men arrived. But it was not Buell's men who turned up in the Union camp at dawn, Sunday, 6 April. It was Johnston's rebel-yelling Confederates, one of whom shot dead an aide standing next to ragged, redheaded General William Tecumseh Sherman.

Just the day before, Sherman had rebuked a colonel for his fearful reports that the rebels were coming. Sherman was known to have a nervous disposition and was full of twitches (unless he was in action). He had previously been relieved of command under suspicion of insanity (he memorably said later, "I took care of Grant when he was drunk, and he took care of me when I was crazy"). But he was intolerant of nervousness in others and fought hard to keep his own dreaded imagination under control. Sherman's anxiety was based in part on his own love of the South. Before the war he had been superintendent of a military academy in Louisiana (what is now Louisiana State University), and he knew the South would submit only under compulsion of massive Union force. His respect for the South's martial strength had kept him worried about Confederate numbers and intentions. But at Shiloh, he, like Grant, was caught unprepared.

Sherman rushed to find reinforcements, as the Confederate assault drove back the Federals. Some Federal officers and men fled headlong, but the bulk of the Union troops again showed resilience and good order in making a fighting retreat, with Sherman, twice wounded, organizing the defense. Sherman held the Union right; General John McClernand, the Union center behind the Shiloh church; and General Benjamin Prentiss, the Union left, which had been driven back until the Federal troops found a sunken road forming a natural trench where they could re-form and mow down charging Confederates, who dubbed the position "the Hornets' Nest."

The Federals continued to give ground. Grant estimated that he was facing 100,000 Confederates, well more than double the actual number, but even so was inclined to fight it out. The Confederate generals leading the assault were, from left to right, along their line: William Hardee, a Georgia West Pointer and author of the widely read *Hardee's Tactics;* the Episcopal bishop of Louisiana, Leonidas Polk; and on the right, the irascible Braxton Bragg and former presidential candidate John C. Breckinridge. The plan of attack had been Beauregard's and Beauregard was commanding the center of the action from Shiloh chapel. But General Albert Sidney Johnston, making up for his indecision at Fort Donelson, was riding along the Confederate lines, directing men into position, and gallantly encouraging them forward. In an effort to break through a heavily fortified peach grove flanking the Hornets' Nest, Johnston took personal command. On horseback, he led a bayonet charge into murderous fire. His inspiration sped the Confederates to victory at the orchard. As he rode back smiling, he sent his own doctor to look after the Union wounded. Johnston's uniform was torn by minié balls, his boot was filling with blood from a severed artery in his right leg, and Johnston triumphant was helped from his horse. A little brandy touched his lips, and then he died.

Beauregard's offensive seemed to be working, though the day before he had wanted to call it off, fearful that he had lost the element of surprise. He hadn't, and now that the Hornets' Nest stymied his progress, he was determined to clear it out by amassing an artillery barrage to obliterate it. The Hornets' Nest held together—but no other part of the Union line did, as Sherman and McClernand continued their fighting retreats. With Confederates encircling the nest, and more than half of his men dead, Prentiss surrendered. As daylight petered out, Beauregard called off any further advances. The Confederates had won the field, but needed to be regrouped; they could finish off Grant's army in the morning.

With their backs to the Tennessee River, thoughts of escape must have played through many a blue-clad soldier's mind. But Grant was resolute—and he had reason to be. A ravine separated the Federals from the Confederates, a formidable obstacle to any rebel assault. And 20,000 fresh soldiers from General Buell's command would be with him in the morning; so would another 6,000 men under General Lew Wallace.[13] Grant intended to counterattack and smash through the disorganized rebels. Though Grant had no accurate numbers to gauge Confederate strength, his reinforcements alone equaled or exceeded the number of Confederate effectives. The one rebel who noticed this was Nathan Bedford Forrest, whose scouts reported on Grant's reinforcements. Forrest passed word to General Hardee, who dismissed the report, and the rebel cavalry commander was left to growl, "We'll be whipped like hell tomorrow."[14]

Lightning was the gun flash of the night, thunder took the place of cannon, and rain pounded the living, the wounded, and the dead. In the morning, the guns opened up again, but to the Confederates' dismay, they were Yankee guns, and the bluecoats were charging at *them*. In a military *danse macabre*, yesterday's battle was repeated, though the roles were switched. The rebels fought on the retreat; the Federals marched past their own wounded and dead, pushing all the way back to their original lines. By midafternoon, Beauregard accepted that he would have to withdraw.

The Federals were too fought-out to mount a pursuit, except for a duel between Forrest's rearguard cavalry and Sherman's men. Forrest, at one point, surrounded by blue-clad soldiers, became a one-man army, his pistol blowing holes in blue uniforms with one hand, his sabre striking blood with the other, and his horse flailing with its hooves. A Union rifle was pressed into his side and fired, but Forrest stayed mounted, kept on fighting, and grabbed a hapless Federal soldier, throwing him behind his saddle as a human shield until he had ridden out of harm's way; then he dumped the Yankee and rode on. It took two operations to dig out the bullet from near his spine, but Forrest would ride again.

A great many Confederate and Union soldiers, however, would not. More than 24,000 men were casualties—about one in four of the troops engaged—with the Federals having taken somewhat the worst of it. There were more casualties at Shiloh than there had been in the American War of Independence, the War of 1812, and the Mexican War *combined*, but Shiloh marked neither victory nor defeat. It was a bloody draw. If the Union was going to be preserved by force, Shiloh would be no unique horror, as Grant now realized: "I gave up all idea of saving the Union except by complete conquest"[15]—a war of conquest against his fellow Americans.

CHAPTER 13

"WAR MEANS FIGHTING AND FIGHTING MEANS KILLING"

ROM SHILOH, THE UNION moved from strength to strength—for a while. Union forces advanced up the Mississippi. On 11 April 1862, Fort Pulaski on the Georgia coast fell to the Federals. New Orleans fell as well, giving the Federals control of the northern and southern ends of the Mississippi River. At Second Manassas, Confederate General Joseph E. Johnston did what he did best—retreating behind the Rappahannock River, destroying valuable Confederate stores and supplies, and all for no reason that Confederate President Jefferson Davis could comprehend save that retreating was Johnston's forte. Off the coast of Virginia, the ironclad USS *Monitor* and CSS *Virginia* (or *Merrimac*) fought to a standstill. And in another colorful—yet ultimately fatal—sideshow, Union soldiers disguised as civilians stole a train from Marietta, Georgia, and tried to escape in a great race, leaving a trail of burning bridges behind them. The train was recaptured and eight of the Federals were executed as saboteurs. Meanwhile, General Henry Halleck, assuming the victory at Shiloh as his own, took the Union Army on a stately progress, punctuated by daily trench digging, to Corinth, Mississippi, where he intended to defeat General Beauregard, but Beauregard didn't wait for him, and there was no battle at all.

The Confederacy seemed imperiled. In Virginia, however, a formidable constellation of military talents emerged to foil Federal ambitions. In the Shenandoah Valley, old Blue Light, Stonewall Jackson, his kepi cap drawn close over his eyes, his troop movements secretive and swift—so swift that Union officers thought they were impossible—kept the Federal forces off balance. Jackson's "foot cavalry" marches and countermarches, which sometimes mystified his own men as much as the enemy, led to battles that repeatedly stung and repelled the Federal commanders sent to seize and destroy the breadbasket of the Confederacy.

Jackson knew his business and later made it plain to another Confederate officer: "Always mystify, mislead, and surprise the enemy, if possible; and when you strike and overcome him, never let up in the pursuit so long as your men have strength to follow; for an army routed, if hotly pursued, becomes panic-stricken, and can then be destroyed by half their number. The other rule is never fight against heavy odds, if by any possible maneuvering you can hurl your own force on only a part, and that the weakest part, of your enemy and crush it. Such tactics will win every time, and a small army may thus destroy a large one in detail, and repeated victory will make it invincible."[1]

In Jackson, word and deed were never separated, and he mystified, misled, surprised, and defeated the enemy throughout the Shenandoah Valley campaign of 1862 in the battles at Kernstown (23 March, a tactical defeat but a strategic victory), McDowell (8 May), Front Royal (23 May), Winchester (25 May), Cross Keys (8 June), and Port Republic (9 June). Not only did he save the valley, he deprived Union General McClellan of tens of thousands of troops he wanted for his offensive against Richmond, as Federal forces in the valley were reinforced and sent to capture Jackson. The only troops that slipped out of the valley to fight near Richmond were Jackson's own, when Robert E. Lee, taking due note of the clever commander of the valley, summoned him to Richmond's defense at the Battle of Seven Days.

On the Union side, McClellan's massive Army of the Potomac finally bestirred itself. McClellan had hoped to assemble 150,000 men, but with troops diverted to defend Washington or fight Stonewall Jackson, his numbers were quickly reduced to a mere 100,000—still more than double the size of any Confederate Army that could be turned against him.

"On to Richmond!" was still the cry, but the route had been altered. Unwilling to face a slog straight down from Washington to Fredericksburg to Richmond, McClellan planned to cooperate with the Navy to land his men at Fort Monroe near where the James River empties into the Chesapeake Bay, an area known as Hampton Roads. From there he had a march of about seventy-five miles to the Confederate capital. McClellan landed in force and brought more than 50,000 men up the York Peninsula to confront the Confederate defenders at Yorktown. McClellan paused. Confederate General "Prince John" Magruder opposed him with fewer than 15,000 men. Such odds—more than three to one in the Young Napoleon's favor—worried McClellan. He habitually inflated Confederate numbers and planned for earth-shattering, historic sieges. Magruder encouraged McClellan's fears by theatrical displays of marching Confederates.

Artillery was brought up and McClellan spent an entire month preparing his siege plans. That allowed Joseph E. Johnston time to arrive and perform another of his brilliant retreats, leaving McClellan to blow hell out of trenches that had already been abandoned. Because the Confederate retreat made Norfolk indefensible, Johnston had the added fillip of destroying Confederate stores and supplies, in this case including the CSS *Virginia*.

Richmond would not be so easily abandoned, chiefly because General Robert E. Lee was there. Union dreams of a naval assault were crushed when Confederate defenders at Drewry's Bluff, seven miles from the rebel capital, convinced the Federals that the James River was impassable as it approached Richmond. Still, the Federal foe, more than 100,000 strong, advanced on land to a point five miles from the city, within sight of its church steeples. Here Johnston fought McClellan at the Battle of Seven Pines (or Fair Oaks) and did the best service he ever did the Confederacy: he managed to get wounded badly enough that Robert E. Lee took command. Lee renamed his army the Army of *Northern* Virginia,[2] for he intended to "change the character of the war" and "drive our enemies back to their homes."[3]

He set his troops to digging entrenchments, work they hated but that the engineer Lee would not neglect. He used these defensive works not simply to secure his position but to hold it with fewer men so that he could move on to the offensive. Beyond building trenches, earthworks, and fortifications, he invented the use of railroad-mounted artillery and reorganized his units of infantry and artillery to make them more effective and mobile. As he rode along the lines, encouraging the troops, he knew he had men eager to fight. His officers were another question.

He called them to a conference on 23 June 1862. He asked his subordinate generals their opinions on what should be done. While Lee kept his own counsel, they each volunteered that the Confederate Army should retreat closer to Richmond. Lee disagreed, telling Colonel Charles Marshall: "If we leave this line because they can shell us, we shall have to leave the next for the same reason, and I don't see how we can stop this side of Richmond." When another general began drawing a diagram to show why retreat was inevitable, Lee admonished him: "Stop, stop! If you go on ciphering, we are whipped beforehand."[4]

Lee would dispel such defeatism and reassign officers who couldn't shake it. He wanted men like Stonewall Jackson, who soon became his "right arm," the dashing dandy Jeb Stuart, the red-shirted fighting aristocrat A. P. Hill, and his "old war horse," the stubborn old army mule James Longstreet.

With the entrenchments in front of Richmond completed, Lee defended them with a holding force of 25,000 men, out of a total Confederate strength of roughly 70,000. McClellan faced Richmond with an army of 100,000 men. But using Richmond as a pivot, Lee hurled his smaller force on an unceasing offensive—like a bulldog taking after a donkey, if unable to seize its jugular, then ripping at its hamstrings—in what became known as the Seven Days campaign (26 June–2 July 1862).

When Lee took command from Johnston, General McClellan had affected to be pleased by the change. "I prefer Lee to Johnston—the former is *too* cautious & weak under grave responsibility—personally brave & energetic to a fault, he is yet wanting in moral firmness when pressed by heavy responsibility & is likely to be timid and irresolute in action."[5]

But McClellan's dispatches to Washington during the Seven Days soon took on a different tone—one of panic. Before the first battle, at Mechanicsville, Little Mac bleated, "I am in no way responsible . . . as I have not failed to represent repeatedly the necessity for reinforcements. . . . If the result . . . is a disaster, the responsibility cannot be thrown on my shoulders."[6] In another dispatch, written in the early morning hours of 28 June, after the Confederates had driven his men back with a frontal assault, McClellan wrote, "I have lost this battle because my force was too small. I again repeat that I am not responsible for the result. . . . [T]he government has not sustained this army. If you do not do so now the game is lost. If I save this army now, I tell you plainly that I owe no thanks to you or any other persons in Washington. You have done your best to sacrifice this army."[7]

One never heard similar words issue from the soft-spoken, gentlemanly Lee. He preferred action, and he turned many a Union braggart into a Union whiner. Indeed, during the Seven Days, Lee kept the army surging forward until General McClellan was driven back a full twenty-five miles, in what McClellan tried to term a strategic withdrawal, but which became known popularly, and more accurately, as "the great skedaddle." It would take the Union three years to bring its troops as close to Richmond as they were before Lee took command.

But Lee was brutally disappointed in his own performance. The Seven Days campaign proved costly: nearly a third of Lee's available fighting men went down as casualties, compared to 20 percent of the Federals. Not everything went according to plan—for this was still a young army, and Lee's orders occasionally asked too much of it. And Lee's trust in Stonewall Jackson must have been sorely tried as Jackson, suffering from exhaustion, repeatedly and without apology failed him, as did many of his subordinate generals, who turned in lackluster performances. (The worst of them would soon be given new assignments. The best of them—hard-driving Jackson and the gallantly impulsive A. P. Hill—would be given a second chance.)

Most important for Lee, expelling the Federals from Richmond had not been the sum of his objectives. His plans were designed to crush McClellan's army. In his report to Jefferson Davis, Lee volunteered that "Under ordinary circumstances, the Federal army should have been destroyed."[8] He writes in this instance of an army far larger than his own, better supplied, with an enormous advantage in artillery, near perfect defensive positions, and that had fought well.

Still, it was a victory at a time when the Confederacy could not afford another defeat. The victory was as symbolic as it was military. It provided an enormous boost to Southern morale and the morale of Lee's new Army of Northern Virginia. The victory had its theatrical side, too, with Confederate cavalryman Jeb Stuart's famous ride around McClellan, circumnavigating the Union Army, developing intelligence, and taking prisoners. And it was demonstrable in terms of territory and initiative regained. Lee had driven the Federals all the way out of Henrico County to Harrison's Landing on the James River. And Richmond was safe.

SECOND MANASSAS TO SHARPSBURG

BUT UNION ARMIES STILL threatened the Old Dominion. In northern Virginia was Federal General John Pope, who bragged that his headquarters would be in the saddle where, Confederates joked, most people kept their hindquarters. Pope came from the western theater and was not popular with the Federal Army of Virginia. General Fitz-John Porter put the common view that Pope was "an Ass."[9] He was an ass with 50,000 men sitting on the railway lines of northern Virginia. Worse, to Lee's point of view, Pope explicitly designated the South's civilian population as a legitimate war target. Pope gave orders that his army would live off Southern civilians, paying recompense only to those who could prove their loyalty to the Union. All Southern male civilians in territory occupied by Pope were subject to immediate arrest. Both men and women, by his orders, could be executed as spies and traitors for as little as attempting to communicate with family members in the Confederate Army.

While Lee had perfectly sound strategic reasons for focusing on Pope, there is no denying that he thought Pope offered an example of uncivilized warfare.

The "miscreant Pope," he wrote, must be "suppressed."[10] The task Lee assigned himself, of getting at General Pope and destroying his army, was no easy one. McClellan, still at Harrison's Landing, outnumbered the Confederate general even more than he had before the Seven Days. Pope's numbers were also greater than Lee's. Yet Lee daringly divided his forces, confident that McClellan would remain at the river until ordered to leave by Lincoln's new general in chief, Henry Halleck. Lee was right.

Lee ordered Stonewall Jackson and 24,000 men north to harass Pope (whose army was roughly three times that size). When McClellan finally responded to Halleck's recall of his forces to Washington, Lee rushed up another 31,000 Confederates under General Longstreet to help Jackson destroy Pope's army.

Lee ordered Jackson to put his troopers between Pope and Washington, a maneuver that was sure to bring the Federal commander to battle. Jackson had already clashed with a portion of Pope's force at Cedar Mountain (9 August 1862), where he had rallied his men by waving his sword in one hand and the battle flag in the other while under heavy enemy fire. Now Jackson maneuvered his army behind Pope's and further annoyed the Union general by burning his supply depot at Manassas Junction. Confederate cavalry commander Jeb Stuart offered his own insult by raiding Pope's camp and making off with Pope's dress coat.

Pope mistakenly thought he had "bagged" the slippery Jackson. "I see no possibility of his escape," said Pope. But Jackson was Lee's bramble bush. While Jackson held Pope, Lee and General Longstreet would ride up to hit Pope on the flank. Jackson, generally the hammer rather than the anvil of Lee's army, tenaciously defended his position in what became the Battle of Second Manassas (28–30 August 1862). Two of Jackson's best commanders (General William Taliaferro and General Richard Ewell) went down with wounds; some of his men, their ammunition expended, were reduced to swinging their muskets as clubs, desperately hurling stones, and lunging with bayonets; but Jackson remained steely eyed and unruffled. He trusted to Providence and to the ferocity of the Confederate commander holding the most heavily engaged part of the line: the swashbuckling Virginian A. P. Hill.

When General Longstreet arrived on the flank, he waited, as was his wont, for just the right moment to strike. He kept his full complement of troops drawn up and made a careful survey of the land, unhurried by the obvious pressure on Jackson or by Lee's repeated suggestions that he expedite his assault. Finally, Longstreet smashed the exposed Union line with an artillery barrage that lifted the pressure on Jackson. Then, at Lee's command, Longstreet sent his troops charging into the Federals, rolling the bluecoats up, while Jackson's own troopers jumped over their defensive positions, screaming the rebel yell. Under attack from two sides, Pope's army broke into flight—running all the way to Washington, where it met McClellan's tardy relief force.

Jackson's and Longstreet's combined corps totaled 55,000 men; they had defeated 75,000 Federals; and in the words of a Union Army historian, Pope "had been kicked, cuffed, hustled about, knocked down, run over, and trodden upon as rarely happens in the history of war. His communications had been cut; his headquarters pillaged; a corps had marched into his rear, and had encamped at its ease upon the railroad by which he received his supplies; he had been beaten and foiled in every attempt he had made to 'bag' those defiant intruders; and, in the end, he was glad to find refuge in the intrenchments of Washington, whence he had sallied forth, six weeks before, breathing out threatenings and slaughter."[11]

Washington was worried. In the three months since Robert E. Lee had held field command, he had broken the imminent siege of Richmond, ended the Confederate retreat, and driven two Union armies—Pope's and McClellan's— across the Potomac. It was the Federal capital that now feared a siege, that was preparing to evacuate government property to New York, and that was readying clerks for the defense of the city.

Lee's success had liberated not only most of Virginia, but also, indirectly, the North Carolina coastline. In the Old Dominion itself, western Virginia was now under only tenuous occupation, and in the words of Lee's Pulitzer Prize–winning biographer Douglas Southall Freeman, except "for the troops at Norfolk and at Fort Monroe, the only Federals closer than 100 miles to Richmond were prisoners of war and men busily preparing to retreat from the base at Aquia Creek."[12]

Having neatly reversed the situation that confronted Richmond in June, Lee could have staked out a defensive position. But Lee did not intend to let the enemy rest; every victory had to be exploited. Lee did not believe that time was on the Confederacy's side—a war of attrition and endurance could benefit only the larger, better-equipped Federal army and its seemingly illimitable resources. So Lee embraced the risky strategy of invading the North.

Lee summed up the situation, with typical honesty and humility (and in marked contrast to so many bombastic Union generals), for Confederate President Jefferson Davis: "The army is not properly equipped for an invasion of the enemy's territory. It lacks much of the material of war, is feeble in transportation, the animals being much reduced, and the men are poorly provided with clothes, and in thousands of instances are destitute of shoes. Still we cannot afford to be idle, and though weaker than our opponents in men and military equipments, must endeavor to harass, if we cannot destroy them. I am aware that the movement is attended with much risk, yet I do not consider success impossible, and shall endeavor to guard it from loss."[13]

Lee did not intend to lay siege to Washington, but to advance into Maryland—a slave state that harbored Southern sympathizers, a state that had already provided Confederate recruits and where his men could find forage unavailable in the devastated wastes of northern Virginia. It was also a state to which he might draw the Federal armies away from their defenses in Washington and defeat them in open battle.

Invading Maryland was the beginning of Lee's plan, which called for striking the railroad at Harrisburg, Pennsylvania, both to disrupt Federal troop movements, and to threaten three major northern cities—Philadelphia, Baltimore, and Washington, in a descending arc. Lee wanted to change the complexion of the war—and end it. This was an election year, and if Lee could bring Confederate troops to Maryland and Pennsylvania, perhaps Northern voters would return a congressional majority that would recognize Southern freedom.

The proclamation Lee issued as his army crossed into Maryland—a state where Lincoln had suspended habeas corpus and imposed martial law[14]—emphasized that the South stood for the principle of freedom, free association, and tolerance: "No constraint upon your free will is intended: no intimidation will be allowed within the limits of this army, at least. Marylanders shall once more enjoy their ancient freedom of thought and speech. We know of no enemies among you, and will protect all, of every opinion. It is for you to decide your destiny freely and without constraint. This army will respect your choice, whatever it may be; and while the Southern people will rejoice to welcome you to your natural position among them, they will only welcome you when you come of your own free will."[15]

To look at the Army of Northern Virginia, as one young Maryland boy noted, was a revelation. They were, he said, "the dirtiest men I ever saw, a most ragged, lean and hungry set of wolves. Yet there was a dash about them that the Northern men lacked. They rode like circus riders . . . were profane beyond belief and talked incessantly."[16] A cavalryman of the Army of Northern Virginia described it as a "voluntary association of gentlemen organized for the sole business of driving out Yankees."[17]

It had thus far been effective in that role, but in one of the great turning points of the war, Union troops found three cigars wrapped in a sheet of paper. The paper was a duplicate of Lee's Special Orders No. 191 belonging to one of General D. H. Hill's staff officers. The orders were delivered to McClellan, who now knew Lee's entire plan of maneuver, and knew how dangerously divided were Lee's forces. Lee, who trusted his ability to read McClellan, was surprised to receive intelligence reports that showed the Union general moving with uncharacteristic rapidity toward Lee's vulnerable army, as though he knew its exact location and where it was heading—which of course he did. "Here is a paper," exclaimed Little Mac, "with which if I cannot whip Bobby Lee I will be willing to go home."

McClellan was bringing 75,000 men to the attack. Lee's full strength was only 38,000 men, and he could bring that number to the field only if Jackson's corps returned in time from recapturing Harpers Ferry. Lee dispatched 15,000 men to impede McClellan's advance through a gap in Maryland's Catoctin Mountains. He brought the rest of his army to the Maryland town of Sharpsburg on Antietam Creek: he would not be chased out of Maryland; Little Mac would have to fight him.

The battle was engaged on 17 September 1862. The odds against Lee narrowed with the clock. Each advancing hour brought more Confederates from the march to the battle line. In the morning, as Lee arranged his men at Sharpsburg, he brought barely a quarter as many troops as McClellan to the field. By afternoon, with the arrival of Jackson, Lee had shaved McClellan's advantage to three to one. And at full strength, which Lee did not have until the battle was nearly over, he was still outnumbered by two to one.

The battle was desperate. In the first four hours of combat, 13,000 men in blue and grey fell as casualties in the bloodiest day of the war.

At one point in the heat and smoke of battle, there was a poignant moment for Lee. An artillery commander reported that a battery had lost three out of four cannons, their crews and their horses dead. Lee ordered the remaining piece back into action. One of its gunners was a begrimed slip of a man who came forward to pay his respects. It was Lee's youngest son, Rob.

"General," he said, "are you going to send us in again?"

Lee smiled and replied, "Yes, my son. You all must do what you can to help drive these people back."[18]

Twice, the Confederate line was almost overwhelmed: first at Bloody Lane, where the Confederates, mistakenly thinking they had been ordered to retreat, nearly allowed their forces to be divided; and then late in the day when Lee's right flank, which he had continually stripped to support his left, began to give way under a fierce, sustained attack by Union General Ambrose Burnside. As the flank finally dissolved under Federal fire, Burnside had a clear field to destroy Lee's army.

Lee, who had been confident in the morning and unruffled throughout, now pointed to the southwest, asking an artillery lieutenant to use his field glasses and identify a new unit marching toward the battle. Were they yet more Union troops? The lieutenant saw the snap of Virginia and Confederate flags, though many of the men appeared to be dressed in blue.

Lee identified the unit immediately: "A. P. Hill from Harpers Ferry." Their uniforms were a way to make do, replacing their own tatterdemalion grey with confiscated Federal stores.

Confederate General A. P. Hill, who had been left to finish the job at Harpers Ferry, had started his men as soon as he could, leading them on a seventeen-mile forced march. Of the 5,000 who started that morning, only 3,000 remained, the others having fallen out or been left straggling behind. With serendipitous precision, Hill arrived exactly when and where the Confederates needed him most, on Burnside's flank. Despite the rigors of the march, Hill's men tore into the Federals, scattering the Union assault. The day of battle was over. But the danger was not.

Lee could have skedaddled, as McClellan had done before Richmond. But he ordered no retreat. His men made camp and rested. The next day, when the sun rose over a grim battlefield littered with grotesque rows of swollen corpses, Lee's army was still in place, bloody but unshaken, daring McClellan to attack.

McClellan declined the opportunity, content to watch Lee's army from afar. Indeed, McClellan feared that without reinforcements, his own army, more than twice the size of Lee's, shod where Lee's army was not, well fed where Lee's army was not, and with an endless supply of arms, ammunition, and other supplies that Lee's army had to conserve, was actually in danger of destruction. McClellan would later report that "at that moment—Virginia lost, Washington menaced, Maryland invaded—the national cause could afford no risks of defeat."[19]

While the engagement at Sharpsburg had blunted Lee's invasion—indeed, effectively ended it—the Army of Northern Virginia had not only survived but achieved what amounted to a brilliant tactical victory. It had held its ground against overwhelming odds, and held it again without challenge the next day. Its honor assured, that night Lee pulled the men out of their lines and led them back across the Potomac to the safety of Virginia, with A. P. Hill smacking a contingent of pursuing Federals into the north bank of the Potomac and providing, in the words of historian Shelby Foote, "a sort of upbeat coda, after the crash and thunder of what had gone on before."[20]

Lee's men were rested, refitted, and fed, while Jeb Stuart raised Southern morale—and increased McClellan's caution—by leading his cavalry in another ride round the Army of the Potomac, taking the Confederate horsemen as far north as Chambersburg, Pennsylvania. Then came more interesting news: President Lincoln had relieved General McClellan from command. Lee greeted the announcement humorously, saying of McClellan, "we always understood each other so well. I fear they may continue to make these changes till they find someone whom I don't understand."[21]

Lee would soon be facing a new threat, as a frustrated President Lincoln and his secretary of war, Edwin Stanton, took a more active role in directing Union strategy. With General Ambrose Burnside they plotted a straight course from Washington to Fredericksburg to Richmond. The only thing that stood in their way was the army of General Robert E. Lee.

FREDERICKSBURG AND MURFREESBORO

THE BATTLE FOR FREDERICKSBURG would close the 1862 campaign in the East. Lee did not want to fight there. It was then only a small city, but for the people who lived there, the hardship of facing a Federal invasion was no less severe. It was a hardship that Lee would rather have spared them, particularly as the city was noted more for its charm and its history (James Monroe, John Paul Jones, and Mary Washington, George Washington's mother, had lived there) than for any militarily useful industry. Lee told the Federals he would consent not to occupy the city, if they would do the same. But the Union's objective was one of subjugation—of waging war on the people of the South to bend them to the Union's will. So, in bitter cold, the women of Fredericksburg, their children, and the men too old to fight gathered their belongings and trudged through the deep snow, evacuating their homes, which the Federals had threatened to shell. As the civilians marched from the looming battlefield, they were pelted by sleet.

Lee looked on the spectacle with wonder, sorrow, and admiration. Lee preferred to keep fighting away from civilians. But when the Federals chose the route of attack, he was given little choice but to meet them there. When the Federals bombarded the city, Lee said, "These people delight to destroy the weak and those who can make no defense; it just suits them."[22]

Fighting at Fredericksburg displeased Lee for another reason. While the ground was easily defensible, it was not ground from which he could maneuver. The Federals, if beaten, would simply return across the Rappahannock and have an easy line of retreat to Washington. Lee prepared defensive positions on the hills to the east of the city, in a seven-mile line facing the Rappahannock River. But rather than rely on trench works, he relied on the high ground and carefully positioned artillery. Lee, as usual, was badly outnumbered, but he was confident of doing Burnside damage and wanted to lure him to battle.

Lee's initial line of resistance was a deployment of Mississippi and Florida riflemen who sniped at the Federals as they bombarded Fredericksburg. The Federals then crossed the river and moved into the city. Lee's Mississippians, under the command of General William Barksdale, were gallant in slowing the Union advance, but by evening the Mississippians and Floridians were withdrawn,[23] and the Federals were, for the moment, uncontested occupiers of Fredericksburg, looting and vandalizing the houses. They would receive a terrible punishment the next day.

The morning opened with a fog so thick that cavalry commander Jeb Stuart and an aggressive Stonewall Jackson thought the Confederates should launch a surprise attack under its cover. But the Grey Fox Lee demurred. Then the Union guns belched smoke and thunder, trying, largely unsuccessfully, to find the Confederates. As the fog slowly lifted, the artillery battle became a duel—a duel between an entire line of Union cannon and a single Confederate artillery officer, Captain John Pelham, with two guns, one of which was quickly disabled. Jeb Stuart sent orders for Pelham to retire, but like the Mississippi sharpshooters before him, Pelham had to be compelled with three sets of orders, before he would withdraw his cannon.[24]

The Federal artillery barrage intensified. Then the Federal infantry began testing the Confederate line, advancing uphill in force. The Confederates waited until the Union soldiers were well in the open before unleashing a deadly artillery barrage of their own. The Federals fell back, only to come again at the Confederate line. It would be a day of slaughter, with the Federals repulsed once, twice. . . . It was here on a hill overlooking the battle that Lee uttered one of his most memorable phrases, "It is well war is so terrible; we should grow too fond of it."[25]

While Jackson had some hard fighting on Lee's right, Burnside massed the bulk of his forces for an almost obsessive assault on Lee's left at Marye's Heights. Lee saw the Federals were taking a horrible beating but warned Longstreet that the Union concentration was so heavy that it might break through. The Federal strength was 120,000 men to 78,000 men for the Confederates. But Longstreet, who preferred to fight on the defensive, was phlegmatic: "General, if you put every man now on the other side of the Potomac on that field to approach me over the same line, and give me plenty of ammunition, I will kill them all before they reach my line."[26] The Union soldiers came on, and were shot down, all day.

As night fell, Lee finally ordered his men to dig in. Burnside, he concluded, would come again. Lee was right about Burnside's intention but wrong about his resolution. Burnside's subordinate officers talked him out of renewing the battle; they had had enough of futile slaughter. Federal casualties for the Battle of Fredericksburg (11–13 December 1862) were more than 12,000 men; Confederate casualties were more than 5,000. A month later, Burnside tried to regain the offensive with what became known as "the Mud March," which went nowhere. He offered to resign and was reassigned to Ohio.

In the West, there was no Lee to turn the tables on the Federal invader. An attempt to retake Corinth, Mississippi (3–4 October 1862) failed, and Braxton Bragg, a foul-tempered favorite of Jefferson Davis, proceeded to invade—and lose—Kentucky at the Battle of Perryville (8 October 1862). Bragg regrouped at Murfreesboro, where he met Union General William S. Rosecrans in battle on 31 December 1862.[27] Bragg had about 34,000 men; Rosecrans about 44,000.

The Confederates moved first, driving into the Federal right, overwhelming it, and swarmed ahead until they ran into Union General Phil Sheridan. Sheridan held the line, counterattacked, and then set up a new defensive line, pivoting his troopers ninety degrees from the one they had to abandon. His men fought hard, but when they ran out of ammunition, they had to fall back again. The Union right was folding onto the Union left. Rebel yells pierced the air, and again butternut and grey uniforms surged ahead, even though many Confederates, their rifles fouled by rain, charged with sticks in their hands instead of guns.

The initial assault on the Federal right had been led by General Patrick Cleburne, "the Stonewall of the West," an Irish-born veteran of the British army, who had immigrated to America to become a pharmacist (and, inevitably, a lawyer), but became one of the western theater's best and bravest Confederate generals.[28] He, like Nathan Bedford Forrest,[29] suffered from having to serve under Braxton Bragg—and Murfreesboro was an example of why that was no honor. The day could have been won by the Confederates had Generals Bragg, John C. Breckinridge, and Leonidas Polk committed themselves now en masse, but they did not. Instead, Bragg ordered Breckinridge's men into the center of a well-defended Union line bristling with artillery, and General Polk, who directed the attack, sent the troops in piecemeal, which is how they were destroyed.

The Union Army survived the first day of battle—and it was the only day that mattered. New Year's Day was a day of inactivity, and an attempt to dislodge the Federals on 2 January was repulsed with heavy Confederate casualties. Bragg then abandoned the city of Murfreesboro. Both sides suffered casualties of about 13,000 men, but the Confederate losses had apparently been for nothing. Had Bragg delivered a Confederate victory to match Lee's successes, the Union, as Lincoln noted in his letter of congratulations to Rosecrans after the battle, "could scarcely have lived."[30] As it was, the combatants entered 1863 with no end of bloodletting in sight.

CHAPTER 14

"FOR EVERY SOUTHERN BOY . . . IT'S STILL NOT YET TWO O'CLOCK ON THAT JULY AFTERNOON IN 1863"

A FTER THE BATTLE of Sharpsburg, Lincoln announced his Emancipation Proclamation, which became effective on 1 January 1863. It was, explicitly, a war measure. By order of the commander in chief of the United States, slavery was to be abolished in all areas in rebellion against the Union, pending the Union's military victory. The proclamation did not abolish slavery in the Border States or in areas (like New Orleans) under Union control. While it might have been dubious as constitutional law and "abolished" slavery exclusively in areas where Lincoln's writ did not run, it did please Northern abolitionists (who were pressing Lincoln for action), put paid to Britain or France recognizing the Confederacy (now that the war had the moral cause of abolishing slavery), and gave some Federal troops an additional reason to fight. It also permitted the enrollment of free blacks in the Union Army.

The Emancipation Proclamation was not universally popular in the North. "Preserving the Union" was far the more effective recruiting slogan; and for some in the North, it was actually a disincentive to fight for the Federals. The immigrant Irish, for instance, blamed free blacks for driving down laborers' wages, and freeing more blacks was not on their agenda. In 1861, Archbishop John Hughes of New York informed the War Department that Irish Catholics were "willing to fight to the death for the support of the constitution, the government, and the laws of the country," but they would not fight "for the abolition of slavery."[1] In 1863, after the Emancipation Proclamation was declared law, Irishmen facing a military draft in New York rioted. The violence raged for four days and pitted Irish mobs against Irish-dominated police and Federal troops (perhaps also largely Irish). The riots, wrote the historian Samuel Eliot Morison, were "equivalent to a Confederate victory," for the pacification of the riots required troops that could have been used elsewhere, and the riots themselves inflicted a million dollars' worth of property damage.[2]

The Confederates did not riot, but they did come to a cynical conclusion about Lincoln's motives: namely, that he cared less about abolishing slavery than he did about encouraging a slave insurrection in the South. Why else would the proclamation be so pointed and limited to the Confederate states? With Southern men at the front and plantations under the management of their wives, such presumed Yankee treachery appeared particularly heinous.

While the proclamation did encourage slaves to leave plantations, seeking the Union Army and freedom, Southern slaves did not rise up against their masters' wives and children. Though fears of slave insurrections ran deep[3] (and might have been a sign of guilty Southern consciences), for most plantation owners the risk had always been small. Many planters—like Jefferson Davis— had grown up in circumstances where slave families were kept intact, where it was a point of pride to treat slaves well, and where the relationship between master and slave was amicable and protective, sometimes in amusing ways. Confederate officer Richard Taylor, son of President Zachary Taylor, recounted seeing Southern planters refuse to let their slaves work as stokers on boats that might draw Federal fire and noted that it "was a curious feature of the war that the Southern people would cheerfully send their sons to battle, but kept their slaves out of danger."[4] Such was the noblesse oblige, martial honor, and, of course, commercial interest of the planter.

Lincoln's next act as commander in chief was to replace Ambrose Burnside with the brash, coarse "Fighting Joe" (a nickname he hated) Hooker as general of the Army of the Potomac. Hooker was reputed a mighty drinker (a florid complexion helped solidify this reputation) and Henry Adams's son Charles, a Union cavalry officer, remarked that Hooker's headquarters was "a place to which no self-respecting man liked to go, and no decent woman could go. It was a combination barroom and brothel."[5] In the tradition of barrooms and brothels, Hooker was boastful: "My plans are perfect, and when I start to carry them out, may God have mercy on General Lee," Hooker said, "for I shall have none."[6]

Nevertheless, the winter and spring were largely quiet. Hooker spent his time rebuilding his army. In Virginia, John S. Mosby led his Confederate raiders in swashbuckling exploits that included bagging a Union general in his bed. In the Tennessee theater, Nathan Bedford Forrest's cavalry kept Union supply lines in tatters.[7] Only on the Mississippi River did the Union make progress and even here it was slow, as Grant began his advance down on Vicksburg and Federals moved up from New Orleans.

When his wagons started, Joseph Hooker brought the largest-yet Army of the Potomac into the field to put an end to the career of Robert E. Lee. The Federals had 134,000 men under arms against only 60,000 Confederates, with one of Lee's best divisions, General John Bell Hood's, and one of his best corps commanders, General Longstreet, reassigned to the defense of Virginia's southern coast.

Hooker's plan was to advance on Fredericksburg and then divide his army, taking the larger portion on a flanking movement on Lee's rear while the smaller portion advanced from Fredericksburg. Lee, under Hooker's plan, would be crunched in a Union vise.

Most generals facing the prospect of being attacked on two sides—and outnumbered on both—would undoubtedly beat a hasty retreat out of harm's way. But Lee merely detached a small force of about 10,000 men to hold the roughly 23,000 Federals at Fredericksburg and turned his attention to confronting Hooker's main force of more than 73,000 men that was coming round behind him. To Hooker's amazement, Confederate General Stonewall Jackson launched an immediate attack on the Federal line. Hooker was so stunned by the Confederates' audacity that he actually ordered his much larger army to retreat, requested reinforcements from Fredericksburg, and began building defensive entrenchments. But Hooker didn't retreat far enough.

That night, Lee, in conference with Stonewall Jackson, mused, "How can we get at those people?"[8] He wanted Jackson to lead an attack on Hooker's flank. The question was how to get around the Union defenses. After scouting the position, Jackson proposed dividing the Confederate Army even further. Lee would retain 17,000 men (and be outnumbered four to one against Hooker's entrenched forces), while Jackson took 26,000 men on a bold flanking movement across the Federal front, shielded by forest, to strike the Federal right. "This," in the words of Lee biographer Emory Thomas, "was audacity to the point of madness."[9]

The conversation between the two generals has been recorded as going something like this:

"General Jackson, what do you propose to do?"
"Go around here."

"What do you propose to make this movement with?"

"With my whole corps."

"What will you leave me?"

"The divisions of Anderson and McLaws."

"Well, go on."

Lee's report to President Jefferson Davis was similarly low-key to the point of madness, noting little more than that "the enemy is in a strong position at Chancellorsville and in large force. . . . I am now swinging around to my left to come behind him."[10] On his "swinging around to my left" hung the fate of the Army of Northern Virginia, and, by that measure, the fate of the Confederacy.

Hooker, meanwhile, admired his men's impressive fortifications and counted his growing troop strength. He expected to take advantage of Lee's aggressiveness. He imagined Lee vainly assaulting his immovable line, after which Hooker would chase the shattered, bleeding Confederates into anemic retreat, catching them, even weaker now, in the pincer movement he had planned originally.

But Hooker's dream was mere fantasy. While he rubbed his hands in eager expectation of Confederate self-destruction, a ragged army in butternut and grey was marching hard in a long arcing movement, racing against the fading day. Near dusk, at 5:15 P.M., General Jackson gave the order.

"Are you ready, General Rodes?" Jackson asked.

"Yes, sir."

"You can move forward then."

Yankee troops were jolted from their campfires by a terrifying scream—the rebel yell—as the sweating, hard-marched Confederates broke into a run, crashing through the woods. The bluecoats scattered in fear, dropping packs and rifles, fleeing with horror-stricken eyes, as the Confederates rolled over the line, hooting, hollering, firing, bayonets lunging forward.

"They are running too fast for us," one Confederate officer remarked to Jackson. "We can't keep up with them."

"They never run too fast for me, sir. Press them, press them!"[11]

The one enemy the Confederates could not beat was time. As darkness fell onto the field, so did confusion. Jackson, however, knew that if Confederate units were disordered, the Federals were in complete chaos, and he was eager to give the Union troops no respite, no chance to re-form and turn their superiority in numbers against him. He intended to press his attack through the night.

Scouting ahead of his own lines to see how he could capitalize on his smashing success, Jackson was shot by Confederate soldiers who mistook him and his staff officers for a Federal patrol. Jackson was badly wounded, but no one yet knew that his wound was mortal.

During the next day's fighting, Hooker was nearly as incapacitated as Jackson. A cannonball struck the porch on which Hooker was standing, and a splintered beam hit his head, leaving him dazed all day, a condition not improved by his ordering himself a supply of medicinal brandy. (Hooker had forsworn alcohol for the duration of the campaign, until the conk on his head returned some sense to him.)

When Lee was informed of Jackson's wound, he replied, "Ah, Captain, any victory is dearly bought which deprives us of the services of General Jackson, even for a short time."[12] Command of the attacking Confederate forces had fallen to Jeb Stuart. Lee admonished him to carry on in the spirit of Jackson. "Those people must be pressed today," he wrote. "It is necessary that the glorious victory thus far achieved be prosecuted with the utmost vigor, and the enemy given no time to rally."[13] Stuart pressed the attack singing "Old Joe Hooker, come out of the Wilderness!"

Hooker's forces continued to fall back from Chancellorsville, but the Federal troops on Lee's other front were shoving hard against Confederate General Jubal A. Early's skeleton defense outside Fredericksburg. Lee reinforced Early with two more divisions, who shifted the tide, driving the Federals back across the Rappahannock River. With that Federal threat cleared away, Lee looked to renew his offensive against Hooker, only to find that the Union commander had also sought the safety of the north bank of the river. One Union officer confessed: "They have beaten us fairly; beaten us all to pieces; beaten us so easily." In New York, in the newspaper offices of Horace Greeley, the reaction was worse: "My God, it is horrible—horrible! And to think of it—130,000 magnificent soldiers so cut to pieces by less than 60,000 half-starved ragamuffins!" Worse still was the reaction in Washington. Senator Charles Sumner of Massachusetts exclaimed, "Lost—lost. All is lost!" Lincoln moaned: "My God! My God! What will the country say?"[14]

On 3 May 1863, when victory was assured but the battle not yet over, Lee rode to Chancellorsville's front lines.

> The scene is one that can never be effaced from the minds of those who witnessed it. The troops were pressing forward with all the ardour and enthusiasm of combat. The smoke of musketry fringed the front of the line of battle, while

the artillery on the hills in the rear of the infantry shook the earth with its thunder, and filled the air with the wild shrieks of shells that plunged into the mass of the retreating foe. To add greater horror and sublimity to the scene, Chancellor House and the woods surrounding it were wrapped in flames. In the midst of this awful scene, General Lee . . . rode to the front of his advancing battalions.

Lee's aide Charles Marshall continues, describing Lee's effect on the men, as his appearance sparked

. . . one of those uncontrollable outbursts of enthusiasm which none can appreciate who have not witnessed them. The fierce soldiers, with their faces blackened with the smoke of battle, the wounded, crawling with feeble limbs from . . . the devouring flames, all seemed possessed with a common impulse. One long, unbroken cheer . . . rose high above the roar of battle, and hailed the presence of the victorious chief. He sat in the full realization of all that soldiers dream of—triumph; and as I looked upon him in the complete fruition of success . . . I thought that it must have been from such a scene that men in ancient days rose to the dignity of gods.[15]

Chancellorsville (1–3 May 1863) was the greatest Confederate victory of the war, won against the longest odds, but for which the Confederacy paid an enormous price in the death of Stonewall Jackson. Lee wrote to his wounded general, "Could I have directed events, I would have chosen for the good of the country to be disabled in your stead."[16] To one of the army chaplains, Lee noted that Jackson's arm had been amputated. "He has lost his left arm, but I have lost my right."[17] Pneumonia claimed Jackson's last breath. The "great and good" Jackson was gone, and with him, perhaps, went the cause of the Confederacy. His loss would be felt immediately, on Lee's next great campaign.

VICKSBURG

IN THE WEST, Grant moved to besiege Vicksburg, Mississippi—the key point in seizing complete control of the Mississippi River from the Confederates. It was the citadel the South could not afford to lose and that Grant was hoping to skirt, because Vicksburg's defensive position was formidable. It was situated on a fortified bluff overlooking the river, and surrounded, on its landward approaches, by soggy terrain that limited an attacker's mobility. Much as he tried, however, Grant could find no way round the fortress city on the Mississippi, and his attempts, in the winter, were plagued by the unyieldingly swampy countryside, malaria, and smallpox. Felled trees, Confederate sharpshooters, and the occasional makeshift fort of cotton bales and a few cannons turned back attempted riverine approaches.

Despite months of boggy failure, Lincoln was certain: Vicksburg must be taken. The president, who could turn a phrase with the best of them, said: "We may take all the northern ports of the Confederacy and they can still defy us at Vicksburg. It means hog and hominy without limit, fresh troops from all the states of the far South, and a country where they can raise the staple without interference."[18] Lincoln wanted to put an end to Southern "hog and hominy without limit."

Resolved to do it, Grant began a campaign of real initiative and daring. He set up two diversions: General Sherman would demonstrate in front of Vicksburg, and Union cavalry would plunge through Mississippi into Louisiana. With the shorthanded Confederates thus occupied, Grant, taking two corps, would cross the Mississippi River from the Louisiana side, well south of Vicksburg's guns, then march east and cut off Vicksburg from Mississippi's capital city of Jackson, before swinging up to join with other Federal troops, rolling back the outlying Confederate defenders, and besieging the city. Marching through enemy territory was dangerous business, but there were far too few Confederate soldiers to make it dangerous enough. King Numbers was Grant's best friend. Assembled for the Vicksburg campaign, in the spring of 1863, were 50,000 Federal troops to a little over 30,000 Confederates, who, with the mismanagement typical of western Confederate generalship, were ineffectually strung out guarding too much with too little.

The first major battle of the campaign was at Port Gibson (1 May 1863), one day after Grant landed his men across the Mississippi River at Bruinsburg. Grant's first objective was to take his 24,000 men and drive out the 8,000 Confederates[19] under the command of General John S. Bowen, commander of Grand Gulf, the next Confederate strongpoint on the river. Bowen—a Georgia-born West Pointer who before the war had served as a frontier rifleman—had smelled out Grant's intentions and warned Vicksburg's commander, General John C. Pemberton. But Pemberton had other things to worry him: defending the northern approaches to the city and coping with raiding Union cavalry. Still, outnumbered as he was, Bowen put up a gallant defense at Port Gibson and retired in good order. Grant, however, now had his foothold twenty-five miles south of Vicksburg.

The Federals moved fast. At the Battle of Raymond (12 May), near Jackson, the bluecoats again outnumbered the Confederates three to one (and in artillery seven to one) and again the Confederates withdrew but only after a stiff fight. The next day, Confederate General Joseph E. Johnston arrived to take command in Jackson. He surveyed the situation and came to his usual conclusion: the city was indefensible and retreat the only option. So the Confederates retreated. Grant then marched into Jackson and destroyed its railways and industry.

The climactic battle before the siege of Vicksburg was at Champion Hill (16 May) twenty miles east of the city. Grant's strength, reinforced to 32,000 men, finally met a Confederate force of some considerable number—22,000 soldiers under General Pemberton. The battle happened by accident. Pemberton's Confederates were marching to combine with Joseph E. Johnston—until they spotted Grant's troops, and rapidly formed a battle line at Champion Hill. The Federal attack nearly broke the Confederate left, but rushing up with reinforcements was the ever-handy General Bowen, whose counterattack was so successful that the Confederates threatened Grant's headquarters. The nobly named General Marcellus Crocker—one of Grant's most trusted officers and leader of "Crocker's Greyhounds"—threw two brigades of bluecoats against the rebels and saved the Federal line. Eventually, Union numbers began to tell, and the Confederates fell back. As they had before, the rebels fought well, but this defeat was costly. The Confederates lost more than 3,800 men as casualties, along with twenty-seven artillery pieces, and the survivors were now bottled up at Vicksburg, where the grim siege would begin.

Grant first tried to take Vicksburg by storm. But he underestimated the strength and stubbornness of the Confederate defenders. After five days of knocking Federal troops against the Confederate wall, Grant decided to shell and starve the Confederates instead, while continuing offensive probes and calling for reinforcements, which soon made him the commander of a host of 77,000 men. The shelling of Vicksburg was so intense that its citizens dug a system of caves in which to live. So when pundits talk about the barbarity of bombing people back to the Stone Age, they should remember that the idea goes back to Grant at least and was practiced against our fellow Americans in Mississippi, who were also threatened with starvation.

By July Pemberton realized how fruitless it was to rely on help from Joseph E. Johnston, who despite having orders and reinforcements to save the city, would take no such risk. Pemberton wanted to fight his way out, but his subordinate generals thought this quixotic, given how ill-fed and badly outnumbered the men were. Pemberton conceded this and on 4 July 1863, nearly 30,000 Confederates—and the city of Vicksburg—were surrendered to U. S. Grant. Ever since, July 4 has not been a day for celebration in Vicksburg, but a day of mourning.

When the news reached Port Hudson, Louisiana, where 40,000 Federals had besieged 7,500 Confederates since 22 May, the Confederate commander, General Frank Gardner—whose men were eating rats and mules—realized the game was up. He surrendered on 9 July.[20] The Mississippi River belonged to the Union.

GETTYSBURG

IN THE EAST, another brass hat was gone. On 28 June 1863, General Joseph Hooker joined the ranks of the defeated—McClellan, Pope, and Burnside— and resigned command of the Army of the Potomac, to be replaced by General George A. Meade. Meade had little time to draw up grand plans for his own great offensive, because Lee's army was already coming at him. Lee had launched his second invasion of the North.

Lee's strategy was similar to his previous invasion of Maryland, which had resulted in the Battle of Sharpsburg the year before. He needed to bring relief to Virginia, to lift the Union's devastation of her farmland. He needed to feed his troops, and there was little food to be had in the war-torn Old Dominion. And finally, as always, he wanted to get at the enemy and defeat him whole. He did not want a situation where the Federals would have their noses bloodied and retreat to safety. He wanted to maneuver the Army of the Potomac into the field so that he could land it a devastating blow, complete its destruction, and give the peace party in the North a signal case to point to, illustrating the futility of the Union's war, urging an end to hostilities.

There were fire-breathing voices in the South who, encouraged by Lee's victories, spurned any talk of peace. Peace talks, they held, would be a sign of weakness. Worse, they would force the South to consider the prospect of peace with reunion, which was heresy. Southern valor alone would hammer the North into accepting Southern independence. Lee was more realistic. Jefferson

Davis, he knew, sympathized with the fire-breathers. Nevertheless, Lee wrote to President Davis that if the people of the North could be convinced that immediate peace might bring eventual reunion, "the war would no longer be supported [in the North], and that, after all is what we are interested in bringing about." It also seems likely that—*contra* the fire-breathers—eventual reunion was Lee's hope as well. Lee advised Davis that there "will be time enough to discuss its terms, and it is not the better part of prudence to spurn the proposition" beforehand.[21]

Diplomatic prudence was not Jefferson Davis's strong suit. He was a man of adamant principle, not negotiation and compromise. So Lee focused on what he could control: his army. One of his first acts after Chancellorsville was to reorganize it.

Lee wrote General Hood, "Our army would be invincible if it could be properly organized and officered. There never were such men in an army before. They will go anywhere and do anything if properly led."[22] The problem for Lee was finding proper commanders. Casualty rates among officers were high and while Lee preferred professionals, of necessity many of his officers were gifted amateurs—men like cavalry commander Wade Hampton, one of the wealthiest planters in the South.

Lee divided his army into three corps and chose as his corps commanders General Longstreet, who already held corps command; General Richard Ewell, "Old Baldy," who had served Jackson, but who was damaged goods: high-strung, minus a leg (lost in action during the Second Manassas campaign), and unlike Jackson, an officer who required detailed instructions rather than invitations to initiative; and the gallant, impetuous A. P. Hill, whose health, however, was beginning to falter under the stress of continuous campaigning. But whatever Ewell's and Hill's failings, they were Virginians, West Pointers, and professional soldiers. As for Longstreet, he too was a professional. He showed it by being careful, cautious, and deliberate. He didn't like taking risks. But he could be a bull in battle. Like a bull, he was stubborn, which served him well when conducting a defensive fight, but it was a problem when his ideas conflicted with Lee's.

As the men marched across the Potomac and into Union territory, Lee again forbade "wanton injury to private property" and ordered that the soldiers pay civilians for what they needed. As always, the Confederate Army was short of virtually everything. Horses and men were ragged. Gettysburg, the climactic battle of the war, would be fought because a Confederate brigade went to the town looking for shoes.

THE FIRST DAY, 1 JULY 1863

THE BATTLE WAS FOUGHT over three days, with the final troop totals equaling close to 95,000 Federals and 75,000 Confederates. As the initial skirmishes began, almost accidentally, Union General John Buford, an old Indian fighter, secured the high ground for the Federals. The Federal line eventually extended from the summits of Little Round Top and Big Round Top on the Union left, straight down Cemetery Ridge, curling in like the base of a J on the Federal right at Cemetery Hill and Culp's Hill.

On the first day of battle, as he rode up to investigate the action that had suddenly erupted, Lee inspected the ground. The Confederates were shoving the Federals from their advanced positions in front of Gettysburg and along Seminary Ridge. As the Federals took up their new line, which would often be called "the fishhook" because of its shape, Lee saw that an assault on the Union right, at the curve of the J, would allow the Confederates to sweep the line. He ordered General Ewell to attack that point "if practicable" without sparking a major battle. The "if practicable" was a common phrase in Lee's orders, leaving discretion to the commander in the field; and in this case, Lee was eager to avoid a full-fledged engagement because so many Confederate troops were still on the march. Nevertheless, as the afternoon wore on, Lee's patience wore thin, as Ewell's front remained remarkably quiet.

Ewell thought it wasn't practicable to take Cemetery Hill and Culp's Hill, though they had yet to be defended by the Federals. Ewell's men had already spent much of the day in combat—Ewell himself received a minié ball in his wooden leg—pushing the Federals back. He was reluctant to ask more of them. But had Ewell acted with a vigorous advance on these vital positions, he almost surely would have succeeded, and the entire Union line would have been in danger. Indeed, one of Ewell's generals had to be ordered four times to halt. As Confederate General John B. Gordon explained: "The whole portion of the Union Army in my front was in inextricable confusion and in flight . . . my troops were on the flank and sweeping down the lines. The firing upon my men had almost ceased. Large bodies of the Union troops were throwing down their arms and surrendering. . . . In less than half an hour my troops would have swept up and over those hills. . . . It is not surprising that . . . I should have refused to obey that order."[23]

Daylight was fading, and Ewell and his subordinates told Lee that it was too late for an assault. Lee pressed them: "Can't you, with your corps, attack on daylight tomorrow?"[24] They demurred. Their men were tired, the hill increasingly fortified. They wanted to hold their line, and take up the defensive. Even Jubal A. Early, a hard fighter, wanted to shift the attack to someone else. He thought the better plan would be for Longstreet to strike the opposite flank, which was yet to be fortified. If Longstreet could take Little Round Top, it would achieve the same result of allowing the Confederates to sweep Cemetery Ridge.

Lee was shocked. His second corps, his offensive thunderbolt, old Stonewall's command, had grown battle weary. He had no objection to Early's plan in principle—indeed, it was the plan he would execute—but he worried about Longstreet, his defensive counterpuncher, having to carry it out. As Lee said: "Well, if I attack from my right, Longstreet will have to make the attack. Longstreet is a very good fighter when he gets in position and gets everything ready, but he is so slow."[25]

Still, Longstreet would have to do it. The land and the disposition of the Union Army favored his assault, and Longstreet was a reliable, professional soldier. There was no reason why he should not succeed. Lee gave orders that Ewell was to demonstrate against the Union right, and, if practicable, turn the demonstration into a full-fledged attack. Longstreet would lead the main Confederate assault on the Union left. Lee was eager for battle. He told General John Bell Hood: "The enemy is here, and if we do not whip him, he will whip us."[26] It was on this field that the Army of Northern Virginia might crush the Army of the Potomac and effectively win the war.

THE SECOND DAY, 2 JULY 1863

ON THE UNION SIDE of the line, there had been a lucky escape. The I Corps had lost nearly 10,000 men as casualties, with some units virtually annihilated (the 24th Michigan suffered casualties of 80 percent). Valuable officers had been lost, like General John F. Reynolds, who was killed by a sharpshooter. Reynolds had been George Meade's superior officer, until Meade was promoted to replace Hooker.

After midnight of the first day, Meade arrived to take command at Gettysburg. Union General Winfield Scott Hancock took him on a tour of the Union lines. Meade liked what he saw: a solid defensive line on the high ground. He expected the morning's main attack would be on his right, with Ewell trying to make up for his irresolution of the day before. But morning came quietly. Ewell was waiting for Longstreet.

Lee's plan was to "attack the enemy as early in the morning as practicable."[27] Longstreet, however, disliked Lee's plan, preferring, according to his later testimony, to maneuver the Confederate Army into a defensive position that would force the Yankees to attack it. Longstreet, as Lee knew, was always slow, but generally had the excuse that he would launch a well-prepared strike when truly needed. At Gettysburg his laggardness betrayed an insubordinate hope that if he moved slowly enough, the whole plan of attack might be called off.

At 8:30 A.M., Lee rode up to Longstreet and told him flatly, "I think you had better move on."[28] Thinking that was clear enough instruction, he rode back to direct Ewell, whose nerves were jangling again. By 10:00 A.M., Lee was back at the center of the Confederate line. To his dismay, Longstreet's guns weren't firing, and his men weren't moving. Lee rode to Longstreet's position. It was now 11:00 A.M. Longstreet had done nothing because with his usual caution he had decided to wait until he could be joined by General George Pickett, and his corps be brought to full strength. "The general," Longstreet explained to one of his officers, ". . . wishes me to attack; I do not wish to do so without Pickett. I never like to go into battle with one boot off."[29] Pickett would not be able to reach the field until the end of the day.

Lee ordered Longstreet forward. Longstreet failed to move. Another brigade under General Evander Law was due in half an hour. Longstreet told Lee he wanted those extra men. Lee reluctantly agreed, though the delay inevitably lengthened until one o'clock. When Longstreet's men finally began their advance, Lee again rode to the center of the line. Once engaged, Lee assumed that the bullish Longstreet would press the enemy. But he was wrong. Longstreet was still sulking, and moving slowly. It was not until four o'clock that his men were in position to launch their attack.

A fierce Confederate artillery barrage smashed into both sides of the Union line. That line had advanced, thanks to independent action by Union General Daniel Sickles. Sickles, contrary to General Meade's orders, had not kept his line along Cemetery Hill but had moved it forward looking for the rebels. It put him in an exposed position. It also put him smack in front of Longstreet's advance in an area known as the Peach Orchard, the Wheat Field, and Devil's Den.

General John Bell Hood, leading Lee's beloved Texans, knew what to do. He dispatched scouts to see if it was still possible to flank the Union left, as originally planned. The answer was yes, if the Confederates moved their attack around to the hills of Little Round Top, which had no more than a Union observation unit, or unoccupied Big Round Top.

Hood reported this intelligence to Longstreet, but if Longstreet was going to execute an order with which he disagreed—after all attempts to foil it by delay had sputtered—he would execute it to the letter so that if it failed no opprobrium would fall on him. Longstreet's generals asked him to reconsider, reminding him that Lee's orders were for an attack in the morning. The situation had changed, but the spirit, if not the letter, of the order could be fulfilled in an easily executable maneuver. Longstreet stubbornly refused. He sent his men charging, in echelon, uphill, into spewing Union fire. Still, the Union line began to dissolve, and the Confederates on the Union left spilled over into a march up Little Round Top.

There they met the hastily formed line of the 20th Maine led by that remarkable officer—a professor in civilian life—Joshua Chamberlain. Chamberlain's thin blue line forced back the Confederate attacks, but Colonel Chamberlain saw that with his ammunition running out he couldn't hold the line. So trusting to courage against numbers, he countercharged, stunning the Confederates into retreat and hundreds of surrenders.

But everywhere else on the center-left of the Union line, furious fighting continued. General William Barksdale, pushing his Mississippians to almost pierce the Union line, was killed. Union General Sickles lost a leg (smashed by a cannonball), but nonchalantly lit up a cigar as though it were nothing. The 1st Minnesota regiment, rushing to plug a gap in the Union line, took 82 percent casualties, but did their duty and held the position. Cemetery Ridge remained in the hands of the bluecoats.

That night, at his council of war, Meade and his officers resolved that they would hold their ground and brace for Lee's next move. Meade suspected that Lee, having attacked the Federals on both flanks, would attack dead center. Meade was the first general to read Robert E. Lee exactly right.

Lee remained optimistic despite the almost blackly comical situation confronting him. His men had fought bravely, even if the assaults had been ill-coordinated, with reserve units that could have made the difference left doing nothing. On Lee's left was Ewell: a fidgety, one-legged general, once a fighter, now wracked by indecisiveness. At his center was the aggressive A. P. Hill with his famous red battle shirt. But Hill was not so aggressive now, as he was recovering from another bout of illness. On Lee's right was his formerly dependable "old war horse" General Longstreet. But Longstreet was behaving like a sulking Achilles. Then there was Lee's beloved cavalry commander, Jeb Stuart, waving his plumed hat in another ride around the Yankee army, returning with wagons full of captured supplies, but too late to be the desperately needed eyes and ears of Lee's army. And Lee himself was unwell.

But Lee thought he had spotted the weak point in the Union line: its center. His plan was for Ewell to launch a diversionary attack on the Union right, while Longstreet made the main attack. At Gaines' Mill during the Seven Days, Lee had done the same: hitting the Union flanks before hitting the Union center with what looked to be a suicidal charge—until it shattered the Union lines and routed the bluecoats. He trusted he had the men who could do it again.

THE THIRD DAY, 3 JULY 1863

IN THE MORNING, Ewell's men were ready. But there was no word from Longstreet. Lee rode to "Old Pete" and found his subordinate again ready to argue with him. Longstreet had decided he wanted either to renew his flanking attack or to shift Lee's entire army to the Union left and establish a defensive line that would compel the Federals to attack. Lee listened patiently, but rejected Longstreet's arguments and told him to get his men into position. The "old Dutchman" made one final verbal sally to stop his commander's plan. "General, I have been a soldier all my life. I have been with soldiers engaged in fights by couples, by squads, companies, regiments, divisions, and armies, and should know as well as any one, what soldiers can do. It is my opinion that no fifteen thousand men ever arranged for battle can take that position."[30]

Lee pointed to the potential strength of the Confederate assault. The infantry would advance under cover of the largest artillery bombardment ever attempted by the Confederate Army. Eight of Longstreet's thirteen brigades would be committed to the attack, leaving a plentiful reserve to be committed later as needed. Among those committed would be three fresh brigades, numbering 4,600 men, under the command of General George Pickett. The soldiers were well aware that the outcome of the war might be determined here. It was impossible that men who had fought so well, and against such odds, in the victories that had led them here would fail when the stakes were so high.

Longstreet was unconvinced. But he had no choice. The troops took up their positions under sheltering shade trees and waited, shielded from the Federals' sight by a short rise in the ground in front of them. As Lee rode along the line, he saw a discouraging number of the 15,000 men he expected to make the charge were wounded—indeed, so mauled had the Confederate forces been that the true number of assembled effectives was no more than 12,000. But the attack, he told them, must succeed.

Shortly after one o'clock in the afternoon, the Confederate artillery barrage began. The artillery was under the command of a talented twenty-eight-year-old Georgian, Colonel Edward Porter Alexander, on whom Longstreet, quite unfairly, attempted to shove responsibility for the coming action.

Longstreet sent him a note with these instructions: "If the artillery fire does not have the effect to drive off the enemy or greatly demoralize him so as to make our effort pretty certain I would prefer that you should not advise General Pickett to make the charge. I shall rely a great deal upon your judgment to determine the matter, and shall expect you to let General Pickett know when the moment offers."

Alexander's response to Longstreet was a simple statement of fact: his job was to execute plans, not draw them up and decide which ones to implement. "General: I will only be able to judge of the effect of our fire on the enemy by his return fire as his infantry is but little exposed to view and the smoke will obscure the whole field. If, as I infer from your note, there is any alternative to this attack, it should be carefully considered before opening our fire, for it will take all the artillery ammunition we have left to test this one thoroughly, and if the result is unfavorable, we will have none left for another effort. . . ."

Longstreet stubbornly kept the pressure on the young man, replying, "The intention is to advance the infantry. If the artillery has the desired effect of driving the enemy off or having other effect such as to warrant us in making the attack. When that moment arrives advise General P., and of course advance such artillery as you can use in aiding the attack."

The colonel submitted. "When our artillery fire is at its best, I will advise General Pickett to advance."[31]

Longstreet ordered the cannonade to begin, and a rain of shrieking, exploding lead burst over the Union lines. It made a splendid racket, but as the smoke thickened, the Confederate gunners were firing blindly and largely overshooting their mark. The havoc they wreaked was largely on the rear of the Union Army, not the men at the front.

Less than half an hour into the bombardment, Colonel Alexander tried to urge Pickett forward. "If you are to advance at all," his note read, "you must come at once or we will not be able to support you as we ought. . . ." Ten minutes later, seeing no movement on the Confederate line, he sent another dispatch. "For God's sake come on quick or we cannot support you. . . ." Alexander knew the danger of charging the Union center, but he saw a glimmer of opportunity, as the Federals were attempting to maneuver their own artillery to safety. If Pickett moved now, he might move under a brief artillery advantage.

But Pickett did not move because he had no orders from Longstreet. Alexander's bombardment continued until 2:45 P.M., when he ordered a cease-fire. By three o'clock the Confederate troops were finally marching forward. They had never received an order from Longstreet to move out. When Pickett requested permission to advance, Old Pete limited himself to a sober nod of the head.

The Confederates now had the challenge of crossing a mile of open ground with minimal artillery support to suppress Federal fire. They did not flinch. Officers to the front, General Lewis Armistead—whose father had been a general and whose uncle had been the lieutenant colonel commanding the defense of Fort McHenry in the War of 1812—shoved his black hat over the tip of his sword and waved his men forward. With him were Pickett's other brigade commanders: James Kemper, a former member of the Virginia House of Delegates whose grandfather had served on George Washington's staff, and Richard B. Garnett, a West Pointer suffering from a bad knee and worse fever. He advanced on horseback, however obvious a target that made him.

Now—now that it was too late—Longstreet joined Colonel Alexander to find out why the Confederate guns were silent. Alexander informed him. He was saving what little ammunition he had left so that he could offer at least some support for the Confederate advance. Pickett's men should have been ordered forward an hour and a half earlier. Now they were marching into a maw of doom. "Go stop Pickett right where he is, and replenish your ammunition," Longstreet commanded.

"We can't do that, sir. The train has only a little. It would take an hour to distribute it, and meanwhile the enemy would improve the time."

Longstreet shook his head sorrowfully and mumbled a mournful confession: "I do not want to make this charge. I do not see how it can succeed. I would not make it now but that General Lee had ordered it and is expecting it."[32]

The Confederates marched forward as if on parade, even stopping at one point to adjust and straighten their lines, oblivious to the holes being torn in their ranks by the Union fire. For the Union troops, the Confederates were marching through a shooting gallery, but they could not believe the grandeur of the spectacle as the troops moved relentlessly forward, their flags held high. A British observer, Lieutenant Colonel Arthur Fremantle of Her Majesty's Coldstream Guards, made the mistake of expressing his excitement and admiration to Longstreet. "I wouldn't have missed this for anything."

Longstreet, who had a streak of gallows humor in him, laughed and replied, "The devil you wouldn't! I would like to have missed it very much. . . ."[33]

The attack, Longstreet told Fremantle, had already failed. Indeed, the unthinkable had occurred. Four exhausted and bloodied Confederate regiments broke and ran under heavy shell fire. Of Pickett's Virginians, Brigadier Garnett was shot off his horse, dead. Brigadier Kemper, calling for Armistead's men to support his brigade, collapsed, shot in the groin.

But Armistead waved his men to come on; they were close enough now to the Union line to break into a jog—and they were blasted by canister. But through the storm of smoke, artillery fire, and minié balls, the Union front *was* suddenly pierced. Chasing a line of retreating Federals was Armistead himself, still waving his black hat on his sword, shouting, "Come on boys! Give them the cold steel! Follow me!" They surged forward into hand-to-hand combat, Armistead and his troopers running straight into two Federal regiments rushing to close the line. Armistead, arm outstretched to a silent Federal cannon, went down, mortally wounded, falling at a point on the battlefield now called "the high tide of the Confederacy." On another part of the front, the University Greys, made up entirely of students from Ole Miss, managed to plant their colors no more than a yard from the Union line before devastating Union fire killed every last one of them.

Now it really was over. The Confederate lines wavered and buckled. As one rebel commander said, "The best thing the men can do is get out of this. Let them go."[34] As the shattered Confederate units drifted back, Lee rode forward to meet them. "All good men must rally. . . . General Pickett . . . your men have done all that men could do; the fault is entirely my own. . . . All this has been my fault—it is I that have lost this fight and you must help me out of it the best way you can."[35] The Confederate soldiers cheered Lee. They even begged another chance. But Lee waved them down, and prepared them—with a newly revitalized Longstreet—for a counterattack that didn't come.

Both sides licked deep wounds. The Union Army had suffered 23,000 casualties. The statistics were even grimmer for the Confederates. Twenty-eight thousand men were lost, more than a third of Lee's army, and among them a high proportion of senior officers whose talents and experience could not be replaced. Lee's officers had sacrificed their lives in the battle they hoped would secure Southern freedom, but the war was doomed to go on.

At 1:00 A.M., 4 July 1863, the Confederate Army began its return march to Virginia. Lee fell into conversation with cavalry commander John B. Imboden and told him: "I never saw troops behave more magnificently than Pickett's division of Virginians did today in that grand charge upon the enemy. And if they had been supported as they were to have been—but for some reason not yet fully explained to me, were not—we would have held the position and the day would have been ours. Too bad! Too bad! Oh, too bad!"[36]

On the victorious side of the battle line, Meade could barely believe his luck. He had succeeded where every other general before him had failed: McClellan, "the young Napoleon"; Pope, who boasted that his headquarters would be in his saddle, and who carried that saddle as fast as he could north of the Potomac; Burnside, commander of the "Mud March"; and "Fighting Joe" Hooker, who had fought his way in frantic retreat from an army less than half his size. Meade had turned back Lee's invasion of Pennsylvania. In gratitude to his men, he let them rest. Lincoln, however, was not satisfied: if Meade pressed on, he could catch and crush Lee's army; and if he did so, Lincoln said, "the rebellion will be over."[37] Meade was harried with telegrams from Washington urging him forward, but Meade waited ten days before he moved. As one Confederate staff officer wrote, the Federals "pursued us as a mule goes on the chase after a grizzly bear—as if catching up with us was the last thing he wanted."[38]

Though he had won the victory, Meade won few plaudits from Lincoln, who held him responsible for letting the Confederates escape. Meade offered to resign. Lincoln refused Meade's resignation, but in a draft letter of congratulations, which he did not send, he could not refrain from writing: "I do not believe you appreciate the magnitude of the misfortune involved in Lee's escape. He was within your easy grasp, and to have closed upon him would, in connection with our other late successes [like Vicksburg], have ended the war. As it is, the war will be prolonged indefinitely. Your golden opportunity is gone, and I am distressed immeasurably because of it."[39]

Both Lee and Lincoln thought Gettysburg was the great event. Both could not understand how the opportunity to win all had been lost. But Lincoln had the final word. On 19 November 1863, he gave remarks to dedicate the Gettysburg battlefield cemetery:

Four score and seven years ago our fathers brought forth on this continent, a new nation, conceived in Liberty, and dedicated to the proposition that all men are created equal.

Now we are engaged in a great civil war, testing whether that nation, or any nation so conceived and so dedicated, can long endure. We are met on a great battlefield of that war. We have come to dedicate a portion of that field, as a final resting place for those who here gave their lives that the nation might live. It is altogether fitting and proper that we should do this.

But, in a larger sense, we cannot dedicate—we cannot consecrate—we cannot hallow—this ground. The brave men, living and dead, who struggled here, have consecrated it, far above our poor power to add or detract. The world will little note, nor long remember what we say here, but it can never forget what they did here. It is for us the living, rather, to be dedicated here to the unfinished work which they who fought here have thus far so nobly advanced. It is rather for us to be here dedicated to the great task remaining before us—that from these honored dead we take increased devotion to that cause for which they gave the last full measure of devotion—that we here highly resolve that these dead shall not have died in vain—that this nation, under God, shall have a new birth of freedom—and that government of the people, by the people, for the people, shall not perish from the earth.

It was by no means clear that government "of the people, by the people, for the people" was endangered by Southern independence. But it was surely true that the twin Federal victories at Vicksburg and Gettysburg ensured that no Union soldier had died in vain. Now it was only a matter of time. Nearly two more years of hard fighting lay ahead, but the outcome had been decided on that July afternoon of 1863 when Pickett's brigade finally charged.

CHAPTER 15

"THE SATISFACTION THAT PROCEEDS FROM THE CONSCIOUSNESS OF DUTY FAITHFULLY PERFORMED"

T HE VIRGINIA THEATER was quiet.[1] General Meade and the Army of the Potomac had no interest in pressing their luck against Robert E. Lee. Elsewhere the Federals had the Confederacy bottled up. The Confederate coastline was effectively sealed to all but a few blockade-runners. So was the Mississippi River, cutting off the Confederate West. So the action focused on the middle theater, where Tennessee and Georgia were the pivotal states. The key point, initially, was Chattanooga, a railroad hub of the Confederacy. Braxton Bragg was in command of the Confederate forces, which meant retreat: Bragg gave up Knoxville and Chattanooga without a fight.

This was supposed to be the setup for a masterful counterattack. Somehow such masterful counterattacks never quite worked for Bragg, but against the hard-drinking, hard-swearing Yankee General William S. Rosecrans ("Old Rosey"), he had a chance.[2] Rosecrans took the bait and chased after Bragg as if the Confederates were in full retreat.

Both commanders had poor intelligence. When the armies collided on 19 September 1863, it was in a deeply forested area near Chickamauga Creek. Visibility and room to maneuver were minimal, and the fighting was fierce with virtually every unit committed to combat. That night, after a bloody but inconclusive opening round, Rosecrans pulled his men back to tighten the Union lines, build up log breastworks, and take up defensive positions.

Bragg planned to flank the Federal left, which, unfortunately for him, was exactly the point that Rosecrans decided to reinforce. Bragg, however, now had another hammer to bludgeon the Federals: James Longstreet had arrived, detached from Lee's command. Longstreet's journey from Virginia had been detoured and delayed because of the Federal capture of the railroad at Knoxville. He finally found the battlefield by riding through the dark and asking directions from Federal troops—neither side recognizing the other in the black night.

The attack on the Federal left was pushed hard but went nowhere. The morning's fighting was another bloody stalemate, until the Federals mistakenly left a gap in the center-right of their line. Confederate General John Bell Hood—riding to battle with one arm in a sling, and suffering a wound that would cost him a leg—led a charge against the Federal right flank. As the Federal right dissolved, Longstreet shifted his own men to the right and charged through the gap.

Hood once said of Longstreet: "Of all the men living, not excepting our incomparable Lee himself, I would rather follow James Longstreet in a forlorn hope or desperate encounter against heavy odds. He was our hardest hitter."[3] He certainly hit hard here, crashing through the forest like a wild bull (hence his new nickname, "Old Bull of the Woods"), shattering the Union line, and driving Rosecrans and the Federal army into flight.

Union Major General George H. Thomas saved the day for the Federals, becoming "The Rock of Chickamauga."[4] He regrouped the Federals on the high ground at Snodgrass Hill, from which the Confederates couldn't dislodge them until dusk.[5] Thomas gave ground so stubbornly that the Confederates, exhausted, finally stopped pressing him. Thomas then withdrew his men in good order to Chattanooga. The only Confederate pursuit came from Nathan Bedford Forrest.

Forrest was convinced the Federals could be destroyed. He fired a string of messages urging the army to follow. Every hour wasted, he thought, was worth 10,000 men to the enemy. But Bragg had fallen into a stupor and refused to budge. He questioned a Confederate eyewitness of the Union retreat, asking him, with his usual charm: "Do you know what a retreat looks like?" The soldier shot back: "I ought to General, I've been with you during your whole campaign." Forrest grumbled about Bragg: "What does he fight battles for?"[6]

At Chickamauga the Confederates for once outnumbered the Federals, 65,000 to 62,000 men. They also took worse casualties: more than 18,000 to more than 16,000. Though a Confederate victory, it was a victory that achieved little, except to reassure the Southern people that all was not lost in Tennessee.

There were a few scalps to be had. Rosecrans had performed badly, fleeing the field and wiring telegrams full of McClellan-like despair. General Ulysses S.

Grant, who never liked Rosecrans, sacked him and several of his subordinate generals. Grant then did the obvious thing and appointed the Rock of Chicka-mauga, General Thomas, to replace the Runner of Chickamauga. General Thomas had the task of holding Chattanooga at all costs—and Lincoln made sure he was plentifully reinforced.

On the Confederate side, rather than drive north and force the Federals to attack him, Bragg laid pointless siege to the city. Longstreet, for one, recognized the idiocy of Bragg's position, writing, "I am convinced that nothing but the hand of God can save us or help as long as we have our present commander. . . . Can't you send us General Lee? The army in Virginia can operate defensively, while our operations here should be offensive—until we recover Tennessee at all events. We need some great mind as General Lee's (nothing more) to accom-plish this." That even Longstreet, a defensive fighter, advocated going on the offensive was telling. So too was Longstreet's assessment of Bragg's incompe-tence: "We were trying to starve the enemy by investing him on the only side from which he could not have gathered supplies."[7]

Bragg was a favorite of Jefferson Davis. Davis thought he could right things by gathering Bragg's subordinate generals and asking them to make their criti-cisms to his and Bragg's face. To Davis's surprise, they did, Longstreet saying bluntly that Bragg "was incompetent to manage an army or put men into a fight" and "knew nothing of the business" of being a general.[8] Faced with such criticisms as these, Davis stood by Bragg, even fêted him by transferring some of his critics—Longstreet, Leonidas Polk, and D. H. Hill—to other assignments (or in Hill's case, to no assignment), and otherwise left Bragg to get along with officers he now knew hated his guts.

In the case of Brigadier General Nathan Bedford Forrest—who was not present at the meeting with Davis—he knew this in the most dramatic way pos-sible. Forrest, fed up with Bragg's interfering with his command, wrote him a stinging missive and followed it up by riding into Bragg's camp, dismounting near his tent, and delivering a stern and imposing speech that concluded thus:

> I have stood your meanness as long as I intend to. You have played the part
> of a damned scoundrel, and are a coward, and if you were any part a man I
> would slap your jaws and force you to resent it.
>
> You may as well not issue any more orders to me, for I will not obey them.
> And I will hold you personally responsible for any further indignities you try to
> inflict on me.

You have threatened to arrest me for not obeying your orders promptly. I dare you to do it, and I say to you that if you ever again try to interfere with me or cross my path, it will be at the peril of your life.[9]

In this case, Bragg understood the wisdom of letting Forrest be.

If Bragg was Davis's man, Lincoln's light shone on a finer figure in Ulysses S. Grant, who by now had arrived in Chattanooga and was awaiting the arrival of his trusted lieutenant William Tecumseh Sherman for a breakout attack. By 23 November 1863, 70,000 Federal troops were amassed in Chattanooga. The breakout began with General Thomas seizing Orchard Knob from the Confederates. The next day, Joseph Hooker led the Federal attack at the Battle of Lookout Mountain, known as the "The Battle above the Clouds," and used his six-to-one advantage in men to defeat the Confederates.

But the key battle was the Battle of Missionary Ridge. It was begun on 24 November and engaged with a fury on 25 November. Again the Federals had six-to-one odds in their favor, but the three Confederate lines ascending the steep ridge threw back Federal attacks all day—at times in hand-to-hand combat.

General Thomas, however, refused to be denied victory. He brought up 23,000 Federals on a two-mile-long line and sent them charging a full mile under fire. The bluecoats crashed into and overwhelmed the 3,200 Confederates in the rifle pits at the base of the ridge. As retreating Confederates scrambled out of the way, fire poured down on the Federals from the Confederate second line: artillery fire, musket fire, an inferno of blazing fire. The Yankee junior officers on the spot thought they had no choice: they had to charge straight up the mountain through that avalanche of artillery shells and bullets.

Grant, seeing the blue uniforms move up, thought it was suicide and demanded to know who had given the order to attack up the ridge. No one knew, but the bluecoats kept moving, dodging behind whatever cover they could find as they made their ascent. Soon they had captured the second line of Confederate rifle pits, the defenders scrambling higher to the final line. Though the fire remained fierce and deadly, the Union troops got a break. A general like Longstreet would have arranged his artillery so that it could sweep the entirety of the ridge; Bragg had instead simply perched his cannon on the top. As the Federals ascended, the Confederate artillery's field of fire diminished to nothing, it being impossible to depress the barrels any farther. The Confederate gunners were reduced to lighting fuses on canister shells and rolling them and cannonballs down the ridge.

Grabbing the flag of the 24th Wisconsin from an exhausted color sergeant, eighteen-year-old Lieutenant Arthur MacArthur led the final charge: "On Wisconsin!" he cried. Soon the Federals were over the top, and as MacArthur planted his regiment's colors in front of what had been Braxton Bragg's headquarters he was greeted with the sight of Confederate uniforms melting away down the reverse slope of the ridge.

Phil Sheridan led the Federals' pursuit, which continued the next day. Only Patrick Cleburne's fighting division allowed the Confederates to escape. The charge up Missionary Ridge had decided the contest. Told that Confederate generals had considered Missionary Ridge impregnable, Grant replied, "Well, it *was* impregnable."[10] But the courage of men like Arthur MacArthur and Phil Sheridan had changed that. Though Bragg tried to blame his troops, the failure was his, and to Jefferson Davis he confessed this. Davis finally replaced him—but with another general who specialized in retreat: Joseph E. Johnston.

ATLANTA

ON 9 MARCH 1864, Ulysses S. Grant became the first lieutenant general since George Washington (not counting Winfield Scott, who was brevetted lieutenant general) made commander of all the armies of the United States. Grant also took field command of the Army of the Potomac, brought Phil Sheridan with him as cavalry commander, and allotted the middle theater to the tender mercies of William Sherman, who prepared his march through Georgia. (The West—aside from an abortive Federal campaign in Louisiana, along the Red River—was essentially a nonissue.) The Confederacy now faced two generals with apparently limitless resources who would not accept defeat, no matter what the cost in casualties or suffering. Grant's orders to Sherman were to "get into the interior of the enemy's country as far as you can, inflicting all the damage you can against their war resources,"[11] or as Sherman famously boasted, he would "make Georgia howl!"

Amassed under Sherman's command were 100,000 excellently supplied men against Joseph E. Johnston's 65,000 Confederate defenders, many of whom suffered shortages of clothing, ammunition, and food. As Sherman pursued them, they proved to be wily opponents, blocking all attempts to flank them and erecting impromptu earthwork defenses.[12] But the salient fact was that the Confederate line kept drawing southward, toward Atlanta. The entire month of May 1864 was spent in fighting retreat from north Georgia to just north of the Chattahoochee River, beyond which was the prize city. Johnston finally drew up his forces at Kennesaw Mountain, where he was prepared to make a stand. As Sherman noted, Johnston had made the area "one vast fort . . . Johnston must have fifty miles of trenches."[13]

Sherman tried to take Kennesaw Mountain by storm on 27 June 1864 and suffered a bloody repulse, losing 2,000 men to 500 Confederates.[14] Unable to break Johnston, Sherman maneuvered around him, crossing the Chattahoochee and forcing Johnston to fall back on Atlanta. Johnston had done what Johnston always did: executed tactically brilliant retreats. Jefferson Davis suddenly awoke to the fact that if this continued, Johnston would be executing his tactical brilliance all the way to the Gulf of Mexico. If the Confederacy was going to survive, Sherman had to be defeated, not parried. Davis relieved Johnston and put the gallant Texan John Bell Hood (now with only one leg and one useful arm) in command. Hood, a West Pointer, had been an aggressive and courageous division and corps commander and knew what was expected of him.

Many of Hood's fellow officers thought he had been promoted beyond his abilities, and Hood's performance argued that they were right. His initial attacks were well planned, but they failed badly in execution and horribly in casualties. He attacked at Peachtree Creek on 20 July 1864 and lost nearly 5,000 men while inflicting well fewer than half that many Union casualties. Two days later, he surprised Sherman with another attack. If delivered properly, it could have been a body blow to Sherman's army. Instead it was an ill-coordinated glancing blow that cost the Confederates another 10,000 men to fewer than 4,000 Federals. Six days later, Hood fought at Ezra Church and lost 5,000 more men. Aggressive he was, but the one-armed, one-legged general was suffering amputations of his army. And it was to no avail. Atlanta was besieged for a month, and then Hood had to evacuate the city. On 2 September 1864, the Federals occupied Atlanta.

As northern Georgia fell to the Federal occupier, so too did the most famous rebel raider of the sea, the sloop responsible for the crimson tide, the CSS *Alabama*. Built for the Confederacy by a Liverpool shipyard, the *Alabama*, under the leadership of Commander Raphael Semmes (a naval veteran of the Mexican War), established an extraordinary record. For twenty-two months she was almost always at sea. She sank the USS *Hatteras*, captured some sixty-five Union merchant ships, took 2,000 prisoners, and suffered no casualties—not even to sickness or accident—among her own crew. Finally putting up for repairs at Cherbourg, France, she was cornered by the USS *Kearsarge* on 19 June 1864. Semmes brought the *Alabama* out to fight. After an hour-long duel—of which the *Alabama* got far the worse—the *Alabama* gulped water and sank. Most of the crew, however, were saved—either picked up by the *Kearsarge* or, the luckier ones (like Semmes), by a British yacht, the *Deerhound,* which tootled them over to England for some proper celebrating. Semmes slipped back home and by the end of the war held dual commands as rear admiral and brigadier general.[15]

Semmes's adoptive hometown, however, felt the fire of Yankee guns. On 5 August 1864 Rear Admiral David Farragut of the United States Navy attacked Mobile Bay, the headquarters of Southern blockade-running. The entrance to the bay was mined, guarded by Fort Gaines and Fort Morgan, and sheltered three Confederate gunboats and an ironclad. Farragut had fourteen ships and four ironclads, an easy advantage in naval firepower, but had to run the gauntlet of the forts and the mines (which were called torpedoes). The USS *Tecumseh* tried to force the passage, struck a torpedo, and went down with ninety-four men. The other ships hesitated; fire poured in on them from the forts; and Farragut barked the order that won the day: "Damn the torpedoes! Full speed ahead!"[16] So they did, and so they won, forcing Confederate Admiral Franklin Buchanan's surrender. The bay was closed to the Confederacy, though Fort Morgan held out until 23 August 1864 and the city of Mobile held out until the very end, surrendering on 12 April 1865.

LEE VERSUS GRANT

WHILE SEMMES RECOVERED from his wounds and accepted toasts from gentlemen in England and Joseph E. Johnston tried to fend off Sherman in Georgia, Robert E. Lee in Virginia was confronted by the most successful Union general of the war, Ulysses S. Grant. After Gettysburg, Lee no longer had the men, the horses, or the provisions to attempt another invasion of the North. He was now compelled to fight on the defensive. His task: repel the invader at every turn. Remarkably, he did.

Grant's plan was simple. Sherman's fiery "March to the Sea" would ravage Georgia and then cut north through the Carolinas and Virginia; Phil Sheridan would go on a farm-burning crusade in the Shenandoah Valley; and the U.S. Navy would tighten its grip on the South's blockaded ports. Meanwhile, Grant and

Meade and the Army of the Potomac, about 120,000-strong, would march relentlessly down to Richmond slugging it out against Robert E. Lee's army of roughly 62,000 men until the Grey Fox was pummeled and beaten into submission.

There was another Union Army, the Army of the James, southeast of Richmond under General Benjamin "Beast" Butler, the infamous Federal occupier of New Orleans. In New Orleans he had issued his notorious "Woman Order" against the loyal Confederate belles who showed their disdain for the Yankee boys. Butler proclaimed: "Hereafter when any female shall by word, gesture, or movement insult or show contempt for any officer or soldier of the United States she shall be regarded and held liable to be treated as a woman of the town plying her vocation."[17] Once again, Southern chivalry was affronted, and rightfully so. Luckily for virtue in Virginia, the courtly General Beauregard bottled up Butler and his 35,000-man army at the Battle of Drewry's Bluff (16 May 1864), removing the Beast from making any immediate threat to the Confederate capital.

Far more dramatic was the clash of arms at the Battle of the Wilderness (5–6 May 1864). Lee hit Grant's army as it marched through "the Wilderness" west of Fredericksburg. The ever-aggressive Lee hoped to trap the Army of the Potomac in this dense forest where its numerical superiority would be negated by the impossibility of maneuver.

Lee's first challenge was that his army was at only two-thirds strength. Longstreet's corps was a day's march away. Nevertheless, Ewell's and A. P. Hill's corps rushed to engage the Federals. On the first day of fighting, Hill—outnumbered nearly three to one—caught and held the Federals at his front. As night fell, the Confederates, tired by hard marching and even harder fighting, drifted to sleep. A. P. Hill had fought well, but again was sick.

Lee was counting on Longstreet's fresh troops to reenact the Confederate victory at Chancellorsville. The thin grey line of Hill and Ewell would hold their positions, while Longstreet launched a flank attack on the Federal Goliath trapped in the Wilderness. But Longstreet was late. At 5:00 A.M., a massive Federal assault tore into the ragged Confederate lines. Grant had seen his opportunity to rip Lee's tired army to pieces.

Lee quickly mounted his horse and rode to rally his men, as butternut and grey uniforms streamed past him.

"My God, General McGowan," Lee shouted, "is this splendid brigade of yours running like a flock of geese?"

Lee was answered not by McGowan, but by Longstreet's lead troops running onto the field. Lee waved them forward.

"Who are you, my boys?"

"Texas boys!"

"Hurrah for Texas!" Lee took his hat and thrust it in the air. "Hurrah for Texas!"[18]

Lee led the men into their positions and refused to retire until one of his aides took the bridle of his horse, Traveller, and forcibly evicted horse and general from the fight.

Longstreet might have been late, but he made up for it by pressing the battle aggressively, not merely repelling the Union charge, but crumpling the Federals' left flank. As one Virginia soldier memorably recalled: "Like a fine lady at a party, Longstreet was often late in arrival at the ball, but he always made a sensation . . . with grand old First Corps, sweeping behind him, as his train."[19]

So effective was the Confederate countercharge that it appeared the momentum would be completely turned—that the moment of absolute Confederate danger might become an amazing Confederate triumph, routing the Union forces. But it was not the flanking movement of Chancellorsville that was reenacted, it was the tragedy of Jackson, as General Longstreet was felled, riding ahead of his lines, badly wounded by friendly fire.

With Longstreet down, Lee again rode to the front to direct the Confederate attack, but he found the forward surge of the Confederate line had already stalled. The moment of redirecting it had passed—yet not before teaching Grant the likely cost of trying to cage Lee's Confederate tigers.

With the smallest army Lee had fielded, he inflicted more casualties than he had on Burnside at Fredericksburg or on Hooker at Chancellorsville. The Wilderness, in fact, was a stunning tactical victory. In the Battle of the Wilderness, Grant lost nearly two men for every one of Lee's (Union casualties were 18,000 to not quite 11,000 for the Confederates). But it was a ratio that Grant knew he could afford and Lee could not.

Lee understood Grant's mind as well as he had that of the other Union generals he had faced. McClellan in these circumstances would have pulled his army out, refitted his men, and entrenched them, calling for more reinforcements. Pope and Hooker would have fled from the nightmarish brambles and fires of the Wilderness and on their way to Washington clamored for more troops. Burnside would have pulled back and marched his men one way and the other outside the forest, stalling for time to see what orders might come from

President Lincoln. Meade, who was actually here under Grant's command, might have held his ground and waited, if the choice had been his.

Lee knew that Grant would choose none of these options. Grant would not withdraw; he would attempt a relentless series of hooks to the body of Lee's army. He would shift his men to the left and attack, shift to the left and attack, forcing Lee to keep moving with him to block the Army of the Potomac from advancing against Richmond. That was Grant's way, and both Grant and Lee fully realized that 1864 was an election year for Lincoln—whose opponent was a dovish Democrat, George McClellan, late Napoleon of the Union Army—and Lincoln needed victories.

Grant's army continued its swing south. Blue and grey clashed again, only two days later in a two-week-long struggle at Spotsylvania Court House, where Lee set his men to digging what his biographer Clifford Dowdey has called "the most elaborate system of field fortifications then seen in world warfare," designing "what amounted to mobile forts."[20] Twice, during the fierce fighting, Lee had to be restrained from charging into the fray. When it was over, the results for Grant were as bad as they had been in the Wilderness. He had lost another 18,000 men out of numbers that had been reinforced to 111,000, while Lee suffered no more than 10,000 casualties out of a troop strength brought up to 63,000. At this rate if Grant hoped to defeat Lee by attrition he would have to sacrifice the entire current strength of the Army of the Potomac, and raise another.

The Spotsylvania battlefield was a grim panorama of what that cost meant: a horror of mangled bodies repeatedly bludgeoned, trenches clogged with dead, blue and grey corpses intertwined in death grips. Among the dead Union officers was Major General John Sedgwick, who was assuring his men that enemy sharpshooters "couldn't hit an elephant at this distance." He said it twice, which was daring fate too much. He was shot below the left eye, and fell smiling, as though he knew the joke was on him. Grant was devastated, asking repeatedly, "Is he really dead?"[21] And Lee too had lost a favorite officer, the plume-hatted Jeb Stuart, in a separate action at Yellow Tavern. "I can scarcely think of him without weeping,"[22] Lee said.

But there would be many more losses and much more weeping. Grant swore that he would "fight it out on this line if it takes all summer,"[23] which it would—and more. Two days after the last fighting at Spotsylvania Court House, Lee checked Grant again at North Anna River (23–26 May 1864) in a well-executed tactical defense that Lee hoped to turn into another trap for

Grant's army, but Lee was too sick to direct his counteroffensive and had no worthy lieutenant to carry it out. So the armies repeated their mirrored shifts to the south, confronting each other at Cold Harbor.

Grant, frustrated at Lee's continual thwarting of his advance, decided to rely on the sheer weight of his two-to-one superiority in numbers to end this bloody minuet. He hurled his men in a straightforward charge against Lee's newly and hastily erected fortifications.

For Grant, at least in human terms, it was a terrible mistake. The Union soldiers ran into blistering musketry and artillery fire, blue uniforms falling in grotesque, bloody clumps. Grant ordered assault after assault, thinking he had shaken the Confederates. In fact, he had only demoralized his own men. The Battle of Cold Harbor (31 May–3 June 1864) was a Union disaster. Federal casualties were 10,000 men to Confederate losses of 4,000 men. While Grant's steady stream of reinforcements kept his army above 100,000 troops, it was *his* men who were wondering how long this could go on and *his* officers who feared political reaction to the staggering bill in casualties. In a month's worth of fighting, Grant had lost 50,000 men. Nearly 1,700 Federal soldiers had sacrificed their lives every day in Grant's war of attrition.

Because of Grant's reinforcements, the odds confronting Lee had not changed. Lee felt compelled, nevertheless, to divide his army in order to bring relief to the people of the Shenandoah Valley. He took advantage of the sudden quiet on his front after Cold Harbor to dispatch Jubal A. Early's corps to drive the Federals out of the breadbasket of the Confederacy. Cadets from the Virginia Military Institute had already done their bit, hurling back the Federal invader at the Battle of New Market (15 May 1864). Old Jube followed up with a Jackson-worthy counteroffensive that went so far as to strike into Maryland (the Battle of Monacacy, 9 July 1864). Early's thrust brought panic to the Federal capital where bureaucrats feared that the Confederate commander might be so crazy (he could give that impression) as to throw his troopers at Washington, D.C.

In the meantime, Lee had only 28,000 men, a provocatively small number to dangle in front of General Grant. But Grant had no interest in refighting Cold Harbor and had given up trying to find a way around Lee to Richmond. Instead, he opted to lay siege to Petersburg and cut Richmond's supply lines to the south.

Lee had foreseen this probability but was powerless to prevent it. He also knew what it meant for the Confederacy. Lee confessed to Jubal A. Early, if Grant were to cross the James River and attack Petersburg, "It will become a siege, and then it will be a mere question of time."[24] Lee would have to buy that time.

THE SHROUDS OF DIXIE

A SIEGE MEANT that Grant's war of attrition would be ratcheted up a notch, but Lee held Grant at Petersburg for ten months, during which time the Union general could spare no men for an attack on Richmond. If this delaying action could be counted a victory, it was certainly a Pyrrhic one, because it was also during these ten months of successful defense that Lee witnessed the rest of the Confederacy wither, put to the torch by the blue-coated foe.

Sherman's men marched from Atlanta, one-third of which lay in ashes, on 16 November 1864. Dividing his men to march on parallel courses, they cut four paths of unimpeded destruction to Savannah. By January 1865, they were marching into South Carolina. By March, they were in North Carolina, fighting their last major engagement at Bentonville (19–21 March 1865), where Sherman defeated the ever-retreating Joseph E. Johnston. Johnston's little force (one-third the size of Sherman's) survived, and he did not surrender. But he bowed to the inevitable by suspending executions for deserters. He would not kill those who could see, as readily as he could, the inevitable outcome of the war.

In Tennessee, a frustrated John Bell Hood recklessly threw his long-suffering, ill-used army at the entrenched Federals at Franklin on 30 November 1864. His men fought with equally reckless bravery, but endured enormous losses— 6,000 men, about 20 percent of his force, including General Pat Cleburne, "the Stonewall of the West." Nevertheless, he moved on to the outskirts of Nashville, where he fought until his army was effectively annihilated. When the Confederate Army re-formed at Tupelo, Mississippi, it had been reduced to 20,000 men. Hood resigned.

In the breadbasket of Virginia, Union General Phil Sheridan executed Grant's orders to reduce "the Shenandoah Valley [into] a barren waste . . . so that crows flying over it for the balance of this season will have to carry their provender with them."[25] By the time Sheridan was done, the fertile valley's wheat, flour, hay, cattle, sheep, pigs, and chickens were either destroyed or in Federal hands; the farmers were left with nothing but burnt offerings; not even their tools were spared.

Grant's initial assault on the defenses around Petersburg in June 1864 led to another bruising engagement, where the Union troops suffered so grievously, despite their overwhelming numbers, that the Union's offensive had to be cut short, General Meade saying "the moral condition of the army" was shattered.[26]

Indeed, the Union troops had suffered such horrible casualties over the long struggle against Lee's army that their offensive spirit was drained to its dregs. A comfortable siege was what suited the Army of the Potomac. If Lee's men were hard-pressed, the Federals' spirit was incomparably lower than that of the Army of Northern Virginia. As Union General M. R. Patterson wrote, the Army of the Potomac "is nearly demoralized and the cavalry is no better than a band of robbers,"[27] preferring to inflict raids on civilians rather than fight Lee's rebel army. In the first two months of the siege, the Confederates, somewhat to their surprise, collected 8,000 Union prisoners, who felt well out of the fighting.

As the siege wore on, the Federal artillery shelling the city, Lee offered his wife a humorous assessment of the situation. "Grant," he wrote, "seems so pleased with his present position that I fear he will never move again."[28] However morally exhausted Grant's men, his was not an inactive siege. He continued to press and probe Lee's army. At its greatest extent, Lee's line of trenches stretched for nearly fifty-five miles.

In the most spectacular incident of the siege, blue-clad Pennsylvania coal miners burrowed beneath the Confederate lines, packed the tunnel with 8,000 pounds of explosives, and on 30 July 1864, detonated it. The blast tore a hole in the Confederate line, the earth collapsing into an enormous crater. The Federals poured into the breach. But with amazing sangfroid—amid the earth-shattering explosion that sent men flying and plunging to their deaths; and with the Federals now charging straight at them—the Confederates re-formed around the lip of the crater, threw back the Yankees in hand-to-hand combat, and opened fire on those who had charged into the pit.

The Battle of the Crater cost the Union another 4,000 casualties to fewer than 1,300 Confederates. Worse than that, from the Union perspective, was the speed with which the Confederates restored their lines. There was no chance to follow up with another attack on the breach. General Grant was appalled. "It was the saddest affair I have witnessed in the war. Such an opportunity for carrying fortifications I have never seen and do not expect again to have."[29]

The Battle of the Crater looked like an act of Union desperation; the repulse another blow to Federal morale. But Grant kept his men in place, and the siege dragged on through the winter and into the spring of 1865. The Union's noose was tightening around Lee. The rest of the South was reeling under the Union's terrible swift sword and purging torch. Virginia was the South's only defensible front, the Army of Northern Virginia carrying the hopes and prayers—the very fate—of the entire Confederacy. And Lee's army had little enough to sustain it. It was critically short of food and ammunition. Confederate soldiers on the line at Petersburg were limited to using 18 percussion caps a day, while the Union soldiers were *required* to fire 100 rounds every day.

Shelby Foote notes that during the siege: "Lee's veterans fought less . . . for a cause than they did for a tradition. And if, in the past six months, this had become a tradition not so much of victory as of undefeat, it had nonetheless been strengthened by the recent overland campaign and now was being sustained by the current stalemate, which was all that Grant's hundred thousand casualties had earned him in this latest On-to-Richmond effort, launched in May. Mainly, though, Lee's veterans fought for Lee, or at any rate for the pride they felt when they watched him ride among them."[30]

Lee knew that his army could not hold the line at Petersburg indefinitely. Grant simply had too many men. One of Lee's recommendations to address this Confederate shortfall was to arm freed slaves for military service. He noted that if the South ended slavery itself, it could "devise the means of alleviating the evil consequences to both races. I think, therefore, we must decide whether slavery shall be extinguished by our enemies, and the slaves used against us, or use them ourselves at the risk of the effects which may be produced upon our social institutions. My own opinion is that we should employ them without delay. I believe that with proper regulation they can be made efficient soldiers."[31]

Lee's belief was never tested—at least in the South; in the North, it was and with success. When the Confederate Congress finally capitulated to his advice and that of like-minded officers, it was too late. Certainly, the thought of the South arming its black population struck no fear in Northern hearts. As Abraham Lincoln said, "There is one thing about the Negro's fighting for the rebels which we can know as well as they can, and that is that they cannot at the same time fight in their armies and stay home and make bread for them. And that being known and remembered, we can have but little concern whether they become soldiers or not."[32]

Lincoln had put his finger on the really crucial issue, which was food. The South's agricultural economy had been blockaded, burned, and derailed. In the trenches at Petersburg, while the Federals ate and drank their fill, Lee found it increasingly hard to scrounge supplies for his besieged men from denuded Virginia farms and warehouses. After Phil Sheridan's defeat of Jubal Early at Cedar

Creek on 19 October 1864, the valley had belonged to the Union. Surviving the harsh winter had been difficult enough, but the spring brought no new source of supply, or hope of any.

Lee finally convinced President Davis that Petersburg and Richmond had to be abandoned. Lee's army—about 35,000 men, roughly one quarter of Grant's strength—had to be freed to maneuver, to find forage to feed itself, and to attempt to unite with Joseph E. Johnston's fragment of an army in North Carolina.

It was a desperate strategy compounded by enormous tactical difficulties. For just how was Lee to disengage from the siege, on lines that stretched more than fifty miles, pursued by a giant, well-equipped adversary, and then race his army—with its skeletal horses and hungry men on the verge of collapse—to find Johnston in North Carolina?

He would have to fight his way out and somehow manage to keep Grant from turning his flank. Lee held the line protecting Petersburg and Richmond as long as he could, keeping the Federals back with occasional offensive maneuvers. But Grant knew that Lee's lines were paper thin, and on 2 April 1865, the Federals punched through. Lee could only stall him now. He could not defeat him here, and he could not hold him. Lee dictated a dispatch to the Confederate secretary of war. "I see no prospect of doing more than holding our position here till night. I am not certain that I can do that. If I can I shall withdraw north of the Appomattox, and, if possible, it will be better to withdraw the whole line tonight from the James River."[33] Petersburg and Richmond were lost.

The Confederate Army—and Lee in his headquarters—were now under continuous bombardment. Lee and his staff mounted their horses, the fire intensifying. As they rode away, their abandoned headquarters exploded under a rain of Union shells, the artillery bursts chasing after them.

The Army of Northern Virginia that left Petersburg numbered no more than 30,000 men. Lee's plan was to march them to Amelia Court House, where he expected to find supplies. The troops were in good spirits—if anything, they were relieved to escape the trenches of Petersburg. But Lee's hopes, and his men's, were quickly crushed. At the railroad station at Amelia Court House, Lee found trains loaded with inedible cannonballs. The food he expected had been sent everywhere but here—to Danville, Virginia, to Lynchburg, Virginia, to Greensboro, North Carolina. The cannonballs on the other hand were worthless to Lee, save to break the backbones of his already weakened supply horses.

The food his men needed was now long marches away. The situation was turning from desperate to hopeless. He sent a message to Danville, the nearest of the supply dumps on his route to North Carolina, ordering that rations be sent on to the railroad station at Jetersville, Virginia, eight miles south of Amelia Court House. He dispatched supply wagons to scour the countryside for whatever else might be available from friendly farmers. The answer, however, was that nothing was to be had, and Federal cavalry under Phil Sheridan were riding to seize Jetersville.

Lee had slipped through Grant's fingers, but it would not be long before the Federal army was upon him. Now came a bizarre reenactment of the Lee versus Grant campaign of 1864, with Lee maneuvering continuously to the west, as Grant had maneuvered south, trying to find a clear road to North Carolina, as Grant had probed for a way to Richmond. Grant's troops shadowed Lee, meeting him at every turn. Where in the 1864 campaign Lee had checked Grant with bloody repulses at the end of every arcing movement, here the Union cavalry pressed the pursuit while maintaining, in Shelby Foote's words, "a respectful distance."[34] But there were also bloody engagements, the worst of which was at Sayler's Creek, where the ragamuffin Confederates were outnumbered two to one. Their casualties, however, were on the order of *seven to one,* including the loss of eight captured Confederate generals, among their number Dick Ewell and Lee's son Custis.

When Lee saw the survivors of Sayler's Creek fleeing to join his part of the army, he exclaimed, "My God, has the army been dissolved?"

The answer came from General William Mahone: "No, General, here are troops ready to do their duty."[35]

Lee ordered Mahone to screen the Confederate retreat, while Lee reassembled his forces. "I wish to fight here," he said.[36]

The united Army of Northern Virginia now numbered about 15,000 men with approximately 80,000 troops under Grant in pursuit. Lee knew that he could not outrun the Union commander. His only option would be to try to fight again. But the end was apparent on 9 April 1865. It was then that General John B. Gordon fought the last engagement of the Army of Northern Virginia near Appomattox Court House. "Tell General Lee," Gordon ordered, "I have fought my corps to a frazzle, and I fear I can do nothing unless I am heavily supported by General Longstreet's corps."[37] General Longstreet anchored Lee's other flank; he could not be moved short of sacrificing the entire army.

Lee had hoped against hope that it would never come to this. Only two days before, Lee had told his son Rooney (a cavalry commander): "Keep your command together and in good spirits, General. Don't let them think of surrender.

I will get you out of this."[38] But now he had to concede there was no way. In discussing the matter with the young artillery officer E. P. Alexander, he rejected the idea of scattering the army so that it could fight a guerilla war; that, he said, would lead only to lawlessness, Federal reprisals against Southern civilians, and the further devastation of the South. Though they could wish otherwise, Lee had to surrender.

And so it was done. On Palm Sunday, 9 April 1865, General Robert E. Lee appeared in a bright, clean uniform with a sword, red sash, and highly polished boots. "I have probably to be General Grant's prisoner, and thought I must make my best appearance," he said.[39]

General Longstreet told his commander, "Unless he [Grant] offers us honorable terms, come back and let us fight it out."[40]

But as Lee mounted Traveller, he knew he would not come back to fight it out.

The surrender was enacted at the Appomattox house of Wilmer McLean, formerly a resident of Manassas. McLean had fled Manassas, and the war, after an artillery shell struck his house during the Battle of First Manassas in 1861. Now, ironically, his house would close the war in a meeting between the immaculately dressed Virginian aristocrat and the mud-spattered soldier from Ohio, Ulysses S. Grant.

Grant later wrote: "my own feelings, which had been quite jubilant on the receipt of his letter [Lee's note agreeing to discuss terms of surrender], were sad and depressed. I felt like anything but rejoicing at the downfall of a foe who had fought so long and valiantly, and had suffered so much for a cause, though that cause was, I believe, one of the worst for which a people ever fought."[41]

Grant attempted small talk, but Lee preferred that the matter be settled. Lee asked Grant to commit his terms to writing, which Grant did with the same concision that marked Lincoln's Gettysburg Address, in fewer than 200 words. Lee read the terms and told Grant, "This will have a very happy effect on my army." Lee asked only that the men be allowed to keep their horses; he added that he wished to exchange the Union prisoners he held as quickly as possible, for he had provisions neither for them nor for his own men. Grant agreed and offered Lee 25,000 rations. The officers shook hands, and it was done. Lee would tolerate no harsh words spoken against Grant after the war.

Grant returned to his headquarters and informed his staff: "The war is over. The rebels are our countrymen again."

Lee rode back into his camp. Rebel yells rose from his men, who asked the inevitable, but, to them, virtually unbelievable question: "General, are we surrendered?"

"Men, we have fought the war together, and I have done the best I could for you. You will all be paroled and go to your homes until exchanged." Then, after a pause, "Good-bye."

"General, we'll fight 'em again. Say the word and we'll go in and fight 'em yet."[42]

Lee shook his head sadly and rode Traveller through the gathering throng, the men reaching up to shake Lee's hand and cheer him.

They "were whipped," as Shelby Foote has noted, "about as thoroughly as any American force had ever been or ever would be, short of annihilation, but it was a part of their particular pride that they would never admit it, even to themselves."[43]

That spirit was captured in Lee's "General Orders No. 9," his farewell to the Army of Northern Virginia. It became the funeral ode for "the Lost Cause," the Gettysburg Address of the South:

> After four years of arduous service, marked by unsurpassed courage and fortitude, the Army of Northern Virginia has been compelled to yield to overwhelming numbers and resources.
>
> I need not tell the brave survivors of so many hard-fought battles, who have remained steadfast to the last, that I have consented to the result from no distrust of them.
>
> But, feeling that valor and devotion could accomplish nothing that could compensate for the loss that must have attended the continuance of the contest, I determined to avoid the useless sacrifice of those whose past services have endeared them to their countrymen.
>
> By the terms of the agreement officers and men can return to their homes and remain until exchanged. You will take with you the satisfaction that proceeds from the consciousness of duty faithfully performed; and I earnestly pray that a merciful God will extend to you his blessing and protection.
>
> With an increasing admiration of your constancy and devotion to your country, and a grateful remembrance of your kind and generous considerations for myself, I bid you all an affectionate farewell.
>
> *Deo Vindice.*

CHAPTER 16

"BUT WESTWARD, LOOK! THE LAND IS BRIGHT"

GENERAL GRANT had been magnanimous at Appomattox, but it was an open question how the conquering Federals would treat the Southern states—especially after the assassination of Abraham Lincoln.[1] Lincoln had proclaimed a policy of reconciliation. The Radical Republicans in Congress had other ideas. They dominated Congress; bullied the new president, Andrew Johnson; and repudiated talk of reconciliation. They were for punishing the South and stripping former Confederates of their citizenship in the now forcibly restored Union. They also wanted to hang a few of the more famous rebels (which didn't happen),[2] maintain martial law in the South (which did), and turn the South into a Radical Republican fiefdom through disenfranchising ex-Confederates and enfranchising newly freed blacks. This was the program known as Reconstruction. It exacerbated Southern bitterness about losing the war.

Under the Reconstruction regime, proud Virginia, which had been governed by an elected legislature since the seventeenth century and was the home of more American presidents—including founders Washington, Jefferson, Madison, and Monroe—than any other state, would become Military District Number One, occupied territory under an imposed military governor.

Such was the temper of the times that there were those in Congress who thought the John Brown strategy of encouraging a slave insurrection against white Southerners was not outdated. Perhaps if the blacks slew "one-half of their oppressors," that would teach the remaining Southern whites just who was in charge now.[3] That was the vision expressed by Senator Benjamin Wade of Ohio in a letter to Senator Charles Sumner of Massachusetts, and such vituperative language against the South was common. Even the British novelist Anthony Trollope—who, from afar, was a staunch supporter of the Unionist cause—thought Reconstruction was worse than any regime that had ever before been put over a fallen people. It was imposed upon a people who had already suffered as no Americans ever had or, by the grace of God, ever will again. *One quarter* of the draft-age white male population of the South lay dead from battle or disease. In material terms, as historian Gary Gallagher notes, the war "cost the Confederacy two-thirds of its assessed wealth . . . killed 40 percent of its livestock, destroyed more than half its farm machinery, and left levees, railroads, bridges, industry, and other parts of the economic infrastructure"— not to mention entire cities—"severely damaged or ruined."[4]

Still, Southerners were loath to concede defeat. At Appomattox, Union Colonel Charles S. Wainwright noted, "The Army of Northern Virginia under Lee . . . has surrendered. During three long and hard-fought campaigns it has withstood every effort of the Army of the Potomac; now at the commencement of the fourth, it is obliged to succumb without even one great pitched battle. Could the war have been closed with such a battle as Gettysburg, it would have been more glorious for us. . . . As it is, the rebellion has been worn out rather than suppressed."[5]

Wainwright spoke with the honor of a soldier, and in admiration for the courage and pride of his adversary. Radical Republicans in the Congress noted the same undiminished Southern pride but without admiration. They worked eagerly to suppress it. If the South's spirit was unvanquished, materially the South was prostrate, and Reconstruction, which did not end until 1877, was the conqueror's heel on its throat.

All of which is not to minimize the sacrifices of the boys in blue, who suffered more casualties, if far fewer in proportion to population. Union dead were more than 364,000; Confederate dead 260,000. All told nearly 625,000 Americans had died in the war to reunite the states—and these are only the military dead, not counting an unknown number of Southern civilians. More American servicemen died in the failed War of Southern Independence than died in World War I, World War II, the Korean War, and the Vietnam War *combined.*

How could such wounds be healed? By turning America's aggressive spirit against others, of course. The first opportunity was in Mexico. In the spirit of the Monroe Doctrine, Fighting Phil Sheridan brought 50,000 troops to the Texas border *pour encourager les français* to *vamos a francia.* Emboldened Mexicans then murdered Emperor Maximilian (Mexico's best emperor since Charles V). Sheridan's action might also have discouraged more than a few Confederates from moving south of the border. Some already had done so, rather than accept

Yankee domination.[6] But what was the point if the Yankees were going to conquer Mexico anyway?

Reconciliation between North and South would truly come only at the end of the century, when the nation united to kill Spaniards in the South's long-desired vacation spot of Cuba and, rather amazingly, in the far Pacific. But in the immediate postwar era there were always Indians: the traditional enemy of choice for Americans since the seventeenth century. Western expansion and killing Indians would do the trick to help Americans shake off the trauma of killing one another. As that admirable tough guy Phil Sheridan[7] once remarked, "The only good Indian I ever saw was dead."[8] On that point, Southerners moving west and blue-clad cavalry officers could agree.[9]

The odds in some ways favored the Indians. There were an estimated 270,000 Indians west of the Mississippi River. The postwar United States Army shrank to just over 20,000 men, of whom 14,000 could be used to patrol the vast western territories. Nor did the American troopers have a technological advantage to bring against the Indian warriors. As most readers know from watching countless westerns, some Indians acquired repeating rifles from Indian traders. Standard issue to American servicemen were single-shot carbines.

What remained the same, from America's long tradition of Indian wars, was that the Indians relied on stealth, surprise, and avoiding set-piece battles. The white man's army emphasized discipline and toughness, which carried U.S. Army troopers through winter campaigns—campaigns that the Indians found hard to endure. Most important of all, the Army was backed by a land rush of civilian settlers and a dynamic culture of conquest and confidence. America would not be denied her continental empire.

Some Indian fighting had occurred during the War Between the States (including with Cochise and the Apaches in the Arizona Territory). But now the postwar onslaught of westward settlers opened up a quarter-century's worth of fighting from the Pacific Northwest to the border with Mexico and across the Great Plains. The Indian wars, from their beginnings 200 years earlier, had always been marked by desecrating atrocities of which scalping was the most famous. These began again. The victims were often civilians. Retaliation, when the U.S. cavalry or territorial militia caught up with the Indian malefactors, was violent. The moralistic Northeast of the United States found this appalling. Then as now moralists and *bien pensants* expressed sympathy for the Indians; but American soldiers and western settlers had no sympathy for either Indian raiders or Boston pantywaists.

There were campaigns throughout the West from 1866 to 1891. Three were crucial. The first began in 1876 when General Phil Sheridan ordered action against the Sioux in the Black Hills of South Dakota and Wyoming. The Sioux, under Chief Red Cloud, had been a problem for a decade, killing miners and settlers, massacring Captain William Fetterman and eighty-one troopers in Wyoming (in 1866), and shutting the Bozeman Trail. When gold was discovered in the Black Hills, the United States government tried to buy the hills from the Indians, unsuccessfully. Then the government ordered the Indians to a reservation where there were other Sioux. They refused to go. That was when Phil Sheridan was told to go to work.

Three Army columns—under the command of Generals George Crook, John Gibbon, and Alfred Terry—set out to locate and crush the hostiles. General Terry was right in guessing that they were camped along the Bighorn River in the Montana Territory. But neither he nor anyone else was aware of just how large the Indian presence was. Reinforced by Cheyenne, Arapaho, and others, there were perhaps 12,000 Indians including 4,000 braves. Among them were Chief Sitting Bull, the elder statesman of the Indians, and the warrior Chief Crazy Horse.

The first to strike the Indians was General Crook at the Battle of the Rosebud (17 June 1876). Or rather, the Indians struck him, as Chief Crazy Horse led more than 1,200 braves against Crook's equally numerous command of troopers and Indian scouts. The six-hour battle ended in the Indians' withdrawal, but it was a tactical victory for Crazy Horse, because Crook's command retired to its base camp.

Eight days later (25 June 1876) the flamboyant Lieutenant Colonel George Armstrong Custer espied the main enemy encampment. Custer had graduated at the bottom of his class at West Point, but he had rocketed through sheer dash and courage to become the youngest (at age twenty-five) brigadier general in the U.S. Army during the War Between the States. By now he was an experienced and dedicated Indian fighter, widely known among the Indians as "Yellow Hair." He held command of the 7th Cavalry.

Though he didn't know the size of the enemy that faced him, he divided his command of roughly 650 men into three battalions. He took one, Major Marcus Reno was given another, and Captain Frederick Benteen was assigned the third. His plan was to strike quickly before the Indians knew he was there. Reno would charge across the river into the Indian camp, while Custer maneuvered to strike the camp from the center, at a ford of the Little Bighorn. Benteen was to move along the western bluffs looking for other hostiles. The plan, of course, came a cropper. Reno's charge quickly turned into a fighting defense. The Indians, initially surprised, re-formed and counterattacked, pushing Reno back into the hills where Benteen reinforced him. The Indians kept Reno's and Benteen's battalions pinned down for two days

Custer never crossed the river. Instead of smashing into the Indians, a raging flood of warriors stormed over his battalion and killed every last man. Though what actually happened at Custer's last stand is a mystery, evidence indicates that Custer was in fact one of the last men fighting. Although his corpse, like the others, was stripped naked, he was not scalped, whether out of respect or because he was starting to go prematurely bald is unclear.[10]

What was clear was that the United States Army had suffered a disaster, and suddenly Eastern sympathy for the Indians seemed a bit passé, with more than 240 American troopers dead, among them a famous commander regarded as something of a cavalier. The task of avenging him was given to Massachusetts-born Colonel Nelson Miles, who had risen through the ranks as a volunteer in the War Between the States. He became the most accomplished Indian-fighting officer in the Army. Already well experienced in fighting tribes along the Great Plains, he beat the Sioux (but did not capture Sitting Bull) at the Battle of Cedar Creek (21–22 October 1876) and beat them again (when the Indians were led by Crazy Horse) at Wolf Mountain (8 January 1877). Fighting continued sporadically and on a small scale, but the Lakota Sioux were no longer a serious threat. Sitting Bull made one last attempt to rouse them, with the "Ghost Dance War" of 1890, but the Sioux found that contrary to the medicine man's visions, they were not impenetrable to bullets. Braves were killed, so was Sitting Bull, and so were women and children. It was the end.

Nelson Miles was involved in the second major Indian campaign as well, which was against Chief Joseph, who led a rebellion of the Nez Percé Indians. Again, Miles assumed command after a couple of stinging Army defeats. The result was a 1,500-mile fighting pursuit of the Indian chief, who finally surrendered on 5 October 1877 just short of the Canadian border over which he had hoped to escape with his people. His noble words of surrender have gone into the history books: "Hear me, my chiefs, I am tired; my heart is sick and sad. From where the sun now stands, I will fight no more forever."[11]

The last major campaign was against the Apaches of the Southwest and their wily guerilla leaders, including Cochise and most especially Geronimo, leader of the Chiricahua, who fought the white man throughout the 1870s and 1880s. Nelson Miles was again tapped to bring the Apaches to heel, superseding General George Crook. Crook had achieved great success in winning Indian trust and gaining Apache scouts, but not in locking up Geronimo. Five thousand American troopers, 500 scouts, 3,000 Mexican troops, and five months of hard pursuit resulted in Geronimo's final capture and the end of the major Apache threat. Geronimo eventually reconciled himself to the white man's dominion. He became a Christian, a farmer, and perhaps even a Republican (he was a member of Theodore Roosevelt's inaugural parade). Before that, he had provided plenty of outdoor exercise for the United States Army.

Among that well-exercised contingent was a cavalry officer named Henry Lawton. Lawton looked like a British colonial officer, perhaps because he admired such men. Tall (six foot, four inches), with a martial moustache and oft-proven courage, he had imported the heliograph—a British colonial invention for sending Morse code by reflected sun flashes—as a means to track Geronimo. Now he and the American Army, having tamed the West, would embark on taming the farther reaches of the Pacific. And Lawton would get to wear the gleaming white pith helmet of his dreams.

REMEMBER THE *MAINE*!

THE WORLD'S LARGEST OCEAN lapped against the shores of California and the Pacific Northwest, beckoning America onward. In 1867 Secretary of State William Seward expanded the nation's western coastline with his purchase of Alaska from czarist Russia—"Seward's Folly"—for an exorbitant two cents an acre. Seward had been looking for other real estate to purchase—including Hawaii and islands in the Caribbean—but the ridicule he received over "Seward's Icebox" discouraged him from such bargain shopping.

Seward would have found a great supporter thirty years later in Theodore Roosevelt. Roosevelt called his own expansive foreign policy "Americanism" rather than imperialism, but he also had a wonderful name for his anti-imperial opponents. He called them "goo-goos," which is as apt a term as any.[12] It was goo-goos who ridiculed the purchase of Alaska.

Even goo-goos, though, could be bellicose in exerting the Monroe Doctrine. President Grover Cleveland (1885–89 and 1893–97), for instance, was very much a goo-goo. The previous president, Benjamin Harrison (1889–93), had approved of an American settler–led coup against the Hawaiian monarchy in 1893 and even sent in Marines to support it. As had happened in Texas and California, the Americans made Hawaii a republic and petitioned to be annexed by the United States. This made sense, not only because of the coup, but because for the last twenty years Hawaii had been a de facto American colony anyway, with an American-driven economy. Moreover, the United States Navy viewed the occupation of Hawaii as a vital national interest. As early as 1867, Admiral David Porter Sr. had concluded that "Honolulu is bound to be the principal stopping place between China and California and a point of great importance to American commerce. . . . We could not afford to let so important an outpost fall into the hands of any European power."[13] President Cleveland, however, squashed the treaty of annexation.

Yet while he temporarily denied Hawaii to the United States—the William McKinley administration (1897–1901) annexed Hawaii five years later[14]—President Cleveland took America to the brink of war against Great Britain over the seemingly irrelevant question of where the border should be drawn between Venezuela and British Guiana. The British, rather dismayed at American bellicosity, submitted the border dispute to arbitration. The arbitrators settled the matter to Britain's satisfaction, as was mete and just as the British are almost invariably right.

Cleveland was not so right. For while he rattled arrows at the Mother Country, he took no action at all when rebellion rocked Spanish Cuba that very same year (1895), though Cuba lay just ninety miles south of Florida and was an obvious target for annexation. But goo-goos were often mulish—or donkeys; Cleveland was a Democrat—with a tendency to kick out at presumed friends; and friends the British and the Americans increasingly were, with the Royal Navy and the United States Navy having a long record of cooperation in the nineteenth century, enjoying captain's quarters toasts and even action together in distant ports of call from Egypt to Hawaii and Samoa.[15]

Indeed, the idea of Anglo-Saxon world dominion (which included the United States as Britain's global partner) was very much in the minds of British imperialists from Cecil Rhodes to Rudyard Kipling; and there were Americans, like young Theodore Roosevelt, assistant secretary of the Navy in the administration of President William McKinley, who agreed. So did the Clausewitz of American naval strategy, Alfred Thayer Mahan, author of *The Influence of Sea Power Upon History, 1660–1783,* who thought it not so much a matter of choice but of inevitability: "Whether they will or no, Americans must begin to look outward."[16]

A goodly number of Americans did look outward, including the Reverend Josiah Strong, a prominent evangelical minister, who saw in Anglo-Saxon America "This race of unequalled energy, with all the majesty of numbers and the might of wealth behind it—the representative, let us hope, of the largest liberty, the purest Christianity, the highest civilization—having developed peculiarly aggressive traits calculated to impress its institutions upon mankind, will spread itself over the earth." Or, to be more specific, he envisaged the United States moving "down upon Mexico, down upon Central and South America, out upon the islands of the seas, over upon Africa and beyond,"[17] and indeed of Anglo-Saxonizing mankind.

The president who took up this white man's burden was the unlikely figure of William McKinley—unlikely because McKinley was a waffler, not a visionary, and instinctively in favor of a quiet administration untroubled by foreign conflict. But he was driven on by young thrusters like Theodore Roosevelt and by the jingoistic mood of the American people. He was very much, in this respect, of a mind with Disraeli: "I must follow the people. Am I not their leader?" And the people in 1898 wanted war with Spain.

Cuba, once more, was the focal point. Cuba had been in a state of imperfectly subjugated rebellion since 1868. War erupted again in 1895. The rebels simultaneously appealed for American aid, threatened American interests on the island, and organized guerillas from Florida. In assessing the rights and wrongs of the conflict it would appear that the Spaniards were more sinned against than sinning, but they were incompetent at articulating their cause and protecting the Cuban people from the insurrectionists. Not so inarticulate were William Randolph Hearst and Joseph Pulitzer, whose competing New York City newspapers—the *Journal* and the *World*, respectively—painted a garish tropical passion play of innocent Ricky Ricardos brutalized by Spanish inquisitors. The great American artist Frederic Remington, sent by Hearst to Cuba, cabled back a report: "Everything is quiet. There is no trouble here. There will be no war. I wish to return. Remington." Hearst cabled back: "Please remain. You furnish the pictures, I'll furnish the war."[18]

One honest reporter was the young Winston Churchill. He reported that having initially sympathized with the rebels, he changed his mind after traveling with the Spanish army in Cuba, meeting Spanish officers, and seeing "how unhappy the Spanish were at the idea of their beautiful 'Pearl of the Antilles' [being] torn from them." But he "did not see how they could win. . . . We knew that Spain was not a rich country as things went then. We knew by what immense efforts and sacrifices she maintained more than a quarter of a million men across 5,000 miles of salt water—a dumb-bell held at arm's length. . . ."

The Spanish soldiery "moved like Napoleon's convoys in the Peninsula, league after league, day after day, through a world of implacable hostility, slashed here and there by fierce onslaught."[19]

Because of the Monroe Doctrine, if nothing else, America had no incentive to intervene on the side of the Spanish. As for intervening on the side of the rebels, there was no point of national interest to do so unless the island was going to be annexed. In any event, there was no casus belli.

Spain tried to be conciliatory to the United States. It had, under American pressure, granted Cuba autonomy in 1897, which, the Spanish said, meant "real self-government," the granting to every Cuban (and Puerto Rican) the same rights as citizens of Spain, and "every concession compatible with inflexible defense of Spanish rule and sovereignty."[20] But the war continued. When mobs—pro-Spanish ones—rioted in Havana, the American Consul General Fitzhugh Lee requested a show of force to protect American interests. The USS *Maine* turned up, Spanish officials nodded politely, and then, after twenty days of doing nothing, the ship exploded on the night of 15 February 1898. Two hundred and sixty-six American crewmen were dead.

The cause of the explosion is a matter of mystery and dispute. The result is not. Ten days later, Teddy Roosevelt—as acting secretary of the Navy Department while Secretary John D. Long took off for a visit to an osteopath—seized America's "Asiatic Squadron" by its smokestacks. He cabled Commodore George Dewey in Hong Kong (where the commodore was enjoying the hospitality of officers of the Royal Navy): "Order the Squadron . . . to Hong Kong. Keep full of coal. In the event of a declaration of war [with] Spain, your duty will be to see that the Spanish squadron does not leave the Asiatic coast, and then offensive operations in the Philippine Islands."[21]

He had to wait a bit. Spain tried to appease the United States in every particular save granting independence to Cuba. On 11 April 1898, President McKinley went to Congress asking that he be authorized to intervene with whatever means, including military, necessary—"in the name of humanity, and in the name of civilization, [and] in behalf of American interests"[22]—to ensure the end of the war in Cuba. McKinley, like the Spanish, did not want war. McKinley, a veteran of the War Between the States, said, "I have been through one war. I have seen the dead pile up, and I do not want to see another."[23] As befits such a man, his speech before Congress was somewhat vague about actually going to war; he asked for that authority, but kept open the possibility that he might not need to use it.

Congress helped force his hand. On 19 April 1898 it took the rather extraordinary step of proclaiming that Cuba was—by congressional declaration—independent, and it authorized President McKinley to guarantee the island's independence. That seemed to settle matters. Two days later, Spain severed diplomatic relations with the United States. Four days after that, 25 April 1898, Congress declared war.

"YOU MAY FIRE WHEN READY, GRIDLEY"

THE SPRING OF 1898 marked the Alaskan gold rush. But the number of volunteers to fight the Spanish was far greater than the number of prospectors with gold fever. By the time these new recruits had signed their names and been issued their gear, the United States had already sunk Spain's Pacific fleet, and President McKinley had won an archipelago of 7,000 islands that he needed help finding on a map.

The president might have been unprepared for this blow struck against Spain, but the Navy wasn't: it had well-developed intelligence (an effective make-do effort organized by Commodore Dewey) and war plans for just this contingency. As Navy Secretary John D. Long said: "Seven hours only were required by the American Squadron to place the Philippine Archipelago at the mercy of the United States, and relieve this government of anxiety for the Pacific slope and its trans-Pacific trade. More than seven years, however, had been needed to provide the ships and perfect the personnel which accomplished the result."[24]

The Royal Navy officers who cheered Commodore Dewey and his nine-ship squadron[25] were convinced the Americans were doomed. Wonderful chaps, of course, but not ready to battle a European navy, especially one supported by land-based guns and mines. They were in for a surprise.

The American squadron encountered scant resistance as it passed by the islands of Corregidor and El Fraile. The Spanish had concentrated their fleet of nine warships—and forty vessels total, including small gunboats—in a defensive line at Cavite naval base in Manila Bay. Powerful shore batteries added to the firepower of the Spanish ships. As the Americans approached, the Spanish batteries erupted. Their shells fell just short, splashing American sailors. At 5:40 A.M., 1 May 1898, Commodore Dewey aboard the USS *Olympia* gave the order: "You may fire when ready, Gridley"[26]—Charles Gridley being the ship's captain. The Battle of Manila Bay began with Dewey's guns belching smoke and hurling 250-pound shells.

The American ships raked the Spaniards, turned about, and passed abeam for the guns to fire again and again. Return fire exploded overhead or shot up geysers in the water below, but to little effect, while shells from the American guns struck home, turning the Spanish ships into funeral pyres. The Americans even took a three-and-a-half-hour break for breakfast, a smoke, and a casual stroll around the decks, while ammunition was redistributed and casualties were counted (only six wounded and no dead). As the smoke cleared from Manila Bay, it was apparent the battle was almost won. At a quarter after eleven, the Americans set to finish it. The battle was over in time for a late lunch. Manila Bay, if not greater Manila, belonged to Dewey.

When the news reached the Navy Department, Commodore Dewey was promoted to rear admiral. When the news reached continental Europe there was shock. A new naval power had burst upon the world, and Germany, in particular, saw this as a threat. If Spain was to be ousted from the Philippines, Germany wanted to make the archipelago its own. Germany even sent ships to cruise into Manila Bay, after Dewey's victory. Dewey, however, with a little gunpowder encouragement, a threat of war, and the support of the Royal Navy, bade them depart. Only the British regarded American sea power, and imperialism, as welcome. As one British regimental surgeon said, toasting the American and British flags, "Their colors never run."[27]

Perhaps that was because the American Army and Navy, though small—the United States had 25,000 soldiers and only a few dozen ships and boats—was an efficient fighting force. The Navy in particular had been modernizing. The Army, if lacking the modern artillery and rifles of the Spanish, had been kept sharp fighting Indians. And both services—considering how rapidly they had to fight a Pacific and Caribbean war and, in the Army's case, train, equip, and ship out thousands of volunteers—were reasonably well primed and ready for action. After the onset of hostilities, Congress agreed to more than double the size of the regular Army and threw open the gates to volunteers. Nearly a quarter of a million men enrolled to fight.

Three weeks after Dewey's victory at Manila Bay, troopers began shipping out from San Francisco. The following month, on 14 June 1898, 17,000 troopers under the command of General William Shafter embarked from Tampa Bay to Santiago, Cuba, where the Navy was hoping to bottle up a Spanish naval squadron—and in the process seize Cuba's third-largest city. One of the units employed was the 1st Volunteer Cavalry, the Rough Riders, officered by Colonel Leonard Wood and Lieutenant Colonel Theodore Roosevelt, who traded his pin-striped suit as assistant naval secretary for a bandana and cowboy hat—and a uniform he had designed by Brooks Brothers. The Rough Riders were an extraordinary collection of men, prototypical TR men, men who reflected Roosevelt's own confidence in a virile America. As Roosevelt noted: "It is as typical an American regiment as ever marched or fought . . . including a score of Indians, and about as many of Mexican origin from New Mexico; then there are some fifty Easterners—almost all graduates of Harvard, Yale, Princeton, etc.,—and almost as many Southerners; the rest are men of the plains and the Rocky Mountains. Three fourths of our men have at one time or another been cowboys or else are small stockmen; certainly two thirds have fathers who fought on one side or the other in the civil war."[28] They were men who knew how to ride and handle a gun, which helped enormously in expediting the training and departure of this quickly mustered force.

On Cuba, the Marine Corps had already established a foothold forty miles east of Santiago at Guantánamo Bay, a piece of real estate the leathernecks liked so much that they have never left. General Shafter planned to land his men on the beaches between Santiago and Guantánamo at the idyllically named Daiquiri. The Cuban rebels were happy to provide intelligence on the Spaniards and promised to strike the Spanish garrison in order to assist the American landing. The Navy, meanwhile, would bombard other points on the coast to keep the Spanish distracted and pinned down.

In the event, the American landings were unmolested, the Spanish forces having retreated to cover the approaches to Santiago. The Americans followed the retreating Spanish, cutting a narrow path through the mosquito-buzzing jungle. They advanced from Daiquiri to their new coastal base at Siboney, and there they waited. General Shafter thought it wise to avoid engaging the first line of Spanish defenses—about 2,000 men, five miles inland at Las Guasimas—until he had drawn up and organized his entire force. Among the lead units were volunteer cavalry under Georgia-born and West Point–educated "Fighting Joe" Wheeler. Wheeler had been a general of Confederate cavalry. After the war, he was held prisoner (with Jefferson Davis) under the supervision of future Indian fighter Nelson Miles. Once Reconstruction was past, Wheeler, a planter and a lawyer, was elected to Congress from Alabama. Now, at age sixty-two, he was a general of volunteer cavalry—the only postwar Confederate general to gain the rank of general in the U.S. Army.

General Wheeler desperately wanted, in his own words, to get at "the Yankees—dammit, I mean the Spaniards"[29] and had sound military reasons for his impetuosity. The Americans were more vulnerable now, on the beaches, than they would ever be. They needed to clear away any potential Spanish threat. Fighting Joe was as good as his name. On 24 June 1898, he took his boys against the enemy. The Americans, including the Rough Riders, dismounted and launched a two-pronged attack at the Spanish front and right flank at Las Guasimas. In an hour's hard fighting—with bullets clipping through the jungle and smacking flesh with sickening thuds—the Americans pushed the Spaniards back. As the old Confederate general saw the straw-hatted Spanish retreat, he couldn't help himself, hallooing: "We've got the damned Yankees on the run!"[30] The Rough Riders had their own excitement, trekking through the jungle under heavy fire and driving the Spanish from a blockhouse and well-defended rock forts.

The Americans seized the Spanish positions, but General Shafter warned General Wheeler to do no more attacking without orders; he did not want his men to outrun their logistics. Shafter, however, was overweight, overheated, and gout-ridden. He was no man to lead eager volunteers and toughened regulars in a tropical campaign. Joe Wheeler could see Santiago, not ten miles distant, waiting to be plucked. What he didn't see were the Spanish positions in the intervening hills. Wheeler was for moving; Shafter was for waiting: so the Americans waited, for a week, doing nothing except shooing away the Cuban rebels. These native allies, they quickly decided, were little more than half-naked, half-savage beggars, more notable for ever-present and insistent outstretched hands—looking to grab any detachable American article of uniform, equipment, or food—than they were for their fighting prowess.

While the Americans waited, the Spaniards dug rifle pits, improved their defensive positions, and trained guns on the jungle trails. On 30 June 1898, Shafter unveiled his plan. The Americans were to capture two fortified positions: first, El Caney to the northeast of the city, so that he needn't worry about his flank, and then San Juan Hill, directly in front of Santiago. There were little more than 500 Spaniards at El Caney. But to make sure they were swiftly swept away, Shafter detached more than 6,600 men under General Henry Lawton.

El Caney was home to a little stone church where Cortez allegedly prayed before embarking on his conquest of Mexico. Perhaps that inspired the Spaniards, for they proved far more heroic defenders than the Americans expected. The Spaniards had superior rifles—smokeless Mausers—and from their blockhouses and every scrap of cover they kept the Americans under merciless fire. If Lawton's troops were dismayed at the hailstorm of Spanish bullets, the Spaniards were astonished at how tenaciously and stubbornly the Americans kept attacking. El Caney inevitably fell, but it was a daylong affair.

Lawton was to have joined the attack on San Juan Hill, but detained as he was at the sticky battle of El Caney, the assault on fortified San Juan Hill would have to be conducted without him and his men. Also missing was General Shafter, who was sick. Teddy Roosevelt was not impressed: "Not since the campaign of Crassus against the Parthians has there been so criminally incompetent a General as Shafter; and not since the expedition against Walcheren has there been grosser mismanagement than in this."[31] Still, there was a battle to be won.

It began with a morning's artillery duel, the puncturing of an American observation balloon, and Spanish fire raking into the jungle road on which the American troops—including the Negro 10th Cavalry under First Lieutenant John J. Pershing—had to advance. The Americans were pinned down in the jungle, suffering heavy casualties, and, most maddening, receiving fire from an enemy they couldn't see, to whose smokeless fire they couldn't reply.

Captain William O. Bucky O'Neill, the Irish-born former mayor of Prescott, Arizona, "had a theory," wrote Roosevelt, "that an officer ought never to take cover—a theory which was, of course, wrong." O'Neill told his men: "The Spanish bullet isn't made that will kill me."[32] A few moments later, Roosevelt wrote, "a bullet struck him in the mouth and came out the back of his head."[33]

The torrent of lead would not stop, but the Americans had to take the two hill positions before them: Kettle Hill and San Juan Hill. They literally crawled forward through the jungle up to the slopes of Kettle Hill until they had cleared the forward defenses. Above them, the Spanish were dug in and triggering a barrage of fire. Though he had seen O'Neill shot through the head, Roosevelt rose up and mounted his horse—you couldn't get more conspicuous than that. Rather than crawl on their bellies, he ordered his Rough Riders to charge. They came running, through the buzzing bullets, and leapt into and overwhelmed the Spaniards. Roosevelt was there, too, on foot; his mount, Little Texas, wounded and left at a gate.

There was more work to do. San Juan Hill lay to their left. Supporting fire came from Gatling guns (or "coffee grinders" as some of the troopers called them) that spat rapid-fire rounds into the Spaniards. The Americans charged again. Their numbers looked sparse going up the tall, slick grass of the hill—apparently no match for the entrenched Spaniards who kept an unending stream of bullets whizzing at them (luckily mostly over their heads). But the blue-clad wave breached the crest and jumped into the lines of enemy trenches, Roosevelt firing a vengeful revolver recovered from the USS *Maine*. The fighting went on until dark, with a thin blue line of Americans—Southerner, Cowboy, New Yorker, New Englander, Midwesterner intermingled—holding the Spanish trenches, and leaving Shafter biting his nails until Lawton's men could come and reinforce the boys of San Juan Hill.

Shafter needn't have worried. No straw-hatted Spaniards—no matter how many—could have shifted these conquerors. They wouldn't have allowed it: the hill was theirs, if just. The next line of Spanish defenses—stronger than those they had just attacked—was a scant few hundred yards away, and far from pressing on to Santiago the Americans were themselves digging in. General Wheeler rejected any thought of retreat, though he conceded the Army's lines were attenuated, the men exhausted, and many troopers had gone to the rear with wounds. Even Teddy Roosevelt thought the American position precarious. It was made worse by Spanish shelling and rifle fire, and shortages of food.

San Juan and Kettle Hills had been taken on 1 July. As the wretched hours passed, Shafter took the counsel of his fears and believed he needed to withdraw his men. On Sunday morning, 3 July, a bold junior officer convinced the sick and prostrate Shafter to instead send a message demanding the surrender of Santiago and, failing that, the evacuation of civilians before he bombarded the city.

What really decided the issue was the Navy. The Spanish fleet at Santiago made a break for it, even though the Spanish officers knew it was futile. One Spanish captain remarked: "The sound of my bugles [calling for battle] was the last echo of those which history tells us were sounded at the capture of Granada. It was the signal that four centuries of grandeur were at an end and that Spain was becoming a nation of the fourth class."[34] He was right. The Spanish fleet was sunk at a cost of one American sailor killed, one wounded. The Americans fished more than 1,800 Spaniards out of the water and made them prisoners. On the evening of 3 July, Rear Admiral William T. Sampson had this wire cabled to Washington: "The fleet under my command offer the nation, as a Fourth of July present, the whole of [Admiral Pascual] Cervera's fleet."[35]

Meanwhile, negotiations between Shafter and the Spanish had the benefit of perpetuating a truce. The truce broke down, however, because the Spanish felt that in order to surrender with honor they needed to be in direr straits. The bombardment of the city for two days and the arrival of General Nelson Miles with reinforcements made the situation sufficiently dire. Spanish honor was assuaged and the surrender was made on 17 July 1898.

With the surrender of Santiago, Cuba was won. Puerto Rico was America's, too, falling to General Nelson Miles, who showed the same mastery over Spaniards that he had shown over Indians. Half a world away, Filipino rebels under Emilio Aguinaldo—who on 1 July 1898 declared himself, rather prematurely, president of the Philippines—continued the fight against the Spanish, while Admiral Dewey held Manila Bay. Aguinaldo kept Dewey informed of his progress and also provided intelligence on the Germans who appeared to be offering minor covert assistance to the Spanish forces.

Americans began landing in the Philippines on 30 June—after having snapped up the Spanish island of Guam along the way. On 13 August, Admiral Dewey and General Wesley Merritt adjudged they were ready to take the city of Manila, and with it, the entirety of the Philippines. The Spanish commander had one objective: to surrender to the Americans, not to the rebels, and Dewey and Merritt tried to plan the attack so that no one would get killed. The rebels, however, didn't cooperate, and then the Spanish didn't either, leaving the Americans with some minor fighting to do. But it was over swiftly, thanks to some coolheaded American officers. The Stars and Stripes was raised over Manila, the Spaniards were made prisoners, and the rebels were locked out of the city. It was a deft conclusion to a war that had actually ended the day before.

On 12 August 1898, the French ambassador to the United States signed a peace protocol on behalf of Spain, relinquishing Spanish sovereignty over Cuba, the original casus belli. The eventual peace treaty, worked out over a process of months, gave the United States formerly Spanish Puerto Rico, Guam, and the Philippines. And in the Philippines the United States inherited the war against the *insurrectos,* the chaps who would become "our little brown brothers."

CHAPTER 17

"HALF DEVIL AND HALF CHILD"

From London, the American ambassador John Hay wrote to Teddy Roosevelt, "It has been a splendid little war; begun with the highest motives, carried on with magnificent intelligence and spirit, favored by that fortune that loves the brave."[1] So perhaps it had been, though there were plenty of postwar recriminations about the failure to protect America's soldiers from tropical diseases, which claimed far more lives than had battlefield casualties.[2]

But Americans would have to get used to the tropics, because they had decided to join in shouldering the "White Man's Burden." Rudyard Kipling's poem of that title, written in 1899, marked America's role in the Philippines and welcomed the United States to the Anglo-Saxon imperial mission to fight "the savage wars of peace— / Fill full the mouth of Famine / And bid the sickness cease."[3] Or as Britain's Colonial Secretary Joseph Chamberlain put it: "It can hardly be necessary to say that the British nation will cordially welcome the entrance of the United States into the field of colonial enterprise, so long and so successfully occupied by themselves. There would be no jealousy of the expansion of American enterprise and influence; on the contrary, every Englishman would heartily rejoice in the co-operation of the United States in the great work of tropical civilization."[4]

It is true that President William McKinley could seem a bit ignorant about the tropical civilization he was building. Among his goals, he said, was to "educate the Filipinos, and uplift and civilize and Christianize them, and by God's grace do the very best we could by them, as our fellow-men for whom Christ also died."[5] A noble sentiment, but it rather neglected the fact that most Filipinos had been Catholics since the sixteenth century, when Ferdinand Magellan and the Jesuits arrived. Still, the idea that Filipinos were our "little brown brothers"[6]—in the famous phrase of the American governor of the Philippines, William Howard Taft—expressed the benign intent of the administration.

The young, handsome Republican Senator Albert Beveridge of Indiana—the only member of Congress to have traveled through the Orient and the Philippines and conferred with America's overseas commanders—struck a similar note to President McKinley's. Beveridge was one of the nation's frankest imperialists, though his youthful bumptiousness was considered a handicap in the Senate, where the Treaty of Paris, which included a $20 million payment to Spain for the Philippines, managed to just slip by with a two-thirds majority.

Beveridge echoed McKinley in saying that America had a duty to the Filipinos. But he also spoke of advancing America's legitimate self-interests. By acquiring the Philippines, he said, the United States had positioned itself to be the dominant power in the Pacific. America could be the greatest beneficiary of trade with China. America could, in fact, become the chief power in the world. He cited America's Indian wars to prove that it was no corruption of American ideals to say that the Filipinos were not ready for self-government; and the Indian wars proved that expansion and imperialism were anything but un-American. Here was a destiny similar to taming the continent; America's expansion was meant not to stop at California but to reach across the Pacific, because God, "has marked the American people as His chosen nation to finally lead in the regeneration of the world. This is the divine mission of America. . . . We are trustees of the world's progress, guardians of its righteous peace."[7]

American policy was, it should be noted, not cynical but sincere in believing that American rule over the Philippines was a necessary duty. Having toppled Spain, the United States could not turn around and either give the Philippines to a European power or allow it to be annexed by one. President McKinley was not an imperialist; he had earlier said he wanted "no jingo nonsense."[8] He had not wanted war with Spain nor had he ever had ambitions for the Philippines. But now he had them, and he and his administration judged the Filipinos incapable of self-government—though the United States intended to lift them to that level—and Emilio Aguinaldo, McKinley was informed, was a factional rather than a popular leader. America had no other choice but to accept the duty of helping the Filipinos.

To prove America's good faith as a colonial administrator, the United States began an enormous program of good works: building schools, hospitals, and sewage systems; providing vaccinations against disease; and laying roads for commerce. It was soldiers, at first, who did many of these chores, becoming schoolmasters and construction foremen. But providing good government meant more than that—it meant fighting, because the Filipino rebel leader Emilio

Aguinaldo did not see things the way that Senator Beveridge and President McKinley saw them.

Aguinaldo was convinced he was the perfect man to lead the Philippines. He was unimpressed by Senator Beveridge's call for an American Pacific imperium, perhaps because he was a former provincial mayor and maintained a mayor's provincial mind. But if he did not understand America's manifest destiny, he did understand power and politics. He kept a cordon around Manila, his men lined up in trenches directly facing the American troops.

The mood was tense, Aguinaldo's men restive. There were knifings and scattered brawls with the Americans. Finally, on 4 February 1899, an American sentry shot two rebels dead—the official starting gun of the Philippine Insurrection, which burst into gunfire that night. The following morning, the rebels, who were happy enough fighting during the cool of evening, were stunned to see the Americans roaring out of their lines in a charge—boys from Kansas, Nebraska, and Montana leading the way; this was a war of true western expansion, with most of the troopers coming from states west of the Mississippi.

Shelled by the American Navy, stunned by the cowboys and farmers coming at them with hard-kicking and outdated Springfield .45-caliber rifles and Krag-Jorgensen .30-calibers (in many ways inferior to the Filipinos' German Mausers and American Remingtons, but they were too surprised to notice), the rebel trenches became mass graves. One American trooper joyfully remarked that it was "more fun than a turkey shoot."[9] Nearly 3,000 rebels were killed. American casualties were 59 dead and 300 wounded. But for all the American skill at arms, driving the rebels farther than forty miles from the city proved a problem, because there were a hell of a lot more of them (about 80,000 rebels all told) than there were American troops (about 21,000), who always had to return to Manila.

Emilio Aguinaldo's strategy was simple. It was to hamper and bedevil the United States, to make it bleed in the Philippines, and by his efforts to give strength to anti-imperial movements in America, movements that incorporated not only "goo-goos," but "mugwumps" (liberal Republicans turned self-righteous Democrats), racists (who didn't want any racial mixing with Filipinos), social Darwinists (who wanted nothing to do with the world's poor), Ivy League intellectuals (who played at Voltairean relativism), New England moralists (who had become the vanguard of American liberalism), and a roster of the rich and famous: from Andrew Carnegie to Mark Twain to former president Cleveland.[10] The result in the Philippines was an ugly guerilla war that lived up to Kipling's billing of a savage war of peace.

The 21,000 American troops in the Philippines were hardly an overwhelming force for an archipelago of 7,100 islands. Nevertheless, in stand-up conventional warfare they mauled Aguinaldo's army to the point that his Filipino Congress voted for peace with the Americans. Aguinaldo ignored his own Congress, took his rebel generals (for whom peace would have brought no spoils or power) into the jungles, and vowed to fight on.

Command of the American land forces was in the hands of Major General Ewell Otis, an insomniac with an insomniac's passion for fiddling over details and micromanaging. With him, however, were good officers, including the punctilious division commander General Arthur MacArthur and General Henry Lawton—the picture-perfect colonial soldier who had once helped track Geronimo. By summer 1899, Otis had amassed 60,000 American troops in the Philippines, a number that would continue to grow.[11] But no matter how many men Otis had, it often appeared that little progress was being made.

In the early days of fighting, Americans easily defeated the rebels in large-scale combined operations of gunboats and flying columns of infantry and cavalry. But the guerilla war ground on, and Otis showed no great aptitude for winning it. It was also full of atrocities, as frustrated American soldiers grew contemptuous of an enemy that mutilated American soldiers and that hid behind civilians so that every Filipino became a suspect. The troopers learned not to trust the natives. The Americans were kept agitated and angry by the intense heat, mosquitoes, and feverish tropical diseases that put a third of them on the sick rolls. And when on occasion they found the corpse of an ambushed American with his genitals severed and stuffed in his mouth, they could become dangerous company to any shifty-eyed Filipino.

The troops in the field spat that Otis didn't have the guts to "smash the gugus."[12] And maybe they were right. He was certainly complacent, unlike the dashing General Lawton, who said he could win the war if he were given two regiments and a free hand; he would hunt down Aguinaldo the way he had hunted down Geronimo. For this constructive criticism Otis laughed Lawton out of his headquarters at Malacañang Palace in Manila. Later, Lawton told journalists that the alternative was garrisoning the Philippine Islands. Lawton estimated that would take 100,000 men, but at least it meant progress and victory. Lawton—in every way Otis's superior (except in rank)—died in the field (an area where Otis was notably absent), shot through the lungs by a Filipino sharpshooter named . . . Geronimo.

The Americans were making more progress than perhaps they realized.

Aguinaldo's forces were melting away. Factionalism—including the assassination of a rival general—had consolidated Aguinaldo's power but had weakened his reach. Many Filipinos preferred peace to independence under Aguinaldo; and the Americans were successfully establishing local governing bodies that combined elected Filipinos with U.S. military advisers. In April 1900, President McKinley shipped to the Philippines his secret weapon, the 300-pound judge William Howard Taft.

Like McKinley, Taft was not a jingo, and while he thought such imperial holdings like the Philippines were constitutional he didn't think them necessary or wise. For that reason alone, McKinley was inclined to trust him. They also agreed on the future: now that the United States was saddled with responsibility for the Philippines, America owed the islanders the sort of tutelage that would eventually lead them to self-government. Taft brought other advantages as well. He was a hard man for critics to assail; he was a man not only of girth, but of stature and rectitude—a federal circuit judge no less (and by taking over as governor of the Philippines had guaranteed himself the quid pro quo of a nomination to the Supreme Court). So Otis departed and American authority in the Philippines rested on the twin pillars of Taft and General Arthur MacArthur.

MacArthur considered Taft a rival. The general—an imperialist and realist—understood not only the grim reality of guerilla war but the psychology of the Filipinos, who "acted openly in behalf of the Americans and secretly in behalf of the insurgents, and, paradoxical as it may seem, with considerable apparent solicitude for the interests of both."[13] As such, the only way to win the war was to annihilate the insurgents as a military force. As befitted their experiences, MacArthur saw the insurrection as a military problem (an enemy to be obliterated) while Taft saw it as a legal one (murderers to be incarcerated so that peaceable people could go about their business), but the result was much the same: a determination to win the war.

Taft expanded and accelerated the good works programs that MacArthur thought were so much self-deceiving hearts-and-minds mollycoddling. Taft took a low view of the Filipinos—most, he thought, were barbarous, and the tiny, educated elite were schemers—but his colonial administration successfully oversaw the creation of a pro-American political movement. This movement's gravest setback came not in the Philippines but when Secretary of State Elihu Root told them plainly that the Philippines would never become a state of the Union. Still, Filipinos became more prominent in the American administration of the islands. American intelligence gathering benefited enormously from

Filipinos turning against the increasingly isolated insurgents. When President McKinley was resoundingly reelected in 1900, Aguinaldo's hope of an anti-imperialist administration vanished.

More than that, the Americans finally pinpointed Aguinaldo's lair, and Frederick Funston launched a daring scheme to capture him. Funston was a stocky Kansan adventurer who had fought as a soldier of fortune for the Cuban rebels, and then gone back to Cuba as a colonel of Kansas volunteers. He was in the Philippines from the start of the insurrection and led from the front. Promoted for bravery, he was now a thirty-five-year-old brigadier general of United States Volunteers. In his hands, he held a decoded captured dispatch from Aguinaldo requesting reinforcements. Funston decided his Macabebe scouts would pose as these reinforcements and Funston and his men would pose as their prisoners. Together, they would walk into Aguinaldo's camp and capture the rebel leader. Arthur MacArthur approved the plan saying, "Funston, this is a desperate undertaking. I fear that I shall never see you again."[14]

The desperate undertaking worked. Funston returned with his prisoner and acted the nonchalant hero. But the normally formal-minded Arthur MacArthur was jubilant in his pajamas, congratulating Funston and treating Aguinaldo with every military courtesy. Aguinaldo publicly announced that he accepted American rule over the Philippines and called on his followers to surrender. Many did, though some did not, including, on the island of Samar, a band of *insurrectos* who—with bolos they had smuggled inside of coffins—hacked to death forty-eight American troops who had sat down to breakfast. It was the sort of incident that made for bad newspaper stories. It also made for angry American soldiers, who found the bodies of their comrades grotesquely desecrated.

The American administration wanted action. The massacre on Samar was regarded as the greatest American military catastrophe since Custer's Last Stand. Three weeks earlier, on 6 September 1901, President McKinley had been assassinated. The new president, Theodore Roosevelt, was the American imperialist par excellence and wanted stern retribution to end the war.

The answer was obvious—send in the Marines as part of a special brigade to root out the insurgents on Samar. In overall command was Army Brigadier General "Hell-Roaring Jake" Smith, a veteran of the War Between the States and the Indian wars. Commanding the Marines was a gung-ho major from an old Virginia family, Littleton W. T. Waller, who had seen action around the world, from Egypt to Cuba to China. And tagging along was a Marine captain from an old Navy family, David D. Porter, whose grandfather was Admiral David

Dixon Porter of Vicksburg fame (slightly farther back was Captain David Porter of the war against the Barbary pirates). "Hell-Roaring Jake" gained a new nickname when he issued his orders. He wanted Samar turned into a "howling wilderness." And he added, "I want no prisoners. I wish you to kill and burn, the more you kill and burn the better you will please me. I want all persons killed who are capable of bearing arms in actual hostilities against the United States"—which to his mind included anyone over the age of ten.[15]

"Howling Wilderness" Smith admonished Major Waller, whose southern chivalry recoiled at these orders, to remember: "Short severe wars are the most humane in the end." In the meantime, as a matter of prudence, said General Smith, every Filipino should be "treated as an enemy until he has conclusively shown that he is a friend."[16]

From a purely military point of view, the campaign was a success. But when it was revealed that American troops had tortured Filipinos and that prisoners had been shot, Waller and Smith were forced to stand trial. Waller, who was far less at fault, behaved honorably and tried to protect Smith. Smith, however, dishonorably tried to blame Waller. Justice was served: Waller was acquitted and Smith was forced into retirement, though he remained a hero to the troops who believed he had done what needed to be done against a treacherous enemy.

Despite the trial, and the howls of the anti-imperialist press—Mark Twain thought the stars in the flag should be replaced by skulls and crossbones—the war was pressed aggressively. Filipinos were relocated from hostile areas into garrisoned camps while American troops thoroughly scoured the countryside of rebels. While sporadic fighting continued, especially with the Moros (Muslim Filipinos) and occasional headhunters, the insurgency was finished as an organized movement. The last rebel commander surrendered on 16 April 1902. On 4 July 1902, Teddy Roosevelt felt it was safe to say the war was over and won. Five years later, the Filipinos had the first elected legislature in Asia. The ideal of Filipinos becoming our little brown brothers was actually fulfilled, as the vast majority of Filipinos found American rule beneficent and benevolent, and Americans began to think that the gugus—that is, the Filipinos, not the goo-goo American isolationists—had their good points, too.

Elsewhere in Asia, America divided Samoa with the Germans—after a bit of fighting of course—and Secretary of State John Hay issued his "Open Door" (1899) policy for China, demanding free access of all powers to Chinese markets. The Open Door policy also committed America to a sort of Asian Monroe

Doctrine, declaring that the United States stood fully in support of the territorial integrity of an independent China. Quite how the United States could give effective force to this policy was open to question, which might help explain why the European powers recognized it as a diplomatic formality to which they could agree and as a patent, polite falsehood that they could ignore.

Indeed, America and the other imperial powers in China quickly became military allies. American interests in China were not just those of trade but, more important, the physical protection of Christian missionaries. When the anti-Christian, anti-European Boxer Rebellion broke out in China (with covert support from the imperial Chinese government) in 1900, the United States Marines helped defend the besieged European and Japanese delegations in Peking and then cooperated with the other powers in smashing the rebels of "the Fists of Harmonious Righteousness."

Elsewhere, Teddy Roosevelt, with his motto of speaking softly and carrying a big stick, sent the U.S. Navy's "Great White Fleet" on a goodwill mission around the world, promoting diplomacy and displaying the hardware with which he could carry it out. He also used his big stick to dig out the Panama Canal after recognizing Panamanian independence from Colombia in 1903—an independence movement the administration had quietly encouraged. And in the spirit of the Monroe Doctrine, somewhat expanded, the United States became the policeman of the Caribbean and Latin America.

Teddy Roosevelt's chosen successor as president was William Howard Taft. But the fat Unitarian so disappointed the Rough Rider colonel that TR ran against him in 1912 as a third party Bull Moose candidate. The unfortunate result was the election of a Democrat: the prim, Presbyterian, Princeton professor Woodrow Wilson. Wilson did not believe in speaking softly and carrying a big stick. He believed in delivering sermons on international morality, every so often punctuating them with the force of a ruler across the knuckles, while posing as a man too proud—and too proper anyway—to fight. So it was in 1914 that Wilson felt obliged to teach the government of General Victoriano Huerta the error of not achieving power the proper way, through a ballot rather than a coup, though the latter was a Mexican tradition. So the U.S. Navy and Marine Corps—and Frederick Funston, now a U.S. Army brigadier general—were dispatched to seize Vera Cruz, which they did with their usual éclat, the Marines led first by Colonel John A. Lejeune and then by Colonel L. W. T. Waller, the conqueror of Samar.

Having taken Vera Cruz, the American forces waited three months for Huerta to resign, and then another five months while Wilson conducted diplomacy over their heads. They were not, alas, ordered to finish the job of the first Mexican War and annex the country—another opportunity missed. And Wilson would pay for it in 1916 when the thug and revolutionary Pancho Villa began murdering American citizens in Mexico and even raided Columbus, New Mexico. General "Black Jack" John J. Pershing of the United States Army—an Indian fighter and Moro tamer—was assigned the task of tracking him down. Pershing brought more than 6,500 men 300 miles into Mexican territory along the eastern side of the Sierra Madres. Pershing didn't find Villa, but American troops did tangle with Mexican ones. Wilson, ever too tentative, held back from declaring war.

As it was, the punitive expedition to Mexico merely provided outdoor amusement for the Army, including a couple of young, daring, handy-with-a-pistol lieutenants named Douglas MacArthur and George Patton. Patton had the right idea when he led a raid against a Villaist headquarters, gunned down a Villa general, and saw two other rebels get dropped as well. Patton strapped the banditos to his cars like bagged deer and drove back to camp, demonstrating the good stewardship of a hunter and sheriff. The bandit dead were given all due respects, an American sergeant saying the words over the graves: "Ashes to ashes and dust to dust, / If Villa won't bury you, Uncle Sam must."[17] Aside from these religious services, nothing much was achieved. Patton blamed President Wilson: "He has not the soul of a louse nor the mind of a worm or the backbone of a jelly fish."[18]

All true, of course, but Wilson did use the Marines to rap nasty boys in Haiti, the Dominican Republic, and Cuba, and he followed up on a plan, which former secretary of state William Seward had earlier proposed, to annex the Virgin Islands. The Marines patrolled, essentially governed, and fought in the Caribbean for the next two decades. In Haiti they built up an infrastructure that, when the leathernecks departed, the natives destroyed, but it included "1,000 miles of roads constructed, 210 major bridges, 9 major airfields, 1,250 miles of telephone lines, 82 miles of irrigation canals, 11 modern hospitals, 147 rural clinics, and on and on. . . . All built by the occupiers at little cost to U.S. taxpayers . . . [because] the administrators of Hispaniola were expected to finance their governments out of customs revenue."[19] Such was the sordid result of imperialism. For the Caribbean islanders, glorious independence—and poverty, hunger, and disease—would follow.

CHAPTER 18

"COME ON, YOU SONS OF BITCHES! DO YOU WANT TO LIVE FOREVER?"

I N   A U G U S T   1 9 1 4, Armageddon came to Europe. Most Americans thought it was none of our business. The United States Army War College warned otherwise.

In a report, issued in 1914, it stated: "The safeguard of isolation no longer exists. The oceans, once barriers, are now easy avenues of approach by reason of the number, speed and carrying capacity of ocean-going vessels. The increasing radii of submarine, the aeroplane, and wireless telegraphy, all supplement ocean transport in placing both our Atlantic and Pacific coasts within the sphere of hostile activities of overseas nations." The report added: "The great mass of the public does not yet realize the effect of these changed conditions upon our scheme of defense."[1]

Naval guns sounded immediately in the Western Hemisphere—proving the War College's point—as German and British ships contested Latin American neutrality rights. In November 1914, the British met their first naval defeat in a hundred years—not in the North Atlantic, but off the coast of Chile, when a German squadron under the command of Vice Admiral Graf Maximilian von Spee sank two British ships, killing 1,600 men, at the Battle of Coronel. The British had their revenge off the Falkland Islands, sinking six German ships, and killing 2,200 German sailors, including von Spee and his two sons.

Lurking beneath the surface were the German U-boats (*Unterseeboots*). At the outset of the war, the British blockaded the European continent, just as they had done in the war against Napoleon. In retaliation, German U-boats (submarines) threatened to sink ships at will in the waters around Britain and Ireland. In April 1915, Germany informed the United States that the British luxury liner the *Lusitania* would be carrying not just passengers from New York to Britain, but munitions for the British army and more than sixty Canadian soldiers.

The German government took out an advertisement—approved by President Wilson's secretary of state, William Jennings Bryan—in the New York papers warning Americans not to book passage on the ship. Would-be passengers scoffed at the German threat: on the passenger list were such prominent Americans as the millionaire Arthur Vanderbilt. The *Lusitania* was big, fast, and outfitted with guns as a precaution. No one showed fear; no one, indeed, could imagine that the Germans would, in the event, fire on a luxury passenger ship.

But off the coast of Ireland, a German U-boat launched a single torpedo that sank the *Lusitania,* killing 1,195 passengers and crew, including 95 children and 124 Americans. The Americans killed aboard the *Lusitania* were not the first whose lives had been lost to U-boats, but they tipped American opinion decisively against Germany.

The sinking of the *Lusitania* fit a broader picture of German conduct in the war—conduct that appeared guided by Nietzschean amorality,[2] beginning with the German invasion of Belgium in August 1914.[3] When Britain declared war over the violation of Belgian neutrality,[4] German Chancellor Theobold von Bethmann-Hollweg professed himself stunned that "Just for the sake of a scrap of paper Great Britain is going to make war on a kindred nation."[5]

It is fashionable to write smirkingly about the "myth" of the German "rape of Belgium" in 1914. The "myth," however, is a fact,[6] and the German war against Belgian civilians registered heavily in Anglo-American public opinion. So did the German destruction of the city of Louvain (August 1914), including its celebrated library; so did the German bombardment of Rheims Cathedral (September 1914); and so too did the execution of the British Red Cross nurse Edith Cavell (12 October 1915), who was convicted of helping wounded Allied prisoners escape into neutral Holland.

The idea that the First World War was a war—in the West at least—pitting humane liberal democracy against unbridled Prussian militarism had facts in its favor,[7] and Britain made a powerful rhetorical case to that effect in the United States. The sinking of the *Lusitania* was another—and characteristic—charge on the bill of indictment. It was as much—or more of—a casus belli than had been the explosion of the *Maine.*

But President Wilson declared: "There is such a thing as a man being too proud to fight."[8] And such, most demonstrably, was he. Wilson's secretary of war, Newton D. Baker, was a pacifist. So was Wilson's secretary of the Navy, Josephus Daniels. Newton Baker was, in addition, a lawyer, a Wilsonian idealist, and a man without military experience; Josephus Daniels was a newspaperman, not a Navy man (though his father had been a shipbuilder), a Democrat Party cheerleader, and a temperance agitator who encouraged sailors to drink coffee ("hence a cup of Joe") rather than rum.

Then there was Secretary of State William Jennings Bryan, another pacifist, whom Teddy Roosevelt accurately pegged as "a third rate revivalist preacher . . . and a not wholly sincere revivalist preacher at that."[9] Bryan purported not to see any difference between a country sinking ships loaded with civilian passengers and Britain's maintenance of a naval blockade against Germany—a moral blindness perhaps made clearer by the difference between Lincoln's blockade of the South and an imagined Union policy of blowing up Southern passenger ships.

In comparing Wilson to Bryan, Teddy Roosevelt noted, "The President, unlike Mr. Bryan, uses good English and does not say things that are on their face ridiculous. Unfortunately, his cleverness of style and his refusal to face facts apparently make him believe that he really has dismissed and done away with ugly realities whenever he has uttered some pretty phrase about them."[10]

Wilson's pretty phrase about being too proud to fight was couched in a demand that Germany apologize for sinking the *Lusitania,* pay reparations, and "prevent the recurrence of anything so obviously subversive of the principles of warfare." A month later he added a specific first principle that America would insist upon: "The lives of noncombatants cannot lawfully or rightfully be put in jeopardy by the capture and destruction of an unresisting merchantman."[11] Bryan thought this far too harsh. It would, he warned, goad Germany into war with the United States. Wilson stuck by it, and Bryan resigned. The Germans were less apoplectic than Byran was and agreed to Wilson's demands.

Teddy Roosevelt blamed the sinking of the *Lusitania* on the Wilson administration's lack of big stick diplomacy earlier in the war and its failure to condemn German atrocities. The Rough Rider colonel railed against Wilson's "abject cowardice and weakness" and said that Wilson "and Bryan are morally responsible for the loss of the lives of those American women and children. . . . They are both of them abject creatures and they won't go to war unless they are kicked into it."[12] Roosevelt thought America should already be at the side of Britain and France. He wrote his son Archie that "Every soft creature, every coward and weakling, every man who can't look more than six inches ahead, every man whose god is money, or pleasure, or ease, and every man who has not got in him both the sterner virtues and the power of seeking after an ideal, is enthusiastically in favor of Wilson."[13]

William Jennings Bryan feared Wilson was far too belligerent and joined with pacifist congressmen to agitate against military preparedness. He opposed the voluntary officer-training program, paid for by the volunteers, known as "the Plattsburgh movement," and pushed for Congress to prohibit free American travel on the merchant ships of combatant powers.

Americans continued to be killed at sea. In March 1916, a German U-boat sank an unarmed British steamer (the *Sussex*) without warning. Eighty civilians, some of them Americans, went down with the ship. On 1 April 1916, an American steamer (the *Aztec*) was torpedoed, and the Wilson administration and the kaiser's government redid their mutual demands and pledges stemming from the sinking of the *Lusitania*.

But Wilson did something else, too. He recognized that if he was going to continue lecturing the world—which, as a professor, he was fond of doing—and if he was going to adequately defend the United States at a time of world war among the European powers, he needed a Navy that could deliver his message in words that everyone understood. With two vast coasts and commerce that extended across the Pacific and the Atlantic, the United States needed the largest Navy in the world and a greatly enlarged Merchant Marine.

The 1916 Naval Appropriation Act and United States Shipping Board Act proposed to give the United States just that: a Navy bigger than the combined forces of any two other navies and fifty million dollars that would be devoted to building and buying for the Merchant Marine. To those of an Alfred Thayer Mahan disposition, this was simple common sense, even if it rattled the large pacifist tendency in Wilson's Democrat Party. Wilson campaigned for reelection in 1916 as "the man who kept us out of war." As such, enlarging the Navy and the United States Merchant Marine were only acts of prudence. German U-boats coursed through the Atlantic. German saboteurs were widely suspected (and much later proven) to have blown up an American ammunition dump on Black Tom Island, New York, damaging the Statue of Liberty and shattering windows in Brooklyn. On more than one occasion in 1916, German U-boats turned up in American harbors and sank ships just off America's coastal waters. Documents were found proving a network of German subsidized propaganda and subversion, including paying American union leaders to organize strikes.[14]

The Wilson administration wanted to be neutral in thought and deed—that was its platform. Wilson was so wedded to it that his secretary of state, Robert Lansing (Bryan's replacement), feared that the president might actually intervene on the side of the Central Powers after the British suppression of the Easter

Rebellion in Ireland in 1916, British and French interception of American mail, and British blacklisting of American firms that traded with Germany.

Reelected in 1916, Wilson began 1917 by announcing his eagerness to negotiate "peace without victory," a proposal that was inevitably treated contemptuously by all sides in the European struggle. On 31 January 1917, Wilson was informed that Germany was renewing its policy of unrestricted U-boat warfare. Wilson, in protest, severed diplomatic relations with Germany.

The Germans, however, had calculated that they could win the war before the Americans roused themselves to intervene. In 1914, the kaiser had dismissed the British Expeditionary Force (BEF) as "a contemptible little army," a name the BEF adopted as its own, as the "Old Contemptibles." Now the kaiser made the same mistake of dismissing what on paper seemed an even smaller and more contemptible little army, that of the United States. When the kaiser and his generals looked at Wilson, how could they not sneer: a commander in chief who was too proud to fight, who believed in peace without victory, and who refused to put his army and navy on a war footing lest this be thought provocative. Such a man did not impress those who put their trust in "reeking tube and iron shard."[15]

Wilson now spoke in favor of "armed neutrality," which meant armed American merchant ships, something that became rather more pressing after the Germans sank the American merchant vessel the *Algonquin* on 12 March 1917. Three more American merchant ships were sunk less than a week later. And then British intelligence handed Wilson the proverbial bombshell: the transcript of a cable sent from the German Foreign Secretary Alfred Zimmerman to the German minister in Mexico. The "Zimmerman Telegram" proposed a German-Mexican alliance, encouraged Mexico's seizure of Texas, New Mexico, and Arizona, and importuned Mexican diplomats to convince Japan to end its alliance with Britain and attack the United States, perhaps, though this was unstated, with Hawaii, the Philippines, or even California as a prize.

Wilson made the note public in March—the same month the czar abdicated his throne, granting Russia a brief interim of liberal (actually, moderate socialist) government. The departure of the czar made Russia a more palatable potential ally to American democrats,[16] and the sensation of the Zimmerman Telegram made the Allies' cause inescapably America's cause.[17] It had, for some Americans, been America's cause from the beginning. These feelings were particularly strong in the Anglophilic educated classes of the South, the East Coast, and the West Coast, some of whose sons crossed the border into Canada to join the

Canadian armed forces. Others went directly to France and enlisted in the French Foreign Legion or signed up as pilots, forming the Lafayette Escadrille, or volunteered to drive ambulances. Fifteen thousand Americans were in the war before the United States was. The U-boat sinkings and the Zimmerman Telegram won over the masses, and American opinion shifted dramatically in favor of joining the war on the side of Britain and France.

On 2 April 1917, President Wilson issued his "War Messages," affirming that the United States had "no quarrel with the German people," but only with the German autocracy that had forced war upon the United States and Europe. "The world," Wilson proclaimed, "must be made safe for democracy."[18] And it would be the doughboys of the American Expeditionary Force who would be charged to do it.

OVER THERE

THE AMERICANS ARRIVED just in time. The Russian front had collapsed; Bolsheviks had seized power from the gormless provisional government of Alexander Kerensky. The Bolshevik government sued for peace and was bludgeoned into accepting the harsh terms of the Treaty of Brest-Litovsk, which stripped Finland, the Baltic states, Poland, the Ukraine, Belarus, and the Caucasus from greater Russia. The Italian front, too, was in danger. The Italian army had collapsed, and Italy was held only through the efforts of Britain and France, who rushed troops to Italy's defense. On the western front, the battered Allies now faced a stronger Germany. France's northern fields were a trenchwork of desolation, the killing grounds of millions—and the French were facing mutinies within the ranks of the *poilus*. The American Rear Admiral William Sims, meeting with Britain's first sea lord, Admiral Sir John Jellicoe, discovered that the toll of the German U-boats on Allied shipping was so great—and accelerating at such a devastating pace—that Britain was "within measurable distance of strangulation," adding that for the British: "It is impossible to go on with the war if losses like this continue."[19] The German Admiral Henning von Holtzendorff was equally confident of Germany's U-boat prowess. He predicted: "England will lie flat on the ground before a single American soldier sets foot on the Continent."[20]

America was—thanks to the power of the pacifists in Congress—forced to raise, train, and deploy a mass army nearly from scratch. Wilson signed the Selective Service Act—initiating military conscription—in May 1917. The Army grew, during the course of the war, from 200,000 men (including National Guardsmen) to nearly 3,700,000 men who had to be equipped, trained, and (half of them at least) transported overseas. That the Americans arrived safely in France was a tribute to Vice Admiral Sims, who was able to teach the British a thing or two about antisubmarine precautions: both in the laying of mines and, most important, arranging protective convoys around merchant ships and troopships. It was the United States Navy that finally dispelled the terror of the U-boats.

Leading the American Expeditionary Force (AEF) was General "Black Jack" Pershing, who kept an iron grip on his independent command. His men were not to be offered as piecemeal replacements for devastated Allied units. As the ever-diffident President Wilson required, they were to be the forces of an "associated" rather than an "allied" power,[21] and therefore were to remain the independent, unfungible AEF. The first American troops arrived in France in time for a Fourth of July parade in Paris, where Colonel Charles Stanton announced to the joyous Parisians: "Lafayette, we are here!"[22]

The demoralized French *poilus* were stunned to see American troops marching down dusty roads belting out songs, most especially George M. Cohan's "Over There"; they were astounded at the Americans' confidence, their belief that one could "pack up your troubles in your old kitbag and smile, smile, smile," and their certainty that they would win the war for the Allies. The French were equally amazed that American officers were charged with keeping their men clean from foreign debasements of the skirted and bottled variety. Lieutenant Colonel George S. Patton sided with the French on this issue: "We are getting full of virtue here. I don't think much of it. The French do as they please so why not we."[23]

But when it came to fighting, the Americans came at it with a relish the French had long forgotten. When Americans filed into the trenches of a quiet sector along the Swiss border, where the French and German troops had arranged an informal armistice, the Americans lit things up, sending shells into the German lines and not playing the game of "run away" when the Germans retaliated by charging the American lines.

For the Americans, the real fighting began in the spring of 1918, when German General Erich Ludendorff—de facto ruler of the Reich with General Paul von Hindenburg—launched the most vigorous western offensive since 1914.

Ludendorff had achieved stunning success against the Russians, ripping a third of Russia's territory and half its industry from the hands of the Bolsheviks and retaining it for the Reich. This came, however, at the cost of keeping fifty German divisions (one million men) in the east to occupy these territories and expand them. German hubris—a long-standing problem in German history—led the Reich to overplay its hand. Had Ludendorff been content with merely putting up a defensive front against a prostrate Russia, he could have diverted half of his eastern divisions to the western front for his spring offensive. Even without them, the offensive nearly succeeded.

In March 1918, Ludendorff attacked the British, and, at heavy cost, began driving them back. The British bent—indeed, bent badly. In the course of Ludendorff's repeated assaults, the British fell back nearly to the French General Headquarters at Compiègne and within five miles of Amiens, a railway center and British supply depot. But unlike the Russians, the French, and the Italians, the British did not break under the relentless German pounding. British Field Marshal Douglas Haig stiffened his troops with his famous "Backs to the Wall" order, which read in part:

> Three weeks ago today the Enemy began his terrific attack against us on a 50-mile front. His objects are to separate us from the French, to take the Channel ports and destroy the British Army. . . . There is no other course open to us but to fight it out! Every position must be held to the last man: there must be no retirement. With our backs to the wall, and believing in the justice of our cause, each of us must fight on to the end. The safety of our homes and the freedom of mankind alike depend on the conduct of each one of us at this critical moment.[24]

The Tommies held. In May, Ludendorff shifted his attack—as American intelligence had warned he would, though the French generals ignored the warning—against the French Sixth Army. The Germans exploded through the French lines, driving to within forty miles of Paris. Ludendorff's lunge had broken the deadlock of the trenches;[25] the French government prepared to flee. Demoralized French troops pillaged the homes and farmhouses of their own people. It appeared to be the end.

But now, at the second great battle of the Marne, the Americans joined with French troops ordered into the front lines by General Ferdinand Foch—the newly elevated and first supreme Allied commander. Foch ordered a counterattack. American Army units plugged the gap at Château-Thierry, and the United States Marine Corps was sent against German positions at Belleau Wood. Fleeing French troops yelled at the Marines to retreat. Marine Captain Lloyd Williams responded: "Retreat? Hell, we just got here."[26]

On 6 June 1918, the Marines began their assault. The leathernecks had little artillery support and faced a hailstorm of lead from German machine guns. As he leapt toward the enemy and waved his men forward, veteran Marine Gunnery Sergeant Dan Daly growled the immortal words: "Come on, you sons of bitches! Do you want to live forever?"[27] His Devil Dogs responded, charging into the storm of steel. It took the Marines twenty days, nearly 5,000 casualties (more than 1,000 killed),[28] and some usually unremarked-upon assistance from U.S. Army infantry to wrest Belleau Wood from the Germans. But wrested it was in the bloodiest battle in the Corps's history, to be surpassed only in World War II.

The Americans certainly impressed the Germans. German intelligence noted: "The Second American Division [Army and Marines] must be considered a very good one and may even be reckoned a storm troop. The different attacks on Belleau Wood were carried out with bravery and dash. The moral effect of our gunfire cannot seriously impede the advance of the American infantry. . . . The qualities of the men individually may be described as remarkable. . . . [T]he words of a prisoner are characteristic—'WE KILL OR WE GET KILLED.' "[29]

The Germans probed for another opening to reach Paris, but the Allies were now wise enough to practice defense-in-depth, which meant that German artillery barrages fell on thinly manned front trenches, and any advance of German infantry would be halted by unscathed secondary lines. It worked well, save when—as happened to one Pennsylvania National Guard unit—the French abandoned the Americans, leaving the Yanks to fend for themselves: the Americans did, in a heroic rearguard action, though only a few managed to escape capture.

On another part of the line, the 38th U.S. Infantry of the 3rd Division under the command of Colonel Ulysses Grant McAlexander—a bottom-of-the-class graduate of West Point but experienced in the Indian Wars and the Philippines—repelled no less than six German attacks, and in the process virtually eliminated the German 6th Grenadiers as a unit. The Americans had achieved this even though the French (seemingly as usual) had abandoned them, leaving the Americans surrounded on three sides and under such intense fire that Captain Jesse

Woolridge's uniform bore fourteen bullet holes (though Woolridge was miraculously unscathed). From this action, the 38th won the nom de guerre "The Rock of the Marne."

The Germans pressed on, squeezing out more ground, but it was a last gasp that set them up for General Foch's counterstroke: French, American, Moroccan, and Senegalese troops, as well as French Foreign Legionnaires, charged into the Germans, shoving them back across the Marne River. When the Moroccans failed to keep pace with their assigned targets, it was the Marines of the 2nd Division of the AEF who filled in, attacking the German positions. Elsewhere, when a battalion commander of the 1st Division said the Germans had stopped him, General Charles Summerall rebuked him: "You may have stopped for reorganization. If you ever send a message with the word *stopped* in it, you will be sent to the rear for reclassification."[30]

Foch's counterattack—and the American part in it—was so sweeping that it turned the Germans from expecting victory to expecting defeat. Said German Chancellor Georg Hertling: "At the beginning of July, 1918, I was convinced, I confess it, that before the first of September our adversaries would send us peace proposals. . . . We expected grave events in Paris for the end of July. That was on the 15th. On the 18th even the most optimistic of us knew that all was lost. The history of the world was played out in three days."[31]

The German army had eviscerated Russia. It had crumpled Serbia, Romania, and Italy. It had demoralized the armies of France. And yet, on the western front—now the decisive front—the bulldog British and the hard-charging Americans had held the line and then advanced, shifting the tide so that imminent German domination of the European continent became imminent German defeat. Berlin had no counter to Pershing's men: doughboys, more than a million of them were training with mock rifles stateside and then roaring onto French battlefields with an élan long lost by the French. In this war the United States was not the arsenal of democracy—that honor belonged to Britain and France, who supplied many of the guns, supplies, and transports, as well as many of the engineers and doctors for the AEF. But the United States was the unmatchable source of manpower that was the despair of the German General Staff.

All along the line, British, French, and American troops pushed ahead. The German troops fought well in retreat, but on 11 August 1918, Ludendorff confessed to the kaiser that victory was impossible. The challenge for the Germans was to hold the Hindenburg Line[32] running from Belgium through northern France to the Swiss border. The line often ran to a depth of three miles and could include three or four lines of fortifications. If the line held—and the Germans thought it impregnable—the battlefront would be kept in France, and peace could be negotiated on German terms. But the Allies smelled blood. They expected another year of fighting—into 1919—but they no longer had their backs against the wall; they had visions of their bayonets piercing into Berlin.

Pershing made meticulous preparations for a campaign to crush the St. Mihiel salient of the Hindenburg Line. The French were to divert the German center at St. Mihiel, while the Americans struck both flanks. The battle began 11 September 1918 when the Allied guns opened up, including giant U.S. Navy guns, transported on French rail lines, and sited by future Nobel Prize winner and telescope builder Captain Edwin Hubble. The Americans, blessed by fog, charged under its cover and through a storm of fire. They had other support too. Nearly 1,500 planes—the largest number of aircraft ever assembled in the war, British, French (half of the planes were French), Italian, Portuguese, and American (about a third of the force was American)—were put under the command of Brigadier General Billy Mitchell of the U.S. Army Air Service. Included among his pilots was the American ace Captain Eddie Rickenbacker, who would notch twenty-six kills in the war. Mitchell's mission was to hit both sides of the salient, strafe the Germans, destroy German airfields, and offer support to the infantry. The American planes flew 3,300 sorties.

Another innovation was tanks. They were deployed for battle but quickly became mired in mud, much to the disgust of their American commander, Lieutenant Colonel George S. Patton. Before America had entered the war, Patton had requested leave to serve in the French cavalry (he admired the French more than the British). That plan was foiled, and instead of commanding horseflesh he was commanding steel—steel that was now stuck in the mud. So he marched across the battlefield, erect through shell fire, and berated a soldier for lying in a trench, not realizing the soldier was dead. He also met Brigadier General Douglas MacArthur of the famous 42nd "Rainbow" Division (so named because its men came from all across the country). The two officers stood while enemy shells crept up on them. Patton acknowledged: "We stood and talked but neither was much interested in what the other said as we could not get our minds off the shells." MacArthur remembered that he admonished Patton: "Don't worry, major [sic]; you never hear the one that gets you."[33]

The St. Mihiel campaign lasted a week, liberated 200 miles of French territory that had been occupied for four years, and stunned the German high command. The Germans had been in the process of withdrawing when the Americans attacked. German war-planners expected an orderly fighting withdrawal; they never expected to see their troops routed. German morale was obviously slipping. Sergeant Harry Adams of the 89th Division herded 300 Germans out of a trench with an empty pistol.

The victorious Americans were immediately pulled from St. Mihiel and thrown into their biggest battle of the war, at the Meuse-Argonne. Colonel George C. Marshall was charged with the logistical nightmare of getting them there, and General Pershing was made personally responsible to General Foch for the AEF's success in this next campaign. In the vast Allied advance, the Americans had the hardest part.

THE MEUSE-ARGONNE

THE AMERICANS WERE ASSIGNED to spearhead an advance along the Meuse River through the Argonne forest—a sector held and heavily fortified by the Germans for four years. General Pershing noted: "In my opinion no other Allied troops had the morale or the offensive spirit to overcome successfully the difficulties to be met in the Meuse-Argonne sector. . . . The entire sector of 150 kilometers was accordingly placed under my command, including all French divisions in that zone."[34]

The Meuse-Argonne campaign began on 26 September and would be fought to the end of the war. The initial American attack stalled with heavy casualties—including Patton, who suffered a severe wound to the thigh—but with notable moments of heroism: including Corporal Alvin York's single-handed capture of more than 130 Germans, killing 25 others, and destroying 35 German machine gun nests; Captain Frank Williams's liberation of an American prisoner by quick-drawing his pistol (he was a western sheriff) and shooting four of the five Germans who were guarding the captured doughboy; First Lieutenant Samuel Woodfill's solo adventure that eliminated four enemy machine gun nests (when he ran out of ammunition, he showed Yankee ingenuity, fighting with captured enemy pickaxes until his company caught up to him); and the Lost Battalion of the 77th Division that was trapped behind enemy lines but refused to surrender (it was finally rescued).

Hampered though the Americans were by heavy battlefield losses and an epidemic of influenza, the Yanks kept driving forward even if the gains were modest. They were too modest for General Foch, who upbraided General Pershing for not keeping up with the rest of the Allied advance (which included American units operating with the British and the French to crack the Hindenburg Line). Pershing pointed out that his troops faced the toughest sector of all; Foch countered that he cared only for results. Foch's hauteur was diplomatic and reserved compared to that of French Premier Georges Clemenceau, who wanted Pershing sacked. But Pershing, unruffled, knew exactly what was up: with victory in sight, the French were looking to discredit the Americans and reap the laurels for themselves.

The return of the 2nd Division to Pershing's command—it had been loaned to the French to attack Mont Blanc—helped provide the breakthrough in the Meuse-Argonne. By 3 November 1918 most of the German entrenchments were breached in a spectacular American advance against what Pershing admiringly called the Germans' "desperate tenacity and . . . rare skill of experienced soldiers."[35] The Germans did not fall into headlong flight; they retreated, in the words of war correspondent Floyd Gibbons, "as a Western 'bad man' would back out of a saloon with an automatic pistol in each hand."[36]

The tide, however, was rising against the Germans. At the end of September, the Central Powers had lost their ally Bulgaria. At the end of October, the Ottoman Empire had been defeated. And on 4 November 1918, a rejuvenated Italy had—with Allied help—compelled Austria's surrender. The Germans were alone, and even their troops were showing signs, here and there, of the Bolshevism that had toppled the czar. German sailors mutinied; mutiny spread to the army; revolutionaries waved the red flag; and Bavaria declared itself a republic. With Germany teetering, Prince Maximillian von Baden began a reluctant correspondence with the United States government to achieve an armistice under the terms of President Wilson's "Fourteen Points"[37] (which the Allies, especially the French, had already repudiated). But Wilson refused to deal with the German regime, demanding its dissolution and its replacement with a civilian government.

He got his wish. The kaiser abdicated on 9 November, and Germany became a republic with a socialist government. The French and the British handed German representatives their armistice terms on a railway car in Compiègne, France. The Germans signed, and the armistice became a reality on the eleventh hour of the eleventh day of the eleventh month in 1918. Pershing did not celebrate. The failure to press for unconditional surrender, he said, was an enormous mistake. In a week or so, the Allies could have bagged the German army and Germany would have been truly defeated. As it was, the Germans signed an armistice, as they had hoped to do, while still holding enemy territory. That made the armistice not so much a surrender—indeed it was not a surrender—but a concession that the war should end for political reasons. It could and would be renewed when the political seasons changed.

ADVENTURE IN SIBERIA

AFTER THE BOLSHEVIK REVOLUTION, the British asked President Wilson to join them in sending troops to Russia. The goal was to keep Russian supplies out of the hands of the Germans, and incidentally to help the counter-revolutionary "Whites"—whose disparate, squabbling forces included everything from czarists, to moderate socialists, to freebooting Cossacks—fight the Bolshevik "Reds." Wilson characteristically refused. He agreed that Bolshevism was "the poison of disorder, the poison of revolt, the poison of chaos," and "the negation of everything American."[38] But in his liberal, professorial way, Wilson thought military intervention wouldn't help. He believed the Russian people would and should decide their own fate. Yet after definitively ruling out any military intervention, Wilson definitively ruled it in.

Pershing and his staff growled about politicians sending troops to nonrelevant sideshows when they needed every man jack on the western front, but nevertheless a few thousand doughboys packed their bags for northwestern Russia and Siberia. Few were as prescient as Winston Churchill, who recognized that it was not the kaiser but the Bolsheviks who were the great threat to the West. Russian Bolshevism, Churchill said, was "a ghoul descending from a pile of skulls." Again: "It is not a policy; it is a disease. It is not a creed; it is a pestilence." In 1919, with the kaiser safely packed off to exile in the Netherlands, Churchill advocated a policy of "Kill the Bolshie and Kiss the Hun"[39]—one of the most endearing slogans in political history. Further, he thought Britain should encourage a German invasion of Communist Russia; failure to crush the Communists now, he warned, would lead to "a union between German militarism and Russian Bolshevism . . . which would be unspeakably unfriendly to Britain and to the United States and France, and to all that those free democracies stand for."[40]

One could not expect such wise and robust language—or policy—from Wilson. Indeed, such talk was the sort that affrighted him and befogged his spectacles. But there was one thing that could unite the Cavalier Churchill and the Puritan Wilson: "the Czech Legion." The Czech Legion was a body of 50,000 to 70,000 Czechs and Slovaks who were ready to fight on the side of the Allies at the western front—if they could get there. Some were citizens of Russia; others were deserters from the Habsburg Empire. None of them wanted anything to do with the Bolsheviks. They wanted an independent Czechoslovakia as part of the postwar carve-up of Central Europe—something that fit Wilson's Fourteen Points and its call for national self-determination over multinational empires.

The Czech Legion tried to fight its way through the Bolsheviks. First it appeared that freedom lay in northwest Russia, where British General Frederick C. Poole was commanding an expeditionary force that hoped to aid the Legion. British policy even considered that the Czech Legion might be the makings of a new eastern front. The Legion had proved it could fight by seizing control of the Trans-Siberian Railway.

The Czechs soon decided, however, that the northwest offered a less likely escape route than did using their control of the railway to trundle east 6,000 miles across Siberia to Vladivostok, where they could be evacuated on Allied ships. Waiting for them was a force that included troops from all the major Allied powers. The British, French, and Italians had sent token forces. The Japanese, however, deployed more than 70,000 men in Vladivostok. They had more in mind than helping the Czech Legion. Only a decade before, the Japanese had fought the Russians—indeed, annihilated the Russian fleet—and the idea of slicing off a bit of Siberian acreage for sushi cold storage sounded like just the thing for Dai Nippon.

The American detachment in Vladivostok was 9,000 men under the command of Major General William C. Graves. Secretary of War Newton Baker had informed Graves that this mission to Russia would be the equivalent of "walking on eggs loaded with dynamite."[41] In between Graves and the Czech Legion was a wasteland of roving armies: divided between Reds, Whites, unaffiliated independent warlords, Cossacks, freed prisoners of war, and raiders. Graves was a West Pointer and Philippine veteran—and as upright an officer as Wilson could have found. Graves arrived on the scene in September 1918. His orders were to help rescue the Czech Legion but avoid all other entanglements in chaotic Russia. He obeyed these orders scrupulously—to the dismay of the French and the British, who recognized the Whites as de facto Allies. Graves dismissed the local White Cossack leader as a "murderer, robber, and a most dissolute scoundrel."[42] The Old World Allies said this might be true, but it takes all kinds. The Czechs themselves had no qualms about fighting side by side with the Whites against the Reds.

Even when the war against the kaiser was won, the battle to help the Czechs fight their way home continued. They finally made it, but only after the chaotic collapse of the Whites, in 1920. The unstained banner of the Czech Legion emerged a little muddy by the end. The Legion bought off the Bolsheviks by giving them the White leader, Admiral Alexander Kolchak, and a train full of gold.

Meanwhile, in northwest Russia, British General Frederick Poole had assembled not just Royal Marines and Royal Scots, but Canadians, French troops (including members of the French Foreign Legion), and American Marines, soldiers, and sailors. Together they occupied the White-held city of Archangel in August 1918 and beat back the neighboring Reds. Because the Americans commanded by Colonel George Evans Stewart served under the authority of the British, they served Britain's forcible anti-Bolshevik policy rather than Wilson's policy of piety and waffle; and given that Archangel's chief attraction was disease, fighting the Bolsheviks[43] was something of a relief.

Nevertheless, morale was terrible. The British troops were men who had been declared unfit for duty elsewhere. The French were typically war weary. The American troops had little training, but enough pride to resent being under British control. With the Allied forces coming to dislike each other as much as they disliked the putative enemy, the British sent General William Ironside[44] to take command in the fall of 1918. Likewise, the Americans superseded Colonel Stewart with General Wilds Richardson, who could at least approach General Ironside as an equal.

The new commanders faced trouble immediately. When the Great War officially ended, many of the troops in Archangel (especially the French) wondered what the hell they were doing in Russia. (Of course, by winter they were icebound anyway and couldn't leave.) There were mutinies, which began as refusals to accept orders and ended in open rebellion. In the Slavo-British Legion of allied Russian troops, British and Russian officers were murdered. The doughboys never mutinied in any serious sense. They grumbled, they sometimes needed prodding, but they stuck it out and fought well when called to do so, until the Allies eventually decided to leave the defense of Archangel to the White Russians. The Americans were fully withdrawn by June 1919, though General Ironside and 8,000 British volunteers stayed on for another three months to keep the Reds bloodied and at bay. After that, the Whites held Archangel on their own, until 21 February 1920.

So it was all, apparently, for nothing—though it needn't have been. Had the initial Allied landings at Archangel, argues historian Richard Ullman, "been carried out by two or three divisions—the number which [British envoy R. H. Bruce] Lockhart and the military attaches at Moscow had insisted was the bare minimum necessary for success—instead of the 1,200 troops who actually occupied the port at the end of July [1918], there is little doubt that they could have forced their way to Moscow and overthrown the Bolshevik regime."[45] If Teddy Roosevelt had been in the White House that might have happened, but with Woodrow Wilson no such determination and vision could be expected.

It was thus that American involvement in the Great War finally ended—with victory in the West and a less than halfhearted failure to overthrow the Bolsheviks in the East. The doughboys had done their bit—and done it well. But the politicians would treat the peace as they had treated the Allied intervention in Russia—with a failure of nerve, vision, and commitment. It was their failure that made the doughboys the fathers of the next generation's GIs.

CHAPTER 19

A WORLD MADE SAFE FOR WAR

I N 1919, PRESIDENT WILSON sat with the leaders of France, Great Britain, and Italy to redraw the map of Europe in order to make the world safe for democracy. A century earlier, in the wake of the Napoleonic Wars, a rather different set of statesmen had gathered at the Congress of Vienna to make the world safe for monarchy and stability. The conservative aristocrats of the Congress of Vienna succeeded in preventing a continental European war for a hundred years. President Wilson's Fourteen Points and his plan for a League of Nations, which guided the Treaty of Versailles after the Great War, created a peace that lasted barely twenty years.

Wilson failed where Viscount Castlereagh, Prince Klemens von Metternich, and the Duke of Wellington succeeded, because Wilson was guided by liberal idealism and spite (which often go together) while the aristocratic statesmen of the nineteenth century were guided by reactionary prejudices: the restoration of monarchies, with peace guaranteed by a balance of power. Future peacemakers should note that the reactionary model works better than the progressive one.

The reactionary model could—with difficulty—have been employed at the end of the Great War. The reactionaries of Vienna would have been in Churchill's camp. They, too, would have kissed the Hun and killed the Bolshie; they would have agreed that Europe could not tolerate a Communist state, the first principles of which were international subversion and revolution. They would have pressed Allied intervention against the Bolsheviks all the way to Moscow, founded a new royal house—taking the place of the murdered Romanovs—and elevated a new "Czar of all the Russias."

So too they would have restored the Habsburg Empire. This would have been more difficult still, as its constituent parts were already rapidly unraveling. But a loose federation of states—united by open borders, internal free trade, and the crown of the double eagle—could perhaps have been stitched together. In the postwar chaos of Germany, where right-wing Freikorps battled Bolsheviks on the streets, a new royal family, chosen from the many princely houses of Deutschland, could have been elevated to provide a sense of national unity, continuity, and normalcy. As for Turkey, long the sick man of Europe, Castlereagh, Wellington, and Metternich might very well have accepted Kemal Atatürk as a man they could do business with. They would have kept the peripheries of the Ottoman Empire partitioned, as they were, among the great empires of France and Britain as both a necessity and a fait accompli. But otherwise they would have conciliated the Turks.[1]

Most of all, the statesmen of Vienna would not have created a League of Nations, a powerless talking shop. They understood that peace is maintained by regimes that cherish stability, by a concert of recognized national interests, and by a backing of force. And in their revived concert of Europe, the New World would indeed, in George Canning's phrase, have been called to redress the balance of the Old.[2]

Woodrow Wilson, however, approached the challenge of the peace from an entirely different direction. Not for him the restoration of multinational monarchies, but the call—echoed by the Bolsheviks with whom he competed in progressive rhetoric—for national self-determination. So he rewarded the very passion that had led to murder in Sarajevo, the incineration of Europe, and the hecatomb of millions in the First World War.

In the postwar (1932) novel *The Radetzky March*—written by Joseph Roth (who was born in the Austro-Hungarian Empire)—a Polish nobleman speaking shortly before the Great War laments:

> This era wants to create independent nation-states! People no longer believe in God. The new religion is nationalism. Nations no longer go to church. They go to national associations. Monarchy, our monarchy, is founded on piety, on the faith that God chose the Hapsburgs to rule over so and so many Christian nations. Our Kaiser is a secular brother of the Pope, he is His Imperial and Royal Apostolic Majesty; no other is as apostolic, no other majesty in Europe is as dependent on the grace of God and on the faith of the nations in the grace of God. The German Kaiser still rules even when God abandons him; perhaps by the grace of the nation. The Emperor of Austria-Hungary must not be abandoned by God. But God *has* abandoned him![3]

Whether God had abandoned the Habsburgs, Woodrow Wilson certainly had. His goal was redrawing the map of Europe rather than restoring it, which naturally created new jealousies and new irredentist claims. Rather than balance-of-power politics—which Wilson rejected as corrupt and cynical—he preached disarmament and an international League of Nations to arbitrate disputes on the basis of international law.

European politicians felt steamrolled by Wilson. His idealism, they knew, was politically potent. But they also tended to think he was mad. British Prime Minister David Lloyd George thought Wilson's "most extraordinary outburst" was when he said: "Jesus Christ so far [has] not succeeded in inducing the world to follow His teaching, because He taught the world without devising any practical scheme to carry out His aims." Lloyd George noted that French Prime Minister Georges "Clemenceau slowly opened his dark eyes to their widest dimension and swept them around the Assembly to see how the Christians gathered around the table enjoyed this exposure of the futility of their Master."[4]

The bill of indictment against Wilson as a statesman is long: his failure of nerve against the Bolsheviks,[5] his endorsement of the nationalism that had turned Europe into an abattoir, his careless redrawing of the map of Europe, and his repudiation of balance-of-power politics. Every item in this bill of particulars contributed to the dégringolade of postwar continental Europe.[6]

So did Wilson's domestic political stupidity, which doomed the Versailles Treaty in the United States Senate. In the 1918 elections, the Republican Party regained its majority in the House and Senate, yet Wilson refused to compromise, even modestly, with Republican senators or include them in his Versailles delegation. And he was unable to articulate to the American people (as Teddy Roosevelt could have done) that the United States was the necessary guarantor of the peace of Europe.[7] For the first time in American history, the Senate rejected a peace treaty. Refusing to ratify the treaty did not, of course, erase the reality that America was a necessary world power. All it did was ensure that America had no internationally recognized legal right and responsibility to preserve the peace.

That the peace would be overturned was almost inevitable after Wilson's litany of failures. Pershing had been right. Germany did not feel like a defeated power; she merely thought of herself as a wronged and abused power that the Allies had subjected to political and economic chaos. And so weak was France (which had suffered horribly in the Great War), and so guilty did Britain feel after Versailles, that there was little to stand in Germany's way—certainly not the League of Nations, certainly not the isolationist United States, and certainly not the spirit of Wilson's Fourteen Points—when German nationalism reasserted itself. Wilson's very principles were the stuff of appeasement. For in the spirit of Wilsonian national self-determination, there were German-speaking peoples all across central Europe to be reunited with the *Vaterland*. Instead of Wilson's promised peace, Churchill's warning of a Bolshevist-German militarist alliance became fact with the Treaty of Rapallo (1922), when Russia conspired to assist German rearmament and plot against Poland.

The Western Allies backpedaled from some of the exactions of Versailles: the French withdrew from the occupied Ruhr, reparations payments were made less stringent, and Germany was brought into the League of Nations. Though the Great Depression hit Germany especially hard, it did not crush the German people so much as become a goad to their determination to come marching back. They did so not behind a crusty old monarch or the aged Field Marshal Paul von Hindenburg, but behind an entirely new kind of leader, a leader who proclaimed himself the political master of the new age: the leader of the National Socialist German Workers Party, Adolf Hitler.

GLOBE AND ANCHOR

WHILE POLITICAL AND ECONOMIC STORMS intensified over Europe, the United States followed a foreign policy of traumatized isolationism. So bitter was the fallout from Wilson's bollixed postwar diplomacy—and his failure to deliver a promised impossibility: "a war to end all wars"—that politicians of both parties decided that European affairs were a bane and a curse. The cynical Europeans were either to be ignored or enrolled—while held at arm's length—in programs of Wilsonian moral uplift to which no well-meaning American could object. The American government, led by Secretary of State Frank B. Kellogg, thoughtfully outlawed war with the Kellogg-Briand Pact of 1928 (during the administration of President Calvin Coolidge). With Britain, the United States followed a course of disarmament, including most particularly, naval disarmament—and in the process helped ensure Japanese naval supremacy in the western Pacific. The Japanese—who had inherited most of Germany's Pacific island territories—were signatories to the Kellogg-Briand Pact, but apparently thought its provisions did not apply to Manchuria, which Japan invaded in 1931.

To members of Congress it only made sense, during so calm a period of rising fascism and revolutionary communism, to slash the defense budget and focus the armed forces on protecting banana plantations in Hispaniola and Nicaragua, while practicing occasional gunboat diplomacy in China. For these duties, the Marines were the service of choice. The Marines didn't operate alone, of course—the 15th United States Infantry, for example, was on permanent deployment in Tientsin—but the Marines were the spearhead of American foreign policy. This was in part because of their undeniable efficiency with foreigners and because China was, from an American military point of view, a province of the United States Navy. The Navy patrolled the Yangtze River, kept China's open door properly propped open, and could deliver Marines from Guam and the Philippines if things got hot. The main task of the Marines was to protect American lives and property as China devolved into a chaos of civil war—between Nationalists, independent warlords, and Communists—and war against the invading Japanese. The Marines did not leave China until 1941, by which time the Japanese had so mutilated the country and cornered its Western residents that the Marines' position was untenable. The Marines were withdrawn to the Philippines. They would soon be seeing much more of the army of the Rising Sun.

In Nicaragua, a scene of intermittent Marine intervention since 1909, the Devil Dogs had the pleasure of chasing down a bandito generalissimo, Augusto César Sandino. He was a short man—barely five feet tall—with all the associated power neuroses. The would-be Napoleon led a band of rebels whose cause was troublemaking for the sake of Sandino. In a country violently divided between Liberals and Conservatives, Sandino was the only Liberal general who refused to accept the American-brokered Treaty of Tipitapa (1926), which aimed to reconcile the two camps. Though offered a governorship, he turned it down.

Among its provisions, the Treaty of Tipitapa established an agreement for elections in 1928 and created a united national army to be trained by the United States, the Guardia Nacional. In Nicaragua in the past, politics had meant dictatorship punctuated by coups. Until the treaty, the rival political parties—essentially rival family dynasties—maintained their own armies, with predictable results. America tried to introduce the idea of peaceful politics that respected the rule of law, including the right to private property. America had a threefold interest in providing such civic education: to help stabilize a southern neighbor, to protect American investment in Nicaragua, and to inoculate Nicaragua against international communism, which already had a foothold in Mexico.

To Sandino, the Treaty of Tipitapa was an outrage. He was a political outsider, not part of the Liberal elite, who became a Liberal general simply by showing up with a band of armed men; he was not interested in the usual party politics of the country. He was, by preference, a revolutionary socialist and welcomed the support of Communists, though his socialism was centered on the idea that revolution and socialism could bring him power. He put Sandino first—that was his cause; he was a Sandinista. Initially he demanded that more U.S. troops be brought to Nicaragua to enforce immediate elections. The United States declined, and from that refusal Sandino's demands hardened to a fierce cry of opposition to the *Yanqui*-imposed peace. On 16 July 1927, Sandino's guerillas attacked barracks housing United States Marines and Nicaraguan troops. Two Marines went down—one killed, one wounded—but the leathernecks inflicted such severe casualties on the enemy that it appeared the Sandinista rebellion might be crushed at first battle.

In fact, Sandino was only just building his rebel army. The Marines were preoccupied far more with ensuring free elections, keeping the peace, and reconciling the Conservatives and Liberals than with worrying about Sandino's rebels. But Sandino became a celebrity, the political beneficiary of radical chic. The revolutionary government of Mexico praised him. American radicals, Communists, and anti-imperialists portrayed him as a hero. And with his fame, his numbers grew. Yet Sandino was never popular in Nicaragua, and he was no hero. When he captured Marines or Nicaraguan Guardias, he executed them—or more accurately, murdered them. His men developed a system of torture—different machete strokes for different folks—to punish peasants who refused to support him. His seal of office bore the image of a machete-bearing peasant murdering a Marine. His goal was not a national Nicaraguan peace—that was America's goal—but a sanguinary socialist revolution for Sandino's benefit.

The result was that the Marines and Guardias found themselves in a guerilla war in the jungle-choked mountains of northern Nicaragua, where Sandinistas lay in ambush. Supporting air strikes—strafing and bombing by Marine pilots—was the Marines' way to make up for the disparity in numbers between the Sandinistas and themselves. Fixed-wing aircraft were used to evacuate Marine wounded. Marines also ran to the rescue of American-operated mines, timber companies, and plantations when these became targets of Sandinista raids.

Sandino was certainly troublesome, but few Nicaraguans rallied to his cause. In 1920, 90 percent of the country's population ignored his demand for an electoral boycott and braved his attacks on polling places. In an election universally judged as fair and free, the Liberals were elected. Both parties demanded that

American troops stay to keep the peace. President Calvin Coolidge, who had sent the Marines on this latest adventure to Nicaragua, agreed. Coolidge, however, was a lame duck, paddling his way out for Herbert Hoover. Hoover, a Quaker, didn't like Coolidge's policy, but reluctantly accepted it. Sandino, though not a Quaker, was no fan of Coolidge's policy either. With so little support for his revolution in Nicaragua and with the Marines picking off his lieutenants, he sought help from socialist Mexico, but the Mexican government of President Emilio Portes Gil was more cautious than revolutionary in its foreign (if not domestic) policy and showed little interest in socialism beyond Mexico's own borders.

Meanwhile, the Marine-trained and -officered Guardia Nacional took over the bulk of the fighting against the Sandinistas in the countryside. Marines not in the field with the Guardia Nacional defended Nicaragua's cities. The ongoing fighting—and the ongoing casualties—wore down Hoover's patience with the Marines' mission. He cut the Marines' Nicaraguan manpower from 1,500 men to 1,000, set a target for total withdrawal after the 1932 Nicaraguan election, and his secretary of state, Henry Stimson, publicly declared that American property owners who feared Sandinista attacks should move. Congress was if anything more eager than Hoover to get the Marines out of Nicaragua, especially after the stock market crash and the Great Depression made foreign deployments seem unnecessary expenditures.

The 1932 Nicaraguan election—again universally regarded as fair—resulted in another Liberal victory. The Liberals had campaigned against American business interests in Nicaragua, but given that Secretary of State Henry Stimson had dismissed American businessmen in Nicaragua as "a pampered lot of people"[8] this hardly bothered the Hoover administration. American businessmen could fend for themselves in Nicaragua or they could come home. The Marines were ordered out in January 1933, and Sandino took their departure as an invitation to reconcile with the Nicaraguan authorities. He signed a cease-fire in February, and though Sandino was officially now at peace with the Nicaraguan government, the Guardia Nacional still hated him—and he still verbally abused them whenever he had a forum. In 1934, the Liberal General Anastasio Somoza conspired with other Guardia Nacional officers to rid Nicaragua of the Sandinista annoyance. The Guardia captured Sandino and some of his leading officers, lined them up, and shot them down, in traditional Latin American fashion. The Guardia made short work of rounding up the last of the Sandinista rebels—and it was over. The Marines no doubt regretted not being in on the kill. But it was mission accomplished nevertheless.

President Franklin Roosevelt, elected in 1932, agreed with Hoover that Nicaragua should not be a training ground for American Marines. Under his "Good Neighbor Policy," America was no longer the policeman of Latin America. Thus General Somoza overthrew the elected government of Nicaragua and set up a dynastic dictatorship that lasted until 1979, under the impression that good dictators make good neighbors. FDR did nothing to dissuade him of that impression. And Marines of the Old Breed, like Chesty Puller, were left to reminisce about how "The Constabulary Department, where I saw it in both Haiti and Nicaragua, was the best school the Marine Corps has ever devised."[9] That school was closed, but the Marines would find more demanding employment in the following decade.

A FORMER NAVAL PERSON

ON 12 DECEMBER 1937, Japanese planes repeatedly dive-bombed until they sank the USS *Panay,* one of the Navy's Yangtze River patrol boats.[10] On board were embassy staff and American civilians the *Panay* was evacuating from Nanking. Of the seventy-three people on board, three were killed and forty-eight were wounded. The *Panay* incident was one small part of the infamous "rape of Nanking" committed by the invading Japanese army. The army of the Rising Sun was divided between old-style officers who had some—to Western Christian eyes—sense of restraint and usually younger ideologues who were committed to a Japanese version of National Socialism, though centered on the Shinto religion and the bushido code of the samurai. It is they who believed that the conquered deserved no mercy. In Nanking they treated civilians as vermin to be hunted, women as objects to be raped, and slaughter as the price of surrender. It is estimated that 200,000 to 300,000 Chinese—the city was full of refugees—were killed.

The massacre of Nanking was widely reported in the United States, in part because of the sinking of the *Panay.* The attack on the *Panay* was not an isolated occurrence. British merchant ships had been attacked as well. And throughout their undeclared war in China, the Japanese had made especial targets of American missionaries—their churches, schools, and hospitals. Though Japanese diplomacy routinely treated such attacks as regrettable mistakes, they were in fact part of the Rising Sun's ambition to eradicate Western influence in Asia—and American sailors aboard the *Panay* were sure the Japanese attack was no accident.

The Japanese tried to make amends, officially apologizing for the attack and paying an indemnity of more than two million dollars. Japan was dependent on American oil and scrap iron, and so could not afford a total breach with the United States (at least until the Japanese seized—as their ambition made likely—the Dutch East Indies, which had oil). American anger was further assuaged when the American embassy in Tokyo reported being inundated with Japanese condolences and donations because of the incident.

The bloody Japanese invasion of Shanghai, a major international city, in the summer of 1937, had made a breach much more likely. Repeated "incidents" against Americans in Shanghai appalled even American isolationists and allowed President Franklin Roosevelt to threaten economic repercussions against the Japanese. Aside from the China-based Marines and Navy patrol boats, trade was the only weapon Roosevelt had.

The United States was the obvious naval rival to Japan in the Pacific, but continual congressional budget cuts had left the United States Navy high and dry. In the four years of his presidency, Herbert Hoover (1929–33) had not permitted the Navy to build a single ship. In fact, after 1921, the United States did not lay the keel of another battleship until 1940. Though the administration of President Warren G. Harding (1921–23) had negotiated the Treaty for the Limitation of Naval Armament, neither he nor his presidential successor Calvin Coolidge (1923–29) bothered to keep the Navy up to the levels permitted by the treaty. Albert B. Fall, secretary of the interior for the Harding administration, even leased naval oil reserves to private business. To Harding, Coolidge, and Herbert Hoover, defense spending beyond a bare minimum was unnecessary, immoral, or both. It was not just the natural parsimony of small government and free enterprise men that made them think so, but the very same idealism that led to the Kellogg-Briand Pact negotiated during the Coolidge administration. Coolidge (one of whose hobbies was translating Dante from the Italian) famously said, "the chief business of the American people is business" (self-evidently true), but, in the same speech to the American Society of Newspaper Editors he also noted:

> We make no concealment of the fact that we want wealth, but there are many other things that we want very much more. We want peace and honor, and that

charity which is so strong an element of all civilization. The chief ideal of the American people is idealism. I cannot repeat too often that America is a nation of idealists. That is the only motive to which they ever give any strong and lasting reaction.[11]

President Franklin Roosevelt (1933–45), thankfully, broke from naval parsimony. He was an aristocrat, a jaunty Machiavellian, and a spendthrift, who was also a former secretary of the Navy (and a distant cousin of Teddy Roosevelt). During World War II, British Prime Minister Winston Churchill (a former First Lord of the Admiralty) began a correspondence with the American president. He chose as his own code name "Naval Person," eventually amended to "Former Naval Person," as a bow to his and Roosevelt's having once held similar briefs in their respective governments.

Roosevelt had as his campaign theme song "Happy Days Are Here Again," and for the United States Navy this was certainly true. For the first time since Theodore Roosevelt's administration, the United States had a president who believed in spending money on the Navy. Of course, he believed in spending money on everything else, too, trusting that federal dollars would put Americans back to work and claw the country up from the Great Depression. The economic theory might have been dubious, but for the Navy the immediate results were not. In 1933, the president, by executive order, ensured that $238 million of federal spending authorized by the National Industrial Recovery Act was directed to the Navy. The Navy's orders were to build thirty-two ships in three years—to which the admirals were happy to say, "Aye-aye, Mr. President."

The nation as a whole, however, did not share Roosevelt's fondness for spending money on the Navy. Harding's, Coolidge's, and Hoover's administrations had reflected popular opinion, which deprecated military preparedness. Such-minded Americans believed there was no need or expectation that the United States would fight another large-scale foreign war. That sentiment was exacerbated for left-leaning people by the revelations of a sensationalistic report by Senator Gerald Nye, a progressive Republican from Iowa. Senator Nye was so progressive a Republican that he favored higher taxes on the wealthy, was deeply suspicious of big business, disapproved of Calvin Coolidge's and Herbert Hoover's economic policies, and thought Franklin Roosevelt's New Deal didn't go nearly far enough. He also wanted to demonstrate that munitions industries—the "merchants of death"—operated a racket. Their interests had compelled American entry into World War I, he said, and from the blood of

the doughboys they extracted obscene profits. Nye assembled a Senate committee to investigate and issue a report supporting his beliefs—which it duly did.

While the United States kept warning itself of the dangers of spending
money on its military, Hitler's regime was overthrowing the Versailles Treaty—
not to mention the Reichstag and the German constitution. Under Hitler's leadership Germany rearmed, occupied the Saar, remilitarized the Rhineland, and
sponsored a pro-Nazi coup in Austria. Italy invaded Abyssinia (Ethiopia) in
1935—further exposing the feebleness of the League of Nations, of which
Ethiopia was a member—and two years later allied itself with Germany and
Japan in the Anti-Comintern Pact. The Japanese, meanwhile, had abrogated
their commitments under the naval limitation treaties they had signed and were
pillaging China. Spain, torn apart in a horrific civil war, became an international battlefield, with the Soviets intervening on the side of the anticlerical Republican (Socialist) government and Germany and Italy intervening on the side
of General Francisco Franco and the Nationalists. In Bolshevik Russia, state-
engineered famines were followed by periodic fanatical purges that killed
millions—including the bulk of Russia's officer corps—while the Comintern
(the Communist International) insinuated Bolshevism into the politics of every
country in which it could find a crack.

Behind this storm of international tension and violence, a much greater war
was looming—one had to be blind not to see it. But to speak the truth was to be
denounced as a warmonger. In 1937, President Roosevelt said: "Let no one imagine that America will escape, that America may expect mercy, that this Western
Hemisphere will not be attacked,"[12] if the march of militarism continued.

Isolationism and pacifism had sprung up like weeds after the disastrous
presidency of Woodrow Wilson, but they were not an American tradition. As
the historian Samuel Eliot Morison wrote, "Never since Jefferson's time had
America, and never in recorded history had England, been in so pacifist a mood
as in 1933–39."[13] For America's survival, Franklin Roosevelt would have to lift
that mood. America's Former Naval Person would have to become a war
leader—albeit a war leader, at first, by subterfuge, for the United States was
pledged to neutrality.

The Neutrality Acts, passed by Congress between 1935 and 1939, prohibited not only American arms sales to countries at war, but *private* commercial
or financial transactions within war zones, and American ships were forbidden
to enter belligerent waters. In other words, freedom was to be sacrificed in the

name of isolationism. Roosevelt had signed these acts into law—facing a congressional fait accompli—but worked carefully around their terms to make such preparations as he could without the isolationists noticing.

BLITZKRIEG

BY 1938, THE ROAD TO WAR—at least for Europe—was as swift as an autobahn. In March, Hitler executed the *Anschluss*, the reunion—that is, the annexation—of Austria to Germany. Then he annexed the Sudetenland of Czechoslovakia to reunite its ethnic Germans with Germany proper. British Conservative (and First Lord of the Admiralty) Alfred Duff Cooper saw where this was leading and had the appropriate rejoinder: "There are Germans in Switzerland, in Denmark, in Alsace; I think that one of the few countries in Europe in which there are no Germans is Spain, and there are rumors that Germany has taken an interest in that country."[14]

Though Czechoslovakia had an army worthy of the name, British Prime Minister Neville Chamberlain and French Premier Edouard Daladier congratulated themselves on forcing Czechoslovakia to surrender the Sudetenland to Herr Hitler. Chamberlain called this "peace in our time." Duff Cooper thought Chamberlain's Munich Agreement with Hitler a disgrace and resigned. Winston Churchill called it "a total and unmitigated defeat. . . . [T]he German dictator, instead of snatching the victuals from the table, has been content to have them served to him course by course."[15] The German army—still small—had doubted its ability to pierce Czechoslovakia's defenses; and Germany's conservative generals might have launched a military coup against Hitler if France and Britain had threatened war (this intelligence had come to Churchill). But Chamberlain's appeasement made all that moot. Hitler then decided, of course, that he needed to annex all of Czechoslovakia, because it seemed a shame to leave the rest of it dangling out there defenseless.

Benito Mussolini, getting into the spirit of the thing, had joined Chamberlain and Daladier in approving the annexation of the Sudetenland. Now he decided to do some annexing of his own, choosing Albania—which proved, if nothing else, that Hitler had better taste in countries than did Il Duce.

No European power—or for that matter, the United States—was inclined to stop the fascist dictators from gobbling up their neighbors: until Poland and Romania. Here Britain and France drew the line. If Hitler invaded Poland it meant war.[16] Hitler played his trump card, announcing the Hitler-Stalin Pact. Poland, trapped between the jaws of the Nazis and the claws of the Communists, was doomed. Czechoslovakia had been Britain and France's last chance to stop Hitler short of world war. Now Armageddon had come again.

On 1 September 1939, Germany invaded Poland. Two days later, Great Britain and France declared war on Germany.[17] With Britain came soldiers and sailors of the empire and the white dominions: Canadians, Australians, New Zealanders, Indians, Rhodesians, South Africans, and others of every color and religion, from every continent. But not yet the United States, the imperial possession that got away.

American neutrality did not guarantee American safety. On 3 September 1939, the Glasgow-based ship *Athenia* was mistaken by a German U-boat for an armored cruiser and torpedoed without warning. One hundred and twelve of its passengers and crew were killed, including twenty-eight Americans. The Germans feared they had just propelled the United States into war, but American isolationist sentiment made it a diplomatic trifle. In 1812, the United States went to war rather than allow its merchant vessels to be boarded and searched in international waters. In 1939, the Germans proclaimed they would board and search American vessels in international waters—and American neutrality did not budge.

So the war continued without us. Poland was ripped apart by the German wolf and the Russian bear. Then Russia attacked Finland, the Baltic states, and Romania. Hitler waited until April 1940 before he swept the Germanic peoples of Denmark and Norway into the Reich. France hid behind its supposedly impervious Maginot Line, but collapsed when the Germans stormed through neutral Holland, Belgium, and Luxembourg and into France in May 1940. Within a month, the Gallic rooster was plucked, and "Vichy France" became a German client state.

Continental Europe belonged to Hitler and his allies. Across the English Channel, Britain alone stood defiant. The Battle of Britain began, as British Spitfires and Hurricanes battled the Luftwaffe, German bombs rained on British cities, and Winston Churchill, now elevated to prime minister, stood before the House of Commons and announced his policy:

> Even though large targets of Europe and many old and famous States have
> fallen or may fall into the grip of the Gestapo and all the odious apparatus of
> Nazi rule, we shall not flag or fail. We shall go on to the end, we shall fight in

France, we shall fight on the seas and oceans, we shall fight with growing confidence and growing strength in the air, we shall defend our island, whatever the cost may be, we shall fight on the beaches, we shall fight on the landing grounds, we shall fight in the fields and in the streets, we shall fight in the hills; we shall never surrender, and even if, which I do not for a moment believe, this island or a large part of it were subjugated and starving, then our Empire beyond the seas, armed and guarded by the British Fleet, would carry on the struggle, until in God's good time, the new world, with all its power and might, steps forth to the rescue of the old.[18]

While Churchill roared the British Empire's defiance of Nazi tyranny, President Franklin Roosevelt debated with Congress about amending the Neutrality Acts so that Britain could buy war materials on a "cash and carry" basis. Congress reluctantly acceded, but only after affirming the important principle that if you're going to sell goods to the lone defender of Western civilization at its hour of greatest peril, you need to get the cash in hand first.

On 27 September 1940, Hitler, Mussolini, and the government of the Emperor Hirohito announced the signing of the Three-Power Pact. The Pact's purpose was "to establish and maintain a new order of things calculated to promote the mutual prosperity and welfare of the peoples concerned,"[19] which sounded very benevolent, with Germany and Italy managing western Europe and Japan supervising matters in Asia. Though Soviet Russia was not a signatory to the Three-Power Pact, it was acknowledged in Article Five, which affirmed that the Hitler-Stalin Pact remained operative. The most important article for President Roosevelt was Article Three, which stated that an attack on any of the Tripartite Powers by a state not currently at war would be considered an attack on all three. So, for the three fascists, it was all for one and one for all, to rape, murder, and steal, with Soviet Russia playing the role of a proletarian D'Artagnan. Franklin Roosevelt—not without some justification—was cast in the role of Cardinal Richelieu and warned not to try overturning the new world order of the fascist powers in Asia and Europe.

That this new world order would inevitably impinge on the United States was obvious to all save the majority of the American people. An anti-Western, fascist, Japanese-dominated Asia could not be viewed kindly by the United States, which had been a Pacific power since the mid-nineteenth century. China was disappearing into the Japanese maw. America's Pacific territories—including the Philippine Commonwealth (well on its way to independence under

American tutelage), Hawaii, and Alaska's Aleutian Islands—were at obvious risk. In fact, on 28 November 1938, the U.S. naval attaché in Tokyo reported that Japan "would not hesitate to undertake offensive operations but not beyond supporting distance of her strategically excellent geographical position. By this is meant that Hong Kong, Singapore, Dutch East Indies, Philippines, Borneo, Guam, Aleutian Islands and possibly the Hawaiian islands would be in jeopardy."[20]

In Europe, the battle between Britain and the fascists had consequences just as dangerous for the United States. On 18 June 1940, Winston Churchill declared that:

> Upon this battle depends the survival of Christian civilization. Upon it depends our own British life, and the long continuity of our institutions and our Empire. The whole fury and might of the enemy must very soon be turned upon us. Hitler knows that he will have to break us in this island or lose the war. If we can stand up to him, all Europe may be free and the life of the world may move forward into broad, sunlit uplands. But if we fail, then the whole world, including the United States, including all that we have known and cared for, will sink into the abyss of a new Dark Age made more sinister, and perhaps more protracted, by the lights of perverted science. Let us therefore brace ourselves to our duties and so bear ourselves that, if the British Empire and its commonwealth last for a thousand years, men will still say, "This was their finest hour."[21]

To support Britain in her finest hour, Roosevelt needed all his Richelieuean cunning in working around the political constraints of an isolationist country and Congress. He did so masterfully, especially after the fall of France, which shocked Congress into realizing that Roosevelt might be right: that the nation needed to be prepared for war. In June 1940, he won Congress's approval to rebuild the United States Navy into a fully-fledged two-ocean fleet, in the largest naval construction project in American history. When the president declared a state of national emergency, Congress empowered him to ban the sale of militarily relevant products and raw materials—most specifically to Japan, a ban that would be tightened over the next year and a half.

Roosevelt shot new life into the Monroe Doctrine, declaring that the United States would protect the entire Western Hemisphere from fascist aggression and conquest. The United States and Canada (already a belligerent power) reached an agreement on sharing naval bases. President Roosevelt, on his own initiative, became an arms trader, swapping World War I–era U.S. Navy destroyers to the British in exchange for naval bases in the Western Hemisphere (in Bermuda, the West Indies, and Newfoundland).

In September 1940, Congress approved the first peacetime military draft in American history. In December, Roosevelt urged American industry to become the arsenal of democracy. Roosevelt rang in the new year of 1941 by asserting "the moral order" of the four freedoms—freedom of speech, freedom of religion, freedom from want, and freedom from fear—against the amoral world order of the fascists. He also asked Congress to go beyond "cash and carry" and permit a policy of presidential "lend-lease" so that the president could sell, trade, loan, or give war materials to Great Britain and let the British use American shipyards. Churchill had said: "Give us the tools, and we will finish the job."[22] Roosevelt was eager to oblige and won the necessary fight in Congress. After the Nazi invasion of the Soviet Union, Roosevelt immediately extended lend-lease to the Soviets.

Neutrality was now more of a pretense than a policy. Axis shipping was barred from—and seized in—American ports. The United States Navy moved from conducting "neutrality patrols" to officially defending shipping lanes across the Atlantic. In April 1941, Greenland was put under America's protective umbrella, and by July the Marines were patrolling Iceland. To protect Allied shipping, the Navy was freed to shoot on sight German U-boats and any Axis ship within twenty-five miles of the American coastline. By the end of October, Roosevelt could note in his Navy Day speech:

Hitler has attacked shipping in areas close to the Americas in the North and South Atlantic. Many American-owned merchant ships have been sunk on the high seas. One American destroyer was attacked on September fourth. Another destroyer was attacked and hit on October seventeenth. Eleven brave and loyal men of our Navy were killed by the Nazis. We have wished to avoid shooting. But the shooting has started. And history has recorded who fired the first shot. In the long run, however, all that will matter is who fired the last shot.[23]

Four days later, a German U-boat sank the U.S. Navy destroyer the *Reuben James,* killing 115 men.

The shots were coming closer. In a reminder of the Zimmerman Telegram of the First World War, Roosevelt declared he had received "a secret map" made by the Nazis that showed South and Central America divided into "five vassal states" and that one of these states would possess "our great life line—the Panama Canal." Roosevelt revealed another Nazi document in his possession, which offered a "detailed plan" to eradicate religious freedom. "In the place of the churches of our civilization, there is to be set up an International Nazi Church. . . . In the place of the Bible, the words of *Mein Kampf* will be imposed and enforced as Holy Writ. . . . A God of Blood and Iron will take the place of the God of Love and Mercy."[24]

In Asia, the fascist march was abetted by French (now Vichy) Indochina joining the Axis. In 1941, it became a colony of Japan, bringing the Philippines, the Dutch East Indies, and British Singapore and Burma within quick striking distance of the army and navy of the Rising Sun.

President Roosevelt absorbed the Filipino armed forces into America's and made General Douglas MacArthur—former Army chief of staff, now military adviser to the Filipino government—America's Far Eastern commander. Japan was treated as a de facto enemy. Its assets in the United States were frozen; and the United States made Japan's withdrawal from China and Indochina a condition for removing economic sanctions.

Japan, however, had no intention of abolishing—it had every intention of expanding—its "Greater East Asia Co-Prosperity Sphere." Indeed, it was polishing its war plans against Dutch Indonesia, the British, and the United States. In late November, U.S. Admiral Harold R. Stark, chief of naval operations, told the Japanese ambassador to the United States, Admiral Kichisaburo Nomura, "If you attack us, we will break your empire before we are through with you . . . we shall crush you."[25] The warning went unheeded. On 26 November 1941, the Japanese fleet began its stealthy approach to Pearl Harbor.

CHAPTER 20

INFAMY

J APANESE VICE ADMIRAL Chuichi Nagumo watched the Zeros fly off the decks of the aircraft carriers *Akagi, Kaga, Soryu, Hiryu, Shokaku,* and *Zuikaku* as dawn broke over the Hawaiian Islands. Behind these fighter planes flew his bombers. Beneath the seas, Japanese midget submarines were sneaking into the battle zone. And surrounding him was his battle fleet of two battleships, a light cruiser, two heavy cruisers, and nine destroyers. The Zeros' objective was less than two hours away: the American naval base at Pearl Harbor and the United States Army Air Base at nearby Hickam Field. The Japanese plan—drawn up by Admiral Isoroku Yamamoto—was to lay a devastating blow against the American Pacific Fleet, leaving it crippled long enough for Imperial Japan to make lightning strikes of conquest across the Far East. By the time the United States Navy rebuilt itself, the Greater East Asia Co-Prosperity Sphere would be too enormous an octopus for it to harpoon.

The Japanese attack was daring, yes, but its success was virtually assured. Twice before in training exercises, the United States Navy had successfully "attacked" Pearl Harbor (in 1932 and 1938). Admiral Husband E. Kimmel thought his base at Pearl Harbor was poorly defended and continually—and without success—asked for more antiaircraft guns.

Tensions with Japan were taut; to many in the armed services and in Washington war seemed inevitable, and a Japanese surprise attack was judged likely. Still, the Navy was under orders not to antagonize the Japanese with aggressive surveillance operations. Japan had to fire the first shot, and there had to be no provocations. That shot was *not* expected to come at Pearl Harbor. There were American targets easier for the Japanese to reach—most notably, the Philippines.

In any event, 7 December 1941 was a Sunday. The post slept late, a third of the base's sailors were on leave, and the Japanese pilots cheered when their torpedo bombs and machine guns burst upon that lazy Sunday morning. Their gamble had worked. Japanese Commander Mitsuo Fuchida, flying a bomber, shouted jubilantly into his microphone: *"Tora! Tora! Tora!"* (Tiger! Tiger! Tiger!). Surprise was Japan's, as explosions ripped across the calm Sunday morning. Stinking clouds of flaming petrol mushroomed into the sky, machine guns cut through runways, and stunned American servicemen hurriedly grasped their gear to fight back.

When Navy Lieutenant Commander Bromfield "Brum" Nichol first heard the guns, he said, "My God, the army has gone crazy, having antiaircraft drill on Sunday morning." Army Major General Walter Short, however, was inclined to blame the Navy, thinking Sunday morning a peculiar time for having "some battle practice." Meanwhile Army Captain Brooke Allen at Hickam Field stood in his bathrobe shaking a fist at the storming Zeroes: "I *knew* it! I *knew* the little sons of bitches would do it on a Sunday! I *knew* it!"[1] And by "little sons of bitches" he meant the Japs, not the Navy.

Actually, the fight back had begun a bit earlier. First blood had been to the Americans when the destroyer *Ward* sank a Japanese midget submarine with depth charges. That action was at 06:30. It was not seen as presaging a full-scale Japanese onslaught. Japanese submarine probes were expected, and it was expected that American naval officers would terminate the midget submarines with extreme prejudice. It was the naval equivalent of pig sticking.

But with the torpedo bombs falling, the battleship *Oklahoma* torn apart like a sardine tin, and Battleship Row a seared vista of blazing steel and dying men, the official words echoing across Pearl Harbor seemed self-evident: *"Air raid, Pearl Harbor! This is no drill!"*

The men at the antiaircraft batteries fired back hard, the guns so hot from action that they burned the flesh off their hands. So many counterblasts spat from the guns of the battleship *Pennsylvania* that the Japanese planes veered away, landing only a single bomb. But other ships on Battleship Row took a beating, including the *California,* the *West Virginia,* and famously and horribly the USS *Arizona,* which became the watery grave of a thousand men. The battleship *Nevada,* trying to sail through the channel and escape, was chased by Japanese bombers and ran aground.

Just as the battleships were all lined up in perfect order, so were the American planes at Wheeler and Hickam Air Fields. The planes were secured against possible Japanese saboteurs on the island rather than against aerial attack. Under armed guard and with their ammunition carefully locked away, they were the proverbial sitting ducks. The Japanese feasted on them.

The devastation was immense: 18 ships sunk or battered, including 8 battleships; nearly 170 planes destroyed, another 130 badly damaged; more than 2,300 America servicemen were dead. All this destruction purchased at the cost of 29 Japanese planes and 6 submarines (5 of them midgets). But there was another price to be paid. For a decade, the Japanese had ravaged China and plotted a course of aggression in the Far East without meeting any armed opposition from the United States other than the odd Marine standing athwart their path saying: "Sorry, Charlie, no bayoneting Yanks." A bigger response was due now; and the final price to be paid for the infamous attack on Pearl Harbor was by the Japanese. Fatally for the Japanese Emperor Hirohito's men, the United States had not lost a single aircraft carrier—none, to the attackers' surprise, was at Pearl Harbor. It would be the carrier, not the battleship, that would be the weapon nonpareil for the Navy in the Pacific War.

When a bullet crashed through the window of his quarters at Pearl Harbor, and bounced harmlessly off his chest, Admiral Kimmel said: "It would have been merciful if it had killed me."[2] Perhaps, but when President Roosevelt declared 7 December 1941, a date that would live in infamy, the American people felt more like dealing out death than accepting it. Isolationism was sucked out of America's soul by the oily, black fires of Pearl Harbor. Congress voted all but unanimously for war with Japan; the sole dissenter was a feminist, pacifist Republican, Jeannette Rankin of Montana. She was not reelected.

On 11 December 1941, Hitler and Mussolini, honoring the Tripartite Pact, declared war on the United States, saving Roosevelt the trouble of declaring war on them. Winston Churchill rejoiced that with America in the fight, the Axis was doomed: "How long the war would last or in what fashion it would end no man could tell, nor did I at this moment care. Once again in our long island history we should emerge, however mauled or mutilated, safe and victorious. We should not be wiped out. Our history would not come to an end. . . . Hitler's fate was sealed. Mussolini's fate was sealed. As for the Japanese, they would be ground to powder. . . . I went to bed and slept the sleep of the saved and thankful."[3]

So trusted all good men as they tucked themselves abed that Advent season, but the Japanese were not yet powder. Indeed, armies of the Rising Sun were besieging British Hong Kong (which surrendered Christmas Day), invading British Malaya (and thereby threatening Singapore), and attacking Siam (Thailand). Japanese bombers, nine hours after the wrecking of Pearl Harbor, tore through Clark Field in the Philippines, incinerating Douglas MacArthur's air force, which the great general—apparently dazed by the disaster in Hawaii—had unaccountably left on the ground, arranged wingtip to wingtip for the bonfire. Two days later, the Japanese were invading Luzon and would soon be besieging the general himself.

On 10 December 1941, British naval power in the Pacific sank with the battleship *Prince of Wales* and the battle cruiser *Repulse*: 840 British officers and sailors perished, making it a minor Pearl Harbor for America's chief ally in the Pacific. A week later, the Japanese moved into British Burma. More ominous, perhaps, was the Japanese invasion of the Dutch East Indies, which would give the Rising Sun access to a wealth of raw materials—paramount among them oil for Dai Nippon's navy.

The Japanese rolled like a tsunami over the Pacific. On 19 February 1942, the Japanese struck at Fort Darwin, Australia's lone northside naval base. On 27 February, in the Battle of the Java Sea, the Japanese defeated a grossly outnumbered and outgunned Dutch-led Allied fleet of Dutch, British, American, and Australian ships, and made the 9 March surrender of the Dutch East Indies a fait accompli, giving the Japanese control of Indonesia (Dutch Borneo, the Celebes, Sumatra, Java, and Bali). The Japanese swept over British Borneo, the British Gilbert and Solomon Islands, and the Australian protectorates of New Guinea, New Britain, and New Ireland. On New Britain the Japanese constructed the fortress of Rabaul, which became an enormous naval and military base. Dai Nippon's warriors were now in striking distance for an invasion of Australia, most of whose fighting men had been called to the defense of the British Empire against the Nazis.

To the northwest, on a line extending from Pearl Harbor west, the Japanese had overwhelmed the small and nearly defenseless Navy and Marine garrison at Guam on 8 December 1941. That same day, they blasted the airfield at Wake Island, destroying all but four planes and killing half of the air maintenance crewmen. The entire garrison numbered fewer than 500 servicemen, more than 400 of them Marines. But when the Japanese tried to land their invasion force on 11 December 1941, they caught Marine hell. The Marines managed to sink two Japanese destroyers, damage seven other vessels, and throw the Japanese back into the sea. For nearly two weeks, the Marines ducked and covered under Japanese bombs. Their sole hope was a relief force expected from Hawaii. But fearing the Japanese naval gauntlet it had to pass, the relief force turned back (against the wishes of the officers and crewmen, who were nearly mutinous at the order), and the Marines were left in their island Alamo under their extraordinary officers: Navy Commander Winfield Cunningham, a Naval Academy graduate and pilot; Marine Major James Devereux, a Cuban-born, American- and Swiss-educated "mustang" (an officer who came up from the ranks) with previous service in China and Nicaragua; and Marine Major Paul Putnam, a naval aviator and Nicaragua veteran. On 23 December 1941, the Japanese launched another invasion, backed by cruisers and destroyers. The first wave of Japanese was turned back, but the end was inevitable for the outgunned Marines, who were finally ordered to surrender.

The Army had its own desperate defense in the Philippines. As the British commander at Hong Kong had surrendered in order to save the lives of civilians, so Douglas MacArthur declared Manila an "open city" hoping to spare innocent lives. The Japanese, however, did not share such concern for civilians—as they had proven already in China. They believed in samurai pride, domination, and contempt for the weak and the inferior.

MacArthur drew his troops south into the mountainous jungles of Bataan, from which the Japanese invaders, to their embarrassment, could not budge the Americans. MacArthur's men were wasted by disease, famished from lack of supplies, and embittered that no reinforcements had come to save them. But they hung on.

Sixty-one-year-old General Douglas MacArthur had his headquarters on the island of Corregidor, "the Rock," where he, his wife, and three-year-old son lived in a tunnel that would become the last redoubt of the defenders. As a result, his troops called him "Dugout Doug" and called themselves "the battling bastards of Bataan."

> We're the battling bastards of Bataan;
> No mamma, no papa, no Uncle Sam;
> No aunts, no uncles, no nephews, no nieces;
> No rifles, no planes, or artillery pieces;
> And nobody gives a damn.[4]

Their commander cared more than they knew and was more courageous than they credited him. The general was, in his warrior spirit, the same man who wouldn't budge when German artillery shells plowed the ground before him and Patton in World War I. Now MacArthur stood amid the Japanese bombing at Corregidor, disdaining a helmet in favor of his famous soft cap. During one bombardment, a Filipino aide removed his own helmet and stuck it over MacArthur's head as a bomb exploded nearby, deflecting shrapnel and perhaps saving the general's life. The general could only remark on how the bombing had ruined the family garden.

MacArthur didn't want to abandon his battling bastards. President Roosevelt, however, personally ordered him to Australia. MacArthur delayed as long as he could, but on 11 March 1942, he boarded a PT boat, along with his family and staff. They were exhausted and sick and had to evade a Japanese blockade to escape. Taking over command at Corregidor was tough and wiry General Jonathan Wainwright. MacArthur told him: "If I get through to Australia you know I'll come back as soon as I can with as much as I can. In the meantime you've got to hold."

Wainwright told him he'd hold on and assured MacArthur, "You'll get through."

"And back," MacArthur insisted.[5]

When MacArthur reached Australia, he announced that he had been withdrawn at the order of the president in order to lead the war against Japan and liberate the Philippines. To the Filipinos he promised: "I shall return." MacArthur's promise became the rallying cry of the Filipino resistance.

Meanwhile, the battling bastards were running out of ammunition, food, and hope. On 9 April 1942, Bataan was lost and a month later, Corregidor succumbed. A bone-thin Wainwright surrendered rather than see his tunnel become a scene of massacre. Chivalry was part of it, because the tunnel housed American nurses. But chivalry, like mercy, was a Western concept, a Christian concept, not held by the samurai of the Greater East Asia Co-Prosperity Sphere, and the samurai were angry. The reduction of the Philippines had taken far longer than expected. General Masaharu Homma was five months behind schedule on the Japanese army's timetable for conquest and the prisoners of war were an encumbrance.

The Corregidor prisoners were packed off to a prisoner of war camp, where 2,000 men died in two months. The battling bastards of Bataan fared even worse. They were harried into the sixty-five-mile Bataan Death March to their prison camp. They were kept on starvation rations, but that wasn't the worst of it: Japanese officers drew their swords (on horseback or on foot) to practice the artful decapitation of prisoners; men who collapsed from hunger, fever, injury, disease, thirst, or exhaustion were bayoneted and sometimes buried alive. The horrors of the march were unspeakable, and to the Japanese, dead prisoners were seen as an advantage: one less weakling to look after. Some 750 Americans and 5,000 Filipinos died horribly on their way to the internment camp. There, 16,000 men died after only two months of captivity. If Nazism represented barbarism guided "by the lights of perverted science," as Churchill had it, the fanatics of Dai Nippon represented barbarism guided by a culture of death and cruelty.

The Americans were intent at striking back at that cruelty. Vice Admiral William "Bull" Halsey lived up to his bullish name and sailed the South Pacific fighting the Japanese wherever he could find them in the winter of 1942, pounding the Japanese navy at the Marshall Islands, bombing Japanese-held Wake Island, and hitting Japanese bases on New Guinea. MacArthur, too, having arrived in Australia, worked to immediately make good on his promise to the Filipinos and planned an American-led invasion of Port Moresby on New Guinea's southern coast.

But most dramatic of all was Jimmy Doolittle's raid over Tokyo. Doolittle combined brains—he had a Ph.D. in aeronautical engineering—with a daredevil streak, as a man who flew for speed. Doolittle and his men trained—in deep secret—to do something that had never been attempted before: launching big, medium-range B-25 Mitchell bombers from the short flight deck of an aircraft carrier. There would be no turning back. Once launched, the planes would bomb targets in Japan and then land in China. Doolittle's mission had been hatched by Franklin Roosevelt himself and was to be launched from Bull Halsey's carriers.

Inevitably, the dangerous raid became even more so once the men were aboard ship. When Halsey's carriers spotted Japanese picket boats—Admiral Yamamoto's early warning system—the pilots learned they would be launched 150 miles farther out than they had expected. They might not even make China. But Halsey was from the "damn the torpedoes" school. Doolittle and his men benefited from the body English of every sailor on the USS *Hornet* who urged them successfully into the sky.

Tokyo was hit—the targets were military-industrial targets—but for the pilots the bombing run was only the middle point in the adventure. All but one of the planes made it to China—albeit with crash landings. The other plane landed in the Soviet Union, where its crew spent more than a year interned by the not-yet-allied Communists. The Japanese tracked down and captured eight airmen, executing three of them, and imprisoning the remaining five in brutally—and for one of the airmen, fatally—inhumane conditions that included torture. More than sixty of the raiders were smuggled to safety by Chiang Kai-shek's

Chinese Nationalists. But the Chinese paid a terrible price in Japanese retribution. The Japanese had suffered about fifty dead from the Doolittle Raid; they
slaughtered an incredible 250,000 Chinese to make sure that no peasant would
ever again think of helping an American flyer.

To Americans, the raid was a daring pull on the noses of Admiral Yamamoto and Emperor Hirohito. It buoyed morale, when the entire Pacific theater
seemed to have bowed to imperial Japan's Rising Sun. Asked whence the planes
had been launched, Franklin Roosevelt jauntily replied: "Shangri-La."

Less than a month after the Doolittle Raid came an encounter far more substantial in its military impact: the Battle of the Coral Sea (7–8 May 1942). From
their base at Rabaul, a Japanese invasion force advanced under the command of
Vice Admiral Shigeyoshi Inoue. Their target: Port Moresby, New Guinea. But
American naval intelligence had cracked Japanese communications, and Admiral Chester Nimitz[6] rushed a naval task force to intercept the Japanese. Vice Admiral Frank Jack Fletcher was the man on the spot. He had two carriers, the
USS *Yorktown* and the USS *Lexington*. With them, he not only blocked the
Japanese invasion, but also conducted the first naval battle in history fought entirely by aircraft carriers and their Navy and Marine pilots (the ships never even
saw each other). The *Lexington* was sunk, and Admiral Fletcher lost a tanker, a
destroyer, 66 planes, and 543 men; but 77 Japanese planes became fireballs,
more than 1,000 Japanese were killed, a small Japanese carrier was sunk, and
the Japanese invasion of Port Moresby was called off. Coming just after General Wainwright's surrender of Corregidor (6 May 1942), it was the first defeat
of Japan's samurai blitzkrieg.

An even bigger blow was struck against the Japanese aggressor at the Battle
of Midway. Admiral Yamamoto had previously targeted Midway Island—
halfway between Wake Island and Hawaii—as a strategic target for the Japanese Imperial Navy. Midway lies 1,100 miles from Hawaii and is only two miles
long, but it offered this one great temptation to Yamamoto: it was the western-
most island still in American hands. From that strategic point, the Japanese admiral believed he could sweep the Pacific of his only naval competition: the
Americans, who were still not finished after the attacks on Pearl Harbor, the
Philippines, Wake Island, and Guam. From Midway, the Japanese would be
placed to threaten Hawaii and the tempting target of America's West Coast,
which was nearly defenseless.[7]

After the jolt of the Doolittle Raid, Yamamoto's argument for action
against Midway overwhelmed any previous doubts in Japanese war councils.

But Admiral Nimitz had guessed—from the U.S. Navy's excellent intelligence operations, led here by Lieutenant Commander Joseph Rochefort—that Midway was his next chance to meet the Japanese in a major battle.

Admiral Nimitz was a naval Robert E. Lee, a southerner (a small-town Texan) who wanted to go to West Point to get an education. He went to the Naval Academy only because there were no openings at the Military Academy and he didn't know where else to apply. Once immersed in the traditions of the Navy, it became his life and his love. He was a man devoted to duty who turned down commercial offers to capitalize on his engineering knowledge during his service and on his fame after. He was a calm, humble man who initially declined command at Pearl Harbor (which went to Admiral Kimmel) because he thought he was too junior, and in his retirement declined to write his memoirs. Most of all, he was a man who knew talent; who appreciated aggressive, fighting admirals like Bull Halsey, Frank Jack Fletcher, and Raymond A. Spruance; and who proved, as commander in chief of the Pacific Fleet, to be an instinctive, aggressive, daring commander himself. Serving under the overall naval direction of Admiral Ernest King (commander of the U.S. Fleet, comprising all naval forces), Nimitz was perfectly placed to capitalize on his strengths as a leader.

He faced heavy odds this time. Admiral Yamamoto was bringing 162 ships to the battle. His goal was to utterly destroy Admiral Nimitz at Midway, land an invasion force of 5,000 men, and roam the Pacific hunting down any surviving American ships. Yamamoto himself was with the fleet, aboard the massive battleship (the largest in the world) *Yamato*. With his armada would be Japan's aircraft carriers *Kaga, Okagi, Hiryu,* and *Soryu*. Midway, in Yamamoto's mind was to be the battle that finished the job that began at Pearl Harbor. Unknown to the Japanese, the United States Navy knew Yamamoto's target and line of approach. There would be no mistakes about U.S. Navy or U.S. Army gunnery practice this time. Instead, the Japanese hunter would find himself the hunted; indeed Midway radioed disinformation (to be picked up by the Japanese) that the installation was running short of fresh water: it was leading prey to the salt lick.

With Admiral Halsey in sick bay, the American forces were under the command of Admirals Fletcher and Spruance. The Americans had less than a third as many ships as Yamamoto, but included in their task force were the American aircraft carriers *Enterprise, Hornet,* and *Yorktown*. The *Yorktown* had been rapidly—and incompletely—patched up at Pearl Harbor after its heavy fighting in the Coral Sea.[8] Nimitz wagered that as at the Coral Sea the battle would be an aerial one. The key was to have carrier-based planes to fight in the air, destroyers to sink Japanese submarines, and submarines of his own to infiltrate the Japanese fleet. He was right.

On the morning of 4 June 1942, Vice Admiral Chuichi Nagumo, commanding the Japanese carrier fleet, launched his attack, dropping thirty tons of bombs on Midway. It wasn't enough, and Midway's defenders fired back. More important, the American carriers had pulled into range to counterattack. The results were deadly—for the Americans. Thirty-five of forty-one American torpedo bombers were shot down. They inflicted no damage at all. The entirety of Torpedo Squadron 8, launched from the *Hornet,* was blown from the sky; only one of its members survived, Ensign George Gay, who watched the battle, bobbing in the sea, after he ejected from his plane.

But with the Japanese Zeros chasing after the torpedo bombers, American dive-bombers, under the command of Lieutenant Commander Wade McClusky, began their sorties against the Japanese aircraft carriers. Three great prizes burst with flames as bombs ripped through the decks of the *Akagi, Kaga,* and *Soryu.* As Admiral Spruance and Captain Miles Browning (of Nimitz's naval air staff) had hoped, the Japanese carriers were packed with planes refitting for a second run at Midway. The Japanese suddenly went from enjoying a turkey shoot, to suffering a disaster. *Akagi* and *Kaga* sank in the night, and an American submarine delivered the coup de grâce to *Soryu.*

Yamamoto's remaining carrier, *Hiryu,* turned its planes on the *Yorktown.* The *Yorktown*'s guns cleared the skies of all but a handful of Japanese planes, but Japanese bombers—flown with kamikaze desperation—badly battered the *Yorktown* and forced her to retire. Aboard ship was Vice Admiral Fletcher, who transferred overall command of the battle to Rear Admiral Spruance. The *Hiryu*'s attack on the *Yorktown* was like a bee's sting—fatal to itself. As Admiral Spruance directed the American counterattack, bombers raked the deck of the *Hiryu* with devastatingly accurate hits, forcing the Japanese to scuttle her. On 7 June, a Japanese submarine sank the *Yorktown.* But the gallant *Yorktown* had been abandoned, and killing that wounded lion was small comfort to the Japanese who had suffered a naval catastrophe. Aside from the *Yorktown,* the Americans had lost a destroyer, 150 planes, and 300 dead, but they had inflicted 5,000 Japanese casualties, sunk 4 Japanese aircraft carriers and a heavy cruiser, severely damaged several other Japanese ships, and downed more than 320 Japanese planes.

Admiral Yamamoto had known that time was not on Japan's side. He had spent two years at Harvard and two years as naval attaché in Washington, and unlike the militarist general and prime minister Hideki Tojo, he respected the latent power of the United States. Before the war, Yamamoto had warned that to defeat the United States, the Japanese had to understand that victory meant not taking Hawaii or the West Coast but marching all the way to Washington. He opposed allying Japan with Nazi Germany and fascist Italy, about whom Tojo was enthusiastic. Yamamoto had not wanted to fight the United States, but when ordered to do so, he tried to deliver a knockout blow at Pearl Harbor and then again at Midway. Having failed in both attempts, he foresaw Japan's doom, though it still lay three years away—three years of intensely brutal fighting on the islands and in the jungles of the Pacific that would close in two horrible explosions and a shower of radioactive dust.

MERCENARIES, MARINES, AND MACARTHUR

THE AMERICAN COUNTERATTACK went beyond the naval battles of the Coral Sea and Midway. It included, colorfully enough, American mercenaries. These were the Flying Tigers of Major Claire Chenault. Chenault, in his retirement from the U.S. Army Air Corps (in which retirement he had privately promoted himself to colonel), became an adviser to the Chinese Nationalist forces of Chiang Kai-shek in 1937. In 1941, Chiang Kai-shek helped Chenault put some teeth into his advice by hiring the American Volunteer Group, better known as the "Flying Tigers"—300 former American servicemen (many of them released from current service), of whom 100 were pilots, including a future Marine ace, the brawling, heavy-drinking "Pappy" Boyington, whom Chenault loathed and gave a dishonorable discharge from the Tigers.

The swashbuckling Tigers flew obsolescent P-40B "Warhawk" fighters—with little or nothing in the way of spare parts—but in less than a year managed to shoot down 286 Japanese planes while suffering only a dozen losses. While Jimmy Doolittle had his raid, Claire Chenault's flyboys kept up a consistent harassment of the Japanese in the China-Burma theater from 20 December 1941 until the unit was disbanded on 4 July 1942 when the Twenty-third Fighter Group of the U.S. Army Air Corps took over.

On the ground was another American adviser, Army General "Vinegar Joe" Stilwell. Stilwell was an old Asia hand. He had served in the Philippines and in China since 1935. He spoke fluent Chinese and Japanese but had no time for ornate Oriental diplomacy or saving anyone's "face." He was hard, blunt, and independent-minded, and he hated the man he was advising: Chiang Kai-shek, whom he considered corrupt. He served, at the direction of the American government, as Chiang Kai-shek's chief of staff. In 1942 Stilwell was named U.S. commander of the China-Burma-India theater, where, unfortunately, he spent most of his time organizing the retreat of the Chinese Nationalists. But he was a frontline general—in the steaming, malarial, and snake-infested Burmese jungle—sometimes to be seen with a tommy gun slung over his shoulder.

The Allied land-based counteroffensive in the Pacific started in New Guinea, with brave and effective Australian troops prying the Japanese from their latest invasion prize. How anyone could consider New Guinea—populated by headhunters; choked by stinking, prehistoric jungle and swamp that could swallow a man in its mire; infested by disease, "jungle rot," leeches, biting insects, poisonous snakes, and crocodiles—a prize was a mystery. It was certainly a mystery to the American troops who joined the Australians in the campaign to retake the island. It took two years and roughly 34,000 combined Australian and American casualties to conquer this green hell from the Japanese. But, at length, the combined Allied effort of hard-slogging infantry, land-based airpower, and naval support succeeded.

The Battle of the Bismarck Sea was one of the turning points in the campaign. When the Japanese tried to reinforce New Guinea in March 1943, American and Australian land-based bombers—the Americans commanded by General George Kenney, the Australians by Group Captain Bill "Bull" Garing—swept in low and machine-gunned and skip-bombed the enemy into oblivion: sinking four destroyers and every Japanese troop transport. In April, the Americans bagged Admiral Yamamoto—shooting down his plane as he flew out to the Solomon Islands to raise Japanese morale. And the Americans developed the strategy—originated by Admiral Bull Halsey—that served them for the rest of the Pacific war: island-hopping. It meant avoiding Japanese strong points (like Rabaul) and simply going around them, advancing up the Pacific, hitting the Japanese at more vulnerable points. By the end of the New Guinea campaign the Allies had killed 123,000 of the enemy, secured Australia's defensive perimeter, and made possible MacArthur's triumphal return to the Philippines.

Elsewhere the U.S. Marines led the way on the island-by-island advance up from the South Pacific, beginning at Guadalcanal, part of the Solomon Island chain, and as hellish a place as New Guinea. The 1st Marine Division under Major General "Archie" Vandegrift (another veteran of Haiti, Nicaragua, and China) splashed ashore on Guadalcanal and the surrounding islands of Gavutu,

Tanambogo, and Tulagi on 7 August 1942. The Marines seized Guadalcanal's airfield—just completed by the Japanese for their land-based bombers—and named it after Marine dive-bomber pilot Major Lofton R. Henderson, killed at Midway. This auspicious beginning presaged a roaring battle, because whoever controlled Guadalcanal and Henderson Field controlled the shipping lanes between the United States and Australia.

With those stakes at risk, the Japanese, from their base at Rabaul, threw everything they had at retaking the island. Samuel Eliot Morison wrote of the experience: "For us who were there [he was the Navy's official historian for the war], Guadalcanal is not a name but an emotion, recalling desperate fights in the air, furious night naval battles, frantic work at supply or construction, savage fighting in sodden jungle, nights broken by screaming bombs and deafening explosions of naval shells."[9]

Vice Admiral Frank Jack Fletcher, a hero of the Coral Sea and Midway, worried that his supporting carrier force that had seen the Marines onshore was vulnerable to Japanese attack. In a single day's fighting against the Japanese, he lost 20 percent of his airpower. So he pulled out. The Marines were bombarded by the Japanese and did not have the luxury of leaving—indeed, they had not even completed their landings. They watched as the Navy withdrew—taking away their naval air support, the Marines' source of resupply, and 2,000 not-yet-landed Marines. That was at dusk on 8 August 1942.

At 1:40 A.M. of the following morning, the Japanese navy caught American and Australian naval forces—the Southern Group, commanded by British Rear Admiral Victor Crutchley—in the dark, off the coast of Savo Island and Guadalcanal. A Japanese carrier group commanded by Admiral Gunichi Mikawa had raced down the "the slot," the New Georgia Sound running between the Solomon Islands, to make the assault. Admiral Mikawa achieved total surprise—and the results were devastating. One American cruiser—the USS *Chicago*—managed to limp away, badly beaten. But three others—the *Astoria, Quincy,* and *Vincennes*—were sunk. So was the Australian cruiser the *Canberra*. These ships laid the keel for what became "Iron Bottom Sound"—the Davy Jones Locker of the naval battles of the Solomon Islands. More than 1,000 Allied sailors went to their rest—some ripped apart by sharks—from the Battle of Savo Island. Admiral Mikawa sailed back to Rabaul with a tremendous victory in his pocket—a victory that could have been even greater had he pressed on. But Mikawa was content. He did not want to tangle with Admiral Fletcher's carriers, not knowing they were steaming away. Only an American submarine that nailed a Japanese heavy cruiser, sinking it with a single torpedo, ruined the otherwise perfect art of Mikawa's attack.

The battle now centered on Guadalcanal, which Marine Corps Pacific veteran William Manchester thought was worse than New Guinea, which "at least had the Kokoda Trail." On Guadalcanal "the green fastness was broken only by streams. . . . The forest seemed almost faunal: arrogant, malevolent, cruel: a great toadlike beast. . . ."[10] In that green fastness, the Marines stubbornly held Henderson Field for six months so that Marine pilots could fight the Japanese and provide cover for Navy resupply vessels. What they could not do was stop the "Tokyo Express" between Rabaul and Guadalcanal, which allowed the Japanese to massively reinforce the island. Trying to stop the Tokyo Express was the Navy's job, and the Navy had a hard time doing it until Bull Halsey simply demanded it, no matter what the risks or costs.

The biggest of these engagements was the Battle of the Santa Cruz Islands on 26 October 1942. The Japanese brought four battleships, four aircraft carriers, ten cruisers, and twenty-nine destroyers against two American carrier groups led by the USS *Hornet* and USS *Enterprise*. While the Japanese claimed a tactical victory—they sank the *Hornet* (though only after ten hours of fighting, and after it had been abandoned) and badly damaged the *Enterprise*—the overall naval situation was one of shared custody: the United States Navy (and Marine air cover) ruled during the day; the Japanese navy kept the Tokyo Express running through the night.

The turning point was the naval Battle of Guadalcanal, fought 12 November 1942. American Rear Admiral Daniel J. Callahan brought his own badly outnumbered ships—five cruisers and eight destroyers—against a Japanese task force of two battleships, one light cruiser, and fourteen destroyers. The Japanese ships were the artillery of a new Japanese offensive that intended to land 10,000 troops on the island. They never got to land those men or attack Henderson Field. Fighting at close quarters, Admiral Callahan's ships slugged it out with the Japanese in the most furious naval battle of the war.

The battle, fought at night, lasted less than thirty minutes. Admiral Callahan and Admiral Norman Scott were killed. So were the five Sullivan brothers, whose familial sacrifice became a rallying point for the American war effort (and strengthened Navy prohibitions against family members serving together). In total, more the 700 Americans died, four American destroyers were sunk, two were damaged, and one cruiser was scuttled (the rest were badly damaged).

The Americans claimed two Japanese destroyers sunk (and three damaged), and the scuttling of the battleship *Hiei*.

Reverberating naval battles from this initial showdown were fought until the morning of 15 November. Under cover of darkness on 13–14 November the Japanese slipped in to bombard Henderson Field, but when they tried to land infantrymen in the morning, the U.S. Navy sank seven of eleven Japanese transports hurrying to the island—and the survivors were hammered on the beaches. The Japanese tried to strike again in the night, but this time the Navy was waiting for them. Vice Admiral Willis Lee brought four destroyers and two battleships—the USS *Washington* and USS *South Dakota*—to the action. His ships were mauled: he lost two destroyers to the ocean bottom and the other two were battered. The *South Dakota,* suffering from an electrical power outage, spun out of formation and became a floating target for the Japanese. She survived—and kept fighting—even after taking forty-two direct hits. With the *South Dakota* distracting the Japanese, the *Washington* landed roundhouse punches. The Americans' combined efforts forced the Japanese to scuttle their battleship *Kirishima*. The Japanese again tried to land troop transports in the morning, but it was a second bloody shambles for the troopers of Dai Nippon.

The island battle still wasn't over, but the Marines now had the indisputable upper hand. The Marines had fought for months not only against the Japanese, but against sickness, debilitating heat, wretched bugs, and rations that had been condemned yet given to them anyway—not to mention shortages of all kinds thanks to bolshie longshoremen on strike and naval caution. The average Marine logging up the months at Guadalcanal lost twenty-five pounds. If they wanted to eat, Marine Raider Colonel "Red Mike" Edson told his men, they should steal food from the Japs. As William Manchester lamented, "One reason the struggles in the Pacific constantly teetered on the brink of disaster is that they were shoestring operations. At one point, the United States was spending more money feeding and housing uprooted Italian civilians than on the Americans fighting the Japanese."[11]

Aside from the elements and Washington's parsimony, the Marines had endured repeated Japanese bombardments, defended Henderson Field against stiff odds (the most celebrated battles were the night fights at Bloody Ridge, where the outnumbered Marines inflicted heavy losses on the Japanese), raided Japanese positions, collected Japanese heads and ears (in retaliation for Japanese atrocities), and tried to root out a fanatical enemy entrenched in the jungle (and test-fired flamethrowers). The Marines' hard fighting achieved its reward. In the first week in February 1943, the Japanese reembarked their surviving soldiers—about 13,000 men—and evacuated Guadalcanal. The Japanese losses were severe, including more than 24,000 soldiers and 2,300 pilots. The Marines suffered about 1,600 dead. If Marines were instructed to tell St. Peter at the Pearly Gates, "Another Marine reporting for duty, sir. I've spent my time in Hell," they could take consolation that their efforts had sent many more Nipponese to the nether regions.

BLOODY TARAWA

THE PACIFIC THEATER included not just steaming jungles but the frozen wastes of the Aleutian Islands. There, American forces regained the islands of Attu and Kiska—to the relief of civilians in Alaska and the Pacific Northwest, who feared these were the jumping-off points for a Japanese invasion. At Attu, the fighting was savage. Only 29 Japanese were taken as prisoners; 2,400 were killed, some blowing themselves up with hand grenades rather than be taken alive—a mass suicide they committed after running through a hospital and killing all the patients. The battle at Kiska was less ferocious. The American and Canadian troops found the island deserted save for some dogs and fresh brewed coffee. When this report arrived in Washington, the secretary of the Navy, Frank Knox, asked Admiral Ernest King what it meant. King replied: "The Japanese are very clever. Their dogs can brew coffee."[12]

Such was the war in the north. In the South Pacific, not only had the Japanese banzai charge been driven back on its heels and evicted from Guadalcanal and New Guinea, but by 1943 American shipbuilders had made the United States Navy larger than the combined fleets of every other combatant nation. Now that the United States naval forces were bigger and better, Admiral Nimitz was intent they should strike harder and faster than the Japanese could withstand.

The first test was at a Japanese island fortress in the middle of nowhere: Tarawa, a speck—or more accurately a collection of thirty-eight coral island specks surrounding a lagoon—just north of the equator, 2,400 miles southwest of Hawaii. The key island of the Tarawa group was Betio, two miles long and about half a mile wide. It had an airstrip and was as heavily fortified as any such speck can be, with 4,600 well-armed and elite Japanese troops dug into well-prepared and reinforced trenches, pillboxes, and bunkers behind razor-sharp coral reefs, concrete obstacles, mines, and barbed wire. The Japanese were to be supported by land-based bombers from Rabaul and from Japanese island bases like Truk in the Caroline Islands just west of the Marshall Islands. Additional support would come from Japanese surface ships and submarines. Rear Admiral Keiji Shibasaki was charged with fortifying and defending the Gilbert Islands, of which Tarawa was a part. Japan believed the Gilbert Islands, covering a twenty-two-mile triangle, were crucial to guarding the southwestern approach to Japan through the Marshall Islands. Admiral Shibasaki believed the approach was sealed. He boasted that not a million men in a hundred years could take Betio.

The American commanders were well aware how important the Gilbert Islands were and how formidably they were defended. Vice Admiral Raymond Spruance brought to the task the most powerful fleet ever assembled by the United States: seventeen aircraft carriers, twelve battleships, a dozen cruisers, sixty-six destroyers, as well as troop transports bearing 35,000 Marines and U.S. Army infantry. Spruance divided his fleet into three Gilbert Island task forces: one targeted Tarawa, one targeted the island of Makin, and the third was the carrier task force that would give the United States supremacy in the sky.

On 20 November 1943, the big guns of the American fleet opened up on Tarawa and blew the hell out of it, with American B-17 bombers completing the desolation of the island. Just as Admiral Shibasaki was certain Tarawa was impregnable, Admiral Spruance believed nothing could have survived the bombardment he had just inflicted. Both men were terribly wrong, but Shibasaki was more wrong—he was dead, killed during the bombardment.

The Japanese positions had been built to withstand heavy shelling, and though the Japanese had lost their big guns and their commanding officer, they were ready for the Marine assault. As the Marines tried an approach through the lagoon the Japanese defenders crept out of their holes, threw off the safety catches on their weapons, and arranged their fields of fire. The initial Marine invasion force came aboard amphibious tractors that could climb over the coral reef and land on the beaches with machine guns blazing. Japanese fire came whizzing back, and the beach became a storm of lead. Some of the amphibious vehicles caught fire and burned black. Other landing vehicles got stuck on the coral reef or were hit by mortars or artillery, forcing the Marines to wade ashore amid a buzz of bullets cutting through the water. The survivors struggled onto a beach blanketed with Marine dead. Behind them, the lagoon was literally turning red with blood. Five thousand Marines landed the first day; 1,500 became casualties.

But three Marine heroes began bringing order out of the bloody chaos. On the northwestern end of the island, Marine Major Michael Ryan gained a foothold with 200 Marines who were able to take the fight to the enemy and clear a new landing area on "Green Beach." At the main landing site, Major Jim Crowe pushed his Marines up the beach, cigar between his teeth, shotgun in his hands, shouting: "Look, the sons of bitches can't hit me. Why do you think they can hit you? Get moving. Go over that wall and kill some goddamned Japs."[13] Colonel David Shoup, who won the Medal of Honor, directed the battle on the beach while wounded and under constant fire.

That first night on the beach, the Marines had orders to kill Jap infiltrators with their knives—because to open fire in the dark on a beach full of Marines was to invite disaster. Though there was no banzai charge in the night, the Marines were still pinned down, and the second day's landings were even worse than the first. As the landing craft reached the coral reef and dropped their ramps, shells exploded in the water directly in front or on top of them.

But the Marines began advancing from the west with Marine Major Michael Ryan. Once they could move off the landing beaches, they developed a way to clear Japanese positions. They called it "blind 'em, blast 'em, burn 'em"—blind them with a wave of covering fire, blast them with satchels of explosives hurled into their blockhouses, and burn them to hell with flamethrowers. When the Marines took Betio airfield, they named it after Marine Scout Sniper William Deane Hawkins, who was a one-man demolition crew until he was killed by Japanese mortar fire.

The Marines crossed a landscape of shattered palm trees, shell-scarred earth, bullet-cracked concrete, twisted metal, reeking smoke, and the wreckage of the dead. Tanks had finally landed successfully, as had bulldozers driven by Seabees, and half-tracks with 75-mm guns, all of which assisted in the blind 'em, blast 'em, burn 'em operations. The Japanese would not surrender. As at Kiska, they preferred suicide or, at dark, they charged in an all-night-long banzai melee, won by the U.S. Marines. On 23 November 1943, the Marines secured Tarawa and took Makin Island. The butcher's bill of Tarawa proved—if proof were needed—the ferocity of the fighting. All but 17 Japanese defenders were dead. The Americans suffered 1,000 dead and more than 2,000 wounded. It had been four days of unremitting close quarters fighting that the Marines remembered as "Bloody Tarawa."

When the Japanese captured the Gilbert Islands in December 1941, they had forced the natives—British-catechized Christians, Protestants and

Catholics alike—to desecrate their altars and churches. Now the Marine chaplains came to reconsecrate the island, and to offer dead Marines, who were buried by sand-pushing bulldozers, the last rites. As the surviving Marines watched, they offered prayers of their own: for the souls of their departed buddies and for the destruction of Japan.

CHAPTER 21

"THE GREAT CRUSADE"

J APAN HAD STRUCK the first blow against the United States, but Nazi Germany, in declaring war against America, became the primary target. The German war machine was an awesome vehicle of conquest and destruction. Yet when it invaded the Soviet Union and declared war on the United States the same fateful year of 1941, Hitler's Germany overreached.

The challenges confronting the United States were still enormous. Like Britain, the United States was now called to fight against the Axis powers on two fronts: two, if one considers Africa, the Middle and Near East, and Europe a single front, and the Far East from India to Australia to Hawaii to Alaska a single front. Britain could call on the manpower strength of its empire, but that empire had been fighting for better than two full years. And after the Hitler-Stalin Pact and the fall of France, it had been fighting alone against the combined weight of Nazi Germany, Fascist Italy, Imperial Japan, Stalin's Russia, Vichy France, and other Nazi collaborators.

The United States' entry into the war united the English-speaking world—in fulfillment of Winston Churchill's ardent hope. America's enormous industrial capacity would be revved up for the Allied war machine. America's prewar military would be massively expanded—the greatest military mobilization in American history—bringing under arms a people committed to peace but whose military effectiveness had been decisive in the last great war. The American armed forces this time would not be facing a Germany nearly exhausted. They confronted a Germany that was the master of Europe and a Japan that was the master of Asia. If the outcome to Churchill and Roosevelt seemed certain, the getting there, they knew, would be bloody, arduous, and dangerous—a gargantuan undertaking that, in the end, would leave more than a million American servicemen killed or wounded.

Having committed to making victory in Europe the priority, President Roosevelt wanted to mount a cross-channel invasion in 1942 or at the latest 1943. But the British—even the bulldog Churchill—deemed this impossible. First, the United States had to secure the Atlantic. It also had to build an army of a size and quality to face the Wehrmacht. And it would be best, the British thought, to gain a foothold in North Africa and approach Germany from the Mediterranean rather than begin with a head-on assault.

If Pearl Harbor had been a stunning blow to the American Navy, the Atlantic held dangers of its own. In the first four months of 1942, German U-boats sank 87 ships in American coastal waters, and by June 1942 nearly 400 ships had been sunk by U-boats in waters patrolled by the United States Navy. Five thousand merchant seamen and other servicemen—twice the number of dead at Pearl Harbor—died in the first six months of the Battle of the North Atlantic. In the entirety of the war, the Merchant Marine and the United States Marine Corps had the highest casualty rates.

Admiral Ernest King, commander in chief of the U.S. fleet, thought the "situation approaches the 'desperate.' "[1] Not only were the German U-boats devilishly effective—Churchill thought they were the greatest threat to the Allies during the war—but the United States did not have an adequate number of ships and planes for escort duty to sweep the U-boats aside. Despite British pressure, King refused to mount convoys until he was sure he had enough ships. Only the courage of captains and the expectation of bristling production from the arsenal of democracy—production that had to outpace the launching of new German U-boats—could win the Battle of the Atlantic.

In the meantime, Americans risked the hazards to bring supplies to Stalin's Russia and land troops and materiel in Great Britain, America's fellow arsenal of democracy. American troops and supplies began arriving in Britain as early as January 1942. The Americans thought of Britain as the island platform for a cross-channel invasion. But the British pointed out the possibilities for an American landing in Vichy North Africa. From their bases in Egypt, the British were already engaged in fighting the German Afrika Korps. If the Americans landed in the west, the combined Allied forces could crush the Afrika Korps, control the Mediterranean, and then turn against Fascist Italy.

American generals, led by Dwight David Eisenhower (whom General of the Army George Marshall appointed as commander of the European theater of operations), thought Africa was a sideshow—and many American generals, politicians, and bureaucrats suspected that the British were more interested in advancing their own imperial ambitions than in taking the direct route to beating Hitler. General Marshall thought a second front in Europe was vital to appeasing Stalin, who was facing the ferocity of Hitler's Operation Barbarossa. Roosevelt was inclined to agree. And Eisenhower had prepared a plan—named Sledgehammer—for the invasion of France in 1942. He followed it up with another plan for invading France in 1943. But in the argument over North Africa, the British won, with President Roosevelt casting the deciding vote. It was, in fact, the only practicable point where American ground troops could be brought to battle relatively quickly—and without risking disaster. The British were well aware of German military prowess. The Americans would discover it at Kasserine Pass.

FACING *DAS DEUTSCHE* AFRIKA KORPS

EISENHOWER, THE MOST VEHEMENT OPPONENT of a landing in North Africa, was chosen to lead it. Churchill gave the operation its name: Torch. It was meant to be an American show, but in the event, America provided the bulk of the ground forces, the Royal Navy contributed most of the naval forces, and responsibility for achieving air superiority was shared. The Americans would land in Vichy-controlled Morocco and Algeria. The hope was that the Vichy French—who regarded the British as hostile belligerents—would more willingly, with little or no fuss or bloodshed, surrender to the Americans.

The massive convoy of 650 ships and transports for Operation Torch eluded the Germans, who were fooled as to the Allied destination. From 8 November to 12 November 1942—with Hitler threatening Vichy France with occupation if its colonies did not resist—65,000 Allied troops jumped onto the Mediterranean shores of North Africa and Morocco's Atlantic coast. The colonial forces of Vichy France did indeed resist—for three days, until Vichy Admiral Jean Darlan had negotiated his way into a North African governorship. With Gallic pride assuaged, most Vichy resistance ended, save for a few units that joined the Germans.

The objective now was Tunisia, where the Germans prepared to fight the combined British and American forces. The British had evicted the Germans from threatening Egypt at the Second Battle of El Alamein (23 October to 4 November 1942). But the Germans would not surrender Africa as easily as Vichy France had done; they reinforced the Afrika Korps with units from France and

Italy. And they still had Field Marshal Erwin Rommel, the Desert Fox, who had so troubled the British and who now pounced on the Americans as vulnerable prey.

On 14 February 1943, German Stuka dive-bombers came screaming out of the skies against the United States II Corps. The II Corps—like virtually all the green American troops—was ill-disciplined, ill-trained, and unserious. It was done no favors by its commanders, including Major General Lloyd Fredenhall, who far out-dug "Dugout" Douglas MacArthur, building a command post in a cave distant from the front lines. The German bombers hammered war's deadly reality into the Americans. So did the German army that followed on the bombing. Trusting to the impregnability of his eastern defenses at the Mareth Line—and to British General Bernard Montgomery's caution—Rommel rushed at the Americans with vigor. His men poured through Kasserine Pass, his panzers eviscerated the American Sherman tanks, and he looked to rout the American Army. But when Eisenhower hurried American reinforcements to plug the German advance, Rommel sounded recall. Rommel had badly stung the Americans, yet he knew better than to overextend his troops. He had inflicted 6,000 American casualties at minimal cost to himself—nine tanks and perhaps a thousand dead or wounded.

The II Corps would not be so mauled again because it gained a new commander—General George S. Patton. The II Corps was taken from a cave-dwelling commander and given to an ass-chewing one who strode about his command wearing cavalry boots and ivory-handled revolvers, letting loose a stream of profane rebukes and encouragement, and seeking out battle all the time everywhere. With the aggressive and brilliant Patton roaring at him from the west and his nemesis Montgomery coming in strength from the east, Rommel faced what he had already predicted would happen. Before the Battle of the Kasserine Pass, Rommel had wanted to withdraw his troops from Africa. He could see, if Hitler could not, that to reinforce Africa now was to reinforce failure. But Hitler would hear nothing of defeat; the Afrika Korps was to fight to the last man. The last man would not be Rommel, who was recalled to Germany. The battle for Tunisia was fought in its rugged, mountainous north, where the Germans dug in, shielded by minefields, and with well-positioned fields of fire. Here the Americans who had been embarrassed at Kasserine Pass showed they had the stuff to beat the Wehrmacht. On 3 May 1943, the German forces in Tunisia surrendered.

Africa belonged to the Allies, who matched that victory with victory in the Atlantic. By the summer of 1943, improved Allied convoys, radar, and aerial bombing had turned the battle against the U-boats: the naval lifeline between America and Britain was secured, the passage finally safe, the Battle of the Atlantic won. By war's end, nearly 3,000 Allied ships (175 of them warships, the rest merchant ships) had been lost to U-boat torpedoes. But if the Merchant Marine had paid a terrible price for braving the stormy Atlantic, the U-boat crews suffered on a catastrophic scale—two-thirds of them were dead; only 109 of Germany's 863 U-boats survived.

By 1943, the Allies had tamed an ocean and conquered a continent. The next step was the liberation of Europe.

A N Z I O

FOR ITALY TO HAVE BEEN the soft underbelly of Europe it needed to be garrisoned solely by Italians. Unfortunately for the Allies, it was the Wehrmacht that defended Fascist Italy. That made things infinitely harder. The German soldier was the best there was, and the German army clung to Italy with the tenacity of a wrestler. The Germans would not be pried from the Italian boot until Berlin surrendered in 1945.

The stepping-stone across the Mediterranean from Africa to Italy was Sicily, a prize sought by both General Montgomery and General Patton, and defended by Luftwaffe Feldmarschall Albert Kesselring, whose ferocious nickname was "Smiling Albert." Patton grumbled that the Allied plan shortchanged his army; he was assigned to climbing the west coast of Sicily and guarding Montgomery's flank, while Monty claimed the glory of capturing Messina, the port city across whose narrow straits was Italy. But Patton moved faster. He liberated Palermo. He took Messina. But what the Allies had failed to do was seize the straits, which would have trapped 300,000 German and Italian troops on the island. Instead, more than a third of them escaped to fight again. That failure aside, Patton's hell-for-leather conquest of German-fortified Sicily—it was accomplished in thirty-eight days—knocked Montgomery off center stage and put paid to British doubts about the fighting ability of American units. Under Patton at least, the American Army was a winner.

With the Allies at their doorstep, the Italians folded. King Victor Emmanuel of Italy maneuvered Mussolini into resigning and replaced him with Marshal Pietro Badogli. Though Marshal Badogli was that rare Italian who could claim battlefield success (he had been the conqueror of Ethiopia), his task was to cut a deal with the Allies, not to fight them. On 3 September 1943, the Italians signed an armistice and officially left the war, though the war did not leave Italy. The Wehrmacht dug its heels into the country. The Germans seized control of the government in Rome. Allied POWs, who had been freed by their Italian guards, were rounded up. Italian soldiers, the Germans' former allies, were deported to slave labor camps—except for Mussolini, whom Hitler had rescued by the SS and installed in northern Italy as Il Duce of a fascist rump state. In addition, Hitler ordered the SS to kidnap the pope—an order the SS quietly ignored as impractical and unwise.

It could also be argued that the Italian campaign itself was a mistake. The Alps, which the Allies were not about to cross, separated Italy from Germany. That made Italy a diversion rather than a direct assault on the Reich. It was one thing to force the Germans to garrison and defend the peninsula, but there was no practical military value—except to divert German troops from the eastern front—in fighting up the mountainous, heavily fortified center of Italy, where hardened German troops could inflict massive casualties on the Allies. Having swept North Africa and taken Sicily, the Allies had done all they needed to do in the Mediterranean—cleared the sea (the Italian navy joined the Allies) and knocked Italy out of the war. If it was still too early—and the military planners knew it was—to launch Eisenhower's cross-channel invasion, the campaign in Italy was merely a massive effort to do something, however costly.

So Montgomery jumped across the straits to the toe of the Italian boot and American General Mark "Wayne" Clark led the main Allied invasion at Salerno, where Kesselring was waiting. German artillery and the Luftwaffe pounded the Allied—largely American—landing parties. The Americans stubbornly clung to the beachhead. Once the Americans gained a foothold, Kesselring unleashed his panzers, and for a moment Clark's invasion faced being ground to pieces and hurled into the sea. But Clark had friends of high caliber: big guns roared from the Navy's offshore batteries, American land-based artillery drove back the panzers, Allied planes dominated the sky with seemingly endless sorties, and the 82nd Airborne reinforced the troops on the beaches. The Germans withdrew in the direction of Cassino, where they established the Gustav Line about a third of the way up the Italian boot, well behind Naples, which the Allies occupied on 7 October 1943; the city had been left a vandalized wreck.

The soldiers discovered that Italy was not all sun and spaghetti—a better description would have been mud, rain, snow, stony hills, and German shells. And like many soldiers in the field, they felt somewhat abandoned. The big generals—Patton and Montgomery—had been called to England; supplies were stacking up in English warehouses, while the soldiers in the Italian campaign shed their rain-sodden, mud-caked gear and were resupplied by pack-bearing mules. Yet the ragged, tired, unshaven troopers kept slogging on, climbing hills, ascending mountains, to get at the enemy—but the enemy could not be budged from the Gustav Line.

So the Allies planned a landing behind it, at Anzio. The troops would be landed on 22 January 1944. They would cut off the road to Rome and flank the Germans defending the Gustav Line while Mark Clark's men smashed through the line at Cassino. The landing came off like a charm, the very opposite of the near-run thing at Salerno. It was utterly unopposed. Yet General John Lucas moved cautiously. Throughout the planning and preparation for the assault, he assumed that the cockamamie scheme would end in disaster. His caution helped make it so. Carpe diem—not caution—was the appropriate byword, and it was the German commander Albert Kesselring who seized the day, rushing 100,000 troops to the high ground surrounding the beach, forming a noose around the neck of the Allied army, which, had it moved quickly, could have seized those very heights.

Now Lucas really was trapped. German artillery pounded the troops on the beach. There was no cover, no place to hide, no safe rear lines; Anzio beach was a flat, barren artillery range. The Allied soldiers' only effective defense was their own artillery, which, to his credit, Lucas had arrayed to retaliate in force. The fighting became as desperate as it had been at Salerno, as the Germans tried to smash the Allies on the beachhead. Allied naval batteries and air sorties counterattacked, and if they saved Lucas's men from being driven into the sea, the Allied infantry still could not advance against the German ring of steel around them. The battle became an artillery duel, the beach a no-man's land where Lucas's army was trapped for four months and 59,000 Americans became casualties. Winston Churchill, who had ardently pressed for the landing at Anzio, best expressed its failure: "We hoped to land a wildcat that would tear out the bowels of the Boche. Instead we have stranded a vast whale with its tail flopping in the water."[2] When the Allied army finally got itself off the beach in May 1944, it was under the command of the Patton-trained General Lucian Truscott, who had replaced Lucas at the end of February.

Meanwhile, it had taken General Clark all of January—against German counterattacks—to gain a position north of the Rapido River, which brought him up against the Gustav Line, centered on the ancient abbey of Monte

Cassino. Clark ruled out trying to maneuver around the abbey, because too much time had been lost already. He threw everything he had on a full frontal assault to break the line—and failed, wearing out his American troops. In February, Clark reluctantly gave the lead to Commonwealth troops commanded by the tough New Zealand General Bernard Freyberg. Freyberg was convinced that the abbey—one of the treasures of Christendom—had to be destroyed. Freyberg believed the Germans were occupying the abbey and using it to guide their murderous artillery fire on Allied troops. He was, at best, half right. The abbey itself was deserted, save for its elderly abbot, a handful of the abbey's monks, and a few hundred civilian refugees. German officers had ensured that many of Monte Cassino's literary and artistic treasures were trucked to Rome and safety. The Germans had, however, fortified the entire area around the abbey. With Allied casualties running high, the press—and American Catholic laypeople—shouted for the destruction of Monte Cassino; they backed Freyberg. So did British Field Marshal Harold Alexander, supreme Allied commander in Italy, who gave Clark, at his request, a direct order to destroy the abbey. Artillery couldn't do the job, so Allied bombers did on 15 February 1944. The result was not only the destruction of the abbey founded by Saint Benedict but the making of rubble and ruins that actually abetted—as Clark feared it might—the Germans' tenacious defense of the Gustav Line, which they held for three more months.

When Kesselring withdrew his men, it was to the north of Rome, forming up eventually in a second massive line of defense, the Gothic Line above Florence. The Gothic Line was even stronger than the Gustav Line, and to get there, the Allies had to slug their way up the boot of Italy, up the Apennine mountain range. Progress was slow, casualties were high, and it was a campaign made tougher by the Germans' orderly fighting withdrawal.

After Clark had cracked the Gustav Line, Field Marshal Alexander had wanted him to cut off the German retreat, but the American general instead drove straight to Rome, claiming it as a prize for the U.S. Fifth Army. Caesar's city, the pope's eternal city, now belonged to General Mark Clark of Madison Barracks (near Watertown, he was the son of an infantry officer), New York. The New World had most definitely arrived in the Old, and Clark had his moment of glory. But that glory was fleeting. Clark turned down joining the invasion of France in order to see the Italian campaign through to its completion. He stayed in Italy, fighting all the way, until the Germans' surrender in 1945.

D - D A Y ,   A R N H E M ,   A N D
T H E   B A T T L E   O F   T H E   B U L G E

MORE THAN A MILLION AND A HALF American soldiers were coiled to launch from England across the English Channel and onto the beaches of France. If they succeeded, Nazi Germany would be trapped between the Anglo-American forces to the west and south, and the Soviet masses to the east. Out of such calculations, anti-Hitler sentiment was rising among many in Germany's professional officer class. Hitler's insane ambitions and orders were as much Germany's enemy, they thought, as the combatants they faced on the battlefield. But there was another school of thought. If the Allied invasion of France could be turned back, if it was an Allied failure, the results would be stunning. The Reich's western borders could be secured indefinitely, the Allied advance up Italy could be parried for a long time—and thus the Wehrmacht could hurl itself in renewed force against the Soviets, and crush that horrendous enemy that united all Germans, both pro- and anti-Hitler.

Operation Overlord, the invasion of Normandy, was far from a sure thing. It would be the largest military landing ever attempted—and it would be attempted against the toughest military force in the world, an army that had repeatedly proven its superiority whenever it fought on anything like equal terms. The German Feldmarschall assigned to prepare the defense of France was Erwin Rommel. No Allied general needed to be reminded of Rommel's skill.

Eisenhower showed some skill of his own in navigating the military politics of his leading generals. He overruled British Air Marshal Arthur "Bomber" Harris, who believed in bombing German cities. Instead, he redirected American and British airpower to bombing the Luftwaffe into oblivion, to forcing German fighters into the skies where American P-51 Mustang fighters could shoot them down, and to hitting bridges, roads, and railways that would disrupt the German defenses.

American bombers flew very much in harm's way. Between the dangers of fighter aircraft and antiaircraft flak, fighting in the air over occupied France and Nazi Germany was more dangerous than fighting as an infantryman in Italy. But the courage of American pilots, their skill, and their effective aircraft, defeated the Luftwaffe. By D-Day, 6 June 1944, Eisenhower could declare to his men: "If you see fighting aircraft over you, they will be ours."[3] The skies over France belonged to the Allies.

Just as crucial was that Eisenhower had managed to fool the Nazis into thinking the invasion would come at the Pas de Calais, the channel's narrowest point. That German miscalculation diverted the bulk of the Wehrmacht's panzers away from the real invasion site at Normandy. And then there was the weather: on 5 June 1944, a gale force storm had ripped through the channel. The decision to go on 6 June was a risk: would the clearing weather hold for the unparalleled air and sea operations of Overlord?

The Allied armada slipped from the coast of England to Normandy unnoticed until they were just offshore—and then the Germans could hardly believe it; the big guns of the supporting Allied naval batteries shook them into belief. The troops in the landing boats had five target beaches. From north to south, they were Sword (assigned to the British), Juno (assigned to the Canadians), Gold (assigned to the British), Omaha (assigned to the United States), and Utah (assigned to the United States). The first troops in, landing behind enemy lines, were parachuting airborne units and troops delivered by glider. Their task was both to finish the job begun by the Allied bombing—blowing bridges and rail lines—and to harass the enemy from the rear. The key thing was to do everything possible to advance the troops off the beaches, where they were vulnerable, and get them inland and reinforced.

At Utah Beach, the 4th Infantry Division, supported by bombers, was able to move inland fairly quickly and unite with units from the 101st and 82nd Airborne Divisions that had landed on either side of St. Mère-Eglise. Twenty-three thousand men landed at Utah Beach, suffering fewer than 200 casualties. At "Bloody Omaha" it was a different story. Where Utah Beach had been lightly defended, Omaha was heavily defended. Where the Allied bombardment at Utah had been effective, at Omaha it was not, with many bombers missing their targets and naval gunnery not having nearly enough time to do its job. The nightmares of Anzio and Tarawa seemed to have struck again. German shells demolished landing boats before they hit the sand. Men floated between sea and shore as bullets ripped past them. On the beach, German fire cut down rows and rows of Americans.

The only luck the Americans had at Omaha—and it certainly didn't seem like luck to the GIs pinned on the beach—was that the Germans did not storm Omaha and clear the Americans away. Instead, by sticking to their entrenchments, the Germans allowed the Americans a foothold—a gruesome foothold to be sure, but it kept the Americans on French soil; and thanks to Brigadier General Norman Cota (and officers like him) who urged his men up the cliffs and off the bloody beach, the foothold became an advance, a costly one, but an advance that German counterattacks couldn't throw back.

From the beaches the Allies moved inland to the next stage of fighting in the *bocage,* a patchwork of French farmland separated by thick hedges that slowed any hope of a rapid advance, as did the German army, which put up a stubborn resistance wherever it was engaged. In the *bocage,* the Germans rigged up a defensive net that made every field a fortified position with machine guns, mortars, and riflemen. Sometimes artillery or panzers were hidden in the *bocage* ready to belch forth flame and death. In all the planning for the Normandy invasions, neither the Americans nor the British had thought for a moment about how the *bocage* would aid the German defense. For the infantrymen involved every field was a small-scale siege. Every field had to be cleared. Allied mobility on the narrow country roads was minimal, and snipers, mines, and antitank *panzerfausts* were a constant danger.

But American troops showed savoir-faire as well. During the Allied advance after D-Day, General Maxwell Taylor, commander of the "Screaming Eagles" 101st Airborne Division, saw a young soldier, perhaps only sixteen years old, eating his rations with his feet propped up against a dead German. Taylor quipped: "I guess we don't have to worry about our untried division any more."[4]

The "Battle of the Hedgerows" was finally broken by a massive Allied bombardment near Saint-Lô. It was the greatest tactical bombing run in history, and it had its due effect, blasting German defenses, communications, and men to smithereens (including more than 600 friendly-fire casualties). American infantry and tanks (some mounted with hedgerow chompers) now charged through the devastated landscape, and the U.S. Third Army under General George S. Patton raced through the gap, marking fifty miles a day, reducing German armies to surrender, and liberating huge swathes of France, from Brittany through the Loire Valley.

Patton had the enemy on the run. The Germans' second disadvantage was that Graf Claus von Stauffenberg's attempt to assassinate the Führer had failed, and in its failure had left implicated some of Germany's finest officers, who were ruthlessly hunted down, tortured, and killed. Among those implicated was Field Marshal Erwin Rommel, who, in order to save his family from Hitler's vengeance, was convinced to commit suicide by drinking poison. The high command of the Wehrmacht had come to realize that Hitler was mad, bad, and dangerous to know; his power over them relied on terror, yes, but it relied even more on their personal oaths of loyalty to the Führer, which they felt honor-bound to uphold. Nevertheless, Hitler's generals were equally convinced that the war was lost, that peace had to be made in the west, and that all Germany's military resources must be shifted against the Communist menace in the east. President Roosevelt's casual, spur of the moment announcement at Casablanca in 1942 that the Allies were committed to a policy of unconditional surrender had momentous consequences, blocking any hopes of peace in the west short of the destruction of the Reich.[5]

So the war in the west could not be won by diplomacy. It had to be won by force. And in July 1944, it appeared that Allied force would soon be triumphant. Half of the German Seventh Army was cut off and trapped in "the Falaise pocket" and pummeled from the air, battered by artillery, and chased by tanks: 10,000 Germans were killed, 50,000 were taken prisoner. Paris fell to the Allies on 24 August. Hitler had ordered the city's destruction, but General Dietrich von Choltitz ignored the order, and the monuments of Paris were left intact. French wine touched American lips, and unfortunate French girls who had been romanced by German soldiers had their heads shaved by their nasty sisters. The U.S. Seventh Army cleared southern France of any remaining Germans, the U.S. First Army drove through northern France, Patton's Third Army swept into eastern France, and Allied armies entered Belgium.

The breakout from the *bocage* had been spectacular. Now it stalled, as a matter of logistics. Allied supplies could not keep up, despite the best efforts of the truckers of the "Red Ball Express," who drove night and day to keep the Americans supplied. Tanks ran out of gas. With the advance slowing until the supply train could catch up, Eisenhower approved a plan of British General Bernard Montgomery to win the war by Christmas.

It was an invasion of the Netherlands code-named "Operation Market-Garden" and was the largest airborne operation ever attempted. Thirty-five thousand paratroopers (including Americans of the 82nd and 101st Airborne) were to be landed behind German lines in the Netherlands. They were to seize and hold the bridges along the route to Arnhem until the infantry and tanks of XXX Corps linked them together. From Arnhem, the Allies could invade Germany over the Ruhr. The plan, in execution, was a noble failure—and that failure meant the war would not end in 1944. Instead, Eisenhower planned to slug it out, pressing along the broad front of the Siegfried Line—or *Westwall,* the stout, initial defenses of Germany built opposite the Maginot Line—in a battle of bludgeoning firepower.

Among those that Patton threw into the fight were the 761st Tank Battalion—

a unit of white officers and black troops. Patton treated all his soldiers the same—he was the first to integrate rifle companies—and when he greeted his new black tankers, he gave them a Pattonesque welcome:

> Men you are the first Negro tankers ever to fight in the American Army. I would never have asked for you if you weren't good. I have nothing but the best in my army. I don't care what color you are, so long as you go up there and kill those Kraut sonsabitches! Everyone has their eyes on you and is expecting great things from you. Most of all, your race is looking forward to you. Don't let them down and, damn you, don't let me down.[6]

The fighting was a brutal war of attrition. Aachen fell to the Allies after three weeks, but led to no breakout. There was, instead, progress by inches through the snow, the sleet, and the entrenched German army in the Huertgen forest. The Americans finally emerged from the wilderness to take the city of Huertgen in early December 1944. Around the same time, to the south, Patton captured the fortress city of Metz after a prolonged siege.

With these victories, an unwarranted optimism wafted through the American high command. Eisenhower bet Montgomery that the war would be over by Christmas. The western Allies had complete air supremacy. The British and Americans could support their infantry from the air and were bombing the German homeland. The Soviets were rolling like Mongols through eastern Europe. German losses were catastrophic. The von Stauffenberg plot showed cracks in German unanimity that rose through an officer corps that had previously considered mutiny unthinkable. Surely the Germans knew they were beaten; surely the Nazi regime was on the brink of collapse.

The weary, toughened, damn-all GIs who had fought the German soldier at Metz and in the Huertgen Forest might have thought otherwise and been warier of rosy predictions of imminent victory. Patton—a nearly lone voice, though there were intelligence reports supporting him—predicted the Germans would unleash a ferocious counterattack. When the Germans did in fact strike, it was with thunderclap surprise, bursting through the Ardennes forest. The Americans thought an attack there was impossible and were using this presumed quiet sector as a place to park fresh-faced arrivals and units needing to recuperate with uninterrupted sleep and warm meals.

The Germans punctured those dreams with steel and lead. Their goal was to strike through the forest, cross the Meuse River, seize Antwerp, and thus slash

British and American supply lines. Hitler argued that he could then divide, reduce, and evict the Anglo-American forces, and effectively undo the Normandy invasion. In its grandest scheme the plan was pure fantasy, but as a tactical maneuver to throw the Allies into disarray it was a masterstroke.

On 16 December 1944, in the worst winter storm in memory, the Germans attacked along a fifty-mile-long front that narrowed like a funnel as they poured through the Ardennes Forest. They came hurling grenades and unleashing a hailstorm of bullets. They were supported by panzers. And they sowed confusion with commando troops dressed in American uniforms, speaking American-accented English, and infiltrating American lines. American confidence suddenly froze into fear and panic. Stunned to find German troops swarming past them with guns a-blazing, thousands of American troops surrendered—especially the newcomers and the battered units that expected to rest and refit. For two days the Germans lunged forward knocking a sixty-mile-deep bulge in the American lines.

Trapped behind the German avalanche were pockets of American units who continued to fight hard. They slowed the German advance and threw it behind schedule. They also played a crucial role in the defense of Bastogne, a communications, transportation, and supply hub, whose hastily gathered American defenders were reinforced by the 101st Airborne. The Germans surrounded Bastogne; capturing it was a major German objective. But when the Germans demanded the surrender of the trapped, outgunned, and outnumbered Americans, 101st Airborne General Anthony McAuliffe gave his memorable reply: "Nuts!" An American officer kindly informed the puzzled Germans that this meant, "Go to Hell!"

Eisenhower's reaction to the German attack was calm, rational, and swift: he directed a quarter of a million Allied soldiers to destroy the exposed German forces. Three divisions of General Patton's Third Army raced to the rescue of Bastogne. And as the weather cleared on Christmas Eve, and Allied planes again took to the skies, the Germans' Ardennes blitzkrieg was driven back. Two days later, on 26 December 1944, Patton relieved Bastogne. Patton wanted to press on and encircle the retreating Germans. That, however, was not Eisenhower's style. He continued forward on a broad front, pushing to restore the American line. It took another month, and nearly 40,000 additional American casualties (there were more than 70,000 American casualties in the battle as a whole), but by the end of January 1945 the bulge was gone, and so were perhaps 100,000 German effectives. Victory, at last, seemed in sight.

CHAPTER 22

"ANOTHER MARINE REPORTING FOR DUTY, SIR. I'VE SPENT MY TIME IN HELL"

THE GREATER EAST ASIA Co-Prosperity Sphere was looking a little rickety. Japanese forces were still in Burma, Siam, French Indochina, and northeastern China, and entrenched in an island sweep from the Dutch East Indies up past the Marianas in the central Pacific all the way north to the Kuriles. But in 1944, America was rolling up the Japanese Empire in the Pacific. The Marshall Islands of Kwajalein and Eniwetok were captured in February, using the element of surprise (the Japanese did not expect attacks here), massive naval and air bombardments (the United States achieved total naval and air superiority and obliterated the defenses and defenders on the narrow coral atolls), and improved landing vehicles that made the future look grim for the Rising Sun. The Japanese suffered more than 8,400 dead at Kwajalein; American dead were 334. At Eniwetok, more than 2,000 Japanese died, while the American dead were virtually the same number as at Kwajalein. It was still tough fighting, but Kwajalein and Eniwetok were nothing like Tarawa, and were a tribute to growing American firepower, mobility, and technological superiority.

From the conquest of the Marshall Islands, the Americans could spring across to attack the Mariana Islands—themselves the springboard to both the Philippine Sea and the Japanese home islands. From the Marianas, American B-29 bombers could begin bombing the paper-and-wood houses of Japan— something the American high command regarded as necessary to break Japan's will to fight.

To the south, MacArthur's Allied forces had bypassed the Japanese fortress at Rabaul, leaving it isolated, helpless, and bombed into irrelevance, while clearing the rest of New Guinea of any significant Japanese resistance. From his capture of the Admiralty Islands in February to the Morotai Islands in September, MacArthur hopped from point to point, surprising the Japanese. From Morotai, at the southern tip of the Philippine Sea, MacArthur was only 300 miles away from fulfilling his pledge to the people of the Philippines.

In the China-Burma-India theater, "Vinegar Joe" Stilwell—and then his replacement General Albert C. Wedemeyer—pushed Generalissimo Chiang Kai-shek to focus on beating the Japanese, rather than the Chinese Communists. With General Frank D. Merrill's "Merrill's Marauders" to the fore, Stilwell invaded Burma from the north, while the British came from the west and drove south in a long, hard fight to push the Japanese out of Burma.

The crucial campaign, though, was for Saipan—the largest and most heavily defended of the Japanese-occupied Mariana Islands, about a hundred miles north of Guam. The Marianas anchored Japan's Pacific supply lines. Take Saipan, and you pulled the Pacific linchpin of the Japanese Empire. The Marianas were not coral atolls—of the sort that had been blown to pieces at Kwajalein and Eniwetok—but settled islands with towns, civilians, and varied landscapes of mountains, caves, jungles, and sugarcane fields that the Japanese tried to turn to their defensive advantage.

The first task, though, was for the U.S. Navy to blow the hell out of Truk Island. Truk, in the Caroline Island chain to the south, was a fortress like Rabaul—and like Rabaul it was left standing but stripped of any purpose: its air force destroyed, its ships sunk, its ability to reinforce the Marianas nil. The Navy then closed in on Saipan, cutting it off from resupply. But the biggest chore belonged to the Marines. They faced the prospect of storming onto beaches that the Japanese had meticulously divided into fields of fire, with Japanese artillery and mortars expertly targeted on every landing zone.

What the invasion of Normandy was to the European theater, Saipan was to the Pacific. The Japanese looked out at an American armada of 800 ships. Aboard this fleet were 130,000 Marines and U.S. Army infantry. They were assigned to take the islands of Saipan, Tinian, and Guam. On 15 June 1944, after two days of Navy shelling, General Holland M. "Howlin' Mad" Smith's Marines hit the beaches. Navy frogmen with demolition charges had blown away many of the obstacles to the Marines' landing, but the Navy's big guns firing from offshore—and bombers—couldn't dislodge the Japanese artillery positions. As the landing craft approached, Japanese mortar rounds and shells burst into the water. The fire was deadly accurate, but the Marines jogged through the surf and onto the beaches through a rain of incessant explosions. The Marines clung to the beach—though it offered little or no cover—and threw back Japanese counterattacks, including one led by tanks.

The Japanese planned to crush the American invasion on the beaches, while the Japanese First Mobile Fleet—rushing to Saipan—drove the U.S. Navy Fifth Fleet into a watery grave. American Vice Admiral Raymond Spruance, commanding the fleet, fretted about a replay of Guadalcanal: the Navy drawn off into a battle that left the Marines abandoned. In the event, Japanese hopes and American fears were unfounded. The resulting Battle of the Philippine Sea—spearheaded by the carriers of U.S. Vice Admiral Marc Mitscher's Task Force 58—is better known in American naval history as "The Great Marianas Turkey Shoot." Japan's First Mobile Fleet counted on support from land-based aircraft on Guam—not knowing that the U.S. Navy had already annihilated these forces. In the battle of carrier planes, American Hellcat fighters cleared the skies of the Japanese. The Japanese losses were catastrophic: nearly 400 Japanese carrier-based planes were shot down; three of their carriers and two oilers were sunk; and another six Japanese ships were badly damaged. The Japanese fleet could, perhaps, have been completely eliminated, but Vice Admiral Spruance let the Japanese limp away in order to return to supporting the Marines and soldiers on Saipan.

With their navy eliminated from the fight, the Japanese soldiers and marines on Saipan were doomed. But they would not surrender. The enemy withdrew to the island's volcanic caves, from which he spewed venomous fire. The Marines cleared these caves with grenades and flamethrowers, or with whatever else was handy (including, sometimes, tanks). Finally, Saipan's Japanese army commander General Yoshitsugu Saito and his naval counterpart Admiral Chuichi Nagumo ordered their men to prepare for a climactic banzai charge. Neither the admiral nor the general would lead it. They committed hara-kiri (General Saito helped by an assistant who shot him in the head).

Their men charged before dawn on 7 July 1944. More than 3,000 Japanese—including hobbling, wounded men armed with knives affixed to poles—screamed their way into the American lines, breaking through a couple of Army battalions, and killing, in a frenzy, anyone within reach, including medical personnel. Marine artillery fired into the Japanese at point-blank range, but the Nipponese demons kept coming until they met the Marines in ferocious hand-to-hand combat; Japanese who were lamed blew themselves up with grenades.

The banzai charge met its inevitable end. But the horror wasn't over. Two days later, dumbfounded Marines watched as hundreds upon hundreds of Japanese civilians committed mass suicide with grenades, or hurled themselves off cliffs, or drowned themselves, or murdered their own children, or were shot down or beheaded by Japanese soldiers.

The Americans lost 3,500 dead and 10,500 wounded at Saipan; Japanese military casualties were 29,000 dead (1,000 were taken prisoner). Among the casualties, in a political sense, was General Hideki Tojo, Japan's prime minister, who fell from power. A new military regime, under General Kuniaki Koiso, took command. For the U.S. fighting man, getting rid of Tojo was another notch on the rifle barrel, but nothing more. He expected—and he was right—that the war would go on and on, from one damn island to another against a crazed, suicidal enemy.

Next up were Guam and Tinian. Guam was bigger than Saipan, with more people, and for forty years had been American territory before the Japanese seized it and brutalized the island's native Chamorros. The battle began, as always, with a naval bombardment. Then the Marines went in under fire to take the beaches on 21 July 1944. The 19,000 Japanese defenders had plentiful stocks of alcohol to fuel their banzai charges. Some of the Japanese strapped themselves with explosives, becoming walking bombs. The Marines used lead to ignite these human fireballs at a safe distance. By 10 August, the Marines had reclaimed Guam for the United States, at a cost of 3,000 American and 18,000 Japanese dead. In joy at their deliverance, the freed Chamorros sang the "Marine Hymn" as well as their own composition:

> Early Monday morning
> The action came to Guam,
> Eighth of December,
> Nineteen forty-one
>> Oh, Mr. Sam, Sam, my dear Uncle Sam,
>> I want you please come back to Guam.
> Our lives are in danger—
> You better come
> And kill all the Japanese
> Right here on Guam.
>> Oh, Mr. Sam, Sam, my dear Uncle Sam
>> I want you please come back to Guam.[1]

Amid the Chamorros' singing and dancing, the Seabees turned Guam into a major airfield for B-29 bombers.

Quicker to fall was Tinian, where on 24 July Marine General Harry Schmidt fooled the Japanese defenders with a feint at the heavily fortified southern beaches—the only beaches the Japanese thought were suitable to attack—and instead landed his Marines on tiny beaches on the northern side. There the Marines came ashore against minimal resistance. The Marines used a new weapon to inhibit Japanese reinforcements—napalm, which scorched the pathways to the beaches. The requisite banzai charges failed, and the Japanese innovated the art of hara-kiri by exploding themselves with mines rather than grenades. (At Guam they put live grenades inside their helmets and strapped the helmets on—a recipe for scrambled egghead.) As shreds of Japanese flew through the air, the Marines said: "Thanks for sharing," and toasted their good fortune with hot cups of Joe. Tinian was declared captured on 1 August 1944, though the last Japanese defender was not found until 1953.[2] The Marines suffered fewer than 330 dead; Japanese dead were virtually the entire garrison of Tinian, 8,000 men.

MACARTHUR RETURNS

PLOTTING AMERICA'S ADVANCE, the Navy, led by Chief of Naval Operations Admiral Ernest King, believed the Philippines should be bypassed for a strike at Japanese-occupied Formosa, far to the north, directly threatening the southernmost islands of Japan.[3] Opposing him was Douglas MacArthur. He had given his word that he would return to the Philippines, and with that word, he said, came an American moral obligation to liberate the Filipinos. President Roosevelt agreed. MacArthur had his way, and another leapfrog campaign began.

U.S. naval intelligence discovered that Japanese air defenses at Mindanao, in the southern Philippines, were weak. So Mindanao was bypassed in favor of a strike at Leyte Island, smack dab in the center of the Philippine Islands. To secure the strike, the Navy moved against the Palau Islands—Angaur, Ulithi, Peleliu—not quite midway in a southern sweeping arc between Saipan and Leyte. Marines pulled the long straw and were assigned the toughest of the three, Peleliu, while the Army handled Angaur and Ulithi.

There were more than 10,000 Japanese troops on Peleliu. Their defenses included an elaborate system of caves interlocked by a series of tunnels. Some of the caves were single-man entrenchments, others were enormous with fortified artillery positions and capable of holding up to 1,000 men. Retractable steel doors sheltered the artillery caves, and the Japanese commanders had the island crisscrossed with fields of fire. At Peleliu, the Japanese had no intention of hurling themselves at the Marines in banzai charges (though Japanese tanks on the island made one ill-advised charge into Marine bazookas, Sherman tanks, and Avenger bombers flying air support). Instead, the Japanese intended to use every scrap of Peleliu rock and coral for a defensive firefight. Despite the Japanese fortifications, the impatient and prideful Marine Major General William Rupertus planned to overrun the island in a matter of four days or less. It would take two months.

The island smoldered under a U.S. Navy bombardment and smoldered again as the Marines fought their way to shore. The Marines came under fire from the moment their amphibious tractors approached the beaches, navigating past mines, barbed wire, and other obstacles. The Marines' landing sites were pounded by the deafening blasts of Japanese mortars and artillery that shot out shards of death. Ahead of the bloody beach, the Marines saw a burning, shell-torn landscape, dotted with shorn palm trees and jungle, hotter than hell, the air hissing with bullets, the ground sharp with coral that made it impossible to dig a foxhole. Stubborn as ever, they advanced off the beaches and clambered to ascend the rock and coral of Bloody Nose Ridge, braving fierce Japanese fire, while sweating, cursing, bleeding, and lacking supplies and clean water (their water came from improperly cleaned oily drums and was near poisonous).

The Marines made frontal assaults on entrenched Japanese positions—and did so while outnumbered by the Japanese. The U.S. Marine 1st Division—"the Old Breed," led by Colonel Lewis B. "Chesty" Puller—was mutilated by enemy fire, oil-poisoned water, and heatstroke with temperatures soaring well over 100 degrees, and with humidity so high that the Marines could literally pour sweat out of their boondockers (boots). General Rupertus wanted no help; but he was eventually forced to accept it. It took support from the air to begin breaking the stalemated firefight on the ground. Like flying angels of vengeance, Marine Corsairs arrived shooting out flaming napalm on the Japanese positions. That was the first break the land-based Marines—and reinforcing U.S. Army infantry—got. Then came more reinforcements with the 7th Marine Division, and it became a matter of relentlessly blasting the Japanese from their caves.

The Japanese knew they could not win at Peleliu, but they were committed to inflicting massive casualties on the Americans. At night, they crawled into American lines and cut Marine throats. They desecrated corpses. They made Peleliu as notorious as Tarawa and gave evidence to one Marine's justification for why he hated the Japanese: "Because they're the meanest sonsabitches that ever lived."[4] When the battle was declared won on 25 November 1944, nearly 11,000 Japanese were dead, while the Americans had taken close to 7,000 casualties, 1,300 of them dead.

A month before Peleliu was over, the battle for Leyte had begun. Admiral Bull Halsey set the stage for MacArthur's return by cruising his Third Fleet[5] around the northwestern boundaries of the Philippine Sea—from Okinawa to Formosa to Leyte—obliterating everything in his path, but most especially hundreds upon hundreds of planes in follow-up turkey shoots. Self-deception now became the enemy of the Japanese; the generals in Tokyo, believing their own propaganda, expected a smashing victory in the Philippines that would end American pretensions in the Pacific.

Once again, they were wrong. MacArthur's landing at Leyte caught the Japanese by surprise. When the American general came ashore, "our beachhead troops were only a few yards away, stretched out behind logs and other cover, laying down fire on the area immediately inland. There were still Japanese in the undergrowth not many yards away." His trousers wet from the ocean surf, MacArthur made one of the most famous broadcasts of the Pacific War: "People of the Philippines: I have returned. By the grace of Almighty God, our forces stand again on Philippine soil. . . . The hour of your redemption is here. . . . Rally to me. . . . Rise and strike. Strike at every available opportunity. For your homes and hearths, strike! For future generations of your sons and daughters, strike! In the name of your sacred dead, strike! . . . The guidance of Divine God points the way. Follow in His name to the Holy Grail of righteous victory."[6]

The Japanese were far from conceding MacArthur his victory. The garrisons at Leyte were swiftly reinforced with another 45,000 Japanese troops; Japanese planes darkened the skies in dogfights with the Americans; and a Japanese naval group sought to draw the American Third Fleet—the largest fleet the world had ever seen—out of supporting the invasion of Leyte and into battle. With the Third Fleet thus occupied, the Japanese planned to shoot a naval task force into Leyte Gulf to exterminate the invasion. Japan's naval attack was a noble gesture but rested on frank hopes for a miracle. No miracle was delivered.

The Battle of Leyte Gulf—the largest naval battle in history—was fought over a period of four days (23–26 October 1944) and was really four battles: the Battle of the Sibuyan Sea, the Battle of the Surigao Strait, the Battle of Cape Engaño, and the Battle of Samar. The Japanese planned to take advantage of Admiral Bull Halsey's bullishness and lure him north with the Northern Force of their fleet, while the Japanese Central and Southern Forces struck from the west and south to destroy the Americans in the Leyte Gulf. Admiral Halsey took the bait, racing Task Force 38 (Halsey's carriers) after the Japanese. Meanwhile, Rear Admiral Jesse Oldendorf caught the Japanese Southern Force in the Battle of the Surigao Strait and hammered it to scrap metal.

The Japanese Central Force, however, sailed through the San Bernadino Strait, which had been left unguarded. The Central Force had been strafed by naval aircraft in the Battle of the Sibuyan Sea (24 October), and in Halsey's haste to catch the Japanese Northern Force and his assumption that the Japanese Central Force was retreating, no ships had been left to block this passage. At the ensuing Battle of Samar (25 October), Rear Admiral Clifton Sprague, commanding six escort carriers and a few destroyers, suddenly found himself confronting a Japanese task force of four battleships, eight cruisers, and ten destroyers. Sprague's escort carriers were designed to provide air support to Leyte; they were not naval combat ships; and his destroyers were a light covering force for his carriers. But Rear Admiral Sprague threw everything he had at the enemy, and sent the Japanese—who packed more than ten times his firepower—paddling away in fear.

As for the dangled Japanese Northern Force, it was caught and its four carriers sunk. American losses were one aircraft carrier, two escort carriers, three destroyers, and a cruiser; and 3,500 Americans were killed. But the Japanese losses were far worse; indeed they were fatal to the Japanese navy: four aircraft carriers, three battleships, six heavy cruisers, four light cruisers, and twelve destroyers, not to mention the flaming symbols of Japanese desperation, kamikaze suicide planes, which made their debut here. All told, 10,000 Japanese were killed.

On land, the Leyte campaign meant fighting through stubborn Japanese, inhospitable jungle, three typhoons, and an earthquake. Officially the campaign ended with the year 1944. Unofficially, and in truth, it last lasted through the spring of 1945. Japanese dead were 49,000; American dead were 3,500. The odds were getting better.

The new year saw the American invasion of Luzon, the main island of the Philippines, and its capital, Manila. MacArthur eventually landed 280,000 troops on the island. Opposing him was Japanese General Tomoyuki Yamashita—the Tiger of Malaya, the conqueror of impregnable Singapore—who had nearly an equal number of men. He was confident of victory, which he thought would be achieved not in the cities (though his men would fight to the death in Manila) or on the beaches, but in the countryside, where it would be impossible for the Americans to root him out.

The Americans landed in Luzon on 9 January 1945. MacArthur's men liberated the survivors of the Bataan Death March and then raced to rescue Manila. The battle for the city, which began on 3 February 1945, was fierce and horrible. The Japanese went on a rampage of gruesome obscenity, destruction, mutilation, and murder against the Filipinos. In their anti-Western animosity, the Japanese especially targeted anything Spanish or Catholic, including the city's cathedral, the University of St. Thomas, and the city's enormous network of Church-sponsored hospitals, schools, and religious houses. The Japanese raped women, gouged the eyes out of children, strapped hospital patients to their beds and set them alight, and sacked and torched the city; almost 100,000 Filipinos died during the siege.

The fighting was street by street, building by building, even room by room. The Japanese lodged themselves in sewers, as if they were the caves of Peleliu. It took until the end of the war to completely flush the Japanese from the Philippines. When it was over, 400,000 Japanese soldiers were dead. Though the fighting would go on for months, at the end of February 1945 General MacArthur restored the independent government of the Philippines at Malacañang Palace, which had somehow escaped the Japanese rape of Manila. The Japanese responsible for that rape were now either dead or on the run. MacArthur had kept his word: he had returned; the Filipinos' vicious oppressors were gone; the Philippines were free.

ENDGAME IN EUROPE

IN FEBRUARY 1945, American and British bombers leveled the picturesque German city of Dresden. Other cities were bombed to rubble as well, including Berlin (seat of the German government), Bremen, Cologne, and Hamburg. In the past, American bombers had focused on obvious military targets, including the Nazi war machine's oil fields in Romania. But the strategic bombing of Germany had shifted from military-industrial targets narrowly defined to incorporating the punishment of the German people. The aim was to break their will to fight. In this, the bombing failed. But Franklin Roosevelt had another objective. He wrote to Secretary of War Henry Stimson that it was of "the utmost importance that every person in Germany should realize that this time Germany is a defeated nation. . . . The fact that they are a defeated nation, collectively and individually, must be impressed upon them that they will hesitate to start any new war."[7] In the end, it was not the bombing that proved this; Allied occupation did.

Allied occupation depended on the foot-slogging infantry who were shattering the Siegfried Line. Between February and March 1945, German resistance broke. On 7 March, the Americans seized the Ludendorff Bridge at the central city of Remagen on the Rhine. The Germans had been wiring it for demolition when the U.S. 9th Armored Division stormed across the bridgehead. Elsewhere along the Rhine, Americans built their own bridges, and the Allies poured into the Reich. Victory was at hand.

Few if any Germans feared the British or the Americans, but they feared or hated the Russians, whose rapaciousness was infamous. So for the first time in the war, masses of Germans surrendered on the western front, thinking it better to surrender to the civilized Anglo-Americans than to the barbarous Soviets. The Wehrmacht continued to fight, but not as it had in the past. As German Feldmarschall Walter Model recognized, it was near kaput. With his army isolated in the Ruhr, he shot himself rather than surrender. Only the SS could bring zealotry to combat in the West.

Eisenhower remained cautious. He had intelligence reports of fanatical volunteers re-forming in the mountains of Bavaria, preparing to fight the Allies for every foothold. There was another political calculation, too. At Yalta, in February 1945, Churchill, Roosevelt, and Stalin had reaffirmed their commitment to unconditional surrender and agreed on partitioning Germany for a postwar Allied occupation. East Germany, including Berlin, was in the Soviet sector—and the Soviets flooded the western Allies with a litany of complaints and suspicions that they were not being given their due. Eisenhower, to keep the political peace, had no intention of racing to Berlin ahead of the Soviets, a campaign that would have been costly in any event. For Eisenhower, the point was simply to defeat Nazi Germany. Neither Roosevelt nor Eisenhower saw in Soviet Russia a threat to the United States or to the West. There were wiser heads, including British Prime Minister Winston Churchill, his annoying Field Marshal Bernard Montgomery, and hard-driving General George S. Patton, whom Eisenhower ordered to halt at the border of Czechoslovakia—a country that his pit bull general wanted to occupy. Churchill, Montgomery, and Patton knew the Soviets for what they were and wanted to keep them out of as much of Europe as possible. But like Roosevelt (who died 12 April 1945), Eisenhower suspected the imperial motives of his British allies and put more trust in the Russians; the Russians were common folks, he thought, just like us.

Patton reached the Czech border on 23 April 1945. The U.S. Seventh Army captured Nuremberg on 20 April and Munich on 30 April, the day that Hitler committed suicide. The Anglo-American Allied forces weren't trying to move fast; they were trying to slow down so that the Soviets could reach the Elbe, where the western and eastern Allies met on 25 April. On 2 May, the Soviets took Berlin and went on a spree of rape and murder. Hitler's Thousand Year Reich was finished; it had lasted a dozen years; its official surrender occurred on 7 May 1945. Its crimes in the death camps—sights so horrible that a hardened soldier like Patton had to excuse himself and was sick—were its lasting legacy. After touring the concentration camp at Ohrdruf, Eisenhower ordered: "I want every American unit not actually in the front lines to see this place. We are told the American soldier does not know what he is fighting for. Now, at least, he will know what he is fighting against."[8]

IWO JIMA, OKINAWA, AND THE EMPEROR'S SURRENDER

THE FIREBOMBING OF JAPAN had begun. General Curtis LeMay—an Air Force wunderkind—had developed a system that meant flying low, at night, stripped of unnecessary weight (such as rear-gunners and their ammunition), and dropping batches of napalm-loaded "firesticks." On 10 March 1945, LeMay's crews laid fire to Tokyo in the most devastating aerial bombardment of the war, killing an estimated 100,000 Japanese, making it a hundred times worse than all previous bombing attacks on Japan combined. For ten days, LeMay kept up the bombing until there were no more bombs to be dropped. When more bombs arrived, he started up again. If the Japanese government trusted to the indomitable will of the Japanese people, LeMay was prepared to incinerate every industrial city in Japan, if he could find the bombs to do it.

The Marines assisted LeMay by attacking Iwo Jima, which was a reconnaissance and communications hub that warned the Japanese mainland of approaching B-29s and alerted Japanese antiaircraft batteries and fighter squadrons. In addition, the island had three airfields from which the Japanese launched raids against America's Saipan-based bombers. And B-29 pilots saw something else in Iwo Jima. It was perfectly sited as a potential staging area for P-51 Mustang fighters that could fly protection duty for the bombers, and it was an ideal place for exhausted pilots (with exhausted gas tanks) to land on the long Saipan-to-Japan-and-back bombing route. What the flyboys desired, the Marines delivered. The Marines' conquest of Iwo Jima is credited with saving the lives of nearly 27,000 airmen who would otherwise have plunged into the sea. But taking the island inflicted a bloody toll of its own: nearly 29,000 American casualties, almost 7,000 of them dead, for an island of eight square miles.

The volcanic ash of Iwo Jima (which translates as "Sulfur Island") had been bombed to wasteland, which wasn't saying much as it had been a wasteland before. It was an eerie place wreathed in volcanic smoke, shaking from volcanic tremors, blanketed by volcanic ash, and studded with Japanese guns and men. By now the leathernecks knew that bombing could not exterminate well-dug-in Japs. Navy frogmen—"the naked warriors"—swam to the beaches to draw fire so that American naval artillery could draw a bead on the Japanese guns. The frogmen's valor helped, but at Iwo Jima there were 22,000 Japanese troops in the biggest and most elaborate underground fortifications yet—concrete bunkers and caves bristling with firepower. The Marines were sent in on 19 February 1945. Military planners expected they might take 40 percent casualties. Marine General "Howlin' Mad" Smith replied: "We have taken such losses before, and if we have to we can do it again."[9] The Marines' first objective was the high ground at the southern tip of the island: the fortress at Mount Suribachi.

The Marines landed on beaches that were raked by Japanese mortars, artillery, and machine guns—most them sited by watchers on Mount Suribachi. The incoming fire was some of the most ferocious of the war, but the Marines kept coming. In the course of a week, 70,000 Marines invaded Iwo Jima, yet in the first few days they could only crawl by yards, under buzzing bullets and ducking shrapnel thrown up by the Japanese guns.

Offshore batteries and bombing freed the Marines to move inland. They advanced behind tanks, cleaning out pillboxes one at a time, including at the base of Mount Suribachi, where the Marines began a fighting ascent. On 23 February, the Marines raised the Stars and Stripes over Mount Suribachi and the Marine Corps gained one of its most enduring images of perseverance and valor. It was a symbol that every American fighting man recognized immediately. The cheers of sailors, Marines, and even ships' horns erupted into a roar.

After the first flag was raised, a second larger flag—the scene captured on the Marine Memorial—reaffirmed the conquest.

From Suribachi, the Marines had to fight their way up the island against linked concrete blockhouses. To clear them took blasts of tanks, bazookas, and flamethrowers, as well as grenade-throwing, bayonet-stabbing leathernecks. Helping to direct air and artillery strikes on the island were the Navajo code-talkers, whose unwritten Indian language was never cracked by the Japanese.

It took until 26 March 1945 to complete the capture of Iwo Jima. Even on that day, there was a banzai charge of 300 Japanese, and mopping up operations went on for months. The Marines killed 21,800 Japanese on Iwo Jima, took 200 prisoners, and won Admiral Nimitz's plaudits for a campaign where "uncommon valor was a common virtue."[10] More than a quarter of the Medals of Honor won by World War II Marines were awarded for action on Iwo Jima. After the battle, Secretary of the Navy James Forrestal remarked, "I can never again see a United States Marine without a feeling of reverence." It was reverence shared by an American pilot who spoke for many: "Whenever I land on this island, I thank God and the men who fought for it."[11]

The Marines' next assignment was Okinawa, only 350 miles from the main Japanese islands. Okinawa had more civilians—450,000 of them—and a far more significant size (463 square miles) than the other island fortresses of the central Pacific. Ranged against it, the United States assembled a fleet invasion as big as the one that had been launched against Normandy the year before. Once taken, Okinawa would be the base for the assault on the Japanese home islands (Operation Downfall). The trick was seizing Okinawa from the 110,000 Japanese soldiers and militia who would fight to the death for it. There was also a question about the native Okinawans. They were a subject people and not ethnically Japanese, but might they launch suicide attacks themselves? The Marines leading the invasion were briefed to expect 80 to 85 percent casualties on the landing beaches—and the Marines were not alone. With them for the invasion were divisions from XXIV Corps of the United States Army. Overall command of the operation belonged to U.S. Army General Simon Bolivar Buckner Jr. (son of Confederate General Simon Bolivar Buckner). At sea, Admiral Nimitz expected Japanese kamikaze pilots to attack in force from Okinawa's airfields. Kamikazes had already scorched the Navy: at Iwo Jima, the Navy had suffered higher losses than it had at Normandy. Every expectation was that Okinawa would be worse still.

At first, it wasn't. The Marines landed unopposed on 1 April 1945. The weather was mild, even delightful. The Marines marched through well-kept farming communities without hostile signs from the Okinawans. As the soldiers and Marines moved inland, they met resistance, but nothing as fierce as they had expected. American forces captured the two airfields (Kadena and Yomitan) in northern Okinawa, and within three weeks had secured the northern three-quarters of the island. Then came the surprise.

Japanese General Mitsuru Ushijima had concentrated his forces—including the most formidable artillery the Japanese had—in the south, honeycombing his troops across the terrain so that the GIs and Marines had to fight for every yard they gained. Okinawa became a process of grinding slaughter, the fiercest fighting of the Pacific. So too for the Navy: Nimitz's fleet faced not individual kamikaze pilots, but a suicide arsenal: underwater suicide divers strapped with bombs, the giant battleship *Yamato* running to beach itself and become land-based artillery (before the *Yamato* hit the beach it was sunk, along with its accompanying cruiser and four destroyers), and air fleet armadas of Japanese bombers and kamikazes, striking hundreds at a time, piercing through the sky like angry hornets, willing to die themselves but yearning to incinerate American sailors and ships in the bargain. The naval air war over Okinawa was a spectacle of high-speed explosive death between American fighters, antiaircraft guns, and the Japanese fighter-bombers: the Japanese lost nearly 8,000 planes, but sank 36 American ships and inflicted more than 9,700 casualties on the American Navy.

On land, GIs and Marines slugged the Japanese along the Shuri Line across the southern bulb of Okinawa. So much firepower (both artillery and small arms) and so many fighting men were concentrated here that the entire line was one vast, charred, corpse-stinking, maggot-ridden, earth-rumbling, ear-pounding, nerve-shattering battlefield of unparalleled intensity. And at night, whenever the shell fire let up, the Japanese would come crawling over for hand-to-hand combat. The nature of the fight at Okinawa was described by a *Time* magazine war correspondent: "There were fifty Marines on top of Sugar Loaf Hill. They had been ordered to hold the position all night, at any cost. By dawn, forty-six of them had been killed or wounded. Then, into the foxhole where the remaining four huddled, the Japs dropped a phosphorous shell, burning three men to death. The last survivor crawled to an aid station."[12]

The Marines clawed their way back up Sugar Loaf Hill and punched across the Shuri Line. It was perhaps the most dearly bought scrap of real estate in the war. With the Japanese in fighting retreat, the Marines returned to cave-clearing: blasting and flame-throwing Japanese from their hidey holes, and learning—from Japanese who faked surrenders or dressed as civilians and exploded grenades—the virtues of suspicion and quick firing.

Okinawa was the biggest land-air-sea battle in history; it was declared won on 21 June 1945, though fighting went on to clear out pockets of Japanese. The estimated number of Japanese killed was 107,000. American dead were 12,500, among them General Buckner, killed by an artillery shell near campaign's end. Civilian casualties numbered perhaps 130,000. Catechized by the Japanese into fearing the Marines, many of the civilian casualties were suicides. The southern end of the island—torn apart by the fighting—was by far the most populous. The Marines did everything they could to save civilians, but they had to fight against the Japanese-inculcated culture of death.

Now came the sobering task of preparing for the invasion of Japan. The Japanese high command conceded that the Greater East Asia Co-Prosperity Sphere was over, but was confident that the home islands of Japan would not fall to the United States. That tiny Okinawa could last for three months and inflict such casualties proved the point. Now with every Japanese citizen a potential suicide bomber, with a stockpile of kamikaze planes, with the greatest possible concentration of Japanese military force, it was inconceivable that Japan could be defeated. The American admirals and generals thought otherwise. They never considered any outcome but total victory and Japan's unconditional surrender; the only question was the cost—and that final calculation was changed when President Harry S. Truman considered using the newly developed atomic bomb, which was first tested at Alamogordo Air Base in New Mexico on 16 July 1945. Potential military targets were chosen, including Hiroshima (a military supply center and headquarters of the Second Japanese Army) and Nagasaki (a military port). The decision of whether to go ahead was the president's.

The United States military had not sought the atomic bomb; scientists had cajoled the generals and admirals into accepting it as a possibility. But now that it was available it offered the prospect of saving hundreds of thousands of potential American casualties. Civilians would inevitably be killed, but they were being killed in General LeMay's firebombing raids already. Moreover, the long and growing record of Japanese atrocities erased what little American sympathy they might otherwise have had.

On 6 August 1945, the *Enola Gay* flew from Tinian with a target of Hiroshima. The bomb was dropped. The aircrew wasn't sure the *Enola Gay* would survive the blast—the mushroom cloud rose three miles above the aircraft. On the ground, Hiroshima was no longer a city; it was wreckage. Perhaps 70,000 people were killed.[13] The Japanese did not surrender. So on 9 August, in part to convince the Japanese that the United States had a stockpile of atomic weapons (which it did not), the second and only other existing atomic bomb was dropped on Nagasaki. On 10 August, the Japanese surrendered on condition that the emperor remained sovereign over Japan. President Truman accepted that proviso on condition that the supreme authority in Japan not be the emperor but the supreme Allied commander who would be in charge of the American forces occupying Japan. After three days of silence, Truman ordered a massive air assault on the Japanese mainland. That did it. On 14 August 1945, the Second World War was over.

For American soldiers, sailors, and Marines preparing for the assault on Japan, the morality of dropping the atom bombs was self-evident. Two bombs had ended the most terrible world war in history; they saved millions of lives (most of them Japanese). They ended not only the necessity of invading Japan, but the prospect of a British invasion of Malaya and a siege of Singapore. Paul Fussell was a U.S. Army infantryman detailed for the invasion of Japan. After the war, he became a professor of literature. An acerbic liberal, he wrote an essay and a book entitled *Thank God for the Atom Bomb*.[14] He took the phrase from Pacific War veteran (a combat Marine and Kennedy Democrat) William Manchester, who also believed in the morality of the atomic blasts. On the British side of things, Burma veteran (and brilliant novelist and crotchety conservative) George MacDonald Fraser agreed that dropping the bomb was right, even if barbaric, though if the men he led in combat had been told of the alternatives—the horrific atomic annihilation of two cities or the prolonged and deadly continuation of the war:

> They would have cried "Aw, fook that!" with one voice, and then they would have sat about, snarling, and lapsed into silence, and then someone would have said heavily, "Aye, weel," and got to his feet, and been asked, "W'eer th' 'ell you gan, then?" and given no reply, and at last the rest would have got up, too, gathering their gear with moaning and foul language and ill-tempered harking back to the long dirty bloody miles from the Imphal boxes to the Sittang Bend and the iniquity of having to do it again, slinging their rifles and bickering

about who was to go on point, and "Ah's aboot 'ed it, me!" and "You, ye bugger, ye're knackered afower ye start, you!" and "We'll a' git killed!", and then they would have been moving south. Because that is the kind of men they were.[15]

So, too, had they been called upon to do it, the Raggedy Ass Marines and the Dogfaces of the U.S. Army infantry would have slung their own rifles and done what they expected to do. But Truman's decision spared them—and for that, they thanked God for the atom bomb.

On 2 September 1945, the Japanese signed the surrender documents aboard the USS *Missouri*. As the generals, admirals, and dignitaries organized the documents into leather folders, a GI aboard ship said: "Brother, I hope those are my discharge papers."[16] Symbolically, at least, they were. The war was over. The boys would be coming home, save for those who would now garrison the outposts of American victory, which spanned the globe.

CHAPTER 23

"RETREAT, HELL—WE'RE JUST ATTACKING IN ANOTHER DIRECTION"

I T IS SAFE TO SAY that for the fighting men of the American armed forces, who had destroyed fascism in Germany, Italy, and Japan, the liberation of British imperial possessions from Britain—America's wartime ally—was hardly a consuming issue. But it had been high on the agenda of President Franklin Roosevelt. At the Yalta Conference in 1944, Roosevelt, in front of Winston Churchill, cordially invited Uncle Joe Stalin for a "just the two of us" conversation to deal with a pressing political problem. That problem was not restraining Stalin's appetite to swallow Eastern Europe but to get the British imperialists out of Hong Kong. Roosevelt thought that he could see eye-to-eye with his Russian contemporary, because, as he put it: "Of one thing I am certain, Stalin is not an imperialist."[1]

No, Stalin was a Communist, which to Roosevelt was a much lesser problem. As Robert Nisbet noted, during the war, "India was Roosevelt's most consuming obsession. From the correspondence between Roosevelt and Churchill one might conclude that second only to the defeat of Germany, the independence of India from the British Empire was Roosevelt's fondest aspiration. His ignorance of the real problems and issues in India was gargantuan."

Roosevelt told Churchill that he had an "injection of a new thought" to offer on India, which was that the Indians were the same as the American colonists in 1776 and should be treated to a similar independence. To Roosevelt, the Soviet Union fit in well with the world's democratic future, but the British Empire did not.[2] Roosevelt, like Wilson before him, had become a full-fledged adherent of the idea that colonialism and imperialism are bad, and that the United States is an anti-imperial power.[3]

But it was a strange sort of nonempire that in 1945 had troops stretched from North Africa to the Philippines and from New Guinea to Great Britain. Its general in command of all U.S. forces in East Asia during World War II—Douglas MacArthur—had previously been in charge of training the Filipino army (a rather imperial sort of position) and was now reigning over Japan as a de facto Caesar.[4] The United States Marine Corps had a word for going crazy, which was "Asiatic," from the Marines' long service in the Orient. And American troops were garrisoning western Germany—as they would do for the next half century and beyond—making America the most important power in Europe. From the facts on the ground, the United States was as imperial a power as Rome or Great Britain.

Roosevelt was an anti-imperialist, but he also believed in the creation of a global *Pax Americana*. This odd dichotomy occasionally made a hash of American wartime and postwar foreign policy. During the war, American generals often worried about British imperial ambitions—rarely about Soviet ones. Eisenhower naively thought the ordinary Russian bore "a marked similarity to what we call an 'average American,'" and averred that the Russians and the United States "were free from the stigma of colonial building by force,"[5] which showed an appalling misreading of Russian history.

American leaders could show an amazing lack of self-knowledge as well. In the summer of 1944, Roosevelt hosted Charles de Gaulle and, as Christopher Hitchens notes, according to de Gaulle's memoirs, "the President proposed a 'permanent system of intervention' with a chain of American bases occupying what had been French and British possessions in Africa and Asia. By including China and France in his plan [as part of what would become the United Nations Security Council], Roosevelt demonstrated a preference for what he had termed 'the United Nations' over Anglo-Americanism," and the traditional imperial policies of Western Europe.[6] *Pax Americana* was assumed to correspond with the peace—and interests—of the world's United Nations.

One upshot of such anti-imperial imperialism was that in the postwar world the United States applauded the dismantling of the British and other European empires, only to find itself, by necessity, taking over many of their responsibilities while hardly noticing—or wanting to acknowledge—that it was doing so.

As the Soviet Union tightened its grip on Eastern Europe, as Winston Churchill gave his warning about an iron curtain descending from "Stettin in the Baltic to Trieste in the Adriatic,"[7] as Communist insurgencies began fanning out into Western Europe and Asia, the United States adopted an ever more imperial foreign policy, shoring up its Allies with aid, drawing up regional alliances (like NATO, founded in 1949), and taking on the duty of restoring the world's economy and keeping the world's peace.

It began with President Harry S. Truman's address to a joint session of Congress on 12 March 1947. Though Truman had earlier fallen under Stalin's spell, the litany of consequent Soviet treachery had shown this Missourian which end was up. Truman saw the Soviets treating their sector of eastern Germany rapaciously. He saw Stalin wrapping Eastern Europe in chains. And most of all, he saw Uncle Joe supporting Communist insurrections in Turkey and Greece, which opened up the possibility of Soviet Russia stretching its paws down into the Mediterranean and the Middle East. The former World War I National Guard artilleryman said to hell with that.

"The peoples of a number of countries of the world," he told Congress, "have recently had totalitarian regimes forced upon them against their will. The Government of the United States has made frequent protests against coercion and intimidation, in violation of the Yalta Agreement in Poland, Rumania, and Bulgaria. I must also state that in a number of other countries there have been similar developments." Truman said that while Great Britain had done what it could to stave off the Communists in Greece and Turkey, it could no longer bear the burden. "I believe," Truman declared, announcing the doctrine that would bear his name, "that it must be the policy of the United States to support free peoples who are resisting attempted subjugation by armed minorities or by outside pressures."[8] From this came America's policy of containing Soviet expansion; and to do that immediately, American aid was rushed to Greece and Turkey.

On 5 June 1947, General George C. Marshall, now secretary of state, announced the Marshall Plan for aiding the economic recovery of Europe. As a gesture of goodwill, the United States invited Communist Russia and its satellites to participate in the Marshall Plan. Poland and Czechoslavakia showed interest. But the Soviet Union refused for itself and for them—indeed, the Russians did more than refuse; in February 1948, they sponsored a coup in Soviet-occupied Czechoslovakia, toppling its marginally independent and democratic government and installing a Communist puppet. As a further sign of their good faith, in June 1948 the Soviets blockaded Berlin, hoping to absorb the entire city, which had been divided into American, British, French, and Soviet occupation zones. The city itself was deep within Soviet-occupied East Germany. But Truman responded with the Berlin Airlift, which was joined by the French, the British, and the "White Dominions" of Australia, New Zealand, South

Africa, and Canada. The airlift fliers brought food, coal, and other supplies, sometimes in such quantities that planes were landing minute by minute. Stalin lifted the blockade in May 1949. For the West it was a stupendous, bloodless victory in a year that would otherwise be filled with ominous news.

In 1949, China fell to the Communists led by Mao Tse-tung and supported by Stalin. America's ally Chiang Kai-shek fled with his army to the island of Formosa. China had long loomed in American sympathies as the victim of Japanese aggression, as an enormous field for Christian missionary endeavor, and as a potential giant trading partner. Now it was locked behind the Communist "Bamboo Curtain," where atheism, communism, and febrile anti-Western—and especially anti-American—propaganda were enforced in a belligerent totalitarian state. If the loss of China was not shock enough, America's monopoly on the atom bomb ended when the Soviets test-exploded one of their own.

After the Second World War, the United States had rushed to disarm and demobilize. Yet the United States now confronted global communism. From Berlin to Shanghai a tyranny every bit as vile as the National Socialist menace stretched its barbed wire dominion. The Communists railed against the United States, threatened global revolution, and were developing atomic weapons. President Truman faced these facts, reinstated military conscription, and only five years after having won the biggest and costliest war in the history of the world, America's legions were sent to another distant Asian battlefield.

INVASION

STALIN HAD AGREED at both the Yalta and the Potsdam Conferences (1945) to a free and independent Korea. The Japanese had occupied Korea since 1904, taking it from the Russians who had taken it from the Chinese who had taken it from the Japanese who had taken it from the Koreans. The United States was designated to accept the surrender of Japanese troops south of the 38th Parallel, the Russians north of it. But while American troops were fighting at Okinawa, Soviet troops flooded into Manchuria and Korea, stripped these territories of whatever industry they had, and sent it to Russia. They also rounded up Japanese soldiers—600,000 of them—to serve as Siberian slave labor. The Soviets then fortified the 38th Parallel, cut northern Korea off from southern Korea, and installed a Communist government in their sector. The Soviets put Korean Communist faces—rather than Russian faces—in every public place so that at least the people of North Korea could feel nationalist pride. Korean Communists who had fought for Mao or Stalin became the leaders of northern Korea, including one who took the name of Kim Il Sung—after a Korean folk hero who had fought against the Japanese decades before.

When United States troops finally arrived, they found a country forcibly divided, spewing anti-American hatred in the North, and in the South suspicious of American military occupation. The United States tried to do the right thing, which was to achieve United Nations' supervised elections in a united Korea. But the Russians said *nyet*. As Germany was divided, so now was Korea. Free elections in the South elevated the longtime nationalist Syngman Rhee as president of the Republic of Korea, which was, officially, all Korea. But the North proclaimed Kim Il Sung as its leader, adopted a constitution based on the famous Bulgarian model, and staged a propaganda exit of Russian troops.

The last point was meant to pressure an American departure, which happened in June 1949. Not only did American troops leave, but so did American enthusiasm for Syngman Rhee, who took a hard line with dissenters and who boasted that with American military support he could reunite Korea in a matter of two weeks. Rather than supplying Rhee with the military hardware and seeing if he could pull it off, the United States kept most military items—certainly ones that could easily be put to aggressive use—off South Korea's aid docket. The United States did not want another flash point with the Soviets.

What the Soviets and their Communist allies wanted was another thing entirely. The Russians flooded North Korea with military hardware—tanks, guns, and planes—and Kim Il Sung was just as eager to come to blows as Syngman Rhee was; all he needed was an opening. American Secretary of State Dean Acheson appeared to give him one. On 12 January 1950, Acheson, in a major speech to the National Press Club, drew the outlines of America's defensive perimeter in the Pacific. It ran he, he said, "along the Aleutians to Japan and then goes to the Ryukyus. . . . The defensive perimeter runs from Ryukyus to the Philippine Islands. . . . So far as the military security of other areas in the Pacific is concerned, it must be clear that no person can guarantee these areas against military attack. But it must also be clear that such a guarantee is hardly sensible or necessary within the realm of practical relationship."[9]

Notably missing from the defensive perimeter were Korea and Formosa. Acheson had already written off Formosa and testified to Congress, in a closed-door session, that South Korea was indefensible against a North Korean attack backed by the Soviets and the Red Chinese. Acheson did not believe in American intervention to save South Korea, should it be invaded, and added that the

Soviets would block any action from the United Nations. In May 1950, Democrat Senator Tom Connally of Texas, chairman of the Senate Foreign Relations Committee, said publicly what Acheson had said in private: Korea was unimportant; the Soviets could take it without sparking American intervention. These statements were nothing new. As early as 1948, it was President Truman's official policy that a Korean war need not involve the United States.

On 25 June 1950, artillery shells suddenly burst among unsuspecting South Korean troops. Led by charging tanks, 90,000 North Korean soldiers stampeded into South Korea. The South Korean troops (or the ROKs, as their American instructors called them) were well trained and had fought Communist guerillas in the South, but they were no match for the northern hordes. Outnumbered, outgunned, and outwitted, they were routed.

The spotlight fell on the United Nations. It had earlier recognized the government of the Republic of Korea as the legitimate government of *all* Korea. With that government now threatened with extinction, what would the United Nations do? The Soviet Union had a permanent seat on the Security Council and could veto any United Nations military action. That permanent seat, however, was empty. The Soviets were boycotting the Security Council because Formosa (Taiwan) held the seat that Roosevelt had reserved for China. In Russia's absence, the Security Council voted for a cease-fire and the return of North Korean troops north of the 38th Parallel.

Truman took more forceful action. He told Acheson, "Dean, we've got to stop the sons-of-bitches no matter what!"[10] He ordered Douglas MacArthur in Japan to deliver arms, supplies, and hardware to the South Koreans; to use all necessary force to make sure it got there; and to go to South Korea and report on the situation. The president alerted the U.S. Seventh Fleet to be prepared to sail between Formosa and Red China, should Kim Il Sung's surprise attack be part of an all-out Asian Communist offensive. And Truman acted elsewhere: he junked FDR's anticolonialism and agreed to send aid to the French in Indochina and to the Philippines, where the government was fighting its own Communist rebels, the Huks.

Suddenly, with South Korea in peril, both Democrats and Republicans argued for swift American intervention. Truman told Senator Connally: "I'm not going to tremble like a psychopath before the Russians and I'm not going to surrender our right or the rights of the South Koreans." Connally encouraged Truman to act as commander in chief and not get bogged down in congressional debates: "If a burglar breaks into your house, you can shoot him without going down to the police station and getting permission."[11] Bold words from a Texan to a Missourian, but the Democrats had so savaged the defense budget that MacArthur doubted how quickly and effectively the United States could act.

The Communists paid no heed to UN resolutions and scoffed at Truman. They lunged for the South Korean capital of Seoul, just fifty miles south of the 38th Parallel. In an act of military desperation, the South Koreans decided to blow the bridges over the Han River, directly behind Seoul. The Americans were horrified. Blowing the bridges would kill hundreds, if not thousands, of refugees, and strand the bulk of the South Korean army. The Americans demanded that the order be rescinded. A ROK general rushed to the bridges, his jeep pushing through floods of refugees, but arrived just in time to see an almighty blast and the deaths of hundreds upon hundreds of South Koreans.

Without the bridges, the South Korean troops' only hope was to clamber through the eastern mountain country, which meant abandoning all heavy equipment. The ROK army was isolated, disorganized, broken up, stripped of its minimal artillery, and, in MacArthur's estimation, finished as an organized fighting force. All right, Truman told MacArthur, then give the North Koreans hell via American air and naval power on any enemy targets south of the 38th Parallel. It was too late to save Seoul, but MacArthur's orders were to save South Korea.

The Soviets, meanwhile, proved slow learners: they continued their boycott of the Security Council, which met again on 27 June 1950 and authorized United Nations members to "render such assistance to the Republic of Korea as may be necessary to repel the armed attack and to restore international peace and security to the area." Eleven days later, the United Nations Security Council vested President Truman with the power to appoint a commander for all United Nations forces committed to the "police action" of evicting the North Koreans from South Korea.[12]

Truman chose MacArthur. No Pacific commander could rival his prestige and knowledge of the Asian theater. No one could dismiss his success in transforming Imperial Japan into Irenic Japan or deny that MacArthur was the man on the spot (only the Tsushima and Korean Straits separate South Korea from Japan). MacArthur, however, was no self-effacing Eisenhower. He was, as his biographer wrote, an *American Caesar*. In Caesar's view, enemies were to be crushed. In Truman's view, the Korean War was not a "war"—it was a "conflict," a "police action"—words that carried little weight with the general behind the teardrop sunglasses and corncob pipe.

Falling under MacArthur's command were soldiers from Britain, Canada, Turkey, Australia, the Philippines, New Zealand, Thailand, Ethiopia, Greece, France, Colombia, Belgium and Luxembourg, South Africa, and the Netherlands (in order of troop strength). But it was an overwhelmingly American force—ten times as much—reaching, at its peak, 348,000 Americans, with the next largest contribution coming from the British—the first to join the coalition—with more than 14,000 troops. The first troops to hand were Americans, too, shipped from their bases in Japan. Few of them were World War II veterans, and as they had been garrison troops, they were poorly equipped and unprepared for combat. But there was no time for retraining and re-equipping. In the emergency, they were thrown into action. They were told to hold the line against the Reds. Like so many green troops, they were in for a shattering introduction to the reality of war.

Disaster loomed. The North Korean forces were racing—from the west and from the mountainous northeast—to the southern port city of Pusan, on the Korean Straits. If they could reach it, MacArthur would lose his lifeline. Pusan was the chief shipping port from which arrived guns, men, and materiel. Without Pusan, the Americans would lose the peninsula and be forced offshore. U.S. Navy guns helped slow the Reds coming from the northeast, but aside from his fresh American troops, MacArthur had little on the ground to stop the Communists. What little he had—the 400 men of "Task Force Smith" under the command of Colonel Charles "Brad" Smith—was rushed to the front line, wherever Colonel Smith might find it. Korean drivers were unwilling to take him there, so Smith's men took themselves, finally digging in between Suwon (where there was an airfield) and Osan, the next major city south of Seoul. Task Force Smith's first combat was against a convoy of Soviet T-34 tanks. The Americans had no effective antitank weapons (save for six armor-piercing shells) or air support and could not stop the tanks. Smith held on as long as he could, but in danger of being enveloped, he ordered a withdrawal, and the shattered task force—it took nearly 40 percent casualties—fled south. So did the 34th U.S. Army infantry, which was next in line, as the North Koreans came storming down. The badly outnumbered Americans had assumed their very presence would intimidate the North Koreans. The North Koreans simply slashed through them.

A new field commander—General Walton "Johnnie" Walker, one of Patton's men from the last war, and a veteran of the First World War—arrived and drew up a new defensive line in the west, trying to hold a position between Osan and Taejon, which was sixty miles farther south. He didn't have much luck, in part because he didn't have many men—but any success he did have came from American valor and air strikes.

MacArthur delivered some blunt truths to the Joint Chiefs of Staff:

> The situation in Korea is critical. . . . [The enemy's] armored equipment is of the best. . . , as good as any seen at any time in the last war. . . . [T]he enemy's infantry is of thoroughly first class quality.
>
> This force more and more assumes the aspect of a combination of Soviet leadership and technical guidance with Chinese Communist ground elements. While it serves under the flag of North Korea, it can no longer be considered as an indigenous N.K. military effort.
>
> I strongly urge that in addition to those forces already requisitioned, an army of at least four divisions, with all its component services be dispatched on this area without delay and by every means of transportation available.
>
> The situation has developed into a major operation.[13]

To meet the challenge of this major operation, defense secretaries from Washington to London, from Ottawa to Canberra, were wondering where the men, the planes, the ships, and the guns would come from, so complete had been their postwar demilitarization. Had the United States not had advanced bases in Japan, the United Nations war to save South Korea would have been lost before it began. The green American troops—many of them poorly trained for combat and even lacking in such basic skills as competent marksmanship—were thrown at the enemy to try to impede him, like speed bumps.

MacArthur knew the limitations of America's peacetime Army and Navy, but he had to buy time to undo the politicians' folly if he was to save South Korea. In the east, the mountainous terrain and the guns of the U.S. Navy slowed the Communist charge. But in the west, the Americans retreated behind the Kum River and fell back on the city of Taejon. Here General William Dean led the defense—trying to inspire his men by roaming the battlefield with a team of bazooka-equipped tank hunters. But Taejon was doomed. The city was flanked and then overrun on 20 July 1950, and Dean, after a marathon escape attempt, was eventually captured when South Korean civilians betrayed him.

As the Americans dug in again—thirty miles east of Taejon—they assessed their enemy. The North Koreans were, if anything, more ferocious than the Japanese. Like the Japanese, they came in human wave attacks, but the Korean waves were not kamikaze acts of suicidal desperation; they were waves of an apparently unceasing supply of well-armed Communist fanatics; they resembled more the relentless surging of army ants than they did a banzai charge.

The Americans also noticed that North Koreans didn't play by the rules: they infiltrated American lines dressed as civilians; they used human shields (advancing behind mobs of refugees); they shoved captured South Koreans into their first wave attacks. They committed atrocities, binding the wrists of captured Americans with barbed wire and shooting them in the back of the head. Most of all, the North Koreans spread panic among American troops who perpetually found themselves flanked, outnumbered, lacking support, and wondering what the hell they were doing in a land they had never heard of, a land that literally stank of human feces (which Korean farmers used as fertilizer), facing an army of crazed Communist hordes. The South Koreans learned something, too: fear of the Communists. That fear, mostly theoretical before, became very real in the summer of 1950 when, according to United Nations estimates, the Communists executed 26,000 South Korean civilians.

As the South Koreans were brutalized, the Americans were shell-shocked, and the United Nations retreat continued until, in the south, the North Koreans were within thirty miles of Pusan. Here the line was drawn. The Americans could retreat no farther; they had to brawl it out in a geographical box that became known as the Pusan Perimeter, established on 31 July 1950. It was a rectangle bordered on two sides by the sea. Its landward sides marked a front 130 miles long. The defensive line running north to south followed the natural defensive border of the Naktong River and continued east of the southern coastal city of Masan; east to west it ran north of the coastal city of Pohang to intersect the road between Kumchon and Taegu. These were the lines defended by the United Nations forces, still almost all American.

The North Koreans tried to crush this remaining box of resistance, hoping to drive the Americans into the sea. The American line along the Naktong River bent but was re-formed thanks to Marine reinforcements. American airpower—and the arrival of American artillery—took its toll, too, on the North Koreans. The North Koreans assaulted the line the entire month of August, and temporarily pierced it. Then they coiled and struck in full force along the entire perimeter on 31 August 1950, hurling themselves at, and occasionally through, the Americans. Within a week, American troopers—sometimes down to their final rounds—and American artillery were driving the Communists back; the American lines re-formed; and the North Korean lunge for victory had failed.

And there was something else. General MacArthur was preparing a devastating—and extraordinary—counterstrike.

INCHON

AT HIS HEADQUARTERS in Tokyo, MacArthur had developed a daring battle plan: he would strike the enemy deep behind its lines in South Korea, making an amphibious landing at Inchon on the west coast, nearly parallel with Seoul. Other senior American commanders opposed the plan: too dangerous, too deep in enemy territory, the tides made it virtually impossible, the Marines would have to wade through mudflats and then face a harbor wall, no chance for surprise, the landing force would be pinned down and trapped just as the rest of the army was isolated within the Pusan Perimeter.

But MacArthur was certain. He saw Inchon as the surprise attack that would win the war; he cited the example of Wolfe at Quebec; he asserted his confidence in the Navy to meet any challenge; and he told his commanders that: "It is plainly apparent that here in Asia is where the Communist conspirators have elected to make their play for global conquest. The test is not in Berlin or Vienna, in London, Paris or Washington. It is here and now—it is along the Naktong River in South Korea."[14] With such stakes in the balance, he was certain his commanders and their men would not fail. Though some of the commanders remained doubtful and continued to press for alternatives, they pledged their support. It was made clear to everyone that responsibility for the Inchon landings rested squarely on MacArthur and Truman. If the landing failed, MacArthur and his commander in chief had to take the blame.

Responsibility also rested on the 1st Marine Division, to whom MacArthur had entrusted the landing and—to his mind—the winning of the war. Other postwar military planners had considered the Marines—despite their extraordinary valor in World War II—a virtually expendable service. MacArthur saw them for what they were: the best amphibious force in the world. The planners believed that technology had made the leathernecks irrelevant—but planners always make that mistake. Men like MacArthur do not.

Despite the almost contemptuous lack of secrecy about the Inchon plan, the scrounging and make-do spirit that put together the landing fleet, and the fact that, as one Marine said, "The whole thing was a rusty travesty of World War II amphibious operations,"[15] it came off as a brilliant masterstroke. The Marines went in after a naval bombardment on 15 September 1950 watched by

MacArthur aboard the flagship *Mount McKinley*. The Marines' first objective was Wolmi-do Island, which guarded the entrance to Inchon. The Marines took it from its North Korean defenders without losing a single man. Then they seized the beaches at Inchon with ease and secured the city. At the end of the day, the Marines had suffered fewer than 200 casualties and only 20 men killed.

The ROKs were left to guard Inchon while the hard-charging Marines—so hard-charging that the Army thought the Devil Dogs were longer on courage than on brains—seized Kimpo Airfield. The unstoppable leathernecks raced to strike Seoul from the north, while the Army supplied an uppercut from the south—their combined massive firepower blasting the North Koreans from the city in street-to-street fighting. Simultaneously, General Walton Walker—nicknamed "Bulldog" for his looks, his previous service under Patton, and his defense of the Pusan Perimeter—began a fighting advance out of his corner. The North Koreans suddenly broke and ran: the United Nations collected 130,000 prisoners. On 29 September 1950, MacArthur ceremoniously returned the capital of the Republic of Korea to Syngman Rhee. "We love you as the savior of our race," said Rhee.[16] But MacArthur already knew that.

His mind had leapt from the deliverance of another Oriental race to how he could finish the job and sweep away the shattered remnants of the North Korean hordes. On 7 October 1950, the UN General Assembly authorized MacArthur to proceed to crush the armed forces of North Korea. It was the objective of the United Nations to achieve a unified, democratic Korean state—though the American government warned MacArthur to be careful around the Chinese and Russian borders, and in no circumstances was he to strike across the Yalu River into China, whatever the provocation. MacArthur chafed against these restrictions and regarded them as folly. Nevertheless, he pursued his course of expected victory. United Nations ground troops surged across the North Korean border; in one week, South Korean forces that had been humiliated three months before gleefully advanced a hundred miles into North Korea.

President Truman decided that it was time to share the limelight with his general and summoned MacArthur to Wake Island for a meeting. There, on 15 October 1950, MacArthur told the president that the Communists would be defeated by Thanksgiving and American troops could begin withdrawing at Christmas. If the Chinese or Russians intervened, he added, he now had sufficient firepower to deter them. Four days later, American and South Korean troops captured Pyonyang, the capital of North Korea. Even pessimists thought North Korea's capitulation was imminent.

They were wrong. Unaware to them or to anyone else in the UN command, the Communist Chinese were crossing the Yalu River into North Korea. Later in the month, there were brushes with Chinese units. MacArthur discounted them as isolated incidents: it would be foolish for China to intervene now, with Kim Il Sung in hiding behind the Yalu, and his forces routed; and the North Korean dictator was more an ally of Stalin than Mao, in any event. But the news grew ominous. In the last week of October, South Korean units were so badly mauled by Chinese units that they fled south, fearing another Communist flood into their country. Soviet MIGs appeared in the skies. The North Koreans stopped retreating. The warnings were there, but when the Chinese struck, it came as a thunderclap.

The North Korean human wave attacks were miniature versions of what the Chinese now mounted. A rumbling, shouting, bugle-braying horde rolled out of the dark on 1 November 1950. Supported by mortars and rockets, the Chinese came on like a roaring dragon. Hurling grenades and spitting bullets, they chased American troops of the U.S. 1st Cavalry Division into disorganized flight. Still, MacArthur regarded the attack as a Chinese face-saving gesture; he did not know that behind these units were another 300,000 Chinese troops; and he was reinforced in his mistaken belief by the fact that suddenly on 6 November, the Communist troops withdrew. The Chinese Communist thrust appeared to be over. The front grew quiet, and as American troops settled down to a frozen Thanksgiving on 24 November, it appeared once again that the war was nearly over.

But on 25 November the Chinese Dragon reappeared with all its bugles, cymbals, whistles, and shouts, breathing gunfire—it had only recoiled to strike again. The ROKs had a special terror of the Chinese and the ROK II Corps disintegrated as a fighting unit. The Americans were driven back, some cutting and running ("bugging out" was the phrase the GIs used). The Chinese waves were not mindless swarm attacks but were designed to funnel UN retreats onto roads lined by Chinese guns and capped by Chinese roadblocks—with predictably terrible results for units that were trapped. One such gauntlet was the "Death Ride" faced by the American 2nd Division, which took 3,000 casualties as it raced six miles through the Kunu-ri Pass, where, luckily, British troops rather than Chinese waited at the end.

In the west, the U.S. Eighth Army was in swift retreat. On 5 December 1950, the great prize of Pyongyang was abandoned. But in the east, where the American advance had gone farther—at one point nearly reaching the Yalu

River—the retreat of the U.S. Army and ROK forces was orderly, pulling back to the sea for evacuation. One segment of the withdrawal became the stuff of legend: the 1st Marine Division's stubborn heroism as it moved out from the Chosin Reservoir.

THE FROZEN CHOSIN

THE WEATHER FOR THE MARINES was atrocious—down to thirty degrees below zero—and the Chinese forces outnumbered the leathernecks five to one. The Marines were arranged to make their final big push to the Yalu River, linking up with the Eighth Army. But the Eighth Army was now heading toward Seoul.

On 27 November, the Marines took the village of Yudam-ni, northwest of the Chosin Reservoir. That was easy. What came next were ever-bloodier firefights with Chinese troops, lots of Chinese troops, in a conflagration of close-quarters combat. The Marines had run into the eastern wing of the Chinese Communist charge. While the Marines were hit north of the Yudam-ni, the Chinese leapt from the snow to attack U.S. Army units that had been advanced on the opposite (northeastern) side of the reservoir.

General Mark Almond, commander of X Corps (the United Nations forces in the east) was reluctant to call the Marines into retreat. A favorite of MacArthur, Almond wanted to deliver victory, the reward of Inchon. The commander of the 1st Marines, General Oliver P. Smith—whom Almond detested for his caution, which in the event turned out to be realism and prudence—demanded that Almond order a withdrawal. His Marines were under massive assault at Yudam-ni, and at Hagaru (where he had his headquarters) and Koto-ri (where Chesty Puller was in command), in a line heading south along the road to Hungnam. The Marines endured two days of savage fighting before Almond agreed to withdraw them. By then, General Smith faced the prospect of being surrounded.

The Army units to the east of the reservoir formed themselves into "Task Force Faith," under the command of Lieutenant Colonel Don Faith, and tried to escape. Faith himself was killed less than five miles from the Marine lines at Hagaru; what was left of his shattered command staggered into the Marine camp. The Marines, meanwhile, had to retire down a road that was completely flanked by Chinese units. Not only did these units have plenty of firepower and plenty of men, but as American pilots had found when they struck Chinese convoys, they had a hearty willingness to accept casualties, as though they were of little or no consequence. The intervention of the Chinese Yellow Peril seemed to imply a bottomless reservoir of Communist troops. The Marines had to hack their way through these troops.

The Marines' plan was to consolidate their forces. The Marines at Yudam-ni would link with the Marines at Hagaru; then these combined units would join Chesty Puller's men at Koto-ri, and from there the 1st Marine Division would retreat to Hungnam and a seaborne evacuation. This fighting withdrawal was as much a masterpiece of the military art as MacArthur's stroke at Inchon. The Marines fought their way in freezing weather that was itself a mortal hazard (a third of the casualties suffered in the retreat from Yudam-ni to Hagaru were from frostbite; that proportion rose to half, once they reached Hungnam).

The Marines seized surrounding hills from the Chinese so that United Nations units could pass down the road. These were small-unit actions: fierce and deadly in the bitter snow. And the Marines won them. When reporters asked General Smith whether his Marines were retreating for the first time in the history of the Corps, he replied, "Gentlemen, we are not retreating. We are merely attacking in another direction." That was true. Smith was insistent on fighting his way out, keeping (rather than abandoning) his equipment, clearing the Red Chinese from his path to the sea, not leaving any wounded or dead Marines behind. Smith's remark was translated into Marine Corps legend as "Retreat, hell—we're just attacking in another direction," a better quote to be sure, but out of keeping with Smith's reserved demeanor.[17]

From Hagaru to Koto-ri the Marines had to pass through "Hellfire Valley," though that didn't faze Chesty Puller, who announced: "I don't give a good goddamn how many Chinese laundrymen there are between us and Hungnam. There aren't enough in the world to stop a Marine regiment going where it wants to go! Christ in His mercy will see us through."[18] Christ in His mercy did indeed appear to prefer Marine regiments to Red Chinese laundrymen, which in the circumstances was understandable, given that the Red Chinese laundrymen were atheists and known to be rather nasty.

One shouldn't dismiss Puller's bravado. He was a tough, hard leatherneck, to be sure, but a thoughtful one, too. He left VMI (the Virginia Military Institute) after one year in order to enlist in the Marine Corps, hoping to see action in World War I. He missed that war but completed his own education in the field, starting in the banana wars, but also in the library with books on military history. He was astounded that his fellow officers hadn't read up on the Russo-Japanese war (which involved Korea). While proud of his own Marines, he was appalled at, in his view, the lack of leadership, unspeakably low morale, miserable training, and poor performance of the Army in Korea. He was disgusted at its long tail of rear-echelon paper shufflers and coffee sippers, whose jobs were unnecessary and who should have been infantrymen. He was contemptuous of the Truman administration for being all mouth and no stick: its budget cuts having reduced the armed forces to a travesty of what they should have been. He was so infuriated at this that he thought the United States should withdraw from Korea until it had the army it needed to do the job. He rated the Chinese soldier higher than the North Korean and even the Japanese. Finally, perhaps because of his pride as a Virginian with Confederate forebears, he was mindful of trying to limit the impact of hateful war on civilians, for whom he was always concerned. Chesty Puller was bullet-headed, barrel-chested, and belligerent, but he was far from being a lout.

The Marines at Hagaru, harassed by the Red Chinese, trudged through the snow and ice to reach the eloquent Colonel Puller. From there, a ready-to-assemble bridge was airlifted to replace the already thrice blown bridge at Funchilin Pass, through which the Marines had to exit. The Marines assembled the bridge, plowed a path, and marched all the way to Hungnam—and civilian refugees from the Communists followed their trail. The Marines had performed superbly. Chesty Puller underlined General O. P. Smith's view when he reminded reporters: "Remember, whatever you write, this was no retreat. All that happened was we found more Chinese behind us than in front of us. So we about-faced and attacked."[19]

Now it was the Navy's turn to do equally splendid work as it evacuated 105,000 men, 91,000 refugees (thousands more North Koreans were lined up at the docks hoping to escape the Communists), and hundreds of thousands of tons of equipment. By Christmas Eve, the last of the troops were safely aboard and the harbor was blown. It was an American Dunkirk. But a successful evacuation was far from the triumph MacArthur had sought only weeks before; and many Marines, including General Lemuel C. Shepherd, General Edward A. Craig, Lieutenant Colonel Raymond L. Murray, and Puller himself thought the withdrawal was unnecessary and only proved that MacArthur and his war planners were demoralized. Hungnam, they thought, could have been held; it was easily defensible; and the Chinese could have been beaten. Colonel Puller said: "Why the hell they [withdrew] I'll never know, gave up all that ground we paid so much for. Not all the Chinese in hell could have run over us."[20]

CHANGE OF COMMAND

THE EIGHT ARMY HAD RETREATED to the 38th Parallel, and the depressing scuttlebutt was that the United Nations forces would not bother to dig in there; they had to be ready to move out again. On 23 December 1950, the Eighth Army's harried commander, General Walker, was killed in a road mishap, bringing an immediate change of command—the arrival of a new general who intended to give the Eighth Army a new attitude. General Matthew Ridgway, a World War II airborne commander, wore grenades on his combat webbing, demanded that officers lead from the front, and thought the Korean "police action" was more a matter of killing the enemy than capturing his territory: charging the Yalu had brought in the Chinese; to do it again could bring in the Russians. For all the deficiencies that Chesty Puller had seen in the Army, Ridgway seemed the perfect corrective. He wanted to take the battle to the enemy, but recognized, after inspecting his troops, that they weren't ready—at least not yet. Ridgway found the Eighth Army sorely lacking in commitment, courage, and tactical competence.

All that added up to a lack of leadership. Ridgway designed a system of defense in depth so that units no longer feared being swarmed and flanked by the enemy. He repudiated the mood of panic he thought gripped the Army—all the way up to MacArthur. There was no reason why the United States Army with its superior firepower and command of the sea and air should not dominate the Korean battlefield. MacArthur's answer to the shock of Chinese intervention was to accept a showdown with the Communists: to bomb China and deploy Nationalist Chinese troops from Formosa. MacArthur's best-case scenario was that he could liberate China from the Communists (whom he thought were vulnerable) and thereby knock international communism back on its heels. At worst, he could achieve permanent victory on the Korean Peninsula by sealing the Korean-Chinese border with nuclear weapons.

But MacArthur's plans were the stuff of war games rather than real war. It didn't matter whether his ideas were good or bad; they were completely at odds with the foreign policy of the Truman administration, which explicitly wanted to avoid a showdown with China. In the famous words of General Omar Bradley, chairman of the Joint Chiefs of Staff, attacking Red China, as MacArthur wanted to do, would be "the wrong war, at the wrong place, at the wrong time, and with the wrong enemy."[21]

MacArthur's grand strategy failed to keep in mind that he was the servant not the designer of American foreign policy. He had reconfigured his own position beyond a military into a political one, and even had a congressman insert a letter from MacArthur into the Congressional Record announcing that "There is no substitute for victory." True enough, but since the heady days of the race to the Yalu, the Truman administration had reassessed its objectives; the goal now was to limit the war and prevent its expansion against the Communist Chinese. MacArthur needed to formulate a strategy that fit the strictures of his commander in chief. Ridgway could do that; MacArthur in the winter of 1950–51 could not, because of his conviction that the strictures needed to be removed.

At first, in the early days of January, all Ridgway could do was organize retreat: retreat from Seoul, Inchon, Suwon, Osan, and Wonju, to a line running roughly fifty to sixty miles south of the 38th Parallel. Here he stopped and prepared his counterthrust. American airpower and naval guns tore into the lines of Chinese troops. On 15 January 1951, the counterattack began. Ridgway gave the lead to one of the best-performing Army regiments in the war: the Wolfhounds of the 27th Infantry. The Wolfhounds' reconnaissance in force discovered that the Chinese, under the slightest pressure, would pull back; their lines were overstretched, and America's air and sea bombardment had weakened them.

Ridgway was ready to take advantage. United Nations forces began advancing up the peninsula, with Ridgway's objective being not speed but using America's overwhelming firepower to destroy enemy units. It was the right match of capabilities to objective: destroy the enemy, advance; destroy the enemy, advance. And it had another compensating factor for the troops executing it: it kept United Nations casualties low. By 14 March, Seoul was back in South Korean hands. By April, Ridgway's men had advanced beyond the 38th Parallel.

And by then President Truman had relieved MacArthur of command. There could be only one commander in chief, and Truman was tired of sharing the stage with MacArthur. So on 11 April 1951, the old soldier had to pack his bags, and Matthew Ridgway, the frontline combat leader, was sent to an office in Japan to take MacArthur's place as theater commander.

The objective of the United Nations forces was murky. Reunifying the peninsula was now quietly dropped, an armistice along the 38th Parallel quietly raised; and to the soldiers in the field, it was all a muddle. All they knew was that MacArthur's strategy of rolling the Communists back beyond the Yalu was over. In the meantime, they were kept focused on Ridgway's limited objective: killing the Communists in front of them.

Eleven days after MacArthur's dismissal, the Chinese rebounded with a spring offensive. The new commander of the Eighth Army, General James Van Fleet,[22] was Ridgway's man to stop it. Asked what the goal was for United Nations forces in Korea, Van Fleet was resolute: "I don't know."[23] But he did know how to fight the war the way that Ridgway and Truman wanted it fought. When the Chinese Communists came pouring down, he had his men arrayed for defense in depth, ready to slaughter the Communists with massive firepower, which they did. An infantryman expressed the revived spirit of the Eighth Army: "I was attacked by two hordes, sir, and I killed them both."[24]

The Chinese hoped to regain Seoul, but the United Nations forces, though they were forced back, merely moved down a notch on the battle maps on a range of ten to twenty-five miles south of the 38th Parallel. There they held the Chinese, and Van Fleet, sensing an opportunity, counterattacked and threw the Chinese back. With the rival combatants' starting lines reestablished, a stalemate appeared to be in the offing. But the Communists weren't done: they were stockpiling men and materiel for another lunge south.

On 15 May 1951, the Communists threw a haymaker at the eastern side of the battlefront, like a punch-drunk boxer who thinks one big blow will deliver a knockout. This, they rejoiced, was to be the final campaign. Only it wasn't. The Communists pushed a salient twenty miles into the United Nations lines, but after four days, they found themselves stalled. Worse, from their point of view, the western portion of the United Nations line began moving northeast. The Americans were advancing to envelop them. The Americans and ROKs regained the 38th Parallel; in June they were up to the Iron Triangle whose pinnacle was Pyongyang. And with the arrival of July 1951, the Communists accepted an American offer to negotiate an armistice.

Though fighting continued, there was no second race to the Yalu River by United Nations forces. If there had been, it had a better chance of succeeding now than before, because there was no Chinese rabbit to come jumping out of the Communist magician's hat. The Chinese had intervened, and they had been beaten. In June it was announced as official American policy that a return to the prewar status quo along the 38th Parallel was a sufficient objective for an armistice.

Negotiating with the Communists proved to be an exercise in frustration: a theater of the absurd showcasing Communist propaganda, bellicosity, abuse, irrationality, delay, and intransigence. Piddling negotiation details were routinely seized as opportunities for Communist lectures or attempts to humiliate American negotiators. And the whole charade at first came to nothing. By the fall, however, United Nations troops were again shellacking the Communists, and negotiations were reopened. On 27 November 1951, the Communists agreed to accept an armistice if the United Nations troops would advance no farther and would end any further operations. The Americans agreed, and then watched while the Communists stalled at the negotiating table and created a massive network of tunneled fortifications manned by more than 850,000 Communist troops. This time it was stalemate indeed—a fortified stalemate.

Small-unit actions and United Nations bombing runs continued, but there were no major campaigns. In the summer of 1952, General Mark Clark replaced Ridgway as theater commander, and in February 1953, a frustrated General Van Fleet—who had wanted to press on to victory—gave way for a new Eighth Army commander, another airborne man like Ridgway, General Maxwell Taylor. In between, there had also been a change of president, as Dwight David Eisenhower took over the White House and fulfilled his promise to go to Korea. There was, alas, not much to see.

The war had been reduced to holding symbolic hills. The Communists tried to seize them for propaganda victories or negotiating gambits. Some of these actions took on a sort of miniature epic glory—as in the heroic American defense, near-loss, and recapture of Pork Chop Hill, a battle that began in April and lasted through mid-July of 1953, inflicting heavy Communist casualties. Then, on 10 July, General Maxwell Taylor ordered the hill given up. Pork Chop Hill was emblematic of the latter stages of the war: American blood and courage expended on temporary tactical—and largely symbolic—objectives.

But the Communists were losing heart. In the first week of March 1953, Stalin died, and with him, apparently, died some of the Communists' confidence; at the end of March, the North Koreans and Chinese suddenly accepted a Red Cross–brokered prisoner exchange that they and the Soviets had earlier rejected. The Chinese, so keen on propaganda victories, suffered a major black eye when the prisoners of war they turned over were found to be half-starved and in miserable condition. It was common knowledge that the North Koreans were barbarous, but people assumed better of the Chinese; that was no longer the case.

Worse than propaganda defeats were psychological ones. The new administration had a new secretary of state, John Foster Dulles, who talked openly of the possibility of using newly developed tactical nuclear weapons; he spoke of basing American foreign policy on the principle of massive (nuclear) retaliation rather than limited police actions. What, the Chinese had to wonder, did that portend? Already, American air strikes were increasing. With a general as the American president, a hawkish secretary of state, and Syngman Rhee angrily inveighing against any settlement short of a united anti-Communist Korea, could the Americans be preparing for a second charge at the Yalu?

The Chinese tried to improve their negotiating position by launching another massive offensive in the summer. While it might have dented American hopes that the rapidly expanded ROKs were the Communists' equal, it nevertheless underlined that massive American firepower could halt and repel any Chinese attack. That was it for the Chinese. On 27 July 1953, an armistice was signed ending the war, though Syngman Rhee offered only passive consent; he would not sign the agreement or allow a ROK military presence at the ceremony. The United Nations forces didn't care. It was typical of the bloody war that in the final negotiations their ally had been as troublesome as the enemy. But even General Mark Clark, who signed for the Americans, was disappointed. He, like MacArthur, believed there was no substitute for victory; and for him, the restoration of the status quo ante was not victory; the war ended not with fireworks but with a damp squib.

For the American military, it was a sobering welcome to the Cold War.

CHAPTER 24

THE LONG TWILIGHT STRUGGLE

AT THE END OF MOST WARS, there is a chorus of "never again." But after the Korean War, it was not clear whether "never again" meant never fight another land war in Asia, or never fight a limited war with a goal of peace without victory, or never inflict such swingeing defense cuts as to effectively ruin the Army.

President Eisenhower, the man who gave us the phrase "the military-industrial complex," did his best to ruin the Army, inflicting—again—draconian defense cuts. He and his secretary of state, John Foster Dulles (whom Churchill accurately pegged as "dull, duller, and Dulles"), preferred relatively cheap atomic bombs stacked away for the threat of "massive retaliation" rather than an expensive standing army of men, bases, materiel, and the upkeep they required. The operative phrase was "more bang-for-the-buck." American foreign policy relied on "brinksmanship"—threatening massive retaliation—and downplayed the idea of limited interventions across the world.

But there were plenty of chances for interventions. When the French faced defeat in Indochina in 1954, the administration decided to steer clear. Uncle Sam was already picking up 80 percent of the costs of the French war effort. Having just finished the Korean police action, the administration was loath to send American boys into an Indochinese gendarmerie action.[1] Instead, the administration accepted the division of Vietnam along the Korean model of a Communist north and a non-Communist south, and the creation of an independent Laos and Cambodia.

To the Communist Chinese, the French defeat in Indochina appeared as yet another omen of the eventual triumph of communism over the West. They probed for more weaknesses, bombarding the islands of Quemoy and Matsu, property of Chiang Kai-shek's regime on Formosa. But the Eisenhower administration affirmed that it would defend Formosa from attack and faced down Red Chinese threats against the islands in 1954 and 1958.

America also reshuffled its own diplomatic cards. In 1954, the United States created the Southeast Asia Treaty Organization (SEATO) of the United States, Great Britain, France, Australia, New Zealand, the Philippines, Pakistan, and Thailand. President Eisenhower put forward the "domino theory" that if Indochina fell to the Communists, the other countries of Southeast Asia might fall one by one into the Communist camp. SEATO was the buttress to prevent that. But, like most treaties, it proved of little use, honored by the participants when they believed it served their national interests, ignored when it didn't.

Despite Eisenhower's and Dulles's anticolonial prejudices, the United States and Great Britain collaborated on a covert operation in Iran, helping Iranian royalists overthrow the socialist (and, it was feared, Communist-inclined) Iranian Prime Minister Mohammed Mossadegh in 1953. It was one of the most important Cold War victories of the 1950s, swinging oil-rich and Soviet-neighboring Iran into the Western camp. Closer to home, Eisenhower and Dulles again showed they were not above a little imperial (or Monroe Doctrinesque) skullduggery. In 1954, the United States helped fund and organize Guatemalan exiles to overthrow the Communist-leaning dictator Jacobo Arbenz.

In 1956, however, Eisenhower's and Dulles' anti-imperial prejudices betrayed them—and betrayed the West—during the Suez Crisis. British Prime Minister Anthony Eden warned that Egyptian dictator Gamal Abdel Nasser was another Mussolini; Dulles, skeptical of British imperialism, thought Nasser was another George Washington. When Nasser illegally nationalized the Suez Canal and closed this international waterway to the Israelis, the British and French intervened militarily[2]—without consulting the United States. In a huff, Eisenhower and Dulles threatened to initiate a run on the British pound and bankrupt Great Britain, humiliating America's closest ally, and doing nothing positive for our relationship with France. Shamefully, the United States found itself siding with the Soviet Union (which was simultaneously crushing the Hungarian uprising against communism and threatening missile attacks against France and Britain) in demanding a cease-fire and an Anglo-French withdrawal. It was a blundering diplomatic fiasco based on Eisenhower's and Dulles's reflexive and misguided "anticolonialism."

Fresh from his victory at Suez (and the resignation of Eden), the Communist-leaning Nasser fulfilled Eden's fears. He led Egypt to annex Syria and Yemen, aided and abetted the 1958 coup that killed King Faisal in Iraq, and prepared to destabilize the rest of the Middle East—most particularly Lebanon and Jordan. Eisenhower and Dulles had by now shed their illusions about Nasser. The United States Sixth Fleet and a force of 10,000 troops (Marines and U.S. Army airborne) were sent to Lebanon, while the British sent troops to Jordan. This was the first employment of the "Eisenhower Doctrine," proclaimed in 1957, pledging the United States to protect the independence of Middle Eastern countries from the threat of global communism.

The American show of strength defused the situation in the Middle East, but another crisis arose just ninety miles south of Florida in 1959 when Fidel Castro overthrew the dictator Fulgencio Batista. Castro was fêted throughout the United States, applauded by liberal opinion everywhere, and handed fistfuls of American dollars after his successful revolution. Nevertheless, he chose to ally himself with the Soviets, sent thousands of Cubans (and some American expatriates) to their deaths before firing squads, nationalized property (including American property), established a police state, exported terror and revolution, and in due course made Cuba a temporary base for Soviet missiles. The Eisenhower administration planned to oust Castro, using a plan similar to what had worked in Guatemala. But the plan had to be executed by the incoming Kennedy administration.

President John F. Kennedy declared in his inaugural address: "Let every nation know, whether it wishes us well or ill, that we shall pay any price, bear any burden, meet any hardship, support any friend, oppose any foe, in order to assure the survival and the success of liberty."[3] He even added: "To our sister republics south of our border, we offer a special pledge—to convert our good words into good deeds—in a new alliance for progress—to assist free men and free governments in casting off the chains of poverty. But this peaceful revolution of hope cannot become the prey of hostile powers. Let all our neighbors know that we shall join with them to oppose aggression or subversion anywhere in the Americas. And let every other power know that this Hemisphere intends to remain the master of its own house."[4]

But while the president authorized Cuban exiles in Florida to go ahead with their CIA-supported invasion of Cuba, at the last minute he withdrew American support, leaving them stranded and under fire at Cuba's Bay of Pigs in a humiliating catastrophe. It was only partly redeemed when, in 1962, Kennedy faced down Soviet Premier Nikita Khrushchev during the Cuban missile crisis, convincing the Soviet leader to withdraw nuclear missiles the Soviets had planted in Cuba.

Despite his cold feet at the Bay of Pigs, President Kennedy was an avid reader of Ian Fleming's James Bond novels, took a special interest in counterinsurgency strategies, and believed in the efficacy of Special Forces units.[5] The Kennedy administration dropped John Foster Dulles's strategy of massive retaliation and brinksmanship in favor of "flexible response."

It was surely an act of benevolence tinged with irony that flexible response would be tested not in nearby Cuba, but 8,000 miles away from California, 5,500 miles away from Hawaii, to save South Vietnam from communism.

LAND OF THE BLUE DRAGON

AMERICAN MILITARY ADVISERS had been in Vietnam since the 1940s, when anti-imperialist American officers of the OSS (Office of Strategic Services, the forerunner of the CIA) helped a Vietnamese Communist known as Ho Chi Minh topple the pro-French king of Vietnam, something American policymakers soon regretted. Advisers stayed on into the 1950s, advising the French and then the independent South Vietnamese.

As a United States senator in 1956, Kennedy had declared that Vietnam "represents the cornerstone of the Free World in Southeast Asia, the keystone to the arch, the finger in the dike. Burma, Thailand, India, Japan, the Philippines, and obviously Laos and Cambodia are among those whose security would be threatened if the red tide of Communism overflowed into Vietnam." Vietnam, Kennedy said, was the "proving ground for democracy in Asia." One million Vietnamese had fled the Communist North for the democratic-leaning South. America stood as "the godparents" to "little Vietnam." It was our responsibility— upon which stood our credibility in Asia—to make South Vietnam a success.[6]

As president, Kennedy upped the American military presence in Vietnam from fewer than 900 men to more than 16,000 by the end of 1963. Nikita Khrushchev pledged to support Communist insurgencies everywhere; President Kennedy committed the United States to foiling them. He drew the line in Vietnam.

The situation in Southeast Asia was unstable. The British were waging a long—and ultimately successful—anti-insurgency campaign against the Communists in Malaya. In neighboring Indonesia, President Sukarno—leader of the largest Muslim country in the world—was tilting toward the Communist camp. And the government of South Vietnam was fighting Communist insurgents, who were supported and often infiltrated from North Vietnam.

The president of South Vietnam was Ngo Dinh Diem, an authentic Vietnamese nationalist and a Roman Catholic, with all the ardent anticommunism that implied. But he ruled a land where 90 percent of the people were Buddhist, and did so, increasingly, with the same authoritarianism that had made Syngman Rhee an uncomfortable American ally in South Korea. When Buddhist monks immolated themselves in protest at Diem's regime, Diem was unmoved. His brother (and chief political adviser) Ngo Dinh Nhu even raided Buddhist pagodas to crack down on dissent. More worrisome to American military advisers was Diem's distrust of his own military. As a check against potential military coups, Diem broke up and interfered with the military chain of command; he disapproved of successful commanders who might rival him in power and popularity.

The Kennedy administration let it be known in South Vietnamese military circles that it would not oppose a coup against South Vietnam's president—and inevitably it happened, though Kennedy was shocked when Diem and his brother were murdered. Diem had been an imperfect leader for an emerging democracy, but he also had more legitimacy and political skill than any other potential leader—and certainly more than any military officer seizing power in a coup. Without Diem, the government of South Vietnam lost much of its stability and respect and suffered a series of coups and even an uprising of the Montagnards—a mountain people loyal to America's Special Forces but disdainful of Saigon—which only added to the chaos of a country fighting for its life against a Communist invasion and insurgency.

Three weeks after Diem's assassination, a Communist named Lee Harvey Oswald assassinated President Kennedy. The new American president, Lyndon Baines Johnson—a man who lifted dogs by their ears, conducted conversations from the toilet, and demanded that staffers (at least in theory) be willing "to kiss my ass in Macy's window at high noon and tell me it smells like roses"[7]—accepted Kennedy's commitment to South Vietnam and greatly expanded it, making it a far-flung outpost of his Great Society, dedicated to the civil and economic well-being of Vietnam. The United States Military Assistance Command Vietnam (MACV) became, in the words of historian Walter McDougall, "less like a comrade-in-arms to the Saigon regime than a nagging social worker."[8]

Plenty of troops were on the way, too, especially after U.S. ships were fired upon in the Gulf of Tonkin on 2 August and (more ambiguously) 4 August 1964, the latest in a long series of targeted attacks on American forces. With a congressional resolution in hand "to take all necessary measures to repel any armed attack against forces of the United States and to prevent further aggression,"[9] President Johnson escalated American involvement in South Vietnam's war against Communist guerillas (the Viet Cong) and their supporting units of the North Vietnamese Army (the NVA). Standing behind both Communist forces with arms and materiel were Communist China, the Soviet Union, and the Soviet bloc (even Communist Cuba). By the end of 1965, there were more than 180,000 American troops on the ground in South Vietnam.

The American commander in charge of MACV was General William C. Westmoreland, a South Carolina–born West Pointer with a stellar record of command in World War II (serving in North Africa, Sicily, and Normandy) and Korea (where he led an airborne infantry regiment). Westmoreland recognized, as any military commander would, that the key to victory was taking the battle to North Vietnam and eliminating the prime source of subversion in Indochina. But this the politicians would not countenance. So, as a veteran of Korea, and knowing what was expected of him, Westmoreland did what appeared to be the right thing—only it wasn't.

Westmoreland decided, as Matthew Ridgway had done in the Korean War, that success lay in American firepower: pin the enemy and destroy him. Thus began the American strategy of search and destroy in a war of attrition. But Ridgway had fought a conventional army in a conventional war. In Vietnam, the enemy disappeared into the jungle. Search and destroy missions often meant unleashing devastating firepower to little useful purpose.

Instead of reproducing Ridgway's success, Westmoreland was saddled with some of the worst military baggage of Korea. Soldiers were on one-year tours of duty, so that, as Colonel Dave Richard Palmer put it, the U.S. Army wasn't in Vietnam for twelve years, it was there for one year a dozen times.[10] The corporate managerialism that came in with Secretary of Defense Robert Strange McNamara—a devotee of "quantitative systems analysis"—made it worse. Officers rotated through Vietnam to punch their tickets, many of them staying only a matter of months. Achieving statistical goals on paper rather than leading men into battle became a corrupting temptation.

As in Korea, but worse, the length of the Army's rear-echelon tail was an embarrassment. The cornucopia of rear-echelon perks meant to raise morale actually undercut it. The indiscipline and drug abuse, which riddled the Army in the last three years of the war (years of course marked by antiwar fervor, drug abuse, and spiking racial and criminal problems at home among the draft-age population)[11] were all strikingly higher the farther away one got from combat.[12] What the troops needed was better training and leadership, not more dollops of ice cream and beer; more discipline and focus on combat arms, not more rear-echelon billets where troops punched clocks and marked time.

The emphasis on overwhelming firepower, bureaucratic managerialism, and high-tech solutions meant that combat basics were too often overlooked. Army Colonel David Hackworth was a hard charger who turned a hopeless battalion into a hard-core battalion. In June 1969, he noted the weakness of the Army's green infantry lieutenants, who were, he wrote, "extremely weak in troop leading, practical knowledge and small-unit combat operations" and "almost without actual field experience."

The affluent civilian society at home bred "nice guy" lieutenants who often failed as combat officers:

> In Vietnam, good guys let their people smoke at night and take portable radios to the field. Good guys allowed night ambushes to set up in abandoned hooches so they wouldn't get wet and left only one guard by the door so everyone else could get a good night's rest. They let their men leave their boots on for several days and didn't inspect their feet, resulting in immersion foot. They didn't make sure their men kept their weapons and magazines perfectly clean or protected themselves against mosquitos or took the required malaria pills and salt pills.
>
> Good guy lieutenants ended up killing their men with kindness.[13]

Another problem for Westmoreland and his commanders was the political micromanagement of the war. It was worse than any American commander had ever suffered, to the point that President Johnson liked to brag that he approved every bomb that fell in Vietnam: "I won't let those Air Force generals bomb the smallest outhouse north of the 17th parallel without checking with me."[14] He even approved the bomb weights. When the president wasn't available, Secretary of Defense McNamara was on hand to do the micromanaging.

Facing the Americans, on the other hand, were dedicated Vietnamese Communists—people who had been at war for generations, who were willing to endure every hardship to win, and who took the long view. They were under no misapprehension that they could defeat the Americans in a stand-up fight, and in the early years of the war, they relied primarily on guerilla forces, the Viet Cong, rather than North Vietnamese regulars. The Vietnamese Communists believed, rightly as it turned out, that the Americans would tire of the war long before they would.

WHAT WOULD CHESTY PULLER DO?

THERE WAS AN ALTERNATIVE to Westmoreland's strategy. It was captured in Army Colonel David Hackworth's insistence on "out G-ing the G"— fighting a better guerilla war than the guerilla. Americans from the days of Rogers' Rangers, and almost always in the Marines, had been adept and effective in small-unit combat. Marine General Victor "Brute" Krulak knew this, and at the beginning of the Vietnam War put forward what he called "the spreading inkblot strategy." He took as his historical starting point not the conventional war in Korea but the guerilla war against the Philippine insurrection. General Krulak proposed a spreading inkblot of small-unit actions to pacify South Vietnam village by village, province by province, beginning with the Mekong Delta in the south, where 80 percent of the population lived. When big units or NVA were encountered, Westmoreland's firepower could be employed. Otherwise it was a matter of foot patrols. The goal was to secure South Vietnamese villages, and train and support the villagers to defend themselves.

In addition, Krulak believed that North Vietnam should pay a heavy price for supporting the insurgency. He wanted to mine Haiphong Harbor near Hanoi, which was the prime entry point for Chinese and Soviet military supplies, and he wanted North Vietnam bombed so that its port areas, railways, power stations, fuel docks, and heavy industry were utterly destroyed.

Krulak's plan was rejected. Such bombing, W. Averell Harriman, assistant secretary of state for Far Eastern affairs, told him, would provoke Soviet and Red Chinese intervention. The United States intended to limit itself to carefully calibrated retaliatory air strikes. Krulak had the support of Army generals Maxwell Taylor and James Gavin but was opposed by General Westmoreland. Westmoreland believed in hammering the enemy into submission through superior firepower. The inkblot strategy might work, he conceded, but it would take too long, and he did not have the luxury of time. "I suggested," wrote Krulak, "that we didn't have time to do it any other way; if we left the people to the enemy, glorious victories in the hinterland would be little more than blows in the air—and we would end up losing the war."[15]

Though the inkblot didn't spread, there was plenty of bombing to be sure. It is a commonplace that America dropped more bombs in Vietnam than it did in World War II. Less well known is that most of these bombs fell on the South, in what might be called VC-hide-and-American-bomb-go-seek, or the bombs were otherwise wasted in churning up the mud of the Ho Chi Minh supply trail that ran through neutral and unstable Laos (which was fighting its own Communist insurgency) and Cambodia into South Vietnam.

As for boots on the ground, General Westmoreland had plenty. From 1965 to 1967, he assembled an Allied force that included 60,000 non-American and non–South Vietnamese troops (more than turned up for the police action in Korea). Especially notable were some tough ROK units as well as the ever-handy Australians and New Zealanders. All told, forty-five countries pledged some sort of support for South Vietnam. Westmoreland's American force numbers rose to 540,000 men. It was a massive, if rear-echelon-heavy, host. He suffered no shortage of men or materiel, though he thought he did, and that was part of the problem, too.

Before 1964, the main accomplishment of America's military advisers and military aid had been to improve the confidence, mobility, and firepower of the South Vietnamese Army (the ARVN) and put the Viet Cong on the defensive. A de facto version of the spreading inkblot strategy known as the Strategic Hamlet program had some success, too. In fact, at the end of 1962, many American military advisers thought that South Vietnam could be secured within three years.

What put paid to optimistic assessments of defeating the insurgency in 1965 was the rapid escalation of Communist forces sneaking across the border: both guerillas to reinforce the Viet Cong and regular NVA regiments. Together, they were inflicting severe losses on the ARVN, and tilting the war dramatically toward a Communist victory. General Maxwell Taylor, who in 1964 became American ambassador to Saigon, said, "Viet Cong units have the recuperative powers of the phoenix . . . [and] an amazing ability to maintain morale."[16] Westmoreland reported, "Whereas we will add an average of seven maneuver battalions per quarter, the enemy will add fifteen."[17] While he waited for reinforcements, Westmoreland tried to shore up ARVN units with close air support, and he used helicopters to aid mobility and firepower.

Democrat Senator and Majority Leader Mike Mansfield of Montana toured Vietnam and presciently noted that it "was not too early to begin to contemplate the need for a total of upward of 700,000 men"—which in due course Westmoreland would request.[18] It was also the figure that General Earl Wheeler of the Joint Chiefs of Staff told President Johnson would be necessary to win the war: 700,000 to a million men and seven years. General Wheeler made this prediction before Johnson's massive escalation. Such predictions begged the question, however, of whether there wasn't a better way to fight the war.

In August 1964, President Johnson pledged that he would not be "committing American boys to fighting a war that I think ought to be fought by the boys of Asia to help protect their own land"[19]—though if he really believed that, there was no reason to go beyond deploying military advisers, Green Berets, and some Marines, and employing the sort of bombing program advocated by Admiral Ulysses S. Grant Sharp. Admiral Sharp, U.S. Pacific commander from 1964 to 1968 (and a supporter of General Krulak's inkblot strategy), lamented: "We could have flattened every war-making facility in North Vietnam. . . . The most powerful country in the world did not have the will-power to meet the situation."[20] Instead, the Johnson administration followed a course of carefully graduated escalation. The aim was not victory or the return to any status quo ante, it was to punish the Communists when they killed Americans and to pressure them to negotiate a peace.

When the Viet Cong attacked American advisers at Pleiku on 7 February 1965, Johnson sent bombers to rap North Vietnam's knuckles; when the Viet Cong attacked a hotel a few days later, killing twenty-three Americans, Admiral Sharp rapped North Vietnam's knuckles again, and President Johnson gave his approval for the sustained, if limited and measured, bombing of North Vietnam, an operation known as Rolling Thunder that would last more than three years. The goal was, in the words of Air Force Chief of Staff General J. P. McConnell, "strategic persuasion." Or as soldier and historian Dave Richard Palmer put it: "It was a far cry from 'bombing them back into the stone age' [as General Curtis LeMay had wanted to do]—it was more like trying to bomb them into the Age of Reason."[21] The North Vietnamese met President Johnson's policy of "graduated response" by importing Soviet technicians to give them one of the best air defense systems in the world, and by otherwise shrugging off Johnson's explosive pinpricks—something they couldn't have done had General Curtis LeMay (who retired in 1965) been in charge.[22]

A month after the attack on Pleiku, on 8 March 1965, the Marines waded ashore at Danang to protect an American air base. They also established an airstrip and base at Chu Lai. There, in August 1965, the Marines fought their biggest battle since the Korean War. It was known as Operation Starlight, a weeklong fight in which the Marines used helicopters, an amphibious landing, air strikes, offshore naval gunnery, and cooperation with the ARVN to kill nearly 700 Viet Cong and destroy their networks of caves and tunnels (caves and tunnels that could have reminded older Marine officers and NCOs of the Japanese). Civilian villages, however, were also in the fire zone, and it was any

Marine's guess, in many cases, whether the dead Vietnamese he found was a Viet Cong, or VC sympathizer, or merely a villager caught in the crossfire. Distinguishing friend from foe was, for the infantryman, one of Vietnam's most troubling dilemmas, though it was certainly not a dilemma unique to this war.

Civilians weren't in the way at Ia Drang in the Central Highlands, where the Army had its first major battle of the war. Ia Drang stood across a line, parallel with Pleiku, drawn by North Vietnamese General Vo Nguyen Giap. It was the line along which he hoped to cut South Vietnam in half. He planned to deploy three NVA divisions (supported by Viet Cong), destroy American and South Vietnamese units at Pleiku, conquer the Central Highlands, and inflict such a shattering Communist victory as to convince the Americans that the war was hopeless, that South Vietnam should be left to its fate.

American intelligence, however, had figured out what Giap was up to, and in September 1965 General Westmoreland placed as his counterforce the First Air Cavalry. Under the command of Major General Harry Kinnard, a Texan, it had, he reckoned, the mobility and firepower to be sent anywhere and do anything. From its base at An Khe, the Air Cav patrolled the highlands. General Giap and Westmoreland played true to form. Giap wanted another Dien Bien Phu—a climactic battle that would defeat the United States, as Dien Bien Phu had defeated the French. Westmoreland wanted to find and destroy the North Vietnamese invaders.

On 1 November, the Air Cav found a small NVA force and defeated it. More important, they found a map marking the retreat routes for NVA forces withdrawing from a successful ARVN counterattack elsewhere in the highlands (at Plei Me). Kinnard hunted down the NVA and placed Air Cav units on their paths of retreat. Sharp battles followed, and over the ensuing days, the NVA forces were harassed, suffered heavy casualties, but were not destroyed. The Air Cav were reluctant to pursue the NVA into the jungle, because the jungle was gookland. The Air Cav stuck close to their landing zones (LZs), where choppers could lift them out of a jam, or bring them resupplies and reinforcements.

The NVA commanders re-formed, brought in antiaircraft support to neutralize American helicopters, and waited for a moment to counterstrike. That was when Lieutenant Colonel Harold G. Moore of the 7th Cavalry came knocking at their door. Inserted with the 7th Cavalry's 1st Infantry Battalion into the Ia Drang valley, Moore sent forward a company to reconnoiter for the enemy; the Americans ran smack into them and into a firefight. Mortar shells exploded on the LZ and North Vietnamese fire poured into his position.

Pulling his battalion back into a defensive perimeter—except for one platoon that was cut off and decided to dig in—Moore called in air strikes, asked for reinforcements, and held on, repelling successive NVA attacks in fierce fighting. On the second day, the NVA again tried to overrun the 7th Cavalry. Moore's men refused to buckle. Reinforced, they retrieved the survivors of the cutoff platoon, while supporting American artillery and air strikes pounded the NVA positions. By the morning of the third day of battle, the NVA had had enough and were again in retreat. The NVA had suffered more than 2,000 casualties, more than a thousand of them dead. Seventy-nine Americans had been killed. The victory was marred somewhat, when the next day a relief column—the 2nd battalion of the 7th Cavalry—was ambushed and suffered virtually twice as many dead.

But the key thing was that General Giap's great offensive was foiled. Even the ARVN had fought well—both at Plei Me and in chewing up NVA units as they tried to slip across the Cambodian border. Westmoreland had won the battle he sought to win, a battle of kill ratios. But the Air Cavalry clung to no territory; there were no geographical markers of advance and success. When the airmobile infantry remounted their helicopters, it was to fight wherever they were needed: and that could be anywhere the enemy chose.

JOHNSON'S QUAGMIRE

IN 1965, AFTER THE BATTLE of Ia Drang, Secretary of Defense Robert McNamara toured South Vietnam. When he returned to Washington he warned the president that because the North Vietnamese were willing to pay any price and bear any burden to conquer the South, the United States ran the risk of an escalating stalemate. What no one in the Johnson administration was willing to do was break the stalemate by threatening the existence of the government in Hanoi. Had General Westmoreland been allowed and encouraged to launch an Inchon-like invasion of the North, had Admiral Sharp been given approval to conduct bombing that was meant to cripple the North's ability to fight (rather than to persuade it to negotiate), victory on the Korean model would have been achievable. But to allow the enemy, in essence, to dictate America's strategy and commitment—to allow it sanctuaries not only in its own country but in Cambodia and Laos—was an absurdity that only a politician could endorse. Johnson appeared to regard North Vietnamese dictator Ho Chi Minh as merely an especially recalcitrant congressman who with the right amount of pressure and cajoling would fall into line. Former president, and of course general, Dwight Eisenhower told Johnson he was fighting the war entirely the wrong way; the North Vietnamese, he advised, should have no sanctuaries free from American bombing and attack. Defense Secretary McNamara's answer to the sanctuaries problem was not to invade them or destroy them, but to build a fence. "McNamara's fence," like McNamara's military education, was never completed.

Between 1964 and 1968, Johnson offered no less than seventy-two peace initiatives and ordered sixteen bombing pauses to convince Uncle Ho that they could cut a deal. Johnson at one point offered to extend the Great Society programs to the people of North Vietnam—an outlandish offer that even the liberal Arthur Schlesinger felt compelled to ridicule as "a form of imperialism unknown to Lenin: sentimental imperialism."[23] Unfortunately, realism appeared to be in short supply at the White House. The result was that, as Vietnam veteran Colonel Dave Richard Palmer noted, "political considerations left military commanders no choice other than attrition warfare, but that does not alter the hard truth that the United States was strategically bankrupt in Vietnam in 1966."[24]

Within that bankruptcy, General Westmoreland did everything he could to find and kill the enemy in South Vietnam. As the "kill ratios" attested, American troops did this extremely well. But fighting a war of attrition relied on the assumption that America had more patience for a protracted and costly war than the North Vietnamese had—an assumption that was patently unwarranted. Colonel Harry Summers, another Vietnam veteran, recounted a conversation he had with a North Vietnamese colonel in 1975. " 'You know you never defeated us on the battlefield,' said the American colonel. The North Vietnamese colonel pondered this remark a moment. 'That may be so,' he replied, 'but it is also irrelevant.' " Summers called what happened in Vietnam "tactical victory, strategic defeat."

> As far as logistics and tactics were concerned we succeeded in everything we set out to do. At the height of the war the Army was able to move almost a million soldiers a year in and out of Vietnam, feed them, clothe them, house them, supply them with arms and ammunition, and generally sustain them better than any Army had ever been sustained in the field. . . . On the battlefield itself, the Army was unbeatable. In engagement after engagement the forces of the Viet Cong

and of the North Vietnamese were thrown back with terrible losses. Yet, in the end, it was North Vietnam, not the United States, that emerged victorious.[25]

In that context, it is even more remarkable that for all the political restrictions that tied his hands and left him "strategically bankrupt" General Westmoreland not only waged an aggressive war, but brought the United States to the brink of victory. This was despite the obvious frustrations of operations like "Cedar Falls" in January 1967, which attempted to block and destroy the enemy in the "Iron Triangle," a major Viet Cong nest forty miles from Saigon. The United States evacuated the 6,000 villagers of the region, Allied forces swept the area, capturing loads of arms and equipment, and destroyed the VC's complex of sophisticated tunnels. But the VC themselves had escaped, and when the Americans left, they returned.

More satisfying was the Battle of Dak To. NVA General Vo Nguyen Giap aimed to eliminate the Special Forces outposts dotting the South Vietnamese border with Cambodia and Laos. But it was not the Special Forces who had to pick up and run; it was the Communists. American airborne and infantry units spotted the enemy forces and in a series of battles in the Central Highlands near Dak To, from June through November 1967, the North Vietnamese troops were driven from hill to hill all the way back to their Cambodian sanctuary. The most intense period of fighting (from 3 November to 22 November) had American forces attacking heavily fortified Communist bunkers with artillery, aerial bombardment, napalm, flamethrowers, grenades, and guts. In the end, more than 1,600 of the enemy were killed for American losses of 289 men.

While this in terms of the Vietnam War was a major set-piece battle, it was in some ways small beer. In 1968, Vietnam would be rocked by a bold, massive Communist invasion. Westmoreland finally had his enemy in the open. He was about to achieve his greatest success of the war—and it proved, ironically, to be his undoing.

THE TET OFFENSIVE

THE VIET CONG WERE fingering their collars. Bearing the full brunt of America's awkward but massive military might, the VC were none too optimistic about the future. The optimism came from Hanoi—and from Hanoi's assessment of growing domestic opposition to the war in the United States. The

North Vietnamese politburo pointed to this as hard evidence that America would lose the war of wills. The Viet Cong scoffed at the armchair generals in Hanoi: they did not have to endure the horrible casualties the VC did, casualties that were now outpacing the arrival of North Vietnamese recruits.

The Communist strategy that emerged was for a massive New Year's uprising—an offensive that might win the war, and that even if it didn't, would so shock American public opinion as to make an American withdrawal a political necessity for the White House. In the last months of 1967, General Giap ordered large-scale attacks near the DMZ (the demilitarized zone separating North and South Vietnam) and other areas that would draw American troops away from South Vietnam's major cities. The Communists suffered terrible losses, but Giap was willing to sacrifice these men for what he trusted would be a bigger gain.

Among these actions, NVA troops gathered against a remote Marine outpost, Khe Sanh, in northwestern South Vietnam, near the Laotian border, where initial skirmishes led to a heavy firefight between a Marine patrol and the NVA on 21 January 1968. The next day the North Vietnamese bombarded Khe Sanh, blowing up an ammo dump and pinning the Marines down in their foxholes. The NVA poured men, mortars, artillery, antiaircraft guns, and even tanks into their cordon around Khe Sanh. Western reporters began to mutter darkly about Dien Bien Phu repeating itself. Westmoreland, though, was not so worried. He was convinced that the Marines at Khe Sanh were the flypaper—and now he had a perfect chance to sweep in and exterminate the flies, which he did with air attacks and Marine and Air Cavalry reinforcements. The siege of Khe Sanh lasted seventy-seven days, and it was certainly not Dien Bien Phu.[26] It was, for General Giap, another hugely expensive diversionary attack. American casualties—dead, wounded, and missing in action—were 650 men. The NVA lost more than 15,000 casualties during the siege. Khe Sanh was game, set, and match to Westmoreland.

Neither that battlefield nor the men lost there mattered to General Giap. He had Washington obsessed with an apparent replay of Dien Bien Phu. Now he would show them that the situation was even worse than they could have imagined—the Vietnamese people would rise up in a Communist revolution in the South, the ARVN would collapse, and the war—for the Americans—would be lost.

Tet, the most important holiday in the Vietnamese calendar—one that is celebrated for a week—fell on 30 January 1968. And that was when the Communists struck. Despite all their careful preparations, their importing and stockpiling of arms, their distribution of propaganda, and their amassing and infiltrating of guerilla cadres (some, disguised as ARVN, even hitching rides on American military vehicles), they achieved virtually complete surprise. The Viet Cong, typically, had announced a holiday cease-fire, as had the Allies, except where reality, as at Khe Sanh, intervened. Half the ARVN went on holiday—and when they absented themselves, the Viet Cong leapt upon all the major cities of South Vietnam in an offensive to win the war.

Villagers across the country raised their fists and grabbed their weapons—but unfortunately for the Viet Cong, they raised them against the Communists. The ARVN rushed to defend their cities. The fighting was fierce. For the Viet Cong, this was the great all-or-nothing climactic battle; Westmoreland had his enemy fully out in the open, in urban combat. If he relished the chance to wipe out thousands of Viet Cong, the images broadcast to the people and politicians back home were devastating to the idea that Westmoreland had victory nearly in hand.

Saigon remained relatively secure throughout the Tet Offensive, so secure that the Tet celebrations continued with public parties. But a team of Viet Cong saboteurs pulled off a propaganda coup when they blew their way into the American embassy. It took all of four hours to kill the saboteurs, but early wire reports about the embassy attacks, and about attacks around the country, evoked palpable shock in American newsrooms and in Washington. The results on the ground were rather different: in the course of roughly a week the Viet Cong assault on Saigon was utterly crushed.

In the former imperial capital of Hue—which was still regarded as the cultural capital of South Vietnam—the Viet Cong, the ARVN, and the United States Marine Corps fought one of the toughest battles of the war. The Viet Cong had seized the Citadel—the former imperial palace and a fortress walled city within Hue. The battle became, in part, a struggle to push the VC out of the Citadel. Because the palace was a cultural landmark, heavy weapons were forbidden; and the under-strength Allies—who did not have enough men to surround and cut off the Citadel—had to fight the easily reinforced enemy in intense house-to-house, street-by-street combat. On 14 February 1968, jets were given the go-ahead to strike the Citadel. But it was not until 24 February that the enemy evacuated the city. The Allies lost 500 men in the retaking of Hue; they killed perhaps ten times that many Viet Cong. More shocking was that the Communists had come prepared to assassinate their class enemies and had murdered 3,000 people.

By the time Hue was cleared, the stark military fact was that General Giap's Tet Offensive had not only failed, but failed spectacularly—so spectacularly as to eliminate the Viet Cong as a military threat. An estimated 45,000 of the 85,000 Viet Cong committed to battle had been killed; the VC's popular support was exposed as paltry. Westmoreland had won the victory he had wanted. He asked President Johnson for an additional 200,000-plus troops so that he could launch a counteroffensive to wipe out the remaining VC.

Johnson's weary, heavy-bagged eyes betrayed his lack of confidence. The media and political opponents—not Republicans, but fellow Democrats, fellow liberals—were pummeling him, declaring the war unwinnable, as were some in his own cabinet; and he was coming to believe it. On 22 March 1968, he kicked Westmoreland upstairs, appointing him U.S. Army chief of staff, and turned MACV over to General Creighton Abrams. Then nine days later, the president committed political suicide: he announced he would not run for reelection. In the meantime, he was imposing further bombing restrictions—a partial halt— and would seek a negotiated settlement with the North Vietnamese. But there was no need for negotiations—Johnson had already surrendered.

In South Vietnam itself, even without reinforcements, the Allies were fanning out and attacking the retreating Viet Cong. To try to stave off a complete rout, and to improve their negotiating position, the North Vietnamese rolled the dice again, launching a May offensive, an attempted replay of the Tet Offensive to further sway American public opinion. They succeeded in bringing the fighting back to Saigon, but at a horrific cost. Between January and June 1968, the Communists lost more than 100,000 men. Allied losses were one-fifth that number. But the continued heavy fighting encouraged American opponents of the war—and for the North Vietnamese, the antiwar movement in the United States was the essential pivot to swing the outcome of the war from defeat to victory.

NEW COMMANDERS AND A NEW STRATEGY

THE AMERICAN PEOPLE did their part to win "peace with honor." In November 1968 they elected a new president, Richard M. Nixon. The phrase "peace with honor" was his, and he appeared to have a good deal more nerve and character than the hapless, bullying dealmaker from Texas. The commander in the field whom the new president inherited, Creighton Abrams, was a Massachusetts-born West Pointer, a World War II tank commander (admired by Patton), and had served as Westmoreland's deputy at MACV. Abrams was the man responsible for the impressive performance of the ARVN during the Tet Offensive. So he was the perfect executor of Nixon's strategy of "Vietnamization"—of gradually withdrawing American troops, while the ARVN picked up the load. Abrams was also committed to a strategy of rural pacification, and he implemented both these policies extremely well given the political constraints upon him.

His commander in chief, Richard M. Nixon, was in an ironical position. Nixon had been vice president to President Eisenhower, who had declined to intervene in Vietnam when he had the chance in the 1950s. Now Nixon was left to extricate the United States from a commitment made by the ticket that beat him in 1960 in his first race for the presidency. In contrast to Kennedy's pledge to "pay any price, bear any burden, meet any hardship, support any friend, oppose any foe, in order to assure the survival and the success of liberty," Nixon propounded his own doctrine, which enunciated a much more restrained version of the national interest. On 3 November 1969, Nixon delivered his "Address to the Nation on the War in Vietnam," in which he set out three principles that would guide American foreign policy:

- First, the United States will keep all of its treaty commitments.
- Second, we shall provide a shield if a nuclear power threatens the freedom of a nation allied with us or of a nation whose survival we consider vital to our security.
- Third, in cases involving other types of aggression, we shall furnish military and economic assistance when requested in accordance with our treaty commitments. But we shall look to the nation directly threatened to assume the primary responsibility of providing the manpower for its defense.[27]

If America's willingness to bear burdens on behalf of others was reined back a bit in the name of prudence, by no means did Nixon intend to abandon the South Vietnamese. His goal was an independent South Vietnam that could defend itself. He did the best he could to achieve that while facing a Democrat Congress that opposed him, radical leftists who were leading riots in the streets and on college campuses, and then a reelection scandal that led to his eventual resignation. Hanoi's leadership suffered from no such distractions and no self-imposed constraints. Hanoi remained committed to victory at all costs.

Nixon's Vietnamization policy was conscientiously applied—within its first year, American troop levels were drawn down by 100,000 men, and the rate accelerated dramatically in 1970, 1971, and 1972. Westmoreland had wanted to do more with more; Nixon asked Abrams to do more with less—and Abrams succeeded. In the aftermath of the Tet Offensive, the Viet Cong were driven from the South Vietnamese countryside, many of the Communist cadres were infiltrated and their leaders killed, and 70 to 90 percent of the country was considered pacified.

With the Viet Cong hobbled, the NVA, operating from its border sanctuaries, became the main threat—and turmoil in Cambodia gave Nixon the opening he needed to launch an incursion against the Communist safe havens across the border. For nearly a decade, Cambodia's Prince Norodom Sihanouk had pursued a policy of "neutrality" that gave the North Vietnamese a virtual free hand in eastern Cambodia (though he gave the Americans an equally free hand to begin bombing across the border in 1969). The fellow-traveling prince's compliance with the Communists eventually led to a Cambodian populist backlash. In 1970 a new Cambodian government under Lon Nol effectively stripped the prince of his powers. The new government demanded that the hated Vietnamese no longer run roughshod over the Cambodian people. But with no army to speak of, the Cambodians were helpless when the North Vietnamese swiftly annexed (de facto) eastern Cambodia. Lon Nol then turned to the United States, and President Nixon sent in the Air Cavalry.

Nixon did not undertake the protection of Cambodia as a war aim; the purpose of the American incursion was to raid and destroy the cross-border base camps of the Viet Cong and the NVA. First into action were the ARVN, and on 1 May 1970, the Air Cav joined the mission. In the area of Cambodia known as the Fish Hook, the Air Cav discovered a Viet Cong supply and training base so elaborate that it became known as "The City." The Air Cav sacked The City.

As with every other military operation in Vietnam, there were tight political constraints: in this case, the incursion was restricted to a twenty-mile range and a two-month time limit. Within those limits, the ARVN and American forces hit the enemy hard, the ARVN gained confidence, and the Americans chalked up a necessary victory to expedite Vietnamization and the safe withdrawal of American troops. The mission was a success, but the Nixon administration took a political scorching for it. There were more street protests and riots. Congress responded by forbidding American troops—or even advisers—from operating in Cambodia and Laos. Thus military victory was turned into a political humiliation for the United States—while American negotiators were still trying to bring Hanoi to a peace agreement. Congress's slapping down of the president and slapping handcuffs on the military meant that the greatest ultimate beneficiaries of the Cambodian incursion were Soviet-bloc arms merchants. After the sack of The City, the Communist Vietnamese placed vast orders for military supplies—and planned another massive attack. The Communists had deposed one American president in 1968 with the Tet Offensive; they planned to do the same to Nixon in 1972. Nixon, however, was a far tougher customer.

General Giap's plan was Tet revisited, but with regular NVA forces taking the place of the now crippled Viet Cong. The Communists infiltrated the South with men and heavy weaponry, including Soviet tanks. The NVA assault came on 29 March 1972, with Soviet tanks crashing across the demilitarized zone—the first thrust of an all-out, twelve-division conventional force attack. Initially, the NVA overwhelmed the ARVN, forcing them back on Hue. But from Hue the South Vietnamese refused to budge. ARVN troops were engaged everywhere. As with Tet, the entire country was a battlefield. The ARVN fought the Communists to a standstill, though the ultimate outcome remained in doubt until Nixon intervened. He ordered the bombing of NVA supply lines and military-industrial sites in North Vietnam. He ordered the mining of Haiphong Harbor (where Soviet supplies arrived). And Americans flew air support for the ARVN. The NVA felt the crunch—in severed supply lines and enormous casualties. When North Vietnam's Spring Offensive was over, the NVA had suffered more than 100,000 dead; ARVN losses were about 25,000.

And to Hanoi's surprise, Nixon showed no fear at all of the electoral ramifications of the Spring Offensive. In fact, he pulled his negotiators from the Paris peace talks—which the North Vietnamese had used solely as a stage for political theater in any event—and continued bombing the North. If the North wanted a peace accord—if it wanted an end to the bombing—it would have to prove that it would negotiate in good faith. The climax came with President Nixon's "Christmas bombing" campaign in December 1972 that hammered out Hanoi's remaining resistance to a peace agreement, which was signed in January 1973. The British counterinsurgency expert Sir Robert Thompson—who had helped achieve the British victory against the Communists in Malaya—said: "In my view, on December 30, 1972, after eleven days of those B-52 attacks on the Hanoi area, *you had won the war. It was over!* . . . They would have taken any terms. And that is why, of course, you actually got a peace agreement in January, which you had not been able to get in October."[28]

Nixon had won his peace with honor—or at least he had for the United States. He and his secretary of state, Henry Kissinger, were equally convinced that they had won the war. They were shocked that South Vietnam's President Nguyen Van Thieu regarded the peace as a prelude to disaster. Kissinger told Nixon that the paradox was that "North Vietnam, which had in effect lost the war, was acting as if it had won; while South Vietnam, which had effectively won the war was acting as if it had lost."[29]

President Thieu was not alone in his assessment. Sir Robert Thompson, who had declared American military victory, called the Paris Peace Accords a diplomatic defeat because the "cease-fire agreement restored complete security to the rear bases in North Vietnam, in Laos, in Cambodia, and in the parts of South Vietnam that it held. It subjected the South Vietnamese rear base again to being absolutely open to military attack."[30] Australian Brigadier General F. P. Serong was typically blunt, calling the agreement "a shameless bug-out."[31]

To assuage such fears, Nixon repeatedly assured Thieu that the United States would punish any North Vietnamese violations of the agreement. On 5 January 1973, he told Thieu, "you have my assurance of continued assistance in the post-settlement period and that we will respond with full force should the settlement be violated by North Vietnam."[32] Nixon's commitment was not the problem. The problem was Congress's commitment.

The North Vietnamese, of course, refused to surrender their goal of taking over the South. Fighting between the ARVN and the NVA continued. With the Americans gone, the North Vietnamese redoubled their preparations for a great offensive. In January 1975, the NVA tried again with a massive blitzkrieg across the demilitarized zone. President Nixon was no longer in office to order American bombers into the air. Congress had driven Nixon to resign and it would certainly not allow his successor, President Gerald R. Ford, to renew America's commitment to South Vietnam. It had, in fact, spent the last two years severing it.

In the summer of 1973, the Democrat-controlled Congress voided Nixon's written pledge to the South Vietnamese that the United States would respond militarily to a Communist invasion. As a further kick at America's ally, Congress denied funding for any American military purpose in Indochina; and Congress slashed every request for American military aid to South Vietnam: aid that covered everything from ammunition to spare parts. In November 1973, Congress passed the War Powers Act, giving Congress additional oversight on American troop deployments. When he referred to "a shameless bug-out," Brigadier General Serong certainly had Congress pegged.

When the NVA struck, Congress refused to allow American intervention on behalf of the South Vietnamese. So the country stood by and watched while embattled American Marines and flyers evacuated American nationals and tens of thousands of South Vietnamese who clambered for freedom. America's role in South Vietnam was over, but the tragedy for South Vietnam had just begun. The "domino theory" that American leftists had mocked came bloodily true, as Cambodia, Laos, and South Vietnam all went Communist.[33] More than one million people fled Indochina after North Vietnam's victory, including the so-called boat people—hundreds of thousands of them—who risked death to flee from their new Communist masters. In Cambodia, the Khmer Rouge, in a frenzy of Maoist class genocide, killed a third of the population.

Other dominoes fell, too. With America vowing "no more Vietnams," the Soviet Union and Communist Cuba began seeding communism in Africa. Newly installed Communist regimes bracketed the Red Sea in Ethiopia and South Yemen. In 1979 the Soviet Union invaded Afghanistan, the Communist Sandinistas took power in Nicaragua, leftist guerillas threatened the government of El Salvador, and radical Islamists toppled the shah of Iran and held employees of the American embassy hostage for 444 days. Most of these setbacks happened under the watch of President Jimmy Carter, elected in 1976. He did next to nothing about them, assuming at first that the Communist Sandinistas and the radical Iranian Ayatollah Khomeini were people we could do business with. He recoiled at the very thought of neo-imperialist intervention to save our ally the shah or our less than salubrious ally Anastasio Somoza Debayle, of whose father FDR had famously said: "he may be a son of a bitch, but he's our son of a bitch." Carter took no such robust view. He wagged his finger and said that Americans had an inordinate fear of communism, which he did not share—until he was shocked by the Soviet invasion of Afghanistan.

Six months into the Iranian hostage crisis President Carter authorized a military rescue mission, "Desert One," that had to be aborted in the Iranian desert, leaving eight American servicemen dead. President Carter's answer to "stagflation" (a stagnant economy of high unemployment and high inflation), an "energy crisis," a demoralized military, and a foreign policy of drift and humiliation was to declare that the American people were suffering a deep "malaise." They cured it in 1980 by electing Ronald Reagan in Carter's stead. The hostage crisis ended immediately. So did American patience with the expansion of communism in the Western Hemisphere, as the Reagan administration supplied aid to the Contras (the anti-Communist forces in Nicaragua) and in 1983 invaded

Grenada to overturn a Communist revolution that frightened its Caribbean neighbors, threatened to turn the tiny island into a Communist air base, and endangered the lives of the 1,000 Americans (many of them medical students) who lived on the island. In a joint operation (partly to ensure that every service got a chance to perform), United States Marines, U.S. Army Rangers, the Air Force, the Navy (including the SEALs), as well as America's Caribbean allies, took on Grenada's homegrown Communists and Cuban troops. In a little over a week, the island was mostly secured—and the days of post-Vietnam retreat were over.

CHAPTER 25

AMERICA RESURGENT

THE INVASION OF GRENADA—Operation Urgent Fury—had, in truth, been less than elegantly done. But the fact that it had been done at all and with a successful outcome was a dramatic break from the Carter years.[1] Britain protested that a member of its Commonwealth had been invaded. President Reagan, however, had responded to the entreaties of the Organization of Eastern Caribbean States and Grenada's governor-general. Among the trophies from the campaign were captured Cubans, of course, but also captured Russians, East Germans, Bulgarians, North Koreans, and Libyans. The enemies of Uncle Sam would no longer be permitted to run wild; and communism, instead of endlessly expanding, would on occasion be rolled back.

After his election in 1980, Ronald Reagan and his secretary of defense, Caspar Weinberger, began the biggest peacetime military buildup in American history, including the proposed construction of a 600-ship Navy; a revitalized Army, Marine Corps, and Air Force; a reassertion of America's nuclear deterrent; aid to anti-Communist military forces in Latin America and Afghanistan; and a plan for a space-based missile defense system, dubbed "Star Wars," that had the Soviets throwing up their hands in despair. The Soviets' sclerotic economy had no hope of competing with the militarily applicable wealth and technology of the United States, especially as America's economy began soaring with the Reagan administration's tax-cutting policy known as "Reaganomics."

No administration ever did more for America's armed forces than the Reagan administration did—a commitment that went across the board, from improving morale to improving training and weapons systems. That investment paid off, not only in little expeditions like Grenada and the chastising bombing of Libyan dictator and terrorist-sponsor Moamar Gaddafi in Libya, but in the biggest victory of all: a peaceful and sudden victory in the Cold War, when

Soviet leader Mikhail Gorbachev could no longer withstand the pressure of Ronald Reagan's challenge in Berlin: "Mr. Gorbachev, tear down this wall!"[2] The Berlin Wall—erected by the Communists during the presidency of John F. Kennedy—came down in 1989, during the presidency of George Herbert Walker Bush, Reagan's two-term vice president and one-term successor.

With communism cast into "the ash heap of history"—as Reagan predicted it would be[3]—the United States took up arms against global thuggery dressed in other guises. One of those was "Pineapple Face"—Manuel Noriega, the dictator of Panama. Noriega was a known accomplice in drug trafficking, and though he had worked for American intelligence in the past, it was suspected that he was also working for the Cubans and the Soviet Union. In fact, it was widely suspected—both in Panama and in the United States—that if there was chicanery or crime afoot in Panama, Noriega had a hand in it. But it was the charge of drug trafficking that initially raised serious American ire against the dictator. America had taken on the role of global narcotics cop, trying to slash the supply of illegal drugs to the United States (where it was devastating inner-city communities in particular) and to shore up the political stability of Latin America, where the "narco-terrorism" of the drug cartels threatened governments.

Noriega responded by harassing American military personnel in the Canal Zone and tightening his political chokehold on the Panamanian people. Astoundingly, he had Panama's assembly declare that a state of war existed with the United States. As an apparent proof of that, Panamanian forces murdered a United States Marine at a roadblock and seized an American naval officer and his wife.

President George H. W. Bush, a former Navy flyer himself, ordered Pineapple Face to be harvested. On 20 December 1989, Operation Just Cause stormed into Panama with Navy SEALs, U.S. Army Rangers, the Air Force (it was the first combat use of the F-117A Stealth fighter), the Marine Corps, the 82nd Airborne Division (which made its first combat jump since World War II), and other Special Forces and regular troops. With men already positioned in the Canal Zone, and with the help of the Air National Guard, which had the cover of regular training deployments there, launching the invasion was relatively easy, and the Panamanian forces were subdued in a matter of days. Noriega was taken into custody on 3 January 1990, tried, convicted, and thrown into a Florida pokey on drug-trafficking charges, while Panama recovered through free elections and the tidy step of abolishing its own corrupt military.

THE MOTHER OF ALL BATTLES

A RATHER MORE DANGEROUS dictator was Saddam Hussein, the Stalin of Iraq. Like Stalin, he considered himself a man of steel: a political operator without a conscience, whose chief method of operation was murder and terrorism against his own people. The party that he led—the Baath Party—was consciously styled as a pan-Arab National Socialist Workers' Party, and though he was a votary of Stalin, he almost equally admired Hitler. Like Hitler, he was a warmonger who suspected professional military officers (he was not one; he was a political hit man). Like Stalin, he trusted that he could eliminate his every opponent (real or suspected, including in the military) and make the entire state apparatus utterly dependent upon himself. And like Stalin, he thought he could get away with anything; he did not envisage dying in his bunker like Hitler.

Saddam Hussein came to power in 1979—the year that saw the Soviet invasion of Afghanistan and the Iranian revolution—and plunged his country into a series of wars and conflicts. He instigated the Iran-Iraq War (1980–88), launched the invasion of Kuwait that lead to the First Gulf War (1990–91), battled the United Nations during the period of the "No-Fly Zones" that were meant to offer some protection to Iraqi Kurds and Shiites from his attacks (1991–2003), and was finally deposed in the wake of the Second Gulf War (2003). He was, in addition, a sponsor of terrorism, fought internal wars against his own people (the Kurds and Shiites), and was ardent in his pursuit of chemical, biological, and nuclear weapons. He used chemical weapons against the Iranians in the Iran-Iraq War and against Iraqi Kurds in 1987–88. His nuclear ambitions had led to an Israeli preemptive strike on the Iraqi nuclear reactor at Osirak in 1981; and his surprisingly advanced nuclear weapons program had been destroyed (virtually by accident, through lucky air strikes) during the bombing of the First Gulf War. Nevertheless, his weapons programs were so worrisome that the United Nations slapped sanctions on Iraq and tried to monitor his access to chemical, biological, nuclear, and other weapons systems (between the two Gulf Wars, from 1991 to 2003).

Even in a part of the world synonymous with terrorism and political violence, Saddam Hussein was the most militarily aggressive tyrant in the region. He was, however, long regarded in the West as a bulwark against the spread of radical Islam from Iran, a much larger, more powerful, more dangerous, and more strategically located country. Saddam Hussein threw aside that reluctant Western goodwill—the goodwill of Realpolitik—when he invaded Kuwait on

2 August 1990. The invasion of a friendly, oil-rich, sovereign emirate of the Persian Gulf was exacerbated by the threat that Iraq immediately posed to Bahrain, Qatar, the United Arab Emirates, and Saudi Arabia. Saddam rushed troops to the Kuwait-Saudi border—whether to seal it or continue his blitzkrieg, racing down the littoral of the Persian Gulf, was unclear. Three hundred thousand refugees fled Kuwait, reports of Iraqi atrocities against Kuwaitis stacked up, half the world's oil supplies potentially lay within Saddam Hussein's reach, and the Saudis cried for help.

President George H. W. Bush's first instinct was to resolve the crisis by diplomacy, though diplomacy had failed already. Before the war American diplomat April Glaspie had told Saddam that the United States had "no opinion on the Arab-Arab conflicts, like your border dispute with Kuwait." But, she added, "we hope that you solve this problem via [the Arab League] or President Mubarak [of Egypt]."[4] While that was less than deft diplomacy, she surely had no intention of approving Saddam Hussein's invasion; the dictator knew what he wanted to do, and he did it.

The United Nations condemned Iraq's aggression and demanded the immediate withdrawal of Iraqi troops from Kuwait. Saddam refused and British Prime Minister Margaret Thatcher prodded President Bush to assemble a coalition to drive Saddam out of the emirate. The British prime minister had more than force of character on her side. British interests in the area dated back to the eighteenth century. American interests were more recent and related to oil, the general stability of the region, and support for pro-Western Arab regimes, such as Kuwait, which the American Navy had guarded during the Iran-Iraq War. But when Mrs. Thatcher admonished President George H. W. Bush not to "go wobbly," the president responded to his nanny's voice.

In a masterpiece of diplomacy, the president organized an international blockade of Iraq and assembled a coalition of twenty-five combatant nations: Afghanistan, Australia, Bahrain, Bangladesh, Belgium, Canada, Czechoslovakia, Egypt (40,000 troops), France (18,000), Germany, Honduras, Hungary, Italy, Kuwait (11,000), New Zealand, Niger, Oman (25,500), Poland, Qatar, Romania, Saudi Arabia (118,000), South Korea, Syria (17,000), the United Arab Emirates (40,000), and the United Kingdom (43,000). Leading them into battle was General "Stormin'" Norman Schwarzkopf[5] and 540,000 Americans.

As this mighty host assembled to expel the Iraqis from Kuwait—with the full authorization of the United Nations as well as the United States Congress (though most Democrats voted against the authorization, despite the UN's approval)—Saddam Hussein refused to back down. The United States warned Saddam that if he used his stockpiles of WMD (weapons of mass destruction) against American troops, Iraq would cease to exist as a modern society. That was one threat that Saddam Hussein did heed.

When the United Nations–designated deadline of 15 January 1991 passed, Allied bombers flew over Iraq in the first of 106,000 sorties that were tasked with eliminating Iraq's means of making war—from chemical, biological, and nuclear weapons development sites, to airfields, air defenses, communications centers, transportation networks, military bases, and troop concentrations. American airpower was decisive. Smart bombs sliced through targets, and in the battle of Khafji, on 29–30 January 1991, Iraqi invaders into Saudi Arabia were trapped in "kill-boxes" from which American airpower and Saudi and Qatari troops inspired them to flee.

Chairman of the Joint Chiefs of Staff General Colin Powell gave the press a memorable summation of General Schwarzkopf's battle plan: "Our strategy to go after this army is very, very simple. First we're going to cut it off, and then we're going to kill it" as well as "rip up the [Iraqi] air force in its entirety."[6] The Iraqi air force escaped to Iran, but after thirty-eight days of pounding Iraqi targets, General Schwarzkopf decided to kill the Iraqi army. A student of military history, he planned to reproduce Hannibal's crushing envelopment at Cannae. On 24 February 1991, he unsheathed his "Desert Sabre," the land component of Operation Desert Storm. Allied troops smashed across the Kuwaiti border while a flanking attack struck into Iraq and behind the Iraqi army. In four days' time, the Allies had liberated Kuwait, fought one of the largest tank battles in history (without a single loss),[7] and shattered the Iraqi army (the fourth-largest army in the world, more than 80,000 of whom surrendered to the Allies). The retreating Iraqis laid fire to Kuwait's oil fields and committed yet more atrocities on Kuwaiti civilians.

Desert Sabre lasted only 100 hours. President Bush, watching Allied planes incinerate Iraqi trucks on the "Highway of Death," saw no need to continue beating a fallen foe. His mercy took Saddam Hussein by surprise. Saddam expected the Allies to march on Baghdad. Given a reprieve, he declared victory in what he had called the "Mother of All Battles." His regime had not fallen and his nuclear weapons program would continue.[8]

The First Gulf War was one of the most lopsided wars in history, and a vindication of America's Reagan-revived armed forces. In the entire campaign, the United States suffered 148 battle deaths;[9] the combined Allied killed-in-action total, exclusive of the United States, was 63. The Iraqis lost an estimated 60,000 men killed.

It seemed a smashing victory, but the endgame became controversial. President Bush had rejected the temptation to march on Baghdad, though he did encourage the Iraqi people to overthrow the hated regime. When the Kurds in the north and Shiites in the south rose in rebellion, the Allies did nothing to assist them. Saddam bought off the Allies by quickly agreeing to their peace terms so that he could turn his army to wreaking a bloody vengeance on those who challenged his authority. To provide some protection for Saddam's victims, the United Nations enforced an Iraqi No-Fly Zone over the Kurdish north, while the Americans, the British, and the French carved out a No-Fly Zone in the Shiite south. Moreover, the United Nations imposed a regime of arms inspections and sanctions on Iraq to try to prevent Saddam from keeping or obtaining chemical, biological, nuclear, or other threatening weapons systems. The inspections, No-Fly Zones, and sanctions annoyed Saddam but they did not undo his bottom line: he had survived to fight another day.

DEPLOYMENTS OF DISTRACTION

PRESIDENT GEORGE H. W. BUSH had come to office hoping to enjoy the "peace dividend" expected from the end of the Cold War. The war to liberate Kuwait had put the peace dividend on temporary hold. It was President Bush's successor, President William Jefferson Clinton, who turned the peace dividend into a machete against the defense budget, while at the same time deploying American troops all over the world—and with little, if any, apparent regard for American national interests, and much more regard given to serving United Nations operations and media spin. Where previously American military deployments had been in the cause of carving out an empire (including the War for Independence, the War of 1812, the War with Mexico, the War with Spain) and national interest (preventing the domination of Europe by the kaiser or the Thousand Year Reich, the domination of Asia by Imperial Japan, the domination of the world by communism, or the domination of the Persian Gulf by enemies of the United States), President Clinton's military deployments seemed to be driven by what one serving officer, Lieutenant Colonel "Buzz" Patterson (who was deployed to meet them), called "CNN Diplomacy." By Patterson's count President Clinton sent American troops to more than forty countries, including Somalia, Rwanda, Haiti, Macedonia, Bosnia, Ecuador, East Timor,

Kuwait, Liberia, Albania, the Congo, Gabon, Sierra Leone, Afghanistan, the Sudan, and Iraq.[10]

For a president who had avoided military service during the Vietnam War and who had protested against the war, an imperial or national-interest-driven foreign policy was simply not on, but a policy of using the military as social workers and handing them over as a plaything for liberal social engineers certainly was. Indeed, President Clinton's first step as commander in chief was to call for the integration of homosexuals into the services. His first act of foreign policy was to turn the American military over to the United Nations; and his foreign policy was forever guided by the reporting on television news.

Such CNN diplomacy took American troops to Somalia. The mission had begun under President George H. W. Bush, who had sent American forces there as part of a United Nations–led effort to deliver food to millions of starving Somalis. The military was needed because food distribution was being blocked and harassed by Somali warlords. President Bush saw this military deployment as a humanitarian one with a clear end. It was similar to other military deployments that had helped out during natural disasters in delivering aid and food. President Clinton, however, inherited the mission and expanded it into one of "nation building" in cooperation with the United Nations.

There is, in principle, nothing wrong with nation building if one is willing to take on the imperial burden it implies. But whereas Victorian imperialists were realists and understood the costs of sending "forth the best ye breed— / Go bind your sons to exile / To serve your captives' need,"[11] President Clinton's idealism was rather shallow and could not stand the sight of American blood for fear of the political impact it might have. So dreams of nation building in Somalia evaporated after two Black Hawk helicopters were shot down and eighteen Americans were killed in fierce fighting during a raid on the warlords. The Rangers fought courageously and well, but with televised images of an American soldier being dragged through the streets by a Somali mob and the revelation that Clinton's secretary of defense, Les Aspin, had denied American troops the armor their officers had requested, the Clinton administration decided to pull the troops out after a decent interval. Four months after the "Black Hawk Down" battle of Task Force Ranger on 3 October 1993, American troops were withdrawn from Somalia.

American troops were then deployed to Haiti as part of a peacekeeping operation officially known as "Operation Uphold Democracy" but known among the troops as "What the hell are we doing here?"[12] They were also deployed to

the Balkans, where the former Yugoslavia had divided into six separate republics and swiftly fallen into ethnic conflict. The Haitian operation seemed a
distraction, as there was little, in truth, for the American troops to do; but it
was at least a deployment in the Western Hemisphere on an island formerly po-
liced by the United States Marine Corps. What the Balkans had to do with
American national security was never explained.[13]

What was clear, however, was that the United Nations and the European
Union had failed utterly to restore order in the region, and if anything was to be
done, it had to be done with an American lead. United States military involvement began under the aegis of another United Nations humanitarian intervention, delivering aid and food. Later, though, the United States provided the bulk
of the men and materiel for a NATO-coordinated bombing campaign to stop
Serbian aggression. The United States intervened militarily against the Serbs in
1995—with 20,000 American ground troops, following in the wake of the air
campaign, as peacekeepers—and again in 1999 with a successful seventy-eight-
day air campaign. That latter campaign fatally weakened the government of
Serbian President Slobodan Milosevic, a Communist who after the fall of the
Berlin Wall had declared himself a more socially acceptable Socialist, but who
remained at heart a thug. In 2000, under pressure, Milosevic agreed to hold
elections, his government fell, and Milosevic himself was arrested and put on
trial for war crimes.

While the Clinton administration dealt American troops like cards around
a global card table, it did so without ever thinking in terms of national security.
There were, however, other peripheral attacks, directly on Americans, that
loomed much larger but that received far less attention, and certainly far less action and commitment. These fell under the heading of radical Islamic terrorism,
led largely by the organization al Qaeda, founded and bankrolled by Osama bin
Laden.

Unlike Haitians or Serbians, the al Qaeda terrorists deliberately targeted
Americans. Bin Laden had declared a jihad—a holy war—against the United
States in 1996, and he reaffirmed it year after year, attempting to prove his bona
fides with terrorist attacks killing Americans. In 1993, radical Islamists linked
to al Qaeda car-bombed the World Trade Center in New York City, killing six
and injuring 1,000 people. In 1993, the Somalis who shot down the two Black
Hawk helicopters were al Qaeda trained. That the Americans had been so easily
driven from Somalia made a profound impression on bin Laden. The terrorist
financier later told ABC News: "Our boys went to Somalia and prepared them-

selves for a long war. . . . Our boys were shocked by the low morale of the American soldier, and they realized that the American soldier was just a paper tiger. He was unable to endure the strikes that were dealt to his army, so he fled, and America had to stop all its bragging."[14] Bin Laden was wrong about the American soldier—as he would eventually discover. It was the commander in chief in Washington who was a paper tiger, not the U.S. Army Rangers.

In 1995, al Qaeda attacked the Saudi National Guard building in Riyadh (where American military officers worked). In 1996, al Qaeda bombed a U.S. barracks in Dharan, Saudi Arabia, killing nineteen Americans. In February 1998, bin Laden issued a *fatwa* ordering the killing of Americans around the world. Six months later, al Qaeda truck-bombed the American embassies in Nairobi, Kenya, and Dar es Salaam, Tanzania, killing 220 people. In 2000, al Qaeda attacked the USS *Cole* off the coast of Yemen. With the exception of Somalia, where he withdrew American troops, President Clinton treated these attacks as a legal-criminal matter and made no effective retaliation, bombing an aspirin factory in Sudan and a tented camp in Afghanistan.

Osama bin Laden was not the only foreign terrorist attacking America. There was also Saddam Hussein. The Iraqi dictator had tried to assassinate George H. W. Bush when the former American president visited Kuwait in 1993. Clinton responded with a slap-back missile attack. Firefights between Iraqi antiaircraft batteries and Allied planes patrolling the No-Fly Zones were a near daily occurrence.

In August 1998, Saddam Hussein upped the ante by throwing out the United Nations weapons inspectors who were trying to investigate and restrict his weapons of mass destruction programs. At first President Clinton dithered over what to do, but in December, with a looming impeachment vote against him, he launched a twenty-four-hour air attack on Saddam Hussein's Republican Guard units. When the smoke settled, nothing much had changed.

In the meantime, the Iraqi dictator was continuing to enrich himself and fund his arms programs through the extraordinary corruption of the United Nations "Oil for Food" scheme, which, as one U.S. Navy pilot described it, worked this way: "Saddam ships oil to Bahrain in the UN Oil-for-Food Program. We buy the oil from the UN and refine it into jet fuel. We put the jet fuel in my F-18 and I go bomb Iraq for violations of UN resolutions. It's nuts."[15] Nuts it was, but it was also United Nations and Clinton administration policy.[16]

After two terms in office, President Clinton's vice president, Al Gore, was defeated in the 2000 presidential election by George H. W. Bush's son

George W. Bush. He faced an array of challenges: China was projected as a looming superpower threat; North Korea claimed it had nuclear weapons; Iraq continued to shoot at American planes; and Osama bin Laden plotted his campaign of terrorism to get America's attention.

He certainly got it on 11 September 2001 when al Qaeda terrorists hijacked four American planes, crashing two into the World Trade Center and one into the Pentagon. The fourth plane crashed into the Pennsylvania countryside, as the passengers fought against the hijackers. It was the worst act of terrorism in American history, a day far more infamous than Pearl Harbor. Nearly 3,000 people were killed—600 more than died on 7 December 1941 at Pearl Harbor—in a cowardly, sucker punch attack on civilians and Pentagon employees.

Stunned at first, the United States quickly came roaring back—and this time, it would not be with lawyer's briefs, FBI investigators, and pinprick missile attacks, which had been President Clinton's response to terrorism. President Bush announced that America was at war, a war that he intended to take to the enemy, a war against the terrorists.

"LET'S ROLL"[17]

THE TARGET WAS AFGHANISTAN: home to the Islamic fundamentalist Taliban and host of Osama bin Laden and al Qaeda. Marine General Michael "Rifle" DeLong (deputy commander at Central Command under Army General Tommy Franks) noted that "Afghanistan did not merely sponsor terrorists—it was run by terrorists, with al-Qaeda giving integral support to the regime."[18] Plans for war were drawn up immediately, and when the Taliban refused to turn Osama bin Laden over to the United States, the American military prepared to invade Afghanistan.

Of all the places for the United States to find itself at war, remote, primitive, and landlocked Afghanistan would have ranked low on anyone's list; its place in Western military history lay in the nineteenth century with the British Empire, the defense of British India, and the "Great Game" between Britain and czarist Russia in Central Asia. The United States had, of course, been involved with Afghanistan from 1979 to 1989 after the Soviet invasion and occupation of the country. But the American role had been limited to helping supply the Afghan mujahideen in their war against the Soviets.

Now as America prepared to retaliate for the 11 September terrorist attacks, an expansive coalition of governments offered to help. Officially seventy nations signed on as allies in the war on terror, and so many countries wanted to contribute troops to the invasion of Afghanistan that United States Central Command had to turn them away.

American strategy, as drawn up by Generals Franks and DeLong and Defense Secretary Donald Rumsfeld, was to have a small Allied land force, leaning heavily on Special Forces who would work with Afghan allies—most especially the Afghan Northern Alliance, which had been fighting its own war against the Taliban. The first troops into Afghanistan were British and American Special Forces, but later included Canadians, Australians, New Zealanders, Germans, and Frenchmen, among others, with the French, in particular, being eager to participate. Naval support came from Britain, Italy, France, Germany, Canada, Australia, Bahrain, and even Japan. Other European nations, like Denmark and Norway, joined the coalition with air support.

The bombing campaign of Operation Enduring Freedom began on 7 October 2001, with British and American planes. One challenge was minimizing "collateral damage," because the task of building a new Afghanistan had already been accepted. Aid to the Afghan people began, in fact, at the very start of the war. Another challenge was that there were not that many command, control, and communication targets to hit after leveling Afghanistan's air defenses and terrorist training camps. So the United States used its high technology for air support strikes. Allied bombers and AC-130 gunships went after enemy troop concentrations, while Northern Alliance and Special Forces units on horseback fought the enemy on the ground. It was, in short, war as it was meant to be.

Within a month's time, the Northern Alliance began winning over deserters from the Taliban—a sure sign of the tipping balance of power—and the Allied-Afghan campaign picked up speed. From the first major victory—at Mazar-e-Sharif, where United States Special Forces, American airpower, and Afghan fighters on horseback stormed to victory on 10 November 2001—to the last, the war was far from the quagmire that countless left-wing commentators had predicted, citing Soviet and even British experience.

President Bush gave American commanders something they had not enjoyed in a long time: complete presidential confidence, support and trust to get the job done in what they, in their professional judgment, thought the most effective way. Can-do commanders, rather than political spinmeisters, called the shots. The results were stupendous, as American military professionalism put on a magnificent display of the military art. United States casualties were kept extraordinarily low. Over the course of the war and peacekeeping duties from October 2001 to April 2005, 180 Americans were killed in Afghanistan. In the war itself, victory came swiftly. American generals who had begun their careers in Vietnam—like the innovative war planner Tommy Franks, a tough, hard, artillery-trained Oklahoman/Texan—showed that they knew their business, and the professionals at their command proved that they knew theirs.

On 13 November, the Northern Alliance entered Afghanistan's capital of Kabul, which the enemy had virtually deserted. With Kabul in Allied hands, the Taliban collapsed, save in its northern stronghold of Konduz, its southern stronghold of Kandahar, and its redoubt in the caves and mountains of Tora Bora near Jalalabad along the border with Pakistan. But these were only momentary holdouts. Konduz surrendered on 25 November. At Kandahar, Mullah Mohammed Omar, leader of the Taliban, escaped just before the city fell on 7 December 2001 to Afghans under the command of royalist Hamid Karzai and United States Marines. That left Tora Bora, where American Special Forces and Afghan troopers had to climb glacial mountains to get at grips with the enemy. By 17 December, most of the enemy fighters had been cleared—but Osama bin Laden, like Mullah Omar, had escaped.

Still, the Taliban was gone and a new interim government under Hamid Karzai had been installed through negotiations among Afghan tribal leaders. Afghanistan, miraculously, became a constitutional democratic republic, with Karzai elected president in January 2004. The fighting, however, continued, as the United States worked to protect the new Afghan government and keep the pressure on al Qaeda, which was an around-the-world assignment for American intelligence, Special Forces, Marines, and other units who deployed—sometimes openly and sometimes stealthily—to close al Qaeda's terrorist shops.

The biggest American military operation in Afghanistan actually happened after the war in March 2002. The purpose of Operation Anaconda was to shatter regrouping Taliban and al Qaeda fighters. Previous operations had relied heavily on Northern Alliance ground forces, but with the Northern Alliance disbanded and the official Afghan army still in the process of being assembled and trained, Operation Anaconda was an American show.

It was in this fierce mountain fighting that Navy SEAL Petty Officer First Class Neil Roberts, a handsome, grinning Californian, one of nine children, and a recent father himself, fell out of a chopper after it was hit by a rocket-propelled grenade. In the darkness, no one saw him fall out or noticed he wasn't aboard until it was too late. When Special Forces went back to rescue him, they were pinned down and the small unit suffered six killed and eleven wounded, but the field was littered with dead al Qaeda. Neil Roberts himself, alone and surrounded, fought his own personal Alamo, winning fame among the SEALs for dying hard. His sacrifice and that of pro football player (and fellow Californian) Pat Tillman—who turned away millions of dollars to enlist in the Army, become a U.S. Army Ranger, and serve in Afghanistan, where he died a victim of tragic friendly fire—epitomize the valor of the American servicemen who serve in this theater.

POUR ENCOURAGER LES AUTRES

NEXT ON THE AGENDA was Iraq, where Saddam Hussein could no longer be regarded as a penned-in regional irritant. Iraqi attacks on Allied aircraft patrolling the No-Fly Zones were increasing, while at the same time Iraq was testing chemical sprayers and having Chinese engineers install fiber-optic cables for Iraqi military command-control-communication systems. More worrisome were reports, in the files of every intelligence organization in the region and in the West, that Saddam Hussein's weapons of mass destruction program was moving rapidly ahead: weapons were being stockpiled and tested. So, too, it was reported that the Iraqis were working with al Qaeda. Iraqi and al Qaeda leaders had been in contact for a decade and al Qaeda terrorists had been training in Iraq since 1997.[19]

Moreover, a casus belli already existed in Saddam Hussein's violations of the armistice ending the Gulf War of 1991[20] and in his firing on Allied aircraft. There was also, after 11 September 2001, little stomach in the Bush administration to wait and see if the combative Saddam Hussein struck again, this time with chemical, biological, or even nuclear weapons. President Vladimir Putin of Russia had, in fact, repeatedly warned the American president after 11 September 2001 that Russian intelligence indicated the Iraqis planned terrorist actions against the United States.[21] In the White House's view Iraq remained a hostile power firing on Americans every day, it was an open supporter of terrorism, it was likely planning further hostile actions against the United States, and it was, in President Bush's own words, one of three key countries in an "axis of evil," the other two being Iran and North Korea.

A statesman might have kept one last matter in mind. In the battle against global Islamist terrorism, centered largely on the Arab world, to oust the government of Saddam Hussein might very well be an *alternative* to perpetual war.

Attacking al Qaeda and its Taliban hosts in Afghanistan was necessary, but likely insufficient, to put the wind up Arab and Islamist governments that collaborated with terrorists. It was a mere ratcheting up of tit-for-tat, better and more effective by far than President Clinton's bombing of the odd aspirin factory, but not enough to stop the sponsors of the jihadists.

To win the war against al Qaeda and radical Islam the United States needed to make an object lesson of a hostile Arab regime. Iraq was the obvious choice. Take down Saddam Hussein and make it clear to terror-harboring governments that if they didn't want to be hit by America's big stick they must rapidly clean up their own backyards or be held accountable—that, a statesman might wager, was a strategy for winning the war against terrorism at less ultimate cost in blood, treasure, and risk.

President George W. Bush tried mightily to win the approval of the United Nations Security Council for the war against Iraq, but the United Nations refused to stand behind its own resolutions against the regime of Saddam Hussein. So President Bush went it alone—or went it, rather, with Great Britain and a coalition of twice as many countries as supported the United States in the Korean War, though France was so bellicose in its opposition as to virtually qualify as a hostile power.

While American troops waited in the Kuwaiti desert, Special Forces penetrated behind enemy lines. On 27 February 2003, the United Nations declared that Saddam Hussein was still not cooperating with United Nations weapons inspectors. On 17 March 2003, President Bush delivered an ultimatum: Saddam Hussein had to leave Iraq or we would come get him. Saddam Hussein called President Bush's bluff. Forty-eight hours later, bombs were bursting in Baghdad.

This time, Iraq would not be softened up by a lengthy bombing campaign. The air and ground wars were nearly simultaneous. Speed on the ground was the objective. American General Tommy Franks thought it imperative to seize the oil fields in southern Iraq before Saddam Hussein had a chance to fire them, which would have created an ecological disaster zone. The United States forces charged across the Kuwaiti border into Iraq, the 1st Marine Division and British commandos took the wells and shut them down, while Special Forces disarmed the Scud missile sites in western Iraq and worked with the Kurds to grab the oil wells in northern Iraq.

With Turkey having refused to be a staging area for a northern front, the race for Baghdad came from the south, with the 1st Marine Division coming from the southeast and the 3rd U.S. Army Infantry Division coming from the southwest. General Franks's ground forces were less than a quarter of the size of what General Schwarzkopf had in Operation Desert Storm. Operation Iraqi Freedom, like the war in Afghanistan, was fought a new way, with extremely precise airpower and a heavy emphasis on Special Forces, as well as with swift-moving armor and hard-charging infantry. The professionalism of the British and American units was exemplary.

Within two days, the American columns were halfway to Baghdad; then sandstorms kicked up and proved a far bigger hindrance, if a less lethal one, than the Iraqi forces. The Iraqi regulars, as well as Saddam Hussein's Republican Guard, were simply destroyed; other pests were irregular fedayeen and Iraqi fighters who dressed as civilians. Both of these latter groups were essentially terrorists, but they too were mowed down once they exposed themselves. Captured Iraqis revealed that Saddam Hussein had never expected the invasion; at worst he was braced for a Clinton-like missile attack. But the allies also found stockpiles of chemical warfare suits and antidotes, which made worries about weapons of mass destruction all the sharper. The Americans wanted to keep close to the enemy—not only to destroy him quickly but to make it difficult for him to use these weapons except at risk to himself.

When the storm let up, the race was on again. By 4 April 2003, Saddam International Airport was taken. On 5 April American troops began their "thunder runs" into Baghdad. And four days later, Baghdad fell, though rough neighborhoods remained. The main campaign ran twenty-one days—from 20 March to 9 April 2003, a swift and conclusive contest.

Military success was followed, as the statesman might have envisioned, by foreign policy success. Libyan dictator Moamar Gaddafi surrendered his weapons of mass destruction program, citing as his reason, to Italian Prime Minister Silvio Berlusconi, that he did not want to end up like Saddam (who was later arrested, dirty-bearded and disheveled, hiding in a "spider hole"). Iraq's fellow Baathists in Syria made accommodating noises and eventually pulled their troops from Lebanon (which they had occupied since 1976). The Lebanese Druze leader, Walid Jumblatt, a former enemy of the United States, told a reporter from the *Washington Post*: "It's strange for me to say it, but this process of change has started because of the American invasion of Iraq. . . . I was cynical about Iraq. But when I saw the Iraqi people voting three weeks ago, 8 million of them, it was the start of a new Arab world. . . . The Syrian people, the Egyptian people, all say that something is changing. The Berlin Wall has fallen. We can see it."[22] Normally sabre-rattling North Korea went temporarily silent. Pakistan—an ally threatened with instability by its own large radical Islamic population and former alliance with the Taliban—shut down A. Q. Khan, a national hero and the scientist behind Pakistan's own nuclear weapons, but who was also working on proliferating them to "rogue" regimes.

There were, however, some political failures, too. In western Europe, among liberal opinion in the United States, and even in victorious Britain, there seemed an obsessive desire to steal defeat from the jaws of victory. Pundits who had predicted that Iraq would be a disaster for Western arms were not so ashamed by their wrongful predictions as to forgo screaming calamity, disaster, and quagmire at every act of looting, terrorism, or insurgency that followed the Allied victory. Lack of UN support was cited as evidence of the war's criminality; the nondiscovery of stockpiles of weapons of mass destruction was regarded as proof that "Bush lied and people died." Failure to turn Iraq instantaneously into a prosperous, peaceful, democratic state was regarded as negating the entire moral force of the war. Iraq was better off, allegedly, under the secret police and mass graves of Saddam Hussein.

Such voices, which became widely dominant opinion in the West, ensured that other dictators didn't feel the pressure that Moamar Gaddafi felt in the immediate aftermath of the war. But by 2005, the United States had performed a massive—and continuing—rebuilding effort in Iraq, supervised no less than three national, peaceful, free and fair elections, and vouchsafed Iraq a democratically elected constitutional government.[23]

The United States has achieved this while simultaneously fighting an insurgency that the Islamists now see as their main battle front. Defeating the insurgents could be accelerated if the United States deployed more troops and ran the military less with an eye toward business efficiency and more with an eye toward the application of maximum force to crush the jihadists and Saddamites. But there is no reason that America's longer-term strategy of training Iraqi troops to do the job themselves cannot work. All that stands in the way of success is the antiwar party in the West, which bleats incessantly about the inevitability of failure in Iraq, the need for the immediate withdrawal of Western troops, and the heinous stupidity of toppling venomous anti-Western dictators—rather disconcerting rhetoric, it must be said, to the soldier in the field or the Iraqi emerging from a voting booth.[24]

The pessimism and self-hatred of the post-Christian West, however, should not color our vision of what the Allied forces achieved in Iraq: a stunning victory, the destruction of a cruel and vicious terror-allied regime, and a new breath of hope and life for the Arab world, where the idea of free elections will now be harder to suppress and Arab hostility might be directed against their own city councilmen, mayors, and parliamentarians rather than the phantasms of conspiring international Jewry and the Crusaders of the West.

As the distinguished British military historian John Keegan has noted, "Reality is an uncomfortable companion, particularly to people of good will. . . . The reality of the Iraq campaign of March–April 2003 is, however, a better guide to what needs to be done to secure the safety of our world than any amount of [international] law-making or treaty-writing can offer."[25] And for that victory, we should thank the American military and our allies.

"GO TELL THE SPARTANS"

R OGERS' RANGERS FOUGHT INDIANS, but they did so in the context of a world war between France and Britain. Two hundred and forty years later, the United States has fulfilled the founders' dreams of becoming a mighty empire. And today we are involved in another global struggle. This one requires us to put a stopper into Islamist terrorism, cap the spread of weapons of mass destruction, and maintain the security and free trade prosperity of the Western world, even as demographic shifts, a militarily emergent China, and terrorism threaten it.

That the United States maintains such a *Pax Americana,* and does so while hardly breaking a sweat, is an extraordinary achievement, a testimony to the industry, optimism, and resourcefulness of our people. But most of all, it is a credit to the American military. Whether the task is fighting the global war on terror, policing Afghanistan and Iraq, or delivering aid to tsunami victims, the American military leads the way.

If America is not breaking a sweat, our armed forces are working plenty hard. More than a third of our active duty National Guardsmen and Reservists have been deployed in Iraq and Afghanistan. America guards the freedom of the seas with less than half as many ships (288) as Ronald Reagan's projected 600-ship Navy.[1] We are fighting a global war on terror with a military that is half a million men smaller than the armed forces that President George H. W. Bush had at his command during the First Gulf War. Between 1992 and 2000, military spending was slashed by $50 billion.

It is also a military in which women—who enter the military under "dual standards" and are less deployable because they are subject to combat restrictions and can become pregnant—make up roughly 20 percent of the force. Soldiers of the past would not consider this welcome news, nor do many soldiers of the present, for whom wartime brutality and young women and mothers seem worlds apart.[2] As Lord Byron rightly observed, "War's a brain-spattering, windpipe slitting art,"[3] and no civilized society has thought, or should think, that it is an art to which young women and mothers should be subjected. For the sake of readiness and combat efficiency if nothing else, we need a military focused like Rogers' Rangers. Every soldier, sailor, airman, and Marine should be capable and ready to take up a rifle and file into the front lines.

And we need a larger military. To achieve that, we do not need military conscription. A free society can run its military as it runs the rest of its affairs. We need only to pay and support our fighting men so that while they risk their lives for freedom they do not have to worry that they are also risking the economic well-being of their families.

To be an "imperial grunt,"[4] an American centurion on the frontiers of freedom, can be a lonely business. What sustains him is pride in his profession—which he executes so very well—and a cultural confidence that too many of his fellow Americans on civvy street lack. Confidence in America and her mission has been a constant of our history—it is what drove the War for Independence, the rapid expansion south and west, manifest destiny, the setting right of Europe in two world wars, and the defeat of global communism. It is also crucial to the defeat of Islamo-bolshevism.[5] In a war of civilizational self-defense, moral and cultural relativists—the sort who think Osama bin Laden's Islamic fundamentalism and George W. Bush's Christian evangelicalism are merely two sides of the same coin—are obviously weak sisters, historically illiterate, morally bankrupt, and about as useful as a capon in a chicken coop. Thankfully, the fighting men of the United States are of a different stripe.

These are the men who have brought us so far. They have given us our freedom and prosperity—and more than that, they have helped secure the peace, prosperity, and freedom of huge portions of the globe, toppling some of the cruelest tyrannies known to man.

The Marine Corps motto is *semper fidelis,* always faithful. Our armed services have kept their faith with us; let us keep our faith with them.

NOTES

PROLOGUE: THE SUMMONS OF THE TRUMPET

1. This is a paraphrase from Charlton Ogburn, who served with the Marauders. See Charlton Ogburn, *The Marauders* (Harper and Brothers, 1956), p. 227.
2. The Marauders were losing a hundred men a day to sickness after taking the airstrip. Merrill himself had to be evacuated after suffering a second heart attack and recurrent malaria. See Joseph W. Stilwell, *The Stilwell Papers* (William Sloane Associates, 1948), p. 301.
3. Quoted in Barbara W. Tuchman, *Stilwell and the American Experience in China, 1911–45* (Grove Press, 1985), p. 449.
4. Charles N. Hunter, *Galahad* (The Naylor Co., 1963), pp. 1–2.
5. The phrase is Thomas Jefferson's. He referred to America as an "Empire of liberty" in a letter to George Rogers Clark, dated Christmas Day 1780, and the United States as an "empire for liberty" in a letter to James Madison on 27 April 1809.
6. Julian P. Boyd, ed., *The Papers of Thomas Jefferson: Volume 8, February to 31 October 1785* (Princeton University Press, 1953), p. 427.
7. The words *undaunted courage* were used by Peachy Gilmer and Thomas Jefferson (who reversed their order) to describe the soldier and explorer Meriwether Lewis. See Stephen E. Ambrose, *Undaunted Courage: Meriwether Lewis, Thomas Jefferson, and the Opening of the American West* (Simon and Schuster, 1997), pp. 27 and 484.

CHAPTER 1: THE GENTLE ART OF SCALPING

1. Quoted in David Horowitz, *The First Frontier: The Indian Wars & America's Origins, 1607–1776* (Simon & Schuster, 1978), p. 86.
2. Both sides had practiced such severing and displays before they knew each other.
3. The "Pilgrims" were the residents of Plymouth Colony; the "Puritans" were the residents of the Massachusetts Bay Colony.
4. Perhaps this affection for barbarian adornment is the reason so much of the English population is tattooed these days.
5. Samuel Eliot Morison, in *The Oxford History of the American People: Volume One, Prehistory to 1789* (Mentor, 1972), p. 93, estimates at least a third. David Horowitz, op. cit., estimates a quarter. David A. Price, in *Love and Hate in Jamestown: John Smith, Pocahontas, and the Heart of a New Nation* (Alfred A. Knopf, 2003), p. 208, bridges the two estimates saying between a quarter and a third. Horowitz says black slaves were spared the massacre; Price thinks they just might not have been appended to the list of casualties.
6. Later, during the English Civil War, Virginia would pledge itself as a haven for royalists, hence the tradition of the "Virginia Cavaliers," seeking refuge from Roundhead tyranny.
7. Quoted in Horowitz, op. cit., p. 66.
8. His Indian name was Metacom or Metacomet.
9. Morison gives the Indian strength as 3,000 and the Indian losses as two-thirds of their number, pp. 159–60. Horowitz puts the Indian losses at one-third of the "Narragansett Nation," p. 73. Robert Leckie, in *The Wars of America* (Castle Books,

1998), cites Cotton Mather as writing that 600 Indians were "terribly barbkew'd," p. 11. Allan R. Millett and Peter Maslowski, *For the Common Defense: A Military History of the United States of America* (The Free Press, 1994), more vaguely assert that Indian casualties were "in the hundreds," p. 16.

10. This figure comes from Morison. Historian Tony Hayter in David R. Chandler and Ian Beckett, eds., *The Oxford Illustrated History of the British Army* (Oxford, 1994), p. 113, puts the American contribution at 4,163, with 1,463 survivors, and the number of British soldiers at 10,000, of whom only 2,600 survived: "A little over 600 had died in action; disease killed the rest."

11. Quoted in Paul Johnson, *A History of the American People* (HarperCollins, 1997), p. 124.

12. Quoted in Walter O'Meara, *Guns at the Forks* (Prentice-Hall, 1965), p. 89.

13. The French wrote the document in their own tongue.

14. Most Indians were unreliable—they obeyed orders, fought, and chose or changed sides as it suited them.

15. Quoted in Sir John Fortesque, *A History of the British Army, Volume II* (Macmillan, 1899), p. 279. To prevent Braddock's body from being desecrated by the Indians, Washington had him buried beneath the road, and had wagons pass over the gravesite to obliterate the traces.

CHAPTER 2: WOLFE'S TRIUMPH AND PONTIAC'S REBELLION

1. The lake's name came from Johnson, who christened it after his king; the French called it *Lac Saint Sacrement.*

2. Some of those forcibly expelled settled in Louisiana, where they would eventually enter American history as the Cajuns. Indians weren't the only peoples in America sent on trails of tears, exiled as likely hostile combatants.

3. One baby was rescued and returned to its mother by a French Catholic priest who was able to trade a scalp (given him by a sympathetic Christian Indian) for the child.

4. Anywhere from 70 to 1,500.

5. Quoted in Edward P. Hamilton, *The French and Indian Wars: The Story of Battles and Forts in the Wilderness* (Doubleday, 1962), p. 198.

6. Quoted in Geoffrey Treasure, *Who's Who in Early Hanoverian Britain* (Shepheard-Walwyn, 1992), p. 224. He also lent his name to Amherst, Massachusetts, and Amherst College.

7. Louisbourg had been captured by a force of British and New Englanders in 1745 (King George's War) and then returned to the French in the Treaty of Aix-la-Chapelle.

8. Treasure, op. cit., p. 226, gives fourteen as his age. Francis Parkman, *France and England in North America, Volume II* (The Library of America, 1983), p. 1322, says fifteen.

9. In response to the Duke of Newcastle, who was among Wolfe's doubters, King George II replied: "Mad is he? Then I hope he will bite some of my other generals." Quoted in Parkman, ibid., p. 1327.

10. Quoted in ibid., p. 1325.

11. All quoted in ibid., pp. 1325–26.

12. Quoted in ibid., p. 1323.

13. The Royal American Regiment was made up largely of Swiss and German immigrants to Pennsylvania.

14. Thus was founded Pittsburgh, not because it is the pits, but after William Pitt, the Elder.
15. Quoted in J. D. Lock, *To Fight with Intrepidity: The Complete History of the U.S. Army Rangers, 1622 to Present* (Fenestra Books, 2001), p. 85.
16. Lock, op. cit., puts the number of Indian dead between 65 and 140. Hamilton, op. cit., says that the Rangers "killed some two hundred Indians," p. 267.
17. Among the British naval officers was Captain James Cook. On the French side was Louis Antoine de Bougainville, who was at this time serving in the army. He accepted a commission into the navy in 1770. Both would find fame in the South Pacific.
18. Robert Leckie, *The Wars of America* (Castle Books, 1998), pp. 72–73, makes an interesting case for the possibility that among the Frenchmen at Quebec, the Marquis de Vaudreuil betrayed the French commander, the Marquis de Montcalm, not only countermanding Montcalm's instructions on defending what became the British point of attack but actually alerting Wolfe to the footpath's existence in the first place.
19. Quoted in Geoffrey Regan, *The Guinness Book of Decisive Battles* (Canopy Books, 1992), p. 135.
20. The Louisbourg Grenadiers were a scratch unit consisting of the grenadier companies of three regiments—the 22nd, 40th, and 45th Regiments of Foot—that garrisoned Louisbourg.
21. Quoted in Parkman, op. cit., p. 1400.
22. Quoted in ibid., pp. 1407–8.
23. Quoted in ibid., p. 1408.
24. Quoted in Regan, op. cit., p. 135.
25. Quoted in Parkman, op. cit., p. 1419.
26. Ibid., p. 1423.
27. All three of Wolfe's brigadiers were men of higher social standing than Wolfe himself.
28. Some estimates put the number above a million.
29. Quoted in Fred Anderson, *Crucible of War: The Seven Years' War and the Fate of Empire in British North America, 1754–1766* (Knopf, 2000), p. 740.
30. Spare the French and spoil the Frog was the strategy.
31. Colonel John Bradstreet, who preferred the pen to the sword, the treaty to the musket, met with less success in the Great Lakes region.
32. This estimate comes from Paul Johnson, *A History of the American People* (Harper-Collins, 1997), p. 132. John Steele Gordon, *An Empire of Wealth: An Epic History of American Economic Power* (HarperCollins, 2004), estimates that the relative tax burden on British taxpayers was twenty-six times higher.
33. Quoted in David Horowitz, *The First Frontier: The Indian Wars & America's Origins, 1607–1776* (Simon & Schuster, 1978), pp. 203–4.

CHAPTER 3: "DISPERSE, YE REBELS!"

1. Quoted in Major General J. F. C. Fuller, *A Military History of the Western World* (Funk & Wagnalls, 1955), Vol. II, p. 270n.
2. Though he was already commander of the Continental Army, in the winter of 1775–76 George Washington was still toasting the health of King George III.
3. An image and slogan apparently first displayed on the drums of the Continental Marines in 1775.
4. Compared with the budget deficits of modern welfare states, it was but a trifle.
5. C. R. L. Fletcher and Rudyard Kipling, *Kipling's Pocket History of England* (Greenwich House, 1983), p. 240.

6. Henry delivered this sentiment in a speech before the Virginia House of Burgesses on 29 May 1765. Accounts of the speech differ. What appears here is a composite version.

7. Quoted in Samuel Eliot Morison, *The Oxford History of the American People: Volume One, Prehistory to 1789* (Mentor, 1972), p. 257.

8. The Revenue Act (the Townshend duties) was passed by Parliament in 1767.

9. Or actually Benjamin Franklin's petard; he had used this distinction in arguing for repeal of the Stamp Act. As early as 1761, James Otis had raised the bar to a higher standard when he said, "Taxation without representation is tyranny."

10. Some working-class Bostonians resented that the poorly paid soldiers moonlighted and competed with them for jobs.

11. John Adams, quoted in Morison, op. cit., p. 269.

12. Such tabloid journalism played an enormous role in the Patriots' cause.

13. The Canadians declined the American offer to join the rebellion.

14. Samuel Johnson, *The Yale Edition of the Works of Samuel Johnson, Volume X, Political Writings,* edited by Donald J. Greene (Liberty Fund, 1977), pp. 439, 429, 454.

15. David Horowitz, *The First Frontier: The Indian Wars & America's Origins, 1607–1776* (Simon & Schuster, 1978), p. 224.

16. Quoted in ibid., p. 206.

17. Quoted in Don Cook, *The Long Fuse: How England Lost the American Colonies, 1760–1785* (Atlantic Monthly Press, 1995), p. 123.

18. Francis Parkman, *France and England in North America, Volume II* (The Library of America, 1983), p. 1478.

19. Walter Carruthers Sellar and Robert Julian Yeatman, *1066 and All That: A Memorable History of England* (The Folio Society, 1999), p. 63, reminds us of "the *utterly memorable Struggle between the Cavaliers (Wrong but Wromantic) and the Roundheads (Right but Repulsive).*"

20. Quoted in David McCullough, *1776* (Simon and Schuster, 2005), p. 11. The king also noted "that to be a subject of Great Britain, with all its consequences, is to be the freest member of any civil society known to the world."

21. As usual the numbers vary. Because of the various deployments so, too, do the numbers on the later retreat.

22. Quoted in Robert Harvey, *"A Few Bloody Noses": The Realities and Mythologies of the American Revolution* (Overlook Press, 2002), p. 160.

23. Whether he actually said this is open to some debate. Allen became a well-known deist and skeptic. His daughter, however, became the first New England–born Catholic nun.

24. Some credit the famous phrase to Colonel William Prescott.

25. James Thomas Flexner, *Washington: The Indispensable Man* (Little, Brown, 1974).

CHAPTER 4: FORGED IN BATTLE:
FROM 1776 TO VALLEY FORGE

1. Quoted in Harrison Clark, *All Cloudless Glory, Volume One: The Life of George Washington from Youth to Yorktown* (Regnery, 1995), p. 244.

2. Ibid., p. 238.

3. Quoted in Robert Harvey, *"A Few Bloody Noses": The Realities and Mythologies of the American Revolution* (Overlook Press, 2002), p. 183.

4. While the use of Indian allies was traditional in North American warfare, it was a propaganda coup for the Patriots and a disincentive for frontiersmen to be Loyalists.

5. Both colonies, Georgia especially, might actually have had Loyalist majorities.

6. Harvey, op. cit., p. 203.

7. As with most great quotes, some think this apocryphal, though it is based on an eye-witness *British* account.

8. Letter from George Washington to Lund Washington, 17 December 1776.

9. Gates, an Englishman, had been an officer in the British army. So had the Welchman Charles Lee. Neither officer proved worthy of the Continental Army, and both conspired against Washington.

10. This account is contested. James L. Stokesbury's excellent *A Short History of the American Revolution* (William Morrow and Company, 1991), pp. 152–53, offers the traditional account, which blames Burgoyne's Indians, not the Patriots. The pro-British account comes from Harvey, op. cit., p. 250, using evidence from McCrea's exhumed body. While Burgoyne had cautioned his Indians to behave themselves, he had set himself up for a propaganda defeat by publicly threatening to unleash the Indians, which made the likelihood of an Indian outrage against Jane McCrea all the more believable and infuriating; it was compounded by Burgoyne's refusal to punish the Indians allegedly guilty of scalping McCrea.

11. Quoted in Harvey, op. cit., p. 257.

12. Technically, it was not "surrender." Burgoyne had bluffed Gates into agreeing to "the Convention of Saratoga," which allowed the British and German troops to return to Europe, British officers to retain their luggage (unsearched) and small arms, and liberty to the Loyalists and Canadians. The generals and their officers sanctified the convention with a banquet. George Washington convinced the Continental Congress to abrogate the Convention, and the 4,000 British and German troops who had reached Boston were made prisoners of war.

13. In Victor Brooks and Robert Hohwald's rather fun book, *How America Fought Its Wars: Military Strategy from the American Revolution to the Civil War* (Combined Publishing, 1999), generals are given academic letter grades. Howe receives an "'A' for overall tactical success," but which "must be combined with an 'F' for his contribution to British strategic objectives to produce a 'C' grade." Clinton receives a C+. See pp. 148–50.

14. Lee was court-martialed and eventually dismissed from the Army.

15. He is buried in the crypt of the U.S. Naval Academy Chapel, where his remains were interred on 26 January 1913. A Marine honor guard stands duty over the grave. His fame has rather overshadowed that of "the father of the American Navy," John Barry, a towering six-foot, four-inch, Irish-born Catholic who rose from Irish cabin boy to American commodore. Made a captain in the Continental Navy in 1776, he fought as a Marine at Trenton and Princeton and was a true fighting captain at sea. In 1794, President George Washington appointed Barry "Captain of the Federal Navy" to create and lead the navy of the new republic. Barry died in 1803, but to him belongs much of the credit for the gallant seamanship and military success that attended the U.S. Navy from the beginning.

CHAPTER 5: THE WORLD TURNED UPSIDE DOWN

1. Tarleton would later serve as a member of Parliament for Liverpool, in which capacity he was an ardent defender of the slave trade. As for his military career he claimed

to have "butchered more men and lain with more women than anybody else in the army." In other words, he was a man of accomplishment.

2. His baronetcy was self-awarded.

3. Quoted in Harrison Clark, *All Cloudless Glory, Volume One: The Life of George Washington from Youth to Yorktown* (Regnery, 1995), p. 467.

4. Quoted in Robert Harvey, *"A Few Bloody Noses": The Realities and Mythologies of the American Revolution* (Overlook Press, 2002), p. 342.

5. Quoted in Dan L. Morrill, *The Southern Campaigns of the American Revolution* (The Nautical and Aviation Publishing Company of America, no date), p. 103.

6. These were the "long rifles" used by hunters. They had impressive range and accuracy, but were slower to reload than muskets.

7. Quoted in Harvey, op. cit., p. 377.

8. Quoted in Morrill, op. cit., p. 126.

9. Quoted in Burke Davis, *The Campaign That Won America: The Story of Yorktown* (Eastern Acorn Press, 1997), p. 107.

10. Though Sir Henry Clinton was the son of an admiral, this didn't seem to help.

11. Quoted in Davis, op. cit., p. 272.

CHAPTER 6: THE FOUNDERS'
FOREIGN ENTANGLEMENTS

1. The British withdrew from Wilmington in January 1782, Savannah in June 1782, Charleston in December 1782, and New York in November 1783.

2. This was especially true after Admiral Comte de Grasse was defeated—and captured—by British Admiral George Rodney at the Battle of the Saints in the West Indies on 12 April 1782. After that, there was no question of French naval support for Franco-American combined operations. The French admiral's defeat reversed the tide in the Caribbean war, where the British had been left holding only the islands of Jamaica, Barbados, St. Lucia, and Antigua. Serendipitously, de Grasse's defeat occurred on the same day that negotiations began between Benjamin Franklin and the British in Paris. The Netherlands recognized American independence a week later, thanks to the diplomatic efforts of John Adams.

3. Clark's younger brother William became an Indian-fighting soldier and later joined Captain Meriwether Lewis on the famous expedition, sponsored by President Thomas Jefferson and funded by Congress, that took the explorers from St. Louis to the Pacific coast of the Oregon Territory.

4. A key point for the British negotiators was protecting the Loyalists and restoring their property. This was agreed to on paper, but widely ignored in practice, with the result that 80,000 to 100,000 Loyalists chose to emigrate—the equivalent of about 8 million Americans today. J. M. Roberts in *The Pelican History of the World* (Penguin, 1985), p. 693, adds this rather provocative note: "there were fewer emigrants from France during the Revolution than from the American colonies after 1783." Perhaps the food had something to do with it.

5. Quoted in Paul Johnson, *George Washington: The Founding Father* (HarperCollins, 2005), p. 78.

6. Britain had gained the two Floridas in exchange for Havana, Cuba, at the end of the Seven Years' War. The British Floridas stayed Loyalist.

7. Quoted in Warren W. Hassler Jr., *With Shield and Sword: American Military Affairs, Colonial Times to the Present* (Iowa State University Press, 1987), p. 48.

8. Baron von Steuben had his own plans and proposals for a nascent American military establishment. They went far beyond Washington's, with regional commands, a much larger standing army, and reserves of well-trained militia—a combined force that could rapidly expand to 42,000 men. Such ambitious schemes had no hope at all.

9. Quoted in Johnson, op. cit., p. 76.

10. Dickinson had protested against Britain's right to tax the colonies but had refused to support independence—until the war drums sounded. Then he accepted a commission in the Continental Army and served briefly in uniform. More important, he drafted the Articles of Confederation.

11. Quoted in Samuel Eliot Morison, *The Oxford History of the American People: Volume One, Prehistory to 1789* (Mentor, 1972), p. 355.

12. While men like Hamilton and Dickinson worked to enact a new Constitution, Noah Webster worked to develop a distinct American language, because "America is an independent empire, and ought to assume a national character." He described his book *American Spelling and Grammar* as "designed particularly for the youth in the American Empire." Quoted in Christopher Hitchens, *Blood, Class and Empire: The Enduring Anglo-American Relationship* (Nation Books, 2004), p. 138.

13. Wayne's army was abetted by about 1,000 Kentucky militiamen.

14. Lee served as governor of Virginia from 1791–94. In 1794, he led 13,000 militiamen—ordered to arms by the authority of President George Washington (and a larger force than he had ever personally commanded)—to suppress the "Whiskey Rebellion" in western Pennsylvania. The rebels violently opposed Alexander Hamilton's tax on their hard liquor, but whether because of or in spite of their fondness for whiskey, the rebels were easily dispersed.

15. Pennsylvania, despite being Quaker country, supplied a good number of troops to the army of the new Republic.

16. Quoted in Hassler, op. cit., p. 61.

17. Quoted in Stephen Howarth, *To Shining Sea: A History of the United States Navy, 1775–1791* (Random House, 1991), p. 55.

18. Also sometimes known as the Democratic-Republicans.

19. Quoted in J. F. C. Fuller, *Decisive Battles of the U.S.A.* (Thomas Yoseloff, 1942), p. vii.

20. In addition, Washington cites religion and morality as necessary buttresses of good government, recommends fiscal responsibility, and acknowledges the potential dangers of an "overgrown military establishment."

21. George Washington's Farewell Address, 1796.

22. Quoted in Samuel Eliot Morison, *The Oxford History of the American People: Volume Two, 1789 Through Reconstruction* (Mentor, 1972), p. 68.

23. At this time, the vice president was the presidential candidate who received the second-highest total of votes in the Electoral College, with each elector casting two votes. The system was changed with the Twelfth Amendment to the Constitution in 1804.

24. Quoted in Howarth, op. cit., p. 59.

25. Quoted in Morison, op. cit., *Volume Two*, p. 71.

26. The Republicans deemed these acts a "Federalist Reign of Terror." Unlike the real Reign of Terror in France, the "Federalist Reign of Terror" led to the prosecution of fewer than two dozen individuals who received fines or minor jail sentences. More serious were the objections of Virginia and Kentucky—in resolutions written by

Thomas Jefferson (Kentucky) and James Madison (Virginia)—which asserted that the Sedition Act violated the First Amendment. Jefferson had also included a proviso that state legislatures could nullify federal laws within their own borders. Though this part of the resolution was not passed, Jefferson supported the principle of nullification. Madison opposed it. It would become a major constitutional issue in the decades to come.

27. The Marine Corps, originally founded in Philadelphia's Tun Tavern in 1775, was officially revived on 11 July 1798.

28. Quoted in Howarth, p. 60. The British applauded the creation of an American Navy as an ally against the French.

29. Ibid., p. 72.

30. One evidence of this was another tax rebellion—Fries's Rebellion—in Pennsylvania in 1799 that had to be put down by the American Army.

31. Before the War of Independence, the Royal Navy had paid the tribute on behalf of American ships, which also received the military protection of the Royal Navy. The French briefly took over this protector role for the Americans, but soon the young Republic found it had to make its own way in the sordid world of commerce.

32. During the subsequent blockade and battles, Decatur's brother was captured and murdered by a pirate captain. In a later naval battle, Decatur sought the captain out during the fighting and personally killed him.

33. Quoted in Joseph Wheelan, *Jefferson's War: America's First War on Terror, 1801–1805* (Carroll and Graf, 2003) p. 195.

34. Eaton and O'Bannon wanted to continue on to Tunis. Toppling Bashaw Yusuf, wrote Eaton, "would very probably be a death blow to the Barbary system," while stopping now would be "a wound to the national honor." (See A. B. C. Whipple, *To the Shores of Tripoli: The Birth of the U.S. Navy and Marines* [William Morrow and Company, 1991], pp. 234–35.) Eaton's protests were dismissed, to his everlasting regret. Captain Bainbridge, for one, took Jefferson's side on this issue, thinking further military action would endanger his men and inflame rather than subdue the Muslims of the Mediterranean. Eaton and O'Bannon became ardent anti-Jeffersonians.

35. Quoted in Alexander DeConde, *A History of American Foreign Policy* (Charles Scribner's Sons, 1963), p. 77.

36. Thomas Jefferson letter to John C. Breckenridge, 12 August 1803.

37. Some misfit New England Federalists, like Senator Timothy Pickering of Massachusetts, supported secession as a way to "exempt" themselves "from the corrupt and corrupting influence and oppression of the aristocratic Democrats of the South." Quoted in Richard Brookhiser, *Alexander Hamilton: American* (Free Press, 1999), p. 202.

38. Hamilton, though born in the West Indies to a Scotch father and a Huguenot mother, could have been elected president under Article 2, Section 1, Clause 4 of the Constitution, which allows the election of a foreign-born American if he was "a citizen of the United States at the time of the adoption of this Constitution."

39. There was in fact an early-nineteenth-century brawn drain from British ships to American ones, because the wages were higher on American ships; there was also an Anglo-American dispute over who was "British" and who was "American." The British boarding American ships were less particular about these differences than were the Americans.

CHAPTER 7: MADISON'S WARS

1. The flag of the Republic of West Florida gained greater fame as the "Bonnie Blue Flag" of the Southern Confederacy.
2. Wellington's army in Iberia, for example, was largely nourished by American flour.
3. Madison didn't know this, unfortunately, because of the lag time in communications.
4. Quoted in Samuel Eliot Morison, *The Oxford History of the American People: Volume Two, 1789 Through Reconstruction* (Mentor, 1972), p. 110.
5. Quoted in Victor Brooks and Robert Hohwald, *How America Fought Its Wars: Military Strategy from the American Revolution to the Civil War* (Combined Publishing, 1999), p. 162.
6. John R. Elting in his book *Amateurs, to Arms! A Military History of the War of 1812* (Algonquin Books of Chapel Hill, 1991), p. 25, says of Hull: "On the basis of Revolutionary War service, he was the best qualified of all of Madison's generals."
7. President Madison eventually rubber-stamped the popular will and made Harrison commander of American forces in the "Northwest."
8. Elting, op. cit., p. 51.
9. Quoted in Morison, op. cit., *Volume Two,* p. 115.
10. These figures come from Robert Leckie, *The Wars of America* (Castle Books, 1998), p. 255.
11. Procter's name is, in some sources, spelled Proctor.
12. Quoted in Glen Tucker, *Poltroons and Patriots: A Popular Account of the War of 1812, Volume One* (Bobbs & Merrill, 1954), p. 231.
13. Native American medicine at this time followed the "kill and cure" principle, though unlike many Native American folk remedies this one seems to have few modern admirers. It had few British or American admirers at the time, either. Colonel John R. Elting points out that most "Englishmen feared their savage allies as much as the Americans did, and were occasionally killed by them." See Elting, op. cit., fn. on p. 63.

CHAPTER 8: THE GUNS OF OLD HICKORY

1. Quoted in Robert Allen Rutland, *The Presidency of James Madison* (University Press of Kansas, 1990), p. 101.
2. Barney was able to join the fight at Bladensburg because, at the order of the Navy Department, he scuttled his gunboat flotilla (with which he had been harassing the British) above Pig Point on the Patuxent River.
3. The British admired Barney's bravery and paroled him.
4. The Navy Yard's destruction was actually started by the Americans, who wanted to avoid having its stores, ships, and ammunition fall into the hands of the British. The British finished the job.
5. The vandalism meted out to Washington proved a public relations disaster in Britain, criticized by no less than the *Times* of London.
6. The quote is from John Parton, an early Jackson biographer. It is cited in Robert V. Remini, *Andrew Jackson and His Indian Wars* (Viking, 2001), p. 13.
7. Quoted in Edward Pessen, *Jacksonian America* (Dorsey Press, 1978), p. 181.
8. We also have Crockett's testimony that the next morning Jackson's hungry volunteers found a potato cellar beneath a burned Indian cabin. The volunteers ate the potatoes "though I had rather not, if I could have helped it, for the oil of the Indians we had burned up on the day before had run down on them, and they looked like they had been stewed in fat meat." See David Crockett, *A Narrative of the Life of David Crockett* (University of Nebraska Press, 1987), pp. 88–90.

9. The boy's name was Lyncoya, and Jackson treated him as a much beloved son. Instead of becoming a cadet, Lyncoya became a saddler, but died prematurely at sixteen.
10. Quoted in Remini, *Andrew Jackson and His Indian Wars*, p. 75.
11. Spain was a British ally, though officially neutral in the War of 1812.
12. Ironically, Pakenham shared Wellington's view of the war.
13. The Jackson quotes come from Robert V. Remini, *The Battle of New Orleans* (Viking, 1999), p. 70.
14. Quoted in ibid., pp. 75–76.
15. Quoted in ibid., p. 77.
16. One of the earliest and most important diplomatic achievements was a mutual policy of disarmament in the Great Lakes, which made the settlement of the northern border of the United States and the southern border of Canada easier to negotiate, with fewer opportunities for friction.
17. Elizabeth Longford rightly points out: "The battle of New Orleans illustrates the waste of war with peculiar vividness. . . . It is impossible to imagine Wellington accepting the desperate battleground on which the British Admiral irresponsibly landed the army in front of New Orleans, for the sake, according to Wellington, of plunder." See Elizabeth Longford, *Wellington: The Years of the Sword* (Harper & Row, 1969), fn., p. 382.
18. Quoted in Robert Leckie, *The Wars of America* (Castle Books, 1998), p. 312.
19. Quoted in Remini, *The Battle of New Orleans*, p. 152.
20. Quoted in Leckie, op. cit., p. 312.

CHAPTER 9: THE EMERGING COLOSSUS

1. Quoted in Max Boot, *The Savage Wars of Peace: Small Wars and the Rise of American Power* (Basic Books, 2002), p. 28.
2. Calhoun's martial southern spirit was more powerful—thank goodness—than his Republican worry about military establishments. He was a strong backer and reviver of the United States Military Academy at West Point.
3. Quoted in Robert V. Remini, *Andrew Jackson and His Indian Wars* (Viking, 2001), p. 135.
4. Quoted in ibid., p. 148 "our mutual savage enemies" and p. 143.
5. Congress, as ever, feared an American Caesar and saw one in Jackson. Though former War Hawks, Henry Clay made this accusation and Secretary of War John C. Calhoun was for disciplining the successful general.
6. Great Britain had an obvious interest in keeping France from the New World, but also, because of the growing financial power of the city of London, the British believed that the combination of British loans and the Royal Navy would make Latin America a de facto client region of the British Empire.
7. Russell F. Weigley in his influential book, *The American Way of War: A History of United States Military Strategy and Policy* (Indiana University Press, 1973), p. 68, sums up these lessons by saying: "In the end, a kind of victory was achieved through treachery and brutality: the policy inaugurated by Brevet Major General Thomas S. Jesup of making captives of the Indians who came under a truce to parley, as Jesup captured Osceola, and the policy of destroying Indian villages and crops to deprive the enemy of sustenance."
8. The United States had outlawed the importation of slaves—though not slavery itself—in 1808. Under the Treaty of Ghent, which ended the War of 1812, the United States agreed to cooperate with the British against the slave trade. The Royal Navy

was the enforcer that broke the back of the slave trade, though the United States assisted, declaring it piracy in 1820 and detailing the United States Navy to patrol the West African coast against it.

9. See H. W. Crocker III, *Triumph: The Power and the Glory of the Catholic Church, A 2,000-Year History* (Prima/Crown/Random House, 2001), pp. 394–99, for a quick overview.

10. Quoted in Samuel Eliot Morison, *The Oxford History of the American People: Volume Two, 1789 Through Reconstruction* (Mentor, 1972), p. 146. It must be said that Adams did not help Mexico much when his minister to Mexico, Joel R. Poinsett, helped foment a Mexican civil war between rival Masonic lodges—a rather perfidious Protestant plot.

11. The various flags of the Texas War for Independence would suit the ambiance of a biker bar, especially Captain William S. Brown's flag of independence, which in place of the stars in the traditional Stars and Stripes design features a blood-soaked Bowie knife (or sword) dripping blood onto the suitably muscular white arm bearing it. For those who prefer a cleaner look, Captain Philip Dimmit's Goliad flag has a dark, earthy red sword and sword arm dripping blood in an otherwise white banner.

12. In due course, some northerners would arrive as well, including volunteers from New York.

CHAPTER 10: MILITARY HOLIDAY IN MEXICO

1. So many volunteers poured out of Tennessee that it became "the volunteer state."

2. Quoted in Edward J. Nichols, *Zach Taylor's Little Army* (Doubleday, 1963), p. 35.

3. There was also the matter of women: Mexican women proved to be an effective recruiting sergeant of American soldiers for the Mexican army. Such has always been the strategy of the nefarious papists—conversion by the skirt.

4. John O'Reilly (also spelled "Riley" and "Reilly") had been a sergeant in the British army, served as a private in the American Army, and was elevated to a lieutenant in the Mexican army.

5. Quoted in K. Jack Bauer, *The Mexican War: 1846–1848* (Macmillan, 1974), p. 85.

6. Quoted in Robert Leckie, *The Wars of America* (Castle Books, 1998), p. 341.

7. Lieutenant (later General) George Meade certainly did. He called the volunteers "Goths and Vandals . . . laying waste the country wherever we go, making us a terror to innocent people. . . ." Quoted in ibid., p. 350.

8. The fort was renamed Fort Brown after the death of its commanding officer, Major Jacob Brown, who also posthumously gave his name to Brownsville, Texas.

9. Quoted in Lloyd Lewis, *Captain Sam Grant* (Little, Brown, 1950), p. 147.

10. Quoted in ibid., p. 176.

11. Quoted in John S. D. Eisenhower, *So Far from God: The U.S. War with Mexico, 1846–1848* (Random House, 1989), p. 160. Such doggerel is far better than the stuff that issued from the pens of such pallid antiwar scribblers as Henry David Thoreau (bailed out of jail by his aunt), Northern abolitionists, Unitarian divines, and other dissenting New Englanders. Interestingly, Nathaniel Hawthorne, whose daughter Rose became a Catholic nun, supported the Polk administration. Good fellow.

12. Quoted in ibid., p. 173.

13. Quoted in Leckie, op. cit., p. 351.

14. General John S. D. Eisenhower compares the American position to that of the Spartans at Thermopylae. See footnote in Eisenhower, op. cit., p. 182.

15. Quoted in Leckie, op. cit., p. 351.
16. Quoted in Eisenhower, op. cit., p. 188.
17. Quoted in Leckie, op. cit., p. 365.
18. Quoted in Eisenhower, op. cit., p. 298.
19. Quoted in ibid., p. 295.
20. He was the nephew of Colonel Stephen Kearny, who had conquered New Mexico and California.
21. Quoted in K. Jack Bauer, op. cit., p. 318.
22. K. Jack Bauer writes that of the eighty-five captured Patricios at Churubusco (among whom the executed were taken), only twenty-seven were Irish deserters. He argues that the "myth that the San Patricios were Irish deserters seems to stem from the importance given [Private John] Reilly [whom the Americans regarded as the Patricios' ringleader] and the fact that their unit flag had an Irish harp on it." See Bauer, op. cit., n. 37, pp. 304–5.
23. Quoted in Eisenhower, op. cit., p. 367.

CHAPTER 11: WRECKING THE FURNITURE

1. Another obvious example: there would have been no Cuban missile crisis if the United States had annexed Cuba.
2. The greater Nebraska Territory was in fact Indian land, but that never mattered in the drive of manifest destiny. Douglas had divided Kansas from Nebraska as a concession to the South, raising hopes that Kansas could be another Missouri—that is, a slave state—while Nebraska would be a free state.
3. Preston S. Brooks, speech to the House of Representatives, 14 July 1856. Brooks survived an attempt to expel him from the House of Representatives, but resigned his seat anyway. He was reelected by the good people of South Carolina, and having regained his seat died, though only thirty-seven years old.
4. Another plank in the Republican platform was opposition to polygamy, as practiced by the Mormons.
5. Abraham Lincoln, speech in Springfield, Illinois, 16 June 1858.
6. Harpers Ferry lies in what is now West Virginia.
7. Lieutenant J.E.B. ("Jeb") Stuart was the messenger.
8. The defeated National Democrat and former vice president of the United States John C. Breckinridge became a Confederate general and at the end days, Davis's secretary of war.
9. Quoted in Clifford Dowdey, *The History of the Confederacy* (originally published under the title, *The Land They Fought For*) (Barnes and Noble Books, 1992), p. 69.
10. The textbook was Judge William Rawle's *A View of the Constitution.*
11. Abraham Lincoln, First Inaugural Address, 4 March 1861.
12. Ibid.
13. Abraham Lincoln, speech to Congress, 12 January 1847.
14. Quoted in Dowdey, *The History of the Confederacy,* p. 90.
15. Quoted in Douglas Southall Freeman, *Lee* (an abridgment in one volume, by Richard Harwell, of the four-volume *R. E. Lee*) (Charles Scribner's Sons, 1991), p. 110.
16. Quoted in Clifford Dowdey, *Lee* (Stan Clark Military Books, 1991), p. 120–21.
17. Ibid., p. 135.
18. President Jefferson Davis, First Message to the Confederate Congress, 29 April 1861.

19. Uniforms would be standardized after this battle to avoid confusion. Some Confederates, like "Stonewall" Jackson, were dressed in blue; some of the Federals had grey uniforms. Beauregard also designed the Confederate battle flag—the familiar St. Andrew's Cross—in order to avoid confusion between the Stars and Stripes and the Stars and Bars, the first national flag of the Confederacy.

20. Quoted in James I. Robertson, *Stonewall Jackson: The Man, the Soldier, the Legend* (Macmillan, 1997), p. 264.

21. Jackson was yet another Virginian originally opposed to secession. But, he had said before the war, "If that time comes, then draw your swords and throw away the scabbards." Quoted in Byron Farwell, *Stonewall: A Biography of General Thomas J. Jackson* (W. W. Norton & Company, 1992), p. 146. As a strategist, Jackson held that we "must give them [the enemy] no time to think. We must bewilder them and keep them bewildered. Our fighting must be sharp, impetuous, continuous. We cannot stand a long war." Quoted in Robertson, op. cit., p. 269. Jackson saw the greatest mercy—and the greatest opportunity for Southern victory—in swift, crushing counterstrokes that would shock the North into letting the South go free.

CHAPTER 12: "WAR IS CRUELTY, YOU CANNOT REFINE IT"

1. In England, Methodist and evangelical support for the North, based on an abhorrence of slavery, counterbalanced aristocratic opinion in favor of the South.

2. President Benito Juarez's repudiation of Mexico's debts to European creditors was the original excuse for French military intervention.

3. Camerone Day is celebrated every 30 April. At Legion headquarters in Aubagne, the wooden hand of Captain Jean Danjou, whose 65-man force held off nearly 3,000 Mexican soldiers until every legionnaire was dead or wounded, is the focal point of a military parade.

4. Quoted in Joseph L. Harsh, *Confederate Tide Rising: Robert E. Lee and the Making of Southern Strategy, 1861–1862* (Kent State University Press, 1998), p. 57. Lee's own views on slavery were famously summarized in a letter he wrote in late December 1856, in which he had said, "there are few I believe, but what will acknowledge, that slavery as an institution, is a moral & political evil in any Country," but he believed that "emancipation will sooner result from the mild & melting influence of Christianity, than the storms & tempests of fiery Controversy." Quoted in Douglas Southall Freeman, *Lee* (an abridgment in one volume, by Richard Harwell, of the four-volume *R. E. Lee*) (Charles Scribner's Sons, 1991), p. 92. He did not believe that war was the proper means to achieve emancipation. During the war, Lee recognized slavery as a diplomatic millstone around the Confederacy's neck. He even recommended arming slaves on the South's behalf, believing they were fellow Southerners who would fight for their homes. His recommendation was taken up only when the cause was already lost. Slavery, which the Southern fire-breathers considered essential to the South's way of life, instead ensured its death.

5. Quoted in Harsh, op. cit., p. 57.

6. Quoted in Samuel Eliot Morison, *The Oxford History of the American People: Volume Two, 1789 Through Reconstruction* (Mentor, 1972), p. 414.

7. Quoted in Clifford Dowdey, *Lee* (Stan Clark Military Books, 1991), p. 91.

8. Quoted in Shelby Foote, *The Civil War: A Narrative, Fort Sumter to Perryville* (Random House, 1958), p. 90.

9. Quoted in James M. McPherson, *The Battle Cry of Freedom: The Civil War Era* (Oxford University Press, 1988), p. 396.

10. Stewart Sifakis, *Who Was Who in the Civil War* (Facts on File, 1988), pp. 220 and 508.

11. Quoted in McPherson, op. cit., p. 401.

12. Quoted in Brian Steel Wills, *A Battle from the Start: The Life of Nathan Bedford Forrest* (HarperCollins, 1992), p. 64.

13. Wallace later won fame as the author of *Ben Hur.* To his eternal discredit, after the War Between the States, he accepted a commission to help Benito Juarez's revolt against the kindly emperor Maximilian in Mexico.

14. Quoted in Wills, op. cit., p. 69.

15. Quoted in Foote, op. cit., p. 351.

CHAPTER 13: "WAR MEANS FIGHTING AND FIGHTING MEANS KILLING"

1. Quoted in James I. Robertson, *Stonewall Jackson: The Man, the Soldier, the Legend* (Macmillan, 1997), pp. 447–48.

2. It had been the Confederate Army of the Potomac.

3. Quoted in Clifford Dowdey, *Lee* (Stan Clark Military Books, 1991), p. 217.

4. Quoted in ibid., p. 221.

5. Quoted in John M. Taylor, *Duty Faithfully Performed: Robert E. Lee and His Critics* (Brassey's, 1999), p. 68.

6. Quoted in Frances H. Kennedy, ed., *The Civil War Battlefield Guide* (Houghton Mifflin, 1990), p. 60.

7. Telegram (written shortly after midnight) from General George McClellan to Secretary of War Edwin Stanton, 28 June 1862. Stanton did not actually read these words, because the officer receiving the message thought it best to edit them.

8. Quoted in Emory M. Thomas, *Robert E. Lee: A Biography* (Norton, 1997), p. 243.

9. Quoted in James M. McPherson, *The Battle Cry of Freedom: The Civil War Era* (Oxford University Press, 1988), p. 524.

10. The words *suppress* and *miscreant* dot his correspondence on the subject. Lee's orders to Jackson, for example, were that he wanted "Pope to be suppressed." For Lee's attitude to Pope see Joseph L. Harsh, *Confederate Tide Rising: Robert E. Lee and the Making of Southern Strategy, 1861–1862* (Kent State University Press, 1998), pp. 113–14 and 196, and Thomas, op. cit., pp. 249–50.

11. Quoted in Shelby Foote, *The Civil War: A Narrative, Fort Sumter to Perryville* (Random House, 1958), p. 642.

12. Douglas Southall Freeman, *R. E. Lee: A Biography, Volume II* (Charles Scribner's Sons, 1934), p. 343.

13. Letter from General R. E. Lee to President Jefferson Davis, 3 August 1862.

14. Among those jailed for secessionist sympathies was the grandson of Francis Scott Key, author of "The Star-Spangled Banner."

15. General R. E. Lee's "Proclamation to the People of Maryland," 8 September 1862.

16. Quoted in Clifford Dowdey, *The History of the Confederacy, 1832–1865* (Barnes & Noble Books, 1992), p. 214.

17. Stuart W. Smith, ed., *Douglas Southall Freeman on Leadership* (White Mane Publishing Company, Inc., 1993), p. 54.

18. Quoted in Thomas, op. cit., p. 263.

19. This assessment by McClellan was published as part of his "official report of the operations of the Army of the Potomac while under my charge," as submitted on 4 August 1863.
20. Quoted in Foote, op. cit., p. 703.
21. Quoted in Thomas, op. cit., p. 268.
22. Quoted in Freeman, op. cit., p. 446.
23. Some of the Mississippians had to be removed forcibly, even under arrest, because they were reluctant to yield the ground.
24. Pelham withdrew only after he ran out of ammunition. Lee called him "the Gallant Pelham" and said of his performance at Fredericksburg: "It is glorious to see such courage in one so young."
25. Quoted in Stanley F. Horn, ed., *The Robert E. Lee Reader* (Konecky & Konecky, 1949), pp. 269–70.
26. Quoted in Jeffrey Wert, *General James Longstreet: The Confederacy's Most Controversial Soldier* (Touchstone, 1994), p. 221.
27. The Battle of Murfreesboro (31 December 1862 to 2 January 1863) is also known as the Battle of Stones River.
28. Cleburne offered a plan, in 1864, for abolishing slavery and enlisting blacks into the army. Jefferson Davis, advised by Bragg, rejected it.
29. In Robert E. Lee's opinion, the finest soldier of the war was "A man I have never seen, sir. His name is Forrest." It was Forrest's misfortune—and the South's—that he served under Braxton Bragg. Union propagandists later tried to besmirch Forrest for the "Fort Pillow Massacre" of 12 April 1864. Fort Pillow, a former Confederate fort then manned by Tennessee Yankees and freed slaves, was besieged by Forrest, who threatened that if the fort did not surrender "I cannot be responsible for the fate of your command." This was partly bluff, such as Forrest had used in the past, but partly true because the Confederates considered its blue-clad defenders traitors. In the event, the fort was stormed, and the enraged rebels went on a rampage that Forrest tried to—and finally did—stop. Fifty-eight of the 262 black defenders were made prisoners, as were 168 of the 295 whites. For detailed discussions of the incident, see Brian Steel Wills, *A Battle from the Start: The Life of Nathan Bedford Forrest* (HarperCollins, 1992), pp. 179–96, and Shelby Foote *The Civil War: A Narrative, Red River to Appomattox* (Random House, 1974), pp. 108–12.
30. Quoted in Kennedy, ed., op. cit., p. 107.

CHAPTER 14: "FOR EVERY SOUTHERN BOY . . .
IT'S STILL NOT YET TWO O'CLOCK ON
THAT JULY AFTERNOON IN 1863"

1. Samuel Eliot Morison, *The Oxford History of the American People: Volume Two: 1789 Through Reconstruction* (Mentor, 1972), p. 451.
2. Ibid.
3. Bloodcurdling tales of the 1831 Nat Turner Rebellion in Virginia and the 1791 slave revolution in Haiti exacerbated these fears. Turner and his followers murdered nearly sixty whites—men, women, and children—before they were captured. Events in Haiti were far more cataclysmic: thousands of Frenchmen and their families were killed, the revolution became a full-scale war with France, and whites were driven from the island. Both incidents made a huge impact on Southern thoughts and fears.

4. Richard Taylor, *Destruction and Reconstruction: Personal Experiences of the Late War* (J. S. Sanders & Company, 1998), p. 124.

5. Quoted in Shelby Foote, *The Civil War: A Narrative, Fredericksburg to Meridian* (Random House, 1963), pp. 233–34.

6. Quoted in John M. Taylor, *Duty Faithfully Performed: Robert E. Lee and His Critics* (Brassey's, 1999), p. 117.

7. A tribute to his daring and bravery—and the bad luck of his horses—Forrest had twenty-nine mounts shot from beneath him during the course of the war.

8. Getting at "those people" was a constant desire of the aggressive Lee.

9. Emory M. Thomas, *Robert E. Lee: A Biography* (W. W. Norton & Company, 1997), p. 283.

10. Ibid.

11. Quoted in Shelby Foote, op. cit., pp. 296–97.

12. Quoted in Clifford Dowdey, *Lee* (Stan Clark Military Books, 1991), p. 353.

13. Quoted in Burke Davis, *Gray Fox: Robert E. Lee and the Civil War* (Burford Books, 1956), p. 197.

14. Quoted in Foote, op. cit., pp. 315–16.

15. Quoted in Thomas, op. cit., pp. 285–86.

16. Quoted in James I. Robertson Jr., *Stonewall Jackson: The Man, the Soldier, the Legend* (Macmillan, 1997), p. 739.

17. Quoted in Davis, op. cit., p. 205.

18. Quoted in Carl Sandburg, *Storm over the Land* (Harcourt Brace, 1942), p. 181.

19. The Union's advantage in artillery was even greater, at five to one.

20. One interesting sidelight of the siege of Port Hudson is that among the besieging Union forces were regiments of free blacks from New Orleans. These were blacks who were free before the war, and when the Confederate government refused to arm them, they threw in their lot with the Yankees. As educated men, and Louisianans, their black officers could issue orders in French and English.

21. Quoted in Thomas, op. cit., p. 289.

22. Quoted in Douglas Southall Freeman, *R. E. Lee: A Biography, Volume III* (Charles Scribner's Sons, 1934), p. 16.

23. Quoted in Davis, op. cit., p. 225.

24. Ibid., p. 228.

25. Quoted in Freeman, *R. E. Lee*, p. 80.

26. Quoted in Davis, op. cit., p. 230.

27. Quoted in Freeman, *R. E. Lee*, p. 79.

28. Quoted in Douglas Southall Freeman, *Lee's Lieutenants: Gettysburg to Appomattox* (Charles Scribner's Sons, 1972), p. 113.

29. Quoted in Jeffry D. Wert, *General James Longstreet: The Confederacy's Most Controversial Soldier—A Biography* (Touchstone, 1994), p. 265.

30. Quoted in ibid., p. 283.

31. Quoted in ibid., pp. 288–89. I have altered the punctuation of these notes between Longstreet and Alexander for readability.

32. Quoted in Davis, op. cit., pp. 240–41.

33. Arthur J. Fremantle, *Three Months in the Southern States: The 1863 Diary of an English Soldier* (Greenhouse Publishing Co., no date; originally published by William Blackwood and Son, 1863), p. 272.

34. Quoted in Foote, op. cit., p. 563.

35. Quoted in Thomas, op. cit., p. 300.
36. Quoted in Foote, op. cit. p. 581.
37. Quoted in James M. McPherson, *Gettysburg* (Rutledge Hill Press, 1993), p. 109.
38. Quoted in Thomas, op. cit., p. 305.
39. Quoted in McPherson, op. cit., p. 109.

CHAPTER 15: "THE SATISFACTION
THAT PROCEEDS FROM THE CONSCIOUSNESS
OF DUTY FAITHFULLY PERFORMED"

1. The stillness after Gettysburg and Vicksburg was broken temporarily but dramatically by rebel raider John Hunt Morgan, who led 2,500 Confederate cavalrymen storming through Kentucky, Indiana, and Ohio. Morgan was obviously a good man—his college career was cut short by a duel, always a good sign—he served in the Mexican War, formed a pro-Southern militia in Kentucky in the 1850s, and was a successful businessman, flying the rebel flag over his hemp factory in neutral Kentucky. Later, his factory confiscated, his wife dead, he joined the Confederate armed forces. Morgan rose fast as a cavalry officer and was noted for his daring raids. In true Southern Cavalier fashion, he took time out to remarry (to a girl sixteen years his junior) in a ceremony officiated by Confederate general and Episcopal Bishop Leonidas Polk. At the beginning of July 1863, Morgan crossed the Ohio River, in direct violation of Braxton Bragg's orders—a high recommendation—and raised havoc in Indiana and Ohio. Morgan's escapades boosted Confederate morale after Vicksburg and Gettysburg, but "the Great Raid" achieved little else, and most of Morgan's men, and Morgan himself, were captured. Slapped into a maximum security prison, it took him all of four months to escape. Alas, he was killed—shot in the back—in September 1864, when Federal troops surprised him in Greeneville, Tennessee. His death had two ironies: he had promised his wife that he would never again put himself in risk of prison, so he tried to flee rather than surrender; and the man who shot him was a rebel turned blue-belly.

2. Rosecrans was an intelligent man. He had graduated fifth in his class at West Point, served as an instructor there, invented a few gadgets as an engineer, and was a Catholic convert. His brother also converted and became a bishop.

3. Quoted in Jeffry D. Wert, *General James Longstreet: The Confederacy's Most Controversial Soldier—A Biography* (Touchstone, 1994), p. 273.

4. He had performed a similar rocklike task at Murfreesboro.

5. Braxton Bragg stubbornly refused to reinforce Longstreet's attack.

6. Quoted in Brian Steel Wills, *A Battle from the Start: The Life of Nathan Bedford Forrest* (HarperCollins, 1992), p. 142.

7. Quoted in Frances H. Kennedy, ed., *The Civil War Battlefield Guide* (Houghton Mifflin, 1990), p. 159.

8. Quoted in Wert, op. cit., p. 327.

9. Quoted in Andrew Nelson Lytle, *Bedford Forrest and His Critter Company* (J. S. Sanders & Company, 1992), p. 238.

10. Quoted in James M. McPherson, *Battle Cry of Freedom: The Civil War Era* (Oxford University Press, 1988), p. 680.

11. Quoted in Kennedy, op. cit., p. 173.

12. American fighting men have always been adept at this.

13. Quoted in Kennedy, op. cit., p. 176.

14. Two weeks earlier at Kennesaw Mountain, bishop and general Leonidas Polk was killed in action.

15. One of the great heroes of the South (and a descendant of one of the original Catholic settlers in Maryland), Semmes was reviled in the North, which credited him with so devastating Federal merchant shipping that it would take decades for it to recover.

16. Some say the quote is apocryphal. To hell with them.

17. Quoted in Stewart Sifakis, *Who Was Who in the Civil War* (Facts on File, 1988), p. 96.

18. Quoted in Emory M. Thomas, *Robert E. Lee: A Biography* (W. W. Norton & Company, 1997), p. 325.

19. Quoted in James I. Robertson Jr., *General A. P. Hill: The Story of a Confederate Warrior* (Vintage Civil War Library, 1992), p. 265.

20. Clifford Dowdey, *Lee* (Stan Clark Military Books, 1991), p. 449.

21. Quoted in Shelby Foote, *The Civil War: A Narrative, Red River to Appomattox* (Random House, 1974), p. 203.

22. Ibid., p. 224.

23. Quoted in Robert Leckie, *The Wars of America* (Castle Books, 1998), p. 495.

24. Quoted in Thomas, op. cit., p. 339.

25. Quoted in McPherson, op. cit., p. 778.

26. Quoted in Dowdey, op. cit., p. 485.

27. Quoted in ibid., p. 496.

28. Quoted in Thomas, op. cit., p. 342.

29. Quoted in Kennedy, op. cit., p. 253.

30. Foote, op. cit., p. 630.

31. Quoted in Thomas, op. cit., p. 347.

32. Abraham Lincoln, speech, 17 March 1865.

33. Quoted in Thomas, op. cit., p. 349.

34. Foote, op. cit., p. 909.

35. Quoted in ibid., p. 919.

36. Quoted in Thomas, op. cit., p. 359.

37. Quoted in ibid., p. 362.

38. Quoted in Foote, op. cit., p. 925.

39. Quoted in ibid., p. 939.

40. Quoted in ibid., pp. 944–45.

41. Ulysses S. Grant, *Personal Memoirs: Ulysses S. Grant* (Modern Library, 1999), p. 580.

42. Quoted in Foote, op. cit., pp. 948 and 951.

43. Ibid., p. 955.

CHAPTER 16: "BUT WESTWARD, LOOK! THE LAND IS BRIGHT"

1. Robert E. Lee, with his long-standing horror of violence against civilians, called the assassination "a crime previously unknown in this country," which was true, but in March 1864, he had been equally horrified to learn that a band of Yankee raiders had been captured near Richmond and that on the body of their dead commander were papers indicating a plan to assassinate Jefferson Davis.

2. Except for Swiss-born Captain Henry Wirz, commander of Andersonville Prison in Georgia, who was executed for war crimes. Andersonville was a place of horror. Thirty percent of its prisoners died, and many of the survivors were walking skele-

tons. The camp, built in February 1864, was vastly overcrowded (because the policy of exchanging prisoners had been cancelled by the Federals) and was soon, like the rest of the South, short of food and medicine—in the prisoners' case, desperately so. Prisoners trying to escape could be shot, but the Confederates realized how desperate things were in the summer of 1864 and offered to release prisoners unconditionally if the Federals would collect them. In terms of population, the prison was as large as a Southern city (over the course of the fourteen months of its existence 45,000 prisoners of war were kept there), yet had nothing remotely sufficient in facilities and supplies to care for so many. But neither side ran prisons well; the Federal prison for Confederate soldiers at Elmira, New York, for instance, also had a high casualty rate from disease and starvation, but there was no shortage of food in the North.

3. Quoted in Clifford Dowdey, *Lee* (Stan Clark Military Books, 1991), pp. 610–11.

4. Gary Gallagher, *The Confederate War: How Popular Will, Nationalism, and Military Strategy Could Not Stave Off Defeat* (Harvard University Press, 1997), p. 30.

5. Quoted in ibid., p. 53.

6. Descendants of such Confederate colonists—known as the *Confederados*—still live in Brazil.

7. New York–born Sheridan was the son of Irish Catholic immigrants. He was a true fighting Irishman and a superior soldier. He won a hero's reward when in 1875, at the age of forty-four, he married a beauty twenty-four years his junior, Irene Rucker. She took easily to military life, as her father was General D. H. Rucker, quartermaster general of the Army.

8. Quoted in John Mack Faragher, ed., *The American Heritage Encyclopedia of American History* (Henry Holt, 1998), p. 847.

9. An unlikely dissenter from the anti-Indian prejudices of Phil Sheridan and William Tecumseh Sherman was their boss, President Ulysses S. Grant. See, for instance, the discussion in Josiah Bunting III, *Ulysses S. Grant* (Times Books, 2004), especially Chapter 10.

10. For a discussion of these and other points, see Evan S. Connell, *Son of the Morning Star: Custer and the Little Bighorn* (North Point Press, 1984), especially pp. 373–75 and 409–11.

11. Quoted in Robert Leckie, *The Wars of America* (Castle Books, 1998), p. 537.

12. As Warren Zimmermann points out in *First Great Triumph: How Five Americans Made Their Country a World Power* (Farrar, Straus and Giroux, 2002), p. 328: "Behind their backs he called them 'unhung traitors.'"

13. Quoted in Stephen Howarth, *To Shining Sea: A History of the United States Navy, 1775–1991* (Random House, 1991), p. 241.

14. The United States annexed Hawaii in 1898 and Eastern Samoa in 1899.

15. American sailors and Marines had landed, under British naval cover, in Egypt in 1882 to protect American lives during an Egyptian nationalist uprising.

16. Quoted in G. J. A. O'Toole, *The Spanish War: An American Epic 1898* (W. W. Norton & Company, 1984), p. 92.

17. Quoted in Harold U. Faulkner, *Politics, Reform and Expansion* (Harper & Row, 1959), p. 217.

18. Quoted in Arthur Lubow, *The Reporter Who Would Be King: A Biography of Richard Harding Davis* (Charles Scribner's Sons, 1992), p. 140. Lubow also points out that this famous anecdote relies on a single source.

19. Winston S. Churchill, *My Early Life, 1874–1908* (Fontana/Collins, 1985), pp. 90–91.
20. Quoted in Ivan Musicant, *Empire by Default: The Spanish-American War and the Dawn of the American Century* (Henry Holt and Company, 1998), p. 109.
21. Quoted in Edmund Morris, *The Rise of Theodore Roosevelt* (Ballantine Books, 1979), p. 602.
22. Quoted in Musicant, op. cit., p. 184.
23. Quoted in Morris, op. cit., p. 600. The McKinley Monument at the Sharpsburg/Antietam Battlefield in Maryland has this inspiring inscription: "Sergeant McKinley Co. E. 23rd Ohio Vol. Infantry, while in charge of the Commissary Department, on the afternoon of the day of the battle of Antietam, September 17, 1862, personally and without orders served 'hot coffee' and 'warm food' to every man in the Regiment, on this spot and in doing so had to pass under fire."
24. Quoted in Frank Freidel, *The Splendid Little War: The Dramatic Story of the Spanish-American War* (Burford Books, 2002), p. 10.
25. Seven were warships; two were unarmed colliers.
26. Quoted in O'Toole, op. cit., p. 184.
27. Quoted in ibid., p. 191.
28. Quoted in ibid., p. 225. O'Toole, p. 226, adds: "They were a rare assortment—New York City policemen, Ivy League quarterbacks, bronco busters and polo players, Indians and Indian fighters, sheriffs, deputies, and one former marshal of Dodge City, a national tennis champion, a few professional gamblers, several Methodist clergymen, one man who had been both bookkeeper and buffalo hunter, and an ex-mayor of Prescott, Arizona."
29. Quoted in Musicant, op. cit., p. 376.
30. Quoted in ibid., p. 386.
31. Quoted in Freidel, op. cit., p. 112.
32. Both quoted in ibid., p. 122.
33. Quoted in O'Toole, op. cit., p. 314.
34. Quoted in Freidel, op. cit., p. 151.
35. Quoted in ibid., p. 177.

CHAPTER 17: "HALF DEVIL AND HALF CHILD"

1. Quoted in Frank Freidel, *The Splendid Little War: The Dramatic Story of the Spanish-American War* (Burford Books, 2002), p. 1.
2. G. J. A. O'Toole in *The Spanish War: An American Epic 1898* (W. W. Norton & Company, 1984) estimates that 365 men died in action; 2,565 died from disease and other noncombat causes, p. 375.
3. Rudyard Kipling, *Rudyard Kipling's Verse: Definitive Edition* (Doubleday & Company, 1940), p. 322.
4. Quoted in O'Toole, op. cit., p. 379.
5. Quoted in ibid., p. 386.
6. Stanley Karnow quotes a GI's doggerel that responded to Taft: "They say I've got brown brothers here, / But I still draw the line. / He may be a brother of Big Bill Taft, / But he ain't no brother of mine." See Stanley Karnow, *In Our Image: America's Empire in the Philippines* (Random House, 1989), p. 174.
7. Quoted in Warren Zimmermann, *First Great Triumph* (Farrar, Straus and Giroux, 2002), p. 348.

8. Quoted in Robert Leckie, *The Wars of America* (Castle Books, 1998), p. 544.

9. Quoted in Max Boot, *The Savage Wars of Peace: Small Wars and the Rise of American Power* (Basic Books, 2002), p. 108. Boot calls such sentiments "unseemly." "Honest" might be a better word.

10. The infamous blowhard William Jennings Bryan was another anti-imperialist, though he ended up voting for—and urging his fellow Democrats to vote for—the Treaty of Paris, before he flip-flopped again and opposed the war against the Filipino insurgents. As a presidential candidate against William McKinley's reelection in 1900, he was the great white hope of the *insurrectos*. For the makeup of the Anti-Imperialist League see Zimmerman, op. cit., especially pp. 330–1, 339–42.

11. More than 126,000 American troops served in the Philippines between 1898 and 1902, but there were never more than 69,000 at one time.

12. Quoted in Karnow, op. cit., p. 148. These "gugus" were Filipino rebels, not the goo-goos who were American anti-imperialists, though the troops didn't care much for them either.

13. Ibid., p. 171.

14. Quoted in Boot, op. cit., p. 118.

15. Quoted in Kenneth Ray Young, *The General's General: The Life and Times of Arthur MacArthur* (Westview Press, 1994), p. 299.

16. Quoted in Karnow, op. cit., p. 191.

17. Quoted in Carlo D'Este, *Patton: A Genius for War* (HarperCollins, 1995), p. 176.

18. Quoted in Boot, p. 202.

19. Ibid., p. 180.

CHAPTER 18: "COME ON, YOU SONS OF BITCHES!
DO YOU WANT TO LIVE FOREVER?"

1. Quoted in Byron Farwell, *Over There: The United States in the Great War, 1917–1918* (W. W. Norton & Company, 1999), p. 26.

2. Social Darwinism was also an important factor. As Stephen Jay Gould has noted, it was a commonplace among German intellectuals—and the German General Staff, who spoke these sentiments before the kaiser—that the war was justified by "an evolutionary rationale . . . a particularly crude form of natural selection, defined as inexorable, bloody battle." See Stephen Jay Gould, *Bully for Brontosaurus: Reflections in Natural History* (W. W. Norton & Company, 1991), p. 424.

3. The war had been sparked by the murder of the Austrian Archduke Franz Ferdinand and his wife, Countess Sophia, by ethnic Serbian terrorists. Had Germany limited its war to an eastern front—against Serbia and its ally Russia—it would have been morally right, and it would have won.

4. Belgium's neutrality had for more than seventy years been a matter of common agreement between Britain, France, and Prussia. The British, in particular, regarded Belgian neutrality as a keystone to the European balance of power and peace.

5. Quoted in Correlli Barnett, *The Great War* (BBC Worldwide Ltd, 2003), pp. 29–30.

6. See, for example, the discussion in John Keegan, *The First World War* (Alfred A. Knopf, 1999), p. 82.

7. The idea of Germans as "the Huns" came directly from the kaiser himself. In a speech to German troops embarking for China to put down the Boxer Rebellion in 1900, he said, "When you come upon the enemy, smite him. Pardon will not be given. Prisoners will not be taken. Whoever falls into your hands is forfeit. Once, a

thousand years ago, the Huns under their King Attila made a name for themselves, one still potent in legend and tradition. May you in this way make the name Germany remembered in China for a thousand years so that no Chinaman will ever again dare to even squint at a German!" See Kaiser Wilhelm II's speech to German troops at Bremerhaven, 27 July 1900.

8. Quoted in Samuel Eliot Morison, in *The Oxford History of the American People: Volume Three, 1869 to the Death of John F. Kennedy 1963* (Mentor, 1972), p. 179.

9. Quoted in H. W. Brands, *TR: The Last Romantic* (Basic Books, 1997), p. 750.

10. Ibid., p. 751.

11. Quoted in Morison, op. cit., p. 179.

12. Quoted in Brands, op. cit. p. 756.

13. Ibid.

14. The British, of course, had their own partisans in the press and public life, but relied on common Anglo-American sympathies and assumptions rather than nefarious sabotage.

15. The phrase comes from Rudyard Kipling's poem "Recessional."

16. Wiser heads, like the author's, always supported the czar as preferable to any other trumped-up government for the Russians.

17. Pacifists tried to dismiss the telegram as a forgery, until Zimmerman defended it.

18. Quoted in Morison, op. cit., p. 188.

19. Quoted in Farwell, op. cit., p. 71.

20. Quoted in Geoffrey Perret, *A Country Made by War: From the Revolution to Vietnam—The Story of America's Rise to Power* (Random House, 1989), p. 312.

21. The United States has a tradition of going its own way. America made no binding alliances until 1949, with the creation of the North Atlantic Treaty Organization (NATO).

22. Quoted in Laurence Stallings, *The Doughboys: The Story of the AEF, 1917–1918* (Harper & Row, 1963), p. 15.

23. Quoted in Carlo D'Este, *Patton: A Genius for War* (HarperCollins, 1995), p. 229.

24. Quoted in John Terraine, *Douglas Haig: The Educated Soldier* (Leo Cooper, 1990), pp. 432–33.

25. Trench warfare was not new to Americans, who had faced it in the War Between the States. Before America's intervention in the war, Confederate veteran John S. Mosby said of the stalemated trench warfare in Europe that Lee or Jackson "would have done something long before this. As it is, the forces are just killing. The object of war is not to kill. It is to disable the military power." Quoted in James A. Ramage, *Gray Ghost: The Life of Colonel John Singleton Mosby* (The University Press of Kentucky, 1999), p. 336. For thoughts on how a victorious Confederacy might have changed the course of the First World War, dramatically shortening it, see Sheldon Vanauken, *The Glittering Illusion: English Sympathy for the Southern Confederacy* (Regnery, 1989), pp. 160–61.

26. Quoted in John Keegan, *The First World War* (Knopf, 1999), p. 407.

27. Quoted in Farwell, op. cit., p. 170.

28. If one includes total losses for the United States 2nd Division (Army and Marines) in the operations around Belleau Wood, the casualty totals rise to nearly 9,000 men.

29. Quoted in Allan R. Millett, *Semper Fidelis: The History of the United States Marine Corps* (Macmillan, 1980), p. 304.

30. Quoted in Farwell, op. cit., p. 183.

31. Quoted in ibid., p. 184.

32. Also known as the Siegfried Line.
33. Quoted in William Manchester, *American Caesar: Douglas MacArthur, 1880–1964* (A Laurel Book, Dell Publishing, 1983), p. 115.
34. Quoted in Farwell, op. cit., 218.
35. Quoted in ibid., p. 240.
36. Quoted in ibid., p. 241.
37. The Fourteen Points, enunciated in President Wilson's address to a joint session of Congress on 8 January 1918, were "I. Open covenants of peace, openly arrived at, after which there shall be no private international understandings of any kind but diplomacy shall proceed always frankly and in the public view. II. Absolute freedom of navigation upon the seas, outside territorial waters, alike in peace and in war, except as the seas may be closed in whole or in part by international action for the enforcement of international covenants. III. The removal, so far as possible, of all economic barriers and the establishment of an equality of trade conditions among all the nations consenting to the peace and associating themselves for its maintenance. IV. Adequate guarantees given and taken that national armaments will be reduced to the lowest point consistent with domestic safety. V. A free, open-minded, and absolutely impartial adjustment of all colonial claims, based upon a strict observance of the principle that in determining all such questions of sovereignty the interests of the populations concerned must have equal weight with the equitable claims of the government whose title is to be determined. VI. The evacuation of all Russian territory and such a settlement of all questions affecting Russia as will secure the best and freest cooperation of the other nations of the world in obtaining for her an unhampered and unembarrassed opportunity for the independent determination of her own political development and national policy and assure her of a sincere welcome into the society of free nations under institutions of her own choosing; and, more than a welcome, assistance also of every kind that she may need and may herself desire. The treatment accorded Russia by her sister nations in the months to come will be the acid test of their good will, of their comprehension of her needs as distinguished from their own interests, and of their intelligent and unselfish sympathy. VII. Belgium, the whole world will agree, must be evacuated and restored, without any attempt to limit the sovereignty which she enjoys in common with all other free nations. No other single act will serve as this will serve to restore confidence among the nations in the laws which they have themselves set and determined for the government of their relations with one another. Without this healing act the whole structure and validity of international law is forever impaired. VIII. All French territory should be freed and the invaded portions restored, and the wrong done to France by Prussia in 1871 in the matter of Alsace-Lorraine, which has unsettled the peace of the world for nearly fifty years, should be righted, in order that peace may once more be made secure in the interest of all. IX. A readjustment of the frontiers of Italy should be effected along clearly recognizable lines of nationality. X. The peoples of Austria-Hungary, whose place among the nations we wish to see safeguarded and assured, should be accorded the freest opportunity to autonomous development. XI. Rumania, Serbia, and Montenegro should be evacuated; occupied territories restored; Serbia accorded free and secure access to the sea; and the relations of the several Balkan states to one another determined by friendly counsel along historically established lines of allegiance and nationality; and international guarantees of the political and economic independence and territorial integrity of the several Balkan states should be entered into. XII. The Turkish portion of the present

Ottoman Empire should be assured a secure sovereignty, but the other nationalities which are now under Turkish rule should be assured an undoubted security of life and an absolutely unmolested opportunity of autonomous development, and the Dardanelles should be permanently opened as a free passage to the ships and commerce of all nations under international guarantees. XIII. An independent Polish state should be erected which should include the territories inhabited by indisputably Polish populations, which should be assured a free and secure access to the sea, and whose political and economic independence and territorial integrity should be guaranteed by international covenant. XIV. A general association of nations must be formed under specific covenants for the purpose of affording mutual guarantees of political independence and territorial integrity to great and small states alike."

38. Quoted in Max Boot, *The Savage Wars of Peace: Small Wars and the Rise of American Power* (Basic Books, 2002), p. 207.
39. All quoted in William Manchester, *The Last Lion: Winston Spencer Churchill, Visions of Glory, 1874–1932* (Little, Brown and Company, 1983), pp. 680–81.
40. Quoted in Boot, op. cit., p. 223. That alliance had, in reality, existed during the war, when the Germans had, in Churchill's famous words, turned against czarist "Russia the most grisly of all weapons. They transported Lenin in a sealed truck like a plague bacillus from Switzerland into Russia."
41. Quoted in ibid., p. 211.
42. Quoted in Farwell, op. cit., p. 276.
43. The Bolsheviks proved a barbarous enemy, mutilating the dead.
44. Ironside, a huge man, was nicknamed "Tiny." He later achieved fame as chief of the Imperial General Staff at the outbreak of World War II.
45. Quoted in Boot, op. cit., p. 228.

CHAPTER 19: A WORLD MADE SAFE FOR WAR

1. They certainly would not have humiliated the Ottoman sultanate by handing parts of mainland Turkey over to Greek occupation—as the Treaty of Sèvres (1920) did before the sultan gave way to Atatürk in 1921. Atatürk attacked and defeated the Greeks, and became the first postwar dictator to begin the successful rolling back of the settlement of Versailles and its related treaties.
2. Canning held Britain's foreign policy brief after Castlereagh. A possible concession to draft America into a new concert of Europe would have been to transfer at least some of Imperial Germany's territories in the Pacific to the United States. Instead, these territories became League of Nations mandates. They included German Samoa (to be administered by New Zealand), Nauru and New Guinea (Australia), and Germany's northwestern Pacific holdings, which included the Caroline, Mariana, and Marshall island chains (Japan). New Zealand and Australia had contributed mightily to the British Empire's victory and deserved some reward, but Japan had played a much lesser role than had the United States, and America had its own significant interests in the Pacific. In the Second World War, the United States, Australia, and New Zealand would pay a terrible price to regain these Japanese-held islands.
3. Joseph Roth, *The Radetzky March* (The Overlook Press, 2002), pp. 161–62.
4. Quoted in Marvin Olasky, *The American Leadership Tradition: Moral Vision from Washington to Clinton* (The Free Press, 1999), p. 205.
5. Lloyd George, like his friend Winston Churchill, understood this threat much better than Wilson did.

6. Lloyd George said that the peace conference was "All a great pity. We shall have to do the same thing all over again in twenty-five years at three times the cost." Quoted in Olasky, op. cit., p. 205.

7. President Wilson's health began deteriorating in September 1919 and he suffered a paralytic stroke (which was kept secret) on 2 October 1919. The Senate rejected the treaty on 19 November 1919.

8. Quoted in Max Boot, *The Savage Wars of Peace: Small Wars and the Rise of American Power* (Basic Books, 2002), p. 248.

9. Quoted in ibid., p. 252.

10. The United States Navy patrolled the Yangtse River for two decades, starting in 1920. The Navy's mission was to protect American lives and property, ensure the safety of American commerce on the river, and fight Yangtse pirates.

11. "The Press Under a Free Government," speech by Calvin Coolidge to the American Society of Newspaper Editors in Washington, D.C., 17 January 1925.

12. Quoted in Samuel Eliot Morison, *The Oxford History of the American People: Volume Three, 1869 to the Death of John F. Kennedy 1963* (Mentor, 1972), p. 347.

13. Ibid., p. 343.

14. Quoted in William Manchester, *The Last Lion: Winston Spencer Churchill, Alone, 1932–1940* (Little, Brown, 1988), p. 352.

15. Quoted in David Cannadine, ed., *Blood, Toil, Tears and Sweat: The Speeches of Winston Churchill* (Houghton Mifflin, 1989), pp. 130–31.

16. Hitler had irredentist claims on the Danzig Corridor, which divided Germany from East Prussia. Providing Poland with this corridor to the sea was entailed in Woodrow Wilson's Fourteen Points.

17. Italy joined the war on the fascist side in 1940. Britain declared war on Japan on 8 December 1941, in the wake of the Pearl Harbor attacks.

18. Quoted in Cannadine, op. cit., p. 165.

19. Preamble to the Three-Power Pact of Germany, Italy, and Japan, signed in Berlin, 27 September 1940.

20. Quoted in Stephen Howarth, *To Shining Sea: A History of the United States Navy, 1775–1991* (Random House, 1991), p. 365.

21. Quoted in Cannadine, op. cit., pp. 177–78.

22. Quoted in ibid., p. 213.

23. Speech, President Franklin Delano Roosevelt, on the attack on the destroyer *Kearney*, "Navy Day Address," 27 October 1941.

24. Ibid. The "detailed plan" to eradicate religious freedom did not actually exist (though the Nazis were certainly anti-Christian, and murderously anti-Jewish) and the Nazi map of Latin America had been drawn by the British, not the Nazis, as part of the British war propaganda effort. Roosevelt knew this, but in the famous words of Clare Booth Luce, FDR "lied us into war because he did not have the political courage to lead us into it."

25. Quoted in Howarth, op. cit., p. 382.

CHAPTER 20: INFAMY

1. Quoted in Robert Leckie, *Delivered from Evil: The Saga of World War II* (Perennial Library, 1988), pp. 340–41.

2. Quoted in ibid., p. 342.

3. Winston S. Churchill, *The Second World War: The Grand Alliance* (Houghton Mifflin and Company, 1950), pp. 607–8.
4. Quoted in Donald L. Miller and Henry Steele Commager, *The Story of World II* (Simon & Schuster, 2001), p. 103.
5. The conversation is related in William Manchester, *American Caesar: Douglas MacArthur, 1880–1964* (A Laurel Book, Dell Publishing, 1983), pp. 293–94.
6. Nimitz took command of America's naval forces in the Pacific after Admiral Kimmel was relieved from command on 17 December 1941.
7. It was near defenseless because President Roosevelt had ordered his naval chiefs to make the European theater America's first priority, so the rest of the American Navy was locked up in the Atlantic.
8. The *Yorktown* operated like a steel version of Admiral Lord Nelson, minus an arm, minus an eye, but still a fighter for all that.
9. Quoted in Stephen Howarth, *To Shining Sea: A History of the United States Navy, 1775–1991* (Random House, 1991), p. 417.
10. William Manchester, *Goodbye Darkness: A Memoir of the Pacific War* (Dell, 1982), p. 192.
11. Ibid., p. 210.
12. Quoted in Nathan Miller, *War at Sea: A Naval History of World War II* (Oxford University Press, 1995), p. 375.
13. Quoted in Donald Miller and Henry Steel Commager, op. cit., p. 198.

CHAPTER 21: "THE GREAT CRUSADE"

1. Quoted in Stephen Howarth, *To Shining Sea: A History of the United States Navy, 1775–1991* (Random House, 1991), p. 394.
2. Quoted in Robert Leckie, *Delivered from Evil: The Saga of World War II* (Perennial Library, 1988), p. 634.
3. Quoted in Wesley Frank Craven and James Lea Cate, eds., *The Army Air Forces in World War II, Volume 3* (University of Chicago Press, 1948), p. 163.
4. Quoted in John M. Taylor, *General Maxwell Taylor: The Sword and the Pen* (Doubleday, 1989), p. 90.
5. The policy was reiterated in 1943 after Heinrich Himmler of all people—head of the SS—had tried to investigate the notion of a separate peace in the west. Eisenhower, too, had sought, unsuccessfully, to modify the policy of unconditional surrender in order to save Allied lives. But there was never any official wavering on the issue once it was pronounced. "Black Jack" Pershing would likely have approved.
6. Quoted in Carlo D'Este, *Patton: A Genius for War* (HarperCollins, 1995), p. 726.

CHAPTER 22: "ANOTHER MARINE REPORTING FOR DUTY, SIR. I'VE SPENT MY TIME IN HELL"

1. Quoted in Robert Leckie, *Delivered from Evil: The Saga of World War II* (Perennial Library, 1988), p. 720.
2. The last Japanese defender of Guam was not discovered until 1972.
3. Admiral Nimitz, American naval commander of the Pacific, had drawn up this plan and agreed with Admiral King. The issue was decided in a meeting between MacArthur, Nimitz, and President Roosevelt in Hawaii in July 1944.

4. E. B. Sledge, *With the Old Breed: At Peleliu and Okinawa* (Oxford, 1990), p. 34.

5. This was the renamed Fifth Fleet. The renamed fleet confused Japanese intelligence, which assumed that the United States Navy must be growing even faster than it was.

6. Quoted in Douglas MacArthur, *Reminiscences* (Fawcett Crest, 1965), pp. 252–53.

7. Quoted in Ronald Schaffer, *Wings of Judgment: American Bombing in World War II* (Oxford University Press, 1985), p. 88.

8. Quoted in Leckie, op. cit., p. 904.

9. Quoted in "Iwo Jima: The Famous Battle Offers Lessons for Us 60 Years Later," *Opinion Journal: From the Wall Street Journal Editorial Page,* wsj.com, 19 February 2005.

10. Quoted in Allan R. Millett, *Semper Fidelis: The History of the United States Marine Corps* (Macmillan, 1980), p. 432.

11. Both quoted in William Manchester, *Goodbye Darkness: A Memoir of the Pacific War* (Dell, 1982), p. 395.

12. Quoted in ibid., p. 435.

13. The estimated number of dead varies widely. The Manhattan Engineer District report of 1946 estimated 66,000 dead, which included people who were killed in the blast or died of related causes by the end of 1945. The Hiroshima police estimated 78,150. More recent estimates have been higher. Estimates that rise above 90,000 should be treated with caution.

14. Paul Fussell, *Thank God for the Atom Bomb and Other Essays* (Summit Books, 1988), p. 20.

15. George MacDonald Fraser, *Quartered Safe Out Here: A Recollection of the War in Burma* (Harvill/HarperCollins, 1992), p. 221.

16. Quoted in Donald L. Miller and Henry Steel Commager, *The Story of World War II* (Simon & Schuster, 2001), p. 646.

CHAPTER 23: "RETREAT, HELL—WE'RE JUST
ATTACKING IN ANOTHER DIRECTION"

1. Sir Arthur Bryant, *Triumph in the West: Based on the Diaries of Lord Alanbrooke* (Collins, 1959), p. 304.

2. See Robert Nisbet, *Roosevelt and Stalin: The Failed Courtship* (Regnery, 1988), pp. 100–101.

3. In his 1964 book *Suicide of the West: An Essay on the Meaning and Destiny of Liberalism,* James Burnham identified the statement "Colonialism and imperialism are wrong" as one of the articles of faith of twentieth-century liberalism. Burnham, a former Trotskyite, became an American strategist in the Cold War. See James Burnham, *Suicide of the West: An Essay on the Meaning and Destiny of Liberalism* (Regnery, 1985), p. 40.

4. His father, of course, had performed somewhat similar duty as military governor of the Philippines.

5. Quoted in Robert Leckie, *Delivered from Evil: The Saga of World War II* (Perennial Library, 1988), p. 843.

6. Christopher Hitchens, *Blood, Class and Empire: The Enduring Anglo-American Relationship* (Nation Books, 2004), p. 233.

7. Quoted in David Cannadine, ed., *Blood, Toil, Tears and Sweat: The Speeches of Winston Churchill* (Houghton Mifflin, 1989), p. 303.

8. President Harry S. Truman, Address to a Joint Session of Congress, 12 March 1947.

9. Secretary of State Dean Acheson's speech at the National Press Club, "The Crisis in China—An Examination of United States Policy," 12 January 1950.

10. Quoted in John Toland, *In Mortal Combat: Korea, 1950–1953* (William Morrow and Company, Inc., 1991), p. 37.

11. Ibid., p. 41.

12. This phrase came from a reporter asking, "Would it be correct to call it a police action under the United Nations?" and Truman agreeing. See Max Hastings, *The Korean War* (Simon and Schuster, 1987), p. 60. The UN resolution is also quoted here.

13. Quoted in Robert Leckie, *Conflict: The History of the Korean War, 1950–53* (G. P. Putnam's Sons, 1962), p. 74.

14. Douglas MacArthur, *Reminiscences* (Fawcett Crest, 1965), p. 398.

15. Quoted in Hastings, op. cit., p. 105.

16. MacArthur, op. cit., p. 404.

17. See Leckie, *Conflict: The History of the Korean War, 1950–53,* p. 221.

18. Quoted in Hastings, op. cit., p. 161.

19. Quoted in Lt. Col. Jon T. Hoffman, USMCR, *Chesty: The Story of Lieutenant General Lewis B. Puller, USMC* (Random House, 2001), p. 411.

20. Ibid., p. 410.

21. Quoted in James L. Stokesbury, *A Short History of the Korean War* (William Morrow and Company, 1988), p. 258.

22. Van Fleet had chased banditos in Mexico, served in both world wars, and helped the Greeks fight the Communists after World War II.

23. Quoted in Stokesbury, op. cit., p. 131. The spirit of his men echoed their commander. Korea was the "war we can't win, can't lose, and can't quit." See Leckie, *Conflict: The History of the Korean War, 1950–53,* title page.

24. Quoted in Leckie, *Conflict: The History of the Korean War, 1950–53,* p. 287.

CHAPTER 24: THE LONG TWILIGHT STRUGGLE

1. An interesting "counterfactual" is to ponder what might have happened had the United States intervened full bore in 1954 and stood side by side with the French Foreign Legion.

2. The Israelis attacked the Egyptians as part of the scheme; the British and French officially intervened to separate the combatants.

3. John F. Kennedy inaugural address, 20 January 1961.

4. Ibid.

5. Kennedy authorized the green beret as the official headgear of the U.S. Army Special Forces; every 22 November, the date of Kennedy's assassination in 1963, a Special Forces trooper lays a green beret on Kennedy's tomb.

6. Kennedy's speech is reproduced in Wesley R. Fischel, ed., *Vietnam: Anatomy of a Conflict,* (F. E. Peacock Publishers, 1968), pp. 142–47.

7. Quoted in Paul Johnson, *A History of the American People* (HarperCollins, 1997), p. 872.

8. Walter A. McDougall, *Promised Land, Crusader State: The American Encounter with the World Since 1776* (Houghton Mifflin, 1997), p. 186.

9. Joint Resolution of Congress H.J. RES 1145, August 7, 1964.

10. Dave Richard Palmer, *Summons of the Trumpet: U.S.-Vietnam in Perspective* (Presidio Press, 1978), p. xi. Palmer wrote this book while a U.S. Army colonel. He rose to lieutenant general, served as superintendent of West Point, and retired from the service in 1991.

11. Though these were indeed problems, their prevalence has been grossly exaggerated. For a chapter-length discussion of the subject see Chapter 27, "The Myth of Poor

Morale," in Mark W. Woodruff's *Unheralded Victory: The Defeat of the Viet Cong and the North Vietnamese Army, 1961–1973* (Ballantine Books/Presidio Press, 2005), especially pp. 271–88. Woodruff—a Marine Corps Vietnam veteran and a practicing psychologist—also puts paid to the pernicious and evil myth of the deranged Vietnam veteran: "Vietnam veterans were by then [1986] more likely to have a college education, more likely to own their own home, and more likely to earn above-average incomes than their nonveteran peers." Post-traumatic stress disorders among Vietnam veterans were, in fact, found to be "astonishingly low." See pp. 287–88.

12. The Marine Corps, which took a stiffer line with breaches of discipline, fared better than the Army.

13. Colonel David H. Hackworth and Elihys England, *Steel My Soldiers' Hearts: The Hopeless to Hardcore Transformation of U.S. Army 4th Battalion, 39th Infantry, Vietnam* (Touchstone, 2003), pp. 419 and 421.

14. Quoted in Norman Podhoretz, *Why We Were in Vietnam* (Simon and Schuster, 1982), pp. 84–85.

15. Quoted in Max Boot, *The Savage Wars of Peace: Small Wars and the Rise of American Power* (Basic Books, 2002), p. 298.

16. Palmer, op. cit., p. 51.

17. Quoted in Guenter Lewy, *America in Vietnam* (Oxford, 1978), p. 56.

18. Quoted in ibid.

19. Quoted in Palmer, op. cit., p. 69.

20. Quoted in Johnson, op. cit., p. 882.

21. Palmer, op. cit., p. 73.

22. LeMay's position was supported by most of the military brass and the CIA. "Graduated response" was the choice of the president's civilian advisers.

23. Arthur Schlesinger, *The Bitter Heritage: Vietnam and American Democracy, 1941–1966* (Houghton Mifflin Company, 1967), p. 76. President Johnson was capable of authentic imperialism as well. He sent 23,000 American troops into the Dominican Republic in 1965 to prevent its going Communist.

24. Palmer, op. cit., p. 117.

25. Harry G. Summers Jr., *On Strategy: A Critical Analysis of the Vietnam War* (Presidio Press, 1982), p. 1.

26. For one excellent analysis of how wildly divergent the two battles were, see Peter Braestrup, *Big Story: How the American Press and Television Reported and Interpreted the Crisis of Tet 1968 in Vietnam and Washington* (Yale University Press, 1983), see especially pp. 263–64.

27. Richard M. Nixon, "Address to the Nation on the War in Vietnam, 3 November 1969" (also known as "The Silent Majority Speech"). Nixon had laid out these principles earlier at a press conference in Guam on 25 July 1969.

28. Quoted in W. Scott Thompson and Donald D. Frizzell, *The Lessons of Vietnam* (Crane, Russak & Company, 1977), p. 105.

29. Quoted in Podhoretz, op. cit., p. 160.

30. Quoted in Thompson and Frizzell, op. cit., p. 105.

31. Quoted in Lewy, op. cit., p. 202.

32. Ibid., p. 203.

33. The argument can be—and has been—made (by Singapore President Lee Kwan Yew, among others) that American intervention in Vietnam actually prevented other

Asian dominoes from falling by providing a temporary shield against further Communist subversion. It is certainly true that America inflicted hugely disproportionate losses on the Communists that might have discouraged further adventurism. American battle deaths in Vietnam were a bit more than 47,000 (along with nearly 11,000 nonbattle deaths). The North Vietnamese army lost 1.1 million killed.

CHAPTER 25: AMERICA RESURGENT

1. It also occurred after a terrorist bombing on the barracks of Marine Corps peacekeepers in Lebanon killed 220 Marines, 18 sailors, and 3 soldiers on 23 October 1983.
2. President Ronald Reagan, "Remarks at the Brandenburg Gate, West Berlin, Germany," 12 June 1987.
3. President Ronald Reagan, Speech to the House of Commons, 8 June 1982.
4. Quoted in John Keegan, *The Iraq War* (Knopf, 2004), p. 74.
5. Schwarzkopf is a second-generation West Point–educated general. A Vietnam veteran with two tours of duty—and wounds to show for it—his grandfatherly demeanor has made him one of the most beloved military leaders in American history.
6. Dan Balz and Rick Atkinson, "Powell Vows to Isolate Iraqi Army and 'Kill It,'" *Washington Post*, 24 January 1991, p. A1.
7. This was the Battle of Medina Ridge, which is rivaled for size only by the Battle of Kursk (5–16 July 1943) between Nazi Germany and the Soviet Union in World War II.
8. See, for instance, Shyam Bhatia and Daniel McGrory, *Brighter Than the Baghdad Sun: Saddam Hussein's Nuclear Threat to the United States* (Regnery, 2000), passim but especially pp. 228–29.
9. Tragically, the United States also suffered 145 nonbattle deaths; of the battle deaths, 35 of them were "friendly-fire" incidents.
10. Lt. Col. Robert "Buzz" Patterson, *Dereliction of Duty: The Eyewitness Account of How Bill Clinton Endangered America's Long Term National Security* (Regnery, 2003), in particular Chapter 6 and p. 112.
11. From Rudyard Kipling's "The White Man's Burden" in Rudyard Kipling, *Rudyard Kipling's Verse: Definitive Edition* (Doubleday, 1940), p. 321.
12. See Patterson, op. cit., p. 37.
13. The massacre of Bosnian Muslims, however, would have a major radicalizing impact on Muslims in Europe.
14. Quoted in Richard Miniter, *Losing bin Laden: How Bill Clinton's Failures Unleashed Global Terror* (Regnery, 2003), p. 70.
15. From the introduction by Lt. Col. Oliver North in Lt. Gen. Thomas McInerney and Maj. Gen. Paul Vallely, *Endgame: The Blueprint for Victory in the War on Terror* (Regnery, 2004), p. 30.
16. The ridiculousness noted by the Navy flyer was only the half of it: Saddam Hussein and UN administrators were skimming money from the program.
17. "Let's Roll" was what passenger Scott Beamer said as he helped lead his fellow passengers against the hijackers of the plane that crashed in Pennsylvania. President Bush made it a battle cry.
18. Lt. Gen. Michael DeLong, USMC, Ret., with Noah Lukeman, *Inside CentCom: The Unvarnished Truth About the Wars in Afghanistan and Iraq* (Regnery, 2004), p. 22.
19. See ibid., p. 65, and Miniter, op. cit., pp. 231–41.

20. Iraq had violated more than seventeen United Nations Security Council Resolutions.

21. Iraq was one of the few countries—and the only country in the Arab League—not to offer its condolences after the 11 September 2001 attacks; instead it celebrated them. Iraq had provided refuge, subsidized housing, and a monthly salary to al Qaeda operative Abdul Rahman Yasin, who was involved in the 1993 World Trade Center attacks, and Iraq had a long history of links to al Qaeda. See Richard Miniter, *Disinformation: 22 Myths That Undermine the War on Terror* (Regnery, 2005), especially pages 107–34.

22. David Ignatius, "Beirut's Berlin Wall," *Washington Post,* February 23, 2005, p. A19.

23. The United States ruled out partitioning the country, but if it had practiced *divide et impera,* creating an independent Kurdistan, an independent southern Shiite Mesopotamia, and a central rump state of Sunni-dominated Iraq, its job would have been significantly easier. This is also why, *pace* the war's critics, if Iraq were to fall into civil war along these lines, it would not be a disaster for the United States, and would still be infinitely preferable to Saddam Hussein's regime. Nor would it be a disaster if democracy fails to take hold in Iraq; America's best friends in the Arab world are pro-Western monarchs.

24. The Iraqi insurgency might last longer but meet the same end as the Philippine insurgency of 1899–1902 (which included sporadic fighting for another decade). The Iraqi insurgency is more difficult because it has significant outside support from Iran, Syria, and radical Muslims. Also, the Filipinos are predominantly Catholics, which made their adoption of Western liberal democracy a natural development.

25. Keegan, op. cit., p. 219.

EPILOGUE: "GO TELL THE SPARTANS"

1. Alas, President Reagan's rebuilding program itself fell short, topping out at 530 ships.

2. Pacific War Marine E. B. Sledge provides a telling example of this. Having just survived the hell of Peleliu, he was sent with his unit for rest and rehabilitation at Pavuvu: "There I saw—of all things—an American Red Cross girl. She was serving grapefruit juice in small paper cups. Some of my buddies looked at the Red Cross woman sullenly, sat on their helmets, and waited for orders. But together with several other men, I went over to the table where the young lady handed me a cup of juice, smiled, and said she hoped I liked it. I looked at her with confusion as I took the cup and thanked her. My mind was so benumbed by the shock and violence of Peleliu that the presence of an American girl on Pavuvu seemed totally out of context. I was bewildered. 'What the hell is she doing here?' I thought. 'She's got no more business here than some damn politician.' As we filed past to board trucks, I resented her deeply." E. B. Sledge, *With the Old Breed: At Peleliu and Okinawa* (Oxford University Press, 1990), p. 164.

3. George Gordon Noel Byron, *Don Juan,* canto 9, stanza 4.

4. Robert D. Kaplan, *Imperial Grunts: The American Military on the Ground* (Random House, 2005).

5. Niall Ferguson uses this fitting appellation in *Colossus: The Price of America's Empire* (The Penguin Press, 2004), p. 121.

SELECT BIBLIOGRAPHY

This select bibliography is by no means a complete listing of books consulted but is offered more as a guide to books that are frequently referenced or that might be of most interest to the general reader.

Ambrose, Stephen E., *Undaunted Courage: Meriwether Lewis, Thomas Jefferson, and the Opening of the American West* (Simon and Schuster, 1997).

Anderson, Fred, *Crucible of War: The Seven Years' War and the Fate of Empire in British North America, 1754–1766* (Knopf, 2000).

Anderson, Fred, and Andrew Cayton, *The Dominion of War: Empire and Liberty in North America, 1500–2000* (Viking, 2005).

Atkinson, Rick, *An Army at Dawn: The War in North Africa, 1942–43* (Henry Holt and Company 2002).

Barnett, Correlli, *The Great War* (BBC Worldwide Ltd., 2003).

Bauer, K. Jack, *The Mexican War: 1846–1848* (Macmillan, 1974).

Bhatia, Shyam, and Daniel McGrory, *Brighter Than the Baghdad Sun: Saddam Hussein's Nuclear Threat to the United States* (Regnery, 2000).

Bonekemper, Edward H., *A Victor Not a Butcher: Ulysses S. Grant's Overlooked Military Genius* (Regnery, 2004).

Boot, Max, *The Savage Wars of Peace: Small Wars and the Rise of American Power* (Basic Books, 2002).

Borcke, Heros von, *Memoirs of the Confederate War for Independence: A Prussian Officer with J. E. B. Stuart in Virginia* (J. S. Sanders and Company, 1999).

Boyd, Julian P., ed., *The Papers of Thomas Jefferson: Volume 8, February to 31 October 1785* (Princeton University Press, 1953).

Bradford, James C., *Oxford Atlas of American Military History* (Oxford University Press, 2003).

Braestrup, Peter, *Big Story: How the American Press and Television Reported and Interpreted the Crisis of Tet 1968 in Vietnam and Washington* (Yale University Press, 1983).

Brands, H. W., *Andrew Jackson: His Life and Times* (Doubleday, 2005).

————, *TR: The Last Romantic* (Basic Books, 1997).

Brookhiser, Richard, *Alexander Hamilton: American* (Free Press, 1999).

————, *Founding Father: Rediscovering George Washington* (Free Press, 1996).

Brooks, Victor, and Robert Hohwald, *How America Fought Its Wars: Military Strategy from the American Revolution to the Civil War* (Combined Publishing, 1999).

Brooksher, William R., and David K. Snider, *Glory at a Gallop: Tales of the Confederate Cavalry* (Brassey's, 1995).

Bryant, Sir Arthur, *Triumph in the West: Based on the Diaries of Lord Alanbrooke* (Collins, 1959).

Buchanan, Patrick J., *A Republic, Not an Empire: Reclaiming America's Destiny* (Regnery, 2002).

Burnham, James, *Suicide of the West: An Essay on the Meaning and Destiny of Liberalism* (Regnery, 1985).

Bunting, Josiah III, *Ulysses S. Grant* (Times Books, 2004).

Burke, Edmund, *The Best of Burke: Selected Writings and Speeches of Edmund Burke,* edited by Peter J. Stanlis (Regnery Conservative Leadership Series, 1999).

———, *Reflections on the Revolution in France* (Penguin, 1982).

Byron, Baron George Gordon, *The Poetical Works of Byron* (Houghton Mifflin, 1975).

Cannadine, David, ed., *Blood, Toil, Tears and Sweat: The Speeches of Winston Churchill* (Houghton Mifflin, 1989).

Casey, William, *The Secret War Against Hitler* (Regnery-Gateway, 1988).

Castel, Albert, *Winning and Losing in the Civil War* (University of South Carolina Press, 1996).

Catton, Bruce, *The Army of the Potomac,* three volumes (Doubleday & Company, 1952–1953).

Chamber, John Whiteclay II, *The Oxford Companion to American Military History* (Oxford, 1999).

Chandler, David R., and Ian Beckett, eds., *The Oxford Illustrated History of the British Army* (Oxford, 1994).

Churchill, Winston S., *A History of the English-Speaking Peoples,* four volumes (Dorset Press, 1956).

———, *My Early Life, 1874–1908* (Fontana/Collins, 1985).

———, *The Second World War,* six volumes (Houghton Mifflin, 1948–1953).

———, *The World Crisis* (revised and abridged) (Scribner, 1931).

Clark, Harrison, *All Cloudless Glory,* two volumes (Regnery, 1995).

Clausewitz, Karl von, *On War,* translated by J. J. Graham (Penguin Books, 1984).

———, *War, Politics and Power,* translated by Edward M. Collins (Regnery, 1997).

Cole, Franklin P., *They Preached Liberty* (Liberty Press, no date).

Connell, Evan S., *Son of the Morning Star: Custer and the Little Bighorn* (North Point Press, 1984).

Cook, Don, *The Long Fuse: How England Lost the American Colonies, 1760–1785* (Atlantic Monthly Press, 1995).

Corrigan, Gordon, *Mud, Blood and Poppycock: Britain and the First World War* (Cassell, 2003).

Cozzens, Peter, *No Better Place to Die: The Battle of Stones River* (University of Illinois Press, 1990).

Craven, Wesley Frank, and James Lea Cate, eds., *The Army Air Forces in World War II,* seven volumes (University of Chicago Press, 1948–1958).

Crocker, H. W. III, *Robert E. Lee on Leadership: Executive Lessons in Character, Courage, and Vision* (Prima/Forum, 1999).

———, *Triumph: The Power and the Glory of the Catholic Church, A 2,000-Year History* (Prima/Forum/Crown/Random House, 2001).

Crockett, David, *A Narrative of the Life of David Crockett* (University of Nebraska Press, 1987).

Davis, Burke, *The Campaign That Won America: The Story of Yorktown* (Eastern Acorn Press, 1997).

———, *Gray Fox: Robert E. Lee and the Civil War* (Burford Books, 1956).

———, *Marine! The Life of Chesty Puller* (Bantam, 1991).

Davis, William C., *The Illustrated History of the Civil War: The Soldiers, Weapons, and Battles of the Civil War* (Courage Books, 1997).

———, *Look Away! A History of the Confederate States of America* (Free Press, 2002).

Davis, William C., Brian C. Pohanka, and Don Troiani, *Civil War Journal: The Battles* (Rutledge Hill Press, 1998).

DeConde, Alexander, *A History of American Foreign Policy* (Charles Scribner's Sons, 1963).

DeLong, Lt. Gen. Michael, USMC, Ret., with Noah Lukeman, *Inside CentCom: The Unvarnished Truth About the Wars in Afghanistan and Iraq* (Regnery, 2004).

D'Este, Carlo, *Patton: A Genius for War* (HarperCollins, 1995).

Dowdey, Clifford, *The History of the Confederacy* (originally published under the title, *The Land They Fought For*) (Barnes and Noble Books, 1992).

———, *Lee* (Stan Clark Military Books, 1991).

Eggleston, George Cary, *A Rebel's Recollections* (Louisiana State University Press, 1996).

Eisenhower, John S. D., *So Far from God: The U.S. War with Mexico, 1846–1848* (Random House, 1989).

Elting, John R., *Amateurs, to Arms! A Military History of the War of 1812* (Algonquin Books of Chapel Hill, 1991).

Faragher, John Mack, ed., *The American Heritage Encyclopedia of American History* (Henry Holt, 1998).

Farwell, Byron, *Over There: The United States in the Great War, 1917–1918* (W. W. Norton & Company, 1999).

———, *Stonewall: A Biography of General Thomas J. Jackson* (W. W. Norton & Company, 1992).

Faulkner, Harold U., *Politics, Reform and Expansion* (Harper & Row, 1959).

Ferguson, Niall, *Colossus: The Price of America's Empire* (The Penguin Press, 2004).

Fischel, Wesley R., ed., *Vietnam: Anatomy of a Conflict* (F. E. Peacock Publishers, 1968).

Fletcher, C. R. L., and Rudyard Kipling, *Kipling's Pocket History of England* (Greenwich House, 1983).

Flexner, James Thomas, *Washington: The Indispensable Man* (Little, Brown, 1974).

Flood, Charles Bracelen, *Lee: The Last Years* (Mariner Books, 1998).

Foote, Shelby, *The Civil War: A Narrative,* three volumes (Random House, 1958–1974).

Fortesque, Sir John, *A History of the British Army,* thirteen volumes (Macmillan, 1899–1930).

Fraser, George MacDonald, *Quartered Safe Out Here: A Recollection of the War in Burma* (Harvill/HarperCollins, 1992).

Freeman, Douglas Southall, *Lee* (an abridgment in one volume, by Richard Harwell, of the four-volume *R. E. Lee*) (Charles Scribner's Sons, 1991).

———, *Lee's Lieutenants,* three volumes (Charles Scribner's Sons, 1972).

———, *Lee's Lieutenants: A Study in Command* (an abridgment in one volume, by Stephen W. Sears, of the three-volume *Lee's Lieutenants*) (Charles Scribner's Sons, 1998).

———, *R. E. Lee: A Biography,* four volumes (Charles Scribner's Sons, 1934–1935).

Freidel, Frank, *The Splendid Little War: The Dramatic Story of the Spanish-American War* (Burford Books, 2002).

Fremantle, Arthur J., *Three Months in the Southern States: The 1863 Diary of an English Soldier* (Greenhouse Publishing Co., no date; originally published by William Blackwood and Son, 1863).

Fromkin, David, *In the Time of the Americans* (Knopf, 1995).

———, *Kosovo Crossing: American Ideals Meet Reality on the Balkan Battlefields* (Free Press, 1999).

Fuller, Major General J. F. C., *Decisive Battles of the U.S.A.* (Thomas Yoseloff, 1942).

——, *Grant and Lee: A Study in Personality and Generalship* (Scribner, 1933).

——, *A Military History of the Western World* (Funk & Wagnalls, 1955).

Fussell, Paul, *Thank God for the Atom Bomb and Other Essays* (Summit Books, 1988).

Gaddis, John Lewis, *Surprise, Security, and the American Experience* (Harvard University Press, 2004).

Gallagher, Gary, ed., *Chancellorsville: The Battle and Its Aftermath* (University of North Carolina Press, 1996).

——, *The Confederate War: How Popular Will, Nationalism, and Military Strategy Could Not Stave Off Defeat* (Harvard University Press, 1997).

——, ed., *Lee: The Soldier* (Nebraska University Press, 1996).

Gelb, Norman, *Less Than Glory: A Revisionist's View of the American Revolution* (G. P. Putnam's Sons, 1984).

Gordon, John Steele, *An Empire of Wealth: An Epic History of American Economic Power* (HarperCollins, 2004).

Gordon, Lesley J., *General George E. Pickett in Life and Legend* (University of North Carolina Press, 1998).

Gould, Stephen Jay, *Bully for Brontosaurus: Reflections in Natural History* (W. W. Norton & Company, 1991).

Grant, Ulysses S., *Personal Memoirs: Ulysses S. Grant* (Modern Library, 1999).

Grenville, J. A. S., *A World History of the Twentieth Century, Volume One: 1900–1945: Western Dominance* (Fontana, 1983).

Hackworth, Colonel David H., and Elihys England, *Steel My Soldiers' Hearts: The Hopeless to Hardcore Transformation of U.S. Army 4th Battalion, 39th Infantry, Vietnam* (Touchstone, 2003).

Hackworth, David H., and Julie Sherman, *About Face: The Odyssey of an American Warrior* (Simon and Schuster, 1989).

Hagedorn, Herman, ed., *The Free Citizen: A Summons to Service of the Democratic Ideal by Theodore Roosevelt* (Theodore Roosevelt Association, 1958).

Hamilton, Alexander, John Jay, and James Madison, *The Federalist* (Regnery, 1999).

Hamilton, Edward P., *The French and Indian Wars: The Story of Battles and Forts in the Wilderness* (Doubleday, 1962).

Hanson, Victor Davis, *Carnage and Culture: Landmark Battles in the Rite of Western Power* (Doubleday, 2001).

——, *Ripples of Battle: How Wars of the Past Still Determine How We Fight, How We Live, and How We Think* (Doubleday, 2003).

Harsh, Joseph L., *Confederate Tide Rising: Robert E. Lee and the Making of Southern Strategy, 1861–1862* (Kent State University Press, 1998).

Hart, B. H. Liddell, *Strategy* (Praeger, 1968).

Harvey, Robert, *"A Few Bloody Noses": The Realities and Mythologies of the American Revolution* (Overlook Press, 2002).

Hassler, Warren W., Jr., *With Shield and Sword: American Military Affairs, Colonial Times to the Present* (Iowa State University Press, 1987).

Hastings, Max, *The Korean War* (Simon and Schuster, 1987).

Hattaway, Herman, *Shades of Blue and Gray: An Introductory Military History of the Civil War* (University of Missouri Press, 1997).

Haythornthwaite, Philip J., *Invincible Generals: Gustavus Adolphus, Marlborough, Frederick the Great, George Washington, Wellington* (Indiana University Press, 1992).

Hitchens, Christopher, *Blood, Class and Empire: The Enduring Anglo-American Relationship* (Nation Books, 2004).

Hoffman, Lt. Col. Jon T., USMCR, *Chesty: The Story of Lieutenant General Lewis B. Puller, USMC* (Random House, 2001).

Holmes, Richard, *Redcoat: The British Soldier in the Age of Horse and Musket* (W. W. Norton and Company, 2001).

Horn, Stanley F., ed., *The Robert E. Lee Reader* (Konecky & Konecky, 1949).

Horowitz, David, *The First Frontier: The Indian Wars & America's Origins, 1607–1776* (Simon & Schuster, 1978).

Howard, Michael, *Clausewitz* (Oxford University Press, 1983).

Howarth, Stephen, *To Shining Sea: A History of the United States Navy* (Random House, 1991).

Hunter, Charles N., *Galahad* (The Naylor Co., 1963).

Huntington, Samuel P., *The Clash of Civilizations and the Remaking of World Order* (Simon and Schuster, 1997).

Johnson, Paul, *George Washington: The Founding Father* (HarperCollins, 2005).

———, *A History of the American People* (HarperCollins, 1997).

———, *Modern Times: The World from the Twenties to the Eighties* (Harper & Row, 1983).

Johnson, Samuel, *The Yale Edition of the Works of Samuel Johnson, Volume X, Political Writings*, edited by Donald J. Greene (Liberty Fund, 1977).

Kaplan, Robert D., *Imperial Grunts: The American Military on the Ground* (Random House, 2005).

Karnow, Stanley, *In Our Image: America's Empire in the Philippines* (Random House, 1989).

———, *Vietnam: A History* (Viking Press, 1983).

Keegan, John, *Fields of Battle: The Wars of North America* (Knopf, 1996).

———, *The First World War* (Alfred A. Knopf, 1999).

———, *Intelligence in Warfare: Knowledge of the Enemy from Napoleon to al-Qaeda* (Knopf, 2003).

———, *The Iraq War* (Knopf, 2004).

———, *The Second World War* (Viking, 1990).

Keegan, John, ed., *Churchill's Generals* (Grove Weidenfeld, 1991).

Kennedy, Frances H., ed., *The Civil War Battlefield Guide* (Houghton Mifflin, 1990).

Kipling, Rudyard, *Rudyard Kipling's Verse: Definitive Edition* (Doubleday & Company, 1940).

Kirk, Russell, *The Conservative Constitution* (Regnery-Gateway, 1990).

———, *The Conservative Mind* (Regnery, 1995).

———, *The Roots of American Order* (Regnery-Gateway, 1991).

Kuehnelt-Leddihn, Erik von, *Leftism Revisited: From de Sade and Marx to Hitler and Pol Pot* (Regnery-Gateway, 1990).

Künstler, Mort, and James McPherson, *Gettysburg* (Rutledge Hill Press, 1993).

Künstler, Mort, and James I. Robertson, *Jackson and Lee: Legends in Gray* (Rutledge Hill Press, 1995).

Lancaster, Bruce, et al., *The American Heritage Book of the Revolution* (Simon and Schuster, 1958).

Leckie, Robert, *A Few Acres of Snow: The Saga of the French and Indian Wars* (John Wiley & Sons, 1999).

———, *Conflict: The History of the Korean War, 1950–53* (G. P. Putnam's Sons, 1962).

———, *Delivered from Evil: The Saga of World War II* (Perennial Library, 1988).

———, *The Wars of America* (Castle Books, 1998).

Lewin, Ronald, *Slim: The Standardbearer* (Leo Cooper, 1990).

Lewis, Lloyd, *Captain Sam Grant* (Little, Brown, 1950).

Lewy, Guenter, *America in Vietnam* (Oxford, 1978).

Lock, J. D., *To Fight with Intrepidity: The Complete History of the U.S. Army Rangers, 1622 to Present* (Fenestra Books, 2001).

Long, Jeff, *Duel of Eagles: The Mexican and U.S. Fight for the Alamo* (William Morrow and Company, 1990).

Longacre, Edward G., *Gentleman and Soldier: The Extraordinary Life of General Wade Hampton* (Rutledge Hill Press, 2003).

Longford, Elizabeth, *Wellington: Pillar of State* (Weidenfeld & Nicolson, 1972).

———, *Wellington: The Years of the Sword* (Harper & Row, 1969).

Lord, Walter, *Incredible Victory: The Battle of Midway* (Burford Books, 1967).

Lubow, Arthur, *The Reporter Who Would Be King: A Biography of Richard Harding Davis,* (Charles Scribner's Sons, 1992).

Lukacs, John, *Five Days in London: May 1940* (Yale University Press, 1999).

Lytle, Andrew Nelson, *Bedford Forrest and His Critter Company* (J. S. Sanders and Company, 1992).

MacArthur, Douglas, *Reminiscences* (Fawcett Crest, 1965).

Macmillan Information Now Encyclopedia, *The Confederacy* (Macmillan, 1993).

Mahan, Alfred Thayer, *The Influence of Sea Power Upon History, 1660–1783* (Dover, 1987).

Manchester, William, *American Caesar: Douglas MacArthur, 1880–1964* (Dell, 1983).

———, *Goodbye Darkness: A Memoir of the Pacific War* (Dell, 1982).

———, *The Last Lion: Winston Spencer Churchill,* two volumes (Little, Brown and Company, 1983 and 1988).

Marvel, William, *The Alabama & the Kearsarge: The Sailor's Civil War* (University of North Carolina Press, 1996).

McCullough, David, *1776* (Simon and Schuster, 2005).

McDonald, Forrest, *Alexander Hamilton: A Biography* (Norton, 1982).

———, *E Pluribus Unum: The Formation of the American Republic, 1776–1790* (Liberty Press, 1979).

McDougall, Walter A., *Promised Land, Crusader State: The American Encounter with the World Since 1776* (Houghton Mifflin, 1997).

McInerney, Lt. Gen. Thomas, and Maj. Gen. Paul Vallely, *Endgame: The Blueprint for Victory in the War on Terror* (Regnery, 2004).

McPherson, James M., *The Battle Cry of Freedom: The Civil War Era* (Oxford University Press, 1988).

———, *What They Fought For, 1861–1865* (Louisiana State University Press, 1994).

McWhiney, Grady, and Perry D. Jamieson, *Attack and Die: Civil War Tactics and the Southern Heritage* (University of Alabama Press, 1982).

Messenger, Charles, *The Second World War in Europe* (Smithsonian Books, 2001).

Miller, Donald L., and Henry Steel Commager, *The Story of World War II* (Simon & Schuster, 2001).

Miller, Nathan, *War at Sea: A Naval History of World War II* (Oxford University Press, 1995).

Millett, Allan R., *Semper Fidelis: The History of the United States Marine Corps* (Macmillan, 1980).

Millett, Allan R., and Peter Maslowski, *For the Common Defense: A Military History of the United States of America* (The Free Press, 1994).

Miniter, Richard, *Disinformation: 22 Media Myths That Undermine the War on Terror* (Regnery, 2005).

————, *Losing bin Laden: How Bill Clinton's Failures Unleashed Global Terror* (Regnery, 2003).

————, *Shadow War, The Untold Story of How Bush Is Winning the War on Terror* (Regnery, 2004).

Mitchell, Brian, *Weak Link: The Feminization of the American Military* (Regnery-Gateway, 1989).

————, *Women in the Military: Flirting with Disaster* (Regnery, 1998).

Mitchell, Joseph B., *Decisive Battles of the Civil War* (Fawcett Premier, 1989).

Morison, Samuel Eliot, *The Oxford History of the American People,* three volumes (Mentor, 1972).

Morrill, Dan L., *The Southern Campaigns of the American Revolution* (The Nautical and Aviation Publishing Company of America, no date).

Morris, Edmund, *The Rise of Theodore Roosevelt* (Ballantine Books, 1979).

————, *Theodore Rex* (Random House, 2001).

Mosby, Colonel John S., *Mosby's Memoirs* (J. S. Sanders and Company, 1995).

Musicant, Ivan, *Empire by Default: The Spanish-American War and the Dawn of the American Century* (Henry Holt and Company, 1998).

Newell, Clayton R., *Lee vs. McClellan: The First Campaign* (Regnery, 1996).

Nichols, Edward J., *Zach Taylor's Little Army* (Doubleday, 1963).

North, Oliver, *War Stories: Operation Iraqi Freedom* (Regnery, 2003).

————, *War Stories II: Heroism in the Pacific* (Regnery, 2004).

North, Oliver, with Joe Musser, *War Stories III: The Heroes Who Defeated Hitler* (Regnery, 2005).

Nye, Roger, *The Patton Mind* (Avery, 1993).

Ogburn, Charlton, *The Marauders* (Harper and Brothers, 1956).

Olasky, Marvin, *The American Leadership Tradition: Moral Vision from Washington to Clinton* (The Free Press, 1999).

O'Meara, Walter, *Guns at the Forks* (Prentice-Hall, 1965).

O'Toole, G. J. A., *The Spanish War: An American Epic 1898* (W. W. Norton & Company, 1984).

Padover, Saul K., ed., *Thomas Jefferson on Democracy* (Mentor, 1959).

Palmer, Dave Richard, *Summons of the Trumpet: U.S.-Vietnam in Perspective* (Presidio Press, 1978).

Parkman, Francis, *The Conspiracy of Pontiac,* two volumes (University of Nebraska Press, 1994).

————, *France and England in North America,* two volumes (The Library of America, 1983).

————, *The Oregon Trail* (Oxford University Press, 1996).

Patterson, Lt. Col. Robert "Buzz," *Dereliction of Duty: The Eyewitness Account of How Bill Clinton Endangered America's Long Term National Security* (Regnery, 2003).

Patton, George S., Jr., *War as I Knew It* (Mariner Books, 1995).

Perret, Geoffrey, *A Country Made by War: From the Revolution to Vietnam—The Story of America's Rise to Power* (Random House, 1989).

————, *Old Soldiers Never Die: The Life of Douglas MacArthur* (Random House, 1996).

Perry, Mark, *Conceived in Liberty: Joshua Chamberlin, William Oates, and the American Civil War* (Viking, 1997).

Pessen, Edward, *Jacksonian America* (Dorsey Press, 1978).

Podhoretz, Norman, *Why We Were in Vietnam* (Simon and Schuster, 1982).

Porch, Douglas, *The French Foreign Legion: A Comprehensive History of the Legendary Fighting Force* (HarperCollins, 1991).

Price, David A., *Love and Hate in Jamestown: John Smith, Pocahontas, and the Heart of a New Nation* (Alfred A. Knopf, 2003).

Prior, Robin, and Trevor Wilson, *The First World War* (Smithsonian Books, 2003).

Probert, Henry, *Bomber Harris: His Life and Times* (Greenhill Books, 2003).

Rabble, George C., *The Confederate Republic: A Revolution Against Politics* (University of North Carolina Press, 1994).

Ramage, James A., *Gray Ghost: The Life of Colonel John Singleton Mosby* (The University Press of Kentucky, 1999).

————, *Rebel Raider: The Life of General John Hunt Morgan* (University of Kentucky Press, 1995).

Regan, Geoffrey, *The Guinness Book of Decisive Battles* (Canopy Books, 1992).

Remini, Robert V., *Andrew Jackson and His Indian Wars* (Viking, 2001).

————, *The Battle of New Orleans* (Viking, 1999).

————, *The Life of Andrew Jackson* (Harper and Row, 1988).

Riccards, Michael P., *A Republic, If You Can Keep It: The Foundation of the American Presidency, 1700–1800* (Greenwood Press, 1987).

Roberts, J. M., *The Pelican History of the World* (Penguin, 1985).

Robertson, James I., *General A. P. Hill: The Story of a Confederate Warrior* (Vintage Civil War Library, 1992).

————, *Stonewall Jackson: The Man, the Soldier, the Legend* (Macmillan, 1997).

Roland, Charles P., *Reflections on Lee: A Historian's Assessment* (Stackpole Books, 1995).

Roosevelt, Theodore, *The Naval War of 1812* (Modern Library, 1999).

Roth, Joseph, *The Radetzky March* (The Overlook Press, 2002).

Rutland, Robert Allen, *The Presidency of James Madison* (University Press of Kansas, 1990).

Sandburg, Carl, *Storm over the Land* (Harcourt Brace, 1942).

Schlesinger, Arthur, *The Bitter Heritage: Vietnam and American Democracy, 1941–1966* (Houghton Mifflin Company, 1967).

Sellar, Walter Carruthers, and Robert Julian Yeatman, *1066 and All That: A Memorable History of England* (The Folio Society, 1999).

Shaara, Michael, *The Killer Angels* (Random House, 1993).

Sifakis, Stewart, *Who Was Who in the Civil War* (Facts on File, 1988).

Sledge, E. B., *With the Old Breed: At Peleliu and Okinawa* (Oxford, 1990).

Smith, Stuart W., ed., *Douglas Southall Freeman on Leadership* (White Mane Publishing Company, Inc., 1993).

Stallings, Laurence, *The Doughboys: The Story of the AEF, 1917–1918* (Harper & Row, 1963).

Steinhoff, Johannes, Peter Pechel, and Dennis Showalter, *Voices from the Third Reich: An Oral History* (Regnery Gateway, 1989).

Stilwell, Joseph W., *The Stilwell Papers* (William Sloane Associates, 1948).

Stokesbury, James L., *A Short History of the American Revolution* (William Morrow and Company, 1991).

———, *A Short History of the Korean War* (William Morrow and Company, 1988).

Summers, Harry G., Jr., *On Strategy: A Critical Analysis of the Vietnam War* (Presidio Press, 1982).

Tate, Allen, *Jefferson Davis: His Rise and Fall* (J. S. Sanders and Company, 1998).

———, *Stonewall Jackson: The Good Soldier* (J. S. Sanders and Company, 1991).

Taylor, John M., *Confederate Raider: Raphael Semmes of the Alabama* (Brassey's, 1994).

———, *Duty Faithfully Performed: Robert E. Lee and His Critics* (Brassey's, 1999).

———, *General Maxwell Taylor: The Sword and the Pen* (Doubleday, 1989).

Taylor, Richard, *Destruction and Reconstruction: Personal Experiences of the Late War* (J. S. Sanders & Company, 1998).

Taylor, Walter H., *Four Years with Robert E. Lee* (University of Indiana Press, 1996).

Terraine, John, *Douglas Haig: The Educated Soldier* (Leo Cooper, 1990).

Thomas, Emory M., *Bold Dragoon: The Life of J.E.B. Stuart* (Harper & Row, 1986).

———, *Robert E. Lee* (Norton, 1997).

Thompson, Neville, *Wellington After Waterloo* (Routledge & Kegan Paul, 1986).

Thompson, W. Scott, and Donald D. Frizzell, *The Lessons of Vietnam* (Crane, Russak & Company, 1977).

Tocqueville, Alexis de, *Democracy in America,* translated by George Lawrence, edited by J. P. Mayer (Doubleday/Anchor, 1969).

Toland, John, *In Mortal Combat: Korea, 1950–1953* (William Morrow and Company, Inc.).

Treasure, Geoffrey, *Who's Who in Early Hanoverian Britain* (Shepheard-Walwyn, 1992).

Tuchman, Barbara W., *Stilwell and the American Experience in China, 1911–45* (Grove Press, 1985).

Tucker, Glenn, *Dawn Like Thunder: The Barbary Wars and the Birth of the U.S. Navy* (Bobbs & Merrill, 1963).

———, *Poltroons and Patriots: A Popular Account of the War of 1812* (Bobbs & Merrill, 1954).

Vanauken, Sheldon, *The Glittering Illusion: English Sympathy for the Southern Confederacy* (Regnery, 1989).

Weaver, Richard M., *The Southern Tradition at Bay: A History of Postbellum Thought* (Regnery Gateway, 1989).

Weigley, Russell F., *The American Way of War: A History of United States Military Strategy and Policy* (Indiana University Press, 1973).

Weinberger, Caspar, with Gretchen Roberts, *In the Arena: A Memoir of the Twentieth Century* (Regnery, 2001).

Wert, Jeffry D., *General James Longstreet: The Confederacy's Most Controversial Soldier* (Touchstone, 1994).

Wheelan, Joseph, *Jefferson's War: America's First War on Terror, 1801–1805* (Carroll and Graf, 2003).

Wheeler, Richard, *Gettysburg 1863: Campaign of Endless Echoes* (Plume, 1999).

Whipple, A. B. C., *To the Shores of Tripoli: The Birth of the U.S. Navy and Marines* (William Morrow and Company, 1991).

Willmott, H. P., *The Second World War in the Far East* (Smithsonian Books, 2002).

Wills, Brian Steel, *A Battle from the Start: The Life of Nathan Bedford Forrest* (HarperCollins, 1992).

Wolseley, Garnet, Viscount, *The American Civil War: An English View, The Writings of Field Marshal Viscount Wolseley* (edited and introduced by James A. Rawley) (Stackpole Books, 2002).

Woodruff, Mark W., *Unheralded Victory: The Defeat of the Viet Cong and the North Vietnamese Army, 1961–1973* (Ballantine Books/Presidio Press, 2005).

Woods, Thomas E., Jr., *The Politically Incorrect Guide to American History* (Regnery, 2004).

Young, Bennett, *Confederate Wizards of the Saddle* (J. S. Sanders & Company, 1999).

Young, Darryl, *The Element of Surprise: Navy SEALs in Vietnam* (Ivy Books, 1990).

Young, Kenneth Ray, *The General's General: The Life and Times of Arthur MacArthur* (Westview Press, 1994).

Zimmermann, Warren, *First Great Triumph: How Five Americans Made Their Country a World Power* (Farrar, Straus and Giroux, 2002).

ACKNOWLEDGMENTS

Thanks to Alex Hoyt, Jed Donahue, Mary Choteborsky, and all who helped bring this book to fruition.

INDEX

ABOUT THE AUTHOR

Educated in England and California, H. W. Crocker III hoped to enlist in the Marine Corps out of high school. Lingering asthma and a bad back put paid to that, forcing him to earn a living with his pen. He has worked as a journalist, speechwriter for the governor of California, and book editor. He is the author of *Triumph: The Power and the Glory of the Catholic Church, Robert E. Lee on Leadership,* and the prizewinning comic novel *The Old Limey.* Mr. Crocker lives on the site of a former Confederate encampment in northern Virginia.